Never at War

Why Democracies Will Not Fight One Another

Spencer R. Weart

Yale University Press New Haven and London

Published with assistance from the Mary Cady Tew
Memorial Fund.

Printed in the United States of America.

Library of Congress Cataloging-in-Publication Data

Weart, Spencer R., 1942–
    Never at war : why democracies will not fight
  one another / Spencer R. Weart.
      p. cm.
  Includes bibliographical references and index.
  ISBN 0-300-07017-9 (alk. paper)
    1. Democracy—History.   2. War—History.
  3. Peace—History.   I. Title.
  JC421.W43   1998
  327.1′7—dc21   98-2664
                    CIP

A catalogue record for this book is available from the
British Library.

10 9 8 7 6 5 4 3 2 1

Contents

Preface

This book is a foray into the region between history and political science, a poorly mapped frontier zone. Historians will be annoyed by the effort I spend on defining terms and applying them to historical locales where I have no special expertise. By the end I hope you will agree that this is not pseudo-science but a way to dig out valuable insights. Political scientists will be annoyed by the stories I tell with no precise conclusions. Please bear in mind that (as the historian Charles Gillispie once said) "historians are better than their theories"; narrative gives an understanding of human affairs that generalizations never quite capture.

Chief references on a particular historical locale are given when the locale is first discussed substantially and may not be repeated in later notes. When I cite existing translations I have tried to review the original text and in some cases have made slight modifications toward a more consistent use of key terms; elsewhere the translations are my own.

This work was made possible by generous and understanding support from the American Institute of Physics, the Harry Frank Guggenheim Foundation, and the United States Institute of Peace. Also invaluable was Princeton University's comprehensive library. Kevin Downing, Martha Keyes, Johannes Wolfart, and Drew Arrowwood served as research assistants. This book depends on the work of countless scholars living and dead, but I owe special thanks to R. J. Rummel, Bruce Russett, James Lee Ray, and Michael Doyle for discussions and encouragement.

CHAPTER ONE

Investigating the Puzzle of Democratic Peace

Wither the patient brutality of a beating by mobsters, artillery shells fell one by one into the old city of Dubrovnik. The streets, once busy with citizens and tourists, were strangely quiet in November 1991, aside from intermittent explosions and the occasional crack of sniper fire. Dubrovnik's citizens huddled in their cellars and talked about their enemy, the Serbs.

"I have stones," a Croatian sculptor told a reporter. "I think I could throw them on their heads. I was a kind of pacifist. Never hated anybody. But now?"[1]

People reading the news in Western Europe and America, people who perhaps had only recently come to view Dubrovnik's picturesque streets and massive city walls, could scarcely believe that it was all being battered into rubble. A war between Communist nations would not have surprised them. But this fight had begun after both sides, Serbia and Croatia, held free elections. Somehow a war between democracies seemed horribly wrong.

When Eastern Europe began to turn toward democracy back in 1988, news analysts said the risk of war in Europe was "of course" diminishing. As the Soviet Union also stumbled toward democracy, then "of course" at each step the Cold War dwindled. The democracies would "of course" be good friends even with a nation like Iraq if only it were a democracy too. When troubled nations from Nicaragua to Namibia held free elections, the U.S. government drew back from intervention.[2] Everyone from American presidents to Russian peasants spoke as if increasing democracy must decrease the risk of warfare.

Do democracies really tend to maintain a mutual peace? Or is this a delusion that will endanger any nation so foolish as to trust it? The only way to answer this important question is to look at history.

Dubrovnik is a good place to start. A dozen centuries earlier, when it began to build its mighty walls, the city had needed them for survival. It was an independent republic (named Ragusa) where citizens elected officials and voted in councils, generation after generation, obedient to a carefully crafted constitution. They modeled their regime on Venice, another stable republic—and a great enemy. Bitter competitors for the thriving Adriatic trade, the two merchant cities called each other evil names and now and then found a legal pretext to seize a rich galley belonging to their rival. Yet never once did the republics make war on each other. And down through the centuries, as a hundred wars tormented the region, Ragusa never made war on any other solidly established republic. For that matter, neither did Venice.[3]

That surprising stretch of peace is only one of many such cases that turn up in odd corners of history, wherever there were republics. When states avoid war so thoroughly, can that be a mere accident, or is there some deeper reason? If a general reason exists then we may already have at hand, in peaceful democratic regions like Western Europe, the blueprint for a solution to the problem of war.

Such a solution becomes more essential every year. All sorts of nations are learning to build nuclear weapons. Still more unspeakable devices will someday be easy to make, in the zone where microelectronics and bio-chemistry are converging. Sooner than many people think, any substantial fragment of a nation will be able to do to any city in the world what the Serbs did to Dubrovnik. In the long run we may not survive unless we avoid all wars—not just among some states, but among all of them; not just for the next couple of decades, but for all time. What international order can achieve so much?

The ideas that have guided international policy for generations are bankrupt. Few believe any longer that we will create an overarching world government, under the United Nations or any other organization, that will prevent wars through its own unified rule. Policymakers have fallen back on a traditional answer, the balance of power. They propose to deter war by mustering invincible coalitions of nations to oppose anyone who threatens the status quo. But the failures of that policy litter history. Wars in the Persian Gulf and Bosnia are only the most recent of a thousand examples.

Almost in desperation we turn to the claim that free peoples will not make war on one another. This idea had been developed by 1785, when there were scarcely any democracies in existence, by the great philosopher

Immanuel Kant. A world where every state was a democracy, he wrote, would be a world of perpetual peace.[4] Free peoples, Kant explained, are inherently peaceful; they will make war only when driven to it by tyrants.

Kant was wrong. Democratic belligerence is such a pervasive problem that we find it wherever democracies have existed. For example, as early as the fifth century B.C., the rocky coast where Dubrovnik now stands was the scene of deadly quarrels involving free governments. Already people of the region were sending envoys abroad to make impassioned pleas for help to fight their enemies. Corinth, a Greek republic, seized the chance to take control of a coastal town. Corcyra, a nearby island democracy, took offense and went to war. Before the affair ended the rocky Adriatic shores were littered with shattered ships and the pale corpses of sailors.[5] That is all ancient history, but it is a good demonstration that war will not be restrained by an inherent peacefulness of ordinary citizens. In our own times, democracies have burned people to death by the tens of thousands in the fires of Hamburg and Hiroshima.

Yet in all these wars, one side fell short of what most people would call democracy. The United States, as will be discussed later, never has fought a democratic government basically like its own. Neither did ancient Corcyra; its enemy Corinth was governed by an oligarchic elite that scarcely allowed more freedom to common people than did the elite who led Japan in the 1930s. The governments of Serbia and Croatia in 1991, although elected, were hardly democratic (I will get back to this later). Somewhere there is a line that divides genuinely democratic regimes from those pervaded by authoritarian ways. This line has been a line of battle time and again through history.

Can it really be true that genuine democracies, however readily they attack other types of regimes, do not make war on their own kind? Even if they have never done so in the past, is that owing to any solid reason that will reliably restrain them in the future? And if there is such a reason, can it teach us anything about how in general to conduct international relations in this world where many regimes are far from democratic?

These questions can be answered with the evidence of history. In this chapter I briefly review previous work on the subject and describe my own methods for approaching it. Then I summarize the chief results that are worked out in the rest of this book.

Investigating the Peace Among Democracies

Are democracies more peaceful than other forms of regime? Beginning in the 1960s, scholars devoted thousands of hours to analyzing wars statistically. For a long time they failed to find any general rules. On the whole, democracies were embroiled in wars nearly as often as any other type of regime. In fact, hardly anything seemed to have a major influence on the likelihood of war—not a nation's domestic situation, nor its economic position, nor its ideology, nor any other obvious characteristic. Until scholars looked at the two rival regimes as a pair, they failed to clearly demonstrate any influence of democracy.[6]

Yet several scholars (including me) did notice, independently, a peculiar regularity: during the past century there have been no wars between well-established democracies. The first articles on this were scarcely noticed, but gradually a few political scientists took up systematic study.[7] Their findings remained almost unknown outside academic circles. After all, there were obvious objections. Critics pointed out that there were only a few dozen full-fledged democracies in the world, and most of those had not been around long. Maybe they just had not yet happened upon reasons to fight one another. Or maybe the absence of wars between certain nations was not attributable to their democratic nature at all but to a specific level of capitalist economic development, international trade, or the like.

Scholars had meanwhile compiled lists of the hundreds of conflicts of the past two centuries, assigning numerical codes to sizes of battles and degrees of electoral freedom and so forth. At first only one scholar, R. J. Rummel, approached these with an eye to the question of wars between democracies, compiling data and applying rigorous statistical tests. Gradually he was joined by Bruce Russett and others who confirmed and extended the findings. What was the probability, they asked, that the absence of wars between well-established democracies is a mere accident? The answer: less than one chance in a thousand. That is a level of certainty not often achieved with laboratory rats, let alone in studies of international relations.

These studies ruled out out the most obvious objections. They showed convincingly that the lack of wars between democracies is not an artifact caused by the limited number of such regimes—there have been more than enough to provide robust statistics (even if the democratic alliances of the Cold War are left out). It is not because of the geographical distribution of democracies—they are found mainly in Europe, hardly known for its shortage of wars. It is not because of their advanced economic development—wealthy countries fight wars about as often as poor ones. These and other variables, from alliance structures to trade relationships, certainly influence whether nations will go to war, but none have been found useful in explaining the consistent peace between democracies. Some political scientists now feel that, as Jack Levy wrote, "this absence of war between democracies comes as close as anything we have to an empirical law in international relations."[8]

Others remain skeptical. The data on modern democracies are skimpy, and they tell us nothing useful about territory outside the North Atlantic region from the United States to West Germany, the only area where democracies have a long and varied record. Worse, it is far from clear just when we should or should not call a regime a well-established democracy; it seems that in each particular case, scholars defined the regime according to personal taste. Perhaps the strongest objection to the idea that democracies are inherently peaceful is that it does not fit comfortably with other beliefs that many people hold about the way nations behave. We cannot feel confident about a statistical "law" until we understand the reasons behind it. "Nobody has much idea why this relationship exists," one scholar complained.[9]

This is not for lack of theories. Particular cases of peace have been explained by the international configuration of the times (as democracies kept peace with one another in 1945–1990 while allied against the Soviet Union). I address this idea in cases where it arises (chapter 14, for example), but we will find that peace among democracies has been too widespread for such special explanations to work everywhere. That leaves explanations based on the internal characteristics of democratic nations. The possibilities include almost every kind of psychological, cultural, social, economic, or structural feature. I give a quick overview here, reviewing the main alternative explanations more closely in connection with particular cases (especially in chapter 3).

The explanations are usually separated into two categories: one centered on "structures" and the other on "norms" or, more generally, "culture."

"structure" – but only internal

According to the first type of explanation, democracies might keep mutual peace because of something in the structure of their governments or of their entire societies. In particular, perhaps (1) constitutional checks and balances tie the hands of a leader who would hurl a nation into a needless fight. Or perhaps (2) the whole complex structure of democratic civil society constrains the government. Or perhaps (3) democratic nations, associated through international capitalist networks, find more profit in trading than fighting.

Alternatively, democracies might maintain peace because of something in the way their citizens think about things: their norms for behavior, their values and beliefs, their cultural traditions in general. In particular, perhaps (4) the common people, who in a democracy are able to hold back leaders, do so out of fear and horror of war, seeing little to gain from a fight. Or perhaps (5) the public holds back leaders from war because ordinary people think it disgraceful to attack people like themselves, citizens of a fellow democracy. Or perhaps, more subtly, (6) the leaders of democracies themselves are accustomed to negotiating and making compromises, whereas the sort of people who become tyrants are hungry for battle.

yes

Or perhaps the answer lies in some combination of explanations. The structural and the normative cannot be neatly separated, for they are only two ends of a spectrum of human forces—at one end collective and formalized, at the other end individual and internalized. These forces interact promiscuously. Courts of law and legislatures work hard to shape public ideals of behavior; reciprocally, if people did not hold particular ideals about what is proper, their institutions would be different.[10]

The job, then, is to disentangle the structural and cultural influences, to find which weigh on decisions about war or peace so as to inhibit war between democracies. Such a study requires a large and diverse body of historical evidence. I take up the task in this book—the first to attack the question of democratic peace comprehensively from the historian's standpoint, sifting every land and century for relevant evidence.

We cannot study wars between well-established democracies, for no such wars have existed. But we can look through history for whatever conflicts have come close. There were confrontations in which democracies deployed military force against one another, although they did not quite go to war. And there were wars between regimes that somewhat resembled democracies.

For example, Britain and France came close to battle in 1898 over the outpost of Fashoda on the Upper Nile. And in 1954 the United States covertly supported an armed raid that brought down the democratically elected government of Guatemala. These events were not wars, but they were close enough to make us wonder what was going on. Looking further back, we find outright wars between the French and the Roman Republic in 1849, between the Americans and the English in 1812, and so on back to the ancient Greeks, all involving regimes that had at least something in common with modern democracies. Even the most remote cases have something to tell us, if peace among democracies is truly a universal phenomenon with a deep explanation.

I therefore compiled a list of borderline cases—crises in which regimes resembling democracies confronted one another with military force. After sorting through counterexamples proposed in the political science literature, plus discussions with scholars and my own research into over a thousand works by historians, I believe that the list is essentially complete. Even stretching terms like "war" and "democracy" to unreasonably broad definitions, it turns out to be a much shorter list than one might suppose— of the tens of thousands of recorded armed confrontations between regimes, barely three dozen cases fall into this category, including some quite trivial and unlikely ones. They are listed in the appendix.

Lists of crises have also been assembled by political scientists, who dissect them with statistical tests. These tests are powerful tools, but some things (especially in the "cultural" sphere) are hard to reduce to numbers.[11] Nevertheless, in the following I refer to these studies, and also to related statistical investigations by anthropologists and social psychologists, which draw on data entirely different from mine. The results all tend to confirm the ideas I present—no accident, for I gave up any ideas contradicted by solid studies. Some of the confirmatory statistics that I mention only briefly represent years of scholarly effort.

Here I follow a procedure that avoids statistics: comparative case study. In this well-tried method, selected events are investigated with the tools of the historian until the peculiarities of each situation are understood. The method requires asking the same set of questions for each case and comparing the answers.[12] For a given crisis between two regimes, I ask: (1) How far did they proceed toward war? (2) What particular features of each regime were or were not fully democratic? From crises that at first seem kaleidoscopically diverse one can hope to sift out a set of features that vary in strict relationship with a regime's decision to make war or avoid it.

Most comparative studies look at a sample of all cases, but conflict among democracies is so rare that I have been able to include virtually every significant crisis relevant to our inquiry. A typical social science study would proceed by using features of regimes to sort the regimes into categories (defined according to a preliminary theory); then it would count the percentage of regimes in a given category that acted in a given fashion. I have instead found features that let me classify regimes in categories that give essentially 100 percent results—all or nothing. This is a hunt for truly general "laws" of history. Most historians and social scientists would call such an enterprise quixotic, and almost always they would be right. However, I am trying to study only the most deadly conflicts between certain types of regimes. In this particular subject, one can turn up more consistent laws of behavior than anyone (including me) would have guessed.

Certainly there are cases that at first glance scarcely fit any law of democratic peace: the cases gathered in the appendix. Such exceptions can be used to prove a rule, in an old sense of "prove"—to probe the rule, to test it, to uncover its limits and its essential nature. In ambiguous cases, where affairs are most delicately balanced, the underlying forces at work become especially visible.[13] In the method of comparative case study, apparent exceptions can help us to pin down exactly which features sort regimes into categories in such a way that their mutual peace obeys general rules.

Nobody could do original historical research work on so many diverse cases, and I have relied on historians who have specialized in the various periods. I consulted at least five works even for the most trivial crisis, and usually dozens. Some cases, however, historians have never studied with my questions in mind, and I had to go back to primary sources (which meant reading French, German, Italian, Tuscan, and Spanish, plus a bit of Alemannic, Greek, and Latin). It was startling how often these sources cleared things up: people of the time were acutely aware of connections between war and democracy that later scholars overlooked.

Space constraints allow me to present only a small fraction of the evidence I have found. Any crisis involves thousands of events and decisions, but I relate only a few representative ones. Specialists may find the omissions and simplifications unforgivable, but I do not think that more extensive inspections would weaken my conclusions. Nowhere do I dispute what is accepted by specialists, and where they disagree I have always found enough common ground to address my question about the relationship between democracy and war.

But when people say "democracy" and "war," what exactly do they mean? The definition of such terms is no dull formality. Definitions that divide groups into categories are the backbone of comparative case studies. The quest for categorization leads us to inspect a fabulous zoo of political communities, the more strange and remote from our own the better. As an example and a first step, let us look not at wars but at something still more puzzling: unbroken peace, in the most unlikely places and times.

Definitions of "Democracy" and "War"

Sometime around 1200 a group of mountain folk managed to throw a wooden bridge across the Reuss River in the gorge where it hurtles through the Alps. Before long the track filled with trains of mules bearing goods from the plains of Italy north to Germany. Princes began to notice the peasants and herdsmen who lived in the valleys along the new trade route. What the princes saw was a form of governance so bizarre as to seem unworkable, so unfamiliar that they scarcely knew what to call it. Many since have called it democracy.[14]

For centuries the Swiss mountain communities were only vaguely aware that they had any special political character. Everyone accepted the principle that communities should be subject to a feudal lord, in a hierarchy of nobles that extended up to the Holy Roman Emperor. Yet when one of these lords levied an unpopular tax or appointed an unpopular official, the Swiss would argue endlessly while quietly running their own affairs. Such resistance had not brought much conflict when these were bands of impoverished cowherds. But with the booming new trade through the mountains, princes began to attend to their rights over toll and tax. Certain lords assembled their knights and rode into the forests to teach their obstinate subjects a lesson. Instead they learned one: commoners in rugged terrain, standing alongside their neighbors to defend their freedom, can shatter cavalry. From the mid-1300s we can regard some of the Alpine communities as independent states, acknowledging overlords in principle but scarcely in practice.

There were not a few of these little Forest States. The first independent ones called themselves Uri, Unterwalden, and Schwyz (which would eventually give its name to all of Switzerland). Later came others, such as Appenzell and the remote Gray Leagues, making nine distinct states in all.[15] Each ran its affairs independently; usually each had its own flag and coinage. They combined with one another in a variety of pacts, but for the most part each state could and did govern itself and go to war all on its own.

These Swiss "cantons" did not have the rigorous governmental machinery of the modern nation-state. Yet they had enough government to make sure that the quarrels of clans and factions never went beyond minor brawling. In these heights, where early in the afternoon the cold shadows of mountains settled onto the valleys, the people of a village had to cooperate or perish. It was the community as a whole that managed the irrigation ditches and pastures scattered among the pine forests.

Since time out of mind, the men of a given district had gathered in a meadow one Sunday every spring. These were the most ordinary of people, but they felt entirely competent to speak their minds and elect their leaders and judges. When foreign affairs pressed they would assemble more often, listening to envoys and settling policy by majority vote.[16]

Of course these were not democratic states in the modern sense. After the assembly the men would disperse to spend the summer in high meadows with their cows; they then passed the long winter closed in wooden huts. Effective government of the district meanwhile rested in the hands of a few wealthy and respected families who had time for it. Yet these families were no distinct oligarchic elite. Basic policy was settled in open debate where almost every man had an equal right to argue and vote. Through a half-dozen centuries the Alpine valleys constituted a laboratory of independent states that we may tentatively call well-established democracies.

Not once did any of the Swiss democracies make war on another. This was not because the men of the Forest States were particularly peaceful. Time and again they shouldered their terrible halberds and trudged off to battle a nearby feudal lord, the duke of Milan, the duke of Burgundy, the king of France, or the Holy Roman Emperor himself—and usually beat them. Nor did the Forest States maintain mutual peace because they were culturally similar and had common interests. In a world where peasants from Britain to Japan habitually gathered under the command of their lords to slaughter their nearest neighbors, the Swiss restraint was a phenomenal exception. Such a durable success in maintaining peace must have something to teach us.

If this were a unique case it could be brushed off as a freak occurrence, but the Swiss democracies were not quite alone. At the other end of the Rhine lay a terrain the opposite of Switzerland's: the flat lush meadows of Flanders, dotted with sheep, and here and there with industrial cities whose winding streets clattered with the sound of a thousand looms. In the early 1300s craft guilds seized power in Ghent, Bruges, and Ypres; now commoners down to the poorest weaver or baker helped elect officials. Historians have called these governments, with many qualifications, a sort of democracy.

From the chaotic history of Flanders I extract one important fact. Although these cities had long been bitter commercial and military rivals, once they became quasi-democracies there was no war whatsoever among them. The Flemish kept this up for only half a century, however, before they fell under the control of autocrats; then with scarcely a year's delay the cities took up their old practice of battling one another. In short, looking at Switzerland and Flanders together, we see that the connection between democracy and mutual peace is not a purely modern affair.[17] Regimes could be far from modern democracies yet still reliably maintain peace with their own kind. If we aim to understand that fact, we must try to define "democracy" broadly enough to include these regimes.

To define "democracy" I will begin with a more general concept—the "republic." The old dictionary meaning of the word gives us a start: *in a republic, political decisions are made by a body of citizens who hold equal rights.* Many political scientists see the crucial feature of these rights as "public contestation" over choices, with leaders held accountable for their actions. In all such republics the citizens vote to select and remove officials and otherwise set policy, either directly or through representative councils; in all there is freedom of political expression and association, toleration of politically dissenting minorities, and the rule of law.

A lot is packed into that last sentence. Different scholars make up the list of key features in their own ways, but any brief list like this will do, simply to illustrate what "equal rights" to participate in "public contestation" means in practice.

Not all republics are democracies. The body of equal, voting citizens may constitute only a small fraction of the population. In Switzerland, for example, alongside the mountain democracies there were urban republics where only a thousand or so property owners participated in elections. By the traditional dictionary definition, a democracy is a republic in which "the people" comprise the body of citizens. This "people" is never the entire population, and the name "democracy" has normally been applied even to regimes that denied the vote to women. If required to put the definition in a simple form that fits with common usage, I would begin by calling a republic a democracy if the body of citizens with political rights includes at least two-thirds of the adult males. I explore the workings of this definition more closely in subsequent chapters, beginning in chapter 2 by reaching back to ancient Greece.

The other type of republic is oligarchy. In these regimes an entrenched elite rules over a large body of people who are part of the core life of the community—peasants, for example, or blacks until recently in South Africa, or (as we shall see in chapter 2) most of the population under many ancient Greek regimes. As a starting point, I would call a republic an oligarchy if fewer than a third of the adult males hold political rights. That leaves in question regimes in which between one-third and two-thirds of the men were voters, but these have been rare in history. Eventually I supply a definition that covers every case (chapter 7), but for most purposes the crude count of voters suffices.

The main alternative to republics, of course, are autocracies, shading off into authoritarian regimes, such as military juntas and pseudo-republics with sham elections. Another alternative is a regime in which the central government is nonexistent or counts for little, as seen in many tribes, some medieval communities, and Somalia, Afghanistan, and the hinterlands of Colombia and Cambodia in the 1990s. This is sometimes called "anocracy." I explore the borderlines more closely in later chapters, but in practice most regimes can be quickly classified as either thorough republics or something far different. In the overwhelming majority of cases the answer is obvious to anyone who takes a good look—foreigners, the populace itself, or later historians.

The other term that must be carefully defined is "war." This phenomenon is usually only too obvious, but here also it will repay us to inspect ambiguous cases.

Consider, for example, a crisis in Switzerland in 1490. The instigator was the abbot of the monastery of St. Gall, the theocratic ruler of a mountain territory. He had persuaded democratic Schwyz and other neighboring Swiss states to join him in what seemed an innocuous defensive pact. The pact became a problem when peasants under the abbot's authority resisted his tyrannical rule, and the citizens of nearby Appenzell took up arms to help their fellow peasants win liberty. Other Swiss democracies felt bound by their oath to support the abbot's traditional rights; they declared war and sent an army. The outnumbered Appenzellers held back sullenly behind their frontier, and the rebels of St. Gall gave in without a fight. This paltry and bloodless affair would scarcely be worth mentioning, except that it was the only occasion that I have uncovered between 362 B.C. and 1847 when democratic states confronted one another in arms.[18]

The St. Gall conflict hardly seems to qualify as war. But where should we draw the line? One satisfactory definition of war is *violence organized by political units against one another across their boundaries.* For this study I set the level of violence to include any conflict *involving at least two hundred deaths in organized combat.* I give further examples of not-quite-wars between democracies in chapter 2 and later chapters.

Two Rules and an Explanation

Setting aside the few ambiguous cases, which I deal with individually, from the evidence assembled in this book a few simple rules emerge.

First is an observation only slightly different from what others have reported: *Well-established democracies have never made war on one another.* I defer considering a few ambiguous cases by insisting that democracies be "well established"—I clarify what this means as we look through the possible exceptions. The only new feature of this statement is that it does not explicitly or implicitly specify "modern" democracies. The statement applies to dozens of earlier regimes that have scarcely been studied in this context.

In the vastly distant society of ancient Greece there were a number of democracies, by my inclusive way of defining the term. In chapter 2, I review their history and find not a single unambiguous case of Greek democracies warring on one another. The surviving evidence is so meager that we cannot be sure, yet it is remarkable that no clear-cut example can be found during nearly three centuries of democratic regimes—a period during which we know of many undoubted wars between these regimes and oligarchies or monarchies. Another half-dozen communities that have usually been called democracies were the Forest States of medieval and early modern Switzerland; these definitely never warred with one another. It is surprising that scholars have failed to notice the absence of wars among the Greek and Swiss democracies as well as modern ones. Any rule that holds in such an extraordinary variety of societies should have a correspondingly general explanation.

The search for explanation is advanced by a second result, wholly new and unexpected: *Well-established oligarchic republics have scarcely ever made war on one another.* Almost as completely as democracies, oligarchic republics have historically kept peace with their own kind. For example, in Germany more than seventy autonomous Hanseatic city-republics maintained absolute peace among themselves for three and a half centuries, even as they battled every neighboring autocrat. Oligarchic republics may not seem relevant to modern history, where only a few are found. Yet their amazing success in maintaining peace deserves our respect and attention.

This record imposes severe limits on explanations for republican peace. Oligarchic republics have warred abundantly with every other type of regime, including democracies. Peace has prevailed only between the *same kinds* of republics, oligarchies or democracies, as the case may be. This pattern of war and peace undermines explanations that invoke formal constitutional structures. Oligarchic republics, just like democratic ones, have traditionally had an elaborate array of formal structural checks on policy decisions, yet that has not kept them from fierce wars with democracies. Explanations that invoke domestic or international economic and social structures run into much the same difficulty. At any rate, purely economic or social explanations must be strained to cover societies as radically diverse as ancient Greece, medieval Switzerland, and our own.

A better explanation may be found by turning to the few exceptional cases in which republics did confront their own kind in arms. Whatever it is that normally prevents such conflict must have been weak or absent here. I learned about this especially in the history of Italy up to the Renaissance, a laboratory of wars fought by every variety of regime including cities resembling oligarchic republics. These cities often fought one another—leading to the only substantial set of wars that I have found among apparent republics in any historical locale. In chapters 3 and 4, I review the Italian history and find a striking regularity. The city-republics entirely ceased fighting one another in the latter 1300s, although they continued to battle cities ruled by autocrats. What was the changed factor that brought peace? We shall see that the cities before the change had an ano-cratic character, resembling that of primitive "tribal" regimes—a type of "democracy" that does war on like regimes. Evidence from anthropology as well as from the Italian and other historical cases shows that a condition for republican peace is the existence of governments that can keep private feuding from spiraling into group warfare. When I say peace among "re-publics," then, I mean among republican territorial states.

The early Italian cities had formal constitutions with voting councils. These did not keep peace until people became obedient to the structure, putting their trust in law rather than private vendetta. So we should look beyond structures to norms, and in particular to political culture.

In chapters 4 and 5, I take up this slippery subject. "Political culture," however it is defined, at a minimum includes some set of beliefs about po-litical action—beliefs about how people ideally ought to deal with one an-other, and beliefs about how they really do deal with one another in practice, when groups are in conflict. These beliefs are inseparably linked with customary practices and formal institutions. But in the narrow sense of the term, political culture stands near the normative end of the spec-trum of human forces, among private values and expectations.

What makes a political culture republican? One key element, tied up with equal rights and public contestation, is toleration of political dissent. Another element is allegiance to the republican political process itself (something that is crucially absent in an anocratic regime). Where these ideals are well established, disputes among citizens are settled not by law-less coercion, but by negotiation and mutual accommodation in the name of the common good.

People are conservative about such things. Experiments in social psy-chology show us, and common sense tells us, that we cling to our ways of thinking. We repeat accustomed practices in new situations, unless em-phatic experience convinces us that we must change. This fact suggests a key hypothesis: leaders will tend to act toward their foreign counterparts in the way they are accustomed to act toward rival domestic political leaders.

In particular, leaders of well-established republics are expert in applying the methods preferred in a republican political culture; such leaders deal with their equals at home through negotiation and compromise rather than coercion. We would expect them to try the same methods abroad. The thesis sounds simple, yet it is grounded in facts of social psychology.

This thesis seems to contradict a widely respected way of approaching international relations—the school of "realpolitik" (more recently, "neo-realism"). According to this long-established view, leaders make up their minds about something like war through rational calculations of what will most augment their nation's strength, taking into account the potential costs and gains of attacking or of making a concession and other pragmatic factors. Undoubtedly such calculations do have much to do with war and peace.

There is a straightforward way to reconcile this viewpoint with ideas about political culture. One only needs to accept, as many of the great realpolitik theorists have acknowledged, that the actions of leaders are partly constrained by their political culture. Some painstaking statistical studies (reviewed in chapter 5) have indeed found that, on average, democratic leaders tend to act abroad in a somewhat more accommodating fashion than authoritarian ones.

That is not necessarily a matter of involuntary habit alone. Leaders can rationally choose to maintain a reputation for dealing in a consistent way, whether vengeful or cooperative. The tendency of such leaders to negotiate or to apply force then becomes an objective factor, providing vital information which rival leaders should consider in any calculation. In a confused crisis this approach may be more reliable and efficient than for each side to guess how the other will make realpolitik calculations. The cost of holding true to one's ideals is thus repaid by the benefits of credible communication. When republican ideals are steadily maintained on both sides, the result can be something of the greatest value—mutual trust, where each side counts on the other to negotiate a solution without violence.

This argument so far has a gaping hole. The observed inclination of republican leaders toward accommodation is only a crude statistical tendency. Republics have violated it time after time, launching atrocious aggression against other regimes ranging from tribal peoples to dictatorships. Still more disconcerting, democracies have regularly warred with oligarchic elites, although the leaders on both sides were used to peaceful ways at home. Why didn't republican political culture hold them back? Some factor is missing from the explanation.

To find this missing factor, in chapter 6 I take a closer look at the instructive history of Switzerland, plus a few parallel cases. These show that the republican practice of accommodation applies only where the leaders of a state regard their foreign rivals as people who merit equal treatment, in roughly the same sense as domestic fellow citizens. In particular, oligarchic elites deny that democratic commoners are worthy of political equality, and readily put them down by force at home and abroad.

We meet here the universal human tendency to divide people into "ingroup" and "outgroups"—a tendency that anthropologists and sociologists have long identified as central to war-making. People normally use one set of attitudes and norms for behavior with their ingroup, and a different set, often far more suspicious and belligerent, with outgroups. That makes it crucial to understand just where the political culture of people in republics instructs them to draw the dividing line. Our main task is to locate these boundaries, to check how they compare with the boundaries between various other types of regimes, and to see how those compare with the actual frontiers that men will do battle across.

Distinguishing Types of Regimes

Watching ingroups gives us a sharp tool for dividing regimes into categories. The citizen elite of an oligarchic republic sees the bulk of its population as outgroup, a rabble which must be forced into submission. Democratic nations hold that coercion is legitimate against a much smaller category of their populations—chiefly those who are unwilling to abide by the law, namely "criminals." They may also view foreigners who reject democratic principles (despots or oligarchs who suppress commoners, for example) as virtual criminals, outside the group of "people like us."

This suggests a deep connection between domestic suppression and wars among republics. The two types of coercion almost converge in civil wars. In chapter 7 I take these up, notably that troubling possible counterexample, the American Civil War. It turns out to fit into a larger category of warfare between republics which inhabit the border zone between oligarchies and democracies. On one side of such wars we always find a leadership that lived in dread of rebellion by an internal "enemy," a group or class whose liberty would pose a genuine threat to the authority of the elite—slaves, for example. The other side, distinctly more democratic, had no such problem. We shall find that republics can reliably be separated into two categories in a manner that is consistent with their pattern of mutual peace by stipulating that *the suppression of a crucial domestic "enemy" political group as a body distinguishes oligarchies from democracies.* Throughout history, I find, each category of regime readily warred with the other kind but not its own.

Am I not making a circular argument, arbitrarily calling a regime an oligarchy, for example, only because it has gotten into a war with a democracy? Not at all: I have used the pattern of wars as a tool to discover reliable criteria for dividing regimes into consistent categories. We could call them Xs and Ys, but we may as well call them oligarchies and democracies, the terms generally used by people at the time. If a new regime arises, the criteria will allow us to place it in a category and predict with whom it will keep peace.

The threat of domestic rebellion suggests why the character of a republican regime changes somewhere between having roughly one-third and two-thirds of men voting. The key is not in the exact numbers but in the emphasis given to holding down a domestic group. Oligarchic leaders, living in fear of the "rabble" at home, have readily battled the same sort of people abroad. Democratic leaders have often been equally belligerent with elites that stamped upon common people. Indeed, we will find that the detailed histories of the cases show that the suppression of a domestic group was usually one of the central issues in the crisis that led to war.

Some may find it improbable that criteria based on simple political characteristics could be crucial in a world where so much strife seems to revolve blindly around religious, ethnic, or territorial distinctions. In fact, social psychology experiments and historical and ethnographic surveys have demonstrated that group boundaries are typically set in ways connected with political circumstances. In particular, democrats (or oligarchs) normally define even foreign democrats (or oligarchs) as ingroup, "people like us," at least in terms of what kind of political relations they expect. This manner of defining groups in terms of shared political beliefs and practices is probably an integral part of the political culture of republics.

The border between oligarchy and democracy is only one of the zones of ambiguity. We also need specific criteria to distinguish republics from ambiguous autocracies and other authoritarian regimes. A survey of borderline cases in chapter 8 finds that a definite republic would go to war with a regime whose leader commanded powers like those held by, for example, the Prince Regent of England in 1812 or Kaiser Wilhelm II of Germany in 1914. To be precise, the rulers in question held an uncontested veto over military and foreign policy decisions, and the regime forcibly suppressed domestic dissent that threatened to remove that power. This category of regime may reasonably be called, if not pure autocracy, certainly authoritarian rather than republican.

We are left with only a few other ambiguous cases of wars between regimes that might be called republics of the same kind. In chapter 9 I look these over, and find that historically a republic could war even with a regime that had recently held approximately free elections, provided the government was controlled by a leader or a small junta acting in a despotic manner. While constitutional mechanisms might function on the surface, the manifest political beliefs and domestic practices of the leadership rested on domination by force. Such regimes are easy to identify: the ruling clique executes other leading citizens to suppress their political activity, or throws some into jail and drives others into exile. We can lump these regimes with autocracies in the overall category of authoritarian regimes.

Thus everything falls into place provided we understand that a "well-established" republic is a regime that not only has formal republican institutions to allow for public contestation among equals, but also a political culture among the leadership such that governance actually uses and relies upon those institutions. In short, *we can only call a regime a well-established republic if the leaders customarily tolerate full public contestation among citizens*. We can set authoritarian regimes of every kind apart from republics simply by looking to see whether demands for loyalty are so concentrated on a leader, family, or clique that anyone, even in the citizen class, who works to have the leadership replaced is risking severe punishment.

There still remain a few cases where it is hard to be sure whether or not toleration of dissent was a reliable practice at the time of an international crisis. In chapter 10 I review these cases and find that the problem is usually that the regime was only recently created. It is reasonable not to call any republic "well-established" until it has existed long enough to demonstrate a stable, tolerant character. If required to be specific I would include as many regimes as possible in this category, while preserving the rule of peace among well-established republics of the same kind. *When toleration of dissent has persisted for three years, but not until then, we can call a new republic "well established."* For there have been no wars between democracies more than three years old (aside from a few doubtful ancient Greek cases), and wars between such oligarchic republics have been exceedingly rare (only two or three ambiguous cases exist).

The way this category must be circumscribed is instructive, for protorepublics less than three years old do fight wars with republics. Whatever normally inhibits confrontations between republics is evidently weak when a republic is born, but rapidly becomes stronger. Just what is this thing that was not "established"? The republican constitutional structures, the elections and legislatures, were often operating well before the war broke out. That is further evidence against the proposition that constitutional features necessarily make for peace. They are only a precondition. Another and decisive factor is something set in place more gradually—but not the sort of social, economic, or cultural change that takes decades to develop.

The most likely candidate for this factor is the political culture of the leadership. If there is to be a stable republican government, the new leaders must rapidly learn to make compromises, or give way to people who will. This has the right time scale of a few years: partly through changes in personnel, partly through personal changes, new beliefs and practices for managing conflicts take hold.

One important qualification remains. People may see enemies where the historian is not so sure. There have been cases where regimes attracted more hostility from a republic than seems appropriate in hindsight. In all such conflicts I find that the leaders on one side believed, not without evidence, that the other side refused to behave in the ideal republican fashion, preferring subterfuge and violence to honest compromise. The way historians classify a regime evidently matters less than what each side believed at the time. That reinforces the proposition that the perception of a shared political culture is essential for maintaining peace among republics. Fortunately, misperception has encouraged conflict only in a few cases of especially young and ambiguous regimes.

Keeping Peace Through Diplomacy

The consistent pattern of oligarchic/democratic war and peace, the type of criteria that make the crucial distinctions, and the few exceptions for new-born and misperceived regimes all suggest that the key is the political culture of the leadership. But it is not enough to explain something in abstract terms; we must check whether the explanation fits the details of specific cases. If we look at the actions of leaders in a given crisis, does their diplomatic style reflect their regime's domestic political culture? If so, does the style affect the outcome of the crisis? In chapter 11 I review the few relevant social science studies, which agree that on average these effects are real. But that is only suggestive, and such things are difficult to measure. I approach the problem through the investigation of individual cases. This method does not line up features of cases alongside one another, as in the method of comparative case study, but tries to understand directly the mechanisms at work. My approach is to ask a counterfactual question: "If that regime had conformed to a different political culture, would its leaders have negotiated differently, in such a way as to change the chances for war?"

Such a question can be answered wrongly for a given crisis, but if one finds a plain connection running from the political culture to the negotiating style to the outcome, and finds such a connection in crisis after crisis, then it becomes plausible that political culture provides the explanation for democratic peace. That takes us far enough for practical purposes—in the end the best we can hope for is to find an explanation plausible enough to suggest which factors people should take into account in the real world.

Such anecdotal evidence, displaying political culture as a major diplomatic factor, is presented in cases throughout the book, but I focus on the question in chapters 11 through 13. First I give some examples of diplomacy between republics and autocracies and between autocracies. I picked cases that would provide the toughest test, drawing from my list of borderline cases plus some additional cases that have been exceptionally well documented by historians.

The results can only be impressionistic, but the impression is very clear. In negotiations each regime did tend to behave according to its political culture. Time and again we observe authoritarian leaders undeniably extending their domestic style of behavior abroad by using coercion rather than seeking mutual accommodation, in ways that made war more likely. Republican behavior was plainly different—so much so that in quite a few cases the difference created an "appeasement trap." The republic tried to accommodate a tyrant as if he were a fellow republican; the tyrant concluded that he could safely make an aggressive response; eventually the republic replied furiously with war. The frequency of such errors on both sides is evidence that negotiating styles are not based strictly on sound reasoning.

Republics can turn willfully bellicose. In chapter 12 I offer examples of republican leaders acting belligerently and even abusively from the very outset. In every case, however, this behavior was incontestably connected with their conviction that the rival regime was far from republican, and hence fit to be coerced. Some examples of negotiation among undoubted democracies leave a contrasting impression, obvious and consistent, of a less belligerent style of diplomacy.

There remain a few troubling confrontations—not wars but serious nonetheless—in which democracies acted belligerently toward other democracies. In chapter 13 the problem is identified as a conflict between ways of defining the ingroup. Leaders may decline to see others as "people like us" simply because they are dark-skinned, for example, or Catholic, or born on foreign soil. Such prejudiced identifications may displace the principle of republican ingroup solidarity. The danger is greatest in imperialist situations where local affairs are put in the hands of a hierarchical subculture such as the military. Fortunately, none of this has brought war except where one regime was so poorly established that there were excellent grounds for doubting that its leaders should be considered republicans.

If well-established republics do not fight their own kind, just what sort of diplomatic relationships do they form with one another? Chapter 14 surveys comprehensively a record of republican confederation—hitherto overlooked so far as I know—which reaches back to the ancient Greeks. A remarkably large number of cases can be summarized in a final generalization, new and important: *Republics and only republics have tended to form durable, peaceful leagues.* Wherever in history several republics were found, they surrendered some degree of sovereignty to international councils of representatives who negotiated and voted as equals. The spectacular record of republican confederation is further evidence of a powerful tendency for political culture to extend from domestic into foreign affairs, among those who perceive each other as equals. Republican leaders establish the same kinds of mechanisms for peaceful decision-making internationally that they are familiar with domestically. This confounds realpolitik theory, which sees alliances and other forms of maintaining peace as simply a matter of balancing material forces against some external threat (as NATO countered the Soviet Union). That cannot explain why alliances among authoritarian regimes are far less stable.

It would be easy to conclude that we may find security from war by striving to create more democracies. The idea is an old one, yet even historians seldom recognize how often democracies have thrown themselves into just such efforts, from ancient Greece to our own day. In chapter 15 I give a historical survey—again, to my knowledge the only comprehensive one to date—of the results of such democratic crusades. The policy has often been successful, but more often it was applied with too heavy a hand and failed. Any attempt to impose democratic regimes by force can also undermine a more immediate goal: fostering an international "republican" political culture of peaceful negotiation.

This has been only a sketch of my argument, and much will become clear only as we look over borderline cases. It is there above all that we will turn up all the clues we need to solve the puzzle. The puzzle, that is, of exactly how well-established democracies like the Swiss Forest States could maintain centuries of peace, and precisely where there are defects in democracies that make the streets of their cities shudder with explosions.

CHAPTER TWO

Ancient Greece: Definitions and a Pattern of Peace

In 413 B.C. an army of desperate Greeks set off on their last march. These were men of Athens who had sailed all the way to Sicily to attack Syracuse, the island's chief power. In three years of bloody struggle, the Athenians had failed to penetrate the city's massive walls, and now they were retreating. But Syracusan troops were ahead of them, waiting at the dry mountain passes behind makeshift walls of stones. A number of the Athenians battled through and marched on until they arrived at a river. Possessed by thirst, the men broke ranks and crowded in, trampling one another, drinking even as the water became fouled with mud—and then with blood, for the enemy caught up with them here, charged down the river bank and slaughtered them. Of the tens of thousands of soldiers who had come to Sicily, only a handful ever saw Athens again.[1]

It was a unique case, according to its historian, Thucydides: the only time that Athenians had warred against a "democracy like themselves."[2] Anyone speculating in later years about a rule of peace among democracies might well have been brought up short by that plain phrase in Thucydides' famous history. In the twenty-three centuries since, there has been no better case of a war between well-established democratic states—if that is really what it was.

To use such cases for testing the limits of the rule, we first need a rough agreement on what we mean by terms like "war" and "democracy," looking more closely than I did in the first chapter. Scholars have not been able to agree on specific definitions. However, almost any of the ones proposed over the years would work for our purpose.[3] In all but a small minority of cases, careful observers are likely to agree on whether there was a war, and whether both sides were democracies, if they just take the words as most people use them in everyday speech. Still, we must be precise in order to make sure that we do not arbitrarily rule out genuine cases.

Ancient Greece: War and Not-Quite-War

First, a definition of war. The conflict between Athens and Syracuse was plain enough, but other cases can be fuzzier. Consider the only other conflict in history that seems on the surface to plainly refute the rule that well-established democracies have always kept peace with one another. In 369 B.C. the Athenian democracy declared war on its neighbor, Thebes, well aware that Thebes was also thoroughly democratic, but fearful of its expanding strength.[4] Did calculations about balancing power, this once, bring democracies to war?

That depends on what we mean by war. Ordinarily a Greek battle was hard to mistake. Soldiers in the ranks would find themselves facing a mile-long wall of shields, bristling with sharpened spear blades. The men would be sick with fear, knowing well that to attack would plunge them into a maelstrom of screams and blood. Unless the troops could be filled with the fiercest determination, they would never raise their war chant, break into a pounding trot and throw their bodies against a deadly shield-wall.[5]

This kind of determination was notably absent whenever Theban and Athenian armies approached each other. The war actually began with Thebes invading Sparta, which was no democracy. Athens marched to the aid of the Spartans, but the Athenian commander unaccountably let the Thebans slip away. During the entire campaign they had only one skirmish, resulting in perhaps twenty deaths. The following year Thebes again fiercely warred against Sparta while Athens failed to fight effectively. The only noteworthy engagement between men from the two democracies was a brief melee that neither side had planned; the number of deaths is not recorded but there cannot have been many. So it continued for years, with armies marching back and forth, warily observing one another from a distance. The Thebans also built a powerful navy, but it only skirted cautiously around the Athenian fleet.[6]

At last, in 362, there came a great pitched battle. The Spartans and their allies, including the Athenians, formed their long wall of shields. Facing them stood the Thebans and soldiers from other democracies. The Spartans and Thebans hurled themselves at each other for hand-to-hand sword fighting, awful and unremitting. By the time the valiant Spartans gave way, thousands of corpses lay piled in drifts. By any definition this was war. But it was a war only of Thebes against Sparta: a democracy against a repressive oligarchy. The Athenian infantry had not joined the charge. After some skirmishing they had backed away and watched from a hillside.[7]

So much for the clearest example in all history of a battle in which people on both sides would have acknowledged that they faced an established democracy much like their own. In seven years of confrontation between massive democratic armies and fleets, there were probably no more than a few hundred casualties, and quite possibly fewer. It is a far cry from the central conflict of those same years, the tremendous struggle in which the Thebans destroyed Spartan power forever.

Democratic armies did not confront one another again until the squabble between Appenzell and the abbot of St. Gall in 1490, when, as I described in the previous chapter, nobody was killed at all. There was another gap of centuries before the next such confrontation, in 1847. That one was again between Swiss combatants, who were still arguing over the prerogatives of the Catholic hierarchy.

At the time Switzerland was divided between liberal freethinkers and Catholic conservatives, both so impassioned by political and religious hatreds that some states declared war on others. On both sides were regimes that might be called democratic, although they did not always fit neatly into that category (for details see the appendix). More than a hundred thousand men put on their uniforms and marched, Catholics against liberals, through the fields and forests, shooting off tons of ammunition. They did not take good aim. The maneuvering ended in under a month with the loss of fewer than a hundred lives. As more than one historian has remarked, the so-called battles seemed less like mortal trials than neighborhood brawls.[8]

It is remarkable how these democratic regimes, even after mobilizing powerful forces against each other, failed to actually cause much bloodshed. We find such peculiar reticence in more than a dozen of the military confrontations listed in the appendix.[9] Generally the military activity was an extension of diplomatic threats through a mere display of force. Do these incidents merit the dread name of war?

Political scientists have converged on a narrow range of definitions for war, from which I extract the one given in chapter 1: violence organized by political units against one another across their boundaries. The key factor is the level of violence. Some political science studies have set an arbitrary cutoff of one thousand battle deaths for such a confrontation to be called a war. To be sure of missing nothing of any importance, and to gather a few additional cases for study, I set a lower cutoff of at least two hundred deaths in organized combat among troops of the two nations in question. Any confrontation below that level is not the tremendous international problem called war. To place something like the Swiss civil conflict in the same category as, say, the Korean War would be an insult to the moderate Swiss, and would devalue the suffering of hundreds of thousands of families affected by genuine wars.[10]

We must not forget deaths among the civilian population, such as people starved to death in a besieged city. Historians cannot quantify these deaths with the same precision as those in combat, but I include such cases whenever civilian deaths seem to have climbed above a couple of hundred.

The toughest problem is distinguishing international warfare from domestic strife. In many historical locales, down to modern Yugoslavia, observers have found it hard to say whether a particular army belonged to an independent nation or only to some rebel faction.[11] These conflicts are often grievous, and we should not brush them aside with a narrow definition of war. But neither should we become bogged down in the small everyday violence of dissidents and police, be it the killings in Northern Ireland or the still worse bloodshed in Washington, D.C. I will not call a conflict a war unless there were organized armies in open battle across frontiers, if only the temporary frontiers that appear in the course of a civil war. This is not just an arbitrary way to rule out cases, but essential to determining where the limits of peace are found. For we will see later that understanding a state's control over a territory is central to understanding peace.

Defining the Republic

Suppose for the moment that we really can identify a set of governments that never make true war on one another. The next question is, what are the precise traits that distinguish this fraternity of peace? Here we risk an empty circular argument: "Democratic governments are defined as those that do not make war on one another"! To avoid that, we must find features held in common to all the governments within the peaceful set, traits they do not entirely share with regimes they war upon. Whatever we call the governments sharing these features, the existence of a consistently defined category of regimes keeping mutual peace would be a momentous discovery. I will show that there is such a group of regimes, and that the features they hold in common are what most people would call democratic traits.

It will pay to begin with a more general concept—the "republic." The traditional definition contrasts republics with autocracies, pointing to decision-making by a body of citizens with equal rights.[12] According to a widely used formulation developed by Robert Dahl, the essence of republican decision-making is "public contestation," that is, open competition among political choices. A group critical of those in power must be free to speak out, to propose its own solutions to problems, and to offer themselves as candidates for office. A related definition, favored by some writers, is that in a republic the leaders are "held accountable" to the citizens for their public actions. In practice this means that there exists a regular procedure to remove an unsatisfactory leader from office. We thus define, a little more precisely than in chapter 1: *a republic is a regime where political decisions are made through public contestation by a body of citizens who hold equal rights.*[13]

Athens, whose government was so alien in most ways from our own, provides as good an example as any. Not only were its leaders constantly elected and removed, but most issues were subject to immediate contestation by the citizens as a body. Open debate over foreign affairs was especially prized.[14] A good example was the way the Athenians decided in 415 to invade Sicily. We may picture the citizens gathered by the thousands to sit on a stony hillside, listening to speakers declaiming from a platform below. They hear a report from experts just back from a trip to Sicily, and vigorous debate among leaders of the various political factions. Some ordinary citizens also take a turn, interrupted by applause or heckling. Finally the people raise their hands to vote. The expedition will go forward.

In all such republics we find the citizens selecting their officials and choosing among policies by voting, either directly or through representative councils. Politically dissenting minorities are tolerated; those who lose one election can hope to win the next. Furthermore, we always find rule of law, with the judges at least partly independent of the top executives (in Athens trials were decided by a juries of citizens chosen by lot). On the ideological plane, we find people refusing to pledge obedience to any prince or dictator. The focus of loyalty was what the Romans would call the *res publica*: the "public thing," or the sum of the institutions and laws and the citizen body itself.

There exist regimes that permit quite a wide range of verbal opposition and hold elections, yet use state powers to make sure that no serious opponent can actually be voted into office. That is not the kind of "contestation" that counts. Free speech, voting, rule of law, and the like are only necessary conditions for putting into practice the essential element of a republic: decisions made in open competition among a body of citizens with equal political rights.

Autocracies, and less clearly defined authoritarian regimes such as military juntas, to varying degrees may resemble republics by allowing some public contestation. Such ambiguities need not cause problems of definition. Tightly restricted elections (like those of Iran in the 1980s) fool few people; in nearly every case the populace, foreign observers, and subsequent historians all find it easy to judge whether the regime is a true republic. Yet many writers are uncertain what to call a regime where a strongman has the support of the majority, and could win a fair election, but has clamped down on opposition so that his rule is not truly contested. Our inquiry must find a precise definition of the necessary features of a republic. The exercise will point us to the actual mechanisms that make for peace. From here all the way through chapter 10 we will be occupied with rooting out these features by sorting through a variety of regimes.

The first step is to distinguish the two main types of republic. All democracies are republics, but many republics have not been democracies. The body of equal citizens may constitute a ruling elite made up of only a small fraction of the population, voting among themselves but allowing little say to everyone else. There is a second dimension to democracy, what Dahl calls "inclusiveness": who has the vote and who does not.

The Greeks invented the word democracy, and their definition roughly corresponds to what we find in dictionaries today. In a democracy the *demos,* "the people," comprise the body of citizens with political rights. But just who are these "people"?

In the pure democracy of political theory, the citizen body includes all competent adults.[15] No such democracy exists. People have commonly called a regime a democracy even though it denied the vote to numerous immigrants and migratory workers (like the modern United States) along with their children (modern Germany), or the indigent in general (Britain around 1900), or even women. Such non-citizens may be a minority marginal to the main business of the community, like recent immigrants. Or, like women, they may be so thoroughly integrated into every level of society that the voters can be presumed to fairly represent them—if not for certain issues, like women's rights, which involve the distinction itself, then at least in such matters as foreign affairs. People have usually seen democracy wherever respectable working men, those who spend their day with hammers or hoes, have by right a meaningful voice in government.

If required to put a definition in a simple form, I would say that a republic is undoubtedly a democracy if the body of citizens with political rights includes at least two-thirds of the adult males. Such a definition embraces not only scores of modern nations but also a good many earlier regimes which were otherwise radically unlike modern nations.

The definition becomes clearer when democracy is contrasted with oligarchy. In an oligarchic republic, equal rights apply only to a relatively narrow group, decisively privileged above other important groups who are part of the core economic and social life of the community. The ruling group has typically been an elite of aristocratic landlords and wealthy merchants, defined by some combination of birthright and property. In a few cases political power has been bestowed by right of ancestry alone, as in ancient Sparta, seventeenth-century Poland, modern South Africa (until recently), and Kuwait. We might also include those self-selected elites, theocratic or Communist, who rule through voting councils but are privileged above the masses by their supposed dedication to an ideology.

If required to state a simple rule, I would say that a republic is undoubtedly an oligarchy if fewer than a third of the adult males share political rights. What of regimes in which between one-third and two-thirds of the men have such rights? It happens that in all history there have existed only a handful of such regimes—probably because it is an unstable configuration. We will inspect these few exceptional cases with special care, for we must eventually dig past simplistic numerical definitions to criteria that reflect the underlying human forces.

A good place to begin is ancient Athens. The citizen body excluded slaves and a large group called the "metics," mainly people of foreign or slave extraction. Historians have only the crudest numbers, but a common guess is that among the men there were roughly equal numbers of citizens and non-citizens. That would put Athens in the ambiguous zone between democracy and oligarchy.[16] So we must take a closer look at life in Athens. If you had met an Athenian on the street in those days you might have found it hard to tell his status: this porter in filthy rags is a voting citizen, that elegant banker is somebody's slave. The citizen might someday be enslaved through conquest or debt, the slave might win freedom or even citizenship rights. The metics were even harder to tell from citizens—they marched with them in war, and occasionally won full political rights. Thus metics and slaves were so interwoven through the community that their views on most issues were probably represented by the votes of the citizens, who typically worked alongside them under similar conditions. Some scraps of evidence indicate that in foreign affairs and even in class conflicts, Greek metics and slaves indeed lined up politically with the mass of common citizens. It reminds us of the way nations until very recently could deny women political rights yet still be considered democracies.[17]

The Athenians, in short, had some reason to claim that their government followed the will of "the people." If an Athenian could visit a modern democracy, if he saw how our elections are largely determined by large sums of money spent on advertising, if he learned how policy is made behind closed doors with corporate lobbyists close at hand, he would exclaim that Athens was the more truly democratic regime.

The case remains problematic, and in chapter 7 I seek a more precise distinction between democratic and oligarchic regimes. For the moment, let us call Athens and any similar Greek states democracies, making our definition so broad that we cannot overlook wars between any republics vaguely resembling democracies. The next question is what any of this could possibly have to do with an actual decision to make war.

Syracuse and the Causes of War

When the Athenians sent their forces into Sicily they were driven by a calculus of power. Syracuse had been supporting Sparta, the mortal enemy of Athens, with grain and ships. Besides, a war would create jobs for poor Athenians as soldiers and oarsmen, and victory would open up territory in Sicily for land-starved peasants. The rich were even better placed to profit from the economic stimulus provided by war and from the fruits of conquest. Beyond such practical concerns, humans are easily driven to fight, as the Greeks well knew, by community pride and ethnic hatred, by personal ambitions and fears, and by sheer blood-lust.[18]

In such matters of grand strategy almost any force impelling a democracy toward war—social and economic motives, cultural factors, innate biological drives, and so forth—has a counterpart in an oligarchy, monarchy, or dictatorship. There is no way here to advance our inquiry. When political scientists have attempted to analyze the causes of wars, they have generally found a variety of forces pulling this way and that. For one group of regimes, dynastic marriage alliances seem to have mattered above all else, for others it was the clash of political or religious ideologies, for yet others the key factor was a struggle for overseas trade.[19] Everywhere the "realistic" factors of risk and potential gain, of the balance of powers and alliances, undoubtedly play a leading role. Fortunately we do not need to sort out the manifold possible causes of wars. We seek only a special factor that prevents wars between democracies.

For the attack on Syracuse, all the strategic and economic concerns were old news by 415. But if we look to what the Athenians themselves gave as their immediate reason for going to war, we do find a reference to democracy. The debate in the Athenian assembly revolved around a conflict taking place in the Sicilian city of Leontini. The oligarchic landowners there had been fighting a democratic faction and had called in troops from Syracuse to help them. Now envoys of the democrats of Leontini stood before the men of Athens to appeal for aid. For generations afterwards the Athenians would claim that they had gone to Sicily to fight for the freedom of the people of Leontini.[20] Of course the Athenians' main concern was strategic and economic gain. Yet they had a pragmatic reason for remembering the appeal from democrats.

A war begins only when each side estimates that it has more to gain than to lose by fighting. Around this truism, modern political scientists have developed elaborate theories, but the primary question has always been obvious: what forces could each side mobilize?[21] When the Athenians made this calculation, it was crucial that they expected to find allies on the spot in Sicily—and even within the walls of Syracuse itself.

To capture a Greek city was a daunting task. The Greeks had no effective siege machinery to get through the massive stone walls. Starving out the enemy could take years, if the attackers' own troops didn't starve first. It was far better to have allies within the city who would secretly open a portal to let in soldiers. Greek cities were in fact riddled with factions prepared to seek outside help against their political rivals. In the twenty-seven years of the Peloponnesian Wars, a modern historian counted some twenty-seven overt betrayals of cities.[22]

Thus the Athenians had reason to consider the political conditions in any state they hoped to conquer. The assembly was told that Syracuse was crowded with a heterogenous populace "in a state of violent factional strife." But wasn't Syracuse a regular democracy? So said Thucydides afterwards. However, our historian seems to have stretched the facts in order to make a rhetorical point—namely, a warning against wars between democracies.[23] Only one scholar ever possessed the documents needed to study the constitution of Syracuse: Aristotle. He carefully avoided calling Syracuse as it existed in 415 a democracy. Rather he styled it a "polity," by which he probably meant a mixed regime—one with superficially democratic elections, but with an oligarchic elite hanging onto effective control. Only after the Athenians were defeated was the constitution revised so that democratic leaders were fully in power. What the Athenians saw in 415 was a city in some intermediate state of disunity.[24] That was the weakness they hoped to exploit.

When they arrived outside Syracuse's stone walls the Athenians were not entirely disappointed. Thucydides (partly contradicting himself) reported that Athens did have powerful friends inside the walls, looking for a chance to betray their city. The most likely guess is that they were disgruntled democrats (on every other occasion when cities were betrayed to an Athenian army, it was by a democratic faction). The Athenians might have been deluding themselves if they thought that this faction had a significant role in Syracusan politics; they knew little of that, for the distance between Athens and Syracuse was tremendous and communications rudimentary.[25] Or perhaps the Athenians understood their gamble very well. If democratic conspirators had found a chance one night to open a portal, historians might view the war very differently. In short, the Athenians believed that the men in control of Syracuse were enemies of democrats, and found that to be a pragmatic point in favor of attacking the city.

The possibility that the Athenians were wrong suggests a qualification to our rule. Rather than saying that well-established democracies do not make war on their own kind, perhaps we should say that they do not make war on other states that they *perceive* to be democracies. This is an important point, to which I will return. But first we must look at other cases to see what particular features were consistently decisive.

Democracies Versus Oligarchies

When we turn from the borderline case of Syracuse to the rest of ancient Greek history, relations between democracies become clearer. Greek states were wont to switch from democratic regimes to other forms and back again by coup or conquest. And time after time, hostility switched on and off precisely with the coming and going of democracy.

An exemplary case is the long history of relations between Athens and Thebes, a traditional oligarchy and a bitter enemy of long standing. In war after war the Thebans and Athenians slaughtered one another by thousands. When Athens surrendered to Sparta at the end of the Peloponnesian Wars, a Theban envoy tried to persuade the Spartans to raze Athens, sell its people into slavery, and turn the country into a sheep-pasture.[26]

Soon thereafter relations between the two states changed remarkably. While the triumphant Spartans imposed a repressive oligarchy on Athens, the Thebans were making their own regime substantially more democratic. When Athenian democrats rose in rebellion and the Spartans called on Thebes for help in putting them down, "the whole city voted" against intervention.[27] Soon after—barely a decade after Thebes had proposed to level Athens—the two cities, now both democracies, became formal allies. The sequence was repeated in reverse when an oligarchic faction seized power in Thebes. At once Athens turned against the neighboring regime. But once democracy was reestablished in Thebes, the cities resumed their alliance.[28]

In ancient Greece there were dozens of other occasions when regimes switched back and forth between enmity and democratic alliance, just at the moment when coup or conquest or peaceful evolution turned one from oligarchy to democracy or vice-versa.[29] Certainly there were times when Greek democracies quarreled with one another. But did they make war?

The historian feels like an astronomer looking at remote objects through a defective telescope. Here and there a sentence or two in a surviving history suggests a pair of Greek democracies at war. Yet when we look as closely as our poor telescope allows, we always find cause for doubt. One side or the other cannot be made out distinctly as a well-established democracy, or the events do not look like serious combat. Perhaps there were indeed a few genuine cases; the candidates are discussed in the appendix. But the overall tendency, overwhelmingly clear to the Greeks and to later historians, was that democracies helped one another as allies.[30]

The Greek democracies were not afraid to fight. Alongside scarcely a dozen uncertain cases of hostility between possible democracies, most of them mere skirmishes, we find several dozen unmistakable cases of appalling bloodshed where democracies confronted other types of regimes, including oligarchies and every sort of aristocracy, tyrant, king, and emperor. Often in such struggles they got material help from fellow democracies.[31] The oligarchic republics, meanwhile, got help from fellow oligarchies but virtually none from any democracy, except when they were allied against an autocrat. Aristotle later put the matter in a nutshell: "The Athenians used to suppress oligarchies everywhere, and the Spartans democracies."[32]

This tendency was not owing to the strategic or economic position of a given city, but flowed from the character of its regime. That is clear from the way alliances shifted as soon as regimes changed. For example, in 411 an oligarchic faction briefly seized power in Athens; it immediately began to replace democracies with oligarchies in whatever cities Athens controlled. Such consistent and tireless activity on behalf of one's own type of regime must be a mystery to anyone who believes that nations make friends strictly according to their "realistic" interests of economic gain and strategic position. We will see later how the Greeks explained their choices. First I must finish describing the visible pattern of action, which had another and still more remarkable regularity.

Republics at Peace with Their Own Kind

In a painstaking search I could find not a single clear-cut case of Greek oligarchic republics making war on one another. There are a few minor cases where the surviving scraps of evidence are ambiguous, and large areas of the historical map are simply blank. Yet it is clear that the Greek oligarchic republics were extraordinarily unlikely to fight regimes of their own kind. Meanwhile they regularly battled democracies, tyrants, kings, and so forth.[33]

Looking more broadly across history we find numerous oligarchic republics, providing a rich mine of data. In particular, early modern Europe included over a hundred city-states that were oligarchic republics, from Amsterdam to Danzig to Venice. When I scrutinized their histories in search of military confrontations with others of their kind, I was amazed to find only a bare handful of cases, nearly all ambiguous.[34]

This record yields a new general observation. *Well-established oligarchic republics have scarcely ever made war on one another.* Very nearly as completely as democracies, oligarchic republics have kept peace with their own kind. As with the peace among democracies, this is not a finding of statistical probability but a declaration covering all relevant cases. The appendix lists every exception I have been able to turn up. A detailed look through these possible counterexamples reveals that few have much substance.

Oligarchic republics may seem scarcely relevant to modern history, where only a few are found. Yet their amazing success in keeping at peace deserves our attention. Anything that holds reliably for such a remarkable variety of societies, from ancient Greece to early modern Germany, must have a general explanation which can tell us much about what shapes international relations. In particular, the oligarchic peace imposes severe limits on explanations for the absence of wars between democracies.

Oligarchic republics do war with democracies. Indeed, in virtually every historical locale where a democracy and an oligarchic republic came into contact, they warred fiercely. This constrains still more the range of possible explanations.

Most students of international affairs would look for "realistic" factors involving the balance of powers and alliances, economic relationships, and the like. Such factors can often plausibly explain particular wars, like the Athenian invasion of Sicily. But such explanations depend on specific local circumstances. Only by an incredible series of coincidences could such factors explain peace between oligarchies and between democracies, and only such regimes, for scores of independent states scattered throughout the centuries. Moreover, cities quite often changed their regimes, now democratic, now oligarchic, now autocratic, with factors like the geographical and economic positions remaining the same. How then could such factors explain a pattern of war or peace that corresponded only to the type of regime?

We cannot learn much more by examining ancient Greece. Our evidence is slight, and ends abruptly when Roman legions shut off the Greek democratic experiment. For better evidence we must push forward in time to another group of republics. The next ones we meet are radically different from the Greeks, and almost as strange to modern eyes. They can take us a long step toward conclusions that might hold for every kind of republic.

CHAPTER THREE

Medieval Italy: Wars Without States

In 1257 the city of Bologna concluded a war by sending an embassy to a neighboring town. Bologna was not represented by a nobleman, as was customary, but by a commission: a shoemaker, a leatherworker, a fisherman, and a blacksmith. The idea that a community of ordinary men could manage their own affairs, an idea dead for a thousand years, had returned.[1]

Medieval Italy offers us cases equally distant from the ancient and the modern worlds. An Italian city would have looked as strange to a citizen of ancient Greece as it does to us. An approaching traveler would see, rising behind the city's circling wall, a hundred slender towers soaring like masts in a giant's shipyard. These were the fortress homes of noble clans, who mobilized their retainers to battle through the streets and besiege one another's towers. While the architecture is different, these treacherous attacks would have looked familiar to the factions of ancient Thebes, and likewise to the clans of modern Lebanon.

Alongside the feuding was a less violent tradition of republican ways, which the traveler would notice when he came to the market square. At first his attention is caught by the gestures of mountebanks, the displays of fruits and meats, the cries of a sudden knife fight. But off to the side he sees a clutch of merchants discussing the latest news from Milan and Rome: the duke demands this, the pope demands that, what are we to do? Nearby is a table where a highly bred nobleman is buying gloves from a leatherworker with callused hands—and discussing the news, for these men too are members of the city's governing council.

Many northern Italian cities were run by merchants, apothecaries, craftsmen, butchers, and the like—in short, by burghers. They had gradually forced the nobility to give them a large share of power. Hundreds and sometimes thousands of citizens held equal political rights, with mechanisms in place to prevent anyone from monopolizing power. Officials were selected by fabulously complex systems that included not only voting by the public and by elected councils, but also nomination by trade guilds and the random selection of candidates' names from a bag.

We can see an example of the system at its most developed in 1429, when Florence decided to attack the city of Lucca. War was declared only after separate debates and votes in the "Council of the Public," the "New Council," the "Council of the 131 [Officials]," and the "Council of the Commune." It much resembled the way decisions are made in modern democracies, the men sitting for hours in a chamber while one speaker after another marshaled facts and logic and worked up some passion to fill in the gaps, ending with a vote.[2]

Such equality, however, is only part of what a traveler would have noticed in the town square. There are peasants in drab homespun up from the countryside to sell their produce, and clusters of out-of-work laborers in rags lounging by the walls. These were the common people, and, as a writer of the period remarked, in politics "one does not take them into account at all." The voting citizens, the mixture of noblemen and the *popolo* ("public") of burghers, never comprised more than one-fifth of the men in a city, who in turn were outnumbered two or three to one by the powerless villagers of the countryside. This was a typical oligarchic republic.[3]

Northern Italy from the thirteenth to the sixteenth century offers a matchless laboratory of conflict involving such republics. They bickered with one another and with neighboring cities under many other types of government, from dictatorship to hereditary dukedom to papal theocracy. The cities threw themselves against one another in so many wars that nobody has attempted to count them (one historian added up 1,465 battles for 1190–1250 alone).[4] These cases tightly limit the possible explanations for how republics maintain peace.

The Italian Republics as Allies—and Enemies

Violence in northern Italy usually began at home. A personal dispute over property or status would lead to insults in the street, assassinations, and undying hatred between families. When families sought allies the normal result was exactly two rival coalitions, on the principal that "the enemy of my enemy is my friend." A man was born into a particular faction, with a hereditary duty to avenge old injuries in a perpetual cycle of vendetta. The republican city governments were usually too weak to police the violence. Often the strongest faction would seize the government apparatus as a prize, giving themselves a facade of legality as they fined their enemies and demolished their towers.[5]

Defeated families might retreat into exile by the hundreds, sometimes forming a virtual government on the move, complete with its own elected council and diplomatic envoys. Biding their time in mountain castles or as refugees in neighboring cities, they would now and then launch raids against their homeland. Politics were further internationalized as bands of exiles forged coalitions with one another and with factions holding power in various cities.[6]

The coalitions were polarized by an external conflict—the struggle for supremacy between German emperors and popes. Factions pledged fealty either to empire or papacy, if only to gain support against their neighborhood rivals. Local factional names coalesced into notorious epithets: Ghibellines for the party of the empire, Guelfs for the party of the papacy.[7] The terms were arbitrary, but a group's alignment often reflected deeply felt political preferences.

Most "Ghibelline" cities were governed autocratically—after all, the empire itself was an autocratic hierarchy, and noblemen who derived their proud titles from the empire could imagine no better form of government. Emperors might accept the support of a republic when they could get it, but they always preferred to work with a local hereditary nobleman, or failing that a "signor"—an adventurer who had seized control of a city and would gladly pledge fealty to the emperor in return for the legitimacy of a noble title and material aid.

Meanwhile, the "Guelf" factions tended toward republican councils. Their members were mostly artisans and merchants whose rights would be restricted under the imperial hierarchy. Increasingly they saw their party as the defender of "liberty" against "tyranny." This was no mere propaganda; they had reason to worry as they saw city after city forced to submit to a local tyrant confirmed by an emperor, or even a foreign nobleman directly appointed by him, backed by a garrison of tough German soldiers. The Italian city republics had a distinct tendency in their countless wars: they normally stood together against the emperors and Ghibellines. The rule that oligarchic republics tend to be allies and not enemies thus held in general.[8]

But there were instructive exceptions. Some Italian republics held so much enmity for a neighboring republic that they would align with an emperor in exchange for his support. And when the empire was distracted by internal strife in Germany, each Italian faction would strike out for its own advantage, even on occasion Guelf against Guelf. Genoa fought savage sea battles against Pisa, Pisa fought bloody war by land against Lucca, Lucca fought Florence, Florence fought Pistoia, and so forth—even while each had a republican council.[9]

A closer look, however, reveals that these wars generally arose from enmity between republican and imperial factions. An example (the only well-documented one) is a deadly feud between Florence and Siena in the two decades after 1250. It began when a popular uprising in Florence drove out the Ghibelline nobles, thousands of whom took refuge in nearby Siena. The nobles who usually dominated Siena had recently been forced to share power with burghers in a republican government. Nevertheless, Florence declared Siena an enemy and used the occasion to take control of some valuable country towns.

In desperation, the Sienese government pledged fealty to the empire in return for the loan of some knights. They went to battle, and at the first onset Florence's cavalry broke and fled (some called that treachery by aristocrats sympathetic to the Ghibellines). The Ghibelline exiles returned to Florence in triumph and set up a vindictive aristocratic rule. But a few years later the Guelf burghers of Florence again rose in rebellion, dropping stones from their rooftops onto enemy horsemen, driving their enemies again to Siena. Armies again set forth, but this time the Florentines routed their enemies from Siena, where they set up a thoroughly Guelf regime.

Throughout the grueling war, both Siena and Florence were governed by councils of men who rotated through office and voted as equals. What threw such cities against each other, one historian remarked, "was not the contrast, but rather the resemblance of political forms."[10] The resemblance was not that both cities were republics, however, so much as that both were cruelly divided within. A close look at almost any of the conflicts between Italian republics would find less a war between two unitary states than a civil war between factions, battling within the streets of their own city as often as abroad. In these battles republican burgher factions generally stood as allies against imperial aristocrats.

However, there is a single Italian counterexample where the struggle was unambiguously between republics. This was the long and bloody contest between Venice and Genoa over the rich markets of the eastern Mediterranean. This struggle culminated in 1379, when a Genoese army swarmed ashore on the island of Chioggia, right at the entrance to the Venetian lagoon, only to be starved out after huge slaughter on both sides. This conflict was not to be confused with civil strife. Both cities were governed by republican councils, which were normally dominated by a few noble families but which in the Chioggia crisis gave in to demands from burghers on the choice of war leaders.[11]

The battles between Italian oligarchic republics were the only ones of their kind in the history of the world. In this case at least, whatever might inhibit republics from fighting their own kind lamentably failed to operate.

Factors that Failed to Prevent Wars

What is it that might inhibit republics from fighting one another? As we begin to survey proposed explanations, the simplest that comes to mind is plain affinity. People clearly tend to feel less hostility toward others like themselves than toward peoples of greatly different language, religion, or the like. We shall later find a germ of truth in the idea that republics befriend one another because of a general cultural similarity. But of itself it cannot account for the peace among republics.

Culturally, the warring Italian cities of a given region were almost identical. In ancient Greece and elsewhere through history, we also find wars between culturally similar states—not to mention countless ferocious civil wars within single cities—although only in periods when the warring factions did not share the same type of republican government. Political science studies have failed to find any consistent effect of cultural differences upon warfare. At most, according to one large-scale statistical study of modern cases, cultural factors could account for only a small part (in technical terms, one-fifth of the variance) of a nation's tendency to attack or befriend its neighbors.[12]

If a shared culture is not the decisive factor, then perhaps republics refrain from war out of shared economic interests. The republics of medieval Italy, and most other republics in history, were dominated by the commercial classes, and war does disrupt commerce. A trader of any era might have echoed the cry of a Florentine merchant in 1404 after years of war: "God grant us peace soon, so that merchandise can again come and go as it should!"[13] Italian burghers were not ashamed to say that they would leave martial virtues to noblemen and mercenaries; for commerce they required peace and mutual respect. By the nineteenth century many liberals believed that there would be universal peace once power shifted from military aristocracies to the commercial and manufacturing classes. Recent theorists have developed sophisticated arguments based on the idea that republican groups find international commerce more profitable than conquest and direct exploitation.[14]

This argument cannot be dismissed out of hand, and I will return to the role of trade in a later chapter. But this factor does not solve the puzzle. While there is evidence that extensive trade between nations generally reduces the chances of war between them, it is only a partial statistical correlation in a complex system where dependence on foreign trade sometimes actually increases the chance of military conflict.[15] Some republics have not depended heavily on foreign commerce at all, while many autocracies have relied on it and set aggressive policies according to mercantile pressures. Statistical studies of modern conflicts get solid results only when the investigators look at the domestic political regimes.

In the Italian laboratory, cities such as Venice, Genoa, Pisa, and Florence went for one another's throats not in spite of international commerce but because of it. Let one city seize a mountain pass or an island that controlled a trade route, and swords would be drawn. This predatory pattern was repeated in later centuries as Britain, France, and the Netherlands sank one another's fleets from the Caribbean to the China Sea. We had better not count on the peacefulness of merchants.[16]

It is much the same with other material interests that might have deterred warfare. In most cases almost everyone from factory owners to starving peasants stood to benefit handsomely from a victorious war and to suffer grievously from a failed one. We could make a long and contradictory list of material interests without getting closer to understanding how peace could have depended on which socio-economic groups held political power.

Another common argument starts with the constitutional structure of republics. The basic idea was noted by a medieval Italian chronicler who suggested that in a particular crisis Florence had failed to declare war only because its government "by nature and ancient custom delays things, from having to deliberate in many councils." Other writers since antiquity have insisted that republican rule, with its deliberate complexities, impediments, and constitutional delays, constrains leaders who might otherwise prefer a belligerent foreign policy. It is only when a republic is dangerously threatened or actually attacked by an autocrat, this argument runs, that it can gather itself to fight.[17]

We shall meet this "structural constraint" hypothesis in several contexts, but it fails the Italian test. The Italian republican councils, more intricately entangled with formal checks than any modern government, somehow were able to declare war hundreds of times. The wars were often aggressive, sometimes sparked by no more provocation than a belief that one side had a chance to snatch a village from a neighbor. If anyone doubts that republics can make up their minds to do battle in the absence of a direct threat, it is enough to mention the colonial expansion of nineteenth-century Britain, France, and the United States. Moreover, oligarchic republics share with democracies virtually all the constitutional structures of council meetings and public consultation. That has failed to keep democratic and oligarchic republics from one another's throats on numerous occasions.

A broader structural explanation for the peace among republics is their pluralism. Republican communities are subject to innumerable pressures from independent internal groups, ranging from political parties to neighborhood churches, their memberships cutting across each other's boundaries so that the greed or anger of one group may be internally checked. Looking abroad, if tensions arise between a given group in one nation and a foreign group, a variety of other groups within that nation should have counterparts abroad with whom they want to remain friendly. How can such an entangled community agree upon war, except in dire need for self-defense? In other words, the cross-cutting ties in a "civil society" of overlapping private organizations and networks, dispersing authority beyond the control of central government, can hinder excesses of power—such as arbitrary belligerence abroad—as effectively as formal constitutional mechanisms. This argument resembles the one about unwieldy constitutional checks, but points to the structure of the whole community.[18]

It is a persuasive argument. In chapter 5 I will suggest just what the cross-cutting ties of civil society can accomplish. One thing they cannot do, unfortunately, is guarantee peace.

The anthropologist Marc Ross, studying a wide variety of societies from primitive tribes to unified states, found little evidence that pluralism correlates with war or peace. If anything, tribal societies with strong internal cross-cutting ties were not less but *more* likely to get involved in conflict with outsiders. Possibly pluralism only strengthens a community so that it is all the more ready for external aggression.[19]

Anyway, a society with cross-cutting ties is not the same as a republic. The ancient Greek and medieval Swiss democracies were simple societies, hardly entangled with private organizations, but they kept peace with other democracies. On the other hand, warring early modern kingdoms such as Great Britain and France had wondrously elaborate civil societies, a tangle of largely autonomous networks based on hereditary status, occupation, religion, and so forth, which often sprawled across the indistinct national frontiers. Above all, this explanation will not pass the Italian test. Perhaps no communities in history have been more pluralistic than the medieval Italian cities, with their clans, occupational guilds, far-flung commercial webs, religous confraternities, and more, all up to their elbows in politics, and often urging their neighbors to war.[20]

This survey of factors that the early Italian republics shared with more modern states is not helping us find what the Italians tragically lacked, the factor that inhibits war between republics. Let us look in a different direction. The medieval Italian cases border on another huge class of wars we have yet to inspect, which likewise took place among communities of free men.

Tribal "Republics"

Warfare has been found among nomadic herdsmen in the deserts of North Africa and Tibet, among slash-and-burn farming villages in the jungles of Brazil and New Guinea, among hunting bands in the Australian bush, the American prairie, and the Arctic tundra. Yet many of these tribes could be called democratic, if we were to take commonplace definitions of the word at face value.[21]

Political decisions in these tribes were made by a body of citizens who held equal rights, a body comprised of almost the entire male population.[22] Certain men would be leaders, of course, but they led only so long as others felt like following them. Decisions on weighty matters like war and peace were typically made after many hours of speeches in a council where any man could have his say—debates that would have seemed almost familiar to a politician of a Greek or Italian republic.

Scholars who have surveyed the ethnographic literature have found that tribes with such "democratic" characteristics were significantly less likely to fight one another than were tribes organized on more hierarchical or authoritarian principles.[23] Evidently there is something about a society with public contestation among political equals that restrains war against its own kind. However, the study found only a statistical tendency. Time and again, tribes with free and egalitarian governance have fought to the death against similar tribes.

For centuries some have suggested that democracies must tend toward peace because ordinary people are too good-hearted, or too timid, to fight their own sort, unless an autocrat drives them to it. This comforting belief cannot stand against the melancholy evidence of anthropology or even biology. Violence seems innate in simple human groups; even male chimpanzees have been seen to band together and exterminate the males of a neighboring group, one at a time. The most complete absence of government will not guarantee peace.

Many tribal communities had no lack of cross-cutting relationships, such as kinship, trading partnerships, and secret societies. Men would combine especially as followers of charismatic leaders.[24] Of these relationships, only the universal taboo against harming a relative worked against violence. But who was considered a relative? Often a close study would find no actual blood connection, for people tended to define as "kin" everyone with whom they shared territory and other joint interests. A mythical common ancestry then gave the group the solidarity it needed to compete against outsiders.

Conflict with outsiders might involve community needs such as hunting or farming or grazing rights in a contested territory, but usually it arose out of more personal matters. In most egalitarian tribes each man was free to do as he chose, even if he chose to raid a neighboring tribe. The peculiar idea of making a binding decision by majority vote would have seemed a wicked infringement on individual liberty. No matter what the tribal council decided, any man was free to steal a pig or a horse or a woman from a neighboring group. There was no way to keep even a minor insult from escalating to a bloody fight, followed by retaliation from cousins and friends of the injured party. Such incidents could escalate to permanent hostility between entire tribes and even to a war of extermination.[25] The same process often set tribes against civilized democratic states. The history of relations between native tribes and European settlers everywhere from America to Australia offers countless examples of wars set off by individual injuries, initiated from either side.

Such warfare remains a major problem to this day. Anthropologists commonly define as "tribal" any group in which the principal relationships are kinship bonds extended by personal allegiances to notable leaders.[26] Such groups may be found not only in jungles but in cities, armed not with wooden spears but AK-47s. They have created some of history's worst trouble spots, from ancient times to modern Somalia, Afghanistan, Liberia, Bosnia, and so forth. Political thinkers of the past, preoccupied with great nations, tended to brush such matters aside. But now we are rediscovering that it is crucial to understand how such communities fall into mayhem while better organized republics do not.

To study regimes, we must first place them in categories. Political scientists have found that nearly all regimes can be classified as one of three types. First is the authoritarian state, which includes both one-man autocracies and states run by a narrow clique or junta (more on this in chapter 8). Quite different is the oligarchic or democratic republic, whose citizens have substantial freedom and equality. Here we are concerned with the third type, the divided community where groups are not seriously restrained by any legitimate central authority. One name for this type is anocracy. Anocracy is recognized by the absence of any state, where a "state" is commonly defined as a political body that holds priority over other groupings for the allegiance of the population and for the legitimate use of force within a particular territory.[27]

Anocracy takes many forms, but for this study we can focus on territories beset by feuding groups whose members are bound together by some combination of kinship and allegiance to a leader. A recent example is Lebanon, where clans led by their patriarchs controlled politics even during the period of stable "republican" government around 1960. We find, for example, a landlord so dominant within his bailiwick that he felt insulted when a policeman tried to make him obey the rules as he went to vote—so he shot the policeman. The legal government was too weak to act against the landlord; a little later he was elected speaker of the Parliament.[28]

This looks much like medieval Italy. A map of Italy could not have been divided into distinct colored patches, but would have displayed a hundred overlapping webs of feudal rights and obligations. Even within its walls a city was scarcely more than a location shared by various corporate bodies. On a given street one might have found the factory of a cloth-maker, the cloisters of a monastery, and the palace of a noble clan, the inhabitants of each answering first to the laws of their own corporation. Guild courts closely regulated the manufacturer and his workmen; ecclesiastical tribunals jealously guarded their total authority over churchmen; the noble families acknowledged no authority except the emperor and their own code of honor. In this network the city government was only one more element, and a weak one. A powerful man could often ignore its decrees. What one historian said of Genoa in the 1200s could apply to almost any Italian city in these centuries: the true principle of government was not oligarchy, nor aristocracy, nor autocracy, but anarchy.[29]

The lack of central authority was reflected in warfare, in which the typical activity was raiding. Pillaging bands often set off independently of their city's government, and even official campaigns were largely a matter of militia bands and freebooters invading the enemy countryside to burn farmhouses and rustle livestock.

Tribal characteristics also dominated the sea wars. An example, typical in its grotesque twists, began in the 1330s, when a group of exiled Genoese raised a private fleet to menace their own homeland. Meanwhile they made a living by trade and piracy, ranging as far as the Aegean, where they fell into battle with some Venetians. What had forced the exiles away from Genoa was not the city government, but a fleet raised as a semi-private venture by leading citizens. The exiles' fleet eventually retreated into French service and ended its career fighting in the English Channel. The rival fleet based in Genoa, seeking to recoup its expenses, sailed to the East and seized a strategic island—one of the incursions that eventually drove Venice to war. The problem was not the strength of Genoa's government but its weakness, its incapacity to control the Genoese corsair clans.[30]

The Italians themselves explained their wars in personal terms reminiscent of tribal tales. For example, chroniclers reported that the fierce Chioggia War could be traced back to a squabble over precedence between a Venetian and a Genoese representative in Cyprus. Their resentment had boiled over at a banquet where the supporters of each man hurled bread and insults at one another. The food fight led to brawling in the streets, then a "punitive expedition" from Genoa, and finally war. In all such cases the chroniclers report violence arising originally in private conflicts.[31]

Modern historians believe that the causes of these wars had to lie beyond the merely personal, in a city's struggle for control of territory and the like. Italians of the time would have instantly agreed, yet they would have added that nothing mattered so much as personal kinship, loyalty, reputation, and status—factors which in the incessant feuding were as necessary for survival as bread. The stories of wars begun by an insult may have been legendary, but legends show what behaviors people attend to. The strategic calculations of state governments were not foremost in their minds.

Thus the Italian wars are not truly exceptions to the rule that republics do not make war upon their own kind, provided we make a reasonable distinction. By "republic" we must mean a "republican state." In such a republic people stand as equals not just within certain clans or factions but as citizens of a territorial state. If required to strip this distinction down to a minimum I would focus on the state's ability to restrain private violence such as raids. No matter how egalitarian a tribe or a city may be, without such a government it is no republic in the normal sense of the word.

Have we pinned down the unique factor that Italian cities lacked, which inhibits warfare among republics? The argument seems too indirect. Fortunately, the Italian laboratory gives us a matchless opportunity to pursue the inquiry further. For whatever the inhibiting factor might be, it clicks into place when we move a short step forward in time.

The Cessation of Warfare Between Italian Republics

A citizen of an Italian republic around 1350 would have taken it for granted that warfare with neighboring republics was inescapable. To his son, reaching maturity around 1380, such wars would hardly have been thinkable. In the span of a single generation republics had decisively rejected warfare against their own kind. Citizens continued to die by the thousands in combat, but only when one side was under autocratic rule. This is about as close as history can get us to a scientific experiment. It is as if some unknown chemical were poured into a flask, crystallizing the contents into a new form.

Historians have not previously recognized this curious onset of mutual peace. They report so many wars involving republics that an analysis of who fought whom seemed pointless. It cost me a year of research into the detailed history of each Italian city to recognize this crucial transition. Starting around 1350 I found very few possible cases of war between true republics, and after 1380, among hundreds of conflicts, I found no real cases at all.

The earliest borderline case lets us watch the transition in embryonic form. In 1358 Siena sent its militia to raid the neighboring republic of Perugia, honoring a treaty of mutual support with a local signor who was quarreling with the Perugians. As the armies approached each other, envoys from Florence tried to make peace, claiming it was somehow wrong for two republics to fight each other. The Sienese hoped to avoid bloodshed without dishonor, and ingeniously proposed setting a date for battle a good eight days away. The Perugians, equally disinclined to fight, declared that the Sienese had shown themselves to be cowardly and now everyone could go home. Unfortunately, as the Perugians marched away some Sienese shouted insults at them, and a few infuriated Perugians improvised a raid. Some foreign mercenaries who failed to understand the situation began fighting, and the armies fell together in a confused melee in which a hundred men died.[32]

This tragicomedy was not a dreadful "war" but a magnified village brawl. Perhaps practical questions of territorial control were at stake, but what trapped the citizens was their primitive need to defend their honor. Equally strong now, however, was a reluctance to fight that would have scandalized their forefathers.

Neither republic habitually shrank from real warfare. A decade later Perugia faced papal mercenaries in fighting that culminated in a battle where some fifteen hundred Perugians were slain. Three decades after that the Sienese, then under the rule of an autocratic duke, suffered comparable battle losses fighting Florence. Between republics in the region of Tuscany, however, the petty and unwanted fight of 1358 was the last.

Peace spread, eventually reaching even Genoa and Venice, cities notoriously slow to take up new ways. The Chioggia War of 1379 was their last combat. Although the two cities remained stubborn competitors over Eastern trade, their friendship grew so strong that in the 1430s, when the Venetians warred with the duke of Milan, one of their conditions for peace was that the duke guarantee Genoa's freedom.[33]

The most surprising peace was that between Florence and Pisa, two cities whose cycle of enmity, slaughter, and revenge, generation after generation, had seemed beyond repair. If we look back before 1350 we find Florence and Pisa boiling with medieval factional politics. Each city was governed through republican forms in the hands of a few well-born families, rival clans which maintained traditional vendettas among themselves and also between Florentines and Pisans. A typical war ended with over a thousand dead from Florence alone.[34]

Around 1350, burghers established solid governmental authority in each city. It was the ordinary citizens who worked especially hard to end violence, first of all by suppressing the feuds in their own streets. Next we find the Pisans assembling by thousands in their cathedral and voting for peace with Florence; indeed, the ancient enemies now swore a treaty of alliance.

Changes in government promptly affected international relations. In 1356 imperial troops seized Pisa and placed it in the hands of a narrow Ghibelline clique. The new leaders quarreled with Florence over feudal rights, and serious warfare developed.[35] In 1364 the Pisan populace rose and turned out the aristocratic faction. Peace with Florence soon followed, and then a friendly alliance. That lasted for some three decades, until a band of conspirators seized Pisa. For the next decade Pisa was, as the Florentines loudly complained, controlled by one atrocious despot or another. Almost at once the peace broke down again into raids and grueling sieges.[36] Amid all this confusion we find a clear pattern: amicable relations switched on and off in precise step with the establishment or fall of republican government control.

Some have argued that the belief that republics do not war with one another is illusory, for when rivalry grows dangerous between two republics they turn to authoritarian governance in preparation for combat. The argument sounds reasonable, but is backed up by few historical cases. In the

Pisan story, for example, friction with Florence became intense only after the Pisan government was overthrown by forces that had little to do with Florence.

There were many such cases in the Italian laboratory. Time and again, when broadly-based republican regimes were established in two enemy cities, they promptly made peace, and perhaps alliance. Rankling disputes were then settled by negotiation, compromise, or outside arbitration. Time and again internal politics threw one or another of the cities back into factional strife or authoritarian rule, whereupon external warfare resumed, usually within a few years. Time and again the citizens managed to reestablish a republic, and the warfare punctually ceased. These decisions to make war or peace followed regime changes with clockwork reliability, as I have found in detailed study of the history of relations between Florence and Lucca,[37] Florence and Siena,[38] Florence and Venice,[39] and Lucca and Pisa.[40]

One conflict stands out as an exception to help probe the rule. After a revolution led to the establishment of a republic in Pisa in 1495, a war with Florence developed which continued for fifteen hard years. It looks like a plain case of war between two genuine republican states. For at this point Florence was a model of oligarchy, ruled by an assembly that comprised about one in five of the city's adult males.[41]

But what type of regime ruled Pisa? The new government was the work of commoners who gathered and voted in general assemblies, meanwhile forming well-armed militias which guaranteed that everyone down to the lower classes held some control over decisions. Although little evidence of the nature of Pisa's political structure has survived, there is enough to suggest that it may have approached democracy. Pisa even appears to have granted citizen rights to the inhabitants of its surrounding countryside, a democratic feature found nowhere else in Italy of that period. This does not look like a war between republics of the same type, then, so much as an oligarchy fighting a democracy.[42]

The patricians who led Florence were determined to beat down Pisa, one of them wrote in private, out of fear that it "would escape from the hands of the lords, and live entirely under popular rule and in true liberty." It would be difficult, noted one Florentine writer, for a true government of the people to sustain the cruelty necessary to reduce such an enemy. Indeed, Florentine commoners proved remarkably sympathetic to the Pisans;

fifteen years of raiding barely produced the few hundred deaths that make what I define as war. When patrician commanders urged troops to attack in outright battle, the men stood woodenly in their ranks and refused to advance.[43]

This is not the only example of a battle unexpectedly refused. In 1449 an army from Venice joined the formidable tyrant Francesco Sforza in a siege of Milan, although Milan was a republic which had modeled its government on Venice's. Thus a battle between oligarchic republics was in the making when the besiegers stormed Milan's walls by night. But the only dead were among Sforza's mercenaries: the Venetians held back. They promised to do better next time, and Sforza prepared a new assault. On the chosen night he drew up his troops to await the Venetians, but after several anxious hours a courteous message reached him: Venice was withdrawing its army and making peace with its fellow republic.[44]

So it goes for every affair of the period that historians have called a war between republics. A close look shows either that one regime was not actually a well-established oligarchic republic, or else that the conflict did not reach actual warfare. Consider, as a final example, what historians record as a war between Siena and Florence in the 1430s. In reality, the two republics deliberately confined themselves to raiding farms. My inspection of chronicles of the conflict turned up only one death: a freebooter stabbed in a brawl with his companions over the division of their loot.[45]

It was not that the Italians had forgotten how to fight. In the same year as the Pisan revolution, over three thousand Italians died in a battle against the French king. A few years later the duke of Ferrara routed a Venetian fleet, slaughtering at least two thousand men; a land battle in the same war left some six thousand dead.[46] War followed terrible war, often involving republics, except never between republics of the same kind.

If we move forward in time we begin to exhaust the stock of cases in the Italian laboratory, for cities fell increasingly under autocratic rule. After 1530 the only republics remaining in Tuscany were Lucca and Siena, who in the past had frequently been enemies but were now staunch friends, supporting one another as fellow republics in a world where such regimes were isolated and despised.[47] Then Siena was conquered by a duke, and the only republic left near Lucca was Genoa; as turbulent centuries passed the two remained at peace. Republican government also survived in Venice, which maintained its peace with Genoa and across the Adriatic with the half-Slavic republic of Ragusa.[48]

What was it that changed in Italy in the latter 1300s to guarantee peace between republics of the same kind? From ancient times to the present, some theorists of international relations have insisted that to explain wars, we must look to the international power system. For example, peace may be preserved by the hegemony of a single great power, or by a carefully maintained balance-of-power system. That may well apply to many situations, but an explanation of this nature does not even address the pattern of peace among republics of the same kind. Certainly international systems cannot explain the Italian pattern, for the characteristics of international relations in Italy did not change significantly in the latter 1300s. It was at least half a century later that the farsighted Cosimo de' Medici and others established a balance-of-power system (which anyway did poorly at suppressing wars).[49]

Many theorists of conflict prefer to invoke some combination of economic and social factors. But historians of Italy agree that these factors scarcely changed during the years in question. By the mid-1300s the grand transformations that raised up the cities had run their course. The overall level of prosperity, the methods of commerce and industry and agriculture, the flow of goods and taxes, the relationships among classes—none of these things would change much for another two centuries or so.[50]

Yet historians do find a momentous shift taking place during this period: it was just then that anocratic regimes began to transform into states. The traveler approaching an Italian city around 1400 would no longer see a forest of tall towers, each the redoubt of an independent clan. Parties of burghers, determined to end the feuding in their streets, had torn most of them down. Now the traveler would marvel at city walls far grander than before, and rising behind these, a new cathedral dome and a single soaring tower for the city hall—visible signs of a central government and proud civic spirit.[51] Not only clans, but the guilds and clergy lost their immunities, while in the countryside noblemen were winkled out of their mountain castles. New fiscal controls, enforced by an expanded bureaucracy, put the government at the center of affairs.[52]

These occurrences were not the result of changes in the actual constitutional structure. In each city the republican councils and laws, in all their fantastic complexity, stood much as they had for centuries. The councils, however, were now taking full control. Street fighting dwindled as every citizen was compelled to answer to civil law; private raids continued only where a government found them useful tools. In the countryside each government now ruled undisputed over the surrounding territory.

The coming of the state, with its suppression of anocratic feuds, explains how one cause of war dwindled; it scarcely explains the complete peace among republics and only republics. For that we must look to a more fundamental change which historians have identified in the latter 1300s. This was the emergence of an entirely new approach to handling conflicts, whether at home or abroad.

CHAPTER FOUR

The Rise of Republican States, Ideals, and Alliances

I n 1342 a group of Florentines received the appalling news that Pisa had defeated their city in a battle. A grieving knight turned to the burgher Giovanni Villani and demanded to know how God could have allowed such a thing. After all, the Pisans were notorious sinners, enemies and persecutors of the Holy Church! Villani agreed that there was more charity in Florence in a day than in Pisa in a month, but he pointed to a different kind of explanation. In the maneuvering leading up to the battle, each Florentine faction had acted selfishly, while the Pisans had united for the common good of their city.[1]

The knight's question was medieval; in his mind wars and politics were morality tales resolved by divine command. The burgher's reply was more modern, invoking a rational human process: as reliably as a rainstorm brings a flood, so will arrogant factionalism bring disaster.[2] This was an early sign of a change in political thinking, which historians have traced quite precisely. It spread among leading groups in Italian republics between about 1340 and 1400—that is, exactly when they began to keep peace with one another.

What can something so indistinct as a new way of thinking have to do with the tumult of battlefields? In fact, all acts begin in thought, and any plan of action is channeled by ingrained assumptions and accustomed practices. To understand the decisions of national leaders we must know what principles and assumptions about human relationships guide their thinking. Some of these ideas vary according to the type of regime involved. This chapter explores in particular the ideas that people in republics have held about what principles should guide their behavior—in a word, their political ideals—and how these influenced decisions on war or peace.

Trying to analyze the thinking of modern democratic leaders is like surveying a room of flashing lights and mirrors. We are distracted by the issues of the moment and lose our way among ideas we take for granted.

Better to go back to a wholly different time. If we look at the generation of Italians who brought the republican approach to politics into a hostile world, our task becomes simple. We encounter no convoluted theoretical discourses; rather, here and there we find a phrase launched in the midst of action, the idea stripped to its essence.

Ideals of Equality and Toleration

By the 1370s Florentines had drifted into uncharted political seas. Almost everyone else in the civilized world acknowledged an ideology of cosmic order. From China to Mexico, every person held an appropriate place in a hierarchy headed by a divinely ordained sovereign. Command and legitimacy flowed from the top downward through a tiered pyramid. This is the most practical form of government, according to an argument heard from ancient times to the present day, for only an autocrat can rise above the selfish feuding of facations to impose order and unity.[3] The Florentines had begun to question all that.

In the past, when Florence had made war on an emperor they had argued that he was wickedly opposing the spiritual authority of the papacy. But in 1375 a pope's bid for power drove the Florentines to war against him; now neither emperor nor pope could command their obedience. When a leader of Florence's war council died they buried him in defiance of a papal interdict, and on the gravestone they inscribed a word to say what they stood for: LIBERTAS.[4]

This "liberty" was coming to mean not the traditional hierarchical privileges or "liberties" enjoyed by specific groups, but personal rights inseparable from republican government. The earlier city-republics had not accorded such high value to their practice of using groups of eminent men to work out a consensus. The councils were originally just a convenience for handling everyday matters, like the local conclaves of village elders, found across Europe since deepest antiquity, that settled petty quarrels and chose the village shepherd. Weightier affairs of state were supposed to be made within a hierarchy under emperor and pope. When the councils took to deciding by a majority of votes, that had been only an expedient which nobody could justify in principle, a poor substitute for unanimous consent.[5] But now a few bold thinkers were developing an outlandish idea.

Perhaps political legitimacy and authority could derive from the community itself—indeed from the majority vote of citizens?

The timing of this achievement, within the long evolution of political thought over half a dozen centuries, matches our crucial period with the greatest precision. Hierarchies came into question all across western Europe in the latter 1300s. Perhaps that was because of the emergence of territorial states where overlords seized increased powers; withdrawing a right can show people what they are losing. In town after town workmen took up arms to demand a place in the regime. In Italy, the rebels behind the first of many such uprisings seized Rome in 1347. Their leader, Cola di Rienzi, won a huge (if short-lived) following with his shocking claim that government should be based on the will of the populace.[6]

A new generation of educated youths were drawing their ideas less from religious tradition than from the recently recovered Greek and Latin classics. Should sovereignty in a city, indeed legitimacy itself, derive from the body of citizens? The first extended arguments to this effect were constructed in Perugia and Padua starting in the 1340s. In Florence we find the central idea, that liberty is predicated on the right to vote, clearly stated first in 1357.[7]

These Italians were groping for a set of concepts that would explain and justify their form of government—one based on republican ideals. Their starting point, liberty, was what in modern terms we would call the ideal of equal rights. It returns us to the core definition of a republic—a body of citizens with equal rights to participate in political decisions through public contestation. As one modern historian baldly put it, it was around the mid-1300s that "freedom certainly first reemerged as a supreme political value."

The new republican approach defined itself chiefly by contrast with autocracy. Citizens of republics were coming to believe that any autocrat was necessarily a tyrant swollen with selfish greed, pride and vengefulness—exactly the vices that made factions dangerous. Autocracy did not bring internal peace and justice after all, but only fear and discord. The real key to good governance was the establishment of equal individual rights.[8]

Many ancient Greeks had also believed that only autocratic rule could quell factional strife and bring good government. Democratic Greeks had replied that autocrats, prone to the "disease of never trusting anybody," actually spread fear, conspiracy, and murder. The archetypical Greek tyrant was remembered best for his violent fall. Democrats held that politics would be tranquil only where citizens were free from arbitrary authority. The statesman Pericles put it most eloquently in a famous oration, when he boasted that every citizen of Athens stood equal before the law as "rightful lord and owner of his own person."[9]

When this idea reemerged it spread so readily that we cannot identify its exact origin. After 1300, republican ideals and governments sprouted in a hundred towns from Italy to the Baltic Sea. The towns north of Italy were also shifting toward oligarchic republics under elected councils, and they too were becoming organized states largely free of factional warfare. When the perceptive Niccoló Machiavelli toured southern Germany he deduced that the patricians were at peace inside each town because they lived in equal freedom, "without any distinction among men" except through elected office.[10]

The ideal of equal rights is central to republican government almost by definition, but on its own it is not sufficient. Modern political theorists emphasize at a minimum two additional principles of behavior that are necessary to maintain republics, whether democratic or oligarchic. The most obvious of these is the ideal of toleration of political differences, including overt dissent. For Pericles this was part of a larger principle. "Just as our political life is free and open," he told the Athenians, "so is our day-to-day life in our relations with each other. We do not become offended with our neighbor if he enjoys himself in his own way."[11] In practice, the ideal of toleration means that citizens settle their differences through nonviolent public contestation, using the ballot for public matters and the law courts for more personal affairs. The losers of a vote or a court judgment accept defeat peaceably, knowing they will retain their most essential rights and can keep on arguing their case, hoping for revision if they argue it better.[12]

In modern times it has often been stated that a free press is essential to maintaining the principle of toleration in a republican government. But in medieval Italy or ancient Greece there was nothing like the modern press. The crucial factor is simply whether people can safely criticize their governments.

The ideal of toleration is a corollary to equality, for if you truly regard me as your equal you will not try to prevent me from speaking my mind, nor force me to obey your arbitrary command. When I am in the minority, I trust that governmental power will not become so overbearing that I will be driven to violence to protect my position, and that is exactly why those in the majority feel no need to forcibly suppress me.

All this had been painfully lacking in medieval Italy. There toleration was the least practiced of virtues—indeed, it was scarcely seen as virtuous at all. Ruthless defense of one's honor was essential for survival, if only because there was no state monopoly on the legitimate use of force to safeguard the rights of losers in elections or law courts. As states gained strength in the late 1300s, citizens changed their attitudes. The scholar Giordano Bruno, for example, boasted in an essay modeled on the speech of Pericles that Florence's citizens had become free to criticize their leaders. A Florentine merchant of the subsequent generation described in basic terms the change that had taken place, saying that the times were past when "men fought out their differences more with sword in hand than with the ballot as we do today."[13]

The Ideal of the Commonwealth

To create a functioning state people must transfer some of their allegiance away from family and faction—but to what? In medieval German cities the burghers called for allegiance to the "common weal," and they never tired of explaining that it should outweigh devotion to the private advantage of any individual or subgroup. The common weal, the welfare of all, the public interest: there are many such vague and commanding phrases.

People in all societies show concern for the welfare of their communities, a concern which is probably biologically innate. We commonly feel some responsibility for the welfare of those living in our neighborhood, for example, or for those of our own religion. Where a territorial state has established control over its population, the community to which people owe loyalty and support may become the totality of the state's citizens.

Appeals for allegiance to nation or state are issued by dictators and kings as often as by elected councils. In a republic, however, the appeal can take a special form. Citizens call on one another to subordinate personal and clan and factional ambitions, not just to the "common weal" of the populace but to something more distinctly political—sometimes named the "commonwealth." This is not the state, exactly, and still less the people holding power. People insist above all that their fellow citizens give allegiance to the commonwealth specifically as a republic, to the *res publica,* the political arrangements as such. The survival of republican government requires not only equal rights and toleration of political differences but also this third ideal—allegiance to the commonwealth as a republican political process, including the constitutional structures, laws, and patterns of decision-making.

This ideal of allegiance to the republican commonwealth can be distinguished from allegiance to the state or nation. In modern democracies such as Belgium and Switzerland, the citizens' loyalties to their religious or language group and to their locality may be stronger than their devotion to the national entity. Yet these democracies have kept domestic peace because each party is dedicated to maintaining an intricate balance, making concessions to other groups when necessary to preserve what really counts— the political system.[14]

The need for allegiance to the commonwealth has often been overlooked in modern times. Only recently have people returned to it, as the difficulty of building democracy in formerly authoritarian countries becomes plain, and as fragmentation threatens even old democracies. Citizens must put effort into maintaining equality and toleration in politics. That means managing conflict with elections and law courts—but it means more, for votes and judges can never handle more than a small fraction of our affairs. It is essential to head off conflict as much as possible at its origins, using the political process to establish a consensus on common goals through debate and bargaining with a scrupulous concern for minority rights. Where leaders follow this principle a government might be dominated by a single party for decades yet remain fully republican, as seen in many early city-republics and in modern democracies like Sweden and Japan.

The rise of allegiance to the republican political process was central to the changes in Italian city-republics in the latter 1300s. People who had once been subjects were now "citizens" (a word just then coming into use). Men who had built their lives around clan and guild found their sons more loyal to the republican commonwealth. A historian has demonstrated this abstraction with numbers: by the 1380s the names of people nominated for the ruling councils of Venice were scattered among elite families with no sign of clumping into clan factions.[15]

To list as the defining characteristics of a republican commonwealth the ideals of equal rights, toleration, and allegiance to the political system is only one way to analyze what is really a single complex entity. Some political theorists describe this entity in terms of "rule by law." However, even authoritarian regimes may practice rule by law, if only to maintain consistent administration. A person who offends the sovereign could be prosecuted and chopped to pieces in a rigorously legal manner. What characterizes republics is the rule *of* law. Above the highest official stands a set of laws determined by the citizens, acting as a body in assembly or through representatives. In practice, the rule of law is normally enforced by a judiciary somewhat independent of the executive leaders. Most important is that citizens can hold officials accountable for violating rights, not only by voting them from office, but by impeaching them or haling them into a court of law.

We need not add the rule of law as a fourth independent ideal, for it overlaps with the others. Officials and citizens who adhere to the law are thereby adhering to the commonwealth as a republican political process. The rule of law is also bound up with the ideals of equal rights and toleration, for it is law that restrains leaders from violating rights and persecuting critics. Reciprocally, whenever people abandon tolerance and like principles the courts will instantly be corrupted. Thus I feel it would be redundant to add rule of law to my list of republican ideals. The exact list is a matter of taste, for the system of thought must be understood as an integral whole.

To see the set of republican ideals tied up in a neat package, consider a ritual found in most medieval German city-republics. Every year or so the male citizens would assemble by the thousands and swear an oath of mutual support. Specifically, they promised as equals to "support and obey the laws and council of the town," or in some cases not simply "the council" but "the majority of the council."

These men believed that they were renewing a pact begun centuries earlier, when their forefathers had drawn together to defend their rights against a local despot. Actually, the oath took the men outside history, for they were symbolically reenacting a mythical time of pristine community as a band of equals. The mountaineers of the Swiss Forest States went further, claiming that they had cleared and settled a wilderness owned by no lord, and established a government based on mutual trust. It recalled the myth, cherished since ancient Greece, of the primal natural condition as an egalitarian Golden Age. Venetians, meanwhile, spun a story of ancestors who had fled to uninhabited islands and established a community by a sworn convenant. English Whigs, more recently, imagined that their liberties were established in wild forests where Saxon tribes founded self-governing settlements. The same idea inspired the Mayflower Compact, which later Americans saw as the seed of their democracy: a community of equals on the high seas creating law as an actual written contract. Eventually Jean-Jacques Rousseau converted these simple ideas into the concept of the social contract based on natural law, a theoretical foundation for republics.[16]

The German burghers renewed their oath in the nave of the town's cathedral, for the oath must be sanctified. They saw political rights as a divine gift investing the body of citizens with sacred authority. Legitimacy could flow not just downward from God through a sovereign and his hierarchy, but also upward—or one might say inward—from the public to their council. These men chanting their oath in the solemn light from stained-glass windows were certainly very different from ourselves, and their ideas of liberty involved limitations and obligations very different from our own. The ancient Greeks were more alien still. But what matters for our inquiry is identifying the ideals which are common to every single republic.[17]

To the citizen of a modern democracy, the ideals of allegiance to the commonwealth, equality, and tolerance may sound like syrupy platitudes. Surely it is obvious that everyone should live by these principles? Authorities in other types of regime would disagree. To a king or a Communist, a military dictator or a mullah, the thought of ordinary people directing their primary allegiance anywhere but to the personages in the ruling hierarchy would seem subversive. The notion of building a society on equal rights would strike them as unnatural or even dangerous. And toleration of dissent? Sheer stupidity.

There is also a divergence within republican thought between adherents to the principles of oligarchy and democracy. Those who favor oligarchic elites believe a republic should be ruled only by the few "best men"; sharing power with base commoners would bring arbitrary rule by demagogues, the unjust confiscation of wealth, even anarchy. Democratic thinkers believe in a broader equality, claiming that it is the exclusion of entire classes that brings violence and injustice. The two sides do not disagree on the ideals that republican citizens should adopt, but only on who should comprise the class of citizens.

An Enemy in Common: A Realpolitik Explanation for Peace?

Can we find a link between a republic's ideals and its decisions to make war or peace? The foremost critic of that notion was Niccoló Machiavelli, and his conclusions are worth our notice. With extensive diplomatic and military experience and a broad knowledge of history, he was the greatest of all students of the Italian laboratory of wars. Plain considerations of power, Machiavelli wrote, are what chiefly impel states to fight or befriend one another.

Many other statesmen and scholars have agreed that the driving force behind international relations is each state's solitary struggle for survival and gain. "It is a general and necessary law of nature," said an Athenian spokesman, "to rule whatever one can." This remains the most common view among political scientists, who call it the "realist" approach to foreign affairs (or more recently, "neorealist"). According to this view, sensible national leaders practice "realpolitik," that is, an undeviating pursuit of state interests. They are guided strictly by rational calculations of material factors, such as the strengths and weaknesses and geography of the players in the power game. The nature of the other nations' regimes hardly enters into such a calculation. Only fools or fanatics would allow anything so insubstantial as political ideals to cloud their view.[18]

Yet the most pragmatic, "Machiavellian" calculations of state interests have usually brought republics into alliance rather than enmity. A good example of this surprising realpolitik can be found in the Italian laboratory. The Italians developed a rational argument for republican friendship. Their reasoning relied on a new ideology—that is, a consciously articulated system of ideas and beliefs about human society, consistent with their political ideals. In the mid-1300s the Italian cities had not had any such coherent system, but by around 1400 they had developed a complete ideology. It led to a pragmatic call for republican solidarity.[19]

The way scattered republican notions were assembled into a deliberate ideology was described by the eminent historian Hans Baron. He showed how Florentine writers were driven to this in large part by their desire to argue for alliance among republics. They were reacting against the crafty and vicious duke of Milan, Gian Galeazzo Visconti, who was ruthlessly extending his power abroad. As factions in nearby towns opened their gates to the autocrat's supposedly benevolent rule, Florentines developed the first extended defense of republican governance. Turning to other republics for military help, literate Florentines praised their domestic equality, toleration, and allegiance to the commonwealth, and called on republican states to follow these identical ideals in their international relations as well. Republics, they argued, should treat one another as equals, practicing toleration rather than coercion; indeed, they should join peacefully in an international commonwealth of republics, "free peoples federated in equality."[20]

A rudimentary ideal of mutual Guelf support had already coalesced during the previous century, when city-republics joined against emperors and popes and dukes, sometimes swearing alliance against any and all tyrants. By the 1370s alliance with other republics had become the backbone of Florence's foreign policy. In the council chambers, speakers rose to declare that Florence's liberty depended on sustaining liberty in every neighboring republic. Florentines began working not only to preserve fellow republics but even to convert cities from autocracies to republics.[21]

The defense of liberty at home was coming to seem inseparable from the defense of liberty abroad. For example, Florentines promised to defend Lucca's republican form of government, declaring that it was in their interest to surround Florence with a ring of free cities. As Florentine envoys told the Venetians, they must ally against Visconti—indeed against any tyrant—precisely because both cities were republics; "The defense of Florence is also that of Venice."[22]

All across Europe in these same decades the idea struck republican cities that they should be allies. Formal alliances were sealed in a dozen locales, from Flanders to the Baltic.[23] As I discuss in chapter 14, this urge to form leagues has remained strong among republics, down to the contemporary alliance of the Western European democracies.

Most of these leagues arose out of fear of a common enemy. This demonstrates the principle of balance of power, since Machiavelli's day the central pillar of realpolitik. The Swiss, for example, confederated largely to defend themselves against encroaching emperors. Likewise, in Western Europe after 1945, according to some political scientists and diplomats, it did not matter that the allies were democracies; what counted was that all were threatened by the Soviet Union. Since the collapse of Soviet power the democracies have remained friendly, yet some doubt the friendship will endure. Perhaps peace among republics reflects nothing but a common enemy.

In truth, republics have not generally formed bonds only with fellow republics but with whatever allies they could find. Athens sometimes worked with an established oligarchic regime; Sparta struck an alliance with the king of Persia; early modern Italian republics readily joined forces with one or another signor against a more immediate threat; modern democracies like the United States have struck alliances by the score with reactionary kings and thuggish dictators. During the Second World War, both the American president and the British prime minister not only joined forces with the Soviet dictatorship but said they would ally with the devil himself if he would help them defeat Germany.

Power politics can also work the other way. Republics have frequently found themselves at odds with other republics precisely because of a nearby king or dictator, who cleverly worked to lever his neighbors apart, by offering himself as a better ally, for example. As we look into confrontations between approximately republican states, we will find that well over half were exacerbated by some meddling external autocrat, from King Artaxerxes of Persia (who helped set ancient Thebes against Athens), to King Charles VII of France (who did more than anyone to provoke Pisa and Florence to fight each other around 1500), and Joseph Stalin (who pressed Britain to formally declare war on Finland in 1941).[24]

No matter how important power calculations may be, they still cannot explain away the entire pattern of republican peace. Realpolitik teaches that states ought to form coalitions against the regimes that pose the most menacing threats, regardless of their type. Yet there are hundreds of cases of alliances between like republics, and not one unambiguous case of a well-established republic allying with a despot to make war on its own kind of regime. Moreover, republics have remained friends in the absence of any serious outside danger. The unfortified border that lies between the United States and Canada is the best known of numerous examples.

The Italians themselves could explain their call for peace among republics only by pointing to ideology. Even Machiavelli, when he got down to analyzing events, fell back on this. He said flatly that conquest and rule over equivalent states was incompatible with true republican government. Machiavelli had witnessed the mutual peace of republics in his travels through Switzerland and Germany, noting how the republics there "do not want to harm those who desire, like themselves, to be free." Just so, Machiavelli urged, should Italian cities forge a coalition to protect themselves from despots. Appealing directly to the ideal of equality, he sketched a vision of a league of republics "in which no one of them has preference, authority or rank above the others."[25]

Why did these pragmatic Italians, in the midst of brutal international power struggles, pay such close attention to lofty ideals? Perhaps the answer is that their new ideology was a surface indication of something more fundamental emerging out of the transition of the Italian cities from anocratic enemies to republican allies. We have not identified this vital something, but the early modern Italians have given us some clues. To pin it down we need other cases, as different as possible from the foregoing and from one another, in the border zone where anocratic and republican regimes look almost the same.

Republican States Without Republican Ideals: The War of the Pacific

A gigantic step in time, space, and culture takes us to another locale with a variety of regimes and all too many wars—Latin America in the nineteenth century. Our stay in this laboratory can be brief, for in obedience to the rule, the several dozen serious wars included scarcely any between pairs of republican states. Although there were a fair number of states which at times had somewhat republican constitutions, they normally sent their troops into battle only against an outright monarch, dictator, military junta, or native tribe.

There was a single exception worth inspecting: the War of the Pacific. In 1879 Chile invaded Peru, starting a war that slaughtered many thousands, although each nation was a republic governed under a constitution by a duly elected president and congress. To be specific, these were oligarchies, where perhaps one man in fifty could vote. The governments controlled unitary territorial states (at least in the periods between outright insurrections). Perhaps this case can tell us something about why such regimes might fail to keep peace with one another.

The 1879 war was provoked by an autocrat, namely the dictator of Bolivia, whose lawless depredations gave the Chileans good reason to fight him. An ambiguous secret alliance that he had made with Peru offered Chile an excuse for invading Peru as well. The Chilean leaders seized the chance because their regime was staggering under an economic crisis, and lucrative deposits of guano, valuable as fertilizer, lay in the border territories. Many things can cause a war; this one was fought over bird shit.

What sort of regimes governed Peru and Chile? Like early modern Italians, Latin Americans inherited a legacy of domestic factional violence. They sought to solve the problem through a sort of elected dictatorship. Their constitutions assigned great power to a president, who was supposed to rule for a fixed term followed by a new election. In practice, however, people found the presidency, with its total control of government contracts, offices, pensions, and graft, a prize too valuable to give up. The president and his supporting clique inevitably preferred to rig the elections.[26]

Rivals did not meekly submit to this. In the 1871 Peruvian elections the supporters of one candidate came to the polls with guns and chased away any voter inclined toward their opponents. The election four years later was decided, it was said, when one party arrived at the polls with modern Winchester carbines while their opponents had only revolvers. A show of weapons did not always suffice; sometimes groups seized ballot boxes by storm. In the 1886 Chilean elections forty-six people were reported killed.[27]

If a prominent group could not seize the electoral apparatus, they turned to greater violence. The history of nineteenth-century Peru, Chile, and their neighbors is littered with coups and insurrections. Entire private armies were raised through personal and family loyalties. After each bout the losers typically went into exile, becoming living demonstrations of a regime's inability to make peaceful compromises. At the time of the 1879 war, in all of Latin America only Chile was occasionally held up as a "model republic" with a true constitutional regime, which was all of two decades old. That was a mirage: the next ferocious Chilean civil war was to begin shortly.[28]

These actions faithfully reflected political ideals. Only a few intellectuals spoke up for equal rights and toleration. Most men saw more virtue in attaching oneself to a leader with all the stern authority of a medieval Italian signor, a man who would impose stability and compel unity by rewarding his friends and stamping upon his enemies.[29] A Chilean example was Domingo Santa Maria, who was banished not once but twice for helping to lead insurrections that cost thousands of lives; in due course he returned in honor and was elected president. Equally tenacious was the Peruvian Nicolás de Piérola, who launched private military expeditions against his homeland from Chile, where he was in exile. Piérola's bloody efforts to seize power did not discredit him; after the war against Chile began, Peruvians welcomed him back as dictator.

In short, the leaders of these nations valued shrewd intrigue above frank exchange of opinions, decisive action above compromise, and coercion above the accommodations of pluralist politics. Latin Americans themselves often pointed out that their elites rejected republican governance based on the northern European model. Men related to one another not as equals but within a personal hierarchy of patronage and power, where a willingness to compromise could be viewed as a sign of intolerable weakness. At one point Piérola secretly wrote a supporter that he was seeking men "who know only that they can have confidence in me," men whose primary qualities must be "boldness, decisiveness and loyalty." These are the characteristics stressed in certain tribes and factions, where everything depends on personal relationships and the defense of honor.[30]

This is only one example of a general affinity between certain kinds of authoritarian and anocratic regimes. The sort of anocratic regime in which lawless factions are dominated by chieftains has often alternated with rule by dictator or junta. In such instances the only reliable loyalties are to kin: Italian signors, Latin American caudillos, and modern dictators from Syria to the Philippines have all appointed their nephews or brothers-in-law to key posts, while contemporary Asian and African juntas have more broadly relied on people of their own ethnic subgroup.[31]

The ideal of peacefully abiding by free elections gradually penetrated many Latin American nations, including Chile and Peru. Wherever the nations managed to build reasonably democratic governments, they ceased to war against one another. We can count wars by the dozen where one side was openly a dictatorship, but we find remarkably few between even superficially republican regimes. We do find a few such conflicts, such as the ghastly 1932–1935 "Chaco War" between Bolivia and Paraguay, and the brief but highly lethal 1969 "Soccer War" between Honduras and El Salvador. All four countries, as it happened, had constitutionally elected presidents at the time they went to war, so in formal terms these were wars between republics. But in all four countries the elections had merely ratified the candidate of a ruling faction. The democratic forms were surface decoration on a politics in which rebellions and military coups were recent memories and were expected to continue. Indeed, it was only a few years before coups overturned each of the four governments.[32]

In these cases, as in the 1879 conflict between Peru and Chile, we can speak of a war between republics only if we fix our gaze on the superficial structures of government. Every observer knew that the ideals of the leadership and their actual exercise of power did not provide common citizens the equal rights in public contestation that identify a genuine republic.

Just what this provision entails was especially visible in the single Latin American military conflict in which the warring regimes were both democracies established in passably fair elections. This took place in 1981, when a confusing incident on the border between Ecuador and Peru led to a battle for the possession of some outposts in the Amazon jungles, where oil deposits were suspected. The number of deaths may have been as high as two hundred. Both sides were democracies, but constitutional government had been operating for only three years in Ecuador and less than a year in Peru, and military coups remained an immediate threat to both governments. The president of Peru at the time had himself been yanked from office a dozen years earlier by just such a coup. Under the settlement that had restored elections, the Peruvian military was explicitly left free to act as it chose in all matters of national defense. The civilian government of Ecuador likewise had no power to restrain the country's military leaders, least of all when they felt that the national honor was at stake. Therefore, it was not so much the elected governments that fought one another as it was armies obedient to autonomous and belligerent generals.[33]

For one final glance at anocratic ways in Latin America, consider a private meeting in 1871, when the president of Peru invited the leading candidates in the next election to the presidential palace. He hoped to cut a deal to divide up power in advance and so avoid armed conflict at the polls, but no consensus was reached. When one of the candidates rose to leave, a revolver he had secretly brought with him dropped to the floor. The president took offense that such a thing could happen in his very office, but another candidate soothed him. It was all quite normal, he said—indeed, he too had brought a hidden revolver.[34]

Latin American elites were proud of the domineering, violent way they approached the factional struggle over the authority to exploit their own nation's riches. It hardly seems surprising that they fell into similar conflicts with factions governing neighboring countries. Were republican ideals the missing factor that could have prevented war among these regimes? For an answer we must make comparisons with other cases.

From Anocracy to Republican State

Another gigantic step in time, space, and culture takes us to eastern Arabia at the start of the twentieth century. These men in burnooses, sailing out on the gulf to fish or trade, or journeying with their camels across lands as desolate as the salt sea, were unquestionably tribal. Their politics revolved around feuds and bloody raids. Yet they were also in a sense republican, for the sheik of each clan was no autocrat but a sort of "chairman" who relied on ancient ideals of consultation (with contestation over decisions) and consensus (among leading men who to a degree held equal rights). This made a foundation for a new politics that appeared when oil rigs sprang up like grass after a rain and ramshackle fishing hamlets exploded into cities. By mid-century many of the territories had become something like modern states. Most observers called them oligarchies.[35]

While each state had a ruler who was nominally a thorough autocrat, these men were held accountable for their public actions, for they could rule only with the consent of their families. The families comprised princes numbering in the hundreds or even thousands, for the founding sheiks of each family had engendered a startling number of sons and grandsons. These swarms of princes organized themselves through councils of elders, where the men of highest ability and prestige worked out joint positions on the issues of the day. We know very little about how politics were carried on within these close-knit, close-mouthed elites. But it is known that a consensus was needed to designate the next ruler from a field of princes. And if a ruler turned out to be impossibly self-indulgent, incompetent, or retrogressive, a family council could peacefully force him into retirement.[36] The ruling families also followed tradition in consulting with leading men of the tribal, mercantile, and religious communities. Among this narrow elite, decisions were made through negotiation, compromise, consensus, and sometimes even voting assemblies.

None of the half-dozen Gulf States could ever be called a thorough republic, but many of their ideals bordered on those found in unquestionable oligarchic republics. Each of the many princes had rights that he would defend vigorously. Tyranny was especially restrained by a powerful Islamic tradition supporting the rule of law, whereby jurists through personal merit gained prestige that a ruler had to recognize. Limited toleration of minority rights was also traditional. For example, although the ruling families of Kuwait held to the Sunni branch of Islam, they generally included a minister in their government from the Shia branch.[37]

As states established control over their territories, the oligarchic elites turned away from outright factional violence. Perhaps that was possible only because limitless oil money bought off the disgruntled. Nevertheless, the result was a new domestic politics of peaceful compromise and consensus.

Just at this time, in strict accordance with our general rule, the oligarchies also began to scrupulously keep peace with one another abroad. Among these people renowned for their intransigence and fierce pride, history records only two military confrontations after territorial states developed. One was a trivial squabble between Qatar and Bahrein, settled peacefully through ingenious negotiation (see appendix). The other was a skirmish between two states of the United Arab Emirates over possession of an oasis, which left some two dozen men dead. But this case only confirms with uncanny precision that such problems hardly ever occur between regimes that are anything like well-established republics. For one of the rival states was the only emirate that had not moved past domestic violence; factions of the ruling family clashed in a bloody coup attempt that very year.[38]

We cannot predict that peace will always be maintained among the Gulf States, for they are as much autocratic as oligarchic, and their peace has been largely guaranteed by oil wealth and by the pressure that Saudi Arabia, Britain, and the United States exert on behalf of stability. Nevertheless, they give us another locale where movement away from coercion within each ruling elite meant movement away from war with similar foreign elites.

For another example of such a transition in an utterly different society, we can return to ancient Greece. Although the documentation is sparse, it appears that here, too, the earliest society was an anocracy of clan and faction, based on kinship and vendettas. The Greek regimes also evolved into territorial states, ruled under laws established by the whole body of citizens, applied by leaders who owed their status to their office. Only after this transformation do we find true oligarchic and democratic states in Greece, each at peace with its own kind.[39]

For one more case, we can follow the Boers who trekked into the grasslands of South Africa early in the nineteenth century. Divided into family groups under rugged patriarchs, relying only on their Bibles and their rifles, they set up isolated ranches under the stupendous African sky. The Boers held to principles of complete freedom and equality—in the oligarchic sense, for their livelihood depended on the labor of black men under the lash. Indeed, many of them came to the remote veld precisely so they could practice virtual slavery unmolested by British humanitarians. This unyielding independent spirit kept the Boers apart from one another as well. They gave allegiance chiefly to their clan (a group of families allied by marriage), and sometimes to charismatic military chiefs. Their own historians have called them a "white tribe."

The Boers did set up formal republican governance; indeed, they formed half a dozen pocket countries, each with a carefully written constitution, a legislature, and law courts. But few citizens bothered to pay taxes or trusted a judge to settle a dispute impartially. The so-called governments scraped along feebly in dusty shanty towns, staffed by a handful of part-time officials. They were incapable of preventing the Boers from falling into turbulent conflicts of clan and faction, "feuds and rivalries worthy of medieval Italy," as one writer put it. There were bloody skirmishes and tense confrontations between large armed bodies that nearly developed into full warfare. In 1881 some Boers did get into a war against a genuine republican state, Great Britain (see appendix). A generation earlier a party of Boers had fought a pitched battle against British troops supported by other Boers. In sum, here was another case of regimes with republican forms but anocratic ideals and behavior, where the citizens saw one another as equals yet rode off to fight one another.[40]

Here, too, external and internal violence faded away simultaneously. Aroused by the 1881 conflict with Britain, Boers shifted their loyalties from local factions to the states. An outside menace can indeed unite people, but what especially motivated the Boers was less a need for allies than a realization that they had better put their own house in order. Farmers began to pay their taxes and respect the law courts. At just this time the communities ceased altogether to skirmish with one another (even as the British menace faded).

Putting the cases side by side—ancient Greeks, medieval Italians, Latin Americans, Boers, and Arabs—we find a strikingly consistent pattern (and I have found no counterexamples in history). After a transition to territorial states which could suppress private raiding, and only after that transition, republics maintained peace with their own kind. The common factor was not a formal republican constitution; warfare ended only after men turned from tribal feuding to reliance on the councils and courts of law.

Government structures do not by themselves guarantee peace, of course. When people created state organizations it was usually so they could battle foreigners more effectively. Around the same time republican states developed in western Europe, so did autocratic states from France to Russia, with no reduction in warfare. Even a tribe under a dominant chief can abstain from domestic feuding while warring on its neighbors. On the other hand, some tribal societies with no hierarchical control have managed to curtail private raids through the pressure of community consensus, traditional deference to cautious tribal elders, or the like. Broad anthropological studies have shown that the incidence of warfare is roughly constant no matter what the complexity of social, economic, and political organization.[41]

In short, while there can be no reliable peace without a territorial state (or other means of suppressing private raids), something more is needed. We are now ready to identify this crucial thing, which in all these transitions brought mutual peace among republics. Machiavelli would not have been surprised to hear that it lies in the realm of principles and ideals.

CHAPTER FIVE

The Political Culture of Peace

W hen Dante journeyed through Hell, one of the most horrible things he saw was Count Ugolino of Pisa and the archbishop Ruggieri frozen together in ice up to their shoulders. The count was bending his head over to gnaw on the archbishop's scalp, taking eternal revenge on the enemy who had ordered him and his young sons locked up together until they starved to death. The wrathful Ugolino was a shocking image of the effects of enmity. Dante himself, near the lowest point of his journey, indiscriminately cursed the entire population of iniquitous Pisa. It was typical of the Florentines of his day to lump the Pisans together as enemies in the spirit of the vendetta—the will to destroy a rival clan down to the babies.[1]

If we move forward past 1350 we find people beginning to make distinctions between a city's rulers and its general population. Florence and Pisa were fighting one of their recurrent wars, yet a Florentine chronicler wrote that the Pisan people were not to blame. The real enemy was their rulers, a despotic clique that most Pisans themselves hated. Another Florentine burgher said that if only Pisa had a more republican government there would be peace, benefitting everyone "and most of all the Pisans." He even claimed that Florentines only sought to live "as brothers and neighbors of all . . . on the same level."[2] That "same level" is a reference to the ideal of equality, voiced for almost the first time since antiquity—and already it was seeping from attitudes toward domestic relations into attitudes toward relations abroad.

The burghers' newfound ideals are near the heart of that crucial something necessary for republics to keep mutual peace. We now have in hand almost enough pieces of the puzzle to fit a picture together. To find the additional pieces we need, in this chapter I turn to statistical studies in political science, descriptions of human behavior by anthropologists and sociologists, and experiments in social and cognitive psychology. What ties all this evidence together is the concept of political culture.

Political Culture as Explanation for War and Peace

Scholars have never agreed on how to define political culture, but they increasingly agree that something by this name has a role in explaining how nations act. Political culture can include anything from a voting procedure to the thrill that runs through a crowd when a band swings into their national anthem. It is debatable how far one should stretch the definition from the purely political into more private elements of a society's culture.[3] Scholars agree that, at a minimum, political culture involves beliefs. Beliefs influence behavior through mental structures variously called norms, expectations, values, preferences, attitudes, and so forth. All of these operate within a framework of conventional practices and formal institutions, which in return shape what people believe.

For our inquiry it will suffice to concentrate on a simple, core definition of political culture, centered on beliefs about political behavior. To be precise, when I speak of "political culture" I mean the beliefs that a group's members hold about how people ideally ought to deal with one another, and their beliefs about how people really do deal with one another in practice, when groups are in conflict.[4] Everyone knows that people in different communities hold different ideas about how to conduct relations with others. The murderous Archbishop Ruggieri and his insatiable foe did exactly what was expected of medieval Italian noblemen who had a chance to harm their enemies. In a modern democracy, by contrast, leaders are expected to starve or gnaw one another only in a metaphorical sense.

A political culture is a systematic solution to the problems posed by humans living together, and if the pieces comprising the culture cannot be fitted together people will feel distress. Practices cannot consistently and blatantly violate the ideals. Of course a group's grandiloquent descriptions of its virtues never exactly match individual actions. Yet people will not tolerate too obvious and persistent a mismatch between the beliefs they profess and the actions they take. The mental dissonance brought on by such an inconsistency must eventually push them to change either beliefs or behaviors to make a better fit. This suggests why, as we have seen, the ideology announced by a regime (such as republican solidarity) can give hints about the leaders' decisions (such as joining as allies), if never a total explanation.[5]

Practices do not just passively reflect beliefs but reinforce or even impose them. People who have spent their lives amidst free debate will think one way about politics and human relations; people who have spent their lives slavishly obeying commands will think differently. Thus, to define a political culture we can speak of practices and beliefs almost interchangeably. "Republican political culture" in particular can be defined as a specific set of beliefs about behavior, expressed in condensed form as ideals, as summarized in the previous chapter. The corresponding framework of practices, from committee meetings to street-corner harangues, need not be specified in detail.

This sort of workable combination of ideology and practice, arduously assembled and tested, is so valuable that people will try to apply it in all their affairs. This is why medieval writers, for example, praised the feudal lord as the father of his people. Surely, they thought, the well-understood paternalist rule that governed families should conform with the structure of a community under its lord, and likewise for international society under emperor or pope.

This human need for consistency reflects a well-documented fact of individual psychology. We tend to take what we have found to work in one situation and apply it in others, repeating accustomed behaviors. Only emphatic experience can convince us that we must change our approach—and then we change as little as possible. There is good reason for this conservatism, for nothing can be accomplished without mental categories and rules. We would not get much done if we tried to figure out everything from scratch whenever we turned from one situation to another.[6]

Consistency is not only an internal cognitive drive, but also a rational choice in certain situations. Everyone from Machiavelli to the local banker could explain the value of a reputation. Even if you must make sacrifices to maintain a consistent pattern of behavior, the pattern will add credibility to your promises of cooperation or your threats of vengeance. Just how much people's actions involve rational choice and how much they stem from involuntary habits, social conformity, or unbreakable training need not concern us; the point is that consistency is a prominent feature of human behavior.

That fact brings us to a straightforward and hardly novel hypothesis: leaders will tend to act toward foreign leaders in the same ways they act toward domestic political rivals (at least to the extent that they believe the foreigners resemble such rivals).[7] Under this hypothesis, tyrants, accustomed to the power of threats and imperious demands, would be expected to try such methods against foreign rivals. Citizens of republics, accustomed at home to negotiating compromises, would be expected to try such methods abroad as if out of habit.

The brevity and simplicity of this argument should not obscure the fact that it embodies a strict theoretical formulation, grounded in generally accepted facts of social psychology.

The argument flies in the face of some cherished ideas. For example, the most famous contemporary theorist of realpolitik, Henry Kissinger, held that the only way to preserve peace is to manage an objective balance of power, with the nature of regimes largely irrelevant. If that means making a "cold-blooded" alliance with a cruel dictator, so be it. Acknowledging that regimes with "fundamentally different conceptions of what is just" could have trouble with one another, Kissinger blamed that on misperception—a little problem of communication. Once leaders understand one another's objective needs, Kissinger maintained, they will base their relationships on "substantive" issues, that is, national power.[8]

Yet when Kissinger dealt with real national leaders he showed a keen discrimination. Already in his early writings, as a mere historian, he noted continuities between leaders' behavior at home and abroad. For example, he wrote that "the very qualities which had made Napoleon an autocrat domestically" led the emperor to act belligerently abroad. Decades later, looking back on his worldwide experience in diplomacy, Kissinger made a similar remark about leaders of the Soviet Union. They had "prevailed in a system that ruthlessly weeds out the timid and the scrupulous," he wrote, a domestic struggle that had left them disinclined toward conciliation abroad.[9]

Warrior and Merchant Political Cultures

Consistency between a nation's approach to domestic and international affairs has long been recognized. An ancient Athenian remarked that it would be shameful for a republic to allow any state to set itself up as the master of others, because "we have made it a principle to put down despots" at home. Other Greeks boasted that citizens who had learned to tolerate domestic political differences would always try to settle affairs with foreigners in the same conciliatory fashion. They held that only autocrats (and oligarchic elites, according to democrats), deceitful and domineering abroad as in their own cities, strove for dominion over others.[10]

Northern Italians repeated this claim. Even Machiavelli, while praising the wily and treacherous prince, declared that it was characteristic of republics to bargain more honestly. He held that a republican council, even against its own interests, would be more reluctant to break a treaty than the perfidious signors he had known so well. In fact, according to Garrett Mattingly, the leading historian of Renaissance diplomacy, the "law-abiding" Italian republics were less devoted than princes to cynical intriguing, and more inclined to establish formal, stable relationships. Another eminent historian, William Bouwsma, explained that once the Italian republics had established domestic peace, in which groups balanced and accommodated one another as equals at home, they consciously took this domestic structure as their model for external relations.[11]

The theorists of the Enlightenment developed these crude beliefs into a moral system, holding that relations between states ought to follow the same standards of fair dealing that should prevail in dealings between individuals. They expected republics, where ordinary people held sway, to follow these standards better than autocrats.[12] It was a fact that states could hardly behave worse than the monarchies of early modern Europe. Historians specializing in the period agree that the elites were locked in a status-obsessed political culture revolving around duels and executions, where ministers could only survive by subterfuge and sudden coups against their rivals. The sovereigns themselves were admired by their subjects for using deception and force to expand their "glory." One historian compared these kings with children on a playground, given to calling out insults and shoving one another without warning.[13]

When the United States was born as the world's first large-scale republican government, its leaders expected to do better. American diplomats meant to replace monarchical machinations with trustworthy republican ways. Similarly, the democrats of the French Revolution insisted self-righteously that their diplomats must shun courtly subterfuge.[14] However, it soon appeared that envoys from a republic could be as deceitful and pugnacious as anyone. Meanwhile, the courtiers of monarchs were establishing refined protocols for official exchanges. Monarchists complained that it was the ill-bred democratic demagogues who were unreliable, for nobody was so trustworthy as a sovereign bred to honor and secure in his position.[15]

Opinion swung back only in the 1920s, when government archives were dragged into the light to reveal the origins of the First World War. It was discovered that the sovereigns of Russia, Germany, and Austria had acted with an appalling degree of suspicion and belligerence. Scorn for authoritarian behavior was redoubled by the obstruction and truculence of the new Communist and Fascist regimes. "Their promises are worth nothing," a British envoy said of the Bolsheviks, "as they take a delight and pleasure in breaking them." This was conspicuously like the way the Bolsheviks dealt with their opponents at home. In the 1930s it was similarly noted that the Nazis applied to foreign affairs the same techniques of falsehood and brutish intimidation that they had used to seize power. Experts began to speak of a difference between "liberal" and "totalitarian" styles of negotiation.[16]

In 1939 an urbane British diplomat, Harold Nicolson, summarized his extensive experience in a classic book. He wrote that the approach of a democracy like Britain was founded on the virtues that merchants needed to conduct their trade—the "sound business principles of moderation, fairdealing, reasonableness, credit, compromise." Nicolson contrasted this with the bullying and shameless deception of non-democratic states, which he traced to a "warrior" culture.[17]

This distinction remained prominent during the Cold War. Western scholars and diplomats continued to find Soviet envoys exceptionally secretive and uncompromising, given to diatribes and barefaced lies. That was precisely how the Soviet elite dealt with one another. A diplomat who knew them well remarked that the Russians, having no experience in the rule of law, saw every transaction as a personal struggle for supremacy. Other experts reported that Communist Chinese leaders likewise saw every relationship not as an interplay between equals but as a matter of someone imposing his authority.[18]

Many supporters of autocracy would agree with all this. Some Enlightenment writers held it a positive virtue in kings to deceive their rivals and to expand their state through warfare. Fascists and Communists were still more proud to make a virtue of manipulating, betraying, and dominating their opponents. To someone like Benito Mussolini, Nicolson's claim that British diplomacy was preoccupied with fairness and compromise would sound like an admission of incompetence. The Communist "new man" was likewise glorified as a ruthless and uncompromising warrior. Communists had only scorn for those who considered the viewpoints of both sides—weaklings too timid to shed blood.[19]

The idea that most political behavior falls into one or the other of two distinct types was already familiar in ancient Greece, and Italian city chronicles regularly contrasted vain and combative "lords" with honest and peaceable "burghers." Thinkers of the Enlightenment developed the idea into a doctrine of the divergent ways of "aristocracy" and "commerce." Most modern sociologists and political economists similarly distinguish between command "hierarchies" and cooperative "markets" as basic forms of human organization. Even in studies of individuals, when people are asked to check off choices in lists of statements they tend to fall on a line between two poles, at one extreme authoritarian and hierarchical, at the other tolerant and egalitarian.[20]

An extended effort to distinguish types of political culture was recently completed by the social philosopher Jane Jacobs. She found that she could separate her notes about political beliefs into exactly two piles. One cluster included such precepts as: Respect Hierarchy; Be Obedient and Disciplined; Take Vengeance; Deceive Rivals; and so forth, all compatible with one another. The other cluster included precepts incompatible with the first set but no less consistent among themselves: Collaborate with Strangers; Come to Voluntary Agreements; Respect Contracts; Shun Force; and the like. The first cluster of precepts evidently fits more easily with the political culture of authoritarian regimes, the second with republican ones.[21]

This division of political cultures into two distinct sets of ideals is obviously only an approximation. Everybody uses a mixture of behaviors, since no one cluster alone could serve as a guide for every occasion. A group can function in real life only if it makes a creative synthesis of the various beliefs—the merchant ship erupts with cannon fire, the valiant knight cuts a deal with his rivals. In a given crisis nobody can be certain that an elected president will act one way and a dictator another. And it remains to be verified whether political cultures can be divided so neatly into two types; another investigator might find dozens of overlapping varieties. Still, we do have compelling evidence that, at a minimum, there is more than one type of political culture. People have learned from experience to have expectations about how a given regime will behave, expectations that differ from one type of regime to another. It was not out of delusion that so many canny observers over the centuries distinguished between authoritarian and republican styles.

Does National Character Explain War and Peace?

Most observers have not believed that patterns of behavior derive from political systems, but have supposed that the push goes in the other direction. The behavior of Communists, for example, was nothing new: for centuries envoys of Russian and Chinese emperors had been notorious for their insults, lies, and threats. It seemed that their approach to human relations flowed from obscure depths of the Slavic or the Oriental soul. After all, diplomats are well advised to attend to the distinctions between the bargaining conventions of, for example, a merchant in an Arab bazaar and a London stockbroker.[22] In this view political culture is a simple extension of a timeless "national character."

It is true that the way people behave politically must somehow fit with the way they behave everywhere else—the way buyer meets seller in a shop, the way father meets son at home. This concordance of behaviors may explain the rough correlation between nations with liberal economic systems, including open international trade, and republican regimes maintaining mutual peace. We do not need elaborate technical arguments about the economic efficiency or the "rent-seeking" of elites, when a simpler observation will suffice. Nicolson, Jacobs, and many others have pointed out an affinity between the requirements of republican political life and the merchant's perpetual need for mutual understanding and fair, reliable contracts. Thus, where commerce is strong we are more likely to find a republican political culture.

When we ask about peace, however, it is not our task to explain the economic or social forces that create and sustain a nation's political culture, but only what the political culture makes happen. Is it the intrinsic national character of certain peoples to be comfortable with republican ways at home and at the same time disinclined toward foreign aggression? This would explain peace as the reflection of a nation's low level of internal violence in its foreign behavior.

Powerful statistics show that democracies do have less internal violence than autocratic regimes. R. J. Rummel, tallying the murder of civilians by their own governments, has counted for the twentieth century over 150 million deaths, more than four times the total of combat deaths in the century's wars.[23] These tragedies were not the work of republics but of authoritarian regimes, and the most dreadful massacres were planned and carried out by the most totalitarian regimes, under Stalin, Hitler, Mao Tsetung, and their ilk. Democratic governments are also less liable to fall prey to domestic insurgencies.

Other studies show that democracies tend to be more peaceful toward outsiders than are authoritarian regimes, whether the outsiders are democratic or not. Stuart Bremer calculated that over the past two centuries a pair of autocracies was four times more likely to go to war than a democracy paired against an autocracy. Other scholars have compiled statistics showing that in the twentieth century, far more people have been killed in warfare between totalitarian states than in battles involving democracies. Moreover, democracies have proven less likely than other regimes to initiate violence in a crisis, even against a non-democratic opponent.[24]

These are only partial correlations, however. A tendency to be less violent than other regimes, revealed only by sophisticated analysis, is not the same as no violence at all. The statistical studies demonstrate that there is something special in the way democracies approach their foreign rivals, but they do not point clearly to an explanation.

Anthropologists have looked more broadly at violence in societies, analyzing data on hundreds of groups, from primitive tribes to modern nations. They have also found some correlation between the levels of internal and external violence. But again, this is only a tendency, not an ironclad rule, and still less an explanation. Many societies have been preoccupied with internal feuding while avoiding external wars, while other societies have kept peace internally but violently attacked outsiders. Groups or nations that are internally united may only feel so much the better prepared to jump upon their neighbors.[25]

Even if there is a vague tendency for national character to guide foreign behavior, much that affects this character can change within a single generation—the nation's economic system and prosperity, its social arrangements, even its child-rearing practices. Political thought and behavior in particular are surprisingly contingent. A dramatic example is the transformation in West Germany from authoritarian to democratic attitudes in a single generation.[26]

Nor must a society change to its roots in order to change its diplomatic behavior. Modern nations contain a variety of groups with different beliefs about behavior, as the boy from the suburbs discovers when he goes to Marine boot camp. A group of leaders from one subculture may abruptly displace another in power. And diplomacy is determined not by nebulous national character so much as by the specific political subculture of the leadership of the moment.

Most historians and political scientists agree that the leadership groups in any regime have a great deal of autonomy in stipulating diplomatic offers and threats. To be sure, public opinion plays a role in republics. Many people suppose that what restrains republics from war is the pressure of pacifist public opinion. However, as we shall see, there have been times when a belligerent public helped force the hand of elected leaders who were reluctant to make war. At other times the public was indifferent to a foreign crisis but an aggressive elected leader made war anyway.[27] Of course, in a properly functioning republic the leadership and the public can never be far apart on key issues. Thus, even in republics we can answer our questions without studying the character of the nation as a whole, but only the political culture of the leaders.

More than the public at large, government leaders must have a well-developed set of rules and ideas to guide their political decisions. They must have distinct beliefs about political conflict, and well-tested ways to pursue their goals. Intense domestic experience has taught the leaders a pattern of relationships, and they will be inclined to apply these familiar methods in foreign affairs.[28] Within democracies we see this effect after any election in which one party replaces another in power and promptly changes the nation's domestic and foreign policies in directions that can be predicted by anyone familiar with the differences between "liberal" and "conservative" approaches.

Few nations are as famous for charm as Italy, yet the suave expertise of Italian diplomats went into eclipse when Mussolini and his followers took power. Ordered to adopt "fascist" behavior, the dictator's envoys took to hectoring and insulting opponents, renouncing even normal courtesy. After 1945, when democracy was restored in Italy, its diplomats became cooperative. Similarly, under a relatively republican regime in the 1920s, Japan settled its major international conflicts peaceably, but when the military tightened its control in the 1930s, Japanese diplomacy became starkly intransigent. In the 1950s, with democracy established, Japan returned to resolving foreign disputes through peaceable compromises. In the half-century since, Japan has undergone radical changes in its domestic and international situation but has continued to reject military methods; a study by one scholar found no explanation except in terms of the nation's new political culture.[29] In each case, the proclivity to attack foreigners rose and fell in precise parallel with the use of coercion by leaders at home. Many experts would prefer to explain changing diplomatic methods through realpolitik, the international power relationships. But Japan was scarcely more bellicose as the world's second strongest economy in the 1990s than when it was prostrate and dependent in the 1950s—and defeated nations are not always cooperative.

Consider German foreign relations. Confrontational and deceitful under the kaisers, Germany remained uncooperative during the chaotic years following its defeat in the First World War (see Chapter Ten), then became more accommodating in the latter 1920s as a democratic leadership settled in. When the Nazis seized power, German diplomacy promptly reverted to brazen lies and reckless aggression, long before military power had grown sufficient to back up the belligerence. As if to confirm the effect with a tidy experiment, from 1945 to 1990 Germany was split into two nations, presumably with the same fundamental "national character," and with mirror-image positions in the international balance of power, but under radically different regimes. Democratic West Germany was studiously polite and cooperative with its allies and even wooed its Communist antagonists. Meanwhile, the Communist dictatorship in East Germany was fitfully hostile, attacking even fellow Communists in Czechoslovakia, and secretly supporting a despicable program of terrorism and assassination abroad.[30] To be sure, the East Germans were dominated by the Soviet Union, so let us consider Russia itself.

For a brief period in 1917 a democratically inclined provisional government held power in Russia. It behaved unlike any previous Russian regime, promising full autonomy to regions such as Estonia and Finland. That reversed once Communist rule was firmly established. As Nikita Khrushchev put it, Stalin's "suspicion and haughtiness" toward his own people was mirrored in his domineering approach to foreigners. After Stalin died and the Soviet regime moved toward something more oligarchical, its diplomacy softened. Studies of the period have even detected shifts in Soviet diplomatic style from year to year, correlating strongly with shifts of power between militarist and liberal factions. In the late 1980s Soviet diplomacy became more inclined toward compromise in precise parallel with the relaxation of authoritarian controls at home. The timing of these changes did not match shifts in the international power balance, which had been gradually tilting for decades, so much as the abrupt transformations of Soviet domestic politics.[31]

It is hard to conceive any explanation for these drastic variations in diplomatic style except by arguing that a nation's approach to international relations is powerfully affected by the political culture of its leadership. This important possibility has not been systematically investigated. Few scholars of diplomacy have paid attention to domestic political culture.[32] But once one starts paying attention to the connection, evidence can be found everywhere.

There have been a few systematic statistical studies, noted below, but they are still in an early stage and are limited to a very narrow range of data. At this point in investigating peace it pays to apply the historian's tools, setting cases alongside one another for comparison without losing sight of the complexity of each.

As one brief example, which will help clarify the possible meanings of consistency between domestic and foreign styles of behavior, consider a society utterly remote from any other we will look at: China in the 1500s. This is the Forbidden City, with its labyrinth of high walls, locked doors, and eunuchs conspiring over cups of tea. At the center sits the ferocious Chia-ching emperor, who won power through factional infighting and imposed a despotic rule. When officials remonstrated with him he had them flogged to death by the dozen. The emperor treated foreigners with the same contemptuous intolerance; when the Mongol Khan sent envoys to negotiate trade relations, they were simply killed. As if to demonstrate the symmetry between domestic and foreign relations, Chinese officials who advocated a compromise with the Mongols were likewise executed. The result was unrelenting frontier warfare.

Alongside this case we can set the court of the emperor's grandson, the Wan-li emperor. Now the government was in the hands of scholar-officials who rose on the strength of hard work and political dexterity, who tirelessly drafted memoranda and conferred with one another. While the emperor was kept busy with tiresome ceremonies, real control lay in the hands of a first grand-secretary, who governed through cajolery and consensus. If a preponderant number of officials thought the first grand-secretary was accumulating too much power, they could peacefully depose him. Significantly, the losers in such political contests were not flogged to death, but went into quiet retirement. This was still an imperial hierarchy, of course, yet its political culture overlapped with the practices and ideals that characterize oligarchic republics. All mandarins were equal in their fundamental rights and their duties to the commonwealth, notably the duty to express opinions on policy. If there was not quite rule of law, the mandarin commitment to a strict Confucian code of ethics served almost as well. To decide key issues, the senior officials would convene in a body to debate one another and, in effect, reach a decision through voting.

At one crucial point the majority in such a council endorsed accommodation with the Mongols. Abroad as at home, the mandarins felt that domineering methods would only disrupt their regime's scrupulous balance. This time the negotiations with the Mongols were fair-minded, and a compromise was worked out which brought decades of relative peace on the frontier. "One million lives must have been saved," boasted an official.[33]

Personalities of Leaders and the Statistics of Wars

On the many occasions when a historian or diplomat has remarked that a leader approached foreign relationships in the same fashion as domestic ones, the observer has usually seen this as purely a matter of an individual's personality. This man happened to be a reckless brute, that one shrank from violence. Perhaps the Wan-li emperor presided over a peaceful nation because he was born with an innate distaste for conflict, or because he was imbued with his mother's pious Buddhism?

The human heart is not easily studied, but a few scholars have addressed the issue with shrewd research plans. Laboratory studies find that some people are consistently more aggressive and suspicious than others— and that these people negotiate with corresponding truculence. Meanwhile, numerous public surveys have shown that people who are conservative at home tend to advocate a hard line abroad; these are people who hold consistently to a tough-minded view of human affairs.[34] Historical case studies, delving into biographies or diplomatic memoranda, have likewise indicated that particular leaders expressed a similar personal character in both foreign relations and domestic affairs. The same result has been demonstrated by studies that measured the personal characteristics of heads of state by analyzing their responses to questions in interviews. All of these studies confirm a key point: those leaders who seem most competitive, domineering, uncompromising, and distrustful at home are also the most prone to hostile declarations or actual warfare abroad.[35]

An example is a systematic survey of American statesmen carried out by Lloyd Etheredge, later confirmed by another scholar surveying a different set of American statesmen. Both studies found that leaders who tended to domineer over their subordinates and tried to be in charge of everything at home also tended to advocate the use of threats and force abroad. Another scholar studied four Soviet leaders and likewise found that their different approaches to foreign negotiations closely matched the particular methods they had developed in their rise to domestic power.[36]

All of these scholars were analyzing individual personality traits, but what does that have to do with entire political systems? Some theorists and some scraps of evidence suggest that innately domineering people might be more likely to rise to power in authoritarian regimes than in republics.[37] Perhaps so, but when psychologists have attempted to isolate innate structures such as an "authoritarian personality type" they have found them slipping through their fingers. It appears that complex behavioral tendencies are not formed purely by heredity and early childhood experience, but evolve throughout life in response to the social environment. Most people adapt their behavior to their circumstances.

For our purposes we do not need to know exactly how much the political environment may act as a filter to admit only certain types of personality to leadership, or how much an ambitious person's behavior is learned from the political environment. Either way we come back to the political culture. Without ignoring how much one person may do for good or ill, we can simply look at the beliefs and practices that prevail in the entire leadership group of a given type of regime.

Do leaders of autocracies consistently diverge from leaders of republics in the way they think about foreign relations? Margaret Hermann cleverly approached this question by analyzing speeches of the leaders of thirty-six modern nations. She found that the less opportunity a nation's populace had to take part in politics, the more its leaders' statements displayed chauvinism, distrust, and a drive for power and national expansion.[38] But what about actual behavior? In a path-breaking study, Charles Hermann and his assistants classified thousands of international events according to whether a government showed conflictual or cooperative behavior. The regimes were classified as "open" (somewhat accountable to the citizens through democratic processes) or "closed" (authoritarian). Hermann found that closed regimes were much less likely than open ones to act abroad in cooperative ways.

Another study, covering 278 modern crises, similarly found that authoritarian regimes were more likely than democracies to follow a belligerent strategy, including escalation to violence. Yet another study, covering eighty-eight modern regimes, found that the ones with effective public contestation tended to take more friendly steps abroad and fewer hostile ones. Jumping back several centuries, a study of kingdoms in early modern Europe found that those rulers who least needed the consent of other groups to govern were the most likely to take the first step from talking to fighting.[39]

In short, it is an established fact that the behavior a state's leaders practice at home tends to be reflected in their diplomatic actions abroad. The old liberal saw that republicans generally behave more peacefully toward other nations than do autocrats has been confirmed about as reliably as anything can be in statistical studies of human communities.

None of these studies clearly separated political culture from whatever constraints a set of institutions may place on a leader's actions. Attempting to sort that out, Bruce Russett and collaborators conducted a detailed statistical study of modern conflicts. They found, of course, that conflict tended to be rarer where both sides had republican institutional structures. Peace was much more reliably kept, however, where both sides manifested republican attitudes toward domestic political relationships, as shown, for example, by their avoidance of vehement domestic strife and political executions. The same effect showed up in a parallel study of conflicts in primitive communities with varying degrees of egalitarian institutions and attitudes. These scholars concluded that mutual republican peace relies less on formal legal structures than on precepts for proper behavior—to the limited extent that the two can be distinguished.[40] Beliefs and institutions conform with one another too closely over the long run to be separated cleanly in broad statistical studies.

The Well-Established Republic: A Reputation for Tolerance

Leaders are not mere slaves of their political environments, acting unconsciously against their own best interests. Most people who have studied international affairs agree that wars take place under just one condition: leaders will take their nation to war only if they calculate that they have a good chance of getting the benefits of victory without disproportionate losses. At a minimum they must figure that giving in to the other side's demands without a fight will do more harm to the nation (or anyway to the leaders themselves) than war itself.[41]

One element of this calculation is often overlooked. In real-life power games, when players estimate the probable rewards and costs of attacking or giving in, they also estimate something else: the probable outcome of continuing with peaceful negotiation. Here it especially crucial what each side thinks the other is likely to do. If our side gives in on a point, will your side only pocket the gain and make new demands? Can you be relied upon to keep negotiating toward a compromise, or are you liable to launch a surprise attack?

The political scientist Bruce Bueno de Mesquita has codified such appraisals in a mathematical formulation with an interesting result. Suppose both sides in a conflict prefer negotiation and compromise to fighting, and suppose each knows that the other holds that preference. Then no matter what the stakes and the relative strengths, realistic appraisal of potential costs and benefits must lead both sides away from war. This conclusion sounds like common sense, but it is reassuring to learn that it can be rigorously deduced from plausible axioms.

The key process here is the construction of perceptions through an exchange of information. Peace follows if leaders come to recognize that their preference for negotiation is shared. The process has an old-fashioned but still valid name: establishing mutual trust.[42]

Exchanging information about the way a group is likely to behave has costs. In any power game it would be terribly risky to act without such information, but a thorough investigation takes much effort, and in a crisis there may not be time for it. Rather than try to find out exactly what a particular player will do in the situation of the moment, it pays to develop rules of thumb about how that player is likely to behave. It may be still more efficient to form general ideas about a particular category of player; reputations cling not only to individual leaders but also to political regimes.

Sensible leaders, then, will inquire into a rival regime's political culture, in the sense of asking whether the leadership has shown a consistent propensity for mutual accommodation, or for treacherous attacks. Political theories have only recently come to recognize that such information belongs right at the center of the most hard-nosed calculation, and that the cost of gathering such information strongly influences decision-making processes. The ideals of behavior that a group displays can function as a "communication device," as one theorist put it, cheaply passing relatively reliable information not only among the group members themselves but also to their neighbors.[43]

For this argument it does not matter whether the behaviors that leaders prefer are a reflection of their upbringing, institutional constraints, or anything else imposed by psychology or society. The logic still works if leaders rationally decide to maintain a reputation for being accommodating and trustworthy (or for a prince, perhaps, a reputation for Machiavellian ruthlessness). A leadership group might well make considerable sacrifices just to build up a useful reputation. Keeping true to one's ideals is costly, and the cost itself underwrites the reliability of the information conveyed.

We are beginning to see what can make war unlikely among certain types of regimes. I have said that peace prevails among "well-established" republics, but I have not yet dissected the qualifying term. People normally check whether a regime is republican by looking for a visible framework of free speech, elections, and so forth. However, a few leadership groups (like Peru's in the 1870s) have possessed such institutional structures even while engaging in wanton violence both at home and abroad. These I call republics that are not well-established. We are now ready to start understanding what this means. I find that for a regime to conform to the republican pattern of war and peace it needs not just certain institutional structures, but still more a republican political culture: the leaders must visibly and consistently adhere to republican beliefs about ideal behavior.

Since beliefs must be generally compatible with practices, we can say approximately the same thing by speaking of the behavior itself, which is easier to observe and categorize. Thus I call a republic well-established only when leading citizens are accustomed to treating one another as true political equals, particularly in the sense that they tolerate opposition from their domestic rivals—negotiating mutual accommodations and even accepting defeat at the polls—instead of trying to coerce one another. In short, we can only call a regime a well-established republic if the leaders customarily tolerate full public contestation among citizens.

It remains to be seen just how reliably this classifies regimes into categories with special patterns of war or peace; that will become clear only as we look through historical examples to precisely identify the differences between true republics and more ambiguous regimes. But it should already be clear that my definition of well-established republic is a condensation of republican political culture, of the habits of toleration and bargaining that make republican institutional structures work the way they are supposed to.

It is in exactly this sense that republics became well established during the transitions from anocracy to republican mutual peace that I discussed in the preceding chapter—the ancient Greeks, the Boer republics, the Gulf Arabs, and so forth. These transitions all involved a change in how leaders intended to use government powers. Before the transition, if leaders bothered with the constitutional structure at all, they saw the offices, courts of law, and ballot boxes as a prize to seize, something to use as a weapon against the enemies of their clan or faction. After the transition to truly well-established republics was complete, leaders used the constitutional structure in a manner more consistent with republican ideals.

In sum, comparing a substantial number of immensely diverse cases yields a single decisive common feature: peace settled in where people came to believe that disputes should be settled by getting together and debating as equals, not by riding out to murder. (All of these cases also required a second common factor, the creation of territorial states suppressing feuds and raids, but the state is not sufficient in itself for mutual peace.)

It is only after the transformation of the mid-1300s, for example, that we can call any Italian city a well-established republic in terms of the political culture of its leadership. In the formal sense, the regimes had already been republics for a century. But mostly the politics had proceeded in the way Ruggieri used his official position to annihilate Ugolino's family. The public contestation we have in mind when we speak of a well-established republic is carried on with debates and ballots, not insults and swords. Once leaders had a consistent reputation for choosing negotiation over coercion at home, they rapidly established the same kind of relationship with similarly minded leaders abroad.

The cases so far have narrowed down our attention to one particular feature of political culture, the toleration of dissent. We need to bring together an even wider variety of historical cases before we can be sure whether this is the unique key to peace among republics. A problem is indicated by the fact that democratic and oligarchic republics have warred savagely on one another, even though the leaders on both sides lived in an undeniably well-established republican political culture. What had become of their shared inclination to negotiate and compromise? Evidently we are still missing a crucial piece of the puzzle.

We need another set of cases. They should come from a locale with a good many oligarchic republican and democratic states, in a social and economic setting remote from anything else we have studied, and with plenty of wars. History provides what we need.

CHAPTER SIX

The Swiss Republics: Defining an Enemy

For most of its history Switzerland has been no place for a restful vacation, but a laboratory of wars. Some of these conflicts were between republics, for the Forest State democracies had neighbors of a different stripe. A peasant from a backwoods democracy, carting cheeses down from his stony meadows to sell within the walls of a city-republic like Bern or Lucerne or Zurich, would have felt badly out of place. Hawkers and beggars would have been swarming in the maze of smelly streets while fat burghers strutted past in jackets with silver clasps. At the city's center, the Rathaus, a monumental edifice where the town council met, would have stood foursquare. Such councils drew their members from at most a thousand legal citizens, the cream of the artisans, merchants, and landlords. There was no share of power for at least three-quarters of the men in the city, nor for anyone in the surrounding countryside. In short, these regimes were oligarchies.

The Swiss city oligarchies, as much as the Forest State democracies, had a well-established republican political culture. How could groups of leaders, all accustomed to negotiating and tolerating differences, march to kill one another? The idea of free men attacking one another struck the Swiss as unnatural. Yet oligarchic republics went to war against democratic ones time after time. To explain this pattern, and similar cases in other locales, we need one more piece of the puzzle. We must understand the way republican political culture distinguishes friends from enemies.

Elite Against Rabble

In 1436 the count of Toggenburg died without an heir. The Toggenburg lands commanded a strategic position between Zurich and Schwyz, and both states promptly laid claim to the territory. Schwyz's elected governor was the keenly intelligent Ital Reding, a man of peasant stock. Such a low-born mountaineer could hardly be seen as an equal by a city patrician like Rudolf Stüssi, Zurich's burgomaster. Stüssi's father had come to Zurich from the mountains and made good as a wine merchant, but the burgo-master could boast that he had been knighted by the Holy Roman Emperor himself. Like many a parvenu, Stüssi was quick to scorn anyone whose standing he considered beneath his own. Arrogant and stubborn, he has been blamed by virtually every historian for turning the wrangling over the Toggenburg lands into armed warfare.[1]

Stüssi and his supporters in Zurich replied to offers of compromise with insults, then tried to force the Schwyzers to give way by barring them from the city's markets and roads. Faced with starvation, Reding gathered allies among other Forest States and took them to war. When Stüssi led a foray, his men were routed by troops from the Forest States. Stüssi held his ground: a man of advanced middle age with a grand forked beard, wearing knightly armor, laying about him with his sword as the leathery herdsmen closed in. It was said afterward in Zurich that the Schwyzers barbarously desecrated his body.[2]

Here we see in harsh colors what can allow republics to war on one another, if one side is democratic and the other oligarchic. This was no conflict between people who saw one another as equals. Urban patricians looked with open contempt on the uncouth mountaineers, putting them on the same servile level as their own city's laborers and peasants. In a mocking song the Zurichers likened the Schwyzers to a disobedient cow; these country louts deserved a whipping for opposing their betters. Meanwhile, the mountaineers saw Zurich as a den of luxury-loving merchants and domineering aristocrats who ground down their peasantry, as great a threat to freedom as any prince.[3]

This is a familiar kind of enmity. We find it today between landowners and peasants in Central America, and between urban money lenders and rice-paddy farmers in southern Asia. These modern cases do not involve pure oligarchies, however. For a plainer division we could return to ancient Greece, where democratic states lined up against oligarchic ones in dozens of furious wars. We will later consider the Greeks, but first let us examine a better documented case, remote from anything else we will come across.

The setting was a limitless plain of grass as high as a horse's shoulders. A river wound past bluffs with settlements, each a cluster of huts circled by a stockade. This was the land of the Zaporozhian Cossacks, runaway serfs and outlaws who had fled by tens of thousands to live by the Dnieper

River in these wild plains owned by no lord. As if to demonstrate the myth of republican origins, around 1580 the Cossacks established the purest of democracies. Their assemblies were tumultuous affairs marked by drunken shouting and fistfights, yet they did gather to debate and vote on such complex matters as treaties with foreign powers. They elected leaders and removed them, and respected the rule of traditional law as determined by elected judges. We must call this a democratic state rather than a primitive tribal regime, if only because the refugees claimed none of the kinship ties that are basic to the definition of a tribe; they gave their fierce loyalty to the whole political community of equals.[4]

The nominal suzerain of the Cossack settlements, Poland, was the purest of oligarchic republics. The ruling "nobles," less than ten percent of the population, ardently insisted on complete political equality among themselves, with one vote apiece in their assemblies. At the same time, they despised commoners as literally an inferior race. This distinction was central in bringing Poland and the Cossacks to a grueling war in the mid-1600s. The Polish nobles did not see the Cossack settlements as a fellow republican regime but as an insolent horde of runaway serfs. The Cossacks' elected chief was disdained, inaccurately, as "a common menial." There could be no negotiation with such a barbarous mob, a nobleman remarked, except using an army.

The illiterate Cossacks themselves had little in the way of an ideology. They never questioned noblemen's rights over serfs, but only refused to allow those rights to be exercised over themselves. Yet the Cossacks also stood for a free peasantry, if only because whenever a Cossack army rode forth a swarm of Polish peasants would join them, demanding a policy of liberation (or at any rate of butchering noble families down to the infants). As always, there were many reasons for going to war, with the political enmity reinforced by religious and cultural divergences between Poles and Cossacks. Yet it was the divide between noble and commoner that mattered most. On both sides we might see republics with voting assemblies. What people of the time saw was a war across the line that the Polish nobility had already drawn against commoners in their own land.[5]

The Poles had no such problems when they faced an oligarchy politically resembling their own, although of a totally different language and culture. Toward the end of the 1400s, when Polish leaders first began to take up republican practices, they made peace with Hungary, which also had a vaguely republican oligarchic government. These were all men who knew how to keep their serfs in line, and how to debate in a council of their peers. As Poles and Hungarians adopted more republican ways, their ancient and violent enmity gave way to a durable alliance.

The (Only) Battle Between Well-Established Republics of the Same Kind

Enmity between lord and serf is only one aspect of a more fundamental cause of wars which operates even between comparable republics. This cause is plainly seen in one highly exceptional case, which tests the rule of mutual republican peace to the breaking point and shows what lies inside it.

Three times in three centuries, Lucerne marched with the Forest States against Zurich, Bern, and other cities. Lucerne was undoubtedly an oligarchic republic, long and solidly established, much like Zurich and Bern. These were genuine wars. Two battles in 1531 cost Zurich and its allies over a thousand dead; in 1656 men from Lucerne met a force from Bern and slaughtered over five hundred. The Bernese had their revenge in 1712, when they killed nearly three thousand opponents, including some seven hundred from Lucerne.[6]

If we put these cases under the historical microscope, however, we have a hard time finding battle between oligarchic republics. In 1531 Lucerne took part so half-heartedly that it lost only a handful of dead and wounded; it was the herdsmen of the democratic Forest States who slaughtered the Zurichers. In the 1712 conflict Lucerne's patrician leaders wanted peace, but the commoners rose in defiance of the town council, looted the armory, and tramped off to fight Bern alongside the Forest States; their patrician officers went along only to forestall a full-scale democratic revolution. These cases were really just more of the old story—democratic peasants fighting an oligarchic regime.

Only the 1656 war provides us with a battle truly between oligarchic republican states. Not on the Bernese side exactly, for the city's leaders meant to avoid combat with Lucerne (precisely because it was a fellow oligarchy, they said). Bern's real enemy was again the democratic Forest States. However, the Bernese could only get at them by passing through a district where Lucerne held territorial rights. Counting on Lucerne's neutrality, Bern's army straggled through in disorder, and Lucerne's leaders seized the chance to strike a surprise blow. This almost accidental battle left about seven hundred dead, by my definition a war—the only one I have found in all history between undeniably republican regimes of the same kind, a precious exception to probe the rule.[7]

An exceptional outcome should reflect an exceptional circumstance, and exactly that was present. These were wars of religion. The Reformation had come to Zurich, Bern, and other cities, and its followers would do whatever they thought necessary to propagate the Word of God as they now understood it. The pious folk of the Forest States were no less devoted to traditional Roman Catholicism and threw themselves fervently against the "heretics," exhorted into battle by priests holding their crucifixes high. Of the oligarchic cities only Lucerne remained Catholic, and it was strictly as Catholics that its burghers made war against the Reformed burghers of Zurich and Bern.[8]

As always, there were other forces behind the wars, the various economic, social, political, and strategic factors that often push men to war on one another. But it was religion that counted most, as was demonstrated when the two sides sought foreign allies. Zurich and other Reformed cities looked only to Protestants, including even foreign princes and lords. Meanwhile, Lucerne and the Forest States looked only to Catholics, not scrupling to approach the Habsburg emperor. Autocrats took the opportunity to set republics against one another. Suspicions arose of secret pacts with foreign sovereigns, until each side believed that the other's leaders were not committed to solidarity with fellow republicans—indeed, that they could not be trusted to negotiate in good faith.[9] The traditional Swiss framework of compromise and mediation could not mend this, for both sides rejected negotiation where souls were at risk. For example, when neutral Swiss states proposed a last-minute conference to resolve the conflict of 1712, the attempt turned into a fiasco when Bern and Zurich refused even to attend.

Was this a case where leaders tried to coerce their counterparts abroad even while respecting the rights of fellow citizens at home? Far from it, for they had redefined who was a citizen. In the streets of their own towns, Catholic and Reformed no longer held equal rights.

To Catholics, a man who preached Reform was a heretic who should be burned at the stake. The town council of Lucerne forced some of the Reformation's followers into exile and severely punished others. A Lucerner could be thrown into jail merely for reading religious propaganda leaflets from Zurich.[10] On the Reformed side too, religion overrode the fundamental republican practice of tolerating differences. Once followers of the Reformation won a majority on the town councils, men who did not adopt Reformed ways were barred from politics. In Zurich a council member who broke one of the new laws was executed, and other cities similarly suppressed Catholics, not without bloodshed. When some Bernese officials fled to Lucerne, which refused Bern's demand for their extradition as criminals, it was one of the first steps toward the 1531 war.[11]

Exiles were visible indications of a fracture that began within each state and only later spread to relations between states. The 1656 war, for example, started after Schwyz tortured and executed four of its own Reformed citizens. Their relatives fled to Zurich and mobilized the city against their homeland. Negotiation faltered where leaders could not imagine treating anyone of a "false" religion as an equal. Thus, war entered through a gap in toleration of dissent; in the crucial sense of my definition these were no longer well-established republics. Attacking a foreign republic was possible for men who denied their own neighbors their civil rights—an abstract way of saying they beheaded them or burned them alive.

Setting an Enemy Apart

In these cases, each side felt called to do battle in the belief that the other's religion was literally the work of the devil. Catholic propagandists said the Reformed leaders were "heathens" and "thieves," while Reformed pamphleteers called Catholic leaders "bloodsuckers" and "drunken sows." Reformed townsmen were accused of sodomy, and with a neat symmetry they accused the Catholic herdsmen of bestiality.[12]

The Swiss propagandists were displaying an important human trait which has been unanimously emphasized by the anthropologists, sociologists, and psychologists who study warfare. This is the tendency to separate people into "us" and "them"—what social scientists call "ingroup" and "outgroup." Human thought requires lumping things into categories, and among the first things we separate into categories is one another. Most societies teach their children to behave one way toward members of their ingroup and otherwise toward members of outgroups. Usually people feel more suspicion and animosity toward outsiders, and are less restrained in attacking them. In many tribes it was taboo to spill the blood of anyone classified as kin, but permissible, even admirable, to kill almost anyone else.[13]

Republican communities can set boundaries as strictly as any tribe. In some oligarchic republics, like Thebes, Siena, or Lucerne, the ingroup of equals comprised scarcely a hundred families. Democracies have normally drawn group boundaries more loosely, but here, too, the citizens might refuse to treat certain groups as equals. In particular, just as oligarchs see democratic commoners as contemptible or even dangerous, so do democrats despise elites who trample on the rights of commoners.

Here is the missing piece of the puzzle. The political culture of a republic mandates equal rights and reciprocal bargaining only among particular categories of people—"people like us," the fellow citizens. Leaders are free to coerce everyone else in the community, the domestic outgroups. It is perfectly consistent for leaders to attack foreigners as well, provided they categorize the foreigners as outgroup and not as true equals.

The forces that drive people to distinguish ingroup from outgroups are debated, but social scientists agree on some points. Certainly one reason people associate themselves with a group is because membership helps them get a share of valuable things, from territory to jobs. Studies have demonstrated that the more severe the competition for such things with outsiders, the stronger a group's internal solidarity and the greater its disposition to draw a distinct boundary around itself. People come to feel that "we" are virtuously seeking what is due us while "they" are out to grab more than their fair share. The process can spiral out of control until each side demonizes its rivals. For example, old Swiss propaganda woodcuts showed bat-winged devils whispering instructions in the ears of the Swiss's religious opponents; and during the 1991 Gulf War some American cartoonists drew the enemy dictator of Iraq as a demon with horns and fangs. When the line between "us" and "them" is drawn with such prejudice, people can feel justified in killing those on the other side.[14]

The image that a group holds of a given set of foreigners has been called the "master belief" guiding national leaders in their decisions. Certainly leaders calculate objectively what the other side stands to gain or lose, but that is not all. In the tumult of complex affairs people find it convenient to attribute people's actions to innate characteristics of their group: just another perfidious Englishman (say the French), or prideful Frenchman (say the English).[15] Such stereotypes are not always altogether wrong-headed, for each group does have its own ways of handling conflicts, a political culture. The tactic of judging by group characteristics helps a leader to efficiently take into account regularities in the other side's behavior. This can be crucial when leaders try to calculate whether the other side can be trusted in bargaining.

If republican leaders in an international dispute categorize their rivals as good republicans like their own ingroup, then they will regard them as people who are inclined to negotiate mutually acceptable solutions. Then it would be foolish to risk a war. The calculation is otherwise when a regime confronts rivals that its leaders classify as authoritarian, a type that many consider inherently treacherous and aggressive. War then becomes a natural option: "We can't make a deal with those bastards, they only listen to force!"

This has rarely mattered through most of history, where nearly every conflict has involved an autocrat. Most autocrats have no ingroup beyond their family and often none beyond their own selves. Demanding submission from anyone within reach, many a sovereign has warred to the death even against his brother or son. It is only in republics that there is normally a wide zone of reciprocal nonviolence, namely the zone populated by citizens with equal rights. Thus it becomes crucial just where republicans set the boundary of this zone.

The single most important thing about relationships among republics is that their citizens usually do not set this boundary at the frontiers of their state.

Solidarity Based on Political Beliefs

When the citizens of Florence first shook off their feudal allegiances and took up arms against the pope, they encouraged rebellion in other towns that lay under papal rule. As Florence's army marched to aid the insurgents, they held aloft a banner of a kind the world had never seen. Instead of the lily, the traditional heraldic symbol of their city, they carried a red cloth with seven huge white letters: LIBERTÀ. This army fought in the name of a universal ideal.

The Florentines told ambassadors from Lucca that they would respond to an attack on Lucca's liberty as fiercely if it were an attack on their own. Furthermore, they promised to treat any Luccan on Florentine territory as

if he were himself a Florentine. The newborn ideal of freedom and equality among citizens had stretched across the frontier. Later, when Florence
sought allies against the despotic Duke Visconti, manifestos emphasized
that the aim was to help everyone escape from tyranny and live in fraternal equality. The Florentines said they were "accustomed not only to respect liberty at home, but also to maintain it beyond our borders."[16]

This was wartime propaganda, and Florence often did not scruple to
hold captured towns in subjection. Yet nobody would have thought it
worth the trouble to write propaganda invoking republican ideals unless
many people found the ideals attractive. Respect for foreigners as equals
can be found even in the private records of Florence's councils. For example, when some Florentines proposed making a deal with Visconti, a
speaker argued that peace would benefit the tyrant's Milanese subjects as
well as Florentines. Another speaker replied that if Florence struck an alliance with the despot, the Milanese would "remain altogether without
hope of any freedom . . . they will be crushed." Both speakers were regarding people in the foreign city as the Florentines' equals.[17]

Around this same time the Swiss began to act in much the same fashion, although they could not explain themselves so eloquently. When oligarchic Swiss states took over a domain from a feudal lord they thought it
natural to set it free under an elite government modeled on their own.
Sometimes patricians gave citizenship rights within their own city to the
leading townsmen of a smaller neighbor, extending the domestic oligarchic
equality across the border. Similarly, when democratic Forest States took
over a district they would sponsor democratic peasant assemblies modeled
on their own. The practice first appeared around 1405, when Appenzellers
took up arms against neighboring lords, burning castles and liberating
peasants. One of their enemies exclaimed in disgust that the Appenzellers
"accept everyone as a citizen . . . . even the serfs!"[18]

In ancient Greece, too, oligarchies commonly worked to set up oligarchic governments abroad while democracies worked to establish democracies. Once a like-minded regime was installed they might leave the
foreign state to govern itself, trusting it would remain a reliable ally, almost
as if the foreign republicans were fellow citizens. Here, for once in ancient
history, we can consult primary "documents," treaties carved in stone and
recovered from the dirt by archaeologists. Some of these reveal a democracy sealing an alliance not with another state as such, but with its *demos*—

the democratic masses—each pledging not only to defend the other against foreign enemies but also to maintain democracy in their own states. These stone fragments bring before our eyes men groping toward a single community made up of all who loved democracy.[19]

Certainly, on many occasions republics did impose their will on other peoples. Where Athens, Florence, Schwyz, or the United States held predominant power they were liable to treat foreigners as subordinate clients or outright colonial subjects. This is the ancient story of human imperialism. We should not let it obscure the fact that as republics developed, they began to adopt a new policy—they would extend a measure of equal rights to certain foreigners.

We do not know how people first arrived at this transnational republican ideal. From the ancient Greeks only a few hints have survived (the monks who copied Greek writings had scant respect for such thinking). The best example comes to us in papyrus fragments discovered by luck in the sands of Egypt, like a note in a bottle from some far distant shore. We find that a certain Antiphon argued that even barbarians should be treated equally with Greeks, because all people are created according to the same natural laws. Antiphon voiced an idea so explosive that it would be suppressed for the next fifteen centuries: "We all breathe the air through our mouths and noses, we all eat with our hands."[20]

Somehow the idea revived and spread through Europe in the 1300s. Again, only a few hints have survived. For example, Machiavelli recorded as a historical curiosity that some radicals had argued that all men should be treated as equals, having been created by the same natural laws: "Strip us naked and we would all look alike."[21]

Machiavelli took note of the thought only to scorn it, for he was a patrician and considered commoners unfit to govern. Even patricians, however, could not entirely reject the idea of equal rights derived from natural law. It only needed a little modification to serve as a foundation for oligarchic republican principles. While only the "best men," those of breeding and wealth, ought to participate in politics, this still meant that anyone who reached a certain level of excellence should be treated as an equal. As a logical consequence, one would scarcely have distinguished between the "best men" in one's own state and members of a foreign oligarchic elite.

The ideal of a borderless republican community was nourished by people who were forced into exile and sought allies among like-minded foreigners. When universal rights were first conceived in Greece, and later rediscovered in Italy, some of the stimulus probably came from these transnational swarms of emigrés, numbering in the tens of thousands.[22] The process continues in our own day, where exiles from dictatorships call for help to liberate their fellows back home.

By what criteria, exactly, is a given set of foreigners included or excluded from the republican ingroup of citizens? The answer is crucial. Time and again, what came first was their political stance. Oligarchic and democratic communities both put this qualification in the first rank. Would the foreigners in question, they asked, fight for the liberty of commoners, or would they insist upon the rightness of oligarchic councils, or instead uphold the rule of an autocrat?

Of course, people also made distinctions according to what nation another person lived within, and for that matter according to the person's language, profession, race, and other factors. But where distinctions involving deadly violence were at stake, people most often drew the line by judging whether or not the foreigners adhered to a political culture resembling their own. Commoners and patrician elites each saw their own kind in every nation as natural allies.

When Athenians or Florentines pointed to a common enemy as the reason for a fraternal alliance, or when modern Western Europeans called for unity against the Soviet menace, the question of regime type was still uppermost in their minds. Foreigners who threatened to take a slice of territory were never so feared and detested as those who threatened liberty itself. Often the line between friend and enemy had little to do with national frontiers at all. When we find Greek or Italian republicans talking about solidarity it is often hard to tell if they were aiming for defense against a foreign threat or against enemies at home. The distinction was not always important in these walled cities, where the surest way for a foreigner to get through the gates was to conspire with a like-minded political faction already inside.[23] It is reminiscent of how European democrats feared not just the Soviet Union but domestic subversion by its Communist supporters. In sum, enemies were defined by their political stance, whether they lived across the ocean or across the street.

It may seem peculiar that political criteria should define the crucial group boundary in a world where so much poisonous hatred is obviously determined by religious affiliation, ethnic heritage, economic class, or the geographical location of a national frontier. Such things have often seemed to overwhelm every other human relationship, such as during the recent massacres in former Yugoslavia. There is a serious threat to mutual republican peace here, and in chapter 13 I probe the problems raised by these other ways of defining an ingroup. For the moment it is enough to note that in well-established republics, at least, time and again when people looked abroad, they paid especially close attention to political beliefs.

One reason may be that these beliefs have to do with basic attitudes toward human behavior. In a republic sufficiently established so that blatant inconsistencies between ideology and practice have been smoothed out, principles such as equal rights and reciprocal concessions permeate not only politics but daily social relations and economic life. If you are accustomed to such thinking, a regime built on principles of hierarchical domination and coercion will strike you as wrongheaded or even immoral. You would not see anyone who adheres to such a system as a member of your republican ingroup. On the other hand, anyone who agrees that someone like yourself should be treated as an equal is more than halfway to belonging in your ingroup.[24]

This practical effect has been objectively demonstrated. Polls of the public in the United States, Japan, and Europe have all found that the most trusted foreign nations are democracies, even if their people seem very foreign in other ways, whereas the least trusted nations are those under authoritarian rule. A clever experiment confirmed the importance of regime type in determining people's attitudes about foreign nations. Investigators asked people in the United States and Israel to read an imaginary scenario in which a friendly nation was invaded. Half the readers were told that the invader was a democracy, while the other half were told it was a dictatorship. Those who had been told the invader was a dictatorship were more likely to call for the use of force.[25] To the extent that democratic leaders react in such fashion, or are influenced by public opinion, we must expect their behavior toward a foreign regime to be influenced by what they think of its political culture.

A leading role for political culture can be found even in what seems the most compelling counterexample. When Lucerne's troops threw themselves upon Bern's, it was generally agreed that what set them apart was religion. One might call it war between two unambiguously well-established republics which merely happened to define their citizen bodies in terms of religion rather than, say, wealth or parentage. But exactly what did the Swiss mean by religion?

Historians have long understood that the Reformation was not only a spiritual affair, but had to do with politics in the most essential sense.[26] The Reformation called for a change in the way people dealt with one another not only through government but through authority more generally. In those times religious strictures governed everything in people's daily lives, from money lending to marital sex. Within the Reformed cities, activities that the despised papal hierarchy used to regulate (or ignore)—the appointment of spiritual advisers, attendance at church services, even dancing—were now regulated by the council. The mountain folk were appalled by these innovations. Their democratic decision-making had never extended to such matters, which had traditionally been subject to rules transmitted down through a sacred chain of command headed by the pope, and backed up by the consensus of a community that clung to the hallowed ways of its forefathers.

We can call this a division between different political cultures, provided we understand the term in a broad enough sense. When describing the political culture of a group we must remember that it includes all the beliefs that a group's members hold about how people ought to deal with one another in conflicts. This involves the entire pattern of beliefs about authority—not just votes and laws, but also the allegiance owed to priests and to communal tradition. In this larger sense, the leaders of two Swiss republics with similar constitutional structures could adhere to widely divergent political cultures.

Actually, a map of the spiritual beliefs of the Swiss would have been a mélange of a thousand shades. In a single household one person might lean toward refined theological speculations, another toward rural superstitions, a third toward plain indifference. When the Swiss divided into exactly two groups it was under the influence of strictly hierarchical organizations, for Roman clergy and Reformed councils each claimed the power to determine who was a heretic. Thus the Swiss conflict was not just a question of choosing a personal faith with its daily observances; it was a question of who would have power over such matters (and send you to jail if you disagreed)—papal authority within a traditional consensus, or a council of citizens. In this sense, we could deny that Lucerne and Bern were well-established republics, for the differences they refused to tolerate

were largely political. Still, by their own standards each side allowed political rights to fellow citizens, with citizenship defined by religious faith,
so it would be safer for us to say that warfare between well-established oligarchic republics is possible, albeit extremely rare.

The primary importance of fundamental political differences in shaping conflicts is further demonstrated by the fact that the minor fighting
between Lucerne and other oligarchic republican towns was only an accidental by-product of conflict between groups that held still more widely
divergent political cultures, the old fight of peasants against patricians.
The Swiss democracies never fought one another at all, and that was not
for lack of opportunity. Deep in the Alps lay the Gray Leagues, peasant
democracies which took up the Reformation early, and which adjoined
Catholic Forest States. While atrocious religious warfare blazed through
the region, there was never a war between Catholic and Reformed democratic states. The feeling of kinship among free peasants sufficed to prevent the downward spiral of intolerance into demonization and organized
battle.[27]

Ideological Origins of Republican Solidarity

Followers of realpolitik are bound to notice the effects of political in-
grouping, but they see it only as a deviation from good sense. They hold
that bringing political ideals into a calculation will only muddy the assessment of material forces and provoke costly errors. When crude feelings
are refined into a consistent ideology, that only makes the fallacy more
dangerous. It was to no good end that countless statesmen from ancient
Greece to modern America made speeches about solidarity with fellow republics abroad. If they were not deluded, then they were speaking cynical
propaganda to promote material ambitions.

Either way, it is undeniable that ideology can influence behavior; otherwise why would canny statesmen bother to make speeches? People cannot act strictly according to the objective facts of material forces, which are
never perfectly known. They can only act according to what they believe
to be the facts, relying on their ideas about how the world works. Even the
most cynical leaders may gradually come to believe their own declarations
about their ideological motives, or they can become trapped when their
followers embrace what they say and hold them to it.[28]

When ideas are assembled into a coherent ideology, they exert a redoubled influence on views of reality. An example is the argument that
people in republics, because they treasure human liberty and regard their
own kind as equals, can be relied upon as allies. Such a belief could persuade leaders, rightly or wrongly, to establish and maintain alliances with
fellow republics. In short, we would suppose an ideology can become a
self-fulfilling prophecy.

This supposition is difficult to check, but there is some evidence to
support it. In a survey of recent Middle Eastern alliances, Stephen Walt
found that the "socialist" states (Arab one-party regimes plus the Soviet
Union) made alliances with one another far more often than mere chance
would have predicted. The leaders insisted that their one-party type of
government was the best type; other such regimes would likewise be
"good" and so behave in a friendly manner. Such solidarity was exactly
what their official Marxist-Leninist doctrine predicted. For these leaders,
the belief that ideological soul mates would be reliable allies does seem to
have acted as a self-fulfilling prophecy.

Statistical surveys of modern alliances have demonstrated that regimes,
whether democracies or autocracies, have chosen their own kind as allies
far more often than they would have had they picked partners without regard to the type of government. A self-fulfilling prophecy may be based on
illusion (Arab one-party regimes did not always find one another reliable
allies after all), yet wise statesmen will take such ways of thinking into account as a factor that can sway the decisions of others.[29]

The connection between ideas of republican solidarity and actual alliances has never been so clear as when these ideas were too new to be
set forth in any but the simplest terms. A first essential element in the ideology of republican solidarity was put forth by a Florentine chronicler
around 1350: it is the defining characteristic of tyrants, he wrote, to seek
dominion over all others. "Not content in their perverse iniquity with possession of their own city," tyrants would inevitably betray and attack their
neighbors, "and above all the peoples who live in liberty." For if an autocrat were to accept the legitimacy of any republic, he would undermine
the principles of autocratic rule and lead to his own overthrow. The plain
implication was that a republic should never imagine that it could maintain a reliable alliance with an autocratic regime. When the Florentine
council rejected alliance with Visconti it explained that such a man would

always be a dangerous enemy of republics: "Free peoples and tyrants do not go well together."[30]

Of course, amidst the kaleidoscopic diplomatic maneuverings of a hundred independent parties, Italian republics often found themselves on the same side as one or another signor, combining to oppose a more dangerous tyrant.[31] Yet they saw such an alliance as only a temporary and distasteful expedient which should never get in the way of friendship with fellow republics. By 1400, Italian republicans had an ideology which gave a plausible explanation for these choices. Since the enmity of tyrants for republics was inevitable, republics could not afford to leave their mutual enemies an opening by fighting one another. Moreover, proper republics could be counted on to respect one another's liberties, just as citizens of republics respected one another at home.

The Italians were rediscovering ideas that had been prevalent once before. The ancient Greeks saw that democratic groups tended to ally with democracies while wealthy elites allied with oligarchies. We encounter their explanation in the speeches of the Athenian orator Demosthenes. Warning the Athenians to stay clear of King Philip of Macedonia, the orator explained that the king was necessarily hostile to their regime. Since the ideals and the attractive example of democracy threatened the very foundations of his rule, a democracy could never trust an alliance with such an autocrat.[32]

Greek democracies also had to deal with oligarchies, and here, too, Demosthenes said baldly that enmity was inevitable. "Our hostility toward oligarchies, purely on the grounds of principle," he declared, "is stronger than our hostility toward democracies on any grounds whatsoever." He held that it would be better for Athens to have all other Greeks as formal enemies but under democratic regimes than to have them as allies but under oligarchic rule. For the Athenians could easily make peace with fellow democracies, "but with an oligarchic state I do not believe that friendly relations can be permanent." The orator explained that an elite, as much as an autocrat, could never leave in peace men who lived under equal rights, for "of course they want to destroy the source from which they are expecting ruin to themselves." He concluded by exhorting the Athenians to come to the aid of any threatened democracy, just as they would expect democracies to help Athens.[33]

Oligarchic elites had a parallel ideology, which encouraged them to seek their allies among foreigners of their own sort, men of property and breeding, and never among the rabble-rousers of a democracy. As an Athenian of an oligarchic bent admitted, democrats showed good sense in supporting what he called the "less respectable" side in foreign cities. On the rare occasions when Athens had made an arrangement with "the better classes" in a foreign city, at the first opportunity the foreign elite had turned against Athens. In short, Greek ideology argued that democrats and oligarchs were natural enemies, like cats and dogs, or for that matter like republicans of any stripe and autocrats.[34]

Evidence that this belief acted as a self-fulfilling prophecy can be seen in the earliest days of democracy. In 427 B.C., following a hard-fought siege of the city of Mytilene, the Athenian assembly debated whether to follow the tradition of killing the defeated city's defenders down to the last man. When they finally decided they should not, one reason was a practical concern for the effect such an act might have on relations with commoners in cities elsewhere. "In every city," a politician reminded the Athenians, "you have the common people on your side," and he argued that a massacre would weaken that support. The circle closed: belief in the prospect for solidarity among democrats led to actions that would further encourage exactly that belief.

Yet the Athenian assembly was barely held back from slaughter, for at this early date, generations before Demosthenes, most Greeks had only a vague notion of republican solidarity. That was still true a decade later, when the Athenians launched their expedition against Syracuse. Historians suspect that ideals such as equal rights under law became fixed only in the years after this debacle. The idea that democracy and oligarchy were incompatibly different, and the principle of solidarity among republics of the same kind, may have been forged in the furnace of the wars themselves.[35]

Does republican mutual peace, then, require the construction of a complete ideology of international republican solidarity? The answer can be learned from cases where some components of the republican package were present but not others. Ancient Greece left behind too little evidence to help us, but we can learn something from northern Italy. The wars among those republics disappeared just when generalized ideas of equality and tolerance became popular. But only these minimal generalizations were necessary, for peace settled in among Italian republicans while they were still groping in a haze of disconnected ideals. As noted in chapter 4, a coherent ideology of solidarity was not formally developed until about 1400, a generation after the wars among quasi-republics had ceased.

In other locales where we have seen republican groups stop fighting one another at certain points, the change was likewise independent of any well-articulated ideology. The Boers had no ideology beyond their forefathers' maxims and the immutable text of the Bible. Likewise, for the Gulf Arabs to admit any change in traditional Islamic ideology would have been scandalous. When Arab sheiks or Boer farmers ceased their factional skirmishing they imagined that they were only following hallowed religious calls for brotherhood. As for the unlettered backwoodsmen of the medieval Swiss democracies, they left no record of political discourse at all except some traditional proverbs contrasting the good peasant with the tyrannical lord and a few songs boasting of how commoners could band together to vanquish an army of nobles.[36] This simple political contrast was enough. Wherever an idealized distinction was made between the virtuous fellow republican and everyone else, solidarity followed, even across frontiers.

The self-fulfilling prophecy of republican solidarity is thus less a matter of ideological argument than of something more powerful—the process of drawing a group boundary. Where the boundary is drawn according to shared beliefs in equality and tolerance, the group definition is used in return to predict trustworthy future behavior.

If republican solidarity were no more than a self-fulfilling prophecy, it would scarcely keep peace reliably. Skeptical leaders would see through the illusion and seize advantage for their state by betraying more gullible republics. Republics would sooner or later fall into war with one another, especially where there was no threat from a common enemy. That is not what we observe, for the belief that fellow republics can be trusted is based on more than blind faith. National leaders are generally correct when they count on other republican leaders to pursue nonviolent means with people they accept as their equals.

The general outline of the answer to our puzzle is now complete. We have found that two things are essential to the peace among republics. Both are singular features of republican political culture. The first is the republican practice of drawing the crucial boundary around one's ingroup to include everyone, even foreigners, who shares one's political culture.

The other feature is republican political culture itself, with its predilection for nonviolent negotiation and accommodation within the ingroup. The absence of war between republics of the same type follows almost as surely as a logical syllogism.

Sound thinkers will now declare objections. So far I have not described clear and consistent ways to distinguish republics from ambiguous authoritarian regimes, the quasi-autocracies and juntas with their not-quite-free elections. Nor have I described how to distinguish regimes in the border zone between oligarchies and democracies. Until we have strict definitions we cannot be confident that some of our borderline cases might not really be wars between republics of the same kind. Drawing distinctions between regimes must therefore occupy us for the next several chapters. As a bonus, when we see precisely what criteria determine who keeps peace with whom, it will give us a deeper insight into the underlying mechanisms.

Critics will also point out that the logical argument so far involves only abstractions about groups and ideals. We cannot be confident that we have found the actual mechanism of republican peace until we witness it at work in specific leaders, real people puzzling their way through a variety of crises. Such anecdotal evidence is not to be scorned, for it provides a stringent test of abstract hypotheses. Therefore, I sketch a number of narratives of diplomacy in the following chapters. While space does not allow full details, I have looked into the record of diplomacy for every significant case of military confrontation between republics: these have been so rare that they can be surveyed exhaustively.

In every case for which a substantial record has survived, it is demonstrable that perceptions about the republican ingroup played an important role in real decisions. We will, however, find a few situations where republican political culture failed to guarantee mutual peace. Understanding these cases is vitally important if we are to avoid wars.

The most dangerous opening for war is created by the very fact that people may see others abroad who resemble their own group at home. When people leap to defend fellow commoners from supposed oppression, solidarity across frontiers can inspire not peace but war.

CHAPTER SEVEN

Oligarchy, Intervention, and Civil War

L iberty *and* Union, now and forever, one and inseparable!" The famous maxim that Daniel Webster proposed in 1830 stands as a warning that men who are
ready to die for liberty may follow the same ideology
to kill for union. Republican solidarity is no fanciful
vision, but a conviction so strong that it can drive people to war. Typically
this means civil war—which poses a tough challenge to ideas about mutual peace. When people in a single nation form armies that seize distinct
territorial bases and march against each other, the situation is comparable
to international warfare, and such wars have torn apart countries with freely
elected republican governments. Are these exceptions to the rule of peace
among comparable republics?

Most civil wars pose no contradictions to this rule. Usually, one side
openly fought for autocracy, as in the fascist rebellion that General Francisco Franco led against the democratic Spanish government in the 1930s.
Other wars were insurrections by anocratic groups, as in the Irish Civil
War of 1922, where guerrilla bands scorned to obey the elected Irish government—and sometimes even their own nominal commanders (see appendix). In such cases war broke out at precisely the point where some
people shifted their allegiance either to a dictator or to the chiefs of anocratic bands. Nobody could call such incidents wars between republican
states.[1]

Nevertheless, some of these conflicts raise questions about republican
peace. What if a rigid insistence on majority rule leaves an outvoted minority no legal path to separation, as had happened in Ireland before 1920,
so that people turn to demagogues or guerrilla bands? The problem is uncommon, for it is obvious (and confirmed by statistics) that modern
democracies have been much more successful than other types of regime
in finding nonviolent ways to handle the grievances of minorities.[2] Nevertheless, insurrections have arisen, especially where democracies exercised
imperial rule overseas and refused to give the foreigners citizen rights, and
I return to this in chapter 13. Our main concern in this study, however, is

not internal discord, whether at home or in a colonial possession, but organized warfare between actual territorial states.

History does show us civil wars where the sides separated as full republican states. Generally the alignment was oligarchs against democrats. There were many cases in ancient Greece, and a few in Switzerland, where a democratically minded faction battled an oligarchic elite from its own city, each side setting up a separate government, each drawing military support from abroad. Call them international wars or civil wars, the explanation remains as we have already found it. Democrats and oligarchs will take up arms against people who adhere to contrary political principles, whether they are domestic or foreign.

There remains one major civil war in which both sides called themselves democracies. This case is worth an especially close look, for it draws us into a border zone where oligarchy is hard to tell from democracy, where domestic repression merges with international war, and where the very ideal of republican solidarity fosters deadly enmity. Later in this chapter I look at some related cases of civil conflict where the democratic or oligarchic nature of the warring regimes was ambiguous. We shall find that every case can be described as a war between an oligarchy and a democracy—provided we distinguish between the two types of regime according to one specific and revealing criterion.

Abolitionists Against Slave Power

Abraham Lincoln delivered his last great speech in front of the Capitol, its dome only recently topped off by the gigantic bronze Statue of Freedom. In his second inaugural address the president sought to justify the bloodshed he had reluctantly helped to unleash. Lincoln reminded his audience that slaveholding in the Southern states had constituted a powerful interest. "All knew," he said, "that this interest was somehow the cause of the war."

A century later, contemporary historians have mostly come to agree with Lincoln. Of course the American Civil War, like all wars, had many causes. Few Northerners had set out to win freedom for black slaves, and indeed, most despised them as an inferior people. Yet it is almost certain that if there had been no slavery in the South, the two sides would have resolved their differences peacefully. Historians have even reached a rough consensus on Lincoln's "somehow," the thing that made slavery such a crucial issue. It had to do with political culture.[3]

The central issue was the nature of the Southern regime. Under the simple-minded numerical criteria I offered in chapter 2, defining republics as oligarchies if less than one-third of the males could vote and as democracies if more than two-thirds could vote, the South lay in an ambiguous zone between the two. The enslaved blacks comprised slightly over one-third of Southern males (and a majority in the cotton-growing states that launched the war). So we must look elsewhere than at numbers, and the obvious place is in the attitudes and practices that constituted the South's political culture. So far I have mostly discussed a generalized "republican" political culture, but of course this has two main varieties, oligarchic and democratic. It is now time to explore the difference between the two and its consequences.

The elite who set the tone of politics in the South drew their power from the wealth that flowed from slaves, and that naturally influenced their approach to human relationships. The planters were convinced that only slavery could give them a civilization with true liberty, and indeed more honor than Northern factory owners with their debased workers. Modern scholars agree that slavery shaped Southern culture, but they suggest that it did not confer honor and liberty so much as an obsession with status and violent force. That extended down to the poor white families who, while not slaveowners, aspired to ownership and meanwhile rented a slave from time to time.[4]

The poorer whites noticed that they got little share of the wealth created by slavery, and their discontent put the predominance of the planter elite at risk. Planter power was a central issue in every major political struggle of the times, not only the controversies between North and South. Within the Southern states themselves, the control of politics by wealthy planters was the issue that raised up politicians or destroyed them and split entire parties.[5]

Planters defending their status nourished racism to a venomous extreme. Weaken the power of slaveholders, they exclaimed, and bestial "buck niggers" would break loose to rape your daughter! Such arguments drew most whites together in anxious racial solidarity, to the point where people who cared little for the business end of slavery consistently defended the myth of the innate degeneracy of blacks. Fear of losing their racial supremacy was the principle reason many poor whites voted in 1860 to secede from the Union, even at the risk of war.[6] Even so, the decision to secede was determined in most states by a razor-thin margin of votes.

In some places the outcome might have been different but for the oppressive restraint of certain whites. In some cases supporters of the Union were intimidated or even driven out of town. For decades, slaveholders had refused to tolerate any criticism—not only from outsiders but from disgruntled poor Southern whites—of the institution that gave them their wealth, their political strength, and their very dignity. In the cotton-growing regions dominated by planters, social pressure stifled doubts almost before they could form. Elsewhere, bold men published anti-slavery arguments, but severe legal penalties were available to suppress them. By 1860 censorship ruled everywhere from the universities to the post office. One South Carolina farmer who sent a few copies of an anti-slavery book to his friends was thrown into jail for a year.[7]

Beyond legal sanctions lay personal violence, a key characteristic of Southern culture, with its touchy code of honor. A planter preserved his status not only by holding power over blacks but by dueling with his peers and horsewhipping poor whites, who meanwhile disciplined one another with knife fights and lynchings. To many a Southerner, legal arguments and compromises seemed halfway to corruption and dishonor. Violence was especially necessary against anyone who questioned slavery. For that not only cast aspersions on Southern honor, but might help set loose the rage that smoldered in the slave quarters—and nothing terrified the South like the threat of black insurrection. Hundreds of white men who were suspected of anti-slavery views were therefore forced to emigrate to the North, while many more were driven into silence.[8]

A man is not being treated as a republican equal when he is publicly flogged by vigilantes or hounded into exile. As Polish noblemen scorned to deal with Cossacks, so those who governed the South refused political rights to anyone who argued for abolishing slavery. They were called Abolitionists—a vile and menacing outgroup. Someone who wrote a letter questioning slavery was put in the same category as John Brown, whose violent attempt to ignite a slave insurrection panicked the South. Thus a crucial group boundary was determined not by skin color but by political beliefs. A black who claimed to love slavery would be safer than a white who publicly despised it.

The Southern regime's refusal to tolerate significant political dissent shows it was not a "well-established" republic. I mean this not just in the elementary sense that the Confederate government was newborn when the war began, but in the sense I have defined, that none of the Southern states were accustomed to tolerating full public contestation among their own citizens. In the 1860 election Lincoln's Republicans were not even on the ballot in most parts of the South, and in the first elections under the Confederacy, voters in many areas again had no choice of candidates. Southern leaders might boast of white freedom, but on the central political issue of their generation they tolerated no opposition.[9]

When Lincoln was elected it seemed that the entire Union government was falling into the hands of Abolitionists, fanatic and corrupt "Black Republicans" worse than the blacks themselves.[10] Against such foes, Southern leaders were not prepared to carry on politics in normal republican fashion, accepting the national majority vote and working to do better in the next election. That pattern of competitive politics no longer matched their political experience at home, with its one-party suppression of any talk against slaveholding planters.[11]

The Northern Republicans in return looked upon Southern planters as alien and immoral. Usually they called the South not a republic but an "aristocracy," a word that since 1776 had stood for everything opposed to equality and freedom. Other Northerners denounced the South as an "oligarchy," while some, recognizing that the regime stood outside traditional categories, called it a "slaveocracy." There were disaffected Southerners who also called the planter elite an oligarchy. Other Southerners found their hierarchical system a cause for celebration, calling it a benevolent "republic" to distinguish it from the unruly "democracy" of the North.[12]

All these observers had in mind not just the planters' power over blacks but also their treatment of whites. Republican party propagandists claimed that slaveholding had imbued the planters with such a domineering will that they deliberately kept poor Southern whites ignorant and cowed, oppressed almost as thoroughly as slaves. As one Republican wrote to his son, the South seemed burdened with "the war of a *class*—the slaveholders—against the laboring people of *all classes*." These feelings were reinforced by tales of Southern mistreatment of Abolitionists. But the most incendiary information came from slaves themselves, who escaped to the North and presented themselves as human beings who had been subjected to monstrous injustices. Northerners increasingly saw slaveholders as villains, with views and practices so repugnant that they could never belong to the democratic ingroup.[13]

By the 1850s, Northern Republicans believed that white men stood to lose their freedom almost as much as blacks, and not only in the South. For a start, Southerners were seeking to impose censorship of Abolitionist views throughout the Union. Many feared that the "Slave Power," a privileged class if not indeed a secret cabal of slaveholders, was actively conspiring to extend slavery to every corner of the continent. As one Republican newspaper put it, the enemy looked like a "relentless oligarchy, that is as ready to fasten its manacles upon *our* limbs, as it ever has been upon those of the meanest slave."[14]

When Southern states split off from the Union it only provided a new reason to distrust them. Northern Republicans exclaimed that to accept the principle of secession would encourage any remaining state of the Union to disregard the others. The Union would divide and redivide into petty territories, each a prey to factional strife, foreign intervention, and resurgent autocracy. Exactly that had been the fate of recent republican experiments everywhere from Latin America to the Germanies. Monarchical regimes, sneering that common people were incapable of self-government, eagerly awaited the disintegration of the United States to settle the issue for all time. Worse, Northerners saw secession as a lawless act which attacked the most basic principles of majority rule and constitutional order. As we have seen, the ideal of devotion to the commonwealth is an integral part of the republican package. In rejecting it the Southerners seemed to step outside the boundaries of true republican behavior.[15]

In a greatly different time and place we find similar cases, where people who renounced constitutional means for resolving disputes were likewise identified as enemies of republican principles. When Zurich disputed the Toggenburg lands with Schwyz around 1440, neighboring Swiss states tried to arbitrate, but Zurich's haughty burgomeister Rudolf Stüssi and his supporters spurned the arbitration board's decision and refused further negotiation. This violation of traditional mechanisms seemed so outrageous that the other Swiss states, even oligarchic towns, turned against Zurich almost to the extent of full-scale war. As an envoy from Bern put it, it would be better to cut off a limb than to see the whole Swiss Confederation disintegrate.[16] The Swiss again fought almost to the point of serious war in 1847, when Lucerne and other Catholic states reacted to liberal reforms by forming a "separate league" in defiance of the majority of the Confederation's council (see appendix). Liberals exclaimed that the survival of republican ideals was at stake, and took up arms to force the secessionists back into the fold.

In the United States in 1860, each side believed that the other had abandoned republican principles. In particular, each felt that the other was ready to use force against fellow citizens—planters would coerce not only blacks but free whites, Black Republicans would provoke slaves to rise against their owners. Increasingly, each side felt justified in attacking the other directly. In 1856 factional raiding over slavery in Kansas left some two hundred dead, and violence threatened to spread even in the chambers of Congress. "The only persons who do not have a revolver or a knife," an observer of the congressmen claimed, "are those with two revolvers."[17] This was no longer a nation in which leaders saw one another as equals with comparable beliefs, who could be relied upon to work out differences through peaceful negotiation. In the minds of those who began the war, it was Abolitionists against the Slave Power. Or should we say, as some did, democracy against oligarchy?

How to Tell an Oligarchy from a Democracy

It is obviously simple-minded to say that one republic will war on another because one gives the vote to two-thirds of its men and the other to only a third. The numbers must be tokens of a more fundamental difference which we have yet to fully understand. We can illuminate the real forces by surveying the intermediate zone of ambiguous regimes.

In all history I have found only five significant republican conflicts where one regime lay in this border zone; evidently it is hard to sustain a regime that gives voting rights to roughly half its men. The cases include the United States when it battled Britain in 1812, Britain when it warred on the Boers in 1899, and Lucerne when it fought other Swiss almost at the level of war in 1847. We will glance at these three cases in due course, but our questions can best be answered by comparing the remaining two: the American South in 1860 and ancient Athens.

Historians guess that roughly half the males of Athens were citizens, putting the regime numerically in the ambiguous zone. As we saw in chapter 2, the disenfranchised men were distributed through all but the highest levels of society—they worked alongside citizens and were seldom distinguished in an obvious and permanent way. These non-citizens never constituted a body with a distinct political role, and their status was hardly noticed in political debates. Their role was much like the one that women, who were supposedly represented well enough by their husbands, held until quite recently in many democracies. Thus the Athenians found it natural to say that they had a regime ruled by its *demos,* or "people"—a "democracy." I have not denied them the term they invented for themselves, even if this is bending over backwards to make sure that no real democracy is excluded from our study. Is this way of defining democracy so broad that it would include the old South as well?

The American Southerners would have been disgusted by any suggestion that there was a continuum between black slaves and white citizens. They saw blacks as subhuman, and that radical distinction stood at the very center of Southern politics. In this respect the South looked far less like Athenian democracy than like one of the oligarchic republics (Sparta, Zurich, etc.) in which a citizen class was decisively privileged above commoners and tenaciously held them down as a political body.

Such privileges were also central to the conflict that led Lucerne to mobilize for war in 1847. Somewhat over half the men in Lucerne could vote, putting the regime in the numerically ambiguous zone. What really mattered was that the citizens believed that there was a sharp distinction between them and their inferiors—they considered themselves literally more virtuous, for the citizens were Catholics, who forbade political rights to Lucerne's Protestants and freethinkers. These constituted a politically dynamic minority, so numerous and energetic that after the crisis, when the franchise was extended to everyone, the "Freethinker" party outvoted the Catholics. Here, as in the old South, the repression of a major group was the central preoccupation of domestic politics, and also exactly the issue that mobilized the regime to fight its neighbors.[18]

We can compare Lucerne with a quintessential oligarchy like Poland in the 1600s. The excluded class in Poland could not be specified in the usual way as "the poor," for there were impoverished nobles and wealthy commoners. Nor was the distinction manifestly racial, as in the American South, nor did it rely upon religion or any other such test. The distinction between Polish noble and commoner stood unto itself, handed down from father to son, justified only by a myth of common ancestry in the distant past. What mattered was less how the distinction was drawn than that there *was* a distinction, sharply separating the citizens from the sullen mass of the excluded.

This characteristic of oligarchy was already clear to ancient Greek scholars who studied the region's varied regimes. Aristotle explicitly said that although the Greek word "oligarchy" literally means "rule by the few," what really counted was the special status of the wealthy elite. It was called rule by "the few" only because it happened that the poor always greatly outnumbered their betters. Plato still more clearly explained oligarchy as a regime that had within it two hostile states—the city of the rich and the city of the poor—eternally plotting against each other.[19] If required to put the distinction into a succinct phrase, I would follow his lead and say that the suppression of a crucial domestic "enemy" political group as a body distinguishes an oligarchic republic from a democracy.

These terms must be understood precisely. The suppression at issue is strictly domestic, for we would exclude far too many nations if we denied the name of democracy to ones that treated separate territories as colonial possessions, the way France ruled over Algerians, for example, or the United States over Native Americans on reservations. The suppressed body must be spread throughout the society, playing a crucial economic, social, and political role. Even the best democracies feel compelled at times to beat down groups on the margin of politics, the sort who threaten terrorist attacks or other criminal behavior and who are scorned or ignored by most of the population. What makes a republic an oligarchy is the wholesale control wielded by an elite over a crucial domestic body of people— a body that plays a truly central role in the nation's domestic economy, society, and political configuration.

This is a subjective way to describe oligarchy, and I would prefer a less ambiguous rule. I have found no simple-minded way to separate various regimes into crisp categories, but there are some useful partial tests. First, we should reject any description that differs from the way people at the time drew their lines. Every Greek saw democracies like Athens as fundamentally different from pure oligarchies like Sparta. Similarly, leaders of the American North and South agreed on one thing: because of slavery the two regimes were so different as to be incompatible. We shall find that in the other border zone cases, like the United States against Britain in 1812, observers of the time likewise perceived a fundamental opposition between the regime types of the combatants. This test hints that we should attend to how regimes perceive one another, no matter what we think of their actual character.

A second useful test is to ask whether, in making decisions on war, it would have made a difference if everyone had the vote. In the Southern elections that brought secession in 1860, if black men had somehow been able to vote (or perhaps merely if pro-Union whites had been free to argue and organize), the outcome would probably have been reversed. As for Lucerne, if Protestants and freethinkers had been given the vote in 1847, the whole conflict would have dissolved. It is generally so for the wars of borderline oligarchies. On the other hand, in the cases of borderline regimes that I classify as democracies, like Athens, there is no good reason to suppose that a war decision, such as whether to attack Syracuse, would have come out differently if everyone could have voted. These thought-experiments help us locate cases where the denial of rights to a class of people was vitally important even in foreign affairs.

A final test is especially telling. Oligarchic elites live in dread of rebellion by their internal enemy; a democracy has no such fears. For example, nothing in the surviving writings of the ancient Athenians hints that they ever imagined that their slaves might rebel as a body. Greek democracies sometimes armed their slaves when a war became desperate, confident that they would fight alongside common citizens. The old South, even in its final extremity, did not dare to arm blacks in such a fashion.[20]

This suggests why the character of a republican regime changes somewhere between one-third and two-thirds of men voting. The key is not the exact numbers, but the effort needed for large-scale suppression. The prototypical oligarchy, Sparta, organized its entire society around the need to control its helots (hereditary serfs), down to the ruthless military training of little boys. A citizen body that includes all crucially important groups does not need to bother with such practices.

A neat illustration of this distinction appears in a treaty between Athens and Sparta. All the provisions were scrupulously symmetrical—Athens will support Sparta in this, Sparta will support Athens in that—with one exception. Athens pledged to help the Spartans in case of an uprising by their servile class, but there was no hint that the Athenians themselves would ever need such help. This asymmetry led to the first open quarrel in the great Peloponnesian conflict, when the Spartans suspected that the Athenians, far from helping them to repress helot rebellion, hoped to encourage it.[21]

The fear of rebellion not only helps us to distinguish oligarchy from democracy, but also shows the significance of the domestic "enemy" in an oligarchy. It is a group or class that poses a serious threat to the political authority of the ruling elite. If political rights had been given to the helots of Sparta, the blacks (and anti-slaveholder whites) of the Old South, and the freethinkers of Lucerne, then the Spartan warriors, the Southern planters, and the Catholic traditionalists might well have lost control of the government. In a democracy, on the other hand, even when citizens deny rights to women, immigrants, ethnic separatists, or other groups, it is not because they threaten to oust the governing class as a body.

A Spartan ritual offers us a final illustration of the concept of domestic "enemy." Since the Spartans' safety required them to arbitrarily kill helots from time to time, the government of Sparta annually declared war on the helots to provide legal justification for the killings. This was not the only case where a Greek oligarchic elite officially swore that it would regard its own commoners as an enemy nation.[22]

This startling ritual points us to the center of the problem of war between the two types of republic. It is precisely one side's suppression of a domestic outgroup that opens the door to international enmity. The oligarchic leadership, fearing and despising its domestic outgroup, is in a sense already at war. It naturally stands ready to fight such people abroad, especially if they openly sympathize with the oppressed commoners. The democratic leaders, meanwhile, feel justified in fighting an elite who oppress "people like us." Indeed, when we look closely at serious conflicts between republics, from ancient Greece to modern Yugoslavia, in the majority of cases we find that coercion first became a burning problem domestically and only afterward expanded into international struggle.[23] War was most likely to enter at the precise point where leaders on one side suppressed an important body of their own people. Where both sides are democracies, by definition there is no major suppression that could poison their relations.

Likewise, oligarchies normally find nothing dismaying in one another's domestic arrangements. Apparently their central political experience as elite rulers tends to override other identifications and bind ruling classes of any sort together against commoners. But there is a loophole that in principle allows war between oligarchic republics. What if the sort of people that one state suppresses is exactly the sort that governs the other state? We have seen just that in Switzerland, where the reciprocal intolerance of incompatible religious-political systems brought about our single indubitable battle between oligarchic republics that were in a limited sense well-established. Warfare between such oligarchies is not impossible, but it requires extremely rare special circumstances.

Checking for the presence of oligarchic suppression is a simple and accurate way to separate all republics in history into two categories, which have almost never warred on their own kind but have readily warred on the other. The next question is whether domestic suppression actually plays a significant role, or merely correlates superficially with more important factors. To answer this we must dig into the details of the most difficult possible counterexamples to mutual republican peace, seeking out the role of suppression in actual international negotiations.

A Choice of Oligarchies: Boers and Outlanders

Johannesburg in the early 1890s was an astonishing sight. Sitting amidst mountainous mine tailings, it looked as if a race of human ants had swarmed into the scrubland and built a city against a backdrop of gargantuan anthills. The discovery of gold had turned the lonely veld where Boer clans had once fought into a wealthy state, the Transvaal. Now the Boers had to work out a new relationship with the British who ruled neighboring colonies. Although both Britain and the Transvaal were states governed by republican elites, they failed to work out their differences peacefully.[24]

Reforms in Britain had given the vote to all men who had a permanent residence and minimal property, yet poverty was so widespread that these mild requirements excluded about four-tenths of the male population, putting the republic in the ambiguous zone between oligarchy and democracy. The Transvaal republic was an undoubted oligarchy with a suppressed internal class—two of them, in fact. The larger of these comprised black laborers, a large majority of the population and essential to the agrarian economy. The Boers virtually enslaved blacks, believing that God had ordained whites as masters over an inferior race. When war came, the British would arm many blacks, but the Boers did not dare try. Yet the oppression of blacks did not bring on war by itself, for Britain was still led almost entirely by wealthy aristocrats who had small concern for universal human rights. The central issue, said the British, was the way the Boers treated other whites.[25]

While the Boers stuck to their lonely farms, Europeans had flooded into Johannesburg to work its mines and run its shops and banks. Mostly English-speaking bachelors seeking their fortunes, these "Uitlanders" disgusted the pious Boers with their drinking and brawling. The Uitlanders were central to the Transvaal in a way that immigrants rarely are, and not only because they were so numerous; most of the region's businessmen and professionals were Uitlanders. The Uitlanders were so dynamic and numerous that they might have outvoted the Boers if they had the chance, but the Boers refused to allow that. Not only were Uitlanders a repulsive and impious rabble, but they were liable to support permissive treatment of blacks. It was a unique and unstable situation—a republic that denied the vote to those who were the leaders in ambition, wealth, education, and executive skill. There were two elites in the Transvaal, and only one held political rights.[26]

Uitlander workmen complained of unjust taxation and police oppression, while Uitlander mining magnates denounced the government as a system of obstruction and graft run for the benefit of Boers.[27] Many Boers were equally disgusted by the waste and corruption and agreed that reform was needed. In an 1893 election they challenged the Republic's president, Paul Kruger, a grand, weathered patriarch from the old frontier days who despised everything from outside the Transvaal except his infallible Bible. Kruger's party won the election so narrowly that if only a thousand Uitlanders had been able to vote, they would have tipped the scales. This would have brought a more progressive and flexible government, with every prospect of negotiating an arrangement with Britain. Instead, the Transvaal regime looked more and more like the old South: one-party rule by an elite of landowners who extracted their wealth from the labor of servile blacks, uncompromising in defense of their privileges even over dissenting whites.[28]

The Uitlanders' grievances mattered little to the British government, but the cabinet did worry that the Boer regime was backward and hostile. Not only were they constricting the flow of gold out of the mines and eventually to London, but some Boers were boasting that they would sweep away British rule throughout southern Africa. Suspicions redoubled when Kruger, seeking a counterweight to British influence, approached Germany with visions of an alliance. What if the Boers helped the German kaiser, that belligerent and meddling autocrat, to get naval bases athwart the vital sea route to India?[29]

British leaders expected better from a fellow republic. They expected that they could solve everything by forming a free federation of all the republics of South Africa, cooperating under British guidance—a system that was working well in Canada and Australia. This idea was especially cherished by Britain's envoy in southern Africa, Alfred Milner. With tireless fervor, Milner dedicated himself to the creation of a South African federation. Kruger, who regarded all things from London with open suspicion, rejected the proposal.

To Milner and other British leaders, this rejection was reason by itself to classify the Boer leadership as hostile to their most cherished political ideals. What sort of men would prefer to associate with the kaiser rather than with fellow republics? Here, again, rejection of solidarity seemed to exclude rival leaders from the true republican ingroup.[30]

Democracy was not the issue at this point, for most British leaders sympathized with oligarchic ideals. Milner, for example, believed that a gentleman of his standing was better fitted than the ignorant masses to make decisions. We can imagine him and his colleagues negotiating an accommodation with the Boers, elite to elite. That would have been quite easy if the Boers had been able to reach an agreement with the top Uitlander magnates. A united Transvaal elite, keeping blacks and poor white laborers in place, would not have looked very alien to the British Cabinet.

Negotiations between Boer leaders and Uitlander magnates did in fact begin. But Milner sabotaged the talks by taking up the cause of political rights for all Uitlanders, down to the poorest. He did this partly as a wedge to split the Transvaal regime, but also for reasons related to the nature of Britain's own regime. In the 1890s British politicians, although mostly raised as aristocrats, were learning to talk and act like democrats, for they could not accomplish much unless they had broad support in the electorate. This affected even foreign relations. A threatening diplomatic stance could drive voters fearful of war into the hands of political rivals; moreover, without public backing the threats would not impress a canny foreign leader. Therefore Milner and his London allies were obliged to play the democratic card.[31]

Milner encouraged Uitlander laborers to hold protest meetings and petition Britain for succor, and some of the magnates joined in working to discredit and undermine Kruger's regime. When the Boers struck back with violent repression, Milner and his London allies took the opportunity to stir up British outrage. For example, Milner wrote an official dispatch about "thousands of British subjects kept permanently in the position of helots." For several years some British newspapers had been calling Kruger's regime an oligarchy, by which they meant a regime far from British liberty. Milner himself, with characteristic energy, called the Boers "a medieval race oligarchy."[32]

Once British politicians had mobilized their public against the Boers by focusing on voting rights, they could not reach a tidy elite accommodation no matter what was done about mining efficiency or German naval bases. When Kruger and Milner met they wrangled mainly over Uitlander rights. Even here, a compromise was within their reach, but each man became convinced that the other was treacherously hiding his true motives. Unable to establish trust, the two sides finally placed their bets on military force.

By all our tests, Britain was acting here like a democracy. The disenfranchised poor, although numerous, were politically insignificant. They gave scant consideration to organizing themselves, and hardly anyone feared them as an internal enemy liable to mount mass rebellion.[33] If all of them had been voters, the pressure to liberate downtrodden whites in the Transvaal would only have become stronger. It might seem that there could have been a war even if both sides had been strictly oligarchic republics, for the British imperial elite had plenty of reasons to subdue the Boers. Yet we have seen that the decisive sparks were struck precisely where democracy rubbed against oligarchy. The conflict became unsolvable only when British leaders publicly committed themselves (no matter with what inward reservations) to greater democracy in the Transvaal.

The Boer regime was an undeniable oligarchy in which the Uitlanders were an essential group whose suppression dominated all politics. An even more intractable problem was the Boer dread of anything that might undermine their rule over blacks. This dread explains the behavior of the

Orange Free State, a little Boer republic neighboring Kruger's. The Free Staters had no Uitlander problem, but they too were preoccupied with maintaining control over a large population of blacks. When the Transvaal went to war the Free Staters joined them, certain that a British victory would imperil Boer hegemony in general.[34]

Here, as in the American Civil War, the oppression of blacks mattered chiefly because it led the oligarchic leadership to suppress liberal-minded whites as well. It was this suppression that wrecked attempts at peaceful resolution, for, combined with rejection of republican solidarity, it convinced the democratic public on the other side that they faced an alien and pernicious regime.

The Limits of Oligarchic Negotiation: Czechoslovakia in 1968

From horsemen on the veld we turn to armored tanks on the cobblestones of Prague. Here the feuding regimes were both one-party states ruled by cliques, a common modern type of regime that many observers have called oligarchies. It is important that we investigate whether the international behavior of such regimes is anything like that of traditional oligarchic republics.

In the 1960s the Communist Party that ruled Czechoslovakia edged into an ambiguous zone. As power slipped from its aged dictator, the ruling circles buzzed with increasingly open debate. In January 1968 the Party's central committee chose a new leader through an orderly process of frank discussion, bargaining, and voting. Alexander Dubček was a compromise choice, a quiet, colorless party politician, known for decency and accommodation. This was starting to look like a republican political culture.

In that unforgettable spring people decided to speak their minds fearlessly. The Czechoslovak press began to print long-suppressed facts, including polls revealing that a majority of the populace wanted to change over to a multi-party system. Dubček and his comrades rejected this notion: the Communist Party must keep its undivided command. Yet pressure was building for full debate and secret ballots, at least within the Party itself. Czechoslovakia was becoming a sort of oligarchic republic whose citizen class comprised the Communist Party members.[35]

Their powerful neighbor, the Soviet Union, was already an oligarchy in 1968. That is the term selected by nearly all scholars who have studied the regime. What we might call the "citizen" elite was a tiny, self-selecting clique of a couple of dozen people, including the members of the Politburo and two or three other interlocking committees. In their meetings they debated frankly and vehemently. Usually the Politburo hammered out a consensus, but when necessary it would decide an issue by majority vote, each member holding equal political rights. The chairman, Party Secretary Leonid Brezhnev, held more power than the rest only by virtue of his consummate skills as a mediator. Smoking constantly, talking volubly, smiling a little too easily as he clapped someone on the shoulder, at this point in his career Brezhnev did not lead opinion in the Politburo so much as he smelled out where his colleagues were heading and shifted to take advantage, tirelessly assembling compromises.[36]

It might seem odd to give the respectable name of republicans to these overseers of an empire of prison camps. But recall that Polish noblemen and Southern slaveholders could rightly claim to be republican. The question is not how cruelly the ruling group of an oligarchy treats its subjects, but whether they treat one another as equals. A Communist Politburo is certainly distinct from a classic republic, most obviously in its casual approach to the rule of law. Yet among themselves, the Soviet leaders clung with a ritualistic tenacity to sacred rules of "socialist collective leadership," an ideology which had come to serve somewhat like law itself in the way it regulated their behavior.[37] Scarred by the terrors of Stalinism, members of the Politburo never threatened one another with jail, exile, or execution. Their spirited debates, their bargaining and consensus seeking, would have seemed familiar to the tiny elites who had ruled various Italian and German oligarchic republics back to the 1400s. To be sure, the Politburo was so small and secretive that it might be going too far to call it an oligarchy. But let us stretch the term to see what we can learn.

We would expect the Soviet leaders, renouncing coercion of their domestic political equals, to also avoid coercion in dealing with foreign leaders of their own sort. The question of who belonged in this category became pressing when the Politburo looked at Czechoslovakia. The problem was that Dubček's group hesitated to suppress criticism from common people. True Communists, as the Soviet leaders understood the term, would stamp out any hint of dissent from below their circle, even from the inferior ranks of the Party itself. Dubček's regime was allowing the entire Czechoslovak public to debate, on subjects extending even to the prospects for friendship with the Western democracies. Some speculated about withdrawing from the Warsaw Pact alliance of Communist nations. To permit such talk was an actively hostile act in the Politburo's eyes, an act of secession from their ingroup.

What if "counter-revolutionaries" took over Czechoslovakia and set up a capitalist democracy? What if the infection spread to neighboring Poland, to the Ukraine, to Russia itself? Words written in Prague were being echoed in Moscow by a rising movement of democratic dissidents, the sort of people the Soviet regime tended to ship off to Siberia. Thus the Soviets began to lump the Czechoslovak reformers with its democratic enemies both abroad and at home.

The Politburo's first instinct was to negotiate with Dubček and his colleagues. The key meeting was the most extreme example I have found anywhere of national leaders bargaining collectively. Arriving by train in a border town, almost the entire Soviet Politburo sat down with the entire Czechoslovak Presidium. The negotiations proceeded in republican fashion, complete with conciliation on both sides and hard-argued compromises over the wording of communiqués.

At one point Dubček cited a campaign in which millions of Czechoslovak citizens had signed resolutions supporting his policies. Brezhnev brushed it aside, saying that he could easily issue instructions and get a "ton of letters" himself. No, Dubček replied, this was different: the citizens had truly organized a spontaneous campaign. The Soviet leader was appalled. "How can you claim that you are in control of the situation," he exclaimed, "if the people sign a resolution without your prior knowledge?"[38] Brezhnev and his colleagues increasingly doubted that they were dealing with people who followed their own political principles.

Meanwhile, the Politburo's fears were inflamed by misinformation. The spy chiefs of the KGB and other party hacks, appalled by the spread of reform, doctored reports from Prague so that Moscow heard nothing but ill of the Czechoslovak leadership. Dubček's group was smeared as a "handful of rightists," despised by all good workers. Still worse distortions came from within Czechoslovakia itself, from a hardline faction of holdovers from the former dictatorship. Concealing the fact that they were an isolated minority, five members of the Czechoslovak Politburo wrote Brezhnev a secret letter asking him to intervene to remove the "imminent danger" of a "counter-revolutionary coup."[39] The only actual danger to these men was that they would surely be voted out of office when the Czechoslovak Communist Party held its next congress. Before that could happen, armies from the Soviet Union and other Eastern European states swarmed into Czechoslovakia.

This was no war. There were only a few haphazard civilian deaths, for the Czechoslovak leadership had earlier decided against armed resistance. Some believe that if Dubček's group had been more determined there still would have been no outright war, for Brezhnev and other members of the Politburo had been hesitant about sending troops, and they might have held back if they had seen that Czechoslovakia would fight.[40]

Although not a war, the incident does raise the question of whether this was an approximately oligarchic republic attacking its own kind. That was not how it appeared to the Soviet Politburo, who thought they were rescuing a like-minded oligarchic faction threatened by a democratic coup. The Soviet leaders actually expected the majority of the Czechoslovak Politburo and populace to welcome Russian soldiers as saviors.

What happened next looks still less warlike. When the populace mobilized an impassioned nonviolent resistance, the Soviet leaders were bewildered. They summoned Dubček and other Czechoslovak leaders to Moscow for renewed negotiation, mixing browbeating with effusive expressions of goodwill, making some concessions, searching yet again for a consensus. Finally they restored Dubček and his colleagues to power in Prague. The reformers did not manage to hold their own in the end, but it took the hardliners and their Soviet allies another half year of political pressure to gain full control.[41]

This case only confirms the rule that oligarchic republics shrink from attacking their own kind. Again, a conflict between roughly comparable quasi-republics only turned toward violence at the exact point where one group found the other's political principles incompatible. The case shows how even a warped approximation of oligarchic republican leadership will persist in trying to work out a nonviolent and legally defensible compromise. Once the habit of bargaining among equals gets established it is hard to break.

We can support this argument by comparing this case with another, feature by feature. In 1956 the Polish populace began to demonstrate for democracy while the Polish Communist elite was moving away from Stalinist tyranny. At this point, the Soviet Politburo was acting under the prin-

ciples of "socialist collective leadership," for Khrushchev had not yet con-
solidated his predominance. Dismayed by anti-Soviet outbursts in Poland,
Khrushchev and several other leaders met as a group with the Polish Politburo and threatened military intervention. By contrast with the 1968 case,
however, the Polish leaders made it clear that their nation would defend
itself fiercely; they also convinced the Soviets that the regime would never
give way to real democracy. The crisis ended in amicable compromise.[42]
Thus, even cramped Politburos can resolve their disputes in the peaceful
style of oligarchic councils, if the alternative is war and the threat of
democracy does not seem immediate.

War Brought on by Failures of Perception

If leaders always made clear-headed calculations based on accurate information, international relations would be less turbulent. The 1968 invasion
of Czechoslovakia was an enormous mistake, which halted the Soviet
bloc's last chance to turn gradually away from its march toward a wretched
dead end. Many full-scale wars have been equally wrongheaded, having
started with both sides confident of victory, and ended with both in ruins.
Any discussion of war must give a central place to the role of sheer error.[43]

An especially dangerous but common mistake in a crisis is for leaders
to underestimate the prospects for negotiation. They believe they face an
intractable foe, where the historian, looking back, is not so sure. Perhaps
Kruger was not really an intransigent slave driver, and Milner was not really dedicated to imposing mass democracy, but the decisive fact was that
this was the way they saw one another. And while the Czechoslovak Communist reformers might not really have made way for multi-party democracy, the decisive fact was that the Soviet Politburo believed they meant to
do so. No matter whether leaderships are ones that historians would classify as similarly republican, war can arise if leaders of one state perceive the
leaders of another as an outgroup, as people who cannot be trusted to negotiate as equals.

Fortunately, such serious misperception is uncommon, for regardless
of what leaders believe about the role of material factors, they try to learn
everything they can about how their rivals think. National archives over-
flow with memoranda and dispatches bearing witness to how closely governments scrutinize the domestic political behavior of foreign leaders.

Problems have arisen mainly where the nature of a regime was ambiguous, as in our borderline cases.

In such cases people in a republic often debated the character of the rival regime as if all by itself that would give sufficient grounds for choosing war or peace. Time after time, leaders who wanted war (out of whatever motives) would argue that the other nation's leaders were not true republican equals: those Zurichers are haughty aristocrats, those Czechoslovaks are crypto-capitalists, and so forth. Meanwhile, people who wanted peace would point to whatever republican affinities they could find between the two nations. In a study of major American diplomatic crises, John Owen found that groups nearly always justified their arguments for peace or war partly by identifying the other nation as either "free" or not.[44] Evidently we should include the role of perceptions in any explanation of the outcomes of crises.

The effect that perceptions can have in choosing war or peace seems to open a gaping loophole. Cannot leaders always find an excuse for war in the flaws of a foreign regime? Once they have decided to fight for any of the material reasons that bring rivalry between states, won't leaders indulge in whatever mental self-deception and calculated propaganda they need in order to deny that the others are fellow republicans?[45] Thus Northern politicians ranted about a fictitious "Slave Power" conspiracy while Southern planters painted an equally paranoid picture of rabid Abolitionists; Milner deliberately exaggerated the degree of Boer despotism; Soviet hardliners lied shamelessly about capitalist subversion in Czechoslovakia; and so forth.

In all our historical cases, however, such distortions have only surfaced when a regime was already in an ambiguous border zone. A distinct and well-established democracy or oligarchic republic cannot be mistaken for anything else—at least not by the citizens of true republics, who have reasonably free access to information. Only when there is ample reason for misgivings about the character of a rival regime can leaders convince themselves and other citizens that the foreign leader are not their political equals. When the American Northern and Southern states magnified the differences in their politics, that grew out of the insurmountable differences they had to begin with. The British correctly understood that Kruger believed English-speaking immigrants were godless scum and that the Bible ordained that blacks should be literally whipped into line—this was not a man who would react like a London parliamentarian. In all such cases it was genuine and severe political differences that made possible demonization and then bloodshed.

The importance of perceptions can be seen still more distinctly in the countless conflicts that have pitted republics against autocracies. The power of autocrats has often been limited, along a continuum where it may be hard to decide whether to call the leadership autocratic or republican. In this border zone we find a few wars, exceptional cases that can show us exactly which perceptions are crucial when people draw a boundary separating republic from autocracy, and what special dangers that separation brings.

CHAPTER EIGHT

Republics Versus Autocracies

mericans were pleased to learn in 1811 that King George III was hopelessly insane. Not only was their old enemy laid low, but the Prince of Wales had become regent. The old king had kept as ministers a set of Tories who scorned and abused the upstart United States, but his son's Whig friends were more conciliatory. It turned out, however, that the prince had befriended Whigs chiefly to annoy his father, and as regent he left the Tories in power. It was the last time that British royalty had a chance to exercise decisive power over foreign affairs. The prince was a wastrel and an adulterer; in the dim light of gambling rooms and boudoirs he was throwing away the prestige that his father had husbanded. If a historian had to pinpoint one year when the British regime slid over the line from monarchy to oligarchy, a good choice would be 1812. The war that began with the United States that year can therefore join our short list of wars between regimes approximating republics.[1]

The War of 1812 would conform to the general rule if we could define Britain that year as not a republican but an autocratic regime. This is not special pleading if we define all such borderline regimes according to simple criteria which reliably separate them into classes that do or do not war on their own kind (while falling within the range of what people normally mean by "republic" and "autocracy"). The precise criteria we are driven to use will then help us understand just what it means for a regime to be autocratic and prone to wars.

We have already found criteria that distinguish anocratic regimes from republican territorial states. And we have found criteria that consistently distinguish oligarchic from democratic republics. Up ahead I take up some rare cases where we need to distinguish well-established republics from ambiguously authoritarian regimes. But of all borderlines, the most important has been the one that separates republics from autocracies.

The Borders of Monarchy, Oligarchy, and Democracy in 1812

American and British leaders saw one another as enemies in 1812 largely because of their perceptions about political beliefs. In most respects a Boston merchant had more in common with his London counterpart than with a Virginia tobacco farmer. What all Americans shared was a set of republican ideals, backed up by tales of heroic struggle against the tyrannical King George. The British identity was likewise politically based, only their ideals centered on the royal house.

Few people in either nation would have dreamed of calling Britain a republic. The very word was disgusting to the Tory ministers. Of course George III, like most western European monarchs, had not been an absolute autocrat. The power that he wielded in his prime derived from his affinity with the conservative country squires who controlled Parliament. The king's power had waned with his sanity, while a rising mercantile class had begun to contemplate rule purely through elected councils. Nevertheless, in 1812 the Crown remained the linchpin of British politics. Support for the monarchy had grown after the American and French revolutions demonstrated that republican leveling was a serious prospect. The threatened gentry rallied behind the monarchy, until it became dangerous to flirt with lèse-majesté. One writer was sentenced to two years in jail for publicly describing the Prince of Wales, only too accurately, as "a libertine over head and ears in debt and disgrace."[2]

For an example of the political culture of the British leadership, consider George Canning, who handled diplomacy with the United States during a crucial period. No British statesman of the day had origins so far from the aristocracy. Canning had risen from genteel poverty by winning aristocratic patrons with hard work and razor-edged wit. Shedding the radical ideas of his youth, he had taken on the political coloration of his elite environment. In his diplomatic correspondence with the United States, all revolved around the king: "His Majesty therefore commands me to instruct you . . . . His Majesty expects . . . . His Majesty requires."[3] These phrases were sincere, for Canning was intransigent in defending the Crown's privileges. The haughty would-be nobleman publicly ridiculed democracy and Americans (and also a fellow British minister, provoking a nearly fatal duel).

If Britain was almost an oligarchy but retained the touchy arrogance of a monarchy, the United States was almost an oligarchy but was beginning to think like a democracy. The vote was denied to Americans who lacked real property, roughly a third of the white males plus the black slaves (who made up about one-sixth of the total population). Our numerical criterion thus puts the nation in the ambiguous zone between oligarchy and democracy, so we must look for more fundamental factors.

Did American citizens see those they excluded as a distinct and dangerous enemy political body, as people who could never merit citizenship? Not at all. Only a minority of hidebound conservatives worried about a rebellion of poor whites, a class the voters would soon prove willing to enfranchise. Nor was slavery yet a central issue, when even leading slaveholders saw the institution as an evil which must somehow wither away in a generation or two. The United States, for lack of an internal enemy, was more like a democracy than an oligarchy.[4]

But no matter how a historian might classify regimes today, the real question is how leaders of the time characterized their rivals. President Thomas Jefferson believed that the British political system was "the most corrupted and corrupting mass of rottenness which ever usurped the name of government." Most Americans agreed with him, calling Britain an "aristocracy"— that is, a hierarchical system of repression fundamentally opposed to their own ideals. American statesmen knew in particular that the Prince of Wales had the power to install ministers more friendly to the United States if he chose. They also knew that if a larger fraction of the British had been allowed to vote in 1812, Britain would have been friendlier toward the United States.[5]

see p. 133

Americans had observed how forcefully the British regime stifled dissent. In the 1790s, when a radical movement inspired by the French Revolution had brought shouting mobs into the streets of London and outright rebellion in Ireland, the upper classes had struck back by organizing militias and hanging opponents with scant concern for legal niceties. In 1812 economic troubles brought a return of defiant mobs and shootings; that summer the government deployed twelve thousand troops in the heart of England to suppress what many feared would become an insurrection. Dissidents were driven into exile across the Atlantic, where some became American newspaper editors and even congressmen, spreading their blazing hatred of the British aristocracy.[6]

Nevertheless, the regimes in both nations were ambiguous enough that some declared that they should respect one another as equals. Mostly I have spoken of the leaders of a nation as a uniform group, but sometimes we must make distinctions. During the years leading up to 1812 the United States had been severely divided. President Jefferson and his Republican Party had bitter enemies in the leaders of the Federalist Party, a wealthy elite who were appalled by the advance of mass democracy. The Federalists saw Britain's leadership as an elite with political ideals close to their own, and they argued that two countries with "constitutional" regimes and the rule of law ought to stick together.[7] Britain, too, was sharply divided, and many merchants and workers, unlike most members of Parliament, felt a political kinship with Jefferson's quasi-democracy and abhorred the idea of warring on it.

What counts directly in negotiations, however, is the beliefs held by the leaders who actually hold governmental power. The more Federalists praised British aristocracy as a model, the more Jefferson and his supporters hardened their stance. Some warned of plots for a monarchist coup supported from abroad, further driving democratically inclined Americans to view the British regime as dangerously opposed in principle.

On the British side, government officials uneasy about their restive lower classes could barely hide their repugnance for American democracy. The United States was a "mean disgusting country," one of them remarked, "where you may have to dine with your footman." British statesmen respected only the genteel Federalists, who nourished misperceptions among their British friends by telling them that the Republican Party was a small and unpopular faction of vile radicals. Looking across the Atlantic, the British government saw an uncouth mob led astray by firebrand democrats; in return the U.S. government saw a hereditary clique of monarchists busily oppressing commoners.[8]

In this border zone case, as in the Boer War, the American Civil War, and others, the exact places where the two regimes stood in the continuum were not so important as the distance that lay between them—a wide gap in behavior and ideals, further magnified by misperception. In 1812, as in 1860 and 1899, it was not enough that both regimes had a common heritage of constitutional government controlled by a wealthy elite. What counted was that the men actually in power were convinced, not without reason, that the other regime held dangerously different political principles.

"Republics" Under Emperors, Signors, and a Queen

A single case cannot tell us much, but we can set it alongside others in the border zone between oligarchic republics and autocracies. In a greatly different era we have the interesting Swiss war of the 1440s. The fighting began between the democratic Forest States and Zurich, under its proud burgomeister Rudolf Stüssi, but it spread until Zurich was at war also with Bern and other oligarchic republics. That was because Zurich, hard pressed by the mountaineers, struck an alliance with the Holy Roman Empire. The young emperor Frederic III, seeing a chance to recover some of his ancestral Habsburg holdings, called on the nobility of all lands to help Zurich quell this dangerous uprising of peasants against their betters. As armies of knights converged on Switzerland, cities like Bern and Lucerne took up arms alongside the Forest States. Consequently, armies from oligarchic states confronted oligarchic Zurich.

This conflict did not amount to real war between republics of the same kind, for the armies of Bern and Lucerne tramped off to fight foreign noblemen. As one historian remarked, "it seemed that they sought other foes than the Zurichers." When the Swiss confederates finally laid siege to Zurich they did little but bombard the city with primitive cannon. "Nobody in the city died," boasted Zurich's official chronicler, "except one priest and one old woman." Still, a siege is serious business, and we must extract information from what few cases of republican conflict we can find; we should ask whether the governments of Bern and Lucerne felt that they were warring on an equivalent republic.[9]

Before the fighting began, Stüssi's faction had already stifled dissent in Zurich. Leading patricians who said the city should make concessions to the Forest States had been thrown into prison, and later some "traitors" on the city council who sought a compromise peace were beheaded in the marketplace. Even more repellent to the other Swiss cities was the way Zurichers welcomed Emperor Frederic in person into the city. He appointed an Austrian nobleman as Zurich's military leader, and all the townsmen were assembled in the cathedral to swear to obey their new commander. Zurich's submission was more symbolic than real, for a clique of patricians retained effective control of the city's affairs, but from outside the regime no longer looked like a free republic. Once Zurich's leaders repressed domestic dissent, allied with an autocrat, and indeed pledged fealty to him, they seemed to have seceded from the republican fellowship.[10]

We are beginning to locate the frontier across which republics fight autocracies, but we need a few more signposts. Several useful cases can be spotted in Renaissance Italy, where cities often came under the control of narrow cliques dominated by a single dynamic man. Some of these cities rightly claimed to be republics, for the leading clique was careful to work within the consensus of other patricians. Cosimo de'Medici of Florence set the pattern: living modestly as an ordinary citizen, he held no fixed office, but wielded influence through sheer force of character. Such leaders did not suppress other groups as enemy factions, and any man from the more prosperous families had a fair chance at a stint in office. Thus power did not flow entirely downward from the summit but was at least partially distributed among citizens.[11]

A search through Italian history finds that regimes of this type hardly ever went to war against other republican cities, although they did aggressively battle signors and princes. Evidently people were making precise distinctions in choosing war or peace. As usual, the most useful insight into how they chose can be gleaned from the few counterexamples.

One of these began in 1466, when the ancient rivalry between Venice and Florence at last turned violent. There was only one battle, which was actually a sort of chess game of maneuvers (at nightfall the captains walked into the space between their armies and shook hands). Nevertheless, there were some deaths, and it is worth asking whether both sides could be considered republics.[12]

Not Florence, for the insatiably greedy Piero de'Medici, abandoning the consensus politics of his forefathers, had taken full personal control. He had crushed all opposition with prison and exile, until nobody dared speak ill of the Medici. Piero was the first citizen of Florence ever to be called "the signor." It was his domestic politics that sparked the war, for some of his opponents fled into exile and appealed to the Venetians, as fellow republicans, for help in freeing their homeland from tyranny. While they were no doubt tempted by strategic and economic motives, it was this political appeal that the Venetians cited to justify going to war.[13] A few years later Piero died and his heir restored marginally republican forms. Peace was restored in parallel, and henceforth the two republics entirely avoided war.

Nearly identical features can be found in another case from a century earlier. In the 1360s domestic peace was established in Pisa under the paternal dominion of Pietro Gambacorta, who scrupulously respected republican forms, refused the title of signor, and ruled quietly through the consensus of other leading citizens. We are right at the limit of what could be called a republic, but we still find Pisa at peace with Florence and other neighboring republics. But then Pietro was assassinated, and eventually the Pisans selected his nephew Giovanni to lead them. Giovanni promptly attacked his domestic rivals—so weakening them, a chronicler reported, that "they couldn't sneeze without leaning against a wall." In due course he took the title of signor. Now Pisa warred fiercely with Florence.[14]

The societies we have been visiting are so remote from our own affairs that these cases may seem irrelevant. To check whether they contain features that are truly general we need more modern cases. The toughest test is the Spanish-American War of 1898, for both the United States and Spain had democratic constitutions.

To be precise, Spain was nominally a constitutional monarchy under a legislature elected through universal male suffrage. Actually, an elite group of party chieftains took turns in office in a tidy minuet. As an American ambassador contemptuously explained, corrupt officials manipulated Spanish elections to return to office as many of their own party as they wished, "and if any officious person attempts to object he is simply sent to jail." The balance of factions was regulated by the queen regent, the stolid Maria Christina, whose single passion was to preserve the crown for her little son. Menaced by striking workers and restive peasants, her regime increasingly came to lean on the army, or rather on its aristocratic officer corps.[15]

Authoritarian military officers were especially powerful in Spain's colony of Cuba, where they allied with a domineering planter elite. Elections were held in Cuba, but the names of the winners, as one historian put it, were drawn "not out of the ballot boxes but out of the files of party bosses." When peasants rebelled, guerrilla warfare and savage military repression drove thousands of Cubans to exile in the United States, where they incited public opinion against Spain. Americans increasingly saw the Spanish regime as a corrupt and villainous aristocracy. The Spanish leaders were offended—why didn't the U.S. government stifle the exiles instead of prattling about their right to free speech?[16]

Leaders of the United States, not only appalled by the Cuban atrocities but attracted by prospects of economic and strategic gain, demanded that Spain grant the Cubans their freedom. The Spanish government had good reason to bail out of the Cuban mess. But to yield without a fight would have been dishonorable, and loss of honor can be fatal to a regime based on hierarchical status. Surrender land that the army had bled for at the demand of a nation of low shopkeepers? Bowing to democracy would be dangerous to the Spanish regime in many respects, most immediately because, as everyone knew, officers in Madrid would surely respond with a coup. It was not to save Cuba, but to save the dynasty and its system of privileges, that the queen regent and her ministers jointly determined to fight the United States.[17]

This case is a direct counterexample to the old claim that war results from the personal bellicosity of autocrats, who leap to war where common people hesitate. Maria Christina was a good-hearted woman who only wanted to do right by her little boy. In the queen regent's Spain, as in the prince regent's England of 1812, it did not make much difference who wore the crown. What mattered acutely was the ideal of hierarchical status and the attitudes it inspired on both sides. I come back in later chapters to see exactly how these attitudes affected the details of diplomacy in this situation; the present point is that the leadership on each side perceived the other as politically inimical.

To nail the matter down we have one last regime in the zone where democracy shades into autocracy. Modern historians have studied it more thoroughly than all the rest put together, for the errors in this case brought more death than all the rest put together.

The Kaiser as Autocrat

In 1913 there was turmoil in the German town of Zabern—which had been the French town of Saverne until the Germans seized Alsace a generation earlier. The trouble was the fault of a young lieutenant, Günter Freiherr von Forstner, who was even more pig-headed than the usual Prussian officer. After von Forster told recruits that for all he cared they could shit on the French flag, Alsatian schoolboys took to following him through the streets shouting insults. Other soldiers were drawn in and adolescent insolence spread on both sides. Finally the garrison went out of control, arbitrarily pouncing on youths and grown men and arresting them by the dozen. This asinine affair is worth considering for the glimpse it gives into Germany's political culture.[18]

Some commentators have claimed that the war that began in 1914 between Germany and its Western neighbors can be called a war between democracies. In Germany as in France there was open public debate; the German legislature was elected in an approximately democratic fashion, and by an overwhelming majority it voted support for the war. This was a great disappointment to liberals who had imagined that free people would refuse to fight one another. They had not understood what fundamentally divides autocratic from republican regimes.

If Germany had republican tendencies, Kaiser Wilhelm II opposed them to the utmost of his powers. Those powers were weighty, above all in foreign affairs. All appointments to the bureaucracy, the armed forces, and the diplomatic service were made at the kaiser's sole discretion. The man who held this authority could scarcely have been elected village mayor in a functioning democracy. Oscillating between senseless rages and childish pranks, the kaiser left those who knew him doubting his very sanity. Perhaps more importantly, by upbringing and temperament he was fanatically devoted to the principles of autocracy.

The problem was not just his personality but the system that surrounded him. Wilhelm came into contact with hardly anyone but like-minded aristocrats who flattered him endlessly, mostly military officers steeped in principles of warrior obedience and the furious defense of honor. None of these men saw Germany's elected politicians as partners in negotiation, but as enemies to outmaneuver or destroy. The kaiser and his entourage enjoyed talking about the bloodshed they might unleash someday to destroy their enemies, using much the same language whether speaking of unruly German working-class leaders or entire foreign nations.[19]

These attitudes were displayed after the Zabern incident, for the kaiser fervently backed the garrison's illegal attacks on citizens. Wilhelm was passionate about his army and saw any criticism of officers as a threat to the very foundation of the regime. His public support for martial rule had broad implications, for it was common knowledge that the army was eager to arrest the regime's liberal opponents the instant Wilhelm gave the nod.

Wilhelm was only a constitutional monarch, to be sure; the legal head of Germany's government was a chancellor, the well-meaning aristocrat

Theobald von Bethmann Hollweg. He was privately dismayed by the brutality in Zabern, but he held his nose and supported his sovereign. The German legislature, outraged, passed a vote of no confidence. Bethmann Hollweg refused to resign, explaining that he served at the discretion of the kaiser alone. From this point on the legislature mattered little, for Bethmann Hollweg simply bypassed it and ruled by decree.

A less prominent consequence of the affair is equally illuminating. The crown prince was as much a zealot for authority as his father, and avidly supported the repression in Zabern. When a newspaper editor criticized the crown prince for this he was arrested, tried *in camera* for lèse-majesté, and jailed for six months.

When war approached in 1914 Bethmann Hollweg deliberately waited for Russia to mobilize its armies, then exclaimed that Slav barbarians were descending upon the Fatherland. The legislature was not consulted about Germany's declaration of war, but only informed after the fact that its support was required to approve the allocation of funds for defense against the Russians. The liberals could expect to be arrested if they were recalcitrant, but in any case they feared the tsar even more than the kaiser and voted funds willingly. When the German army now turned to invade the democracies of Belgium and France, the attack had nothing to do with Germany's elected legislature at all.[20]

The kaiser's regime, in sum, shared some key features with undeniable autocracies. These exact features also marked other ambiguous autocratic regimes, from Stüssi's Zurich through Medicean Florence and Georgian Britain to Maria Christina's Spain—in fact, every case I have been able to discover where a regime that bordered on autocracy warred with a republic. From detailed inspection of all such cases (see appendix) I find that the wars happened only where three simple conditions were met.

War could result where one side had a ruler who was (1) predominant in war-related affairs: the ruler exercised a veto over important military and foreign policy decisions such as the appointment of key diplomatic and military officials and the declaration of war, and (2) was irremovable from that office: the ruler could not legally be removed (unless entirely imbecile), and the regime would forcibly suppress domestic opponents whose criticism in any way threatened the security of that position.

This corresponds to the way I already defined a "well-established" republic, as a state in which leaders do not coerce politically dissenting fellow citizens. A regime where the author of a paragraph that insults the crown prince is jailed can hardly be called a republic. Of course every regime may prosecute prominent citizens as common criminals, and even in the best democracies politicians may call the law down on a rival with charges like libel or corruption. How are we to know whether someone is being prosecuted for an ordinary crime or as a political opponent? Fortunately, true authoritarian repression does not fool people. In a genuine republic charges must be openly debated in an independent court of law, so it is hard to miss when a ruling group relentlessly refuses to permit anyone to threaten their position in power.

Along with the pair of criteria above, we can get guidance by attending to the words used by people of the time. In all our cases autocrats were given, or took, a title that signaled unrivaled sovereignty: signor, king, emperor. Such titles are not sufficient to make someone an actual autocrat (Britain has its queen to this day). But they do serve as a warning sign, indicating that a particular individual may claim unchecked authority over key decisions.

What about the juntas or other authoritarian regimes that war on republics yet have no single supreme ruler? To understand these regimes we must look at another set of cases, the most problematic exceptions of all. In these cases republics of the same kind—but somehow not exactly well-established republics—sent warriors to kill one another by thousands.

CHAPTER NINE

Well-Established Republics Versus Authoritarian Regimes

The two navies had been maneuvering warily for years in the gusty English Channel, and tempers were strained. In May of 1652 the Dutch admiral Cornelius Tromp was escorting a convoy of merchantmen when he was accosted by English warships under Robert Blake. Both commanders were bold sea dogs, both held strong political opinions, and both served oligarchic republics. Blake sailed up to Tromp's ship and sent a shot across his bow, to warn the Dutchman to dip his flag in the customary acknowledgment of English sovereignty in the channel. When Tromp failed to respond, the English began to fire cannonballs at the flag on his topmast. Somehow the fighting became general, broadside crashing against broadside. News of the battle angered people in both countries so much that the governments could no longer avoid war. A series of indecisive battles followed, leaving several thousand seamen shot or drowned.

This Anglo-Dutch War was minor by comparison with the titanic struggles for survival that the English and Dutch waged against the monarchs of Spain and France during this period. A historian remarked facetiously that it seemed as if the English and Dutch fought "for want of anything more important to worry about." Yet the affair is worth our attention, for it is the deadliest war I have found between two states with full oligarchic republican structures.[1]

England and the Netherlands each set policy through the votes of councils, which were so far from autocracy that no predominant leader can be identified on either side at the time. Nor was either an anocratic regime, for these were solid territorial states that kept feuding factions in check. The two republics were equally far from democracy, restricting political rights to an elite of high birth and substantial wealth. The only remaining question is, were these republics well established?

As explained in chapter 5, I call a republic well established only if the leaders tolerate opposition from domestic political rivals, negotiating mutual accommodation instead of coercing them. Such an abstract definition might easily be twisted by special pleading. One might categorize ambiguous regimes so as to pretend there are no wars between like republics, hiding real problems. To guide us to more specific criteria we have the Anglo-Dutch War and a few others between republics, wars which cannot be explained by the presence of autocracy or anocracy nor by a gap between oligarchy and democracy; indeed, one case is a serious war between two modern democracies. Identifying the features that these exceptional cases have in common will round out our understanding of just what sort of regimes can be counted on to avoid war with one another. Along the way I will also begin to take note of how these features can influence actual diplomacy.

Republics Not Well Established: The First Anglo-Dutch War

Why did Blake fire upon Tromp's flag? Historians agree that the root of the trouble was commercial rivalry, so we will take one final look at the role of economics in conflicts between republics. The worst friction in the Anglo-Dutch case was over the "great fishery" that supplied all of Europe with countless barrels of salted herring. English fishermen watched jealously as hundreds of efficient Dutch ships beat them to the fish that swarmed in the English Channel—stealing away our wealth, said the English. Englishmen also competed against Dutchmen for trade, from the East Indies to the West Indies. These colonial regions were nurseries of domineering attitudes; as European adventurers habitually dealt with natives, so they dealt with rival Europeans, and the lawless cruelties that resulted aroused outrage back home. International mercantile interests do not necessarily foster peace between republics: they can just as easily thrust them apart.[2]

While historians agree that commerce was central to the enmity between English and Dutch, most of them agree that it did not make war inevitable.[3] Diplomats had been haggling over the fishing and colonial problems for decades. To locate the factor that tipped the perennial quarreling into violence we must look elsewhere—at the nations' domestic political systems.

The Dutch considered their republican system well-established indeed. Long ago, they claimed, their ancestors had literally created a homeland from uninhabited salt marshes with their spades, where they governed themselves in free assemblies. It was the usual republican myth of primordial equality, yet the diked fenlands had indeed served to inspire communal effort and defend against knights. By the 1650s burghers in the Dutch cities were well accustomed to settling their affairs by vote in councils elected from patrician families. Their watchwords were consensus and toleration.[4]

England's Commonwealth was similarly governed by representatives in Parliament, elected by the gentry. Decisions on matters such as international negotiations were worked out by the Council of State, an executive committee with rotating membership, and submitted to vote in Parliament. The Dutch government had even stricter checks, for major decisions could only be made by the States-General, an assembly where representatives of each of the seven provinces held virtual veto power; these representatives in turn voted under instruction from an elaborate structure of provincial assemblies and town councils with their own vetoes. Their decision for war belies the old theory that complex constitutional safeguards keep republics from belligerent decisions.[5]

To see how violence began we must look beyond the structural formalities to the political culture. In England this culture was coercive. The leaders of the Commonwealth had been raised as loyal subjects of a monarchy in which the king, with his great hierarchical authority, was taken as the paradigm of appropriate political behavior. King Charles had tried to grasp still greater supremacy through naked force and secret plots, proving himself incapable of accepting any compromise or even of negotiating in good faith. Parliament eventually followed Charles's example all too well, seizing power through civil war.[6]

The new leaders used force against one another as well. In 1648, troops under Colonel Thomas Pride forcibly barred over a hundred members of Parliament from taking their seats, deliberately excluding those who sought a peaceful accommodation with the monarchists. The group that "Pride's Purge" left in power, later named the Rump Parliament, were the ones dedicated to staying in command by any means. They did not dare hold free elections, for the gentry would probably have chosen representatives who would have restored the monarchy. Instead, the regime smothered political opposition with censorship, prison, exile and from time to time an exemplary execution.[7]

A less coercive regime, in accordance with republican ideals, could eventually have been established if people had paid those ideals much heed. But the dominant ideology of the leaders was a zealous and intolerant Puritanism. Many, like Admiral Blake, thought their time of political struggle was meant to prepare the way for an apocalyptic Millennium. Only a few praised the Commonwealth in earthly terms as a republican regime superior in principle to monarchy. The best official reason the Rump Parliament could give for its claim to authority was that it stood on the only genuine foundation of government, namely, the power of the sword.[8]

Yet there was one key group in Parliament who did see themselves first and foremost as republicans, and it was this group that was most responsible for bringing war with the Dutch. These gentlemen were the friends of Henry Marten, a fiery speaker and great advocate of liberty. He and his circle earned reputations as libertines, if not atheists, finding less inspiration in the Bible than in the works of Machiavelli. The Italian theorist had explained how the ancient Roman republic had mastered the world, and they excitedly laid plans to do the same. The trick would be for England to gather other free peoples under its wing and lead a grand league of republics to the destruction of all monarchy and popery.[9]

That brought the Netherlands to mind. On both sides of the channel some people were saying that in the tremendous struggle against the Catholic despotism of France and Spain, England and the Netherlands were natural allies, not only as fellow Protestants but as fellow republics. As a Dutch envoy told Parliament, "one sees in the two Republics the same principles, and the same form of government, since each has foresworn their Monarch."[10] It was time to settle the rankling old commercial disputes and move forward. In 1651 the Commonwealth sent the Netherlands a special embassy.

This will be our first detailed example of how political culture can be reflected in a style of diplomacy that leads to war. The chief English ambassador, Oliver St. John, was no diplomat by experience, nor by character. Contentious and duplicitous, he was notorious for devising political schemes that led to the use of troops and executions. St. John opened negotiations with the Dutch using his characteristic tactics of aggressive manipulation and obfuscation. He insisted that the two republics resolve their differences by merging in some kind of federal union. The Dutch recoiled, for in such a federation their little nation would always be outvoted by England. Yet St. John stiffly refused to negotiate details, demanding that the Dutch commit themselves to the principle of federation without further discussion. The negotiations jerked to a halt.[11]

As we have noticed already in Switzerland, the United States and South Africa, if a republic appeals for union and is rejected, it may take the rejection as evidence that the other regime is not truly their own sort. The English also had other reasons for doubting that the Dutch leaders of 1651 were true republicans.

Under the strain of generations of warfare against Spain, the Dutch had put military power in the hands of the House of Orange. In 1650 William II of Orange had made a bid for full monarchical power, arresting many patrician leaders and cowing the rest with troops. Republican government would have gone under except that William then met an unforeseen foe: he dropped dead of smallpox. His heir could not take his place, for the future William III was still in his mother's womb. The patricians restored their republic. However, the House of Orange and its followers remained a force to reckon with. A monarchy was attractive not only to noblemen and their deferential peasants, but to the common workmen who swarmed dangerously in the streets of the cities. Under an oligarchy such people have often turned to a famous family for protection from the grinding rule of patricians. The government had to handle the Orangists with care.[12]

This impeded relations with the English Commonwealth. For the mother of the future William III was the daughter of King Charles of England, and when Charles was beheaded in 1649, the stroke of the axe had simultaneously instituted a republic in England and made that republic the hereditary enemy of the House of Orange. While William II lived he had made great efforts to restore his relatives to power in England, and after his death his house kept up public pressure against the English leaders, denouncing them as a pack of impious murderers.

While the States-General exercised a conciliatory republican diplomacy, the Orangists shadowed it with a belligerent monarchist diplomacy. When numerous aristocratic refugees fled England for the Netherlands, the Orangists gave them covert support, helping them sail as privateers to harry English shipping. When the heir to the throne of England, Charles

II, made a bid for reconquest in 1650, he sailed for Scotland from a Dutch port in Dutch ships. Meanwhile, he commanded his friends to use their utmost skill to foster enmity between the Dutch and the Commonwealth. When St. John and the other English ambassadors arrived in the Netherlands in 1651, stones flew through the windows of their residence. The ambassadors were frightened, and with good reason in view of the fate of a previous English ambassador: six monarchists had burst into his room and run him through with their swords. The Dutch government had never caught the assassins, and the English indignantly believed that the Dutch had not even tried.[13]

Thus when St. John reopened the stalled negotiations by making a specific demand, it was to insist that the Netherlands suppress the monarchist exiles. Evidently the main reason the English wanted a federal union was so they could oblige the Dutch to treat monarchists as harshly as the Commonwealth did. The States-General would never dare go so far against friends of the Orangists. Besides, the Dutch had a tradition of tolerance for refugees, and found demands to persecute them unsettling. Watching the Rump Parliament's domestic behavior of bloodcurdling diatribes and barely legal executions of opponents right up to their "lawful sovereign," conservative Dutch patricians greatly doubted that such people were trustworthy republican negotiating partners.

St. John's group returned to England with nothing accomplished, bitter and suspicions. Now it was the Netherlands' turn to send an embassy to England to try again to patch up their quarrels. At its head was Jacob Cats, a venerable man of seventy-five who tried to woo Parliament with a flowery speech pleading for friendship among fellow republicans. Parliament listened in stony silence, for they knew Cats was an Orangist. Worse, members of the Dutch embassy were seen consorting with English families notorious for their monarchist sympathies. The feelings of the English Council of State were summed up by its religious minister, who complained angrily about the Dutch emissaries: "there was not one amongst them who was not entirely devoted to the House of Orange, which was an enemy of this state."

The Rump Parliament's leaders were coming to believe that the entire Dutch government had always been on the monarchist side. The Council of State would not compromise with these dangerous Dutchmen. Negotiations foundered as the English dredged up injuries from decades past, meanwhile returning obsessively to the Dutch refusal to form a federation.[14]

It was not this that brought actual war, however, but a direct exercise of autocratic ways. The English monarchs had long claimed sovereignty over the English Channel; they insisted that foreign ships dip their flags in salute, and this was more than symbolic, for a ship admitting English sovereignty was conceding to a toll on herring and the right to search for contraband. The Commonwealth's leaders, retaining hierarchical habits, based their claims in the channel on ancient royal prerogative. Little had changed since 1622, when King James of England had greeted Dutch ambassadors with an arrogant tirade—a nice example of the autocratic negotiating instinct—calling the Dutch a pack of "leeches, bloodsuckers of my realm," and forthrightly declaring, "I decline to treat with you on equal terms." In 1652 Parliament's leaders negotiated in the same high-handed fashion.

Meanwhile, English men-of-war sank Dutch vessels that failed to dip the flag and pay a toll, and boarded merchant ships to force them into English ports under the pretext that they carried the property of England's monarchist enemies. Over a hundred ships were seized in 1651. English judges promptly declared the cargoes forfeit, with an open disregard for legality that outraged the Dutch.[15]

Modern historians have too little documentation to verify just why Marten and other English leaders pushed their maritime claims so aggressively, but historians who witnessed the events were clear. The chief English historian wrote that the war originated in anger over the Dutch rejection of a republican alliance. The official Dutch historian gave much the same explanation, and went on to suggest that Parliament harrassed Dutch shipping to show the consequences of refusing union. It was as if Parliament, like an angry rejected suitor, fought less to drive away the Dutch than to force them into an embrace. Indeed, right through the furious sea battles the English government kept asking the Dutch if they wouldn't really rather turn against monarchists, English refugees, and the House of Orange together, and become federal partners.[16]

Most revealing of all was the specific way fighting began. The States-General, fearing a monarchist rising if it appeared weak when confronting the English, raised a fleet to protect Dutch shipping and placed it under Admiral Tromp. Tromp and most of the Dutch Navy supported the House of Orange, as the English well knew. The flag at Tromp's masthead, which attracted the first cannon shots of the war, was the traditional standard of the House of Orange, topped with a bold orange stripe.[17]

Thus the English were not shooting at people they perceived as fellow republicans. Their political training had scarcely prepared them to understand the delicate balance between the States-General and the Orangists, and the failures of diplomacy led them to identify the Dutch government with monarchists. These were exactly the sort of people who had engaged Parliament for a decade in a struggle to the death.[18] When the States-General gave refuge to Parliament's mortal enemies and refused federation with the Commonwealth, Marten and his colleagues lumped them together as "outgroup," enemies to be punished until they changed their ways.

The English leaders, seeing monarchist plots everywhere (and not imaginary ones), were ready to kill even fellow English gentlemen who threatened their power. With little experience in tolerance, compromise, or legality itself, their solution to conflict both at home and abroad was violence. The Dutch rightly doubted that they could reach a consensus with such men.

None of this is to deny that the war had the usual variety of causes, from nationalist prejudices to religious fanaticism to salted herring. My point is that the single factor that could have prevented bloodshed was absent. Neither side saw the other as people who shared anything like their own approach to politics.

A Parallel Case: The Franco-American Quasi-War

The conflict between the English and the Dutch, with its peculiar twists, cannot provide general conclusions. Fortunately there is a second case, in a quite different locale, with some curiously similar twists. A comparison of the two cases can indicate just which factors mattered, and these indications can be checked against other, widely different cases.

A century and a half after the Anglo-Dutch War and an ocean away, privateers licensed by the Republic of France harassed the commerce of the United States. In place of the gray English Channel they cruised the azure waters of the Caribbean, where the quiet days were only rarely interrupted by a lone frigate sighted on the horizon. For all the differences in nationality and setting, the problem looked much the same.

Again, the most blatant offenses came from a young revolutionary government, the Directory of France. In its formal structure this was as proper a republican government as the Council of State of the Rump Parliament; it was by no means anocratic, autocratic, or democratic. In actual behavior France was as prone as the English Commonwealth to plots and executions. Its conflict with the United States took a violent turn shortly after some of the directors ousted conservative opponents in a military coup closely analogous to Pride's Purge. In sum, the Directory, like the Council of State, thought little of compromise abroad or at home; they too were so precariously in power and so intent on staying there that they saw anyone who refused to combine against monarchy under their leadership as a mortal enemy. These leaders, again like the Council of State, put pressure on their fellow republic overseas in the hope of forcing it into a close alliance against the English king and all other monarchs. When the United States stood aloof, the French punished them by encouraging attacks on their commercial ships. In 1795 alone, privateers seized over three hundred American ships with only a perfunctory nod to maritime law.[19]

The U.S. government was not eager to join in fighting royalty in the 1790s because in those years (unlike in 1776 or 1812) the country was governed practically as an oligarchy by the Federalists, a wealthy elite with aristocratic sympathies. The Federalists saw the French regime much the way conservative Dutch patricians had seen the Rump Parliament: as a lawless faction who had not only murdered their lawful sovereign but were wont to exile or kill their own fellow citizens. Mob politics seemed to threaten at home too, for the Federalists faced the vehement opposition of more democratically inclined citizens. Rumors spread that demagogues were plotting with the French to sponsor an insurrection. The Federalists prosecuted the editors of leading opposition newspapers for sedition and raised troops who seemed intended less to defend against a possible French invasion than to put down democratic agitation within the United States. Meanwhile, the government armed ships to fight French privateers in the West Indies. To the Federalists, suppression of the "French" party at home and defense against French revolutionaries abroad were two pieces of a single struggle.[20]

Negotiations only increased the hostility. The American government had only recently been established, and had little practice in diplomacy. Like the Dutch long before, the Federalists sent abroad envoys who were overtly monarchist, while cultivating cordial relations with the British Crown. The Directory's diplomacy was not only equally inept and inflammatory, but was actively insulting with its peremptory demands for submission (the "XYZ Affair," summarized in the appendix). Relations bogged down in recriminations.

Setting this case alongside the Anglo-Dutch War reveals parallel features responsible for bringing enmity to a head. In both cases a shaky republic sought an alliance, and when rebuffed it classified the other's leaders as monarchist sympathizers. In both cases the other side, none too stable itself, was alarmed by radical exclamations and lawless maritime depredations. In both cases each side, observing the other's domestic strife and the behavior of its diplomats, found further reasons to believe that their rivals were not the sort who would negotiate on a basis of equality and accommodation.

There was one interesting difference between the two cases. Republican ideology, which in the 1650s had only begun to stir in the English-speaking world, was deeply embedded by the 1790s. Many now insisted that any regimes that had renounced monarchy must stick together no matter what. In fact both France and the United States restricted themselves to what historians call a "quasi-war," a scattering of naval encounters where only a few dozen seamen died. While there were other reasons for restraint, ideas about republican solidarity encouraged it in a self-fulfilling prophecy.[21]

In each of these cases at least one side was not fully a well-established republic in the precise sense I have focused on. The Council of State and the Directory visibly refused to tolerate dissent from their domestic peers. Their insistence on maintaining supremacy, and their readiness to use coercion for this purpose, also made for a belligerent diplomacy which helped bring on international conflict.

In these cases the leaders were members of oligarchic elites. It remains questionable whether the lessons of these cases are so general that they can apply to mass democracies. We need to compare their features with a war between modern democracies. Fortunately for our inquiry, we do have one such case.

Democracies Not Well Established:
The War of the Roman Republic

When political scientists write that "there has never been a war between modern democracies," the scrupulous ones add a footnote: "except the War of the Roman Republic." It lasted two months and took perhaps five thousand lives, worth no more than a sentence in most history books, yet some of the finest historians have studied this exceptional conflict.[22] Here, if anywhere, we will discover how the peace between democracies can fail.

In 1848 the people of Paris rose to force their king from power, and France elected a new government by universal male suffrage. Inspired by the example, the following winter the populace of Rome drove their own ruler, the pope, into exile and elected a democratic government—the Roman Republic. Two months later French troops arrived at the city gates.

The reasons the French marched on Rome were directly connected with features of France's democracy that made it far from well-established. The revolution had brought power to cautious middle-class men who knew nothing of how a mass democracy might function. When radical democrats mobilized the workmen of Paris in the "June Days" of 1848, the terrified government replied with troops, killing thousands and driving thousands more into exile. The bourgeois leaders and their demagogic rivals now seemed equally odious to the mistrustful peasants and laborers who made up the majority of voters. Illiterate and bewildered, they sought a magical solution when they voted for president in a free democratic election at the end of 1848. They were offered a candidate with a tremendous name: Louis-Napoleon Bonaparte.

This nephew of the grand emperor was a vague and stumpy man, so incoherent that conservative leaders made him their candidate in the conviction that they could manipulate him as their puppet. Yet he had been a liberal in his youth, and the name Napoleon stood not only for a well-ordered nation but also for the defense of liberty against monarchy. Crowds rallied in the streets shouting, "Long live Napoleon! Long live the Republic!" while other crowds shouted, "Long live Napoleon! Down with the Republic!" He was elected by a large majority.[23]

A free election does not of itself guarantee democracy. An inexperienced and ignorant electorate may choose candidates who are more committed to discipline than to democracy, like the Muslim fundamentalists who won large majorities when Algeria experimented with voting in 1991. The essence of a regime is not the structures but how leaders use them.

Soon after Louis-Napoleon was elected, the conservatives discovered that this dreamy little man would not be their tool. "We're screwed," one politician warned another. "He knows what he can do, and everything he can do, he will." Louis-Napoleon adopted the heraldic insignia of the old empire and allowed people to address him as "Your Highness." French society retained its traditional hierarchical pattern of patron-client relationships, so few objected when Louis-Napoleon quietly gave positions to men whose chief loyalty was to his person. He would need only two years to fulfill his lifelong dream of grasping absolute power. His Highness never saw the Roman Republic's leaders as fellow republicans and equals, for he never saw himself as a republican nor anyone as his equal.[24]

Many of the representatives elected to the National Assembly did see the Roman leaders as fellow republicans, and in 1849 Louis-Napoleon did not have the power to send troops abroad unless the Assembly voted the funds. But a domineering president of a democracy can sometimes circumvent such obstacles. Louis-Napoleon and his ministers insisted that reasonable people in Rome longed for French intervention. According to information from reactionary Roman emigrés and clergy, "foreign ruffians" had converged on Rome and seized power through murder and terror.[25] Moreover, the pope had taken refuge in Naples and appealed for help. Neapolitan, Spanish, and Austrian armies were mobilizing, and the only question was which would arrive first to crush the Roman Republic and impose a vicious, reactionary rule. Louis-Napoleon's spokesmen told the Assembly that France must send troops to protect the Romans from both internal and foreign despotism. It would be a simple police action with scarcely a shot fired. Despite misgivings, the novice politicians of the Assembly voted for troops to protect Rome.[26]

As the soldiers marched inland they saw placards posted by the roadside displaying Article V of the new French constitution: "France will never take up arms against the liberty of any people." That old ideal has more than once inhibited democratic armies from attacking fellow democrats—but this was no democratic army. The soldiers (most of whom could not read a placard anyway) had been rigorously trained to obey their officers without question. The officers, who had made their careers under the old monarchy, distrusted everything republican, and hoped for glory under a new emperor.[27] The French commanding general informed his troops that their task was to brush aside some disreputable "refugees from all nations" and bring freedom to grateful Romans.

When bells within the city sounded the alarm as the French approached, the general believed they were ringing in joy and expected allies within to fling open the gates.[28] Instead he found revolutionary democrats. Many had indeed converged on Rome, putting on red shirts to show their dedication to freedom, and thousands of Romans joined them. These men, as passionate and inexperienced as children, threw themselves upon the French regulars and in six hours of bloody fighting beat them into ignominious retreat.

Back in Paris, many in the Assembly were shocked to learn that Rome had been attacked against their intentions. But it was too late to act, for the following week a new set of representatives was to be elected. Louis-Napoleon's government covertly instructed local officials to obstruct democrats and help his conservative allies, and the peasantry, with its ingrained deference to authority, duly elected a conservative majority. Yet radicals did well in the elections, and panicky conservatives feared a leftist takeover could not be staved off for long.[29]

These conservative fears involved the Roman Republic, for its leaders boasted that they would make the city a center for a revolution that would reach across Europe. Rumors warned that the radicals driven out of France after the June Days had taken refuge in Rome, where they were plundering churches and sending the silver back to Paris to aid their fellow revolutionaries. The conservatives who controlled the French Assembly thus identified their enemies in Paris with the regime in Rome. Meanwhile, liberals were soothed by the manifest fact that Louis-Napoleon wished to settle the affair through diplomacy by inducing the pope to make an accommodation with moderate Romans.[30]

That put the fate of the city in the hands of France's diplomatic corps. This corps was another elite populated by the monarchist personnel of the former regime. The men sent as envoys to the papal court were personally devoted to reactionary Catholicism and hierarchical social order—people who would hardly force a pope to make concessions. The negotiations failed.[31]

As Austrian and Spanish armies approached Rome, Louis-Napoleon sent the French army forward to finish off the affair. His instructions were deviously ambiguous, for he could not constitutionally launch an attack by himself and he did not dare try a vote in the Assembly. But the army commanders knew what he wanted and gladly attacked. Conquering Rome cost the French army over a thousand lives.

We have not yet investigated why the Romans chose battle against insurmountable odds. That was the work of Giuseppe Mazzini. Ablaze with a dedication to human equality, Mazzini had spent months in jail and years in impoverished exile, his friends captured and tortured; he had known only defeat, yet every defeat had added to the moral power of his movement. In 1849 this personal force gave Mazzini control of the Roman regime. He saw in the Roman Republic not just an earthly city but a symbol of universal liberty, which would only become stronger the more martyrs died in its name. Mazzini did not think like an elected leader negotiating the best deal he could get for his nation, but like a self-anointed prophet calling on the world to follow his star.[32]

As for the Roman Assembly, it contained few of the canny politicians needed to run a well-established republic. The pope had promised to excommunicate any Roman who took part in the "prodigious and sacrilegious crime" of elections, so the government was left to radical enthusiasts.[33] Lifted beyond themselves by Mazzini's appeals, the Assembly shouted its defiance of the French. Their reckless defense of Rome inspired young men everywhere with ardent visions of fighting for liberty; in the long run the victory would be Mazzini's.

In the short run the victory was Louis-Napoleon's, and not only because the conquest of Rome brought him the support he had been seeking from Catholic conservatives and army officers. As a bonus, the attack on Rome flushed out French democrats, who took to the streets in vehement protest. While one battalion of French troops was shooting at men in red shirts on the walls of Rome, another was shooting at men waving red flags on the barricades of Lyon. The government jailed or drove into exile thousands of radical democrats. Critics called the repression "the Roman expedition into the interior."[34]

The War of the Roman Republic thus demonstrates again an intimate correlation between domestic and foreign behaviors. It does not contradict the rule that leaders with democratic ideals will make compromises with their equals, for the elites who directly controlled French foreign relations—government ministers, diplomats, and army officers—despised everything democratic. Louis-Napoleon's attack on democracy abroad was only a maneuver in his campaign against democracy in France.

Recognizing Authoritarian Regimes

What kind of regimes exactly were the Rump Parliament, the Directory of France, and the government of Louis-Napoleon? They point to a common class of regimes that are not autocracies with a single all-powerful ruler, yet that seem far from thorough republics. They may be ruled by a military hierarchy under a junta of generals, by a bureaucratic clique as in some Communist states, by a hereditary aristocracy where dukes hold the fealty of barons and so on down, or by a theocracy like the Teutonic monk-knights of Prussia around 1400 or the mullahs of Iran around 1990. Japan in the 1930s managed to combine all these types of regimes in a military-bureaucratic sacerdotal aristocracy.[35]

It is not easy to distinguish these regimes from oligarchic republics. Members of the tiniest clique may practice something like republican equality and tolerance among themselves, as the Soviet Politburo did in certain years. We would expect such a regime to be correspondingly reluctant to war on its own kind. In fact, the military juntas common in the recent history of Latin America and Africa have had a surprisingly slight record of warfare against regimes of their own kind. South America between 1883 and 1932 and ever since 1942, and West Africa since 1957, have been remarkably quiet zones of peace, where regimes far from democratic, and subject to occasional coups and insurrections, have managed to avoid international warfare. Perhaps within the various nations' officer corps or governing civilian cliques, as within an oligarchic republican elite, conflict among peers was customarily resolved in nonviolent ways, and they extended the method to leaders of their own sort abroad. This is only a hypothesis, for juntas work in such secrecy that we know little of their internal relations.[36]

Political theorists generally categorize juntas and like regimes as authoritarian. The authoritarian principle insists that authority flow downward from the head of government, be it a sovereign or a tiny clique who make their decisions in secret. This is fundamentally opposed to the republican principle, which vests sovereignty in a substantial body of equal citizens who may safely engage in public contestation. Some scholars further distinguish among juntas, totalitarian states, personal dictatorships, hereditary monarchies and so forth. Others persist in calling a regime a democracy—but not a "liberal" one—if the leader wins a majority in elections by secret ballot, even though in the meantime any serious opposition group is brutally and lawlessly suppressed. We can ignore these distinctions and lump all such regimes together as authoritarian. Of course, in oligarchies the elite citizens impose their will on all beneath them. But like many political scientists, I reserve the term "authoritarian" for regimes that practice more comprehensive repression, or in short, for any state that is not a republic as it was defined in chapter 2—a regime where political decisions are made in public contestation by a body of citizens who hold equal rights.[37] (I use the term state as a reminder that there are also anocratic regimes, which are more or less authoritarian, but always capable of warring on their own kind.) I would set the border between authoritarian and oligarchic regimes at about the point occupied by the Soviet Politburo in 1968; with only a few dozen equals whose contestation was scarcely public, it could be classified either way.

In chapter 5 I proposed a way to distinguish well-established republics from other regimes, even ones with formal republican constitutional structures. Just ask whether the leaders customarily tolerate full public contestation among citizens, negotiating with domestic political rivals, or whether instead they forcibly suppress dissent even among the nominal citizen class. In our historical examples the difference has been plain enough. Jail or exile at best was in store for anyone, however highly placed, who advocated the election of monarchists in London under the Rump Parliament or in Paris under the Directory, who promoted full democracy in Louis-Napoleon's France or Maria Christina's Spain, who promoted a government by Catholics in seventeenth-century Zurich or by freethinkers in nineteenth-century Lucerne.

To be entirely specific: those who hold office in a well-established republic permit political activity that might lead to their replacement, if only by rivals within their own elite group. In an authoritarian regime, by contrast, demands for loyalty are so concentrated on a particular leader, family, or clique that anyone who works publicly to have the leadership replaced is liable to be punished. This reduces to primitive, observable events the principle of tolerating contestation that is the core of the well-established republic—the kind of republic, that is, that has virtually never warred on its own kind.

Of course, no republic is perfectly free. The most radical dissidents, whether atheists in a medieval city republic, Communist Party members in the United States in the 1950s, or neo-Nazis in Germany today, might be prosecuted for speaking their minds. We are not concerned with repression that only brushes away extremists who have strayed intolerably far from the general consensus of public opinion. The test is how a regime treats a group of citizens who attempt nonviolent public contestation which might actually lead to the replacement of those in power.

It is easy to tell where repression has gone beyond the bounds of republican behavior. One reliable sign of an authoritarian regime is a flock of exiles, some substantial group of citizens whose political activity has not been tolerated. We have already seen political refugees in the early Greek and Italian conflicts, the Swiss religious wars, the Anglo-Dutch War, and the War of the Roman Republic, and exiles were prominent in over half of the more modern conflicts listed in the appendix.[38] A second useful sign of divergence from republican ways is the threat of a coup. This is the other side of a single coin, a resort to violence not by the leaders who hold governmental power but by their rivals; it indicates an elite with a propensity for settling political affairs through coercion.

These signs not only reveal much to historians who seek to categorize a past regime, but held meaning for leaders of the time watching from abroad. A regime boiling with rival political factions that drive one another into exile or that plot against one another in coups does not look like a set of fellow republicans with an inclination to compromise. Thus domestic coercion is not just a useful criterion for categorizing regimes; in international crises it may influence the choice between negotiation and war.

The domestic hostility between ingroup and outgroup can spread across frontiers. Foreign democrats may identify downtrodden classes as people like themselves, who rightfully deserve better treatment. Oligarchic or authoritarian leaders may make the same identification in return, distrusting foreign leaders who support their rabble as much as they distrust the rabble itself. The internal and external enemies merged bodily in cases where people were driven into exile. When three thousand liberals including many exiles marched upon Lucerne in 1847 in an attempt to overthrow the Catholic government, when John Brown called on escaped slaves to help him launch an insurrection against the Southern slaveholders, when ships manned by Cuban exiles smuggled arms to Spanish Cuba from U.S. ports, it might have been hard to tell who was a foreigner and who was a refugee returning in arms. Foreign leaders could readily turn to war when a political division was already so clearly drawn.

While exiles promote war by carrying the effects of intolerance into the homeland of a foreign nation, threats of a coup promote war by strengthening the intolerant spirit within their own nation. I noted how the danger of a coup helped persuade the Spanish government in 1898 to choose war against the United States. Other shaky republics whose fear of overthrow pushed them toward an unyielding foreign stance include the Netherlands when it faced England in 1652, both France and the United States when they battled in 1797, and Ecuador in its 1981 clash with Peru. A survey of diplomatic incidents in the 1960s found that regimes vulnerable to military coups were exceptionally hostile and assertive in their foreign policies.[39] It is another piece of evidence that a regime's behavior is influenced by the political culture of the entire leadership elite—both those in power and those prepared to replace them.

We have seen how suppression of public contestation reliably points to regimes that will war with one another, but so far we have had only glimpses of the direct mechanisms at work. In the cases above it might seem that the wars involving borderline republics were simply a matter of internal enemies connecting with external ones. This was in fact my own hypothesis, until I found a few conflicts where there was no obvious internal enemy on either side corresponding closely with the external one. We must look at these if we are to identify features that determine war or peace between republics in every single case. The best evidence comes from another military confrontation between two democracies, this one no obscure footnote but a turning point in twentieth-century history.

CHAPTER TEN

Well-Established Republics Versus Newborn Republics

The Ruhr: the industrial heartland of the German Republic, a hundred towns thundering with machinery. In January of 1923 the grimy streets were patrolled by squads of French soldiers. Four years after the First World War ended they had marched into the Ruhr and seized its mines and factories to enrich France. Although not actual war, it was a hostile invasion that left millions of Germans impoverished and humiliated, contributing to the eventual rise of Nazism. Here is an excellent place to search for the exact processes that can push hostility between modern democracies to the point of grave harm.

We shall find again that only one condition need be met for serious coercion, namely that at least one of the republics must fail to be well-established. Earlier I defined the term in relation to the suppression of internal opposition. There was indeed some suppression in Germany—but it scarcely figured in the diplomatic negotiations. We must dig deeper. We shall find that the Ruhr invasion can be understood, in a surprising consistency with the other possible counterexamples, by narrowing down the definition of a well-established republic. The result will clarify how republican political culture determines which regimes are manifestly well-established enough to reliably keep peace with their own kind.

Two Germanies and Their Diplomacies

Every night in the summer of 1920, the lights of Paris dimmed after ten o'clock, for coal shortages forced rationing of electricity. Northern France was a wasteland where the retreating Germans had deliberately wrecked coal mines and much else. With the French government near bankruptcy, politicians promised a painless solution: "Germany will pay!" In the treaty signed at Versailles the Germans had agreed to pay enormous reparations for reconstruction of the devastated territories. Payment was expected promptly, for in the German cities, untouched by the war, the lights shone and blast furnaces roared.

The German government was at this time a parliamentary democracy based on universal suffrage, much like the French government. But the German representatives at Versailles had behaved as arrogantly as when they were officials under the kaiser, and the French concluded that for many years they would be dealing with the old Germany, a criminal nation. To prevent renewed aggression they meant to keep Germany weak. All the better, then, if Germany endured grievous sacrifices in order to deliver the promised reparations to the French and their English and Belgian allies. However, with people in Germany already suffering and mutinous, the shaky new government did not dare to impose the necessary taxes. Ministers insisted that Germany could not possibly make the stipulated deliveries of coal and cash.[1]

The first diplomatic collision came in 1920, at a conference between the Allies and Germany in the Belgian town of Spa. One irritation was the head of the German army, General von Seeckt, who tactlessly came in uniform. The French envoys, with a million dead at their backs, found it hard to receive this rigid Prussian ornamented with medals, glaring severely through a monocle. Von Seeckt was exactly as he appeared, an authoritarian warrior who thought democracy was idiotic. He coolly announced that the German army would not reduce its numbers nearly as much as promised in the Versailles treaty.[2]

Tempers got worse when the conference turned its attention to coal deliveries. The crucial statement came not from any official German representative but from Hugo Stinnes, the most powerful of the German industrial barons, the notorious "king of coal" with vast holdings in mines and a dozen other industries. A restless and untidy man, Stinnes looked (as one diplomat put it) like "a rough-haired terrier just come out of one scrap and in search of another." With studied effrontery he told the Allied representatives that their demands were unreasonable. When the Belgian chairman interrupted to ask him to speak more moderately, Stinnes shot back, "I'm not standing here in service of courtesy."[3]

That was precisely the problem. A German delegate tried to smooth things over privately by explaining that Stinnes was used to addressing his corporate board meetings in such a tone. An uncompromising manner had served Stinnes well in his meteoric rise to the summit of the authoritarian hierarchy of German industry. But an overbearing approach may be more appropriate in a corporate office than in a diplomatic conference. The British prime minister remarked that for the first time he had met "a real Hun."[4]

Stinnes's defiance of the Allies won him enthusiastic praise back in Germany, and not only in his own newspapers. He was already the most visible German industrialist and even held a seat in the German legislature. However, contemptuous of democratic speech-making and politicking, he soon quit that. "A few businessmen sitting around a table," he declared, "could achieve more reconstruction than all the chatter of self-seeking politicians." Stinnes's ideal regime would be a sort of oligarchy run by the wise barons of commerce.[5]

Other powerful Europeans felt much the same. To replace the society the war had wrecked they envisioned a corporate system of almost medieval form. Behind a democratic facade decisions would be made by committees of bankers and industrialists, collaborating where necessary with labor union potentates. Many modern nations show tendencies toward such a guild system, so we should see what it might mean for international conflict.[6]

The problem of reparations was not insoluble. Many people believed that if Germany did its honest best, the Allies could be persuaded to strike a compromise. Such was the conciliatory policy that the German government ministers had brought to Spa. But as the British prime minister noticed, "Herr Stinnes, and those whom he represented," vetoed attempts at accommodation.[7]

Statesmen on all sides set doggedly to work. In the following two and a half years they held seven formal conferences and countless private meetings. The proceedings were typical of the way democracies negotiate with one another, a dull tale of commissions studying payment schedules, thick draft reports, lawyerly speeches, indignant newspaper editorials, private compromises, public votes in one or another body, and then a return to more studies.[8]

To the French, it boiled down to the plain matter of collecting lawful payments from a debtor. Nobody took a more legalistic tack than the French premier, a former lawyer, Raymond Poincaré. Although brought up to regard Germans as congenital militarists, in dealing with them Poincaré was always frank and precise. He expected to win his demands with irrefutable proof that they were just.[9]

The Germans' approach was different. Swearing that the Allies' demands were neither fair nor feasible, they fought with a mixture of rigid refusals, evasion, and delays. The Allies increasingly doubted that Germany was negotiating in good faith. The will to compromise, to keep explicit promises to deliver coal, to tell the truth, even to admit obvious realities, all seemed absent.

These failings were not, the Allies began to realize, entirely the fault of the elected German leaders. The new government, following the old German pattern of deference to authorities, had placed its economic policy in the hands of "experts." A few dozen wealthy businessmen, meeting frequently in committees, worked out policy for the government. Following the unyielding views of Stinnes, their most influential member, the committees made sure that German government proposals for deliveries were set so low as to seem derisory.

The Allies angrily pressed the German government for more generous deliveries, and the ministers yielded, sincerely promising to do their best. The industrial magnates were not powerful enough to make their government formally adopt their chosen policy. But when it came to carrying policy out, the magnates had a free hand. Stinnes and a few others personally obstructed the promised deliveries through endless subterfuge. France got far less coal than it needed.[10]

Before the Spa conference the German prime minister had warned a British diplomat that he must not think of a policy toward "Germany," for there was not one Germany but two. The British diplomat had already noticed two types of German diplomacy. The representatives of the new democratic government struck him as "sincere, straightforward men." But alongside them were unreformed holdovers from the old imperial regime, "overbearing, bullying and tyrannical" men who left an "impression of unabashed unreliability."[11] These old-school Germans constituted a shadow regime with oligarchic or wholly authoritarian ideals, despising democracy and working to replace it. They had room to maneuver in foreign affairs, for government ministers were distracted by domestic turmoil, and revolution had left the diplomatic establishment in disarray. The Allies discovered that they were not negotiating reparations with a democratic government so much as *through* it, with people of a different stripe.

These Germans were manifestly more irritating to negotiate with than leaders of the older democracies. Britain and France, for example, were virtual enemies over issues ranging from huge wartime loans to ambitions for hegemony in the Near East, yet their relations never approached the level of subterfuge and mistrust the French and British encountered with Germany. The exchanges were almost too frank. For example, at one point Poincaré lectured an elderly British diplomat so severely that the latter turned pale with rage and collapsed in a faint. "The two protagonists were separated and taken to different rooms," it was reported, "where they were fanned and flapped by their seconds." Yet after mutual apologies the bargaining resumed as if nothing had happened.[12]

Both France and Britain were confident that no conflict would end without such a reconciliation. The more their foreign policies clashed, the more the French and British leaders assured one another that, no matter what, their governments and their peoples would remain perpetual friends. It sounds like a banal platitude, yet in fact every dispute was either resolved or quietly set aside for later negotiation.

Many in Britain and the United States expected that as the Germans became more democratic, negotiations with them would become smoother. The French did not believe that it would be so easy. They thought the authoritarian character of the entire German nation (what we could call its political culture) was too entrenched to change quickly.

Then why not negotiate directly with the German magnates? A French politician suggested that the Allies bypass Germany's elected government and deal with "the ten or twelve masters of German industry who are in reality financially the masters of Germany." Such an approach, however, was doomed by the contempt that democratic and oligarchic leaders normally feel toward one another. The Spa fiasco was almost the only time any German industrialist talked directly with Allied diplomats, and afterward Poincaré complained that Stinnes had "personally been the obstacle" to reconciliation. Stinnes "is at present setting policy for the German government and industrialists," Poincaré warned; "he is the worst enemy of German democracy and of ourselves." When it was proposed that the French government meet with industrialists like Stinnes, Poincaré said the French public would not stand for it.[13]

Nor did industrialists like Stinnes want to waste their time with jabbering democratic politicians. They worked to bypass elected governments and meet directly with their foreign counterparts, just as they did when they worked out international cartels. Stinnes and his colleagues engaged in secret correspondence and direct visits with London bankers, French ironmasters, and the like, seeking agreements on reparations deliveries— with handsome profits for the corporations on both sides, of course. German ministers supported such efforts, being so unpracticed in democracy that they imagined industrial "experts" would represent the interests of all Germans.[14]

If the French had likewise turned affairs over to their magnates, a deal would probably have been struck; oligarchies bargain well with their own kind. But Poincaré indignantly rejected any scheme not negotiated directly between elected leaders. Financiers were men of limited competence, he said, and he would never accept them as "the arbiters of our rights." The premier was in tune with his supporters, millions of shopkeepers and petty functionaries who distrusted the power of wealth as much in the Paris Bourse as in the Ruhr.[15]

French democrats saw the obstructive German diplomacy as proof that Germany was not led by men sympathetic to their own ideals. A French journalist said Germany was neither a democracy nor a monarchy, but a "Stinnesy." In truth, the German government's final offer on reparations was personally drawn up by Stinnes, and it was again rigid and unrealistic, perhaps deliberately provocative. The French concluded that there was no point in further negotiation.[16]

The policy urged by a few dozen industrial oligarchs could not have wrecked negotiations without broad support among important sectors of the German regime and population. Germany in the 1920s did not have a single dominant political culture, but was fragmented to an exceptional degree. While the new constitution reflected democratic ideals, many Germans openly respected force and obedience, and wished only to leave affairs in the hands of officials brought up in the ways of the old monarchy. People dedicated to democracy were a minority under attack. Right-wing bullies harrassed them and authoritarian officials sent democratic leaders to jail on trumped-up charges. Some of the most prominent democrats fell to assassins, and judges held over from the kaiser's regime gave the perpetrators minimal sentences. The French noted all this with little surprise.[17]

The German government looked still less like a democratic partner when it revealed an affinity with the Soviet regime. Abruptly announcing that they had secretly struck an economic pact with the Bolsheviks, the German leaders not only appeared tactless and underhanded, but aligned themselves with the world's most fearsome authoritarian state. The French suspected (correctly) that the treaty included secret military clauses: General von Seeckt was preparing for the day when Germany could crush France for good. And if Germany's regime was nevertheless democratic enough to remain peaceful, how long would it survive? German elites were debating whom to make dictator—von Seeckt probably. Coup attempts followed one after another, and it seemed that the next might succeed. The French, in short, saw in Germany no leadership they dared trust for long, and felt that in the end their defense must depend on sheer military strength.[18]

The French had repeatedly warned that they would use force if necessary to collect what was due them. "A few battalions sent to Mannheim," a French leader had remarked in 1921, "would bring Herr Stinnes quickly to his senses." Magnates like Stinnes did not fear the French, however, but enemies closer to home. The hated Socialists could win control through elections if workers did not first seize power by force. The magnates were actually inclined to welcome a French incursion, foreseeing that it would drive all Germany into the arms of the nationalist right.[19]

When Poincaré realized that Germany would never compromise, he ordered the French army into the Ruhr. He was under pressures of the sort that commonly bring on wars—dire financial straits, outraged public opinion, fear of a future military threat, and so forth. He did not believe that he was bringing force to bear against fellow democrats; the real adversary was a few wilfull authoritarians. Poincaré exlained that now Herr Stinnes would not need to come to Paris to negotiate: he would speak to Stinnes in the Ruhr, where the conversation would presumably be more fruitful. The premier also understood that this was not actual war. If serious armed resistance had been likely the French would never have marched. French troops, the sometime lawyer explained, were like policemen who help collect a debt.[20]

The invasion nevertheless had consequences as serious as many a war. German workers were driven to destitution, the middle classes were bankrupted by inflation, and the democratic government was discredited. The crisis gave a crucial boost to an obscure splinter party led by a nationalist named Adolf Hitler.[21]

The Ruhr case gives us a check on the role of domestic repression in conflicts between republics. Despite a fairly high level of private and quasi-legal government repression of democratic leaders, Germany did have vigorous public contestation. The Germans' deviation from democratic tolerance was not decisive by itself. Far more important was a perception the French had of the Germans, which was built on memory. Dreadful experiences of war had left the French convinced that Germans were an innately authoritarian people, whose leaders answered only to force. The postwar assassinations and other repression in Germany mattered chiefly because they kept these prejudices alive.

French misgivings were reconfirmed by German negotiating practices. The German government plainly found it harder to deal with democratic politicians than with barons of industry or even Soviet commissars. The endless obstructions, denials, harsh surprises, and preposterous demands gave witness that Germany was in the hands of men who would stamp down their enemies by any means within their power.

Domestic repression is only a common and unmistakable indicator of a more fundamental force. In the Ruhr crisis we see this force stripped down to its essence: the regime's political culture—or rather the political subcultures of the groups that influenced decisions. International relations are not affected directly by domestic actions so much as by the way political culture influences the foreign relationship, particularly by shaping perceptions of the leadership. One common way political culture is made manifest is through domestic repression, but another and more direct way is through the negotiating process itself. Poincaré sent soldiers in place of diplomats because he was convinced that Germany was in the hands of men who would never negotiate fairly except under intense pressure.

Of course there were many unique features in the German case, such as the Germans' oligarchic shadow diplomacy, and it might look as if I am straining to hunt down special circumstances to excuse hostility between democracies. Actually, I focus here and in all cases on what contemporary observers and later historians described as the core political and diplomatic features of the conflict in question. In every crisis that might serve as a counterexample to peace among similar republics, one particular feature is always prominent. Conflict exploded at one point: where there was a conspicuous gap between leadership groups, leading one side to believe that the other adhered to an alien and repugnant politics.

Newborn Republics at War

The Ruhr invasion solved nothing, but the quarrel over reparations was eventually put to rest with the aid of American money. As Germany came to look more like a genuine and stable democracy, its neighbors gradually moderated their mistrust. By the latter 1920s relations between Germany and France had grown so smooth that diplomats were talking about general European disarmament, if not actual federation. War came again only when Germany became a dictatorship; peace and talk of federation returned with German democracy.

This type of change is common and crucially important. Looking over all the cases of conflict between republics, I was struck by the extraordinary timing of restraint. Hereditary foes developed a cordial relationship within a few years after establishing similar republican regimes. On the other hand, states that had kept the peace for generations lunged into war shortly after one of them lost its republican government. We have already seen examples in such long-term rivalries as ancient Athens against Thebes and medieval Florence against Pisa or Siena, as well as modern France against Germany.

Another striking example of enmity switching off and on is found in the way the oligarchic republics of the Netherlands dealt with the comparable city-republics of northern Germany at the close of the Middle Ages. They quarrelled incessantly over the Baltic trade, yet managed to settle each dispute peaceably. Then, in 1428, Philip of Burgundy won control over Holland and began constructing a centralized autocratic state. Just two years later the Dutch and Germans went to war (the main cause was Philip's ambitions). Sea fighting continued intermittently for a century. Then, in the late 1500s, the Dutch threw off their overlords and once again stood as a federation of free republics. Their commercial rivalry with the German republics had grown fiercer than ever, yet the warfare ceased at exactly this point.[22]

Still more significant is the fact that warfare has not always ceased at the very moment when both sides became republics. The appendix lists twenty-one clear cases of full warfare between regimes that could be called, with some stretching, republics of the same kind. In all but seven of these cases at least one of the republics was not more than a few years old; most often it was just a few months old at the time the conflict began.[23] Since republics commonly last several decades or even centuries, it is plain that the probability of conflict with a fellow republic is vastly higher when one regime is newborn. Looking at military confrontations below the level of full warfare, such as the occupation of the Ruhr, we again find a highly disproportionate number of infant republics on at least one side: nine out of my sixteen crises in medieval and modern times.[24]

Any kind of newly formed government will be inexperienced in foreign affairs, and plagued with divisions that may push the leaders to act belligerently abroad or tempt aggressors to exploit its weakness. Statistical studies find that regimes established through an overturn of the existing order, no matter whether the new government is authoritarian or democratic, have a heightened tendency to get into wars during their first five or ten years.[25] Yet nations are not reliably inhibited from war simply because they have long-lasting governments, or history would be more tranquil. It is not simple duration but some special factor in republics that makes for mutual peace. Evidently this factor is weak when a regime is born but rapidly strenghtens as the regime stabilizes.[26] This fact gives us a new way, independent of all the foregoing, to identify the factor that must be "well established" before republics will keep mutual peace.

Changes in a nation's economic and social structures, even those effected through revolutions, usually take place gradually, evolving over decades or generations. These structures cannot be responsible for guaranteeing peace between republics after just a few years. On the other hand, if republican constitutional structures were reliable inhibitors of war, we would expect peace to become certain as soon as the new formal mechanisms went into operation. However, in many of our cases the new laws and councils and elections were operating for months or years before war began.

In a survey of numerous crises, the political scientist James Lee Ray found no wars between modern democratic regimes that satisfied a particular criterion. Peace held where both regimes had at least once transferred power through elections from one group of leaders to an opposing party.[27] Ray's criterion gives approximately the same results as simple duration of the regime, but raises additional questions. The concept of transferring power to an opposition party is inapplicable to many early consensus-driven republics, where formal political factions were seen as wickedly divisive. Even in modern times the criterion has problems of definition, as Ray recognized; for example, Hitler took power in Germany in a constitutional transfer, yet the resulting regime was neither democratic nor peaceful, while nations like modern Italy and Sweden were undoubtedly peaceful democracies although they were governed by a single party for an entire generation. Ray's criterion, like the criterion of duration, is apparently a surrogate for some more fundamental factor.

The only factor I can find which meets every historical test is the presence of republican political culture. In modern Italy and Sweden, but not Nazi Germany, political beliefs and practices made a peaceful change of leadership a real possibility. Ray's criterion of a visible transfer of power to an opposition party is useful because such transfers occur only where public contestation and accountability of leaders exist. Other political scientists point to a free press, honest elections, an independent judiciary, and so forth as indicators of whether or not a regime tolerates public contestation. I get a usable answer simply by checking whether or not political rivals of a given regime have been jailed, exiled, or killed.

A political culture tolerant of dissent is established only with the passage of time. In the first few turbulent years of a newborn regime, nobody can be sure whether dissent is tolerated. Rumors of coups fill the air, old enemies threaten treason and are punished. Even if citizens in fact use the rule of law to settle their disputes, for a while nobody can be sure how reliable the practice is. Until a regime is at least a few years old, it would be imprudent to call it "established" in the most everyday sense of the word.

To identify political culture as the key criterion does not invalidate my definition that a republic is well established provided the leaders tolerate full public contestation, but only addresses a weak point in that definition by stipulating how tolerance is demonstrated. Requiring that a regime be maintained for at least a few years provides a useful shortcut for automatically excluding ambiguous newborn regimes. Many of the conflicts between what seem at first glance to be republics of the same kind can be dismissed out of hand by noting that they were simply too young to have a manifestly reliable republican political culture.

We can rule out only very young regimes, however. We observe not only that wars can occur between newborn republics, but that wars disappear after both sides are a few years old. To check whether political culture could be the key factor we must ask how quickly it can be established.

Establishing Republican Political Culture

Building a republican political culture, many believe, takes generations of work. People must learn from childhood the appropriate beliefs about how disputes should be settled, along with particular customs like voting. Also required is an elaborate civil society with deeply rooted private organizations having traditional networks of overlapping obligations, which reflect and perpetuate political culture through their daily activities. The extensive work required for all this became painfully clear in Eastern Europe after the collapse of Communist rule. One Czech writer said the citizens were like long-term prisoners who had become "jail smart"; they were deceitful and obsequious, hardly prepared for democratic politics.[28]

The leaders of a newborn republic may hold to principles far different from those embodied in the nation's formal constitution. In a new regime like Louis-Napoleon's France or Stinnes's Germany we often find holdovers practiced in the old authoritarian ways dominating key groups such as the diplomatic corps, the army command, the bureaucracy, the managers of industry and finance, the judiciary, and the legislature itself. Recent examples are the newborn quasi-democracies of Croatia and Serbia which warred in 1991; the elected leaders were former Communists, men so accustomed to domineering that they were, as a colleague complained, "simply incapable of compromising."[29]

How long does it take for a republic to become well established, in the crucial sense that its leaders are accustomed to handling conflict through negotiation rather than coercion? We can approach that question by drawing a line of demarcation that sets apart all young quasi-republics that have gotten into wars with republics of their own kind. This is a non-circular way to set a consistent criterion for when a republic is "well established," provided the resulting time limit does not turn out to be so long as to exclude even one regime that in a general sense might be called firmly established as republican.

In fact, this criterion turns out to be highly inclusive. Inspecting all the borderline cases, I find that once toleration of dissent has persisted for three years, but not until then, we can call a new republic "well-established." This may seem like an unreasonably short period, for republican government is often shaky for decades. A regime in its fourth year is often still vulnerable to a coup, for example. Yet it turns out to be well-established enough to maintain peace with its own kind.

History records no real war between democracies that had both been established for longer than three years (setting aside a few ancient Greek cases where we do not know the duration of both regimes). War between similarly stable oligarchic republics has been amazingly rare. The only possible cases I have found among the hundreds of oligarchies down the centuries are the somewhat accidental battles between Lucerne and Bern (both of which could be said to have coerced political dissenters, if we understand that the opposition involved political as much as religious principles), and the War of the Pacific between Peru and Chile (both of which were battlegrounds for autocratically-led factions intermittently prone to using coercion against their rivals).

Three years is a reasonable time in which to establish the elementary rules of republican behavior. Where the political culture and the new constitution are incompatible, before long either the behavior must change or the regime must fall. Behavior often does change, for people are adaptable. Historical, psychological, and social science studies agree that when the rules of a political game shift, many people quickly learn to play by the new rules.

Certainly some leaders are tempted to persist in the old coercive ways. The victors in an election see a chance to crush their rivals for good, and the losers contemplate reversing the outcome by force. Yet to resort to force and lose could mean exile or death. It may seem a better gamble to try the new republican politics, the winners governing within limits while the losers prepare for the next election. In this way republican practices can arrive through prudence without any heartfelt conversion to new beliefs. Perhaps it takes generations for an entire society to change to the core, yet the essential daily practices of frank speech, compromise, and so forth are attractive enough for people to take them up quickly. At a minimum, when old ways have been blown to vapor many people will take refuge in a ritualistic conformity to the new legal constitution. Before long the practices may become second nature.[30]

One demonstration of this is a daring experiment that Italy conducted in the 1970s. The national government in Rome abruptly turned over many of its powers to local, democratically elected bodies. A team of sociologists took the opportunity to interview regional elites, and in their first look they found a striking stability of political culture. Tuscany had retained cooperative and egalitarian relationships since the time of the medieval city-republics, while in Sicily, patronage and subservience lingered as always. Yet when the sociologists returned after a few years, they found that beliefs and practices were changing. Now that external constraints and opportunities had shifted, formerly hierarchical chiefs were turning to more democratic and cooperative ways.[31]

The behavior of a nation's leadership can change even more swiftly when a new group, holding a different subculture, seizes power. The founders of a republic are often people who have debated one another through the night in kitchens or cafés, and published their arguments in foreign journals—who were already living in a "republic of letters" where coercion had no place. They did not need to convert to republican ways so much as learn how to apply them in practice.[32] In sum, the political culture of a nation's leadership will shift as a result of both changes in personnel and personal changes. It seems reasonable that this will take neither weeks nor decades, but a few years.

There is another time interval to consider. No matter how fast the leaders of a new republic adopt republican ways, the character of a regime in its birth throes will not be obvious to foreigners. People hold tight to stereotypes about national character, as the French mistrusted Germans in 1920. The modern cases listed in the appendix include eight conflicts which were brought on in part by exaggerated misgivings about ambiguous regimes, nearly all of them new.[33] But anyone who follows the news has seen that spectacular events can alter the beliefs that we hold about a foreign government. One study found a substantial shift in Americans' perceptions of the trustworthiness of the Soviet Union's leaders (and opinions about how the United States should deal with them) in a single year that was punctuated by an important summit meeting.[34]

A new republic is not only liable to be misperceived, but to have its own naive misperceptions. If many in France believed in 1849 that the Roman Republic was ruled by a gang of criminals, that was not only because the Romans had yet to demonstrate stable self-government, but also because French politicians had not developed the experience and independent sources of information they needed to resist the propaganda of Louis-Napoleon and the papacy. In sum, where either of two regimes is newborn, some time is needed for them to build mutual trust. It seems reasonable that this will take neither weeks nor generations, but a few years.

The fact that regimes with republican constitutional structures can get into wars with their own kind during the first few years after they are born, but not later, gives us an additional reason for looking to the political culture of the leadership, in particular as it is perceived from abroad. This factor, unlike almost any other factor invoked to explain international relations, has exactly the right time scale of change. Note that this line of reasoning is independent in its logical and factual basis from the other reasons I have given for focusing on perceptions of political culture.

My general argument is now complete. I have supplied a few simple, readily observed criteria that consistently distinguish a category of regimes, which may reasonably be called well-established republics, from anocratic or authoritarian regimes. Within this category I have given criteria to differentiate between what may reasonably be called oligarchic republics and democracies. The surprising and highly consistent pattern of war and peace among regimes so defined, and the criteria that prove to define the borders, all point toward one explanation. Leaders of republics behave abroad with the same tolerance used at home towards those they perceive as adhering to their own political culture. This does not explain everything about how and why wars arise, of course, but it fully accounts for how republics maintain peace with their own kind.

This explanation cannot be entirely convincing in such an abstract form. Our next task is to look for political culture actually at work in the details of specific international negotiations. A random sampling of crises should show (or, if the argument is wrong, fail to show) plain and consistent differences between the diplomatic approaches of republican and authoritarian regimes, differences that have directly influenced decisions for war or peace.

CHAPTER ELEVEN

Authoritarian Diplomacy

In 1802 Anthony Merry, a young diplomat just arrived from Britain, rode through Washington City to the President's House to present his credentials. Resplendent in ceremonial dress with gold lace and sword, Merry was appalled to find President Thomas Jefferson lounging in casual clothes, threadbare and not entirely clean. Jefferson was only underscoring his democratic ways, but Merry believed the American was delivering a studied insult. Worse misunderstandings arose at diplomatic receptions in the following months. When the guests proceeded into the dining room Jefferson customarily insisted on egalitarian catch-as-catch-can seating, but the British envoy and his wife felt that only a high position at table would befit their status and scrambled for the proper chairs. Merry felt so humiliated, and became so overbearing, that his government was obliged to call him home. His successors failed to repair the damage to good relations; a dozen years later a British army seized Washington City and burned it down.[1]

It seems ridiculous to suppose that the petty grudges of a stripling ambassador could have anything to do with bringing on war. Yet historians and diplomats have often remarked that a single wrong sentence can affect a crisis. Scholars have increasingly focused attention on how diplomatic style influences negotiations.[2] In diplomatic negotiation, each set of leaders is confronted with the other's approach to handling conflicts—its political culture. Are the others likely to negotiate a fair compromise, or to plot deviously and suddenly attack? In the course of negotiation leaders must decide whether to deal with the other side as trustworthy ingroup or despicable foe. And in the course of negotiation they find information to advise them.

We saw in chapter 8 that the normal maintenance of peace between republics failed in 1812, when each side believed that the other followed antithetical political principles. These perceptions were influenced by diplomatic actions. Merry's attitude reflected a preoccupation with hierarchical status that permeated every act of the British government, giving rise to fatal animosities in the United States.

We have already glanced at other situations where the style of a regime's foreign diplomacy reflected its domestic political culture. The Chia-ching emperor, Party Secretary Leonid Brezhnev, Oliver St. John of the Rump Parliament, and Hugo Stinnes each behaved in the style characteristic of his political upbringing. As I pointed out in chapter 5, many have observed that the diplomacy of "liberals" has regularly differed from that of "totalitarians" (or merchants from warriors, burghers from lords, etc.). I also reported that some meticulous statistical studies have shown that diplomatic style does indeed vary according to regime type.

Our current limited understanding revolves around a simple bipolar distinction. One pole has been called the "conflictual" or "aggressive" style of dealing with rivals in a dispute. Its opposite is what I will call the "cooperative" style, defined as a relatively frank and honest approach, not prone to lawless coercion but to searching for agreement through mutual accommodation. These terms are subjective, but scholars and diplomats have generally been able to distinguish honest offers of compromise from lies and threats.

The cooperative style does not fit easily with hierarchical and authoritarian principles, but it is in strict accord with the basic republican ideals of respecting others as equals, tolerating differences under the rule of law, and working for the public good as a whole. As I reported in chapter 5, several studies have shown that regimes with relatively republican political structures do indeed tend to use relatively cooperative diplomatic approaches, as compared with the more belligerent approaches, of authoritarian regimes. Therefore, I will sometimes refer to "republican" and "authoritarian" styles, while bearing in mind that the connection is only a statistical tendency.

Does a particular negotiating style in a crisis actually affect the outcome? Below I review some social science studies that suggest it does. Then, in the rest of this chapter and the two following, I review additional diplomatic crises that show explicitly how the way republics and authoritarian regimes managed relations with one another led to war or peace.

Here my method of argument changes. Until now I have concentrated on presenting a comparative analysis of a full set of borderline cases. This produced a few simple features that reliably sort regimes into categories that do or do not maintain mutual peace. The features that turned out to be crucial (tolerance, duration) pointed toward an explanation of peace among republics in terms of political culture and ingroup identification. The explanation, however, is indirect and tentative. To validate such an explanation we must use another approach—a detailed study of individual cases.

For every crisis ending in a war, investigation should support a particular conclusion: "If only both regimes had been similar well-established republics, the dispute would have been resolved peacefully." Such a counterfactual statement can never be proved amid the multiple forces affecting human affairs. Yet that does not mean we must give up trying to understand anything. It suffices to check whether an explanation is plausible, or at least is better than other explanations or arbitrary guessing as a practical guide to action.[3]

To check the validity of the political culture explanation, I will take a sample of crises and inspect the details. Where one side was authoritarian we should imagine the leaders adopting a more republican political culture (I mention this counterfactual thought-experiment explicitly in some cases, but it is implicit in all). The question is whether such a change of political culture would have changed their diplomacy in such a way that war would have been less likely. The more cases where such effects are plain, and the fewer counterexamples where nothing of the sort is visible, the more plausible our explanation of peace among republics.

To make the toughest possible test, I will continue to inspect crises between what seem almost like republics of the same kind, working onward through the list of possible counterexamples. (The only such crises I have not examined in depth are premodern ones where little record of the diplomacy has survived.) For contrast, in the present chapter I also look at some wars that involved an undoubted autocracy. Such cases are countless, and as a criterion for selecting a sample I chose those for which the diplomacy has been most thoroughly studied by historians. Finally, and worth especially close inspection, I take a few crises singled out by historians because a republic's actions were the very opposite of cooperative (chapters 12 and 13).[4]

As we will see, the evidence is remarkably consistent. A connection between political culture and the style and consequences of diplomacy is a plain feature in the history of crises. Contemporary observers of a given crisis have almost always described this feature, and later historians usually noticed it as well. I was able to discover no plain counterexample. Apparently this phenomenon is rooted in fundamental human behavior.

Concessions and Hostility in War Games

Many scholars who study negotiations have come to concentrate on one specific feature: how does one side respond when the other makes a concession? They describe the polar alternatives as "cooperative," which means responding with a reciprocal concession, or "exploitative," which means pocketing the advantage and demanding more. Common sense suggests that an inveterate exploiter will drive the mildest opponents to a point where they will risk war rather than yield another inch. Scholars doing an analysis using formal logic with plausible premises have indeed demonstrated that even between perfectly rational opponents, when one side perceives the other as consistently exploitative, war is a likely prospect. And a detailed study of diplomacy in actual crises found that a "bullying" negotiating strategy, where one side escalated its threats above the other's level of belligerence, was much more likely to bring on war than a strategy with reciprocal concessions.[5]

The effect has been demonstrated in experiments by social psychologists. Various experimenters set up games where each player's objective was to win money by choosing between options without knowing the other player's choice. In a given turn both sides would profit a little if both chose cooperative options, but one side could get still more by exploiting the other's attempt to cooperate. If neither side tried to cooperate then nobody would profit. It turns out that some people are inherently cooperative in these games, expecting the other player will also make concessions. Other people see the world as a jungle of cutthroat competitors and try to seize advantage.

When people who cooperate are paired with one another, they find their expectations fulfilled and settle into a mode of mutual concessions. We might say that they have made reputations for accommodation and established mutual trust. Exploiters, on the other hand, create precisely the hostile situation they expect: the other player eventually learns to stop making concessions and both end up losers. It sounds like the spiral of mutual distrust that propels nations through an arms race into war.[6]

An individual's style reflects consistent attitudes, a sort of personal political culture. This was demonstrated in an investigation where subjects filled out a questionnaire about their beliefs. When both players in a game were people who approved authoritarian beliefs, they usually echoed each other's belligerent exploitation. When both rejected such beliefs they tended to cooperate, ending up with higher scores than the authoritarian pairs.

This experiment had more surprising results. As a series of games progressed, the authoritarian pairs recognized their problem and began to cooperate at least part of the time. In the final scores, a pair who both rejected authoritarian thinking still did best, but the very lowest scores—the least cooperation overall—came when someone who held authoritarian beliefs played against the opposite type. "The interaction made both of them punitive," the researchers found, "exacerbating the conflict and desire for power."[7]

The behavior of diplomats exchanging momentous telegrams turns out to have something in common with the behavior of college students playing games. In chapter 5 I noted that Charles Hermann's team, analyzing thousands of international events, found that leaders of "closed" (authoritarian) nations were overall more likely than leaders of "open" (approximately democratic) nations to negotiate with hostility. The way behavior differed according to how regimes were paired off can be extracted from their published data. I found that between pairs of open nations there were about three times as many cooperative acts as hostile ones, but between closed nations, hostile acts were about as numerous as cooperative ones. Between open and closed nations the number of hostile acts markedly exceeded the number of cooperative ones: like the college students in games, mismatched pairs of nations had the hardest time finding a route to cooperation.[8]

This issue was recently studied more directly by Bruce Russett and Zeev Maoz, who analyzed acts such as verbal threats and trade embargoes in modern disputes. They found not only that hostile acts were rare between pairs of democracies, but also that a democracy and an autocracy were marginally more likely than a pair of autocracies to treat one another belligerently. Another scholar looked into territorial disputes and found again that autocrats and juntas managed to settle more peacefully with one another than when one of them confronted a republic. As the authors of a statistical study of recent wars put it, "Simply stated, democracies and autocracies fight like cats and dogs."[9]

Other statistics indicate that over the past two centuries combat has been more likely between pairs of authoritarian states than between an authoritarian and a democratic one, and in any case, warring among authoritarian states has been the most costly in terms of lives.[10] Nobody would call despots peaceful. My point is that in the daily actions of negotiation, republican and authoritarian leaders have special ways of rubbing one another the wrong way.

Most people think they know where to put the blame: surely in a democracy, public debate and criticism constrain leaders from naked aggression.[11] Behind this idea lies the old belief that autocrats are by nature more belligerent than common folk. Yet, as we shall see, the leaders and populace of a republic can also be arrogant and belligerent. We cannot understand the problem without looking at both sides of the negotiating table. Republics have much to learn about dealing with the authoritarian regimes that rule over much of the world.

Social psychologists and common sense tell us that groups with fundamentally different principles of behavior have difficulty communicating with one another. What one side offers as a generous concession, the other may see as a tribute wrung from weakness or cowardice. Leaders raised in different cultures may even disagree on what they are really arguing over.[12] Nevertheless, diplomats of the most divergent backgrounds can usually figure out how to interpret a word or a smile. On the other hand, a shared culture is no guarantee of friendship. The medieval lords of Japan and Germany regularly battled other lords who could scarcely be distinguished from themselves except by the color of their banners. Cultural difference as such is not what makes hostility spiral into war.

To see what kind of differences are indeed crucial, a good place to begin is the diplomacy that led to the War of 1812. Anthony Merry had been selected as envoy to the United States because the young man had seemed *less* vain and uncompromising than other candidates. His fervent concern about status was typical of the aristocratic diplomats of the day, and his successors were equally quick to feel offended by uncouth democrats and to respond with ill-concealed hauteur. One British envoy wrote home, "I came prepared to deal with a regular government, and have had to do with a mob, and mob leaders." His mission of conciliation degenerated into an exchange of insults with American leaders. Another envoy wrote home in disgust that he had to consort with a Congress containing a tailor, a butcher, and several tavern-keepers.

The last British envoy before the war, Augustus Foster, was the first who managed to maintain a cordial facade, but in private letters he too confided the utmost contempt for the boorish backwoods congressmen. He trusted no Americans except a few wealthy and genteel families of the Federalist party. Bitterly hostile to Jefferson and his Republicans, these Federalists told Foster that the president was so unpopular that he would be ousted from power if the British held firm. The envoy accordingly sent dispatches that stiffened his government against any compromise. In the end, even the suave Foster snarled up his diplomacy, when he aroused suspicion by conspiring with Federalists and personally insulting the president.[13]

For their part, most Americans felt that British aristocrats were pompous bullies who lived by preying upon common people. Jefferson said as much directly, and his successor, James Madison, felt much the same. At one point Madison accidentally torpedoed what might have been a settlement between the nations by writing a sharp phrase which the British Cabinet read as a deliberate insult to their king (rumor said that George III personally intervened against a compromise). Meanwhile, the American envoy in London occasionally vented what a British aristocrat called "republican insolence."[14]

Of course bad diplomacy did not of itself cause the War of 1812. Like most wars, it had various causes ranging from party politics to economic pressures. But what people of the time noticed most of all, and what specialist historians have increasingly focused on, was something that the diplomacy accurately reflected: a confrontation between an aristocratic regime and a relatively democratic one. There was the arrogance of British officers hunting for sailors who had deserted their navy, officers who kidnapped thousands of Americans to man His Majesty's ships under the lash. More important were the imperious British Orders in Council, which forbade Americans to trade with Napoleon's empire. British cruisers waited within view of American seaports, forcing every outgoing vessel to wait for inspection. American leaders feared that if they failed to stand up to these insults, their infant democracy, that sacred but fragile experiment, would be seen as so cowardly and impotent that it would be discarded in favor of a return to aristocracy. Meanwhile, more self-confident democrats howled for war so they could "liberate" Canada from monarchical oppression.[15]

Nevertheless, war was almost avoided. The American government tried every means of persuasion from diplomatic concessions to trade embargoes, squirming this way and that. Their actions only convinced the British Cabinet that American "mob leaders" were too divided to dare actual warfare. The Cabinet was more concerned with agitation in Britain itself, where the majority of ordinary people wanted a reconciliation with the United States. Public pressure finally persuaded the Cabinet to suspend its Orders in Council—perhaps the first time since the days of the Commonwealth that a British government paid heed to groups outside the aristocracy. Unfortunately, before the news crossed the Atlantic the United States irrevocably declared war. If the British leaders had been just a few weeks quicker to attend to the views of commoners, no blood would have been spilled. War could also have been avoided if the Republican party had viewed affairs in a manner just a shade more like that of the Federalists, who admired Britain as a champion of liberty against the abominably despotic Napoleon. A different vote by a single senator could have limited the conflict to a mild naval quasi-war.[16]

The tardy suspension of the Orders in Council and the hairbreadth Senate vote strongly suggest that only a little more conciliatory diplomacy and feeling of republican fellowship could have prevented the war. But such a counterfactual statement can never be proved in any single case. Let us move on to cases where it was more obvious who was republican and who was not.

Pugnacious Diplomacy: The Crimean War

In 1835 a young English gentleman, Alexander Kinglake, toured the Ottoman Empire for his pleasure and instruction. He was both amused and instructed to find that his native interpreter did not deal with officials "after the manner of the Parliamentary people." The interpreter met any obstacle by pouring forth threats, boasts, and insults in Kinglake's name. Courtesy, he advised his employer, would not inspire fear and respect, and here only fear and respect brought results.

This advice was tested when Kinglake traveled through the squalid towns of the Levantine coast, menaced that year by plague, in the company of a Russian general. The pair nonchalantly violated quarantine rules and were haled before the local pasha, who threatened them with jail or worse. Kinglake was preparing to beg forgiveness when the Russian general forestalled him, swelling with indignation. How dare these wretches mistreat an officer of the mighty tsar! The pasha recoiled and ended up giving the strangers a lavish feast. This was an authoritarian political culture, in which each person must either command or submit.[17]

Kinglake moved on to visit the cavernous Church of the Holy Sepulchre in Jerusalem, where he found Greek Orthodox and Roman Catholic monks disputing with one another over precedence in the use of sacred niches. These squabbles were to continue for decades, starting a diplomatic imbroglio that culminated with French and British troops storming Russian fortifications in the Crimea. The conflict is remembered today for the Charge of the Light Brigade, a fitting symbol for a senseless disaster in international affairs. We shall find that the errors in diplomacy that led to the war were related to the advice of Kinglake's interpreter.

The Crimean War has fascinated historians because it should have been easy to avoid. The mid-nineteenth century was the heyday of professional diplomacy, yet in this affair the negotiations were punctuated by pointless deceptions, ill-considered bluffs, deliberate insults, peremptory demands, and plain stupidity. I will give a few examples to indicate how this blundering connected with political characteristics of the contending regimes.[18]

The trouble began when each of three emperors staked his prestige on the question of who would exercise influence over the Holy Sepulchre, and by extension wherever the Ottomans ruled. The first step was taken by Louis-Napoleon Bonaparte in 1851, as he prepared to proclaim himself emperor of France and looked for ways to consolidate his standing as a militant champion of French and Catholic interests. He took up the demands of certain monks in Jerusalem, using naval demonstrations to threaten the Ottoman sultan. The sultan was easily cowed. Only by birthright could this amiable and indolent man, deficient in physical, mental, and moral strength, have become ruler of an empire. He quickly granted Catholic monks the key to a disputed portal. After further French bullying he allowed the monks to insert the key and turn it.

This action struck Nicholas I, tsar of Russia and anointed defender of its Orthodox faith, as not only damaging to Russian influence in the Near

East, but personally insulting. Severe and self-absorbed, Nicholas had been raised since infancy amidst military ceremony. He felt most comfortable in uniform, and ruled Russia like a drillmaster preoccupied with keeping his platoon in perfect step. If the tsar's officials had private qualms about his diplomacy, they dared do nothing but flatter him and obsequiously attempt to fulfill his self-righteous demands.[19]

Outraged by the sultan's concessions to France, Nicholas impetuously claimed a right to intervene not just at the Holy Sepulchre, but anywhere he chose, on behalf of the millions of Orthodox Christians scattered through the Ottoman Empire. This brought into the open what has always been a problem in relations between authoritarian powers: just who should hold just what authority over a given body of subjects?

To press his claim, the tsar sent an envoy to Constantinople, no diplomat but a notoriously overbearing military official, the Lord High Admiral Prince Alexander Menshikov. Nicholas instructed Menshikov to belabor Ottoman officials with abuse and threats, and the prince was happy to obey. Soon Russian and Turkish courtiers filled the palaces of Constantinople with an impenetrable web of intrigue and sly affronts. The more the Russian envoy insulted and menaced Turkish officials, the more they smiled and promised eternal friendship. But behind the scenes these same officials, backed up by the French and British ambassadors, stiffened the sultan to resist every Russian demand.[20]

Heading this effort was the imperious Mehmet Ali, who was more the true leader of the Ottoman Empire than his brother-in-law the sultan. Mehmet Ali had once personally quelled a mutiny by drawing his sword and rushing at the soldiers, and he was equally fierce in defense of Ottoman sovereignty. When Prince Menshikov, by turns underhanded and domineering, sought to extract concessions under the threat of war, he converted Mehmet Ali from a negotiating partner to a personal enemy.[21] The Turks grew so suspicious that they refused to make even a bland statement that would save Russian face, fearing it would be interpreted as surrender. Menshikov sailed away from Constantinople empty-handed, infuriated by what he considered the duplicity and intransigence of the Turks and their French and British supporters.

The tsar could have let the whole matter drop with nothing worse than some temporary embarrassment, but such a move was beyond him. "Accustomed to command and irresistible in authority at home," as one historian explained, "he had come to think that high-handed methods would succeed equally abroad."[22] Nicholas sent an army to occupy a couple of Balkan buffer states, in reckless violation of international law.

It would be redundant to wade through the months of complex negotiations that followed, as diplomats sought a way out of the trap the sovereigns had built for themselves. Suffice it to say that the tsar would not withdraw his troops, and everyone else found that unacceptable. Louis-Napoleon could not back down without fatally weakening his prestige, which was the only thing that kept him in power. The sultan was in the same bind, for any rumor of weakness toward Russia incited Islamic zealots to riot in the streets of Istanbul. Nicholas was motivated only by his own exasperation when he could not win even a face-saving accommodation. Of course there were much larger concerns involving the entire European balance of power, which I will touch on later, but at no point did these concerns play a central role in the actual diplomatic exchanges. Whether the issue was a priest entering a sacred corner or an army marching into a minor principality, the real preoccupation was who could push around whom.

This case is a particularly well documented example of continuity between domestic and foreign behavior in autocratic diplomacy—but autocrats are not our main concern. There were errors all around, but the ones important for this study were in the diplomacy of a republic. For there was one republic central to the crisis, and here the relationships were quite different.

The Turks and French did not dare to fight Russia unless Britain stood at their side. British policy depended on "public" opinion, that is, the views of the oligarchic class of well-to-do gentlemen who shared power in mid-century. These gentlemen were increasingly adopting republican ideals, and correspondingly coming to despise Russia, land of the serf and the knout. The Russians were also a nuisance to certain British commercial interests, but what worried the British most was the specter of expanding despotism. Through the entire past century, Russian troops had been aggressively expanding their frontiers into Europe and Asia. That was a danger not only to the European balance of power, but to human liberty itself. It seemed time to stop Russia, if necessary by force.

The British government equivocated. The Cabinet wrangled over the issues time and again in the sober and courteous way Victorian gentlemen handled political affairs. The conversation was not so much directed as moderated by the prime minister, Lord Aberdeen, a mild and sensitive man who saw no compelling reason for war. He and the Cabinet took care to maintain cordial relations with Russia, reassuring the tsar with discreet and ambiguous phrases that a peaceful solution would be worked out.

Nicholas decided that Britain would be neutral, if not an active friend. Observers then and afterward said that if only the prime minister had been quicker to warn the tsar with explicit threats, the Crimean War could have been avoided. "If our pacific determination is too clearly reckoned upon," one British statesmen told a colleague, "we may render war inevitable." Nicholas would later complain that the British had deliberately misled him.[23]

The tsar, ignorant of the role of public opinion and political rivalry in a republic, expected to arrange everything through a personal understanding with a few supreme leaders. He believed that to reassure the British that he had no expansionist ambitions it would suffice to give his sacred royal word to his fellow monarch, Queen Victoria.[24] The tsar was dealing with the British as if their way of governing resembled his own, ignorant of how the British (up to Victoria herself) despised Russian autocracy.

The British public was baffled by the complexities of diplomatic notes and military deployments, but they understood that power and prestige were somehow at stake. Anti-Russian politicians howled against every action of the tsar, well aware that in a republic one can attract voters by taking a strong stance against a "tyrant." Whereas at first the Cabinet had deluded itself that the tsar and his court could be persuaded to back down without even a symbolic concession, now newspapers took up the opposite delusion that Russians had an insatiable lust for conquest. Any politician who failed to stand up to the Tsar would surely be punished in the next elections. In the Cabinet itself, ministers pointed to the hopelessly tangled diplomacy as proof that Russia could not be trusted in negotiation. Aberdeen bowed to the pressure and with profound sadness went to war.[25]

Throughout the crisis the leaders of authoritarian regimes had taken an inflexible and coercive approach. The most belligerent of all was the one whose power was most supreme in his own nation, Nicholas. If we could imagine somehow changing the tsar and his courtiers into people who would behave like Aberdeen and his Cabinet, it is difficult to imagine that Russia would have instructed its envoys to make the humiliating demands that escalated the affair into an angry crisis, nor would it have followed up by invading buffer states, and so forth.

The republican leaders had their own problems in negotiating. The convenient assumption that other people will follow the same behavior we do in daily affairs—precisely the assumption that makes for peace among republics—can harm relations when the other side does not match our expectations. One danger is that republican leaders may assume that an autocrat will find it no more difficult than they would to back down from unreasonable demands. Just as dangerously, when a republic follows its accustomed cooperative approach, an authoritarian regime may misread its intentions.

Preceding both the War of 1812 and the Crimean War, the more authoritarian side saw the more republican side's restraint and efforts to reach a compromise as proof that it could safely keep up its intrusions. In both cases this was only one jaw of a trap. The other jaw was that the republic eventually found the intrusions intolerable and flew into a passion to punish its adversary.

Many a monarch and dictator has been spectacularly erratic, one day a sworn ally, the next a mortal foe. Republics, for all their ponderous councils and checks on power and cooperative political culture, may be nearly as volatile. Numerous observers have remarked that the populaces of democratic nations commonly wallow in placid indifference to foreign affairs, but when at length their anger is aroused they leap to extremes of blind truculence.[26] Some additional cases will show how this impulsiveness tends to develop along a specific, hazardous path.

Kaiser Wilhelm's Diplomacy

To show how regimes reluctantly fall into conflict nothing serves so well as the First World War. This struggle was so devastating and yet so useless that historians have scrutinized countless documents related to the outbreak of war, and in recent years the evidence has driven them to a consensus on key points. These points focus on the political culture of authoritarian regimes. Nearly all scholars now agree that the descent into violence in 1914 was chiefly determined by autocratic emperors and their ministers.[27]

Historians have concentrated especially on Germany. As we saw in chapter 8, Kaiser Wilhelm II and his entourage had no taste for conciliation. They shared the ideas of proper behavior of the pigheaded lieutenant who treated the citizens of Zabern as his enemies until they became just that. In a similar spirit, the kaiser personally affronted French, British, and Russian leaders, and in 1914 his government encouraged Austria to punish presumptuous Serbia. Wilhelm's hostile suspicions, his deceptions, his rejection of compromise, his readiness to apply coercion: these traits were not just expressions of his unhappy personality but were applauded by his courtiers, repeated by his ministers, and supported by the entire political culture of the German aristocracy. Most ordinary Germans acquiesced, for deliberate campaigns of school instruction and propaganda had driven the worship of military force deep into every layer of society.[28]

In Britain, by contrast, leaders had grown accustomed to frank trading of concessions with domestic rivals down to the working classes. When they dealt with Berlin, the British were struck by the different behavior there, prone to threats and deceit. As one writer remarked in 1905, the British began to feel that the German regime was "not the kind of government which we can feel confidence in."

Those British who had the closest contact with German leaders tended to acquire the strongest aversion to their behavior. A characteristic example was the disillusionment of Valentine Chirol, Berlin correspondent for the London *Times* in 1896. Chirol valued discussion and mutual trust, and naturally befriended German officials. But when a diplomatic quarrel arose between the two nations, his highly placed "friends" tried to manipulate him into carrying deceitful threats to London. Chirol went home angry, and when he became foreign editor of the *Times* he helped raise British suspicions of German motives.[29]

Enmity between Britain and Germany was easily aroused in those years of commercial and imperial rivalry, but the kaiser, demonstrating an almost pathological hostility to Britain, did much to make it worse. He convinced himself that his erratic blandishments and bluster had left the British without the will to oppose him. Many in the kaiser's entourage likewise looked at every possible rival with a bizarre mixture of suspicion and contempt. Even Germany's astute chancellor, Bethmann Hollweg, deluded himself with the belief that Britain would not fight.[30]

If Britain failed to deter Germany from going to war, that was not only the fault of the Germans but also, historians agree, of the British foreign secretary. This was Sir Edward Grey, a gentleman deliberate to the point of quiescence, unfailingly tolerant of those who opposed him. Grey found the concept of aggression so alien that it took him several weeks to grasp the fact that Austria and Germany were intent on reducing Serbia to impotence. This was partly because the Austrians and Germans worked unscrupulously to deceive him. Yet even when their intentions became clear, he failed to commit Britain to defend Serbia, worrying that this would seem a provocation.[31]

Grey spent his diplomatic energies on proposals for mediation and conferences—the parliamentarian's characteristic response to conflict—appealing to the better nature of the German leaders. The French ambassador in London remarked that Grey was "a man of peace, one may even say a pacifist. With his generous, idealistic nature he tends to attribute to others the sentiments which animate himself." It is no wonder the kaiser felt he could attack with impunity. Grey finally gave the Germans clear warning only after their military machine had been set in motion beyond recall.[32]

The foreign secretary was free to commit these errors because he was in accord with the feelings of the British Cabinet, Parliament, and public at large. All of them expected protracted negotiations followed by a compromise. For generations the British elite, in step with their retreat from monarchy, had been learning to defuse domestic social strife by drawing rivals into discussion and yielding to gradual reform. Increasingly, they had been trying the same methods abroad. In 1914 many in Britain felt like their prime minister, who, as one historian put it, "assumed that Bethmann would decide a question as he would have decided it himself"— namely through patient discussion and reciprocal concessions. The British Cabinet could scarcely imagine how the kaiser's entourage rattled with wrathful talk about taking abrupt and bloody action to crush their enemies.[33]

To pin down more exactly the character of each side's approach, the political scientist Ole Holsti analyzed the wording of the diplomatic records of 1914. His data show that the democracies expressed less inclination than other powers to employ violence. One reason the German and Austrian leaders were belligerent, the records indicate, was that they perceived their opponents as more hostile than they really were. Their opponents, meanwhile, perceived the Germans and Austrians as less hostile than was actually the case.[34]

German, Austrian, and Russian authorities saw all rivals as malicious enemies who must be dominated or outwitted, and they meant not only other nations but also dissenters at home. The kaiser's entourage spoke fervently of smashing the Socialist opposition; the Austrian court followed suit while still more vigorously attacking nationalist separatists; the Russian court, with a violent quasi-revolution less than a decade behind it, was most nervous of all. For each of the three emperors, the domestic and international crises interacted. While none wanted a great war, each needed the prestige that could come from making foreign enemies back down. A crisis offered each autocracy an opportunity to divert the hostility of its subjects onto a foreign scapegoat, smothering criticism under a blanket of patriotic solidarity.[35]

Such scapegoating has been suggested as a chief connection between domestic politics and foreign wars. Since conflict with outsiders strengthens a group's solidarity, shaky regimes may try to divert attention to an external enemy. Followers of Machiavelli even praised a prince who could "busy giddy minds with foreign quarrels." It is not only autocrats who use the trick, however; some of the best-documented examples of attacking a foreign scapegoat come from unstable republics. A few statistical studies have confirmed that the problem of scapegoating is widespread, if hardly ever central to a particular conflict. In short, it is only one of the countless potential causes of war found under any type of regime.[36]

Like all wars, the First World War had causes beyond counting. To mention only Germany and Britain, we find both nations were prone to scapegoating because of domestic tensions resulting from swift industrialization; both stood in vulnerable geostrategic situations; both were locked in a naval arms race linked with grand imperialist ambitions; and so forth. Historians have demonstrated so many plausible causes for the catastrophe that it is particularly obvious that we should not ask why the war happened, but should only ask what could possibly have prevented it. In several preceding European crises, the diplomats had balanced and contained such pressures, and in July 1914, experienced statesmen expected to succeed again, for all sides knew they could not profit from a great war. Yet somehow diplomacy failed.

It would be wearisome to plod through the famous events of that summer: the shockingly hostile Austrian ultimatums against Serbia; the secret "blank check" from Germany backing up Austrian belligerence; the precipitate Austrian invasion; the dithering and frantic mobilization of the Russians; the unprovoked German invasion of neutral Belgium. Leaving aside the pressures on leaders and looking only at their manifest acts, one conclusion is unavoidable. If the kaiser and his entourage had been inclined toward diplomatic behavior more like the British Cabinet's reassurances of friendship and search for accommodation, and still more if the same had been true of the Austrian and Russian emperors, there would have been a far better chance for a peaceful outcome.

Appeasement

Wilhelm laid the blame for war on the British leaders. He said Britain had completed a long planned "*encirclement* of Germany," and promised to "tear away the mask" of their hypocrisy.[37] The kaiser felt the British had pretended they would stay neutral so that Germany and Austria would plunge in too deep to back out, and had then sprung a trap.

The British leadership's hesitant behavior in the 1914 crisis displayed the inclination toward discussion and mutual accommodation that characterizes republican politics. Unfortunately, what works in domestic politics may fail in international relations. Harold Nicolson, the British diplomat who described the difference between "commercial" and "warrior" diplomacy, also explained the danger of assuming that commercial principles of fair play would succeed in diplomacy. He wrote sardonically of his failure to convince his superiors that foreigners would not necessarily act the way Englishmen behaved in their clubs.[38] Nicolson's worries were confirmed when a British prime minister committed the most notorious of all such errors.

Neville Chamberlain was neither timid nor naive. But he negotiated as if everyone were as deeply moral as himself, and as committed to reciprocal concessions. In 1937 Chamberlain remarked that he had learned a basic lesson while serving on various democratic councils: "there is always some common measure of agreement if only we look for it." When he met Hitler at Munich the following year, Chamberlain clung to that principle, remarking that in the Nazi dictator he had found "a man who could be relied upon when he had given his word." Chamberlain's colleagues in Britain had also built their careers on discussion and compromise; the Cabinet supported all his concessions to Germany, and the British public applauded. Conciliation often does succeed. In the face of Germany's passionate claims against the injustices of the Versailles treaty, appeasement looked like a fair policy, or at least a safe one.[39]

Hindsight suggests that war would have been less likely in the long run if Chamberlain had rejected Hitler's demands. For Hitler only pocketed the concessions and pressed ahead in the belief that the democratic leaders were ineffectual cowards—"little worms" who would yield to his force. When Britain at last stuck by its principles and went to war in 1939, the German leaders were shocked. Like the kaiser, they felt that they had been tricked, for they saw affairs largely in terms of aggression and duplicity. In words eerily similar to those Wilhelm had used a quarter-century earlier, Hitler fulminated that the British had "let fall their mask" to complete a long-planned "encirclement" of Germany.[40]

These errors form a pattern which I will call an "appeasement trap." The key elements are: (1) republican leaders imagine that authoritarian ones are like themselves and can be conciliated; (2) authoritarian leaders imagine that republican ones are like themselves and conciliate only when they are too weak to fight; (3) the republican leaders recognize, perhaps too late, that the authoritarian ones are not following republican ideals, and switch to a far more belligerent approach.

We can check the regularity of this pattern by lining up additional cases drawn from American history. We noticed in chapter 9 how the French Directory was taken by surprise in 1797 when the United States, which had seemed destined to protest endlessly over maritime rights, suddenly lost its patience and took up arms. We saw much the same happen to the British in 1812. Historians further note that a clumsy exchange of authoritarian abuse and democratic appeasement, much like the one that ended in the 1914 collision between Germany and Britain, was repeated between Germany and the United States before the Americans angrily declared war in 1917.[41]

Scholars have argued that ideas of "correct" diplomatic behavior likewise made the United States too conciliatory toward Japanese aggression in the 1930s. Failing to grasp that Japan was ruled by military zealots whose politics revolved around deception and force, American leaders staked

everything on moral suasion as the Japanese army devoured China piece-
meal. At one point President Franklin Roosevelt backed off from promises
to send a stern warning, dropping the word "war" from his diplomatic
note and delivering it casually along with assurances of friendship. The
Japanese leaders saw such actions as evidence of timidity and weakness.
When Roosevelt finally decided that the Japanese could not be trusted to
negotiate fairly and imposed crippling trade sanctions, the ministers in
Tokyo were stunned. Assuming that Roosevelt would drive them into ignominious submission if they made concessions, they determined to strike
out against what they called "encirclement." Some Japanese later believed
they had been deliberately lured into war.[42]

Again: when the dictator of North Korea launched an invasion of the
South in 1950, he had calculated that the United States would not fight.
Evidence from Soviet archives suggests that this was another war that
could probably have been prevented if only the United States had issued a
clear warning. The failure to do so was so glaring that some people suspected that the Americans had cunningly tempted a North Korean attack.
Again: in 1989 American envoys professed outright friendship for the Iraqi
dictator Saddam Hussein, under the delusion that he could be eased into
a moderate position. Nobody warned him explicitly against carrying out
his threat to attack Kuwait. Even Americans were surprised at how violently their government responded to the invasion, and some Arabs would
later say a trap was sprung. Again: diplomatic observers have suggested
that if the United States and other democratic nations had taken a firmer
stance with the Serbs in 1991 and after, they would have been less aggressive toward their neighbors.[43]

The frequency and consistency of the appeasement trap is a strong argument against the belief that negotiating approaches are based strictly on
rational evaluation of objective situations. Evidently, leaders muddling
through the confusion and evasions of diplomacy are often forced to fall
back on their ingrained principles and beliefs. Democrats fail to take into
account the authoritarian leadership's preoccupation with status and power
in any dispute where hegemony may be at stake, but readily believe a dictator will respond only to force. The authoritarians fail to appreciate a
democratic regime's preoccupation with discussion, lawful means, and civil
rights, but readily believe it cannot act forcefully. In sum, the pattern of the
appeasement trap serves as an additional demonstration (a circumstantial

one, but using different evidence than anything else in this book) that domestic political culture has a crucial influence on foreign relations.

The appeasement trap leads to war chiefly where a nation's political culture has not been properly assessed by the rival nation's leadership. The source of error is the human tendency to stick persistently to characteristic beliefs, discussed in chapter 5. "Because fear and conspiracy play no part in your daily relations with one another," a politician warned the ancient Athenians, "you assume that the same thing is true" of other states. The same mental conservatism was recently noted by a seasoned diplomat who complained that American political leaders, reviewing messages drafted by State Department professionals, were wont to insist on changes because the phrasing was "not friendly enough."[44]

The diplomacy of republican regimes in particular is sometimes distorted by these regimes' reliance on negotiation. Even after leaders have decided that concessions are useless and that they must refuse to yield an inch, they often continue to place faith in the negotiation process. After discussions have reached an impasse, a republican government often keeps talking like the lawyers in some interminable court case, expecting that the other side will likewise go on negotiating until the problem is somehow resolved.[45]

This projection abroad of processes familiar at home led the United States astray in 1991, when it dismissed the likelihood of an Iraqi attack on Kuwait even after negotiations reached a dead end. It likewise led Israeli leaders astray in 1973, when they ignored Egypt's repeated demands that Israel must withdraw from the Suez Canal. It led British leaders astray in 1982, when they thought only of punctilious negotiation over legal ownership of the Falkland/Malvinas Islands while the generals who ruled Argentina scornfully prepared to seize the islands by force. Likewise in 1914, 1939, and 1941, after democracies reached the limit of their concessions, they expected that courteous diplomatic exchanges would go on and on. Even where communication scarcely existed, leaders of the United States believed that the Communist Chinese would continue to negotiate as American troops approached their border with North Korea in 1950. In all these cases, the democracies failed to make clear just how far they would go in the use of force, largely because they failed to understand how readily the other side would forsake verbal diplomacy.[46]

Faulty perceptions of the nature of a rival regime are not the only thing that makes the appeasement trap operate. Another mechanism, of special importance to republics, is their public's belief that disputes should normally be resolved through negotiation. If leaders had openly threatened war against the rival authoritarian nation in most of the cases listed above, they would have been loudly criticized in the press and the legislature, at least until the rival's aggression became blatant. Whatever the personal judgment of a republic's leaders, their knowledge of the public's dislike for overt belligerence may hold them back from issuing stern warnings. The result may be that leaders fail to state clearly how they would respond to another nation's transgression (they may not even know themselves, as they trim their sails to veering political winds). A scholar who investigated 1960s foreign policy communications demonstrated that democracies were indeed more prone than other regimes to such hazardous vagueness.[47]

The appeasement trap can be avoided if leaders and their public have a reasonably accurate understanding of the political culture of the rival regime. We have been looking at a few cases where major errors led to major wars, but the overall record of diplomacy is not so grim. A statistical study of recent low-level military interventions (covert operations, mobilization of troops, and so forth) found that regimes of any kind were less likely to resort to a show of force against democracies than against autocracies. Perhaps, the authors suggested, even dictators have often judged that conflicts with democracies can be resolved through reasoned negotiation, without the violent threats that seem necessary to prevail upon autocratic or anocratic rivals.[48] If so, it is more evidence that perceptions of the nature of a foreign political culture are crucial.

The errors of the appeasement trap are fatal only in special circumstances. In most of the cases listed above, the problem arose when a democracy entered as a third party into a conflict already begun between authoritarian states (as the United States, for example, was caught up in 1989 between Iraq and Kuwait, or in 1797 and 1812 between Britain and France, or in 1941 between Japan and China). In such a tangled situation, with accusations, deceptions, inflamed emotions, and outrageous violence on all sides, misunderstandings are especially likely.

The misunderstandings of the appeasement trap can impede relations without leading to warfare. For example, in the 1930s many Americans believed that Chiang Kai-shek and his enemy Mao Tse-tung were both "reformers," in some sense potential democrats. The U.S. government tried to negotiate with Mao and Chiang in the same fashion that politicians dealt with one another in Washington, conciliating to an extent that amazed some observers. The Chinese dictators responded with scorn and duplicity, and few problems were resolved.[49]

Most notoriously damaging was the way democratic leaders expected to befriend Stalin in the 1940s. As one historian put it, "Roosevelt saw Stalin as a Russian version of himself, who, as a fellow politician, could be won over by a mixture of concessions and good will." Whatever Roosevelt's private reservations about the Soviets, the president always insisted that friendship and fairness would eventually wean them from their grotesque suspicions. Winston Churchill, although a hard-headed foe of Communism, also came to believe that he had established a congenial personal relationship with the Soviet dictator and could work out any problem to their mutual satisfaction. When Harry Truman became president, he too began to like Stalin and trust him. Truman once remarked that the Soviet chief reminded him of a former mentor, the boss of the Kansas City political machine.

Truman, Roosevelt, and Churchill were not exceptionally naive; many others held still more extravagant fantasies about the Soviet regime's tendency to adopt democratic ways. Of course Stalin was a genius at concealing, even from his colleagues in the Kremlin, the fact that he was a murderous monster. People can be deceived particularly easily by an authoritarian regime, with no free press or assembly to expose opinions and explore motives. But such deceptions cannot last. Stalin felt free to encroach on other countries until Truman and most others switched to a rigid hostility. Perhaps the appeasement trap should be included among the many causes of the Cold War.[50]

There is one more element of the appeasement trap that deserves our notice—the trigger that snaps it shut when a crisis collapses into war. Kaiser Wilhelm and Hitler were shocked, the Japanese militarists and Argentine generals and Saddam Hussein were stunned, a majority in the democratic nations themselves were taken by surprise, to discover how abruptly a democratic government can turn, how harshly it can demand that the other side back down, and how unrelentingly it can reply to an attack that was not even directed against its home territory. A look at a few other cases will show that sometimes dictators were right to feel that a republic was so hostile toward them that war was unavoidable.

CHAPTER TWELVE

Republican Diplomacy

I t did not look like territory worth fighting over. The strip along the Rio Grande was parched scrubland that barely supported a few tumbledown ranches, and the U.S. Army soldiers who trudged to the river in 1846 were not happy to be there. Mexican troops were gathering nearby, angry because the region had always belonged to Mexico. It seemed likely that somebody would get shot.

That was what President James Polk was hoping would happen. He had ordered troops into this territory, where the United States had only the flimsiest legal claim, on the pretext that the Mexicans were preparing an invasion of Texas to the north. The Texans had recently broken free from Mexico and joined the United States, and the Mexicans were fervently swearing to recapture their land. But Polk did not expect the Mexicans to be so foolish as to attack and be beaten. He counted on bullying them into making a deal.[1]

Polk was a sharp, ambitious man, convinced of his own righteousness and so secretive that to this day historians disagree on whether he wanted a war. Most believe that almost until the last moment the president aimed to settle things peacefully. His plan was to give the Mexican government money in exchange for territories clear to the Pacific. Mexico had little to lose. Texas was already gone and California was preparing to follow the example of breaking free of its corrupt and distant rulers. Besides, the Mexican leaders were desperate for cash. By all reason, they should have agreed to the bargain.

They did not. After months of fruitless negotiations, Polk prepared to ask Congress for a declaration of war. He could not be sure Congress would comply, for he had no better pretext than some unpaid Mexican debts to U.S. citizens. Then word arrived that a troop of Mexicans in the Rio Grande country had ambushed a U.S. army patrol and killed some soldiers. Raging about wicked Mexicans, Polk mobilized every resource of deceit and partisan pressure, and bulldozed Congress into declaring a war of self-defense. Many North Americans were caught up in a patriotic fever, but some recoiled in disgust. A junior officer in the war, Ulysses S. Grant, later called it "the most unjust war ever waged . . . an instance of a republic following the bad example of European monarchies." The 1846 war is an undeniable case of a fight deliberately started by a democracy to grab territory that legally belonged to its neighbor.[2]

Not all aggression can be blamed on monarchs, juntas, tribal chieftains, and other such rulers. Republics from ancient Greece onward have sometimes attacked out of predatory greed. There are many examples in the history of the United States alone, beginning with the slaughter of native tribes. How can these events be reconciled with the claim that republican leaders prefer mutual accommodation and shun coercion?

A closer look will show that even the greediest leaders of republics normally began by expecting, like Polk, to resolve issues through negotiation. Somehow the diplomacy degenerated into violence. I focus in this chapter and the next on crises that historians have singled out as the most egregious documented cases of republican aggression. The cases differ widely in detail, but comparing them will isolate a small set of dangerous features in the political culture of republics. These features, amplified in the negotiation process, can encourage leaders to use coercion—sometimes even against regimes that resemble fellow republics.

Diplomatic Signals, from Procrastination to Genocide

The rule of republican mutual peace requires that if the Mexicans had governed their country more like the United States, negotiation would have settled the matter. We can check whether this is plausible by looking at how political culture affected diplomacy.

Mexican political affairs were a morass of brutal civil wars. This affected U.S. citizens who lost property in the turmoil, often by virtual theft under the protection of crooked officials and judges. The Mexican government grudgingly acknowledged such debts, but in its poverty it balked at actually paying them.[3] North Americans came to see the Mexican regime as violent, corrupt, and faithless. That made it all the more desirable to bring liberty to Californians along with the Texans. Polk figured that if Mexico sold the territories to the United States, part of the money could go to pay the debts, and the issues would all be neatly settled. Unfortunately, the president was applying the clever methods he had developed as a small-town lawyer and back-room politician, failing to realize that the great levers of Mexican politics were not legal settlements and cash, but status and pride.

As his envoy to Mexico City, Polk picked John Slidell, a Louisiana politician with the refined manners of an English squire. When Slidell arrived in Mexico, the government refused to meet him under the formal terms that Polk had defined, for the local newspapers ranted that a government that failed to defy the Yankee envoy deserved to be overthrown, and General Mariano Paredes was camped nearby with thousands of troops. Like most soldiers, the Mexican army officers thought of international relations chiefly in terms of force, and they were scandalized by any hint of selling off the nation's land. Again, the threat of a coup indicates a coercive political culture.[4]

The government's refusal to meet with Slidell could not save it. When the envoy came on his own to Mexico City, General Paredes took the opportunity to denounce the Mexican leadership as traitorous, march in, and take over. Having overthrown the government on the explicit grounds that it was avoiding a "glorious and necessary war" over Texas, the general could scarcely negotiate lest he be overthrown in turn. He promptly expelled Slidell and sent troops to confront the Yankees.[5]

From the outset, the exchanges of diplomatic notes had been rigid, argumentative, and indignant on both sides. In the end, Slidell told his government that the Mexicans had been guilty of "unparalleled bad faith" and "gross falsifications." Their political system, he explained, was a chaos of personal factions that each sought only to loot the country. It was pointless to try to negotiate with such people. "Here, all amicable advances are considered indicative of either weakness or treachery," Slidell wrote to Washington. "Depend upon it, we can never get along well with them until we have given them a good drubbing."[6]

The government that Paredes overthrew had ruled under republican constitutional forms, and some in the United States had felt that it would be wrong to fight a "sister republic." Had the Mexican regime been more stable, it is possible that it could have gradually worked out a deal to exchange land for money rather than blood, for most Mexicans were not eager for war. Such a bargain was impossible for Paredes. However, historians have not absolved Polk of blame, considering the provocative way he deployed military forces to pressure the Mexicans, the rigidity of his demands, and the contemptuous attitude of his envoy. The egregious defects in negotiation on both sides removed any chance of peace only because they reflected a more fundamental incompatibility.[7]

We can isolate this crucial factor by setting this case alongside other republican aggressions. A second example is the Spanish-American War, which I previously described in chapter 8 as a confrontation between a republic and an authoritarian state. The Spanish leaders, unlike Paredes, strove assiduously to avoid war, deploying an expert and mannerly diplomacy; likewise for the American president, William McKinley. In this case, both sides followed the highest professional negotiating standards, sending flawlessly clear and courteous messages. Here we can see beyond formal diplomacy to the actual source of enmity.[8]

Historians have long debated why the United States eventually attacked Spain: they have examined how Cuban rebellion dislocated the sugar industry, how idealists envisioned a democratic mission for the United States to acquire colonies and uplift them, how capitalists sought to open up new markets for their products, and more. But historians generally agree that these forces could not have brought war all by themselves. The war could only start after the American public became outraged by Spanish behavior. To what extent this anger was encouraged by newspapers and politicians need not concern us; what matters is that the nature of the Spanish regime was such that American outrage was easily aroused, and perhaps inevitable.[9]

Spain's government was already notorious for suppressing domestic opposition through quasi-legal trials and outright torture. In Cuba, still worse oppression and corruption had provoked furious rebellion. Now Spanish troops were herding peasants into concentration camps where men, women, and children lay in rags and filth like living skeletons, dying by hundreds of thousands from disease and starvation. Sensational accounts convinced most North Americans that the Spanish elite were not merely aristocratic "dons" but bestial criminals. Outrage climbed to the point where McKinley and his party might have lost the next election had they failed to act. The president's personal indignation might have driven him to act anyway, yet he indefatigably sought a peaceful solution.[10]

The Spaniards could have either granted the Cubans political rights or sold the United States the island, which was costing them far more than it was worth. Spanish diplomats agreed that some such accommodation

could be reached, yet they procrastinated, sliding sideways in their eloquent notes. McKinley's doubts about negotiating with the Spaniards were
confirmed when a personal letter written by a Spanish diplomat was stolen
by a Cuban rebel and published. The diplomat, it was revealed, regarded
McKinley as "weak and catering to the rabble . . . a low politician." The
contempt for democracy was damaging enough, but far worse was what
the letter indicated about Spain's repeated promise to give Cubans civil
rights. Evidently the promise was only a mask for plans to crush the rebellion by sheer brutality. That confirmed what McKinley and most of his
countrymen already suspected: the Spaniards were not negotiating in good
faith, but only engaging in delay and deception.[11]

A week later the U.S. battleship *Maine* blew up on a visit to Cuba,
and many leapt to the conclusion that it was no accident. Newspapers in-
flated the tragedy into a heinous crime, a final reason to go to war.[12] This
public wrath against a supposed crime was much like the response to the
Mexican skirmish with Yankee troops near the Rio Grande a half-century
earlier. Such incidents can be misinterpreted or even manufactured out of
mere rumor. Thus unconfirmed reports of North Vietnamese attacks on
ships in the Gulf of Tonkin in 1964 stampeded the U.S. Congress into en-
dorsing a major military intervention. Equally dubious tales about a massacre of infants by Iraqi soldiers in Kuwait made Congress more willing to
support war in 1991.[13]

Outrage cannot be created out of thin air, however (not in countries
with a free press, at any rate). The North Vietnamese and Iraqi governments each had a well-deserved reputation for unprovoked attacks and
atrocity; in 1846 every North American had heard about the Mexicans'
lawless depredations in their own country and grisly raids against Texan
farmers, and well before the *Maine* blew up, reports from both Spain and
Cuba had convinced people in the United States that Spain was ruled by
a cruel and duplicitous aristocracy. Public hatred is easily provoked in such
cases, particularly because republican ideology and tradition have already
instilled prejudices against authoritarian regimes in general.

The antipathies that poison negotiations between a republic and an
authoritarian regime can be seen still more clearly in one more case of a
breakaway province and a neighboring republic. In 1971 East Pakistan
(Bangladesh) rebelled against the oppressive rule of West Pakistan. As millions of refugees crowded into India, straining the resources of their hosts

and bearing tales of inconceivable atrocities, the Indian public hotly demanded relief. But the military men who ruled Pakistan, coercive and uncompromising even among themselves, thought that reaching for an accommodation with the rebels would only show weakness—which would lead to their own overthrow. They likewise saw no use in negotiating with the democratic government in India, a nation they thought of as an inveterate enemy. Pakistani leaders travelled to the United Nations in New York and to Beijing in search of a solution, but not to New Delhi.[14]

India's president, Indira Gandhi, made it clear that there would be war unless Bangladesh was set free. Pakistan's dictator responded, "If that woman thinks she can cow me down, I refuse to take it. If she wants to fight, I'll fight her!" The Indian president was not impressed. "It shows the mentality of the person," she said tartly. "He is one man who could not get elected in his own country if there were a fair election." From the democratic viewpoint, this could almost be considered a definition of a leader who could not be counted on to bargain reasonably.[15] Indira Gandhi visited Moscow, Washington, and London, but not Islamabad. The Indian army began to help Bangladeshi exiles to make raids into their homeland, and Pakistan replied with full-scale war.

There was no appeasement trap in the Mexican, Spanish-American, and Bangladeshi wars. Presidents Polk, McKinley, and Gandhi, indignant when their neighbors refused demands to set free California, Cuba, and Bangladesh, made their willingness to fight plain from the start. Never mind that the liberation of these territories would improve the economic and strategic position of the presidents' own nations; the presidents believed their motives were pure, and could not imagine that moral people would refuse their demands.

The hostility was reinforced by diplomatic experience, whether the negotiations were polite but insincere, as with the Spanish, or clumsy and antagonistic, as with the Mexicans, or simply nonexistent, as with the Pakistanis. The final step was the same as in the appeasement trap: the republican leaders gave up on negotiation and turned angrily to force. Their final viewpoint was neatly expressed (in another case) by what a British official said of the Boer leader in 1899: "You can't believe a word Kruger says. He has never yielded and never will yield till he feels the muzzle of the pistol on his forehead."[16]

Authoritarians likewise distrust their opponents. What people in a democracy see as a benevolent defense of the rights of an oppressed populace, the dictator or junta or Politburo sees as unjustified meddling in their nation's internal affairs. Authoritarian and oligarchical leaders feel that suppressing domestic dissent is their right and duty; protest by democracies must be a mask for schemes to weaken and humiliate them. They too might decide negotiation is useless.

War Against "Criminals" and "Children"

Difficulties with negotiation redouble when a republican state confronts a regime split among anocratic factions. For example, even after his envoy was expelled from Mexico, President Polk hoped to avoid war by meeting the Mexicans on their own ground (as he saw it) of bribery and rivalry between factions. He sought a deal with a general opposed to Paredes, a general Polk hoped would grab power and then accept cash for California. Or perhaps, he thought, disgruntled Californians could be incited to rebel and break away. When Polk impatiently turned from such tactics to military invasion, it was because he saw the Mexican regime as scarcely an organized government at all. Split by dissension everywhere from the capital to the remote provinces, Mexico looked ripe for reorganization.

Republics have similar impulses when they confront primitive peoples. Around the world, colonial officials have typically believed that the indigenous "savage" tribes, no matter how egalitarian, were incapable of negotiating as equals, and the intruders were quick to apply force. Tribes likewise looked on the outsiders as legitimate targets for petty theft or murderous raids. When violence broke out, leaders of the colonizing nations often saw it not as war but as a sort of police action against brigands.

An exemplary case took place in the Philippines following the end of the Spanish-American War. The United States had joined with native rebels to liberate the islands from Spanish rule, but Filipino jubilation turned to dismay when the Americans proved reluctant to leave. A group of educated Filipinos assembled and demanded that the Americans give them independence, then wrote themselves an oligarchic constitution. The political culture of these men was far from republican, however (see appendix). More conservative upper-class Filipinos, who planned to run the country for their own benefit under American supervision, declared that the self-proclaimed government was a mere coalition of "bandit" factions. Much of the population of the islands was in fact divided into relatively primitive tribal groups. Many Americans felt that, as one senator put it, most Filipinos were "as ignorant and savage as the aboriginal Indians." Like Native Americans and other brown-skinned races, the Filipinos were regarded by white elites as too ignorant and wayward to manage their own affairs.[17]

The United States saw no purpose in negotiation. President McKinley received one envoy from the self-declared Filipino republic, listened in bored indifference to a translation of flowery Spanish, and afterward declined to meet with any Filipinos at all. From what Americans in the Philippines told him, the president was convinced that it would be best for everyone if the islands came under American tutelage.

Some communication took place in Manila, for the American military authorities there had to deal with the Filipino militia that had fought in the rebellion. U.S. Army officers likened them to the Native Americans they had battled in their youth, and told Washington that the rebels were merely a primitive rabble. Officers who met with Filipino envoys rejected any attempts to compromise with evasion, deception, and insults. Finally the U.S. Army commander concocted a pretext for launching a surprise attack against the Filipino soldiers. The result was a dreadful guerrilla war, in which American soldiers killed some eighteen thousand Filipinos in combat and left over a hundred thousand civilians dead from famine and disease.[18]

Here, as in the attack on Mexico and other cases, representatives of a republic went from unyielding demands to sly tricks and finally to naked military attack. What happened to the courteous accommodation that I claim is the hallmark of republican political culture?

In fact, this behavior toward foreigners still matches domestic patterns once ingroup identification is taken into account. Within the most thorough democracy there is an important class of people that citizens regard as an outgroup, who may be legitimately addressed with coercion. These are the people who have placed themselves outside the citizen community by denying law itself—that is, criminals. Any regime will employ armed force against people who blatantly reject lawful ways. These include not only robbers and the like but also extremist political sects or fanatical religious cults who stray far from consensus views on what behavior is permissible.

To the republican way of thinking, any anocratic or authoritarian regime is practically criminal as such. Leaders of tribes or juntas hardly seem law-abiding when they attack anyone outside their own kin or faction. Even a monarchical regime that scrupulously obeys its own laws seems to republicans to be violating the "natural law" of equal citizen rights when it convicts dissidents of lèse-majesté or the like.

This points out a specific mechanism through which domestic repression can arouse belligerence in a foreign republic. Republicans are inclined to identify leaders who stamp on dissidents as criminals, by definition an outgroup which may be met with force. To a republican leader, negotiating with such people could seem like talking with a band of bank robbers holed up with hostages: it may be necessary to bargain, but at any moment one may be obliged to start shooting.

Throughout history, republicans have normally hesitated to exert violent force unless the rival leaders were manifestly in the category of criminals. Ancient Greeks sometimes allowed deposed dictators to quietly step down, and so have democracies of the late twentieth century from Chile to Czechoslovakia. After the Second World War, Nazi leaders were not charged with running a dictatorship but with specific crimes such as murder. A republic generally will not attack even a monstrous tyranny as such; before leaders feel justified in using force they must accuse the other regime of specific criminality—and usually not only against its own subjects but against its neighbors as well.

In a number of our borderline cases there were complaints of personal injustice against the republic's citizens. Diplomats in these cases often spent a surprising amount of time dealing with private lawsuits. By the early 1840s, rejection of just claims for damages had already helped lead North Americans to despise Mexican officials, and there were similar grievances over Spain's treatment of North Americans' rights in Cuba in the 1890s. The failure of British or French admiralty courts to dispense justice when ships were seized was a direct cause of the Anglo-Dutch War of 1652, the Franco-American Quasi-War, and the War of 1812. In each case the flagrant injustice not only inflamed public opinion back home, but helped bring the diplomats themselves to loathe the idea of further negotiation.

Usually the republic invoked a second type of justification as well. In nearly every case I have studied from the Peloponnesian Wars to the present, a republic turned to coercion only after it had occasion to accuse the rival leaders of overtly breaking a treaty or other arrangement of international law. For example, Germany's violation of Belgian neutrality was the chief reason Britain gave for declaring war in 1914; Polk's first reason for declaring war on Mexico was the country's refusal to pay its debts, and so forth. Usually I have skimmed over these details, for pragmatic observers ever since Thucydides have brushed aside such complaints as mere pretext.[19] Yet the breaking of promises has been emphatically invoked at the outset of wars throughout history. It must carry some powerful meaning.

A treaty breaker is a criminal. Such a violation is especially meaningful to republicans, who distinguish the ingroup of fellow citizens largely by their allegiance to the public law. To break a contract is to deliberately step outside the community of people who deal with one another in lawful ways. What is the use of negotiating with people who do not keep their word?

Negotiation also falters where a republic meets an anocratic regime. Primitive tribes in particular may seem incapable of following legal principles, even concerning personal property. The republic's leadership typically sees the tribal leaders as mere "children" or "savages." This puts them in a second large category of people who are subject to coercion in any republic: people who are too ignorant, incompetent, or irresponsible to follow the law. Thus in 1899 political cartoonists showed Uncle Sam as a father admonishing his little brown Filipino wards. The category of child-savage often merges with the category of willful criminal, forming a stereotype of wild "bandit" gangs who can be tamed only by force.

Faced with anocratic groups, republican leaders may turn the problem over to specialists in establishing order—police or military officers. Politicians in the capital may have too little interest or knowledge to address the affairs of some inconsequential native people in a faraway place. The more such a situation is confused by factional chaos, the more officers on the scene must make decisions. These officers will act less in the manner of cultured diplomats than in accord with the customary tenor of their profession.

For example, American officers in the Philippines in 1899, largely beyond the cognizance of people back home, addressed the Filipinos with peremptory orders followed by armed attack. Another example is what happened when France returned to Vietnam after the Japanese surrender in 1945. The restored democracy in Paris was too turbulent to pay close attention to the distant colony, and mostly left it in the hands of colonial officials and military commanders. These authorities tried to take charge in their accustomed fashion, demanding unconditional surrender from the Communist nationalists, whom they called lawless "gangs" and despised for their tyrannical leadership. Refusing to negotiate seriously, sending biased information back to Paris, and losing no opportunity to apply force, the French in Vietnam soon found themselves at war.

This is yet another demonstration of foreign behavior reflecting domestic political culture, in this case the subculture of the military, which differs greatly from that of democratic politicians. Officers who have made their careers in a hierarchical structure of strict obedience are naturally commanding and coercive. We would guess that a nation would be especially inclined to use force when its government is under military influence, whether the generals are actually in power or are standing on the sidelines threatening a coup if their wishes are ignored. This guess is confirmed by statistical studies of diplomatic incidents in the 1960s, which found that the stronger the role the military took in a nation's politics, the more the government tended to make belligerent moves and not cooperative ones.[20] Where the government is thoroughly civilian, belligerence can still infect relationships managed by officers beyond the immediate control of elected politicians. Once again we find that what counts first in foreign relations is not a nation's social or constitutional structures but the accustomed behavior of those who make the actual negotiating decisions.

Many wars began because of this on the Asian, African, and American frontiers of European settlement. In such cases the intruding republic, confronted by a tribal, factional, or quasi-authoritarian regime, left negotiations in the hands of military officers on the scene. Sometimes the responsibility was shared by officials of an imperial bureaucracy, likewise accustomed to hierarchical authority. Often neither the government nor the public back home received accurate information about what was going on before negotiations broke down in mutual suspicion and incomprehension, and the commanders turned to force.[21]

Officials of a hierachical bent can sometimes damage diplomacy even between organized states. We noted how monarchist diplomats and generals sabotaged negotiations between France and the Roman Republic in

1849, and there are a number of other examples.[22] In such cases it was only the elected politicians back home who were thoroughly imbued with republican ways, and sometimes these leaders learned too late that their instructions were not followed in the expected spirit. Fortunately, people in the field have little power to lead a republic into serious violence except where their government already has strong misgivings about the foreign regime.

Anglo-American Relations: Neither Fifty-Four Forty nor Fight

In all these cases my argument requires that no matter how aggressive a republic, if its opponent had been a fellow republic there would have been no war. Such counterfactual experiments cannot be performed, but history does sometimes offer a case apt for comparison. During exactly the same months in 1846 when the United States and Mexico moved toward war, Polk was provoking a second crisis. Again we find the president, driven by territorial greed, making unjust and inflexible demands that seemed calculated to provoke war. But this parallel confrontation was with a republic.

Polk had been elected president on a party platform that called for the annexation of two territories, Texas and Oregon. The Oregon country was the last great paradise on earth, its rivers shimmering with a million salmon, its trees so huge that one fir could yield planks for an entire barn. Britain had a claim here, but thousands of American emigrant families were arriving in their Conestoga wagons, unhitching their oxen and setting them to plow the lush meadows.

Experts thought the legal boundary between the United States and British Canada fell somewhere around the 49th parallel, but in his inaugural address Polk brashly laid claim to everything right up to the Alaskan border at latitude 54°40'. Many Americans made it a passionate demand: "Fifty-Four Forty or Fight!" Polk himself was secretive about just what line he would actually fight over. Against Britain, as against Mexico, he thought bullying would win territory with little danger of war. But he was the pugnacious leader of a pugnacious nation, quite willing to fight either opponent or both together.[23]

Many Americans felt that to enlarge the United States at the expense of Britain, as of Mexico, would be to expand liberty itself. They still saw the British regime as an oppressive aristocracy, and in truth Britain was troubled by democratic agitation and talk of armed insurrection. A Michigan congressman said he would be glad for a contest between the "republican and monarchical systems." In Britain, meanwhile, the elite looked down on the United States as a nation afflicted by the "despotism of democracy."[24]

Britain in 1846 functioned as an oligarchic republic. Although America was certainly more democratic, the Southern states that dominated much of federal policy fitted our definition of an oligarchic republic; Polk himself owned a Mississippi cotton plantation stocked with slaves. Probably the best way to categorize the Oregon crisis is as a confrontation between leaders of an oligarchic bent. In both countries some people rejected the thought of war precisely because they felt this political affinity. Britain and the United States should stand together, they said, as countries sharing a love of liberty and "the same principles of moral action."

British leaders shared enough of Polk's political culture to take in stride his rousing public statements about fighting for Oregon. As one of them remarked, any government that depended on votes must take a stiff public stand during international disputes to forestall criticism from chauvinist opponents. The British leaders well understood such pressures from personal experience. However, most people in each nation felt their political principles were different enough to leave it uncertain whether the other could be trusted. The course taken by the negotiation itself would make up their minds.[25]

In public, the leaders on both sides swore to make no compromise of national honor, yet in private they explored possibilities for an accommodation. The British foreign minister who handled the affair was the gentle Lord Aberdeen, who, as we noticed, hesitated to confront Russia a few years later. Polk deliberately chose as his envoy to London a man equally mild and eager to conciliate, Louis McLane. The two negotiators became good friends. The most dangerous point of the crisis came when Aberdeen warned McLane that Britain was making naval preparations for war, yet the British minister recorded that "nothing could be more friendly and cordial than the whole of our interview." Soon McLane was actively collaborating with Aberdeen to bring Polk around to a compromise. Eventually a boundary was drawn that allowed both governments to declare that honor was satisfied. It was around latitude 49°—a long way from fifty-four forty, and a long way from fighting too.[26]

Why did the conflict with Mexico end so much worse? Some historians have blamed the way the United States was separated from the Mexicans, but not from the British, by a cultural and ethnic chasm. However, during this same generation close affinities did not prevent ferocious civil wars inside both Mexico and the United States. Other historians have noted the difference between Mexico's weakness and Britain's strength. However, both statistical evidence and common sense indicate that a disproportion of forces more often makes the weaker side settle rather than risk war. As for possible gains, from Mexico there was California—but in a war with Britain all Canada would have been at stake. Of course there were a hundred other differences, and no historical experiment can be pure.[27] Nevertheless, if we can imagine Mexico and Britain making an exchange, not of their geographical positions nor their armed forces nor their entire cultures, but just of their political cultures, in effect swapping Lord Aberdeen for General Paredes, it is hard to doubt that the negotiations would have gone differently.

In the Mexican conflict, the Americans explicitly pointed to the character of the opposing regime. Polk's envoy to Mexico City angrily said that the ingrained deceit and corruption there left no option but force; meanwhile, Polk's envoy in London insisted that cooperation was to be expected. One historian who studied both cases contrasted Polk's grudging respect for British responses with his outrage at what he saw as injustice and insults from the Mexicans. Another historian contrasted the resolution of the Oregon crisis with the diplomatic failures that sent Britain into the Crimean War a few years later, pointing to the political culture that Britain shared with the United States but not with Russia.[28]

The contrast could be seen right at the frontiers. Officers along the Rio Grande aggressively provoked one another until the resulting deaths gave an excuse for war. Meanwhile, men with rifles were confronting one another in Oregon too, but British and American officials exercised infinite care and patience to defuse every potentially dangerous incident.[29]

The Oregon crisis can also be lined up for comparison with cases in other times. Looking down the trajectory of relations between the United States and Britain from 1775 to the present, it is striking how they moved from violent enmity to intimate alliance in close step with the extent to which they were comparable republics. It was easier to avoid war in 1846 than in 1812, with the leaderships converging on similar principles. But when the United States split into two different regimes, it opened the way to an exceptionally grave crisis, for the British aristocracy aligned itself with the Southern slaveholders. Britain might indeed have entered the war if its leaders had held their ancestors' power to ignore the views of Britain's commoners, who largely sympathized with democracy and the North.[30]

Particularly informative is the last serious Anglo-American crisis, an 1895 dispute over the boundary between Venezuela and British Guiana. By that time both Britain and the United States could have been classified as marginal democracies. Yet Britain's prime minister, the Marquis of Salisbury, had entered government through one of the old corrupt pocket boroughs and found mass democracy disgusting, whereas President Grover Cleveland had begun as a sheriff and won hard-fought elections as a staunch enemy of privilege. The gap in political culture between the two leaders brought mutual incomprehension and an exchange of insulting diplomatic messages about foreign influence in Latin America. War fever broke out in the United States, especially among Irish emigrés and others who persisted in despising Britain as a repressive aristocracy.

Cleveland's ambassador to Britain, however, saw the British government as honorable and trustworthy, while the British recognized that Cleveland's bluster was at least partly a show for his political audience. At heart, the leadership on each side felt that the other could be trusted to deal honestly and accept a just settlement. Using a variety of formal and informal channels, they negotiated patiently until the dispute over the Venezuela boundary slipped from public attention and could be settled through arbitration. War between the two nations had become unthinkable, just at the point where each recognized the other as following similar political rules.[31]

Normal Negotiation Among Democracies

These borderline crises do not show us how governments manage conflict when each recognizes the other without reservation as a well-established democracy. Searching for the hardest test, the most severe military confrontation between modern democracies that were truly well-established, we find . . . historical trivia.

Perhaps the most severe attack of this kind came in 1940, when Great Britain (by then entirely a democracy) invaded Iceland, sending its troops ashore to the consternation of Iceland's equally democratic government. The British acted out of a fearful expectation that Nazi Germany was preparing to seize the strategic island. The unarmed Icelanders had hoped to get through the war unmolested by anyone, and resented the high-handed infringement of their sovereignty. Even so, their government considered Britain a "friendly nation" and half-accepted the argument that the troops had come in Iceland's own interests. Although it was formally a military attack, there was no sense of violence.[32] A related case was Britain's formal declaration of war on Germany's ally Finland in 1941. Again, the two democracies felt little enmity and never came close to combat (and Finland was not entirely democratic; see appendix). These confrontations were mere echoes of the titanic struggle against fascism. To learn about hostile military confrontation between genuine democracies under more normal circumstances we are left with only a single case in the twentieth century: the "Codfish War."[33]

In 1972 Iceland declared that its territorial waters would henceforth extend out 50 miles, a distance which was then raised in 1975 to 200 miles. The British, however, insisted that they had a legal right to pull fish from those waters. When British trawlers persisted, the Icelanders would not stand for it, for the cod fishery was vital to their livelihood. Iceland unveiled its secret weapon, a hooked steel blade that could be dragged across a trawler's wake and cut the cable to its net. The Icelandic navy—a few tiny patrol boats—charged into action.

The British navy sailed to the rescue. Frigates maneuvered themselves between the Icelandic patrol boats and their trawler prey, a game of checkers only marginally governed by international maritime rules. In these lurching and icy seas tempers ran short, and time and again one of the jockeying ships rammed into another, causing a few accidental casualties. Sometimes warning shots were fired. Yet nobody could imagine Iceland making actual war against Great Britain. The captain of Iceland's flagship disclosed that his command was armed with a small-bore gun of 1895 vintage and "a little pistol for boarding parties."[34]

Other democracies rushed to mediate. In fact, republics ever since the medieval Swiss have regularly turned to third parties to help them talk their way through a crisis. Of course many autocrats have used mediation, but mostly to settle peripheral issues, or after warfare had exhausted everyone; mediation has rarely reduced the level of their fighting. Democracies have done better, notably in the use of binding arbitration by a panel of neutrals (as the Venezuelan boundary question was resolved). Statistics on modern conflicts show that a pair of rival democracies is far more likely than a pair of authoritarian regimes to appeal to the international community for help settling a dispute. As one of the scholars who compiled these statistics pointed out, this propensity of democracies is a demonstration of the importance of a nation's political culture (along lines independent of the other evidence I have assembled). Arbitration between states is a plain extension of the domestic belief in the rule of law and the practice of bringing disputes before neutral judges.[35]

In the Codfish War, as in many other cases since medieval Switzerland, the mediators especially appealed to the principle of solidarity against the enemies of liberty. They reminded Britain that Iceland's airfields would be needed in case of war against the Soviet Union. They also appealed to Britain's respect for law and fair play, pointing out that extended fishing limits were increasingly accepted in international law and that the cod fishery was fragile. The British public felt sympathy for the intrepid Icelanders—which was far from how the public might have reacted to a dispute with a brutal dictator. Finally it was Britain, immeasurably the stronger power, that gave way.

Normally democracies get along so well that the notion of using force hardly even occurs to anyone. How is this valuable attitude sustained? A good place to find an answer is that huge and momentous success at maintaining peace, the European Community. The absence of the least hint of armed confrontation among the postwar European democracies is one of the most encouraging things to be found in all history.

The story of this success began in the European heartland along the Rhine, those rich provinces of forests and vineyards, fought over by commanders from Julius Caesar to Dwight Eisenhower. When the region proved to be loaded with coal and iron ore, industrialists laid plans to integrate industry across frontiers. If economic forces alone could create cooperation it would surely have happened here, but national antagonisms wrecked every would-be international cartel. The issue of control of the mines was pivotal in the battles and aftermath of the Franco-Prussian War, the First World War, the French invasion of the Ruhr, and the Second World War. In 1945 France split off one of the richest regions, the Saarland, which became a new bone of contention with Germany.[36]

Transforming this region from a battleground to a joint venture was the masterwork of Jean Monnet, a bustling man with a neat moustache who looked like the cognac salesman he had once been. The war against Hitler had confirmed his belief that democracies must cooperate. After the war, Monnet, Robert Schuman, and others proposed the creation of an international authority to manage the coal and iron regions efficiently, calling on nations to give up a little slice of their sovereignty. Their real concern lay far from the steel mills. Schuman and Monnet did not see industrial confederation as merely a way to economic prosperity, but as a step toward full political federation.

Monnet and his allies gradually constructed an intricate agreement out of hundreds of delicate individual compromises. Thousands of personages in government and industry had to be satisfied. No less important, public opinion across Europe had to be mobilized to push governments in the direction of confederation.[37] Monnet had the personal vision and gift for handsome phrases that can inspire idealism. However, he had little formal authority, and could work only by weaving together the hundreds of personal contacts that he diligently cultivated as he shuttled from Paris to Washington to Bonn to Brussels. He would carry ideas back and forth, he would provoke debate, he would listen to everyone, then he would haltingly propose a solution that would not trespass on anybody's vital interests. When resistance was too strong he would gracefully accept defeat—and claim a victory for compromise. Negotiators were astonished to hear him argue openly against his own French team, encouraging an egalitarian discussion in search of the common good. This was a different universe from the normal diplomacy of autocracies, with their evasions, obsessive secrecy, and brutal threats.

Negotiators did use one type of threat as a last resort. A delegate would warn: if you persist in your inflexible position the talks will fail. Such failure would have been a severe political embarrassment for the governments, given the public enthusiasm for cooperation that Monnet and his allies had aroused. In the end, six nations agreed to a joint coal and iron authority, which would in time develop into the modern European Community.[38]

Conflict over the Saarland threatened to wreck everything. In 1945 the territory's inhabitants had willingly been separated from the wreckage of Germany. But by the early 1950s, as German democracy and prosperity blossomed, many Saarlanders began to think of reunification. When the local pro-French government tried to prevent such talk, its undemocratic repression embarrassed France. The German government added to the pressure, insisting temperately but tenaciously that Saarlanders had a right to choose their own future. Until the issue was settled, Germany threatened to block European economic cooperation.

France's unquestioned military superiority was beside the point. French leaders who tried to hold the Saarland by force would have poisoned the crucial relationship with Germany and laid themselves open to attack by liberal critics at home. The French's own principles dictated that they had no choice but to allow free speech and a plebiscite, and to acquiesce when the majority voted for reunification with Germany.[39]

International plebiscites are a republican invention. Developed in the nineteenth century, they proved widely useful in helping to set boundaries after the First World War and have continued to serve up until the present. Any nation committed to liberty and self-determination cannot long refuse a well-founded call for a plebiscite. Besides, the mechanism offers a simple way to terminate a rankling conflict, win or lose, without sacrificing honor—just like elections within a nation. They are a transparent example of domestic democratic practices extended to international affairs.

The European Community evolved other mechanisms that followed from the domestic democratic principles of the member states. Everyone involved acknowledged that the member nations must have equal rights. Nobody doubted that to implement these rights would require a standard republican apparatus—voting councils, elected or rotating officials, legal adjudication, and so forth. Western European leaders increasingly dealt with one another as they dealt with rival politicians at home, patiently working out compromises and legal agreements. These rules of behavior, new to some, gradually became established. People learned to trust that when a nation won its way on some issue it would reciprocate with a concession on a different issue, perhaps at a later date. Entire nations learned to defer to committee votes and the rulings of the European Court of Justice. Within a few years such mechanisms worked so smoothly that disputes were eased well before they could provoke a crisis. The experience of the European Community is a paradigm of democratic political culture fostering a style of negotiation that easily maintains peace.[40]

CHAPTER THIRTEEN

Imperialist Aggression by Democracies

I n June 1954 Guatemala City was boiling with rumors of war. A clandestine radio station had come on the air, announcing that a rebel army was advancing on the capital. Mysterious airplanes circled over the city at night, now and then dropping bombs. Meanwhile, the U.S. government reported that the populace had risen to expel the Communist-dominated regime. As the tension became unbearable, generals of the Guatemalan army met with President Jacobo Arbenz. They had never liked his government, and now they told him that they could not defend it—or at any rate would not. Exhausted by the pressures, Arbenz resigned, giving way to a military regime.[1]

Two curious features distinguish these events from the normal Latin American uprising against a dictatorship. First, the Guatemalan government was a democracy. The traditional military dictatorship had fallen in 1944 and Arbenz's predecessor was elected president; in 1950 Arbenz was elected in the first constitutional transfer of government in the long history of Guatemala. Second, the great majority of Guatemalans supported Arbenz's reforming regime and had no thoughts of rebellion. The "rebel army" was a few hundred ragtag mercenaries, paid by the U.S. Central Intelligence Agency, who had crossed the border and then sat down to await developments, fighting as little as possible. The CIA had also arranged for the clandestine radio station and the airplanes that harrassed the capital. The fall of Arbenz was engineered by the U.S. government in a breathtaking feat of psychological warfare.

Some critics who doubt that democracies really keep peace with one another cite the Guatemala intervention and similar cases as "war by other means." They misunderstand what sort of events are actually in question in debates over what can prevent war. In 1954 President Dwight Eisenhower forbade any U.S. military involvement in Guatemala. The brief fighting was between rival Guatemalan groups, and probably cost less than a hundred lives.[2] Anyone who insists on putting a conflict like this in the *how about the next 30 years?*

category of "war" would have to invent some other term to describe what this book addresses, horrific full-scale international warfare.

Incidents like the subversion of Guatemala do give an opening for a more subtle criticism. Evidently there is a weak point in the republican peace, perhaps a flaw so severe that someday it could allow genuine war. If one democracy can act so aggressively against another, what use is the argument about the cooperative political culture of their leaders?

Modern history offers several cases of well-established democracies working to destroy regimes that were at least somewhat democratic. These interventions have not been well investigated, for they are clouded in secrecy and mostly of peripheral significance.[3] Only the Guatemala intervention, which was unique in the relentless power of the foreign intrusion, has attracted enough scholarly scrutiny to give us a clear understanding.

An exceptional case of a different type is still more unsettling. In the 1898 "Fashoda Crisis" two well-established modern democracies, France and Britain, got into such an acrimonious dispute that some historians suggest they might well have gone to war. Critics offer the case as an indication that the historical absence of war between democracies is merely a matter of luck, not of mechanisms reliably making for peace.

Indeed, there is a weak point in human behavior that threatens peace between any regimes, democracies or not. People may identify so strongly with their nationality (with its territory, language, ethnic stock, religion, and so forth) that this loyalty outweighs even the solidarity among fellow democrats. They may then see foreigners as an alien and untrustworthy outgroup regardless of their form of government. This can result in aggressive imperialism, the struggle of a nation to enforce its hegemony over other peoples. Unless we can understand this loophole in the rule of republican peace and plug it, some day we may find our destruction coming through it.

The Subversion of Guatemala

When Eisenhower and other leaders of the United States looked at Guatemala, their first question was the one leaders usually ask: what is the political character of the regime? The dossiers that the U.S. Federal Bureau of Investigation had compiled on Guatemalan leaders bristled with warnings.

Most of the FBI's informants were from elite families who had enjoyed a fat life under the former dictatorship, and they branded all opponents on their left as rabid Communists, even those who only encouraged labor unions and agrarian reform. Exaggerated suspicions were also nourished by another set of people who were denounced by the Guatemalan regime for the wealth they had extracted: executives of the United Fruit Company. The new regime was expropriating some of the unused portions of United Fruit's vast landholdings, and outraged executives made their feelings known to the U.S. government with the aid of crack lobbyists.[4]

The Eisenhower administration was prepared to interpret any attack on U.S. business interests as an attack on the nation and on liberty itself. These were serious matters in a time when Communism had been snatching up nations from Czechoslovakia to China with terrifying speed. The Communists advanced partly through covert subversion, but this was normally accompanied by visible labor agitation, agrarian reform, and virulent propaganda against the United States and its corporations—exactly what the U.S. government was seeing in Guatemala. Were the calamities that befell Eastern Europe and Asia being prepared right next door? Eisenhower's secretary of state, John Foster Dulles, admitted that there might never be evidence tying Arbenz directly to the Kremlin, but Dulles was ready to take action anyway, "based on our deep conviction that such a tie must exist."[5]

Arbenz did believe that Marxism was the best solution to the dire subjugation of Guatemala's peasants and laborers, and like many idealists in those years he became isolated within a tight circle of like-minded Communist friends. Dedicated and hard-working, these friends were the only men Arbenz could rely upon to put reforms into practice, so a few Communists got positions in his government. Their methods were legal and democratic, if only because the Communist militants numbered only a few hundred and were far too weak to seize control.[6]

To Eisenhower and Dulles, even a few Communists constituted a grave threat for a nation like Guatemala. Could democracy be maintained among people who had been mired for centuries in ignorance and subservience, a nation moreover composed largely of "primitive" peasants with dark skins? The sad history of Latin politics combined with racist prejudices to paint a picture of natives prone to anarchy and easily misled by scoundrels. Many Latin Americans themselves insisted that their countries could only be governed by authoritarian methods.[7]

If democracy could not be sustained in Guatemala then it was vital that the right kind of authoritarians wind up in power. A top U.S. diplomat declared, "It is better to have a strong regime in power than a liberal government if it is indulgent and relaxed and penetrated by Communists." Of course, this obsession with fighting Reds was only partly driven by concern for what Latin Americans would suffer under Communist rule. A Communist nation might open its airfields to Russian bombers, threatening the United States itself.[8]

Anxiety grew as the Guatemalan regime wobbled in factional disarray. Tensions had peaked in 1949, when elections pitted Arbenz against the more conservative Francisco Araña. If Araña had been elected he would probably have reached an accommodation with the United States. But shortly before the election he was ambushed and riddled with bullets. Nobody ever proved who was responsible, but the CIA and U.S. military intelligence pointed to Arbenz.[9] Winning the election under these circumstances hardly established Arbenz as a democratic leader. While conservatives furiously plotted coups, the reformists themselves splintered into factions, their leaders drawing pistols on one another and even trying to seize party headquarters by force. If anyone seemed likely to come out on top it was the well-disciplined Communists.

By 1954 Eisenhower and his advisers believed that Guatemala was being captured by a Communist conspiracy controlled from the Kremlin. Neighboring nations clear to Mexico might fall like dominoes. Eisenhower later wrote that "the agents of international Communism in Guatemala" were already working to subvert their neighbors, "fomenting political assassinations and strikes" (he did not indicate which he thought worse). It may seem incredible that well-informed people should fail to recognize that a neighboring country was not in the grasp of a clique of fanatic Communists, but loosely governed by a mixed bag of highly popular reformers. Yet every responsible historian of the affair has noted this misperception. The Eisenhower administration, seeing everything through the prism of the Cold War, believed only the enemies of Guatemalan reform.[10]

Journalists and the public in the United States faithfully accepted the administration's views, with help from the United Fruit Company's public relations experts. Typical was a *Saturday Evening Post* story warning of a "Red beachhead" in Guatemala, where Communism "controls one country and is coming close to dominating some others." Few people in the

United States cared much about Guatemala or could even locate it on a map; they would leave the president free to exert whatever pressure he chose.[11]

At first the administration tried open pressures such as an economic embargo. What precipitated harsher action was a move of a type that, as I have noted in other cases, is readily taken as proof that a nation's leaders are far from republican: a covert alliance with an authoritarian regime.[12] In May 1954 the United States discovered that a ship sailing under false documents had smuggled a load of arms from the Soviet bloc into Guatemala. The administration assumed that the machine guns would be used to support insurrection in neighboring Honduras, or perhaps to eliminate anti-Communists within Guatemala itself. Eisenhower decided to act before it was too late.[13]

When the Arbenz government saw that its enemies were preparing to attack, it suspended civil rights and arrested a large number of people. The United States later claimed that leading opponents of Communism were illegally arrested "and tortured in police dungeons." If the Eisenhower administration had once had doubts, it now felt certain that Arbenz led a criminal conspiracy which could not be restrained by legal democratic processes. Nobody remarked that it was unrelenting pressure from the United States that had driven Arbenz to extreme measures. Guatemalan envoys to Washington had begged for forbearance on the grounds that democracy in Central America was fragile, but to Eisenhower the instability was both a reason to oust Arbenz and a means for doing so.[14]

Arbenz fell easily, because potent forces within Guatemala despised the very idea of rule by someone elected to represent the common people. The military regime that replaced him eventually destroyed tens of thousands of lives through kidnapping, torture, and murder, dealing such a setback to social and economic reform and the prospects for decent government that the region has not yet fully recovered.[15] The United States was also harmed directly, for eventually the facts of the CIA's subversion became public, undermining faith in the United States and casting doubt on democratic government in general. In retrospect it seems that Eisenhower committed a grave error in pulling down Arbenz. A different approach might have nurtured the fragile plant of democracy instead of tearing it out before it could take root.

Prejudice and Subversion in Georgia and Chile

One of the things that led the Eisenhower administration astray was a belief that an impoverished, "primitive" people cannot create a democratic government. This fallacy has been refuted by the crude peasants of ancient Athens and medieval Schwyz, and by modern third-world democracies from Botswana to Papua New Guinea. Nevertheless, many people feel that democracy cannot exist where there are too few schools, for example, or other conditions notably different from those seen in normal democratic nations. In cases where the foreigners' politics are already in doubt, misgivings increase if they have unfamiliar social or religious customs or even a different skin color.

An especially plain illustration of this is the racist arguments used by the U.S. government and the state of Georgia when they destroyed a regime resembling a fellow republic. The Cherokee Nation, inspired by missionaries and its own great chiefs, had transformed itself in a single generation. Cherokees had built log cabins, planted cotton and woven it for shirts and trousers, learned to read and write, then constructed towns with handsome whitewashed houses, founded a newspaper, and finally, in 1827, written themselves a constitution as republican as that of the United States. Nevertheless, the state of Georgia claimed the territory where the Cherokees lived. Whites came to seize the farmlands, backed up by troops who prevented the new government from functioning. Eventually soldiers forced the Cherokees into a dreadful migration in which thousands perished, the "Trail of Tears"—in proportion to population perhaps the deadliest of all aggressions between nominal republics. It was another case where military officers on the scene caused harm far beyond what political leaders intended. Our question is why politicians gave soldiers such power over a neighboring elected regime.

There was reason to doubt that the Cherokees thought in true republican fashion (see appendix). Unpracticed in formal governance, in recent years they had divided into murderous factions. But a main reason for their disarray was that the state of Georgia thwarted every attempt to make their government work. White leaders refused to believe that Native Americans were capable of constituting an actual state and contemptuously banned their legislature and elections. This attitude came naturally in slaveholding Georgia, where any nonwhite was seen as savage and degenerate, and a potential enemy. When Georgia sent troops into Cherokee country it was difficult to say whether it was invading a foreign state or suppressing people within its own territory; either way it was dealing with a despised outgroup.[16]

Wherever we find a republic undermining another regime that is at least partly republican, it is not enough to point to the perceived deficiencies in the subverted nation. Couldn't the attackers instead have helped them achieve better government? The danger here is a failure of democratic ideals, not among the victims but among the aggressors—a failure to acknowledge others as potential equals who are due full political rights.

This is what failed in the case of Guatemala. The Cold War years witnessed a general disease of perception in the United States. Many saw diabolic Communist tendencies in anyone—not just foreigners but fellow citizens—who led worker protests, opposed U.S. foreign policy, or simply attacked its corporations. The group that was actually conspiring to serve Soviet interests constituted only a tiny minority, yet Communists were repressed as if there were a national emergency requiring authoritarian measures. The most notorious cases came in the 1960s, when the FBI illegally harrassed protest organizations (especially black and Native American ones) who were imagined to be bound up with Communism.[17] But the persecution in the 1950s of the Communist Party of America and its sympathizers was still more ruthless.

The federal government also infringed on the rights of citizens who only seemed to serve Communism. For example, the Eisenhower administration secretly undermined the reputation of a *New York Times* correspondent when he revealed some sensitive truths about Guatemala. Groundless charges even drove innocent people from the country—exile, that reliable sign of a deficiency in republican practice. At the same time that U.S. envoys were demanding that Guatemalans forbid their Communist Party from even taking part in elections, the U.S. Congress was preparing a law that would do exactly that in their own country.[18] The United States should still have been called a democracy, since its Communist Party was entirely marginal to the significant politics. But in this one direction the government had a blind spot which permitted repression, with foreign and domestic behavior, as usual, in accord.

We can sort out the factors that are liable to promote aggression by reviewing one more case of subversion by a democracy. In this case nobody spoke of dark-skinned natives mired in ignorance, for the targets were of

European stock, with a modern economy and a democracy that had worked well for decades. This indicates that racial prejudices, while they can be a contributory factor, are not a necessary condition for aggression between republics. It was for other reasons that the U.S. goverment encouraged a military coup in 1973 that killed Salvador Allende, the freely elected president of Chile.

Even before his election, leaders in Washington had been worried about Allende. Executives of multinational corporations were warning them that the Chilean was a convinced Marxist. President Richard Nixon and his adviser Henry Kissinger came to see Chile as another battleground in their worldwide struggle against Communism. After Allende took power, some of his actions resembled those that had turned Eisenhower against Arbenz: expropriation of corporate property, abusive rhetoric that echoed *Pravda,* barely legal suppression of democratic opponents, friendly dealing with foreign Communist states. Weapons were even secretly imported into Chile to arm radical leftist groups. To anti-Communists all this was as damning as the discovery of dried toads would be for a witch hunter.

The Nixon administration worked to sabotage Allende's regime by denying Chile international economic aid and credit and applying other economic pressures, while covertly supporting opposition groups. More dangerously, some U.S. agents maintained secret contacts with Chilean military officers. These officers were increasingly alarmed by the advance of Marxism, as well as by the domestic turmoil that Nixon's pressures helped to encourage. In the end it was the Chilean military that brought down its own government, so this was no armed international confrontation. It is nevertheless another example of one democratic government deliberately working to destroy another.[19]

As usual, there was a symmetry between the U.S. government's actions in Chile and its actions at home. In precisely these years Nixon also secretly dispatched agents to molest U.S. citizens, under the conviction that his opponents were aiding the advance of Communism. Again, the problem was an exaggerated pessimism about the ability of democracy to maintain itself by lawful means. Subversion in Chile was no departure for an administration that condoned breaking into the offices of political rivals in Washington itself.

At home or abroad, some leaders lumped all their leftist opponents together as supporters of the Communists, thereby placing them in a demonized outgroup. This is reminiscent of the prejudices that set Catholics violently against Protestants in Switzerland, and whites against Cherokees in Georgia. In all these cases a plain political disagreement was overridden by stereotypes of inhuman evil, until leaders refused to allow their opponents equal rights and applied lawless coercion.

There is a second feature common to the subversions of elected presidents in Guatemala and Chile (among other cases). The attacks were prompted in part by advice and information given by businessmen, from both local elites and corporations based in the United States. The corporate executives had reasons for encouraging conflict with a regime that despised them. We have seen similar foreign policy interventions by mining magnates who worked to undermine the Boer Republic in the 1890s, and Ruhr barons who welcomed French enmity against their own government in the 1920s.[20]

The political subculture within most business organizations is notoriously undemocratic—a matter of hierarchical power and patron-client relationships. Corporate executives may address executives of other corporations as equals in an oligarchic sense, but their daily activity is remote from more universal democratic ideals. In foreign affairs we would expect executives to resemble not elected politicians, but the career colonial officials accustomed to imposing order, or even the military officers trained to beat down their opponents. We must beware of the influence of such subcultures, no matter how democratic the national government itself.

A still more undemocratic, secretive, lawless, and coercive subculture urged Eisenhower against Guatemala and Nixon against Chile: the CIA. Intelligence agents on the scene filtered the information sent home in order to exaggerate how dangerous the target regime was, and arranged conspiracies in the conviction that any means were justified against Communists. There is a disagreeable similarity to the distortions by KGB officers that, as we saw, helped persuade Soviet leaders to invade Czechoslovakia in 1968.

In all these cases diplomacy, in the traditional sense of exchanges of notes between envoys, was beside the point. Suspicious leaders turned less to diplomats than to corporations, intelligence agencies, and military units. It is no contradiction to the thesis that political culture affects negotiations, but exactly in accordance with it, that the resulting "diplomacy" was in a style far from cooperative.

Hierarchical subcultures are not likely to seriously warp a democracy's foreign relations unless the ground has already been prepared by prejudice. Once rivals are classified as "backward natives," "Communist gangsters," or the like, and thereby thrust into a despised outgroup, their hostile acts are exaggerated and their friendly gestures are brushed aside as duplicitous. For this mechanism to secure a foothold, however, it seems there must be deficiencies in democracy not just on one side but on both. One side, ambiguous in its democracy, is branded as an enemy by leaders who are already abnormally repressive of similar opponents at home.

In these borderline cases we find something more nuanced than a black-or-white rule of war or peace; a limited aggression can be connected with a limited deviation from democratic principles on both sides. If some lucky circumstance could have turned down the level of prejudice—if the leaders could have seen Communists or dark-skinned people (for example) as a bit more deserving of the tolerance due equals—it seems highly likely that military and intelligence agencies would not have been given such a dangerously free hand.

There is another type of prejudice that is even more harmful in international affairs, for it directly blocks the extension of domestic tolerance to foreigners. Another nation may seem to lie beyond the circle of fellowship simply because it is . . . another nation. The gravity of this problem is shown in the final crisis on my list.

Military Plots from Paris to Fashoda

In September 1898 five British steamers loaded with troops chugged up the White Nile to a remote settlement named Fashoda. When they neared the dilapidated mud fort they were annoyed to behold a French flag. The British troops were the vanguard of an army that had fought its way through masses of Sudanese, and they felt that the entire territory belonged to them by right of conquest. But here was the dapper Captain Jean-Baptiste Marchand with a handful of French officers and 150 Senegalese soldiers, obstinately claiming the region for France. With a patriotism bordering on mania, Marchand had come from Paris to lead these men for two grueling years up the Congo River and through the sweltering marshes of the upper Nile. He was not about to surrender his position. The British officers did not dare start a war on their own. The soldiers parted with mutual respect, toasting one another with champagne which the French had somehow managed to carry to one of the world's most inaccessible spots.[21]

News of the encounter brought consternation in Europe. The French officials who had launched Marchand's expedition had hoped to extract concessions from Britain in an old dispute over Egypt, but British leaders felt any French intrusion on the upper Nile was flatly intolerable. Both sides held exaggerated views about the strategic value of these insect-ridden marshes. British newspapers howled that the intruders must be kicked out, while French newspapers exclaimed that national honor required holding Fashoda. The French premier, Théophile Delcassé, warned the British ambassador that his nation would "accept war rather than submit." He begged the ambassador to arrange some face-saving compromise: "Do not drive me into a corner." But British leaders felt that public opinion would not stand for the least concession.[22]

Britain's prime minister was that same Marquis of Salisbury whose aloof diplomacy had recently angered President Cleveland. He regarded public opinion and the noisy press with the misgivings of a gentleman confronted by an unpredictable pack of dogs. To Salisbury the mass of voters were only a distraction for the oligarchic elite that still largely controlled British policy.[23] This lack of respect for democracy may have contributed to the imperious way British leaders approached the more democratic French. However, people of all classes in Britain were belligerent over Fashoda, and politicians with an eye on the next elections expected to be rewarded for a truculent stand. The Cabinet had the public behind them when they took the serious step of mobilizing the British fleet as if for war. In reply the French rushed military preparations of their own.

Salisbury had reason for mistrusting the French democracy. That year France had separated into bitterly opposed camps after Captain Alfred Dreyfus was court-martialled for treason. Where the Left sought to exonerate Dreyfus, the Right saw a conspiracy to defame the army command in preparation for Socialist revolution. When tens of thousands of workers went on strike and street fighting erupted, the fearful government packed the public squares of Paris with encampments of soldiers. The Left mounted mass demonstrations, fearing that a military coup was imminent.[24]

As the Dreyfus and Fashoda affairs moved simultaneously toward their peaks of crisis, the British ambassador in Paris telegraphed London that "a military despotism" might be imminent. A group of generals was said to be plotting to seize power and rally France behind them by using Fashoda as a pretext to start a war. The British Cabinet, with its aristocratic doubts that mass democracy could be stable, found the threat plausible. It was on receiving this warning that they mobilized their fleet—less as a coercive threat than as a defensive preparation in case France did fall under authoritarian control.[25]

British newspapers called the entire affair a plot by a French militarist clique, likening them to common criminals who trampled on Britain's rights with the same malicious disregard for justice that they had showed to Dreyfus. This was quite accurate. Marchand's expedition had indeed been organized in secret by a faction of right-wing military men and ministry officials. These enthusiasts for colonial conquest, supported by mercantile interests, formed a chauvinist subculture in Paris that scorned democratic politics. They had contrived to carry out a foreign policy of their own while the elected politicians were preoccupied with domestic conflicts. The democratic leaders had hardly noticed Marchand's little band until it was too late.[26]

If there were enough deficiencies in democracy on both sides to allow them to reach the brink of war, enough strengths remained to stop them there. So long as the authoritarian party did not seize actual control of France, few people expected war. As a French newspaper said, in a typical expression of the public opinion in both nations, "It would be absurd to suppose a conflict between two great civilized powers over some pestilential swamps."[27] In London we find Salisbury, who loathed anything so disorderly as battle, making sure the Cabinet issued no outright ultimatum. In Paris we find Delcassé, just the sort of man to start a crisis—argumentative and afire with patriotism—but also just the sort of man to end one, for he also had a conservative and practical side. Recognizing that war would be profitless, he ordered Marchand's band to withdraw. Courteously, the British gave Marchand a lift down the Nile. In the end, the crisis scrupulously followed the usual pattern, for there was never a chance of war so long as France remained a democracy.

Yet there is one way this case does seriously undermine common ideas about democratic peace.[28] A look through the public statements on both sides reveals a deficiency: hardly anyone called for peace on the explicit grounds that the other nation was a fellow democracy. Many in Britain seemed actually pleased that they might get an excuse to trounce those arrogant French. People ever since the Greeks had insisted that democracies were natural allies, until the claims became a self-fulfilling prophecy, but in 1898 there were few who talked that way. Like Sherlock Holmes's puzzle of the dog that failed to bark in the night, this absence gives a clue for where death may stalk.

The Problem of Imperialism

By the 1890s aspirations in Europe and the United States had turned from democratic reform at home to imperial expansion abroad. People imagined that they were members of a national team competing in a sort of vast game of Monopoly, with the aim of occupying and extracting profit from as much of the world board as possible. Economic ruin would befall a nation that failed to seize enough squares. It seemed to make no difference whether a rival player was a democracy or not. The fittest, those with the greatest strength and willpower, were bound to seize hegemony.[29]

Historians disagree on how imperialism became an international passion, but all agree that ideology went through fantastic changes. The imperialist game was openly waged for the sake of wealth and military position, but not only that. Many devoted their lives to the hope of bringing benighted peoples the blessings of civilization, perhaps someday including republican self-government. Thus the passionate ideology of imperialism swallowed up democratic ideals. The movement reached its peak in a "scramble for Africa," where military officers and colonial officials, along with their supporters back home, reached irrational heights of greed, racism, and vainglorious fantasy.[30]

In their imperial and civilizing mission people often confused nationality with ancestry. A fad for social Darwinism had turned history into a primal struggle for racial predominance—not just between, say, whites and Orientals, but between the Anglo-Saxon and Celtic or Latin "races." For example, in 1898 the British Cabinet was mainly preoccupied with how to rule Ireland; most English thought the Irish were as incapable of self-government (as Salisbury put it) as the Hottentots. Some called the French a Celtic race, lumping them with the despised Irish; others called the French Latins, a hot-blooded and degenerate folk like the Spaniards. Some French wrote with equal derision about "les Anglo-Saxons" and chattered about their own fight for racial survival. Meanwhile, the dispute with the Boers seemed likely to explode in what a British minister would call a "contest for supremacy" between the English and Dutch "races." At no other point in the history of international relations did lines drawn according to nationality and ancestry matter so much, and lines drawn according to political regime so little.[31]

Even on the Left, the principle of solidarity among democracies was eclipsed by the Socialist credo. Workers of all nations must combine to fight international capitalism, never mind whether the capitalists ruled from behind the facade of a monarchy or of an elected cabinet. The few traditional liberals who still declared that democrats in every land should stand together seemed out of touch with modern principles, namely the advancement of class, race, and imperial power.[32]

It is no coincidence that the two men most responsible for the conflict over Fashoda were both experienced in dealing forcefully with subject peoples. Delcassé, the French premier who held out obstinately till the last minute, had earlier served as France's minister for colonial affairs. A man devoted to hard work, control, and secrecy, he thought the public squabbling of republican politicians was disgusting; privately he called himself "not merely anti-parliamentarian but actually authoritarian." It was Delcassé himself who had first plotted the expedition to Fashoda, along with others who believed fervently that France should rule over lesser races.[33]

In the British Cabinet the only member who found the thought of a war with France truly attractive was precisely the Colonial Minister, Joseph Chamberlain. He was one of those Victorian industrialists who devoted themselves with paternal benevolence to the improvement of their employees but who would scarcely tolerate anyone arguing back. In his personal dealings with other politicians Chamberlain tended toward bullying and intrigue, until many of his colleagues came to distrust "Pushful Joe." Meanwhile, he openly denounced the demagoguery of democratic politics, declaring that elite imperialism was a better way to mobilize the nation and the "Anglo-Saxon race." By appealing to the public's chauvinism and by sheer force of personality, Chamberlain made himself the leading figure in British foreign policy. For example, soon after taking office as colonial minister he unleashed on his personal authority a military expedition that grabbed control of an African tribal kingdom. In France, too, he saw an alien "race" that should be put in its place, if necessary by force.[34]

Delcassé and Chamberlain were only two proponents of a way of thinking that was characteristic of the times. The closing years of the nineteenth century, when the mania for racist imperialism briefly displaced ideas of republican solidarity, were exceptionally hazardous for relations between regimes somewhat like republics. Of our little set of crises throughout history, no less than five took place during this half-decade. Colonial positions were the stakes in the Fashoda and Venezuela border crises, and also when the United States fought Spain in 1898, when it fought the Filipinos in 1899, and when Chamberlain helped foment war against the Boers.

We must look far back for a comparable case. When ancient Athens invaded Syracuse, it was another regime that was only barely democratic. It was led mostly by aristocrats and (like Britain in 1898) forbade the vote to perhaps half its adult males. Here, too, ethnic identity counted, for the Athenians were "Ionians" in dialect and ancestry, which made them traditional enemies of the "Dorians" in Sparta and Syracuse.[35] As we saw in chapter 6, it was not until a decade or so after this war that Greeks developed an ideology of democratic solidarity. It would appear that democracies are safer from one another when their leaders believe that self-fulfilling prophecy. They are at risk if some other ideology takes hold, in which primary allegiance belongs not to fellow democrats but to members of the same nationality. This does not qualify my explanation of mutual peace but directly reinforces it, as yet another body of evidence pointing to the crucial role of ingroup identification as a component of political culture.

The Nation as Ingroup

Humans tend to identify an ingroup when they organize themselves in nations—territorial entities bound together under a regime as a single people. These entities include everything from organized tribal groups like the Iroquois or Zulu "nations" to complex societies like the United States. People commonly set such ingroups apart from others by supposing there is an ethnic or racial divide, even in cases where two peoples are physically almost indistinguishable. For example, in 1898 newspapers in the United States stereotyped Spaniards as swarthy Latins with inborn cruelty. Meanwhile, newspapers in Spain called Americans a mongrel race, too obsessed with money to fight like the pure-blooded Spanish heroes. Around the same time the British described the Boers as cowardly and grasping by nature, while the Boers returned the compliment.[36]

Feelings of racial separation can be reinforced or even displaced by feelings of cultural difference, above all in religious practices. Thus Protestants in the United States despised the Spaniards as Roman Catholics, while Fundamentalist Boers distrusted the British as altogether godless. People imagine a nation as a tightly bound community marked off since ancient times by its unique language, cultural heritage, and bloodline. Believing that international wars are passionate struggles between communities so defined, many doubt peace can be maintained between nations even when both are democracies.

People may despair of understanding violence in rational terms when they hear of an ethnic conflict—Hutus slaughtering Tutsis or the reverse, for example, or even wars between French and Germans. Such problems are dismissed as senseless "age-old enmities." Only recently has a sharper understanding emerged among scholars, chiefly historians studying nineteenth-century Europe and anthropologists studying post-colonial Africa.

The modern map of nations, with its neatly demarcated areas of flat pink or green, is only vaguely related to the actual peoples—a mélange of dialects and genetic types smearing into one another. The tribes which today seem so distinct (like Hutus and Tutsis) were in many cases defined only within the last century or so. European colonial administrators typically selected a category of people to help them rule over others, or just lumped together a scattering of diverse villages under a tractable chief. It was much the same even for nations like France. As recently as the start of the twentieth century, nationhood was imposed with difficulty on peasants in Brittany or Provence, who recoiled when the government in Paris dispatched gendarmes and schoolteachers speaking that incomprehensible foreign tongue, French.[37]

Ethnographic surveys and social psychology experiments show that people are flexible in drawing group boundaries. Depending on circumstances, the types of differences that people emphasize can change with surprising ease. Experimenters may assign people to groups arbitrarily, yet the subjects quickly begin to see members of "different" groups as somehow inferior, less worthy of rewards. This human tendency operates especially when people are caught up in competition. In case after case where rivalries developed, scholars found the coalitions divided along lines that were drawn according to the immediate situation, almost like boys choosing up sides for a game.[38]

In most of these cases distinctions were first brought to the fore by an imperial overlord when it organized its hierachical rule by lumping subjects into ethnic categories under local intermediaries. The tactic of divide-and-rule backfired when people began to fight for independence. Elite leaders discovered that emotional appeals to ethnic identity could bind followers into a political force. Historical studies of nationalist movements find these groups developing where people combine to gain control over resources (jobs, land, education, whatever), to defend themselves against intruders, or simply to maintain a respectable status. Once people coalesced around some definition of themselves as a group, they sometimes managed to win full-scale nationhood, complete with their own territorial state. Divide and rule, the disintegration of an empire, elite leaders seeking a new dominion: these were the forces active in the disintegration of the Soviet Union and Yugoslavia, earlier in post-colonial Africa and Asia, earlier still when the Austrian and Ottoman empires broke up; indeed, almost everywhere that an imperial power collapsed.[39]

In short, normally it has been politics that created national and ethnic identity more than the other way round. The very symbols that rally and define people as a nation—the myths of founders like William Tell, the hallowed texts like the Gettysburg Address, the nation's flag itself—are usually ones that were devised in the course of explicitly political contests. Ingroup definition is a political act intimately linked to political culture.[40]

When people talk about ethnic differences, a close look usually finds that what they really care about most is behavior, as determined by social and political culture. Those other people are more cruel (or craven) than we are, they are too tactless (or secretive), they even eat dogs (or pigs). When someone invokes differences like language or skin color, it is largely because such features can be used as a shortcut to defining a group of people whose behavior seems alien. This logic is well expressed by the Pathans of Afghanistan, who all speak the Pashto language and proudly claim descent from a common ancestor. There are always families on the borderline of group membership, and for such situations they have a useful saying: "He is Pathan not just who speaks Pashto but who does Pashto"— that is, who follows their particular code of behavior.[41]

Of all behaviors, political practices are what count most where groups are in conflict. It is political practices that determine whether you join or fight with others and for what goals—indeed, that tell you where to expect safety or torture. It is practical to ask about the authoritarian or egalitarian tendencies of others before noticing their skin color or religious observances (unless you think such visible features are the safest indicators of likely behavior). An extreme case of nationhood based on political behavior is the United States, whose national self-definition rests chiefly on adherence to its democracy. Republics in general, with their ideals of equality and tolerance, tend to define their ingroup of citizens as those who follow republican practices.

This republican mode of group identification has repeatedly struggled against identification along strictly ethnic, linguistic, or religious lines. Sometimes it was the republican principles that lost. Usually the result was that republics never got established, and a tragic history of warfare continued. One might hope that this could not happen in well-established republics, but in fact it is possible. The proof is the two highly exceptional Swiss cases (Bern against Lucerne and the 1847 civil war) where a strict division was defined by Catholic and anti-Catholic leaderships, each requiring allegiance to its own authority even if republican ideals must be partly abandoned. The result was bloodshed, although it was not very severe. Fortunately, it seems that republican group identification hardly ever fails so badly except in republics that have not yet established themselves.

The initial establishment of a republican group identification often depends on specific political circumstances. In a precarious situation it seems that a single idealistic or power-hungry leader can switch history onto a particular track. Leaders may find that they can rally followers most effectively through ethnic or religious appeals, especially in locales where republican political mechanisms have never been practiced. According to most observers, this is precisely what happened in the case I opened this book with, the tragedy of Yugoslavia, where a few authoritarian leaders used egregious lies to inflame latent antagonisms. As one scholar bluntly said, when economic and political upheavals threatened the power of elites, they diverted attention by "purposefully provoking and fostering conflict along ethnic lines."[42]

The political scientist Ted Robert Gurr, in an exhaustive study of recent group conflicts, found that they were especially likely to break out during the first few years after a political transition.[43] As we have seen, only if a republic survives this initial period should we call it "well-established"—that is, a regime whose leaders have maintained a stable, continuous political culture of tolerating dissent. Republican ideals have not always taken root even where people liberated themselves from oppression by fighting for political rights such as free speech and the vote. These individual rights could get mixed up with something altogether different: demands for the collective rights of a particular group. Groups might insist, for example, on maintaining schools strictly in their own religion, or on conducting government business strictly in their own language. Leaders of a majority group might insist on unbridled "majority rule" and treat individual rights as an obstacle to their group's collective goals. A regime is hardly democratic when it tosses aside ideals of equality, toleration, and allegiance to the process of building a consensus. The consequent domestic and international struggles, prominent today in parts of Africa and the former Soviet empire, have little to do with our inquiry into conflicts between well-established republics.[44]

I have left till last one other way in which people identify their ingroup, a division so obvious that we could almost have taken it for granted: the geographical criterion. Very often people who reside together in a particular locale are seen as members of a demarcated community. Ingroup and outgroups become literal insiders and outsiders, perhaps separated with actual barbed wire.

Humans are territorial, like many other species of animals that fiercely defend particular patches of space. But like most innate human tendencies, this trait is flexible. If a farmer in Vermont was outraged to hear that the Japanese had bombed a harbor in Hawaii, that was no crude, instinctive reaction. The emotions naturally evoked by one's home region are extended to a distant frontier only where a territorial state holds the allegiance of a population—politics and political culture again.

Citizens of republics have often refused to treat certain people as equals simply because they lived outside a geographical border. The mechanism was simple in oligarchic cities, already accustomed to lordship over outlying villages within their territory. An example is what happened in 1405 after a signor who had taken over Pisa sold the city outright to Florence for cash. Thereafter the Florentines felt no compunction about ruling over what they called "our city of Pisa," holding that the Pisans had no more right to self-government than the tenants of a country manor. Medieval Swiss democracies similarly ruled without apology as suzerains of various interstitial domains. A proprietary feeling could arise even without outright possession, as when officials of the United States treated the "banana republics" of the Caribbean virtually as colonies. The spirit was well expressed by Colonial Secretary Joseph Chamberlain, who proudly described the British as "landlords of a great estate." The tenants were to be uplifted, no doubt, but they were not seen as political equals.[45]

This is imperialism, and it is the chief loophole through which conflict has entered to divide approximately republican regimes. Questions of dominion over a dependent, geographically demarcated population were important in more than half of our small list of armed confrontations.[46] The fighting could be against rebellious subjects like the Pisans or the Irish, but outside nations were often involved as well. Foreign leaders might feel justified in intervening because of oppression, while the rulers of a subject domain may be quick to suspect other nations of scheming to displace them as overlord.

This is an extension of a general problem we have seen repeatedly: approximately republican regimes may turn to violence exactly at the point where the principles of equality and toleration are not fully established domestically. In the imperialist cases the readiness of leaders to use force abroad was almost predictable in view of how they coerced people, if not exactly at home, then certainly under their dominion. In colonies the distinction between the domestic citizen and the foreign potential enemy was already blurred.

The Fashoda crisis shows all of this at work. In Britain few elite leaders saw their regime mainly as a democracy: they called it an Empire. British intransigence over Fashoda stemmed directly from an anxious desire to maintain control over Egypt and everything east of Suez—territory populated by a multitude of civilized peoples who had no say at all in the affair. Among both Britain and French leaders, exercising command over subject races had fostered enthusiasm for military means.

Nevertheless, outright war has always been avoided so long as the home regimes were comparably democratic, even when they ruled over empires. Mutual peace has held even when the self-fulfilling ideology of democratic solidarity was absent, not only in 1898 but also in earlier cases where the regimes were too primitive for a developed ideology, like medieval Switzerland. However useful the ideology may be, the democracies must have had something else. What is this last, decisive line of defense against war?

The Diplomatic Solution

In every crisis where both sides recognized the other as a fellow democracy, inspection of their diplomacy finds it aimed to resolve the dispute, not to impose dominance. Even amid the nationalist furor over Fashoda, the negotiators were straightforward and respectful. So long as a military junta did not seize Paris, the British expected that the French would be reasonable and eventually concede that their position was untenable. Meanwhile, the French felt that if they withdrew they could trust Britain not to press for ever more concessions. The whole affair would never even have begun, a French diplomat remarked, if French leaders had not taken it for granted "that England would never initiate hostilities." This mutual respect was built through daily experience. The French found British diplomacy disagreeably firm, but always frank, reasoned, and well-mannered. The British ambassador likewise reported that even in their most heated arguments Delcassé was "courteous . . . very straightforward and explicit." The French premier had said from the start that he wanted to be friends with Britain; he meant it, and the British knew he meant it.[47]

This was how French and British politicians managed their domestic disagreements. Salisbury had risen to the top through a penchant for moderation and compromise, which he now applied in restraining Chamberlain's belligerence. Meanwhile, Delcassé was persuaded to retreat from Fashoda by another government leader, Félix Faure, who promised to publicly share responsibility for the decision—a quintessentially republican tactic.

What if we could go back and replace the French or British leadership with people whose diplomatic approach was more like that of Kaiser Wilhelm and his entourage? A peaceful resolution would certainly have been far harder to reach. That exact contrast was noticed by people at the time, for British leaders were beginning to conclude that German diplomacy was excessively deceitful and predatory. As the London *Times* remarked in 1903, "The dignity and calm of France" stood out by contrast with "the restlessness of the German Foreign Office." Chamberlain, even though he had imagined that Germans should be Britons' racial allies, remarked that

Germany's truculent and peremptory diplomatic notes caused deep resentment, whereas the tone of French notes was unfailingly polite no matter how grave the dispute. The French likewise found German diplomacy consistently hostile and untrustworthy. French liberals in particular, loathing Germany for its authoritarian regime, insisted that the British government was more dependable and moral.[48]

The liberals' viewpoint became French national policy when they took power in the aftermath of the Dreyfus Affair. The feeling grew, as one newspaper put it, that friendship "ought to exist between the French and English, both of whom are devoted to liberty under different forms. It is our natural alliance." In 1904 the two nations began an alliance which stands to this day. Of course every government carried on with a strategy of balancing powers, as when France made an alliance with tsarist Russia. But many at the time recognized that alliance as unnatural and dangerous; imperialist obsessions were waning, and democracies increasingly preferred to join with their own kind.[49]

The same shift affected relations between those old enemies Britain and the United States. Americans did not lag behind Germans as imperial rivals to Britain, but the British were too weak to defend their empire everywhere and had to make friends with somebody. For a time they were uncertain whether to approach Washington or Berlin. Some called for an American alliance on the grounds of racial affinity, a joint "Anglo-Saxon" ancestry. Yet the Angles and Saxons (as Chamberlain noted) had come to Britain from Germany, while the United States was populated by everyone from Irish to Africans. The true affinity was in culture, and especially what Chamberlain called "common laws and common standards of right and wrong"—political culture. Many pointed to love of justice, individual rights and the rule of law as the supreme "Anglo-Saxon" characteristics.

These feelings were supported by the two nations' styles of diplomacy. The British had noticed a stark contrast between President Cleveland and the German kaiser: while the American was agreeing to mediation over the Venezuela border, Wilhelm was aggressively meddling in South Africa. After the turn of the century people focused still more on the political methods of foreign governments. For example, one British statesman declared that Canada was safe from invasion simply because of the "innate justice" of the United States—a trait that few would have attached to Wilhelm's regime. Negotiations over miscellaneous disputes with Berlin kept bogging down in German intrigue and insults, while parallel exchanges with Washington sailed ahead to settlement under smooth and rational diplomacy. By 1905 Britain's leaders had made the leap to friendship with the United States, leading to one of history's most successful alliances.[50]

These and all the other anecdotal cases I have inspected, along with the few but consistent statistical studies of diplomatic exchanges I noted above, point to a simple conclusion. Republican governments generally adopt a more cooperative style of negotiation with one another than is seen where one side is authoritarian. And no matter how severe the differences between rival republics, their style of diplomacy contributes to a mutual trust which moves them toward alliance rather than war. Such a proposition can never be proved with the rigor of a mathematical theorem, but it seems plausible enough to be taken seriously when approaching international relations.

Now to summarize what influences may undermine peace between approximately republican regimes. Biased perceptions are the first factor. These are especially dangerous when one or both of the regimes is ambiguous, verging on authoritarian or anocratic ways or simply newborn. The bias may be political, for example a prejudice against leaders who make rousing Marxist or anti-Catholic speeches, or it may be a stereotyping of people of a different language or ancestry or economic level, or simply of people who are across a border. It is common knowledge that such prejudices interfere with both democracy and peace. To this old sermon we can now add a more pointed warning: we should not pay too much attention to the location, culture, or economic standing of foreign peoples, nor even their rhetorical excesses; our first attention should go to their political culture as manifested in their domestic politics.

A second weak point in the rule of republican peace involves the authoritarian subcultures found within even established republics: colonial bureaucracies, the military, secret agencies, sometimes business corporations. These find a particularly good opportunity to apply their customary domineering practices when their nation rules (or tries to) over a subject territory. In international affairs we must attend not just to overall political culture but to the characteristics of the people making key decisions on the scene. War is especially likely when authoritarian or anocratic subcultures influence the central government itself, so that it is not fully a republic.

A case displaying all the factors that can bring conflict between approximate republics is the war with which I opened this book. Serbs and Croats, prejudiced by virulent propaganda spread through media controlled by their governments, each perceived the other as innately authoritarian. Biased perceptions were all the more likely to arise because the regimes were new, with only brief and fumbling experience in both domestic and external relations. But perceptions of authoritarian ways were not all mistaken, for there were actual and notorious cases on each side of lawless coercion of minority political opponents. On both sides an in-group coalesced along ethnic lines rather than according to republican principles, which had scarcely been known in the region. Promoting this process were the leaders, former Communist Party members and military officers inclined toward authoritarian if not outright autocratic behavior. That attitude was reflected in their uncompromising approach to negotiations, which accordingly failed. Serbs and Croats went to war specifically over the control of intermediate territories which were beset with anocratic factions. Probably no one of these features by itself would have sufficed to open the gates to violence, but each additional weakness increased the risk of war.

Such risks are becoming vastly more perilous as leaders gain the capability to launch violence instantaneously on a global scale. Already by the 1960s a U.S. president had the ability to open his box of missile codes and inflict unthinkable destruction without consulting public opinion or even the Congress. Now the complexities of conflict are stripped down more than ever to the simple question of the leaders' patterns of political behavior. We must take care to monitor just where our leaders get their advice and what they personally believe about the use of force.

The goals of this study have now been met, the puzzle of mutual peace worked through. Yet peace is more than a mere avoidance of war. That much could be managed by any set of states if each built impenetrable walls along its frontiers. Republics, more than any other form of regime, have traditionally deployed more positive forces. To see these we must move beyond the inspection of rare and unusual conflicts and turn to normal behavior—the way republics have gotten along with one another in ninety-nine years out of a hundred. Aside from their avoidance of war, is there something unique about the way republics deal with other states of their own kind?

CHAPTER FOURTEEN

Leagues of Republics

I n the broad market square of Athens, where people from a hundred shores strolled and gossiped in the sunlight, there once stood a statue of Liberty. In 377 B.C. the Athenians erected alongside the statue a marble stele the height of a man. The statue is lost, but modern archaeologists shoveling through the rubble found twenty fragments of the stele and fitted them together to read. The stone bears an invitation to join a league of independent states with at least sixty members—a league of democracies.[1]

As I noted in chapter 6, statistical studies show that modern democracies have chosen other democracies as allies far more often than chance would have predicted. For example, one scholar found that at the start of a military conflict, pairs of democracies were twice as likely to support one another as were pairs where one nation (or both) was an autocracy. In less violent confrontations, where nations took a joint diplomatic stance on matters like trade negotiations, a study of modern cases showed that the higher the proportion of democracies, the more successful the group was at forging a consensus.[2] This cooperation sounds like the exact opposite of war. The manner in which republics stick together offers a way, largely independent of the other evidence we have seen, to improve our understanding of their mutual peace.

Diplomats and political scientists have devoted much thought to alliances, but they have rarely thought that it mattered what types of regimes were involved. Alliances were apparently an expression of realpolitik, based on calculations of military advantage, aimed less at keeping peace than at making successful war. Kings and dictators likewise allied with their own kind (about as often as republics did), while republics from ancient Sparta to the United States frequently allied with autocrats against more dangerous foes. Alliances among republics seemed a mere matter of chance.[3]

But if we turn from alliances held together by temporary pressures and look for more permanent associations, we find something remarkable. The league announced on the Athenian stele was only one of many cases when ancient Greek republics bound themselves to one another in close-knit leagues that endured for generations. Medieval Swiss republics did the same. In the early modern era so did Italian republics, German republics, and Dutch republics. When independent republican states emerged in North America in 1776 they likewise formed a confederation, the first of many such modern cases. As if drawn together by an irresistible magnetic attraction, republics have persistently gathered into tight trade associations, durable military alliances, formal confederations, and complete federal unions. The result might be as loose as the British Commonwealth of Nations or as integrally bound as the Netherlands. But something of the sort appeared everywhere in history where there were at least a few republics. When authoritarian states have attempted to combine in this way they have invariably failed over the long run, and usually over the short run.

Political scientists have long recognized that federalism is a feature of republican regimes and not authoritarian ones, but they have focused only on the domestic political constitutions.[4] They have overlooked the fact that nearly every federation originated in an arrangement among sovereign states, with much to tell us about international relations. For example, certain regimes in the Netherlands and in Switzerland warred bitterly among themselves shortly before they confederated. The very name of the United States reminds us that originally each colony was a fiercely independent political unit; Texas and other states subsequently joined as sovereign nations. The history of leagues and confederations is a rich body of evidence, which so far as I know has never been mined for its lessons on maintaining peace among nations.

In this chapter I survey how republics and other types of regimes have formed leagues, or failed to, throughout history. Since we are not dealing with urgent crises but with stable configurations, our focus shifts from the daily interplay of negotiations to the realm of lasting political principles and institutions. These will bring us back again to my central theme, the tendency of political leaders to deal with foreign counterparts as they deal with one another at home.

The First Republican Leagues

As soon as people devised republics, states began to combine with one another in a manner never seen before. The earliest known example, the Delian League created in 478 B.C., already possessed some key features which I offer as a way to distinguish a confederation from a mere alliance. The member states, scattered around the shores of the Aegean, had created (1) a joint treasury, which gathered obligatory dues; (2) a military force under a unitary command; and (3) an assembly drawn from the member states, which voted to settle disputes and policy. For several decades the confederacy kept peace among its members and protected them against foreign enemies.[5]

Unfortunately, Athens, the strongest member by far, gradually took full command. The Athenians' overbearing insistence on assuming leadership was normal at this early point, when ideas about equal rights were just beginning to form. The league's assembly ceased to meet, and the former allies came to be styled "the states that Athens controls." Resentment grew, and after Athens went to war against Sparta, oligarchic factions sometimes persuaded a state to break with Athens. The Athenians' failure to grant the league members equal rights contributed to their disastrous defeat.[6]

Thanks to Thucydides and other historians, the Greeks and all subsequent peoples could learn the lesson. When the Athenians sponsored a new league a century later, they swore that all members would have complete liberty and autonomy—a promise literally chiseled in stone, the stele that is our lonely witness. This league worked, sustaining its members' independence for some forty years against deadly threats from oligarchies and monarchs. The only thing that ended it was bad luck, for the league stood in the path of the invincible King Philip of Macedon.

This was only one of the confederations that Greek democracies created following the spread of democratic ideals: the Arcadian League, the Acarnanian League, the redoubtable Achaean League, and a dozen more. There was even a confederation of non-Greek people in Asia Minor, who, following the example of their Greek neighbors, combined against local despots and set up an assembly with equal representation, with a separate court to adjudicate disputes between member states. They lived in liberty for over two centuries. In each confederation the constitution mirrored the constitutions of the member states. The assembly, the joint treasury and unified military command, even the names and functions of league officials, all reproduced what was found within individual republics.[7]

These leagues usually originated when a democratic city helped a neighbor overthrow its oligarchy or tyrant. The root idea was that even foreigners deserved civil rights. This evolved into a legal principle, with the citizens of each member state of a league given the right to own property and so forth within all the others (of course they could only vote in their home city). A belief in democratic solidarity led the Greek leagues to keep extending their connections, one league allying with the next. The Arcadian League, for example, eventually merged into the Achaean League, with all the states as equal members. This regime, according to its historian, Polybius, was like a single city except that no wall encircled its thousands of square miles.[8]

Alongside these democratic leagues there were a few combinations of oligarchic republics. The most important, the Peloponnesian League led by Sparta, was not much more than a loose long-term alliance with no common treasury or officials. But it did hold occasional assemblies to vote on matters like war and peace, just like the assemblies within each member oligarchy.[9]

This unprecedented invention, the regular assembly of states, proved highly successful. The Achaean League, for example, defended democracy against formidable enemies for well over a century, while preserving peace among its dozens of autonomous members. The only thing that ended the experiment was more bad luck, for the Greek leagues stood in the path of the invincible Roman legions.

It was not a peaceful time. During the two centuries when Greek republican confederations flourished, there were horrendous wars in every single decade, in which democracies and oligarchies battled literally to the death against one another and against tyrants and kings. Yet in the same period each Greek confederation kept uninterrupted peace not only among its own members, but also with all the other confederations of republics of its own type.[10]

The Hanseatic League

We can find even more remarkable leagues by striding across a millenium to late medieval Europe, where hundreds of cities developed self-governing republican councils and promptly formed leagues. To see the greatest of these in action a traveler would have to visit Lübeck. Sailing from the Baltic into a river mouth one would come to a harbor bristling with hundreds of masts, where ships crowded against a wall of severe brick houses. In these houses the merchants kept both their families and their goods, for as a popular saying put it, "Lübeck is a warehouse." The traveler, disembarking and strolling up the main avenue to the center of town, would confront the monumental Rathaus. Here on certain days of the year could be found a crowd of delegates from across half the width of Europe, haranguing one another with speeches in the great wooden council hall, then sitting along tables in the banquet hall to strike bargains over tankards of beer. This was the nerve center of the Hanseatic League.[11]

At the league's peak such a gathering made decisions for more than seventy important cities and another hundred or so lesser towns. Each of these was an independent oligarchic republic ruled by a council of merchants, the models for the league council. The Hanseatic League maintained total peace among its members and held a common front against outside threats for three and a half centuries. It only ended in the 1600s, when most cities were forced to submit to various princes and kings.

These burghers were not docile men—if they had been, they would have been erased. In various coalitions the Hanseatic cities warred against every sort of baron, bishop, duke, prince, king, and emperor of neighboring German states, Burgundy, Denmark, Sweden, England, Poland, and Russia—in short, every autocrat within reach. Northern Europe was a patchwork of political units fighting more wars than anyone has ever tried to count, and studying it is like watching an unending barroom brawl. Only by close scrutiny can we recognize that scattered throughout the room are men wearing a particular type of hat, so to speak, who furiously fight everybody except one another. This mutual peace of the Hanseatic cities was a fabulous achievement, by far the longest maintained by any group of states in history.

The league's foundation was commerce. The seal of the city of Lübeck, the closest thing the league had to an emblem, depicted a ship on which stood two men swearing an oath. It is again the republican myth of origins, the sworn community of equals in a lordless wilderness. Just such shipboard pacts, under which merchant adventurers from different cities fused into a ship's company, had engendered the Hanseatic League. Merchants could make a reliable living only where trade contracts were respected under some sort of equality and reciprocity. In 1230 the cities of Lübeck and Hamburg swore to treat each other's citizens under identical legal conditions. The idea spread, until in 1366 an assembly of many cities decreed that the citizens of each would share the same basic rights for trading purposes.[12]

This is an outstanding demonstration of the famous affinity between republican principles and commerce. In such cases we cannot determine which came first. Believers in economic determinism would say that commercial relationships make for peace and republican government. The Hanseatic burghers, however, would have said that that only where there are republics making peace can commerce flourish.

Hanseatic decisions about trade and other foreign affairs were made by envoys assembled for the occasion, usually in Lübeck, but otherwise each city was independent. The league had no permanent organs; what little administration it needed was left to the officials of Lübeck. The league's treasury consisted of special dues and tolls imposed for a particular contingency (but not always paid), and its army and fleet comprised whatever forces individual cities might volunteer to send in a crisis. Sometimes one of the league's many republics found itself at odds with another, vexed by commercial rivalry and plain human pugnacity. Without a single exception they resolved such disputes peacefully.[13] They would ask neighboring republics to arbitrate, and if that failed the parties considered themselves obliged to come before a league assembly as a final court of appeal.

The Hanseatic cities likewise kept peace with the numerous other city oligarchies scattered southward down to the Rhineland, although all were commercial rivals. As mentioned in chapter 10, they also kept peace with the republics of the Netherlands (but not when the Dutch were ruled by a duke or emperor). Despite the fierce competition between Dutch and German merchants for the Baltic trade, they cooperated elsewhere—here a joint venture to Brazil, there a shared consulate in Lisbon, even a combined army to drive off a duke who had besieged a free German city.[14]

Hanseatic cities were willing to coerce one of their members if its regime strayed from their principles. For example, in the 1370s common shopkeepers and artisans seized control of Braunschweig and executed a few leading patricians. The patricians of the other cities, appalled by the specter of democratic "mob" rule, excluded Braunschweig from the privileges of league membership. Trading rights were necessary for economic survival, and the Braunschweigers yielded, setting up a compromise regime acceptable to their neighbors.[15] On several other occasions the league used similar moral, legal, and commercial pressures—but never military action—to maintain its preferred type of oligarchic government.

The Hanseatic system was not supported by a political ideology in the sense of a consciously articulated system of ideas. These busy merchants found no time to develop doctrines that would have impressed the philosophers of ancient Greece or Renaissance Italy. Here we find again that the ideology of republican solidarity, however helpful it may be as a self-fulfilling prophecy, is not essential to maintaining peace. It suffices to have a core of traditions and attitudes that constitute a republican political culture. If you had asked a Hanseatic burgher to describe his political principles he would only have been able to say that he lived by "das Recht," a potent word lumping together whatever seemed honest and proper—the rule of law, individual rights, devotion to the commonwealth with its consensus politics. The Hanseatic League, as one of its historians remarked, simply extended such domestic ideals and practices to an international level.[16]

Confederations of Anocratic Regimes

A workable confederation seems to need no more than a rudimentary idea of equal rights. The minimum requirements can be found by looking at medieval southern Germany, where rolling pastures and woodlands were scattered with dozens of cities and towns under many sorts of autocratic, anocratic, and republican regimes. Wherever the burghers experimented with self-government through elected councils, they formed leagues.

The first of these arose in the Rhineland in 1254, with only rudimentary republican ideas to draw on. A mere alliance of convenience against robber barons, it collapsed at the first shove. More stable leagues formed after the mid-1300s, exactly when genuinely republican ideas and the corresponding practices were spreading. Cities that had battled one another without mercy when under the rule of different lords became self-governing communities and promptly set up leagues. Like the ancient Greek leagues, these each had a joint treasury, a joint military command, and an annual assembly of representatives to settle disputes.[17]

Here, too, each league tended to ally and sometimes merge with others of its kind, always reaching for a wider community of equals. The peak came in the late 1300s, after fourteen Swabian cities swore to obey decisions made by a majority vote of their assembly. They began combining with dozens of other leagues from Bavaria to the Rhineland, until it almost seemed that all the cities of Germany would form a self-governing confederacy.[18]

However, most south Germans acknowledged the Holy Roman Emperor as their suzerain, and many also recognized lesser princes as rightful lords. The noblemen used that opening to assert authority, repeatedly breaking leagues back into a scatter of mutually hostile towns. The crucial test came in 1388, when the formidable Count Eberhard II led a coalition of knights into combat against the Swabian League. In medieval battles men bunched together with others of their own locality in bands that surged back and forth over fields of gore and the shrieking wounded. Here nothing was so vital as cohesion and belief in the rightness of one's cause. A chronicler reported that the townsmen were gaining ground when Eberhard's voice resounded across the field: "Look how the enemy are running! . . . We have them in our power!" Some townsmen believed the count and panicked, until group by group their army disintegrated into fleeing individuals. In the following months the whole Swabian League similarly fell apart, as each city sought a separate deal with Eberhard and was separately punished. Their failure demonstrates the debility of a confederation whose people believed in their hierarchical inferiority.[19]

Yet wherever burghers managed their affairs even partly through republican practices, the idea of confederation survived. The phenomenon showed up in many milieus. On into the nineteenth century, every time a few German cities gained a modest degree of autonomy they promptly recombined. As early as 1167, sixteen northern Italian cities that were just beginning to experiment with rule by council formed a tight confederation to defend their liberty against the emperor. The cities were only rudimentary republics, yet each sent representatives on an equal basis to an assembly which settled disputes by majority vote, levied funds for a joint treasury, and maintained a joint military command. This Lombard League and its successors broke the Holy Roman Empire beyond repair, preserving a future for republics everywhere.[20]

A more unexpected locale is medieval Spain, where some cities ran their internal affairs through patrician councils. At times when the Spanish monarchy and nobility were busy fighting one another, the cities could act autonomously—and they quickly came together in leagues. The most powerful of these formed around 1520, when cities of Castile sent representatives to vote as equals in an assembly which adjudicated their disputes and set up the usual joint treasury and military command. The Castilian townsmen would have converted all of Spain into a constitutional monarchy with an oligarchic parliament, only the king and nobles set aside their differences to smash them.[21]

Confederation was not confined to peoples of Latin and Germanic heritage, for at the far end of Europe a comparable confederation held together two nations altogether different in cultural roots and ethnic stock from Latins, from Germans, and indeed from each other. In 1566 the Lithuanian gentry established a system of oligarchic councils; the Poles already had a similar regime, and within three years the two quasi-republics formed a durable constitutional union. Each nation retained its laws and army, but foreign affairs were directed by a joint assembly and a common elected monarch.[22]

These leagues were made up of oligarchic republics, but wherever regimes resembling democracies came into existence they formed leagues just as quickly. After the Greeks we find a solid confederation among the Forest States of Switzerland. A looser confederation, complete with mechanisms for adjudicating disputes, also appeared in Flanders during the few decades in the 1300s when quasi-democracies existed, even though the Flemish had only the barest rudiments of republican ideas.[23]

Confederations, in fact, were not formed only by well-established republics. Noblemen sometimes joined with other noblemen whom they recognized as their peers. Aristocratic Italian Ghibelline clans joined together in leagues with elected assemblies and common treasuries, and the hundreds of petty knights who ruled independent manors scattered across the German countryside organized themselves similarly. For confederation it was sufficient that these feudal aristocrats pledged solidarity with their peers in a spirit of equal rights for all of noble blood.[24]

Confederations could function under circumstances still more remote from those of modern states. There was once a league that extended its sway over a land area greater than all the cities of the Hanseatic League together, and which likewise preserved flawless peace among its members for over three centuries. Yet the people of this league were the most ferociously independent of any in this book; next to them the Hanseatic seafarers seem as docile as sheep. To find them we must travel an immeasurable distance from Europe, to a forestland interrupted by clearings containing fields of maize and clusters of bark-roofed longhouses, each sheltering a dozen families or more. Within the longhouses, squatting around fires in the smoky dimness, the Iroquois maintained a confederation.

With unwavering respect for the total freedom of each individual, the Iroquois reached decisions by consensus in councils. All adults (including women) had a right to speak their minds on any question, directly or through representatives. A proposal would be brought to a clan council, and if approved it would proceed to a council of a group of clans (a "nation"), and finally to the grand council of the confederation. While debate stretched out through days of eloquent speeches, leaders might avoid public confrontation by meeting privately "in the bushes." If you replaced their buckskin shirts with black coats, a conclave of the Six Nations of the Iroquois would have seemed much like an assembly of the seven United Provinces of the Netherlands. It involved the same intricate quest for consensus among autonomous units in a political culture that insisted on equality, toleration and dedication to the common welfare.[25]

Anthropologists have recorded similar cases in tribes that had little in common with the Iroquois, except that they too maintained peaceful confederations by sending delegations to an assembly. In each case the league copied on a larger scale the egalitarian practices that governed local communities. The Iroquois themselves compared their federation to one of their cavernous longhouses with its row of family hearths, autonomous yet sheltered under a single roof.[26]

The Iroquois nations were hardly states in the European sense. The "citizens" of each Iroquois clan were in principle relatives bound by blood and marriage. If a stranger was not killed or held as a slave he could be adopted as family; no other friendly status was imaginable. An entire nearby tribe could be adopted as new "Iroquois," and the amalgamation of several tribes into one was a regular practice when wars and epidemics brought the population dangerously low. The strength of the Iroquois, as one historian put it, "arose less from bellicosity than from hospitality." When the Iroquois swore treaties with neighboring groups, including European colonists, they did not address them as "subjects" or "allies," but as "nephews" or "brothers," expressing what we would call political ties in terms of their familiar social relationships. It was a brilliantly conceived system of keeping peace by extending symbolic kinship regardless of actual blood connections.

The one indispensable requirement for "kinship" was that a person behave like a proper Iroquois in personal relationships, adopting what we might call their political culture. The three centuries of complete peace maintained among the Iroquois nations places them alongside the medieval Swiss Forest States and the Hanseatic League as another remarkable demonstration of how an egalitarian political culture can prevent war even among regimes very remote from the modern state.[27]

Modern anthropologists have found a similar amalgamation among the Xingu of central Brazil. For over a century these rainforest natives have maintained complete internal peace in a confederation of ten villages with highly diverse origins, speaking four distinct languages. Gentle and egalitarian, the Xingu accept their diversity and deplore the use of force or even displays of annoyance among themselves. Thus they share something resembling the principles of equal rights, toleration, and community solidarity. Meanwhile, they have defended themselves stoutly against non-Xingu peoples. Those outsiders with their violent, naked anger, say the Xingu, are little better than animals. Here is something the Iroquois were moving toward but never fully attained: "kinship" bonds defined in terms of shared ways of thinking.[28]

Where such bonds were not extended there was only war. The Iroquois, for example, cared little that their neighbors the Hurons were an equally free people with their own system of league councils. Since the tribes did not mingle as kin, the Hurons made fit rivals in a sport of raids, battles, and the ritual torture of prisoners. When Europeans upset the balance the Iroquois wiped out the Huron villages in a ghastly war.[29]

Egalitarian confederations have readily warred on one another. In medieval Italy and Germany the leagues of noble knights warred frequently on the leagues of oligarchic towns. None of this violates our rule about war between comparable republics, for as we have seen, the rule applies only to territorial states. The European leagues of knights, like the Iroquois, defined themselves by clan and bloodline (sometimes a commission would spend days checking pedigrees to make sure a family claiming noble ancestry was qualified for membership). Such a "tribal" political culture, with equality and tolerance for the ingroup of putative relatives, is sufficient for confederation. But peace can be reliably sustained beyond the confederation only where there is a state authority to suppress raiding by private bands, plus a definition of the ingroup that stretches beyond simple blood kinship.

Autocrats as Confederates

The skeptic will ask, what's so special about republics in all this? Haven't monarchies also formed unions? Indeed they have, but in these instances the external relations of a government once again faithfully duplicated its internal practices. Usually in a monarchical "union" one territory was attached onto another by conquest as merely another subject.

States under hereditary monarchs have also combined in a seemingly equal fashion, following the monarchical principle of inheritance. The marriage of Ferdinand and Isabella drew together Aragon and Castile in 1479, a combination that survives as the core of modern Spain; a more complex mixture of inheritance and politics brought the union of England and Scotland in 1603, and so forth. Most spectacular was the tireless matchmaking that patched together half of Europe under the Habsburgs of Austria. As an old saying put it, while other rulers fought wars, "You, happy Austria, marry." Such autocratic unions looked somewhat like confederations, for different provinces retained their own distinct laws and privileges under the rule of their own local aristocracies. For example, the provincial lords of Japan in the Tokugawa period each governed a quasi-autonomous personal domain, at peace with their neighbors despite their notorious devotion to the military arts.

These were not true confederations, however. The tip-off is how they resolved disputes, for example over how to raise and spend taxes. A confederation is characterized by bargaining and voting in an assembly, or perhaps an appeal to neutral mediators or judges under the rule of law or treaties. In authoritarian unions, by contrast, the regional elites held rights and stood as equals *under* the reigning dynasty. The Austrian emperor or Tokugawa shogun held final say, if only because he could assemble enough obedient provinces to punish a dissenting one. Even combinations formed by marriage functioned much like unions by conquest: everywhere countrymen of the ruling family held sway over the provincials, be they Castilian officials in Aragon, English in Scotland, or Austrians in Hungary.

Autocracy, by its very nature, works against a division of power, and federalism is found only where there is a political culture that respects liberty and equal rights. It is true that a sort of federalism has been practiced in largely authoritarian countries, for example in Germany, Mexico, and Brazil in the late nineteenth century. Yet political thinkers in those very countries insisted that the diffusion of power functioned only to the extent that republican ways were practiced. Wherever regimes of a mainly authoritarian character tried to federate with one another as equals, even in regions like South America and Yugoslavia where culture was homogeneous and the need for a federal solution was dire, they failed disastrously to find a stable way to distribute power.[30]

An outstanding case is Central America, whose history, economy, and geography call so urgently for union that the nations have launched formal attempts at federation on an average of once a decade since the 1820s. A political scientist who analyzed their failure concluded that it was basically "a failure of representative government." Inevitably the dictator of one state or another would refuse to share power or would be too much distrusted by his neighbors. Only now, as genuine democracy spreads through the region, are some Latin American nations building institutions of solid international cooperation.[31]

Federalism is one area where political scientists generally agree that institutional structures count for less than political culture. Some analysts, holding up the example of the modern Swiss, focus on the importance of a tradition of moderation and consultation among all parties. One scholar boiled down the concept of federalism to the fundamentally republican image of free and equal men swearing a mutual oath.[32]

The connection between close cooperation and republican political culture also matters at a lower level of organization, the simple alliance. Republics have historically expected to have friendly relations, and the self-fulfilling prophecy has often done its work. For example, in the early 1600s, while the Netherlands competed ruinously against Venice for the Levant trade, the two states praised one another as fellow republics and enemies of tyranny, joining in battle against the Habsburgs.[33] Wherever people founded a democracy in the past two centuries, the United States consistently stood among the first governments in the world to grant diplomatic recognition, and often sent material aid.

Autocrats have also sworn countless treaties and alliances with one another, usually to make war on a common enemy. These were generally short-lived expedients, sometimes disintegrating before the end of the war. Of course, an alliance of kings or dictators could last for decades so long as both sides continued to find it useful, but reshuffle the pattern of international forces, and immediately any pair might fight to the death.[34] Authoritarian collaborations have not worked well even when they were dominated by a single ideology and a single great power, as Communism and the Soviet Union ruled the Warsaw Pact. This alliance did not last even three decades before it deteriorated so badly that most Eastern European soldiers would probably not have fought Western armies even to defend their own national territories.[35]

The incapacity of authoritarian states to form stable alliances has meant much for the survival of republics. The alliances of German lords against Switzerland, the League of Cambrai that marched to crush the Republic of Venice, the grand coalition of kings against the French Revolution—all these coordinated their military campaigns poorly and quickly fell apart in selfish squabbles. Likewise, when Hitler and several other dictators banded together their military and political cooperation was wretched, in contrast to the intimate Anglo-American alliance. Most republican alliances have cohered well, which may help explain a remarkable and momentous fact: in modern times democracies have been far more successful than autocracies at warfare.[36]

Against all the failures of autocratic confederations, history offers one significant counterexample: the Holy Roman Empire. Through half a millennium, haughty sovereigns sent out representatives or went in person to meet as equals, debating and bargaining in voting assemblies or law courts and accepting the decisions. It provides a tough test for ideas about how peace may be sustained.

In the Holy Roman Empire the emperor was elected by majority vote of the chief princes, and commanded obedience only insofar as he served as a champion of law and the traditional balance. Most disputes were settled in an assembly or in imperial law courts. In a few cases, blatantly criminal rulers of minor states were forced to abdicate by the judgment of their peers. Meanwhile, regional assemblies of bishops and counts and burghers negotiated and voted on local disputes almost independently of the emperor.[37] Napoleon dissolved this convenient arrangement, but from the remains a new German Confederation arose, comprising 39 political units—five kingdoms, ten duchies, and so forth—which carried on with voting by representatives and peaceful arbitration of disputes. This seems to directly refute the idea that autocrats must act internationally following the same domineering principles they practice at home.

But what exactly was practiced at home? Here, for the only time in this book, we must distinguish between different degrees of autocracy. These German rulers were not absolute autocrats like Hitler or Tsar Nicholas I, but had been forced to concede some rights to aristocrats, patrician burghers, and even ordinary citizens. Almost every state in Germany had an elite domestic assembly, which often could restrain its sovereign by refusing to confirm taxes. Historians have found that these legislatures tended to hold their regimes back from military adventures.[38]

Other republican practices ran like threads through the fabric of Germany and helped keep it in one piece. The Imperial Free Cities retained local autonomy under their elected city councils; bishops were elected and supervised by their chapters; landowners elected officers to represent them in leagues of "free knights." Countless committees and boards of arbitration took a hand in handling disputes. Power was deliberately dispersed so intricately and inconsistently that no single person could command or even comprehend the whole.

The empire's political culture, like its formal structure, was not a simple ladder of hierarchical obedience. People were accustomed to handling their affairs through consultation and voting, protracted lawsuits and artful bargains. Even free speech, although not officially permitted, was impossible to prevent, as censorship stumbled amid countless independent jurisdictions. People gradually adopted ideals of liberty, toleration of diversity, and especially the rule of law. In the nineteenth-century German Confederation an ideology of equal rights came into full bloom and did more than anything to bind the confederation together. Liberals fought for still broader rights, and at the same time agitated for a complete federal unification of Germany, as if liberty and union were inseparable. In short, while most member states were formal autocracies, republican elements were pervasive, everywhere promoting peaceful confederation.[39]

The nineteenth-century German Confederation was the core of a larger system, the most successful peacekeeping arrangement that authoritarian states have ever achieved. Styled the "Concert of Europe," it was a set of written agreements among the sovereigns of Prussia, Austria, and Russia, plus less explicit understandings among the other crowned heads of Europe, who managed to avoid great wars for an entire century after 1815. Some historians argue that the European balance of forces happened to be configured in such a way that realpolitik favored peace. Yet people at the time believed, and most historians agree, that warfare could not have been contained so well if statesmen had not figured out something new and valuable.[40]

The Concert of Europe, like the German Confederation, was sustained by republican principles. The original idea had been set in motion by Tsar Alexander of Russia, acting out of an idealistic youthful enthusiasm for human rights and constitutional government. After the tsar retreated into conservatism the spirit was kept up by Great Britain, now governed in a republican manner and insisting that every dispute could be settled in council meetings. Historians suggest that the Concert of Europe succeeded better than earlier attempts to keep peace precisely because it adopted new ideals, including devotion to the common interest, consensus through discussion and reciprocal accommodation among equals, renunciation of the use of force against one's peers, and a reliance on legality (with sovereigns making much of their "legitimacy"). All these were republican teachings.[41]

There is a second reason many historians have given for the cohesion of the Concert of Europe. The leaders had joined against a common enemy: their own rebellious subjects. Many aristocrats were convinced that agitators for democracy had linked themselves in a network of secret societies, coordinated by a central committee hidden somewhere in Paris. When democratic outbursts rocked Europe about once a decade, climaxing with the insurrections of 1848, it was found that some revolutionaries had indeed been making amateur attempts at international coordination.[42] The monarchies felt they had to combine in self-defense, and at a minimum did not dare stress their precarious regimes further by making war. Thus a belief in international democratic solidarity, accepted by autocrats themselves, in a curious inversion deterred them from fighting one another.

This case is not unique. In the shifting combinations of the Middle East from the 1950s forward, conservative monarchies like Saudi Arabia consistently allied with one another, largely out of fear of revolutionary states like Syria, with their agitation for universal Socialist equality.[43] Meanwhile, Communist dictatorships clung together in the Warsaw Pact largely because they foresaw that an outbreak of democracy anywhere in Eastern Europe could rip through the whole region. However, a reactive solidarity cannot be as firm as one based on positive ideas of universal rights. None of these autocratic alliances stood up over the long run.

The Failure of Autocratic Peacekeeping

Through its early centuries the Holy Roman Empire fell apart in war every few decades, as ambitious princes launched armies against one another. Here we can take final leave of the hypothesis that a tangle of constitutional checks and overlapping social networks can hold a society back from war. Human beings have never erected a more impenetrably complicated political system than early modern Germany, a gothic fantasy of cross-cutting loyalties and establishments. They only made the wars more wrenching.

The problem seemed solved at last in 1555 by the Peace of Augsburg, a treaty inaugurating the longest period of internal peace in the history of the empire. Actually, the princes set aside their quarrels partly from exhaustion and partly to combine against Turks and Hungarians; when these pressures lapsed, the Germans again turned against one another. The internal peace lasted a scant sixty-four years, ending in the utter catastrophe of the Thirty Years War. Then came another peace born of exhaustion, the second longest at fifty-three years, punctuated by hostilities close to actual war and ending in a battle where twelve thousand died. The only other long interval of internal peace was under the nineteenth-century German Confederation; that lasted fifty-one years and ended with a severe war. The Concert of Europe had already collapsed in the Crimean War.[44]

In sum, a half-century of peace was about the most that a group of authoritarian regimes was able to maintain even when pervaded by republican influences. As if to provide an experimental control case, in exactly the same territory the Hanseatic League republics maintained perfect peace among themselves for over three centuries.

What were the actual forces that so reliably destroyed authoritarian leagues? We have already seen how the Concert of Europe broke apart be-

cause of disputes over hierarchical authority, beginning in the Holy Sepulchre in Jerusalem and spreading to broader issues of power and status. One
other especially well-studied case is the war that broke up the German
Confederation in 1866—a war that many historians consider a fatal step
toward the European calamities of the twentieth century. This case will be
our last look into the background of a particular war. Here, as everywhere,
I did not select the case because I knew in advance what it would show; I
selected it because it has been thoroughly analyzed by other historians, and
I report what they found.

After the insurrections of 1848 failed, many German sovereigns managed to take power back from their domestic assemblies. Liberals despaired
as the ideology of republican government began to seem discredited and
outmoded.[45] At just this point, as republican spirit and practices receded,
war between princes became more acceptable.

Nowhere did thoughts turn more to armies than in Prussia. King Wilhelm I was by nature a mild and well-meaning man, willing enough to cooperate with his legislature. But personal character can only operate within
the boundaries of culture, and the king's education had been strictly military. Wilhelm loved above all his army, and neither understood nor admired parliamentary bargaining. His advisers were aristocrats whose
thinking had likewise centered from childhood on military affairs. They
urged the kaiser to strengthen the army, indeed to turn it into a national
school to instill his subjects with true obedience. When Prussia's legislature objected vehemently and blocked the plan, Wilhelm dithered. His
sense of honor forbade him to break his oath to maintain the established
constitution. But he could not work with the legislature. Seeing no way
out, the elderly king considered abdicating in favor of his son, who was
prepared to serve as a constitutional monarch on the British model.

Wilhelm's proposal was blocked by the political culture of his class,
the domineering military and landholding families who for centuries had
ruled the serfs of Prussia. The minister of war and other officers rebuked
Wilhelm for his weakness and exhorted him to govern as absolute monarch,
appealing to the king's "soldierly spirit." The aristocrats had their way. Wilhelm put his government in the hands of the most combative and for-
bidding Prussian aristocrat of them all, Otto von Bismarck. Bismarck
promptly brushed aside legality to rule by fiat, telling the legislature that
its "speeches and majority votes" were worthless and must give way to

"iron and blood." As one of the parliamentary politicians remarked, Bismarck was guided by a different logic and different moral rules from theirs—we would say, by a different political culture.[46]

As at home, so abroad. Soon after Bismarck's rise, a grand assembly of the German sovereigns convened at the request of Austria, in hopes of designing a firmer confederation. Bismarck thought the talk of states resolving disputes by voting was childish pretense, and under his stern guidance Wilhelm wrecked the assembly's plans. Precisely as the king had been pushed into defying the majority of his own legislature, so he was pushed into defying the nearly unanimous vote of his fellow sovereigns. Relations deteriorated, and in 1866 Bismarck deliberately provoked war against Austria. This was one war where historians agree only a single issue was at stake: would Austria or Prussia hold hegemony over Germany? The idea of sharing power as equals seemed ridiculous to the Prussian aristocrats, who considered it their duty to fight until their nation was as supreme within Europe as their king was now supreme within Prussia itself. Peaceful confederation was flatly incompatible with the ideals and methods of their political culture.[47]

Democratic Federation

To see what fosters durable peace we must turn to more successful unions. Complete federal union, where states concede ultimate sovereignty to a central government while retaining significant freedom of action, is the very opposite of a set of warring regimes.

Many people suppose that federations are bound together chiefly by a shared general culture, like the English language and customs of the United States. But multi-cultural federations have been just as successful. The oldest extant federation, Switzerland, combines regions of German, French, Italian, and native Alpine languages and traditions; even the food changes from one valley to the next, pasta to potatoes. Modern India is a working federation with more different languages and ways of life than all of Europe, and Papua New Guinea is a federation with more languages than India and Europe combined.[48] There is, however, one element which must be shared by the members of a federation: republican political culture.

Federation does not require full democracy. For example, a set of sheikdoms in Arabia federated as the United Arab Emirates just at the time they moved domestically from tribal regimes to oligarchic politics. Another example followed the Anglo-Boer war, when the British granted autonomy to four provinces in southern Africa, two dominated by Afrikaans-speaking Boers and the other two of British heritage. What they had in common was an oligarchic politics of whites ruling blacks, and they soon federated as the Union of South Africa.[49]

Oligarchies, however, have not typically federated as thoroughly as democracies. From the Hanseatic League to the United Arab Emirates they have in most cases formed looser confederations. Rivalries involving oligarchies broke apart the Swiss confederation on several occasions, and a true federal system was not established until democracy took hold throughout Switzerland. It likewise took civil wars in the Netherlands and the United States to impose both full democracy and full federation. Usually it was democratic forces that fought to create or strengthen a federal system. The key to federation, then, is something found only in oligarchic and democratic regimes, but more fully in the latter. The obvious candidate for this factor is the ideals and practices of toleration and equal rights.[50]

The reverse does not hold: even complete democracy does not require federation. Sometimes an increase in democratic practices has actually disrupted established unions, for in the turbulence that follows when subject groups first win political rights, they may proceed to demand autonomy. In this way the Norwegians seceded from Sweden and the Irish from Britain, British India broke apart in 1947 and the Soviet Union in 1991. It was not democracy itself that split these countries; democracy only gave people a chance to react against a bitter legacy of hierarchical rule from a distant capital. Where the separated countries were both democracies they gradually established relations that were friendlier than they had been in the period of colonial domination.

Republics can be friendly with their own kind without federating. International peace does not require a centralized United States of the World. It would probably be enough if the leaders of all major nations could learn to use something like republican principles in managing affairs, and take it for granted that they would go to settle disputes with briefcases rather than bombs.

It is common for nations to share a set of principles, and these principles can change over time. A few centuries ago, for example, most European leaders believed that slavery was good practice and that dynastic marriages were of utmost importance. A set of shared beliefs about control over other people and methods of handling conflict could be called an international political culture. When nations that share such beliefs develop a corresponding set of formal and informal practices for dealing with one another we can speak of an "international regime," contentious or peaceable as the case may be. We have already seen an example of a somewhat law-abiding international political culture and international regime, the Holy Roman Empire and the German Confederation up until 1866.[51]

The influence of shared ideals was illuminated in an ingenious investigation by two political scientists. They analyzed pronouncements on international law gleaned from treatises written during the past two centuries. In some periods, they found, most writers held that nations should stick by their legal obligations; in other periods, most held that pressing national needs easily justified breaking a treaty. It turned out that serious wars and major international disputes were less widespread during the periods when authorities held that lawful treaties should be honored. It seems that even a diffuse climate of opinion about legality—a rudimentary international political culture—can influence great affairs.[52]

For centuries, many political theorists and diplomats have insisted that peace can only be maintained by an international regime whose essence is the rule of law, formally embodied in a set of mutual obligations woven out of a thousand treaties. It is worth noting that building such international regimes has been the work chiefly of citizens of republics. The idea was invented in the democracies of ancient Greece, where the Delian League members took their disputes to the law courts of Athens. It reappeared in the Hanseatic oligarchies, which turned to the courts of Lübeck to resolve their disagreements. Modern theories and practices of international law were worked out mainly by republican thinkers in the Netherlands, England, and Switzerland. In the twentieth century it was under the lead of democracies that nations converged more than ever toward a single international legal community. One scholar found that when a dispute involving a foreign democracy came to trial in the United States, judges assumed that both parties stood within a global "zone of law," where conflicts are settled according to transnational legal principles; only where an authoritarian state was involved would the decision be dictated by power politics.[53]

A zone of law only provides a framework for actual working relationships. Much of the everyday job of maintaining an international regime is done by international organizations, ranging from private coalitions, like the International Red Cross, to agencies representing governments, like the Universal Postal Union. It is worth noting that building such organizations has been the work chiefly of citizens of republics. As evidence, consider which cities have served as home to the international organizations that arose beginning in the mid-nineteenth century: London for the pioneering International Congress of Peace Societies, Bern for the International Copyright Union, Paris for the International Bureau of Weights and Measures, the Hague for the World Court, Geneva for the League of Nations, New York for the United Nations—and so forth, more every year, almost always in republics.[54]

The best-studied example of a successful international regime is the league first called the European Economic Community and now the European Union. It was democratic ideals and practices that created the Community and made it work. Robert Schuman and others who strove to assemble a union insisted that unless it was democratic it could never work, but once the Community was well established people tended to forget that it was rooted in democracy. They should have glanced at Comecon, the Communist bloc's attempt to build a mirror image of the European Community. Actually, the Comecon councils were largely a front for domination by the Soviet Union, and one might suppose that such centralized decision-making would have made joint action easier. Yet Comecon failed pathetically to achieve much in the way of economic integration or any other cooperative task.[55]

An especially telling counterexample of failed union began when the Spanish government approached the European Community in 1962 to seek formal association. The response was foreshadowed in an earlier report to the European Parliament. "States whose governments do not have democratic legitimation . . . ," it warned, "cannot aspire to be admitted into the circle of peoples which forms the European Communities." That applied to the repressive dictatorship of General Francisco Franco, and despite the potent economic logic of integration, negotiations dragged along with little progress. In 1975 the European Parliament voted for a total freeze in relations until Spain established "freedom and democracy." The next year Franco died; the new Spanish government moved quickly toward democracy, and at each step the European Community permitted a parallel step toward full membership. This case is not unique, for in 1974 the Portuguese, having overthrown their own military regime, immediately sought to join the community, and likewise found a welcome.[56]

One other case illustrates with the clarity of a physics demonstration the connection between democracy and cooperation. In the 1960s the democratic government of Greece began gradually to move toward integration with the European Community, but in 1967 a group of colonels seized power and set up a military regime. Within weeks the community suspended negotiations, and the European Parliament formally resolved that no progress could be made until democracy was restored. In 1974 the Greek military regime collapsed. Within weeks the community resumed negotiations towards union.[57]

After Spain, Portugal, and Greece turned democratic they did not become full members immediately. They had to negotiate touchy questions of imports and subsidies, but no less importantly, a few years had to pass before the European Community would accept a regime as a truly established democratic partner. The same questions showed up decades later, when nations in Eastern Europe became democracies and, inevitably, applied for community membership.

In all these cases the motives for combining were as much political as economic. Democratic leaders from Portugal to Hungary hoped that the European Community's democratic political culture would be inculcated in the new members, "through a process of osmosis," as one observer put it. In fact, maintaining republican government within each member has been an aim of nearly every important confederation in history, and one that has often been made entirely explicit, as when the drafters of the U.S. Constitution guaranteed to "every State in this Union a Republican form of government."[58]

Some observers declared that the European Community was actually created mainly to hold off the Soviet Union. Certainly the founders of the Community hoped that economic integration would strengthen their nations against Soviet Communism. But they had in mind chiefly the internal Communist threat, and they were equally worried about a resurgence of nationalist Fascism. As in many earlier republican alliances, much of the talk about standing together against tyranny had more to do with preserving republican governance at home than with holding off foreign powers.

For physical defense there was the North Atlantic Treaty Organization, which put military alliance ahead of domestic politics. Portugal, under its dictator, had been a NATO member from the start, and Greece and Turkey remained members during periods when they were ruled by military juntas. The organization was a plain demonstration that an external threat can hold nations of any political stripe together in temporary alliance. But it is not external threats that make for true confederation and lasting peace. Study of NATO's exceptionally tight cohesiveness, and the alliance's persistence even after the Soviet army disintegrated, has found no explanation except the predominance of democratic beliefs and negotiating methods among the member nations.[59] Moreover, republican states have federated without any pressure from an external threat at all, for example in South Africa and Australia. The one thing that does firmly bind peaceful international regimes is a shared set of republican ideals and practices, applied in pursuit of shared goals such as avoiding strife, increasing the common prosperity, and, not least, strengthening republican government itself.

The rich but little-known historical record of leagues surveyed in this chapter can be summarized in a few words, adding a new general observation to our "laws" of history. *Republics and only republics tend to form durable, peaceful leagues.* To be precise, by a league I mean an association among several political units with approximately equal privileges and with shared institutions such as a joint treasury and a court or assembly that adjudicates disputes between members under mutually accepted rules or laws. Note that we do not need to distinguish here between oligarchies and democracies. We can even relax the requirement that the republics be territorial states, for egalitarian tribes and clans may form leagues. Yet no group of authoritarian states, even when aided by republican elements, has maintained such an association for as long as a human lifetime.

This simple rule has an important implication. It strongly confirms, using a new and completely different body of historical evidence, the mechanism suggested by the absence of war among republics of the same kind: the powerful tendency of political culture to extend from domestic into foreign affairs. Republican leaders establish the same kinds of institutional structures and everyday practices for resolving disputes with one another internationally that they are familiar with domestically. Nothing else seems remotely capable of explaining the frequency and durability of republican leagues.

This extension of political culture abroad is not necessarily a blind, automatic process. Pragmatic wisdom advises governments to deliberately take into account accustomed patterns of behavior. We have seen that factor in crisis negotiation, and it figures no less in maintaining a league. This is a factor that sociologists and economists who study human associations have recently begun to understand.

Many theorists have argued convincingly, along lines that superficially resemble international realpolitik, that people join associations to get benefits that they could not gain through individual effort; the association will persist just so long as the benefits exceed the costs. But a subtle point enters into calculation of the costs of associating. These include the efforts needed to identify and punish people who misuse the association—the "free riders" who, like exploitative players in diplomatic games, seek to gobble up what others concede while making no sacrifices of their own. No matter what the material circumstances, or the realpolitik of the situtation, we cannot fully understand the outcome until we factor in the cost of getting information in advance about how a potential associate is likely to behave.[60]

Within a nation, adherence to republican political culture and practices is an efficient, reliable, and time-tested way to create and sustain a climate of mutual trust. Each person avoids risk and lays a claim to benefits by maintaining the right kind of reputation. As an important side effect, republican political culture also promotes cooperation in an international regime. The process can become self-sustaining, as institutions such as assemblies and courts are established to regulate the international regime. Using the familiar republican mechanisms of voting and legality, these institutions perpetuate the self-fulfilling prophecy that all players are part of a community of people who can trust one another to work out problems peacefully.[61]

It does work. I have mentioned that historical statistics show that democratic governments are internally more stable than autocratic ones, more safe from civil war and ethnic strife.[62] The splendid record of republican leagues demonstrates that related practices can keep entire groups of states from the horrors of war. These are the only practices we know of with such an excellent history of success. To the extent that we can foster a global regime of the kind maintained by republican leagues, and perhaps only to that extent, we may be able to avoid wars. In short, regardless of what goes on within individual nations, we would do well to establish a democratic international political culture, with democratically oriented international institutions to sustain it.

The easiest and perhaps the only way to maintain such an international regime would be for every important nation to adopt a democratic political culture domestically. Critics note that a totally democratic world has never been seen, and in such a world novel dangers might emerge. In particular, if it is true that people must have an outgroup to define themselves, will not nations be driven to somehow make enemies of fellow democracies? There is no certain answer, but it is encouraging that some republics have gone for long periods with no serious foreign enemy, defining their virtue against such outgroups as "criminals" or "shiftless poor people." A world whose social psychology relies on such divisions has disagreeable possibilities, but they do not include the unspeakable perils of war. A uniformly democratic world offers by far the best chance for permanent peace. Should not democracies therefore actively strive to make other states adopt democratic government?

CHAPTER FIFTEEN

Crusading for Democracy

W hen the French overthrew their monar-chy, people who longed passionately for liberty in their own lands set out for Paris. In 1790 France's newly elected National Assembly welcomed representatives at a ceremonial session. Spaniards, Poles, Greeks, and Turks in exotic costumes took turns declaiming that the French example was inspiring their people to throw off their chains, while the manager of the ceremony, a revolutionary from Prussia, claimed to speak for the "human species" as a whole. The French agreed that a new democratic age was coming: tyrannies everywhere would collapse, undermined by their own vices. Of course it might be necessary to give them a little push.[1]

Thousands of foreign radicals were settling in Paris and lobbying for help liberating their homelands. Italians, Irish, an occasional Venezuelan or Québecois sat writing feverishly by candlelight in garrets or arguing in shabby cafés. Some got government posts, for wasn't a democrat of any nation virtually a citizen of France? When neighboring monarchies combined to march against France the exiles formed entire foreign legions—a unit of Dutchmen, others of Germans and Savoyards, even a threadbare English Legion, all burning to bring democracy to their homelands. Their zeal pushed the French government to take up a bold new policy. What could better satisfy the revolution's ideals, and distress its enemies, than helping foreign peoples to revolt against their oppressors? The enterprise was so enormous that for an appropriate term the French leaders had to hark far back in history. They announced that their nation would sponsor "a crusade for universal liberty."[2]

A fantastic project, yet not a unique one. It was only one instance of a tendency that has been so regular we could almost declare it to be another historical law about the behavior of republican regimes: not only do they ally with their fellows, but they usually seek to replicate their own kind of regime in places where it does not exist.

This tendency first appeared at the exact point when republics first began to emerge, in ancient Greece. As we have seen, the Greek democracies fought devotedly to overthrow tyrants and oligarchic elites in order to set up democratic regimes in their place; Greek oligarchic republics meanwhile fought to replace tyrannies and democracies with oligarchic regimes. To pick randomly among many examples, we hear how an Athenian army marched through Thessaly "setting up democracy and arming the serfs against their masters."[3]

We have also seen how the tendency returned a dozen centuries later with the resurrection of republican government. Italian oligarchic republics battled to expel signors from neighboring cities and put elected councils in power; the democratic folk of Appenzell and Schwyz swarmed out of the Alps to burn castles and set up democratic assemblies of serfs; burghers in a hundred cities from Ghent to Lübeck gave their lives to help other cities maintain republics like their own.[4] The drive to propagate liberty waned in the 1500s, when nearly all city republics were overpowered by the rise of monarchical states, but during the American and French revolutions the sense of mission returned, more ardent than ever.

It is not only republics that wish to reproduce their own form of government. Feudal lords have tenaciously sought to weaken city councils and peasant assemblies in favor of feudal lordships. Where lords rejected the claims of an existing hierarchy they would install another; for example, when the barons who led the Crusades captured Antioch and Constantinople they set up new principalities and kingdoms. The princes of nineteenth-century Europe likewise created princely states, for example in Bulgaria when it was liberated from Ottoman rule. Even Joseph Stalin, whose only principle of government was paranoid absolutism, sponsored little Stalins from East Germany to North Korea.

At first glance this proclivity for propagating one's own type of regime seems to reflect only a desire to create solid allies. Greek democracies expected that any new democracy would join them in opposing oligarchy and tyranny, and they were not disappointed. With equal accuracy the Italian oligarchic republics foresaw that cities they converted from autocratic rule would stick with them against emperors, popes, and signors. The peasants of the Swiss Forest States did not fight for the liberty of neighboring serfs purely out of altruism, but also because they hoped to surround themselves with free communities in permanent alliance against lords; the policy worked splendidly. There are many such cases in more recent times. For example, Britain sponsored independent democracies in Canada and Australia, counting on them to be faithful allies, and the hope was amply fulfilled in both world wars.

Authoritarian states, however, have had far less success in creating reliable allies. For example, soon after the Crusaders set up the principality of Antioch it went to war against neighboring Christian states—at one battle nearly two thousand Crusaders were slain fighting one another.[5] Still more poignant were the events after Bulgaria was set up as a principality in 1879, ruled by a dashing young German nobleman picked by Russia and Austria. The prince offended the Russian and Austrian emperors simply by acting as the leader of his nation, and within five years they encouraged the prince of Serbia to start a vicious war against their own client.[6] More recently the Communist Vietnamese helped to install a Communist government in Cambodia, but soon found it so disagreeable that they invaded and overthrew it; and so forth. Authoritarian regimes cannot reliably keep peace with a similar regime even when it is their own creation.

Yet regardless of the prospects for long-term alliance, leaders try to reproduce their own type of regime. As one ancient Athenian put it, people think it only right for a state to bestow on others the "form of government that it has found best for itself."[7] If a democracy faced no threats from abroad at all, it would desire less than ever to turn over a foreign people to the rule of a tyrant, while noblemen would never conceive of putting a country under a peasant assembly. Leaders everywhere have supported the system that they understood and flourished within. Once again we see, using yet another set of evidence, that leaders tend to approach foreign affairs with the same attitudes they use at home.

Autocrats, however, have most commonly followed their hierarchical principles by fighting to extend their own rule abroad rather than by fostering other autocracies. It is republics, with their doctrine of natural rights extending to worthy people everywhere, that have worked most fervently to create independent regimes like their own. Since the eighteenth century many have argued that converting every state into a democracy is both a moral duty and the path to a world of universal prosperity and peace. In this chapter I visit each case where republics worked strenuously to create fellow republics, examining a range of historical evidence that scholars have not hitherto studied systematically.[8] We need to understand how democracies succeed when they set out to reproduce their kind—or how sometimes they only make things worse.

The Corrupted Crusade of the French Revolution

Audacious thinkers of the Enlightenment, publishing in quasi-republics like Switzerland and the Netherlands, maintained that "the Cause of Liberty . . . is ONE COMMON CAUSE."[9] The radicals who seized power in France took it for granted that men in any nation who loved democracy were natural allies. But initially they hardly thought to take action abroad, expecting that the decadent aristocracies would collapse under their own corruption once their subjects learned and copied the French example. When France got into a war with the neighboring monarchies it seemed a matter of old-fashioned territorial rivalry and domestic tension.[10] Then the pressure of combat itself pushed more extreme ideas to the fore.

Wherever French armies invaded neighboring regions, native radicals leapt up to demand help in overthrowing their rulers, and exiles in Paris rushed to support the idea. Clearly it was to France's military advantage to encourage rebellion in enemy lands, but the ideas of French leaders went beyond pragmatism. In 1793 that ardent revolutionary Maximilien Robespierre pushed through a new official ideology, persuading the French National Assembly to proclaim that whoever denied rights to people anywhere was the enemy of everyone. All peoples should help one another against every despot, Robespierre declared, exactly as if they were "citizens of a single state."[11]

The crusade advanced with stunning success. Armies of French peasants, propelled by revolutionary fervor, routed monarchical troops in battles from the Netherlands to Naples. The French set up freely elected assemblies: a Batavian Republic for the Dutch, a Roman and a Cisalpine Republic for the Italians, and so forth. Old oligarchies were swept aside as well. In Venice, commoners welcomed their liberation with speeches and dancing in the Piazza San Marco, which had been festooned with banners displaying inspirational slogans such as "ESTABLISHED LIBERTY LEADS TO UNIVERSAL PEACE."[12]

Many Venetians, however, watched the ceremony in sullen discontent. In every conquered region not only elites but also the majority of peasants

and laborers, confused and troubled, longed for the return of their familiar priests and princes. The revolutionary creed that ordinary people will
automatically take to democracy was fatally in error. The new governments
were only miniature factions of urban radicals who had to be protected
from their own populace by a fence of French bayonets.

The radicals understood that to survive they had to reshape the entire
political culture of their nations. To inculcate republican ideas, ceremonies
with speeches and banners were only a beginning. The new regimes worked
tirelessly to transform education, suppress the reactionary influence of the
clergy, and foster an outspoken free press. Most importantly, they destroyed forever the web of feudal privileges that had enmeshed everyday
life in hierarchy.

Republican ideals were not taken up so rapidly. The radical leaders
themselves, unaccustomed to tolerance of dissent, would not abide by
compromises and elections. Each of the new regimes split into factions
that displaced one another by lawless coups. Suspicions of fellow citizens
burgeoned; after all, aristocrats were plotting to restore the old order, and
in wartime any whiff of subversion was intolerable. The French government, terrified of secret agents, arrested thousands of citizens and foreign
exiles. The newborn republics all around France likewise stamped upon
suspected counterrevolutionaries.

The government in Paris also used force to control the client regimes.
As the wars dragged on, French armies took to looting the regions they occupied, bursting into houses and seizing everything down to the silver-
ware. Was it not the right of the revolution to have whatever it needed to
defeat the monarchies? Actually, France was now ruled by the Directory
and far from a democracy, but the regime's crimes discredited democratic
ideology in many eyes. Eventually the neighboring peoples all turned
against France and helped defeat it.[13]

The failures of the French democratic crusade should not obscure its
successes. For a little while revolutionary France did surround itself with
devoted allies, and over the long term their destruction of feudal regimes
proved irreversible. The policy only faltered when the leaders themselves
abandoned toleration and legality.

The French had followed the same path as the ancient Athenians when
they forced the allies of the Delian League to become imperial clients, losing their friendship and the empire too. Like Athens, France was tempted

to domineer because it was far stronger than the others; like Athens, it justified its control by claiming that as the chief defender of democracy it
should have its way. This unhappy pattern of a great republic bossing its
neighbors was to reappear, as we shall see, in modern North America.

What drove France (like Athens) to exploit its neighbors was a desperate war. The immense expenses of armament, and the wartime para-
noia against spies, drove both France and its client republics to use
coercion within their own territories. In short, when a crusade for liberty
descends into war it may defeat itself, undermining liberty even at home.

The shabby collapse of French democracy did not destroy the ideal of
international republican solidarity. A new generation of romantic radicals
arose, people like the Roman Republic's Giuseppe Mazzini, who threw
themselves into doomed conspiracies that aimed to liberate everyone, regardless of nationality. The fact that republicans everywhere were allies was
increasingly taken for granted. As a British diplomat remarked in 1832,
"people are much more liberals or the reverse than they are Frenchmen or
Germans or Italians."[14]

When that division brought on the revolutions of 1848, wherever radicals won influence they called for a universal crusade against despots.
Once again exiles swarmed into Paris, armed themselves and launched
raids into their homelands. This time, however, the fragile new French
republic declined to support the bands of exiles, which failed ignomin-
iously. French republicans had learned something from history, and feared
that foreign wars would open the way for authoritarian reaction (Louis-
Napoleon showed they were right after his war against the Romans).[15] In
other lands the revolutionaries were still more uncertain, and they had little energy to spare as they contended with the tradition-minded domestic
majority of peasants and bourgeois. Although radicals of various nations
did try to support their foreign counterparts, 1848 saw no organized international democratic crusade. Soon aristocratic forces routed republicans
across the continent, and the survivors despaired of any grand international movement.

The idea hung on precariously where republican government survived, however, above all in Great Britain. Throughout the nineteenth century the British discreetly promoted what they called "constitutional"
government in foreign regimes, meaning chiefly civil rights and the rule of
law. Some British ministers (mainly those who also supported reform at

home) applied diplomatic pressure, issuing warnings and deploying an occasional warship. By the century's end they were able to claim to have helped increase liberty, or at least stave off despotism, in nations including Spain, Greece, Belgium, and Turkey. The effort was sporadic, for British cabinets usually put imperial strategy well ahead of civil rights in other nations. Conservatives feared anything that smelled of democracy, while liberals distrusted any expansion of governmental power and were the first to oppose any use of military force.

The history of nineteenth-century Europe thus reaffirms the lessons of the French Revolution and ancient Athens. First, that wherever there are people who hold republican ideals they will profess a solidarity with like-minded people everywhere, and some will work energetically to foster republican government abroad. Second, that these aspirations have little room for maneuver: too much zeal for universal democracy leads to self-defeating excesses, and too little surrenders the future to a nation's short-term practical needs.

The United States, Beacon and Bully

The problems raised by democratic crusading have been nowhere so persistent as in the United States. Already before the American Revolution, the colonists had eagerly watched agitation against tyrants in Europe as if each episode was part of a single struggle.[16] But when the United States won independence, it had little ability to act abroad. The only foreign land within reach was Canada, and when ardent bands of Americans attempted to rouse Canada against the British king they were dumbfounded by the lack of Canadian support. Throughout the next century the United States had neither a strong desire to transform other regimes nor the means to do so. Most Americans felt that it was up to foreign peoples to free themselves when they were ready.

In the meantime, the United States would be guided by strategic and commercial interests, for the nation's first responsibility was to survive and flourish. Its historic mission would be to inspire the world by showing how well democratic governance could work. This strategy had considerable success, for countless democrats abroad have indeed taken the United States as a model, even to the point of copying phrases from the Declaration of Independence and the U.S. Constitution.

Americans offered a tainted example, however, so long as many of them owned slaves. Northerners often heard that criticism from foreigners, and some said they must fight Southern slavery to set a better example for the world. Yet when the Civil War began only a dedicated minority aimed to put a quick end to slavery. It was the terrible pressures of warfare that made Northerners grudgingly accept Lincoln's proclamation of emancipation—as a weapon to weaken the South. People also began to realize that blacks who had escaped to the protection of Northern armies could never be driven back into slavery, especially after tens of thousands of them put on the blue uniform and fought heroically. As the toll of war mounted, so did a crusading spirit, a conviction that only some great transforming good could justify the tragic sacrifices. By 1864 the North had accepted the abolition of slavery as a sacred aim.[17]

After the South's defeat, Northern Republicans determined to effect a total change in its politics—a Reconstruction. Their first step was to give Southern blacks the vote, under the protection of troops. Former slaves eagerly took up politics, striking alliances with democratically inclined Southern whites and winning high offices. The North had forced through nothing less than a democratic revolution.[18]

Some Northern radicals hoped to go further, to use land reform to break the planter class and thereby transform the South's entire political culture. However, most Americans rejected such an infringement on property rights. Some thought it sufficed to have national civil rights laws. Others argued for stimulating industry so that rising prosperity would reconcile blacks and whites. Still others pinned their faith on the building of public schools.

These policies would take a long time to work, assuming they were valid at all, and Southern whites moved quickly. In naked acts of terrorism they barred blacks from the polls, murdering thousands they deemed "impudent." Whites who supported black rights were likewise silenced or slain. Only Northern troops could suppress the Ku Klux Klan. But the North was increasingly dominated by industrialists who, with an eye on their own restive workers, denounced any thought of government intervention. Nor were liberals comfortable with the prospect of endless rule by bayonet over the South against the will of the majority (that is, whites). Racism added its poison, for many believed that the failure of blacks to maintain their rights proved their congenital inferiority. By 1880 the North had left the South to its own devices, under the rule of a minority of wealthy whites.

The remarkable fact about the attempt to impose democracy on the South is not that it failed, but that it was attempted at all. Once again the fires of war had ignited a crusading spirit. Once again the enterprise was defeated largely because the political culture in the conquered region was too deeply rooted in coercion and inequality. And once again, what made failure certain was a weakness in the convictions of many of the democratic leaders themselves. Everywhere the spirit of democratic crusade was stifled under racist and imperialist ideology.

That spirit revived with shocking force in 1917. Yet again, a dire war was forcing people back upon the most fundamental ideals. It seemed like a God-sent opportunity to President Woodrow Wilson. This son of a Presbyterian minister was convinced that he had a sacred mission to correct the world's evils, and his polestar was equal rights under law. Wilson launched his vision into history on April 4, 1917, when he addressed the U.S. Congress to ask for a declaration of war upon Germany. In somber tones, Wilson held the crowded hall spellbound as he declared that the standard of equal rights that prevailed among the individual citizens of a democracy should likewise prevail among the nations of the world. To achieve such harmony it was necessary only to beat down the militarist ruling elites that had been the perennial cause of wars. The grand aim of going to war, the president explained, was to "make the world safe for democracy." He slid past the phrase without special emphasis, but the audience caught its import: the hall detonated in applause.[19]

Wilson's vision might have made little headway amid the imperialist struggle for survival and dominion, a creed which the war was only making more vehement, but help came from an enemy. The Bolsheviks who seized Russia that November also believed in worldwide egalitarian liberation, and their thunderous denunciations of oppression aroused subject peoples around the world. Imperialism was further cramped by the demands of war. French and British leaders desperately needed support from every quarter—from neutrals, from Americans, from their own common people—and they appealed to everyone by announcing that the war was a battle for universal self-determination.

The meaning of "self-determination" was not as plain as it seemed. "The phrase is simply loaded with dynamite," Wilson's secretary of state warned him confidentially. "It will, I fear, cost thousands of lives." Millions would have been closer to the mark.

Self-determination had two meanings for Wilson. First, it meant a nation's internal freedom from domination by a militarist aristocracy. That could be achieved short of full democracy, and Wilson did not mean to impose his ideal on others. For his second meaning of self-determination was freedom from coercion by external powers. It would suffice to pull down the militarists and let people choose their own government; surely they would eventually settle down in democracy and peace. Events at the end of the war seemed to confirm this vision, for the Germans rose and chased the kaiser into exile, and other nations likewise spontaneously elected their first democratic parliaments. There was no need for Reconstruction-style military occupation; once Germany was beaten and a European settlement negotiated to Wilson's satisfaction, the main task seemed accomplished.[20]

A weakness in self-determination soon appeared. One must define the people who will do the self-determining, the body of citizens whose majority is sovereign. To define such a body one must draw boundaries, and that can awaken demons. Amid the social wreckage of fallen empires, many people found community and security by clinging together within an ethnic group boundary, exalting their collective rights as Hungarians or whatever. The new regimes, still pervaded by authoritarian political culture, scarcely knew how to maintain individual rights against these group passions.[21] One by one, most of the newborn democracies fell to nationalist dictators.

Although Wilson's crusade for democracy failed in the short run, over the long run he prevailed. By the end of the war entire peoples were freed from the Russian, German, Austro-Hungarian, and Ottoman empires to go their own way. Wilson's rhetoric, oddly teamed up with Communist propaganda, also fired resistance among peoples still held subject. From Ireland to the Philippines, democratic nations faced demands for the self-determination they had themselves called for. Wilson himself wanted only a gradual emancipation of "backward" colonial peoples, under the tutelage of their masters. But Americans and Soviets had accepted, and swayed much of the world to adopt, a new principle: foreign rule was illegitimate except insofar as it would foster self-government.

Meanwhile, there was one region where the president hoped to sponsor democracy more directly. The little nations of the Caribbean had languished for generations in cycles of despotism, corruption, and insurrection, and North American progressives believed they had the power to correct the region's problems. They had already tried out the idea following the Spanish-American War, when the United States felt a responsiblity to set up democracy in liberated Cuba. Shiploads of managers and engineers were sent to improve everything from schooling to sanitation, and to organize elections (taking care to exclude candidates hostile to the United States). For the first time since the French Revolution, a nation had actively planted a democracy upon foreign soil. But the flower did not flourish in Cuba, with its tradition of shameless manipulation of ballot boxes. When fraudulent elections provoked a civil war in 1906, many Cubans called on the United States to return. Once again troops and administrators sailed in to oversee fair elections.[22]

Wilson and other presidents ordered many more such interventions. U.S. Marines tramped ashore with some local support to regulate elections in Panama, the Dominican Republic, Haiti, and Nicaragua. Uninvited, the United States invaded Mexico (twice) and Honduras. Through economic sanctions, U.S. governments also undermined despotism in nations as distant as Chile. The first instance came in 1917, when a dictator seized power in Costa Rica and Wilson refused to grant diplomatic recognition, making commerce so difficult that the dictator had to step down.

Historians argue over the motives behind these interventions. Were North Americans aiming to advance private business interests? To prevent European powers from gaining a dangerous military foothold? Or were they driven by ideology to spread democracy? Few progressives at the time would have seen much difference among these motives. In their view, what Latin America needed above all was plain political stability. That would remove the pretexts that European imperialists had often used to intervene, and at the same time provide the right climate for economic development and public education, with democracy to follow in due course. The idea was to build republican political culture from the bottom up, with paved roads, good schools, and honest officials.[23]

The results were not encouraging. The United States did create democracies in Puerto Rico and the Philippines, but they had limitations, and even that took half a century of economic assistance and paternalistic supervision. Elsewhere, the lofty plans hardly got off the ground. In typical agrarian societies, where nearly all the land was owned by a handful of families, establishing full democracy would have meant overturning the whole social and economic system. That called for more persistence and idealism than could be found in either the local oligarchies or the U.S. government.[24]

Holding elections seemed like a shortcut. North Americans supposed that a fair vote would bring stability by conferring legitimacy on those elected. But to many Caribbean leaders, if an election was worth anything it was to show which faction actually held effective power; holding an election without fraud would be as pointless as holding a war without battles. Sometimes the United States sent in soldiers to keep down the cheating, but foreign supervision did little to encourage democratic self-government. The losing factions would go back to plotting coups, howling that the Yankees had connived to install their opponents. Sometimes these accusations were correct. In Nicaragua, for example, U.S. envoys backed up by Marines dictated who could run for office in 1911, 1912, and 1916. Such elections discredited the idea of democratic intervention.[25]

As these problems became apparent, the United States tried another approach. The incessant coups and caudillos in the Caribbean all came from the military establishments, so the United States decided that these should be replaced with police forces trained in constitutional law. Such constabularies were set up under Yankee tutelage in Cuba, Haiti, the Dominican Republic, and Nicaragua, and they did put an end to civil wars and regional insurrections. But consolidating territorial states was not sufficient. In each country the constabularies themselves took to politics and started their own cycles of coups and dictators.

In the 1930s the United States gave up trying to impose its democratic ideals on the Caribbean. Evidently nothing would work short of forcibly altering entire political cultures, starting with land reform. If that were possible at all (which many doubted for such "backward" peasants), it would be intolerably costly, and would violate liberal ideals of property rights and self-determination. The new dictators with their Marine-trained police forces did maintain a stable order, meeting the most pressing goals: the regimes would offer no pretext for European military intervention, and they would make deals with American corporations, promoting economic progress.[26]

Everywhere, the crusade for democracy seemed exhausted. World economic depression accelerated the rout of democratic governments from Argentina to Japan, and many people decided that the future belonged to more brutally "efficient" forms of rule. The remaining democracies, beleaguered at home, had little energy to spare on advancing their principles abroad. The only thing that could restore the crusading spirit would be another terrible war.

Replacing Fascist Political Cultures

In 1944 some British scholars and civil servants were given time off from the war against Fascism to read schoolbooks. They sat down to stacks of German textbooks, diligently working through the pages. What they read struck them with dismay. Hardly any of these books seemed suitable to place in the hands of children. Even books written well before the Nazis took power reeked of chauvinism, militarism, and racism. Here was evidence that the true enemy of democracy was not just the madman Hitler, but an entire political culture.[27]

Many people in Britain and the United States thought that after the First World War the effort to promote democracy had stopped too soon. They thought it obvious that if, this time, the defeated nations could be turned into solid democracies, that would automatically keep them from starting yet another war. Besides, democracies would undoubtedly be allies against Soviet Communism. But how to establish lasting democracy?[28]

Once victory was won, the defeated nations would have to have new leaders. But to impose a government would flout ideals of self-determination, making more enemies than friends. The solution was to clear the ground so that democrats could rise by themselves. American officers and their allies, ruling as Occupation authorities in Germany, Japan, and other conquered nations, devoted their efforts to purging dedicated Fascists from positions of authority. Hundreds of thousands were removed.

Germany, Japan, Austria, and Italy had all had some practice at democracy in the 1920s, and many citizens remembered how it was supposed to work. In the space cleared by the purges, with Fascism discredited by shattering military defeat, democratically inclined men and women made their stand. Thousands of them came straight from jail. Protected from the violence of their old foes by Occupation authorities, they formed political parties and founded governments.

If the democrats were to hold out after the foreign troops withdrew, they must have a foundation to stand on. Americans and British therefore designed a hugely ambitious plan: they would transform entire political cultures. In the words of Japan's new viceroy, General Douglas MacArthur, the defeated nation would become "the world's great laboratory for an experiment" whose aim was nothing less than a "reshaping of national and individual character."[29] It was a heroic assumption that such a transformation was possible—but that very assumption was central to democratic belief. To be a democrat is to believe that appropriate conditions can make a good citizen out of practically anyone.

In pursuit of their grand goal, authorities did not scruple to set aside civil rights for a time. They purged every teacher and journalist who could be accused of supporting Fascism, in some places well over half the total, and strictly censored Fascist thought in every medium from storybooks to movies. Meanwhile, a new generation of teachers was trained by imported democratic instructors, or sent abroad to interact with teachers familiar with democracy. Entire newspapers and radio companies were confiscated from right-wing owners and turned over to liberals. Occupation authorities also directly pressured educators and the media to celebrate democracy. The most important thing about the censorship and pressures, however, was that they were weak. Schoolteachers, writers, and filmmakers, released from the iron cage of Fascist thought control, were glad to try their wings.[30]

The most forceful measures were taken in Japan, where hierarchical traditions were the most deeply entrenched. To transform the political culture, Americans decided that the Japanese political, social, and economic systems must all be radically changed. The Occupation authorities began by writing an entire new constitution and forcing it upon the Japanese. Next came wholesale land reform (many of the Americans were New Dealers who believed that helping common people could take priority over property rights). MacArthur and his men also sponsored free trade unions, emancipated women, and imposed other revolutionary changes.

In both Germany and Japan, the construction of democratic civil society was aided by many private American organizations. Labor unions, women's leagues, 4-H Clubs, and other such groups each worked to reproduce its kind by sending missions abroad and by bringing foreigners back to watch democracy at work.[31]

These efforts were intense, but short-lived. The Occupation forces kept control for only a few years, far too brief a time to uproot all the Fascists and their beliefs, before attention turned to the Cold War. From the outset, the aim had never been revolutionary democratization in the fashion of the Schwyzers or French, who had helped peasant mobs to drive lords from their manors. The Occupation authorities even discouraged attempts to mobilize workers in the name of radical change, which smelled to them of Communism. Instead they relied on the old elites, not only the moderates but often the conservatives as well. As the Cold War took hold, even former Fascists were sometimes accepted as allies against Communism. This limited approach to changing society was a main reason there was no authoritarian reaction after the troops sailed home.[32]

Democracy did take root, profoundly changing the political cultures of Germany and Japan. Many who had doubted that democracy could ever work in their nation changed their minds when they saw how well it served. Others who had always hoped for democracy now found a chance to stake their careers on it. Polls showed that citizens gradually took to democratic ways of thinking, while leaders settled into practices of tolerating dissent, public contestation, and negotiated compromises.[33] To the surprise of many, the experiment produced exactly what it aimed for. As predicted, all these nations gave up their former predilection for wanton aggression abroad. And as predicted, they all became steadfast allies of other democracies.

One reason for success was that the democrats' combative spirit did not fade away after a few years, but was reinvigorated by the Cold War. After China fell to Communism and Stalin imposed his will upon Eastern Europe, the threat to liberty seemed graver than ever. Democrats responded with furious activity aimed at preserving and spreading democracy.

The most crucial battleground was Italy, where many predicted that the Communists would be voted into power in the 1948 elections and then impose a Stalinist dictatorship. The American government secretly channeled large sums of money to the Christian Democrats. American experts advised Italians on political organization, corporations helped out by financing propaganda, and private groups from Italian-American clubs to the American Catholic Church threw in their support. The Christian Democrats would probably have won the election in any case, but the outside help boosted them to a decisive majority. Through the 1950s the U.S. Central Intelligence Agency continued to give Italian democratic parties massive secret aid.[34]

Americans similarly aided democratic parties all across Western Europe through the postwar decades, and as each European democracy grew strong it added its own forces to the task. European governments withheld economic cooperation in order to weaken dictators and military juntas, as in Spain and Greece, and actively assisted nascent democratic groups by every nonviolent method they could think of. Many private organizations joined in the effort. The deliberate aim was to secure not only reliable allies against the Soviet Union, but a stable European peace. This patient campaign for democracy turned out to be one of the most successful foreign policies in history.

The Destruction of Colonial Political Cultures

To see a different route toward democracy, let us visit one last historical locale. The very thought of democracy was unknown in the wretched fishing village called Calcutta when the British purchased it, inhabitants and all, from its owners. Included in the deal was a malarial swamp, which in time became a parkland with gardens and tree-lined promenades. Overlooking the park to this day is a statue of William Bentinck, the governor-general of India in the 1830s, a progressive gentleman who established a uniform and honest administration for the subcontinent. As the epitaph on his pedestal declares, he was among those "who infused into oriental despotism the spirit of British freedom."[35]

In such colonial possessions, republics had their best chance to fulfill the vision of replacing despotism with freedom. Holding supreme power for generations, it might seem that they could have built whatever political culture they chose. Yet it was exactly here that imperialism impeded democracy most stubbornly.

From the nineteenth century on, many people in republics assumed that their colonies would eventually become republics of some sort themselves. As evidence there were Britain's "white dominions" from Canada to Australia, which the British had yielded up to the inhabitants in a bold and unprecedented gamble. However, it was widely assumed that countries with more alien cultures, immemorially ruled by hereditary power and cruelty, could not govern themselves democratically except in the remote future. Perhaps after centuries of economic progress and education these colonies could mature into social and political duplicates of their mother countries.

This complacent program was shaken by the preachings of Wilson and Lenin, and still more by the rise of native associations in the subject lands. Natives of many colonies had already been educated in equal rights and the methods of public contestation, and they demanded independence without delay. What confidence remained in imperialism disintegrated during the Second World War, when the U.S. government insisted that it was fighting to end imperial rule everywhere and the Soviet Union found new opportunities to foster anti-imperialist groups. Powers like Britain began to realize that they would not be granted the centuries they wanted to uplift their colonies.[36]

If there was barely a single generation to work in, it seemed urgent to give indigenous leaders a democratic political culture. British colonial administrators set up local councils in order to provide experience in self-government. They hoped to gradually transfer power to an educated elite, which would follow British ways down to the powdered wigs worn by judges. French leaders cherished a still grander vision: the Greater French Republic. The natives would be educated into virtual Frenchmen and absorbed into a worldwide federation, voting as the equals of citizens back in France.

These romantic plans ran afoul of the political cultures within the colonies themselves—and not only the cultures of the indigenous peoples. European colonial officials were trained in the ways of military and administrative rule, with habits of arbitrary command that extended down to their house "boys." They had little more experience than the natives in managing affairs through a democratic council. It seemed only natural to go on governing by passing commands down through the traditional tribal chiefs, sheiks, rajas, or sultans. European colonials had a hard time imagining that natives with deep-rooted traditions of despotic rule, ignorant people with outlandish ways and dark skins, could ever be capable of democratic self-government. Such doubts redoubled in territories where groups striving for independence organized themselves into secret societies, terrorist organizations, and entire guerrilla armies under authoritarian leaders. These were immediately scorned as "bandit" gangs, or painted in the demonic red of international Communism.

Here we see how the weaknesses in democracies that have sometimes impeded peace with quasi-democratic neighbors also got in the way of fostering an entirely new democratic state. Racial prejudice and political stereotyping made it hard to recognize that some native leaders might be cultivated as suitable negotiating partners. In consequence, hierarchical subcultures were allowed to pursue their authoritarian ways. Most colonial officials fought the independence movements tooth and nail. When natives who sought to organize peacefully for self-government were obstructed, they sometimes saw no way to reach their goals except by forming violent illegal bands. Democratic governments automatically battled these bands as criminal enemies, closing a vicious circle. The result could be what the British descended to in Ireland and Israel (see appendix)—virtual warfare against people who were prevented from establishing a democracy chiefly by the conflict itself.

The independence movements grew irrepressibly, and European governments found that their attempts to keep a grip on colonies not only drained money but disgusted democratic voters. By the latter 1950s people everywhere generally thought that the denial of self-government was incompatible with ideals of equal rights.[37] In many countries the imperial powers pulled out abruptly, abandoning their half-hearted plans for eventually building democracy. Often they left behind a faction-ridden society that had known only hierarchical governance. Elections were held, but for lack of any tradition of toleration and civil rights, leaders often used the democratic "majority principle" to justify mobilizing ethnic groups to grab everything for themselves. Minority cliques fought back with coups.

Meanwhile, the Soviet Union and Communist China roundly proclaimed the successes of authoritarian socialism, and promoted their system with both open and secret aid. Democracy came to seem old-fashioned at best. The number of democracies around the world had increased when colonies won self-government, but a wave of failures followed. The percentage of the world's independent nations that were democratic fell back below the level of the 1920s. Once again history showed that the spread of democracy was not inevitable.[38]

Nevertheless, on balance, European colonial rule did advance world democracy. Deliberately or not, it had undermined traditional authoritarian structures, and when the colonial officials pulled out, whatever hierarchy remained was drained of prestige and power. The mutilated societies that resulted might have been vulnerable to despotism or pure anocratic chaos, but they were also free, for the first time ever, to seek new configurations. Here and there the colonists had left behind some democratic ideals and institutions; occasionally these were well entrenched, as in India, but often they were only sparks smoldering in the wreckage. Yet in dozens of new nations democracy was stamped out only to flare up again with indestructible vigor.

Centuries of tutelage were not necessary after all to create democratic government. A variety of societies already had their own traditions of the rule of law (written or unwritten), of public contestation holding rulers accountable for their policies, of toleration of dissent, of the protection of minority rights, and of allegiance to a consensus-seeking political community. Applied within institutions modeled on Europe's, these traditions could suffice to sustain democracy. Even impoverished tribal lands like Botswana and Papua New Guinea proved that they could govern themselves in a generally democratic fashion.[39]

Most impressive of all was the almost ungovernable conglomeration of India, which found indigenous roots for the principles of nonviolent public contestation. Mohandas Gandhi combined these with tactics such as the hunger strike and boycott, developed especially by the Irish as they wrested their freedom from Britain while retaining democracy. Gandhi's brilliant contribution was the use of a more spiritual force: he would alter the political culture of the oppressors themselves. The methods that others had used to raise up democracy—furious insurrections, crusading armies, foreign troops guarding the polls, sweeping purges, generations of paternalistic tutelage—none of these was necessary. A tolerant politics could be cultivated as part of the liberation struggle itself. This nonviolent route to freedom has been one of the greatest discoveries of the twentieth century.

In India's advance toward liberty and democracy there is enough credit so that the British can have a share. The final result remains in doubt, for much of the tyranny and corruption that William Bentinck found when he arrived in Calcutta is there still. Nevertheless the British intended to leave India far more democratic than they found it, and this they did.

Stumbling Toward a Democratic World

At the close of the Second World War many nations lacked freedom—not just colonial dominions but the majority of nations from Latin America to Eastern Europe. In all these the United States hoped to nurture democracy. As the world's predominant power it felt more certain than ever that its way of life was best. Foreigners would surely want to "Americanize" themselves, and it was simple morality to help them.

One method for doing this was military intervention. On the occasions when this was tried, however, it generally brought more blame than praise. When the troops came home they might leave behind an approximately democratic regime, as in the Dominican Republic, or a ravaged police state, as in Vietnam. In either case it was arguable that the intervention had done more to impede democratic development than to promote it.

Diplomatic pressure was less risky. The United States and its allies pressed insistently for free elections everywhere from Poland to Brazil, reinforcing their words by granting or withholding trade preferences and military aid. The results were mixed. Some regimes indignantly rejected the pressure, some held elections yet wound up with new authoritarian governments anyway, but some did move toward democracy.[40]

This was no ideological crusade, for American presidents gave more attention to a tough realpolitik that aimed to advance the material position of the United States and restrict the Communist powers. The United States freely bestowed economic and military aid to authoritarian regimes in hopes of improving regional stability and free-market economies; democracy could follow in its own good time. Besides, the only alternative to a dictator or junta was usually an opposition that sought power with its own secrecy and violence; these opponents were promptly branded as Communist conspirators.[41]

Unfortunately, in many lands economic aid only increased the dominance of wealthy elites, while military aid only increased the power of militarists. Democracy spread less quickly than slums and torture. Supporting dictatorships did not even win stability. Just as coercive methods cannot bring permanent peace to a set of nations, so apparently are they liable to bring bitter struggles within a given nation.[42]

By the late 1950s some American leaders saw that their policy was faulty and began experimenting with other approaches. President John F. Kennedy's "Alliance for Progress" aspired to send young idealists and government funding to reform the entire social and economic structure of Latin America, making it more receptive to democracy. In the 1970s the U.S. Congress and President Jimmy Carter focused on demands that foreign nations respect human rights, putting pressure on undemocratic regimes from Chile to South Africa by reducing military, economic and diplomatic support. In some nations these policies helped bring greater democracy. But in others, most notoriously Iran, the fall of an autocrat led only to worse repression.[43]

When Ronald Reagan became president he proclaimed a global "crusade for freedom," partly because he felt more democracy would promote world peace. The means would be to foster "the infrastructure of democracy, the system of a free press, unions, political parties, universities."[44] Although in fact the Reagan administration gave short shrift to unions and universities, and supported some unsavory governments in the name of fighting Communism, it did work to train democratically inclined cadres in political skills. Washington put diplomatic and economic pressure on authoritarian leaders, meanwhile reassuring them that their personal safety could be preserved if they gave way to democracy. These efforts significantly aided the indigenous groups that forced through free elections in the Philippines, El Salvador, South Korea, and elsewhere. Above all with the Soviet Union, the Reagan administration combined tough pressure with affable reassurance in a deliberate effort to help leaders and dissidents in their repudiation of authoritarian rule.[45]

And democracy increased. In 1974 the Portuguese liberated themselves; Spain established democracy two years later. In the following decade the movement swept through Latin America, replacing an entire corps of uniformed tyrants with democratic presidents. The movement continued around the world, perhaps most unexpectedly in South Africa. No less surprising, these transitions were mostly without bloodshed, for Gandhi's discovery had become common knowledge. Lech Walesa made the point plainly on his way from rebel workman to elected president of Poland: through all the arrests and beatings, he boasted, "We did not smash a single windowpane." A wary agreement to not punish former rulers often proved essential for the stability of the new regimes. Where toleration and the search for consensus were genuine, even despots and torturers could safely relinquish power.[46]

Historians will long argue over how much influence the older democracies had in causing these changes. Certainly nothing would have happened but for the intrinsic weaknesses of the juntas and totalitarian parties, and the supreme courage of their domestic opponents. Yet democratic governments had tirelessly sustained pressures such as diplomatic criticism, reliable information broadcast by the Voice of America and the BBC, and overt economic warfare that cut off nations like South Africa and the Soviet Union from vital markets and technologies. Meanwhile, there was the beckoning example of free societies. By this point nearly all of the world's wealthiest and most culturally creative nations were democratic. Had there been no democracies in the world to show a way forward, the disintegration of authoritarian regimes would surely have been far more agonizing and less beneficial.

As a further inducement, most democrats held that international relations would improve precisely insofar as governments became democratic. For example, in 1991 the American secretary of state warned nations emerging from the ruins of the former Soviet Union that the support the United States gave them would depend on their degree of democracy. A chief reason for backing democracy, he said, was that it would make for peace in the region. The new Russian foreign minister went further, declaring that "the United States and other Western democracies are as natural friends and eventual allies of the democratic Russia as they were foes of the totalitarian USSR." President George Bush agreed, saying, "Democrats in the Kremlin can assure our security in a way nuclear missiles never could." After all, as Bush's rival Bill Clinton would declare in his 1994 State of the Union address, "Democracies don't attack each other."[47]

Scholars who have studied modern efforts to promote democracy are beginning to draw general lessons.[48] They admit that direct military intervention can succeed, as in Germany and Japan. But the cost is horrendous and the results uncertain; crusades to impose democracy, from Athenians in the Aegean to Americans in the Caribbean, have usually made more enemies than friends. Entrenched elites were not easily cast out, least of all by people who respected civil rights, while intruding officials could be so domineering that they discredited democracy itself. Tearing down a government by force also undermines the highly desirable goal of fostering an international political culture of the "republican" sort, where problems are resolved through nonviolent public contestation. These arguments for international restraint mirror the advice that experts offer to groups striving for reform within a nation. Studies of recent attempts to construct democracy show that nonviolent pressure, negotiation, and mutual concessions have been far more successful than bloody coups or rebellions.[49]

More often than direct military force, republics have tried using economic sanctions to push other nations to change. Trade embargoes and the like have been common since the days of the Hanseatic League, but the results have often been ambiguous. A regime under economic pressure may become more authoritarian, or fall to a rebellion that only puts a new dictator in charge. One survey of 120 modern cases of trade sanctions, imposed for a variety of purposes, estimated that only about a third achieved their goals.[50] Still, that is something, and a boycott is usually less costly and cruel than an invasion.

A still cheaper, more humane, and more effective method for promoting democratic government is to foster the private organizations and routine public practices that make up a free civil society. The idea of helping local efforts in this direction has been developed since 1945 into an arsenal of tools for modifying political culture. It appears that national transformations can be promoted with expenditures trivial by comparison with military budgets. Moral and material support can nourish democratic political parties, public interest groups and publications, training can improve the work of officials from legislative staffs down to neighborhood policemen, poll-watchers can discourage corrupt elections, and so forth. Much of the funds and personnel for this enterprise can be mobilized from private organizations, which rouse less suspicion than national governments. Many such programs are now underway and a great deal more could be done.[51]

Meanwhile, at the governmental level democratic leaders need to strike a careful balance of advice, assistance, and pressure. Pulling down a dictator may only open the way for a new tyranny; an abrupt lunge toward majority rule may only create conditions for ethnic strife. Outsiders need to help the parties to negotiate revisions in the distribution of power by small, cautious steps. An outside nation can also offer to guarantee minority rights. None of this will ensure success, and scholars who have studied the process of democratization believe that much depends on luck, timing, and the emergence of national leaders blessed with political skill, democratic commitment, and true moral quality. Where such leaders can be found, working with them can offer democracies high rewards for low risk and expense.[52]

Where conditions are not so propitious we must be cautious. With our ignorance of foreign cultures and our tendency to confuse self-interest with altruism, we can end up doing more harm than good. Besides, people have legitimate goals that may be more important to them than civil rights. I do not see a strong duty or interest in pressing democracy urgently upon a nation that is preoccupied with avoiding economic catastrophe or a collapse into genocidal strife. It might even increase the risk of war to change a somnolent autocracy into an insecure and volatile proto-democracy, especially if neighboring autocracies find democratization a threat.[53] Anyway, for a long time to come many nations will be ruled by dictators and juntas, wielding ever more sophisticated and far-reaching means of destruction. To keep the peace we must temper the push for democracy while employing more short-term methods of avoiding war, not excluding alliances with despots and the other tools of realpolitik.

Conclusions

The message of this book is that well-established democracies are inhibited by their fundamental nature from warring on one another. I could find no plain counterexample to this rule, even in remote historical locales. To see what lies behind this rule, I sought simple criteria that would consistently divide regimes into natural categories in such a way that regimes in certain categories did not war with their own kind. The crucial and surprising fact is that such criteria do exist.

The first step is to distinguish republics from authoritarian states. It is reasonable to call a regime a republic if it has a body of citizens who hold equal political rights, meaning chiefly the freedom to engage in public contestation over policies and offices. In most cases it is clear to any careful observer whether or not a regime satisfies this criterion (for example, one might check for regular, fair, and meaningful elections). Scrutinizing the handful of borderline cases refines our understanding: to distinguish between ambiguous regimes it suffices to inquire into their toleration of dissent. In practice, we ask whether a supreme leader or clique (with the power to make war in particular) suppresses citizens who might otherwise manage to remove the leadership from office. The exile, imprisonment, or execution of such political opponents reliably marks a regime as one that can war with a republic, even when their formal constitutions are similar.

Not to be overlooked is the distinction between republican states and "democratic" tribes or other anocratic regimes. Here, the key question is whether there exists a government that commands allegiance above what people give to kinship groups and factional leaders, a government capable of restraining private violence. It is not any "republics," but only republican territorial states that avoid war with their own kind. Some set of consititutional and social mechanisms, sustaining republican governance, are structural preconditions for keeping peace.

We must also distinguish between the two kinds of republic, democracy and oligarchy. In the ambiguous zone between these, we find that an identifying characteristic of oligarchies is that their citizens devote much of their political energy to suppressing an important "enemy" class, much as an authoritarian leadership stamps upon individuals who threaten its rule. Using this definition, we find an almost complete absence of warfare among the hundreds of oligarchic republics scattered through history. Oligarchies did fight democracies, and since both types of republic shared many constitutional and societal features it is hard to imagine a structural explanation for this pattern of peace.

Also noteworthy is the timing of wars. Republics do get into wars with their own kind when one of them is not well-established, that is, when its leaders cannot be fully trusted to practice toleration instead of coercion. But once a regime has been operating with real toleration of dissent for about three years, we can be confident it will not fight a republic of its own kind. Often the regime's formal constitution and other social arrangements do not change much during this time span; what made for peace must have been something else that changed gradually, but not too gradually.

In working through history I chanced upon one more spectacular regularity, which deserves equal attention and respect: republics, and only republics, tend to form durable leagues with their own kind.

All these highly regular generalizations can be explained by a simple proposition. A leadership group relies on a political culture, by which I mean a particular set of beliefs about handling conflicts with others (beliefs stable enough to be linked to compatible customary practices). Leaders tend to take the beliefs and practices that they use domestically with fellow citizens and apply them in conflicts abroad. In particular, republican leaders are inclined to use the practices associated with a republican political culture, namely tolerant, nonviolent public contestation, aiming at mutual accommodation for the common good.

The only additional factor, a crucial one, is whether republican leaders accept a foreign leadership as "ingroup," comparable to their fellow citizens at home. Peaceful negotiation is dependably practiced only among such people. Fortunately, and perhaps surprisingly, republican leaders grant this fellowship wherever they perceive the foreigners' fundamental political beliefs and behavior to be similar to their own. In a number of cases we saw violence enter exactly at the point where this perception was lacking. The important influence that one side's perception (or misperception) of the other's political stance has on decisions to make war or peace is yet another historical regularity that cannot be explained by purely structural factors.

In sum, the political culture of republican leaders brings them to follow as a rule of thumb the expectation that in disputes with foreign leaders who share their principles, they will be able to negotiate a satisfactory solution. It is not idealism that makes them follow this practice. Getting objective information about how foreign rivals are likely to behave is so difficult that rules of thumb can be the most efficient way to cut through the clutter of international relations. As experience shows, the practice works.

I have tested these ideas against three large and independent bodies of evidence. Each comprises works by specialist historians, original historical source materials, and a scattering of recent numerical and experimental studies. The first body of evidence juxtaposes the domestic politics of regimes with their record of wars, revealing almost perfectly regular patterns of democratic and oligarchic republican mutual peace when categories are defined as described above. A few studies by political scientists have statistically confirmed the connection between political culture and international violence.

The second body of evidence is the detailed records of negotiations between regimes confronting one another in crises where war threatens. While no limited selection of cases can be definitive, time after time we find situations where a plausible argument can be made that a change in the political culture of the leaders would have shifted the course of negotiations. Again, statistical studies, supported by experiments, confirm the connection between political culture and negotiating behaviors and outcomes.

The third independent body of evidence inspects friendly relationships. The tendency (again statistically confirmed) of republics to ally as equals, indeed to form international leagues regulated by voting councils, is an undeniable demonstration of the faithful reproduction of domestic behavior in international affairs. Belief in equality as a natural right, leading people to see even foreigners as potential members of the republican in-group, also lies behind another tendency, democratic crusading to bring liberty to foreign peoples. Neither structural mechanisms nor realpolitik calculations of power balances seem capable of explaining these remarkably widespread and important features of the historical record.

Driven by these powerful forces, the zone of democratic peace seems likely to expand. We can be sure that existing democracies will keep striving, prudently or not, to reproduce their own kind, and wherever a new democracy emerges they will tend to support it against its enemies. After two centuries of expanding by fits and starts, approximately democratic regimes now govern over half of the world's population, and some two-thirds of its economic product. It is becoming obvious that each new democracy establishes peaceful relationships with the others, so that nations within the democratic zone of peace can devote their military energies to confronting authoritarian nations. Meanwhile, in their characteristic fashion the democracies have been weaving an ever denser web of contractual relationships with one another, greatly augmenting their combined economic and political strength. Already we may be near some critical point where the preponderance of democracies will transform the entire world system of international relations.[54]

None of this suggests that we should sit back and await an automatic triumph. In important nations from Egypt to China it is hard to imagine the establishment of democracy coming any time soon. And as rising populations crash against the barriers of finite ecosystems, entire regions that are now precariously democratic could fall back into despotism or chaos. Further, new information and behavior-modification technologies may push even the most stable democracies toward different forms of governance, as yet unsuspected and perhaps unwelcome.

If democracy is to survive and expand, many people must devote their lifetimes; many must give their very lives, as millions before us have done. Even with such ardent efforts, no rule of history promises us that we are bound to achieve universal democracy. Yet the goal is worth even more than has commonly been supposed. For if we can attain this, we will at the same time attain universal peace.

Military Confrontations Between Approximately Republican Regimes of the Same Kind

In this list I have attempted to include all but the most trivial cases concluded by the end of 1994. The year given is when armed confrontation or combat began. The descriptions focus on connections among the political culture of leaders, their diplomacy, and their decisions to go to war (documentation for these is deficient for all cases before the modern period). Histories that are treated summarily in the main text are discussed at more length here and vice-versa.

An asterisk (*) indicates "wars": conflicts with at least two hundred deaths in combat organized by political units across their boundaries. This list is wonderfully short: such violence constitutes an exceedingly tiny fraction of the countless interactions that have taken place among hundreds of republics across many centuries.

I omit clear cases of wars between oligarchic republics and democracies. Borderline cases are classified for convenience as either "between democracies" or "between oligarchies," but, following the criteria given in this book, I classify borderline regimes as follows:

[A] a non-republican regime, some combination of anocratic, autocratic, and authoritarian.

[D] a primarily democratic regime.

[N] a newborn, not well-established regime.

[O] a primarily oligarchic regime.

? indicates inadequate sources for definitive categorization.

[O/A] an ambiguous regime at a borderline, for example between oligarchic [O] and authoritarian [A]; most of these cases are in transition or oscillation between the two types.

Between Oligarchic Republics: Ancient World

Oligarchic Rome is not covered here, since no primary sources nor reliable secondary sources survive that describe Carthage or other possibly oligarchic opponents.[1] There were many severe wars pitting Greek democracies against oligarchic republics (including Rome); see chapter 2. Among the dozens of oligarchic republics, there are only ambiguous cases of wars:

479 B.C.—SPARTA [O] ET AL. VS. THEBES [A?]

Sparta besieged Thebes to force the expulsion of a pro-Persian group. At this early date Thebes may have been a semi-feudal anocratic regime under a coalition of aristocratic families rather than a republic. The siege was brief and perhaps without serious bloodshed.[2]

411 B.C.—ATHENS [N, O] VS. SPARTA [O] ET AL.

When a coup in Athens installed an oligarchy it continued the war already underway against Sparta and other oligarchies, but tried to make peace; there were few deaths. Subsequently, under a newborn Athenian regime that tried to combine oligarchy and democracy there was one serious battle. The actual fighting against oligarchies was done by the Athenian navy, overseas troops who rejected the authority of the usurpers at home and remained under democratic leadership; thus the fighting was between oligarchic and democratic groups.[3]

Between Democracies: Ancient World

Among the dozens of democracies, there are only ambiguous cases of wars:

427 B.C.—ATHENS [D] VS. MEGARA [N, D]

Megara converted to democracy in wartime, but the democrats could not feel confident in their rule of what had long been an oligarchy. The Megarans were by tradition violent enemies of the Athenians, who continued to ravage their territory. No serious battle is recorded. (After about three years the Megaran democrats made an alliance with Athens.)[4]

426 B.C.—ATHENS [D] VS. MANTINEA [D]

Mantinea, an established democracy, lay in a region dominated by Sparta. The Spartans forced the Mantineans to serve as their allies against the Athenians; the Mantineans later claimed they were "enslaved." In 426 B.C. a severe battle set Athens against Spartan allies, including Mantinea. There is no record of what role the Mantineans played, but at dusk their troops retreated in good order while the other Spartan allies were in disarray, so perhaps the Mantineans did not fight. The next day Athenians rounded up their enemies and slaughtered them—but not the Mantineans, who were deliberately allowed to steal away unmolested. Evidently they were not considered real enemies. (Five years later, Mantinea came over openly to the Athenian side.)[5]

*415 B.C.—ATHENS [D] AND DEMOCRATIC ALLIES VS. SYRACUSE [D/O?], CONTINUED IN *409 B.C.—ATHENS [N, D] VS. SYRACUSE [N, D]*

It is uncertain to what extent Syracuse was a democracy when the Athenians and their allies attacked it in in 415 B.C. It was most likely a mixed democratic-oligarchic regime and probably not perceived by the Athenians as a full democracy. Conditions in Syracuse seem to have been unstable; possibly the regime was newborn. (See chapter 2.)

After the Athenian invasion failed, the Syracusans revised their constitution to establish what was undoubtedly full democracy. Their enmity against Athens persisted and a small force continued to aid the Spartans in the Aegean, with some combat. In 409 B.C., following the removal of an oligarchic commander—the point at which the Syracusan squadron would have responded to the advent of democracy at home—about four hundred Athenians were killed by a mixed force which included Syracusans.[6]

*412 B.C.—ATHENS [D] VS. MILETUS [N? O?]

Miletus revolted against Athenian suzerainty and thereafter fought as a Spartan ally. The revolt probably resembled events at Chios, where the commoners panicked at the approach of a Spartan force and a combination of persuasion and threats brought the partially oligarchic government over to the Spartan side. Miletus retained some form of democratic government, but probably with only partial internal autonomy, the Spartan garrison keeping it in line.[7]

369 B.C.—ATHENS [D] VS. THEBES [D], BOTH WITH DEMOCRATIC ALLIES

In a war that primarily set Thebes and other democracies against oligarchic Sparta, democratic Athens was a Spartan ally but showed little taste for combat. The deaths in battles fought between democratic forces may have totaled under two hundred, and certainly were not much more. (See chapter 2.)

*431–355 B.C.—ATHENS [D] VS. VARIOUS STATES

In the following cases it would be possible to argue that democracies fought one another, but the evidence is far too limited to be certain. In every case a plausible argument, and often the preponderance of the slight evidence, refutes the existence of real war between well-established democracies.

In 431 B.C. there was skirmishing between Athens and Elis [D?] which was apparently some sort of democracy.[8] Elis was under Spartan constraint and switched sides when it could; there was probably little bloodshed.

In 426 B.C. Athens fought the Aetolians [A], hillsmen who had a voting assembly of warriors but were apparently organized largely along tribal, anocratic lines; see below.[9]

In 423 B.C. an assembly of Scione [D?] voted to war against Athens; the assembly may have been called only to rubber-stamp by acclamation an oligarchic decision, as happened in some undoubted oligarchies.[10] The fact that Athens blamed and later executed all the men of Scione tells us nothing, for Athens did the same with undoubted oligarchies. In some other cases, notably Amphipolis [D?], an assembly did not actually vote to make war against Athens, but only to surrender to Spartan forces that threatened to kill or enslave them. Of course it was understood that with a Spartan garrison overseeing local politics, the state would be on Sparta's side; one of the terms of surrender was that enemies of the Spartans would be allowed to flee.[11] Note how the Spartans did not attempt to overthrow the democracy at Acanthus [D] but were satisfied to persuade the people, with the aid of threats, to withdraw from Athenian alliance into neutrality.[12] In all these cases there was very likely serious popular animosity against Athens, but what matters is whether the management of foreign affairs lay in the hands of democrats or oligarchs. In none of these cities under Spartan control is it probable that democrats controlled of foreign relations.

In the 357–355 B.C. Social War, some historians have suggested that cities rebelling against Athens were democracies. An example cited is Rhodes [O?], but there is evidence that the Spartans had installed an oligarchy there in 391 B.C. The skimpy information for this period (there are no primary sources) contains no good evidence that any of Athens's opponents were democracies.[13]

In 354 B.C., during the Sacred War, Athens and other democracies were formally allied with the Phocians against Thebes [D] and other democracies. However, the only actual combat seems to have been between Thebans and mercenaries from Phocis [A?], most likely a tribal regime.[14]

*THIRD AND SECOND CENTURIES B.C.—AETOLIANS [A] VS. BOEOTIAN LEAGUE [D], ACARNANIAN LEAGUE [D], AND ACHAEAN LEAGUE [D]—SEVERAL WARS.

The Aetolian League was a confederation of "democratic" village communities, divided mainly along tribal lines. They fought minor wars against democratic coalitions, including the Thebans, Acarnanians, and Achaeans. There is no first-hand information about Aetolian politics, but their enemies saw the Aetolian regime as semi-barbarian, not comparable with true Greek republics. Conflict was typically instigated by the raids and piracy of anocratic freebooters (and also by nearby kings promoting trouble between their neighbors). Bands of hillsmen would gather under a renowned leader, heedless of whether the majority of Aetolians wanted peace, and descend on some unsuspecting countryside to pillage and haul off citizens into slavery.[15]

Between Oligarchic Republics: Medieval and Early Modern

With the exception of those listed below, there were no serious confrontations among the hundred or so autonomous republics in the region from Lithuania to the Low Countries, nor among the occasionally semi-autonomous city-republics of France and Spain.

*TWELFTH THROUGH THE FOURTEENTH CENTURIES— PERHAPS A DOZEN CASES IN ITALY (GENOA VS. PISA VS. FLORENCE VS. SIENA, ETC.) UP TO *VENICE VS. GENOA IN 1379; IN TUSCANY, THE LAST CASE WAS SIENA VS. PERUGIA IN 1358. ALL [A].

All the Italian proto-republics had anocratic political culture and governance until ca. 1350–1380; lacking centralized governmental authority, they cannot be called well-established republican states. Even so, in their countless wars the proto-republics usually aligned against autocrats rather than fighting one another. (See chapter 3.)

1431—FLORENCE [O] VS. SIENA [O]

Florence made a grab for Lucca in what historians have described as a war of naked territorial aggression; the Florentines justified their switch to enmity by pointing out that Lucca had just then fallen under the sway of a despot. Siena gave Lucca some aid to prevent Florence from gaining territory. There were raids in the countryside, but no deaths between the two republics.[16]

1443—ZURICH [A] VS. BERN [O] ET AL.

The Toggenburg War. Zurich lost its full republican character as the regime violently suppressed proponents of compromise, rejected the decision of neutral arbitrators, and declared the city loyal to the Habsburg emperor. Even so, the warfare was primarily between Zurich and democratic cantons, and later between Swiss and foreign aristocrats. Swiss town oligarchies joined the war reluctantly in opposition to the emperor; there were few if any deaths in combat between them and Zurich. (See chapters 6, 7, and 8.)

1447—VENICE [O] VS. MILAN [N, O] AND FLORENCE [O]

When the Visconti duke of Milan died, a group of idealists set up a shaky republic. The Milanese had been at war with Venice, but the republicans planned to model their constitution on Venice's and confidently expected to make peace with their sister republic. The Venetians declared that they had only made war on the duke, not on the people of Milan, and they would not only befriend the new republic but stand up "as free men for the freedom of others."[17]

However, outlying towns defined freedom their own way. Taking advantage of the confusion in Milan, Lodi and Piacenza expelled the aristocrats who had ruled them in the name of the Visconti. The rebel towns sought the protection of Venice, pledging obedience in foreign affairs if Venice would respect their internal republican laws and autonomy (Venice already allowed this freedom to the elites of most towns within its domains).[18] When the Milanese demanded that the city's former possessions be returned, the Venetians refused, claiming to defend republican ideals.

The Milanese put their military affairs in the hands of the formidable mercenary Francesco Sforza. He was already signor of several towns in his own right, and when he overcame Venetian forces and captured rebel towns it was only to keep them for himself. At this point the warfare was not directly between republican armies but between Venice and an autocratic adventurer.

When the Milanese continued to seek accord with Venice, the crafty Sforza turned and joined the Venetians to march against his former paymasters. When the Venetian militia joined Sforza in besieging Milan, there seemed a chance for real combat between armies of republics. There may have been a few skirmishes where Venetian and Milanese soldiers killed one another in small numbers.[19] But as related in chapter 3, Venice soon backed away from real combat.

Meanwhile, Florence entered the conflict as an ally of Milan (largely because of the influence of Cosimo de'Medici, who was halfway to being signor of Florence).

Venice and Florence were old territorial and commmercial rivals, but this was the most direct conflict that took place between the two regimes when both were approximately republics. The armies of republics did not meet; Florentine troops only skirmished with Venice's ally, the king of Naples.

*1494—FLORENCE [N, O] VS. PISA [N, D?] AND VENICE [O]

A revolution in Pisa set up a republic and ousted the city's Florentine proprietors. The sparse existing evidence suggests that the Pisan regime may have been democratic. Florentines felt that they had a right to rule Pisa in the way an oligarchy normally ruled subject towns in its countryside; they saw the war as a domestic conflict with a subject group, not initially recognized internationally as an independent state. The oligarchic republic of Florence was also newborn, having expelled its signor in the aftermath of Pisa's rebellion.

The well-established oligarchy in Venice, seeing a chance to take its competitor Florence down a notch, dispatched some mercenary troops to help Pisa. Venetian diplomatic missions and council meetings rang with speeches invoking republican ideals on behalf of Pisan liberty. There seem to have been too few combat deaths to call this a war between Florence and Venice (there was more serious combat involving troops of the French king Charles VII, whose promises to both sides did much to exacerbate the conflict).[20]

Florentine commoners and mercenaries proved reluctant to fight much, so combat deaths between Florence and Pisa in fifteen years of declared war probably added up to no more than several hundred, mostly in skirmishes among freebooting gangs rather than the combat of official armies. However, Pisa's blockade of Florence and Florence's siege of Pisa may have caused the deaths of thousands of civilians on both sides through starvation and attendant diseases. (See chapters 4 and 13.)

1499—SWABIAN CITIES [O/A] VS. SWISS CITIES [O]

The Swiss cities were well-established oligarchies. The status of the Swabian "Imperial Free Cities" was ambiguous, as the phrase itself reflects, but the emperor held final authority over the form of their constitutions and his say weighed heavily in decisions on foreign affairs. In the 1499 crisis Swabian cities formally reaffirmed their fealty to the emperor and left in his hands the negotiations with the Swiss that eventually led to war. During the war an officer from the Imperial Free City of Nuremberg caught the essence of the matter in a letter home: the noble lords, he said, "make war on the Swiss voluntarily, but we do so only in obedience to the emperor's commands."[21]

In fact, although oligarchic Swabian towns occasionally fought democratic peasants, most of the battles pitted Swiss democratic cantons and oligarchic towns against the imperial nobility. The knights got little help from the Swabian patricians, whose troops tended to flee at the first sounds of battle. Throughout this long, fierce, and chaotic war I have failed to discover a single instance of a Swabian oligarchic republic battling directly against a Swiss one. I would guess that there were well under two hundred deaths resulting from conflict between oligarchic quasi-republics, although many civilians perished as armies swarmed through the countryside.[22]

1529—SIENA [O] VS. FLORENCE [N, O]

When imperial and papal forces attacked the new republic of Florence and pressed Siena for aid, the Sienese complied. They dared not risk the wrath of such great powers for the sake of a city that only three years earlier, under the autocratic rule of a Medici pope, had warred ruthlessly to subjugate Siena. Even so, the Sienese helped Florence's attackers only grudgingly; once Florence became a republic the two turned from bitter enemies to near friends. There was some raiding in the countryside but no deaths.[23]

1531, *1656, *1712—LUCERNE [O] VS. BERN [O] ET AL.

The most undeniable case of battle between well-established republics of the same kind. While the warfare primarily set oligarchic against democratic states, as a side effect there was serious combat between Lucerne and Bern, both oligarchies. The 1531 war saw negligible combat between oligarchies. The 1656 fighting took place against the wishes of Bern's leaders, who had counted on Lucerne to stay neutral, but accidentally provoked an attack when they violated Lucerne's territory in their march against democratic peasants. The 1712 battle took place against the wishes of Lucerne's patrician leaders, who were compelled to fight only when the commoners rebelled and forced their hand.

Alongside the usual democratic-oligarchic split, the two sides were divided by religion. With the Catholic side standing for a tradition-bound and hierarchical authority over daily life, this was a political division in a broad sense of the term. Each side repressed fellow citizens of the other religion, and each sought foreign help even from autocracies; thus neither could see the other as a republican regime that tolerated their own political principles. (See chapter 6.)

*1576—POLAND [N, O/A] VS. DANZIG [O]

In 1576 a Polish army besieged the town of Danzig at a cost of several thousand lives. The war was seen by Polish leaders as a domestic conflict with a subject group not recognized internationally as an independent state, but functionally both states were independent oligarchic republics. Poland's regime was not well established, for in 1573 the last of its dynasty had died childless. An assembly of nobles determined that henceforth the "king" would be a sort of chief magistrate, elected for life but closely superintended by an oligarchic assembly. In 1575 an assembly elected the nobleman Stephen Báthory to the post, but a few days earlier another, equally official assembly had awarded the crown to the German emperor; each man now considered himself the rightful king. Danzig sided with the German emperor, if only because he did not come to claim his crown (although he meddled enough to keep enmities strong).

Danzig's patricians had managed to keep sovereigns at a distance when they raised claims against the town's liberties. Báthory took up this old monarchical quarrel once he had established his authority elsewhere in Poland. In the subsequent negotiations the king and his aristocratic entourage approached the Danzigers as lords to subjects, with peremptory demands for submission. Báthory was a skilled statesman, but his training as a nobleman drove him to grasp authority as by right. When some members of the Polish assembly questioned his actions he exploded, "I wish to rule and will not let anyone pick my nose!"

When leading Danzigers came to court to negotiate under a promise of safe-conduct, noblemen put the burghers under house arrest and refused to deal with them. The Polish assembly pressed for compromise, but it was too disorganized at this point to block the king. Eventually he went to war.[24]

*1652—ENGLAND [N, A] VS. THE NETHERLANDS [N, O]
The first Anglo-Dutch War. England was a quite new quasi-republic (three years old), governed by a "rump" clique legitimized only by military force. The leaders avoided elections even among the oligarchic elite and violently repressed political opponents; their diplomacy was equally arrogant and abrasive. The Netherlands was a newly restored republic, having narrowly escaped monarchical rule two years earlier, and its leaders had to tread warily under threat of an autocratic coup. Conservative Dutch patricians looked askance at the English as lawless regicides, and supported exiled English monarchists who (along with the French monarchy) worked deliberately to set the two nations against one another. The English leaders became convinced that the Netherlands was under the control of monarchists, especially as the Dutch rejected pleas to form a republican federation. (See chapter 9.)

Between Democracies: Medieval and Early Modern

Wars between a democracy and an oligarchic republic included the Swiss conflicts and possibly the Florence-Pisa case noted above, and the conflict of 1625 between the Zaporozhian Cossacks and Poland (see chapter 6). There were no military confrontations among the short-lived quasi-democracies in Flanders (see chapter 1). For the six to nine "Forest Cantons" in Switzerland, there exists a single case:

1490—APPENZELL [D] VS. SCHWYZ [D] ET AL.
A brief armed demonstration with no deaths. (See chapter 1.)

Between Oligarchic Republics: Modern

*1775—UNITED STATES [N, D] VS. BRITAIN [A]
The colonists had believed that King George III was misled by evil parliamentary ministers and petitioned him to redress their wrongs, believing he was the final arbiter of British policy. So he was, in matters such as the appointment of colonial officials and the power to declare war. Authority in Britain flowed down from the monarchy in a hierarchical system (see chapter 8). Gradually Americans came to recognize that the

king was even more obstinate than his ministers in demanding that disobedient underlings be taught a lesson by force.[25]

In 1775 America was more democratic than it would be for generations to come. Delegations at the Continental Congress had been elected in meetings where often even the poorest man had had a voice. Everywhere people had broken their bond with the Crown and publicly sworn allegiance to the people as a whole—enacting the republican origin-myth of a citizen body creating itself by mutual oaths.[26]

The war was seen in Britain as a domestic conflict with a subject group, not initially recognized internationally as an independent state. British leaders felt the problem was a conspiracy of a few wicked radicals who misled loyal subjects. The Americans had their own conspiracy theory of an aristocratic plot to enslave all Englishmen. Historians now believe that if leaders on each side in 1775 had not grossly misperceived the other side they might have avoided war. The misperceptions, however, resulted from a genuine contrast between political cultures—one based on egalitarian and the other on hierarchical principles.[27]

1797—UNITED STATES [D/O] VS. FRANCE [N, A]

The Quasi-War. Presidents George Washington and John Adams were notoriously hostile to the French Revolution, and some of the envoys they sent to Paris sympathized with the monarchy (one ambassador even gave active help to French monarchists). French leaders came to feel that the entire American government was in the hands of monarchists hostile to republican ideals. Around the same time, French envoys to the United States behaved like combinations of secret agents and rabble-rousers. Outraged American conservatives came to feel that the French government was in the hands of democratic fanatics who meant to overturn the social order everywhere.[28]

A chance for reconciliation came in 1795, when France adopted a government resembling an oligarchic republic, with a legislature elected by some tens of thousands of wealthy Frenchmen. The deputies in turn selected an executive directory.[29] The American regime could, with some stretching, also be called an oligarchy, using the term in a much broader sense; since the Revolution voting had been increasingly confined to people with property, and the Federalists who dominated the government tended to see the "mob" as an enemy.

France's constitutional structure was not admired in the United States, however, for it was not matched by a republican political culture. A faction would extinguish its rivals only to go in turn to the guillotine. When elections put into power conservatives who sought a gradual return to monarchy (and who also wanted a less belligerent policy abroad), three of the five directors called in troops to throw the two moderate directors in prison, then closed down opposition newspapers and condemned hundreds of opponents to exile or death.

The directors reacted with similar violence when the United States signed a treaty with Britain, which they called "the equivalent of an alliance with our cruelest enemy." They believed that the conservative Federalist government was an aristocratic clique, a "British party" alienated from the American people. The directors authorized privateering in hopes that attacks on American ships would prompt the United States to elect Republicans friendly to France.[30]

When the United States sent envoys to Paris, their chances for making a settlement were slight, as one historian remarked, "in that catacomb of traffickers, warlords and bravoes." The French foreign minister sent anonymous gentlemen (Messrs. X, Y, and Z) to issue threats and demand enormous sums of money for his government and himself personally. Such bribes were a routine part of the old princely diplomacy, but the Americans refused with disgust. When the events were made public in the United States, Federalists eager to discredit their domestic democratic enemies stirred up outrage over the "XYZ Affair." Most Americans took the fiasco as proof that the directors were as mired in arrogance and corruption as any decadent monarchy.[31]

There were more direct reasons for the fighting at sea, ranging from greed for booty to deliberate British policy (a case of an outside autocracy seeking to promote enmity between republics). Yet battle mostly was avoided, and combat deaths added up to only a few dozen.[32] (See also chapter 9.)

*1812—UNITED STATES [D/O] VS. BRITAIN [O/A]

Britain might have been called a new oligarchic quasi-republic after King George III sank into hopeless insanity and the prince regent failed to exert his will in governance. But the prince regent retained the final word on ministers and war, while his regime retained a hierarchical and partly authoritarian political culture, suppressing widespread popular discontent with armed force. The franchise in the United States was becoming increasingly democratic, and the party controlling the government did not see those still disenfranchised as a serious domestic enemy class. The leaders on each side saw the conflict as part of a fateful world struggle between regimes that stood for fundamentally opposed principles, democratic against hierarchical. (See chapters 8 and 11.)

1828—STATE OF GEORGIA [O] VS. CHEROKEE NATION [N, O/A]

The Cherokee Removal. The Cherokees had settled down in farming communities and in 1827 created a republican constitution. Their political culture was mixed, for many traditionalists retained a tribal perspective and had no respect for majority votes. The constitutional regime was controlled by a narrow oligarchy of educated men who had adopted European customs, including slaveholding.[33]

The state of Georgia was likewise an oligarchy of slaveholders, but never accepted the Cherokees as equals. While the Cherokees regarded themselves as a sovereign nation, white Georgians saw them as only a tribe of unruly wards within the state of Georgia. In 1828 Georgia decreed the newborn government dissolved. Whites aimed to appropriate the Cherokees' fertile soil, and their greed redoubled when gold was discovered. Men drifted into the territory to seize land, backed up by state troops. When the Cherokees appealed to the federal government for protection, President Andrew Jackson turned them away. The old Indian fighter held that the Cherokees were "savages" incapable of republican government, doomed to wither away unless they moved far from the more vigorous white race.

In their intolerable situation some Cherokees decided their nation must accept the inevitable and remove to the West. The leaders of the Cherokee government drove this faction out of the national council and excluded their views from the nation's one newspaper. Men who argued for removal were threatened, beaten, even murdered. Meanwhile, troops from Georgia prevented the Cherokees from holding elections. When the leaders announced that they would remain in their offices, the removal faction was able to plausibly denounce the regime as an aristocratic clique illegally clinging to power. A handful of the dissidents signed a treaty with the United States to allow removal westward, claiming that they had the support of the majority of Cherokees.[34]

The factional chaos among Cherokees helped convince whites that this was a "tribal" group which could only be managed by force. The disorder also defeated attempts to negotiate conditions for an orderly migration. In 1838 white soldiers roused over ten thousand Cherokee women and men and children from their cabins at gunpoint, herding them like cattle onto the roads where perhaps one in five died from starvation and disease. (See also chapter 13.)

*1879—CHILE [O/A] VS. PERU [O/A]

The War of the Pacific. It was begun by the dictator of Bolivia, but Peru had a secret treaty of alliance with him, which the Chileans felt gave them reason to attack Peru also. Peru and to a considerable extent Chile had a combination of anocratic and authoritarian political culture and governance, although in formal structures both were oligarchic republics. (See chapter 4.)

*1881—BRITAIN [D/O] VS. BOERS [N, A]

The Britain of the 1870s could perhaps be classed as an oligarchy, although one with an increasingly democratic franchise. The British looked down on the Boers of South Africa as backward slave drivers, and British humanitarian societies pressed their government to protect the blacks. Meanwhile, the frontier region of the Transvaal had only an insolvent and ineffectual shadow of government, beset with factional feuding (see chapter 4). Such disorder seemed hazardous on the flank of Britain's strategic Capetown colony. In 1877 a British commissioner rode into the Transvaal to propose that the region become a colony of Great Britain. The English-speaking merchants in the ramshackle villages cheered him on, joined by a few Boers who hoped British redcoats would help them conquer native tribes. Most Boers, demoralized by the prevailing anarchy, stood glumly aside as the Union Jack was raised.

Once the Boers recovered from their surprise, an overwhelming majority of them signed a petition demanding independence. When Boer leaders came to London to negotiate, the government met them with the sort of condescending dismissal that a banker might give an ignorant farmer who asks to revise his mortgage.

British liberals found all this unsavory, and their leader, William Gladstone, made Boer liberty an issue in the election of 1880. Gladstone won the election, but he hesitated to let the Transvaal go. British agents in Africa claimed that the Boers were becoming reconciled to the orderly and benevolent British administration. Gladstone thought he might eventually negotiate some sort of local self-government for the Boers, perhaps in a republican confederation with other South African colonies. Meanwhile, his government ignored the remote Transvaal.

Assembling in a mass meeting, the Boers elected a triumvirate of military chiefs—more of a tribal regime than a republican state—and moved to eject the British. The British military leader on the scene, Major General George Colley, was contemptuous of what he took to be disorganized farm boys; he dismissed every Boer attempt to negotiate as a mere ruse and marched against them. Given a direct order from his government to open negotiations, Colley set the Boers impossible conditions, attacked yet again, and was shot dead along with many of his soldiers. The deaths in these unnecessary skirmishes totalled several hundred.[35]

*1899—BRITAIN [D] VS. BOER REPUBLICS [O]

Although Britain still denied the vote to a large minority of poor, it had no crucial internal enemy class and now functioned largely as a democracy. The Boers denied civil rights to the majority of blacks and also (in the Republic of South Africa) to the numerous white immigrants. It was the combination of these repressions that made war inescapable once British politicians mobilized their public against the Boer regime by portraying it as a heinous race "oligarchy." (See chapter 7.)

*1899—UNITED STATES [D] VS. PHILIPPINE REPUBLIC [N, O/A]

Corrupt city wards in the United States effectively denied the vote to most blacks and many immigrants, but it was still a democracy by our inclusive definition. When the United States conquered the Philippines during the Spanish-American War a group of Filipinos attempted to set up a republic. Their constitution, hastily adopted at a convention in 1899, was explicitly oligarchical, giving power to a small elite of professionals and landowners.

The political culture of this elite relied on factional and personal loyalties. The shaky new regime awarded temporary dictatorial power to Emilio Aguinaldo, who had scant experience in republican politics, having risen in the murderously conspiratorial world of a secret society fighting for independence from Spain. When Aguinaldo's two chief rivals for power were killed, many fingers pointed to him as the man responsible. Nearly all foreign observers, following what they heard from Aguinaldo's numerous enemies among upper-class Filipinos, saw no chance for genuine self-government, but only regional factions and bandit groups.[36]

President William McKinley thought it would be immoral for the United States to withdraw and leave the Filipinos to fight one another endlessly. Besides, amid such turmoil the islands could fall prey to Germany or Japan. McKinley gave the military commanders on the scene a free hand to attack the Filipinos. (See also chapter 12.)

1968—SOVIET UNION [O/A] VS. CZECHOSLOVAKIA [N, O]
Both countries had a largely authoritarian political culture, but actual governance was in the hands of oligarchic elites who no longer used violence against their peers. The Soviet Union's elite comprised a couple of dozen Politburo members; Czechoslovakia was becoming a quasi-republic where the oligarchic class of voters would soon comprise all Communist Party members. Soviet leaders, relying for information on authoritarian enemies of the reformers, believed that Czechoslovakia was falling into full-scale democracy. This they could never accept, and they resorted to armed invasion. There were about a hundred civilian deaths but no combat between organized forces. (See chapter 7.)

1986—QATAR [O/A] VS. BAHREIN [O/A]
Both countries might be called oligarchies with autocratic tendencies (see chapter 4). They mobilized their armed forces to dispute an island—actually a reef awash at high tide—which demarcated a valuable zone in the gulf. After a few shots were fired, Saudi Arabia pressed the countries to negotiate with mediation. In one of the most ingenious ways statesmen have ever found to satisfy honor without war, both sides agreed to demolish the reef.[37]

Note: As terms are defined in the text, the later Anglo-Dutch wars, the wars of revolutionary France against Britain, and other such conflicts set quasi-republics against quasi-monarchies; numerous wars involving tribal "democracies" set anocratic regimes against republics. The 1861 conflict between the United States [D] and Britain [O] (Trent affair, see chapter 12) set a democracy against an oligarchy. Other diplomatic confrontations, such as the 1846 Oregon border crisis which pitted the United States [O] against Britain [O] (see chapter 12) and the 1956 conflict between Poland [O/A] and the Soviet Union [O/A] (see chapter 7), had inconsequential military activity.

Between Democracies: Modern

1847—ZURICH [N, D], BERN, ET AL. VS. LUCERNE [D/O] ET AL.
The Sonderbund War. The Protestant Swiss cities, transformed by industrial growth and political upheavals, had inaugurated democratic constitutions. In Zurich, which would take the lead in the conflict, a victory by liberals in 1845 brought equal political rights to all. Meanwhile, the Catholic Forest States had turned in upon themselves over the centuries, restricting citizenship to men descended from the original inhabitants. Dominated by their priests and a few old families, in effect they were now almost patrician oligarchies.

In the leading Catholic state, Lucerne, revolutionary change had brought political rights to a majority of the male population. But the fairly new regime (six years old) still denied the vote to non-Catholics. The disenfranchised Protestants and liberal freethinkers were an important minority; they were the most powerful economic and political group within the city itself. They attempted a rebellion, but were handily defeated. Liberal leaders were thrown into prison while others fled what they called a Catholic "reign of terror."

The division was partly the result of traditional religious animosity, but it was also political. Liberals in the bustling commercial regions wanted a strong central government to impose reforms on behalf of social equality. The peasant majorities in Lucerne and the Forest States wanted minimal government, asking only to be left alone under the guidance of their priests and their immemorial customs, ratified by community consensus. To liberal townsmen, however, the Catholic Church and its obedient followers loomed as the great adversary of the democratic spirit. Then Lucerne announced that it would put its educational system into the hands of the Jesuit Order—which democrats feared as a band of conspirators dedicated to imposing authoritarian rule everywhere. Swiss liberals now saw Lucerne not as a republic but as a regime under the thumb of that foreign autocrat, the pope.[38]

Exiles from Lucerne stirred anti-clerical sentiments in the Protestant towns, which turned a blind eye when a private expedition of volunteers marched on Lucerne to "liberate" it. A hundred men died, but the uprising they counted on did not materialize. The raid was the last straw for the traditionalist Catholic states. They formed a defensive military alliance, pointedly called the Separate League (*Sonderbund*). It was a disturbing departure from traditional republican solidarity. A majority of the council of the Swiss Confederation voted that the Sonderbund must be dissolved, and when the Catholics refused to comply, the others felt sure they were not true republicans.

The distrust intensified when the Sonderbund turned for aid to foreign Catholic powers (even the Habsburgs, ever ready to encourage discord among republics). This alliance with autocracy was the last straw for the liberals, who mobilized troops to settle the question of constitutional authority and religious freedom once and for all. The ostensible issue was federalism versus individual state rights, but most historians believe the constitutional dispute turned violent because the political cultures of the two sides were incompatible.

Despite the antagonisms, the maneuvering of large armies produced barely a hundred deaths. (See chapter 2.)

*1849—FRANCE [N, D/A] VS. ROMAN REPUBLIC [N, D]
The only outright modern war between definite, if transient, democracies. The French, particularly the nation's new leadership, had a largely autocratic political culture mixed with oligarchic elements, and the regime increasingly suppressed democrats by force. French leaders saw the Roman Republic as a chaotic regime controlled by radical gangsters; it was not recognized internationally as an independent state. The French assembly was persuaded to send troops to save Rome from supposed anarchy,

and still more from the repressive rule that would be imposed by the papal and Austrian armies that were marching on the city. Actually, Rome was controlled by revolutionary idealists who were even less accustomed than the French to compromise. (See chapter 9.)

*1861 — UNITED STATES [D] VS. CONFEDERACY [N, O]

The American Civil War. The Confederacy was newborn. Its constituent states were older, but they had become one-party regimes in which opposition to the central political principle of slaveholding was met with force. Preoccupied with the suppression of blacks and Abolitionists, the regime was fundamentally oligarchic. Northern democrats saw the Southern leadership as an oligarchic or aristocratic "slaveocracy" that refused to accept majority rule within the Union and denied civil rights even to white liberals. The conflict was seen by the United States as a domestic conflict with "rebels" not recognized internationally as an independent state. (See chapter 7.)

1897 — FRANCE [D] VS. BRITAIN [D]

The bloodless Niger and Fashoda crises. The first was a contest for colonial territory along the Niger River. Detachments of French and British soldiers, acting largely on their own initiative, ran up their national flags over lonely outposts and came close to shooting at one another. Meanwhile, belligerent men in London and Paris spoke of defending the national honor and warned that war might come. It took strenuous diplomacy to settle the complex problem of drawing frontiers.[39]

This pattern was repeated the following year over possession of Fashoda on the upper Nile. The incident was planned by authoritarian and imperialist groups in France, partly stimulated by the territorial designs of the despotic King Léopold of Belgium.[40] Just then the French democratic government came under intense pressure from authoritarian factions as part of the domestic Dreyfus Crisis. British leaders, fearing a military junta might take control of Paris and turn to war, mobilized their navy as a precaution. There was vehement talk of war in circles where the political culture was more imperialist than democratic, but most people recognized that serious combat was unlikely. (See chapter 13.)

*1898 — UNITED STATES [D] VS. SPAIN [O/A]

Spain nominally had a democratic constitutional structure, but was actually controlled by an oligarchic and aristocratic elite under a monarchy that retained important powers. Its colony of Cuba was especially repressed and exploited. When the U.S. government demanded independence for Cuba, the Spanish leaders did not dare yield peacefully for fear of provoking a military coup that would destroy the dynasty. (See chapters 8 and 12.)

*1914 — BRITAIN, FRANCE, ET AL. [D] VS. GERMANY [A]

A case cited by several critics of the proposition that democracies do not war on one another, who thereby display either their ignorance of modern history, or a willful indifference to the explicit meaning of this proposition. Germany had autocratic governance in military and foreign affairs. At the time the war began the chancellor had bypassed the Parliament to govern by decree and was answerable only to the kaiser. (See chapters 8 and 11.)

*1919—IRISH REPUBLIC [N, A] VS. BRITAIN [D];
*1922—IRISH CIVIL WAR [N, A]

Irish representatives to the British Parliament were chosen in free democratic elections, but the English always outvoted them over "home rule." In elections after the First World War the traditional Irish politicians were replaced almost everywhere in Catholic Ireland by men who rejected the hope of winning autonomy through London politics. They gathered in Dublin to organize an independent Irish Parliament. This self-declared government set out to collect funds from citizens, establish its own courts of law and take control of local administration. Many Irish gave their allegiance; British tax collectors, police, and local officials were boycotted and harassed, their orders ignored, their records burned. In many provinces administration broke down, while in some the new Irish government established its own control. The British responded by driving the Irish leaders underground, making sure they could govern only partially and intermittently.

This remarkable experiment in nonviolent transfer of power was further undercut by many young Irishmen who were steeped in a romantic and undemocratic tradition of lawless violence. Bands began raiding on their own initiative. Harsh British overreaction led to a vicious circle of reprisals, until Ireland was virtually at war. Irish guerrilla bands, fragmented by secrecy and frequently out of touch with higher authorities, acted independently and sometimes in direct defiance of their own national leadership. In 1921 the president of the Irish government-in-hiding officially claimed responsibility for the actions of this "republican army," but in actuality the elected leaders were being dragged along in the wake of belligerent local chiefs. The newborn Irish regime was closer to anocracy than a territorial state (see chapter 3). The conflict was seen by British leaders as a domestic conflict with a group not recognized internationally as an independent state—indeed against no government at all, but a "murder gang." There were over a thousand "combat" deaths, but they came chiefly in raids and ambushes involving police and guerrillas rather than organized soldiery.

The undemocratic nature of the Irish guerrillas became plain when Britain finally negotiated an accommodation and the treaty was endorsed in 1922 by the Irish Parliament and electorate. Many of the fighting bands despised "politicians," had no respect for the national constitution, and scorned to submit to the decision of the majority. Declaring that any compromise with the British enemy was treason, they struggled to overthrow Ireland's new government.[41] (See chapter 7.)

1923—FRANCE [D] VS. GERMANY [D]

The Occupation of the Ruhr, an armed invasion without combat. Germany was a fairly new democracy (four years) which retained a partly authoritarian and partly oligarchic political culture. These attitudes dominated its effective diplomacy. The occupation produced a few accidental deaths and widespread civilian poverty and malnutrition. (See chapter 10.)

1941—BRITAIN [D] VS. FINLAND [D/A]

Finland had joined Nazi Germany in attacking the Soviet Union, in hopes of winning back territory lost to the Soviets two years earlier. Meanwhile, Britain was allied with the Soviets against Germany. Joseph Stalin (a dictator making trouble between republics) insisted that Britain declare war on Finland, calling it a test of the alliance. Eventually Britain obliged him.[42]

Both sides had put democracy in abeyance for the duration of the war. In Britain, elections were postponed and Winston Churchill held broad authority over foreign affairs. Such concentration of power is common in wartime republics, and does not necessarily mean that the leadership has rejected democratic ways. In Finland, however, the coalition in power was so authoritarian in spirit that many members admired the Nazis. The wartime government not only postponed elections, but arrested the chief spokesmen for the opposition party, condemning them to prison in a secret and scarcely legal trial. The tiny clique of leaders, such as the foreign minister and the army's Marshal Karl Mannerheim, had little experience in international relations and held politicians in contempt; they did not always consult the Parliament nor even the entire Cabinet. Already in 1940 it was a few such men acting on their own who had secretly given entry to the German army, committing Finland to war in violation of its constitution.

Churchill let the Finns know that he could avoid a declaration of war if Finland would only halt its troops when they reached its old frontier. The imprisoned opposition leaders and a large section of the Finnish public, had they been consulted, would have endorsed such moderation. The Finns, in fact, did not advance much beyond the old frontier, but they failed to make their intentions clear. American attempts to mediate were irritably brushed aside; the foreign minister was evasive and even flippant; Marshal Mannerheim was opaque. In short, this unique declaration of war by one established modern democracy against another could have been prevented if only Finland's leaders had understood how to bargain with their foreign counterparts, and with their own political colleagues, using the frank discussion and accommodation appropriate between equals.

Britain sent bombers to impede mining in northern Finland, but operations there were under German control and the British were not attacking Finns. On their side, most Finns did not consider Britain a "real" enemy. The formal declaration of war meant nothing but some financial restrictions and the seizure of shipping.[43]

*1948—ISRAEL [N, D/A] VS. LEBANON [O/A];
1948—ISRAEL [N, D/A] VS. BRITAIN [D]

Lebanon sent a small contingent to aid the Arab armies that invaded Palestine as the British pulled out. The fighting on this front killed 129 Israelis and probably at least as many Lebanese. The Lebanese government had been a reluctant participant, and in subsequent wars it joined in a still more desultory fashion, if at all. In all cases the trouble began in a conflict between Israel and autocratic regimes such as Egypt.

The Lebanese regime was barely established (four years old) as a formal republic. In actuality, the 1947 Lebanese elections had been fraudulent, giving a veneer of legality to an old coalition of oligarchic elites whose chiefs had struck a secret pact to divide government power. Jews were not cut into the deal; in fighting Israel the Lebanese leaders were not attacking people they had ever seen as equals. Most Lebanese gave their primary loyalty not to the nation as a whole but to clans or factions, which at times attacked one another in vendettas or full-scale clan wars; in short, this was a mixed oligarchic and anocratic regime.[44]

Great Britain was officially neutral, and the government in London never defined a clear policy, but it gave the Arabs armaments and other material support. On the scene, British officers stuck by the Arab Legion they had trained, and some took part in serious fighting on their own initiative (other British officers helped the Israelis).

Israel had become an independent state at the very hour the war began, and had not yet held a general election nor otherwise established republican credentials. Its government was a provisional coalition, which Britain did not recognize as an independent state. British leaders saw the leadership, with good reason, as descended from secret terrorist factions which had been battling the British army for years. There was a single incident of direct combat, when Israel shot down five Royal Air Force Spitfires on a reconnaissance mission.[45]

1954—UNITED STATES [D] VS. GUATEMALA [D/A]

The U.S. Central Intelligence Agency secretly promoted the overthrow of Guatemala's democratically elected government. The U.S. government was convinced that the regime was falling under Communist dictatorship, but actually Guatemala's political culture was largely dominated by anocratic factions. As economic and political pressure from the United States grew intolerable, the goverment resorted to authoritarian repression. The only combat was among Guatemalans, causing probably under a hundred combat deaths plus some civilian deaths. (See chapter 13. For the similar but bloodless 1953 conflict between Britain and British Guiana see n. 3 of that chapter.)

1964—TURKEY [D/A] VS. GREEK CYPRIOTES [A];

*1974—TURKEY [N, D/A] VS. GREEK CYPRIOTES [N, A]

In 1959 Britain, Greece, and Turkey imposed on Cyprus an intricate and misconceived democratic constitution. The lion's share of representation was awarded to Greek Cypriots, who made up four-fifths of the population. To safeguard the minority of Turkish Cypriots there was a fantastically elaborate system of designated representation and vetoes. All representatives were to be elected separately by Greeks or by Turks although the two peoples intermingled all across the island. This gave leaders little reason to build coalitions across ethnic borders by appealing to economic and social issues; they could establish themselves most readily with postures of ethnic chauvinism.[46]

Only experienced leaders dedicated to the arts of compromise could have sustained the system, and the politicians of Cyprus were rank amateurs. The Turkish Cypriot leaders found no way to protect their position except by bringing government to a standstill with their veto power. Many Greek Cypriots were still more inclined to sabotage the regime, and secret Greek militias kidnapped and assassinated not only their Turkish compatriots but also fellow Greeks who did not share their extreme views.[47]

The president of Cyprus, Makarios III, had been chosen in a free election, but he had previously been, and remained, the leader of the Greek community and archbishop of Cyprus. Many still gave him the old Ottoman Empire title of "ethnarch." Makarios retained the ecclesiastical and imperial trappings that went with his titles, holding up a scepter, presenting his hand to Greek politicians to be kissed in token of submission. Affecting to stand above politics, the archbishop ruled Cyprus, as one historian put it, "as an abbot rules his monastery."[48]

The ethnarch-archbishop-president in his black robes stood for Greek power, and Turks felt increasingly alienated from his government. Dissension exploded when Makarios insisted that the constitution be amended to remove safeguards for the minority in order to allow true "democratic majority rule." Turkish Cypriots began to withdraw fearfully into enclaves, barricading their villages off from Greek Cypriot areas. By 1964 there was a shooting war of sorts among semi-anocratic militias.

While Turkey at this point had a full democratic apparatus, barely three years had passed since the country had been under military rule, and officers still dominated. The premier himself was a stern old general who had ruled as a dictator in the 1940s. He and his colleagues were warriors who saw international affairs as a battlefield where power and will counted more than justice and trust. They resolved to come to the aid of their fellow Turks, and fighter-bombers swooped across Greek Cypriot military positions, killing scores of soldiers and civilians.[49]

More serious bloodshed came in 1974. Turkey's democracy was not quite a year old, for military officers had taken over in 1971, then after two years had given back power (or most of it) to an elected government. The new premier was an idealistic civilian, but officers were watching over his shoulder and a coup would certainly restore military rule if the regime failed to stand up to the Greeks.

Meanwhile, the Greek Cypriot government had fallen to a bloody coup that drove Makarios into exile. In this turmoil Turkey saw an opportunity and invaded, meaning to settle affairs as it wished. The invasion brought down the gang that had seized control of Greek Cyprus. In formal terms the old democratic constitution was restored, but its legality was threadbare and men from the militias retained a virtual veto. Negotiations failed and the Turkish troops advanced, bringing a few hundred combat deaths and substantially more among civilians.[50]

1972, 1975—BRITAIN [D] VS. ICELAND [D]
The Codfish War. A dispute between two well-established democracies over fishing rights. Warning shots were fired and there were a few accidental casualties, but actual war was never contemplated. (See chapter 12.)

1981—PERU [N, D/A] VS. ECUADOR [N, D/A]
Both democracies were new (one and three years old), with largely anocratic/author-
itarian political cultures. Border clashes produced perhaps close to two hundred
deaths.[51] (See chapter 4.)

1991—YUGOSLAVIA (SERBIA) [N, D/A] VS. SLOVENIA [N, D];
*1991—YUGOSLAVIA (SERBIA) [N, D/A] VS. CROATIA
[N, D/A]
At the start of the conflict the rump "Yugoslav" government was barely a year old and
verged on autocracy, with anocratic elements taking control in various borderlands.
Yet the outbreak of savagery perplexed everyone. Outsiders might speak solemnly of
"ancient ethnic hatreds," but in fact, antagonism between Greek Orthodox Serbs and
Roman Catholic Croats had not been severe until the 1920s, and serious bloodshed
had only begun during the Second World War. Nazi invaders had raised up a marginal
Croat Fascist group into a puppet regime which massacred Serbs in horrible atrocities,
and Serb partisans had struck back in kind. But peace had been restored, and the next
generation of Serbs and Croats mingled, as for centuries past, with no more quarreling than most neighbors. Fears of violence lingered chiefly in the mountainous hinterlands, where human relationships had been built, since time out of mind, on blood
kinship and savage vendettas.[52]

The latent enmity was a legacy of authoritarian governments. The Ottoman and
Habsburg empires, German Nazis, and Yugoslavia's own prewar monarchy and postwar dictatorship had all exploited the religious distinction between Serbs and Croats
as a divide-and-rule tactic, using one people to repress the other. In the 1980s, when
Serbs thought of Croats they could not forget the monstrous wartime Fascist regime.
When Croats thought of Serbs they remembered the officials and police, dispropor-
tionately Serbs, who had bossed them around through decades of Communist repression. These resentments had not been reconciled, for each regime in turn had
forbidden any frank political discussion or free negotiation of differences. Few social
connections had survived except the most narrow and clannish.

In 1990 free elections were held in Yugoslavia for the first time in more than sixty
years. The public had not learned how to choose wisely in such an election, nor had
politicians learned how to compete democratically. The needs of Yugoslavia as a whole
could not overshadow regional rivalries, for elections were held separately in each
province, not across the entire country. Most provinces were mainly Serb, mainly
Croat, or mainly some other ethnic group. Would-be leaders found that the easiest
way to mobilize support within their province was by appealing to ethnic solidarity—
the only form of solidarity that the Communist regime had not pulverized.[53]

That was how Slobodan Milošević became president of Serbia, the dominant
province of Yugoslavia. A master of the strong-arm tactics of the old Communist bureaucracy, Milošević had put his followers in charge in a number of regions, backed
by crowds of Serbs that he raised to a frenzy with speeches portraying them as the vic-

tims of other ethnic groups. Milošević's election in the Serb provinces was assured by his control of the unmatched organizational and financial resources of the Communist Party, above all its control of Serbian television and other major media. Milošević was elected and ruled in a style, as one journalist put it, "reminiscent of a Latin American caudillo."[54]

A massive protest demonstration in Belgrade was suppressed with bloodshed, but Milošević's opponents would not be silenced, and he was hard-pressed. He mobilized troops by claiming that Serbia's vital interests were threatened from across its borders. Most outside observers agreed that Milošević was deliberately inflaming ethnic prejudices to pressure Serbs to unite under his personal rule. Visitors were astonished to see how easily irrational hatreds spread as soon as political leaders with control over key media switched from suppressing ethnic antagonism to inciting it. With television spewing out fake pictures and barefaced lies about atrocities, even urbane Serb intellectuals insisted that their nation was mortally threatened by bestial enemies.

A parallel process worked in Croatia. When the regime transformed itself through naive democratic elections, nearly dictatorial power settled upon Franjo Tudjman, a sometime Communist general and intense Croatian nationalist. The new president fought to suppress any criticism of his government, which he saw as rank disloyalty. Tudjman did not seem so much anti-democratic as wholly oblivious to democratic ways.[55]

The Serbs who lived within Croatia had always been wary of Croats and desired some degree of independence. Now, aroused by Tudjman's favoritism of Croats and by Milošević's rabid rhetoric, the intermingled Croat and Serb communities began to move apart in mutual fear. As rumors spread that massacres were being plotted, irregular militias organized themselves around local strongmen, while citizens who argued for an accommodation were coerced into silence or murdered.

Of the bellicose factions, by far the most powerful was the officer corps of the Yugoslav Army, a closed little society steeped in authoritarian ways and openly hostile to democracy. There had always been a preponderance of Serb officers, and by mid 1991 most of the others had walked out or been purged. If the federation could not be held together, the officers wanted the fragments to be dominated by a strong Serbia, and they struck a deal of mutual support with Milošević. The generals began to smuggle arms into the remote mountain valleys of Croatia, where self-appointed Serb leaders were setting up their own independent quasi-state. Tudjman and Milošević tried to meet to negotiate a settlement, but the talks were a farce of animosity, inflexibility, and walkouts; each of the pair seemed temperamentally incapable of working out a compromise. Finally, the Yugoslav (actually Serbian) army invaded Croatia outright, bringing deaths, especially among civilians, by the thousands.[56]

Meanwhile, similar fears had led the somewhat more democratic (but also newborn) regime of Slovenia to agitate for its own independence. Yugoslav generals, largely on their own initiative, sent troops to prevent Slovenian secession, expecting a bloodless police action, but militias opposed them. In this case the Serbs were reluctant to fight, and two weeks of skirmishing cost fewer than seventy combat deaths.[57] The Yugoslav regime headed by Milošević saw both fights as a domestic conflict with rebel groups not initially recognized internationally as independent states.

*1994—NORTH YEMEN [N, D/A] VS. SOUTH YEMEN [N, A]

In 1990 the two Yemens formally merged into one nation and planned a democratic regime. But authoritarian leaders dominated politics, personal violence was endemic, and traditional tribal loyalties remained so strong that the army was never integrated. The neighboring Saudi monarchy, worried about a democratic neighbor, took steps to weaken the regime.

In 1993 Yemenis voted in the first free democratic elections ever held on the Arabian Peninsula. Parties under the former leaders of North and South Yemen each won a majority in their own region. But overall the Marxist Southern party was outvoted, and they feared their conservative rivals would now try to crush them. Their leader withdrew and set up a separate government in his former capital. The Northern leader—a military man supported chiefly by his clan—decided to take control by force, probably against the wishes of most Yemenis. The war was seen by the North as a domestic conflict with a Communist group not recognized internationally as an independent state. Chiefly, however, the battles were a resurgence of anocratic tribal rivalries.[58]

Note: Other diplomatic confrontations between democracies had inconsequential military activity, including the United States vs. Britain in 1895 (Venezuela border crisis, see chapter 12), Greece vs. Turkey in 1976 (Aegean crisis, see chapter 12 n. 33) and covert aggression such as the United States vs. Chile in 1973 (see chapter 13). The 1940 military occupation that pitted Britain against Iceland (see chapter 12) was scarcely a hostile confrontation.

Notes

CHAPTER ONE
Investigating the Puzzle of Democratic Peace

1. David Binder, "Dubrovnik Diary," *New York Times,* 16 Nov. 1991, sec. 1; Misha Glenny, *The Fall of Yugoslavia: The Third Balkan War* (London: Penguin, 1992), pp. 135–137. See appendix.

2. For contemporary affairs see the *New York Times Index;* compare Nicaragua and Namibia entries for 1989 and 1991.

3. Luigi Villari, *The Republic of Ragusa: An Episode of the Turkish Conquest* (London: Dent, 1904). For Venice see chapter 3.

4. Immanuel Kant, *Fundamental Principles of the Metaphysics of Morals* (1785), conclusion to part 2 of "Jurisprudence." Addendum in Kant, *Perpetual Peace (Zum ewigen Frieden: Ein philosophisches Entwurf),* 1795, trans. Lewis White Beck (Indianapolis: Bobbs-Merrill, 1957), p. 58. Michael Howard, *War and the Liberal Conscience* (New Brunswick, N.J.: Rutgers University Press, 1978).

5. Thucydides, *History of the Peloponnesian War,* trans. Rex Warner (New York: Penguin, 1954), 1.24–54.

6. A good summary of "peace research" that overlooks the absence of wars between democracies is Seyom Brown, *The Causes and Prevention of War* (New York: St. Martin's, 1987), p. 31. Also Evan Luard, *War in International Society: A Study in International Sociology* (London: I. B. Tauris, 1986), pp. 406–407; David Dessler, "Beyond Correlation: Toward a Causal Theory of War," *International Studies Quarterly* 35 (1991): 337–355. Democracies were found to be as prone to war as other governments, except when dealing with fellow democracies, by Michael Haas, "Societal Approaches to the Study of War," *Journal of Peace Research* 2 (1965): 307–323, and Melvin Small and J. David Singer, "The War-Proneness of Democratic Regimes, 1816–1965," *Jerusalem Journal of International Relations* 1 (1976): 50–69. For more recent and more sophisticated statistics which demonstrate that democracies are somewhat more peaceful on average, see chapter 5. For other mostly negative results see J. David Singer, "Accounting for International War: The State of the Discipline," *Journal of Peace Research* 18 (1981): 2–18, and J. David Singer, "The Political Origins of International War," in *Aggression and War: Their Biological and Social Bases,* ed. Jo Groebel and Robert A. Hinde (New York: Cambridge University Press, 1989), pp. 202–220; Wolf-Dieter Eberwein, "The Qualitative Study of International Conflict: Quantity and Quality? An Assessment of Empirical Research," *Journal of Peace Research* 18 (1981): 19–38; Steve Chan, "Mirror, Mirror On the Wall . . . Are the Freer Countries More Pacific?" *Journal of Conflict Resolution* 28 (1984): 617–648. See also the classic J. David Singer, ed., *The Correlates of War,* 2 vols. (New York: Free Press, 1979–1980); also J. David Singer and Melvin Small, *The Wages of War, 1816–1965: A Statistical Handbook* (New York: Wiley, 1972).

7. James Lee Ray, *Democracy and International Conflict: An Evaluation of the Democratic Peace Proposition* (Columbia: University of South Carolina Press, 1995), reviews studies in chap. 1. The pioneer was Dean V. Babs, "A Force for Peace," *Industrial Research* 14 (1972): 55–58. R. J. Rummel's work is summarized in R. J. Rummel, *Power Kills: Democracy as a Method of Nonviolence* (New Brunswick, N.J.: Transaction, 1996), in R. J. Rummel, *The Miracle That Is Freedom,* Martin Monograph no. 1 (1996), Martin Institute for Peace Studies, University of Idaho, Moscow, Idaho, and in R. J. Rummel, *Death by Government: Genocide and Mass Murder Since 1900* (New Brunswick, N.J.: Transaction, 1994). Also Michael W. Doyle, "Kant, Liberal Legacies, and Foreign Affairs," part 1, *Philosophy and Public Affairs* 12 (1983): 205–235; Doyle, "Kant," part 2, ibid.: 323–353; also Michael W. Doyle, "Liberalism and World Politics," *American Political Science Review* 80 (1986): 1151–1161. Ignorant of this literature, I noticed the peace between democracies while writing Spencer Weart, *Nuclear Fear: A History of Images* (Cambridge, Mass.: Harvard University Press, 1988), pp. 248, 430, and 489n17.

8. "Empirical law": Jack S. Levy, "Domestic Politics and War," in *The Origin and Prevention of Major Wars,* ed. Robert I. Rotberg and Theodore K. Rabb (New York: Cambridge University Press, 1989), p. 88. Statistical significance at the 1% level for the rule of peace between democracies was reported by Babs in the 1972 article cited above.

Recent statistical and other work is discussed in Ray, *Democracy and International Conflict,* and Miriam Fendius Elman, "The Need for a Qualitative Test of the Democratic Peace Theory," introduction to *Paths to Peace: Is Democracy the Answer?* ed. Elman (Cambridge, Mass.: MIT Press, 1997); R. J. Rummel, *Statistics of Democide: Genocide and Mass Murder Since 1900* (Charlottesville: Center for National Security Law, University of Virginia, 1997). See also R. J. Rummel, "Libertarianism and International Violence," *Journal of Conflict Resolution* 27 (1983): 27–71; R. J. Rummel, "Libertarian Propositions on Violence Within and Between Nations: A Test Against Published Research Results," *Journal of Conflict Resolution* 29 (1985): 419–455; Zeev Maoz and Bruce Russett, "Alliance, Contiguity, Wealth, and Political Stability: Is the Lack of Conflict Among Democracies a Statistical Artifact?" *International Interactions* 17 (1991): 245–267; and, for powerful statistics, Bruce Russett, *Grasping the Democratic Peace: Principles for a Post–Cold War World* (Princeton: Princeton University Press, 1993). Also Stuart A. Bremer, "Dangerous Dyads: Conditions Affecting the Likelihood of Interstate War, 1816–1965," *Journal of Conflict Resolution* 36 (1992): 309–341. On proximity, Nils Petter Gledtisch, "Geography, Democracy, and Peace," *International Interactions* 20 (1995): 297–323. The latest refutation of critics is Zeev Maoz, "The Controversy Over the Democratic Peace: Rearguard Action or Cracks in the Wall?" *International Security* 22 (1997): 162–198. More articles will certainly appear in future issues of the journals cited above.

Earlier works include James N. Rosenau and George H. Ramsey, Jr., "External and Internal Typologies of Foreign Policy Behavior: Testing the Stability of an Intriguing Set of Findings," in *Sage International Yearbook of Foreign Policy Studies,* vol. 3, ed. Patrick J. McGowan (1975), pp. 245–262; Jack E. Vincent, "Freedom and International Conflict: Another Look," *International Studies* 31 (1987): 103–112.

9. A recent example of denial of the peace between democracies: Joanne Gowa, "Democratic States and International Disputes," *International Organization* 49 (1995): 511–522. Henry S. Farber and Joanne Gowa, "Polities and Peace," *International Security* 20 (1995): 123–146, is useful chiefly for a finding that the peace between democracies was not statistically significant prior to 1914, when democracies were few. David E. Spiro, "The Insignificance of the Democratic Peace," *International Security* 19 (1994): 50–86 has crippling deficiencies pointed out by Bruce Russett, "And Yet It Moves," *International Security* 19 (1994): 164–177. "Nobody:" Jane Mansbridge in National Research Council, Commission on Behavioral and Social Sciences and Education, *The Transition to Democracy. Proceedings of a Workshop* (Washington, D.C.: National Academy Press, 1971), p. 5.

10. Important studies paralleling my own work are Bruce Russett, *Controlling the Sword: The Democratic Governance of National Security* (Cambridge, Mass.: Harvard University Press, 1990), chap. 5, and Russett, *Grasping the Democratic Peace.* John M. Owen, "How Liberalism Promotes Democratic Peace," *International Security* 19 (1994): 87–125, done in parallel with my own work, has mostly compatible conclusions. See also William J. Dixon, "Democracy and the Peaceful Settlement of International Conflict," *American Political Science Review* 88 (1994): 14–32; Joe D. Hagan, "Domestic Political Systems and War Proneness," *Mershon International Studies Review* 38 (1994): 183–207. Although my work was largely finished when these studies appeared, I have addressed objections from Raymond Cohen, "Pacific Unions: A Reappraisal of the Theory that 'Democracies Do Not Go to War with Each Other,'" *Review of International Studies* 20 (1994): 207–223; and Christopher Layne, "Kant or Cant: The Myth of the Democratic Peace," *International Security* 19 (1994): 5–49.

11. T. Clifton Morgan and Sally Howard Campbell, "Domestic Structure, Decisional Constraints, and War: So Why Kant Democracies Fight?" *Journal of Conflict Resolution* 35 (1991): 187–211; Dessler, "Beyond Correlation."

12. The method resembles multivariate analysis. See Theda Skocpol and Margaret Somers, "The Use of Comparative History in Macrosocial Inquiry," *Comparative Studies in Society and History* 22 (1980): 174–197; also Alexander L. George, "Case Studies and Theory Development: The Method of Structured, Focused Comparison," in *Diplomacy: New Approaches in History, Theory and Policy,* ed. Paul Lauren (New York: Free Press, 1979), pp. 43–68; Charles F. Hermann, Charles W. Kegley, Jr., and James N. Rosenau, *New Directions in the Study of Foreign Policy* (Boston: Allen and Unwin, 1987). My cases are mainly studies of crises, see Richard Ned Lebow, *Between Peace and War. The Nature of International Crisis* (Baltimore: Johns Hopkins University Press, 1961), pp. 10–12.

13. For the method of exceptions ("deviant" and "crucial" cases) see Arend Lijphart, "Comparative Politics and the Comparative Method," *American Political Science Review* 65 (1971): 682–693; Harry Eckstein, *Regarding Politics: Essays on Political Theory, Stability, and Change* (Berkeley: University of California Press, 1992), chap. 4.

14. *Handbuch der Schweizer Geschichte,* 2 vols. (Zurich: Berichthaus, 1972), vol. 1, esp. pp. 402–406, 415–416; Hans C. Peyer, *Verfassungsgeschichte der alten Schweiz* (Zurich: Schulthess, 1978); *Nouvelle histoire de la Suisse et des Suisses,* 3 vols.; ed. Beatrix Mesmer,

Jean-Claude Favez, and Romano Broggini (Lausanne: Payot, 1982), vol. 1, pp. 139–149, 157–158, 299–301. Other standard sources: Johannes Dierauer, *Histoire de la Confédération Suisse,* 5 vols., trans. Aug. Reymond (Lausanne: Payot, 1912–1919); Ernst Gagliardi, *Seit der Reformation,* vol. 2 of *Geschichte der Schweiz von den Anfängen bis auf die Gegenwart* (Zurich: Rascher, 1920); Gottfried Guggenbühl, *Vom Jahre 1648 bis zur Gegenwart,* vol. 2 of *Geschichte der Schweizerischer Eidgenossenschaft* (Erlenbach-Zurich: Rentsch, 1948).

15. Six if we count the three components of the Gray Leagues as one; ten if we count separately the two semi-independent entities of Unterwalden.

16. For political arrangements see *Handbuch der Schweizer Geschichte,* vol. 1, p. 403–404; Peyer, *Verfassungsgeschichte,* pp. 45–55; Ulrich Ernst Gut, *Grundfragen und schweizerische Entwicklungstendenzen der Demokratie* (Zurich: Schulthess, 1983), pp. 46–52.

17. Qualifications: most citizens gave chief loyalty to family factions and guilds; local counts retained important powers; the cities denied rights to people in the countryside. Return to war: notably Ghent and Bruges around 1381. Henri Pirenne, *Belgian Democracy: Its Early History,* trans. J. V. Saunders (Manchester: Manchester University Press, 1915), for an English-language introduction; Henri Pirenne, *Du Commencement du XIVe siècle à la mort de Charles le Témeraire,* vol. 2 of *Histoire de Belgique* (Brussels: Lamertin, 1908); Fritz Quicke, *Les Pays-Bas à la veille de la période Bourguignonne, 1356–1384* (Brussels: Editions Universitaires, 1947); David Nicholas, *The Metamorphosis of a Medieval City: Ghent in the Age of the Arteveldes, 1302–1390* (Lincoln: University of Nebraska Press, 1987), pp. 1–13; David Nicholas, *The van Arteveldes of Ghent: The Varieties of Vendetta and the Hero in History* (Ithaca, N.Y.: Cornell University Press, 1988) for factions and establishment of tyranny in 1381.

18. Wilhelm Ehrenzeller, *St. Gallen im Zeitalter des Klosterbruchs und des St. Gallerkrieg,* vol. 2 of *St. Gallische Geschichte im Spätmittelalter und in der Reformationszeit* (St. Gallen: Fehr'sche Buchhandlung, 1938); Dierauer, *Histoire,* vol. 2, book 5, chap. 3; Johann Caspar Zellweger, *Geschichte des Appenzellischen Volkes,* 3 vols. (St. Gallen: Scheitlin und Zollikosen, 1842), vol. 2, pp. 152–215. For 362 B.C. see chapter 2, for 1847 see chapter 6.

CHAPTER TWO
Ancient Greece: Definitions and a Pattern of Peace

1. Classical sources are cited as noted below from the *Loeb Classical Library* (Cambridge, Mass.: Harvard University Press; London: Heinemann; New York: G.P. Putnam's Sons). General sources include Anthony Powell, *Athens and Sparta: Constructing Greek Political and Social History from 478 B.C.* (Portland, Ore.: Areopagitica, 1988); *The Cambridge Ancient History* (Cambridge: Cambridge University Press); A. W. Gomme, *A Historical Commentary on Thucydides,* 3 vols. (Oxford: Clarendon, 1950–1956); Julius Beloch, *Griechische Geschichte* (Strassburg: Trübner, 1904). Sicilian expedition: Thucydides, *History of the Peloponnesian War,* trans. Rex Warner (New York: Penguin, 1954), 7.70–87, also Diodorus Siculus, *Histories,* in *Loeb Classical Library,* 13.13.13–19; Donald Kagan, *The*

Peace of Nicias and the Sicilian Expedition (Ithaca, N.Y.: Cornell University Press, 1981), third in a set of which the others are *The Outbreak of the Peloponnesian War* (1969), *The Archidamian War* (1974), and *The Fall of the Athenian Empire* (1987).

2. Thucydides, *History,* 7.55.

3. Richard L. Merritt and Dina A. Zinnes, "Democracies and War," in *On Measuring Democracy: Its Consequences and Concomitants,* ed. Alex Inkeles (New Brunswick, N.J.: Transaction, 1991), pp. 207–234; James Lee Ray, "Wars Between Democracies: Rare or Nonexistent?" *International Interactions* 18 (1993): 251–276.

4. Isocrates, *Plataicus,* 17–18, 25, 35 (cf. Isocrates, *To Philip,* 53–55) in *Loeb Classical Library,* trans. George Norkin and Laurie Van Hoole (Cambridge, Mass.: Harvard University Press, 1928–1945); Xenophon, *A History of My Times (Hellenica),* trans. Rex Warner (New York: Penguin, 1966), 6.5.37ff. See J. K. Davies, *Democracy and Classical Greece* (Atlantic Highlands, N.J.: Humanities Press, 1978), pp. 217–18. Athens recognized Thebes as a democracy: see Isocrates, *Plataicus,* 33–35.

5. F. E. Adcock, *The Greek and Macedonian Art of War* (Berkeley: University of California Press, 1957); J. K. Anderson, *Military Theory and Practice in the Age of Xenophon* (Berkeley: University of California Press, 1970); W. Kendrick Pritchett, *The Greek State at War,* vol. 4 (Berkeley: University of California Press, 1985), chap. 1; Victor Davis Hanson, *The Western Way of War: Infantry Battle in Classical Greece* (New York: Knopf, 1989).

6. Xenophon, *Hellenica,* 6.5.51. The accounts of the melee at Corinth in ibid., 7.1.18–20 and Diodorus Siculus, *Histories,* 15.69 cannot be reconciled. N. G. L. Hammond, *A History of Greece to 322 B.C.* (Oxford: Clarendon, 1959), pp. 497–509; John Buckler, *The Theban Hegemony, 371–362 B.C.* (Cambridge, Mass.: Harvard University Press, 1980), pp. 152–161, 170; Jack Cargill, *The Second Athenian League: Empire or Free Alliance?* (Berkeley: University of California Press, 1981), chap. 10. For skirmishes: Xenophon, *Histories,* 7.2.10, 7.5.15–17.

7. Diodorus Siculus, *Histories,* 15.84–87; Xenophon, *Hellenica,* 7.5.21–27. The retreating Athenians fought some Theban allies from Euboea, which there is no reason to suspect was democratic.

8. Reluctance to fight is obscured by a Swiss need to assert martial virtues, e.g., Guillaume-Henri Dufour, *Campagne du Sonderbund et évènements de 1856* (Neuchatel: Sandoz, 1876), pp. 142–143, 171–172. A recent study sets deaths in this conflict at 93; for more on this and "Sunday brawl" see Joachim Remak, *A Very Civil War: The Swiss Sonderbund War of 1847* (Boulder: Westview, 1993), pp. 157–159; similarly "Sie gerauft hätten," Erwin Bucher, *Die Geschichte des Sonderbundskrieges* (Zurich: Breithaus, 1966), p. 518.

9. Cases listed for the years 426 B.C., 369 B.C., 1431, 1443, 1447, 1490, 1529, 1531, 1797, 1847, 1897, 1941, 1964, 1981.

10. My definition closely follows John A. Vasquez, *The War Puzzle* (Cambridge: Cambridge University Press, 1993), chap. 1; I use the more general term "political units" rather than his organized "states." I add up the casualties on both sides. Cases that would be excluded by the higher limit are those listed in the appendix for 411 B.C., 409 B.C., 1948, and possibly 1494, 1499, 1531, 1919, and 1994. The 369 B.C. and 1981 conflicts may

have involved slightly over two hundred deaths. Lowering the limit to, say, fifty would not add many cases. On criteria for "war" see Evan Luard, *War in International Society: A Study in International Sociology* (London: I. B. Tauris, 1986), pp. 6–7.

11. For other examples see Jeremy Black, ed., *The Origins of War in Early Modern Europe* (Edinburgh: John Donald, 1987), pp. 11–13.

12. William R. Everdell, *The End of Kings: A History of Republics and Republicans* (New York: Macmillan Free Press, 1983), chap. 1. Cf. Merritt and Zinnes, "Democracies and War," pp. 207–234, or any dictionary.

13. By this definition Australia is effectively a "republic" despite its pro forma allegiance to the British crown. Robert A. Dahl, *Polyarchy: Participation and Opposition* (New Haven: Yale University Press, 1971), pp. 1–6. This definition incorporates what some call the "classical liberal" regime. To call an illiberal regime a republic (or democracy) confuses the key issues. Cf. Fareed Zakaria, "The Rise of Illiberal Democracy," *Foreign Affairs* 76 (1997): 22–43. For other recent discussion see Philippe C. Schmitter and Terry Lynn Karl, "What Democracy Is . . . and Is Not," in *The Global Resurgence of Democracy*, ed. Larry Diamond and Marc F. Plattner (Baltimore: Johns Hopkins University Press, 1993), p. 41. Cf. Steve Chan, "Mirror, Mirror On the Wall . . . Are the Freer Countries More Pacific?" *Journal of Conflict Resolution* 28 (1984): 617–648, see p. 630; Jack S. Levy, "Domestic Politics and War," *Journal of Interdisciplinary History* 18 (1988): 653–673, see p. 662n.

14. See Herodotus, *The Histories,* trans. George Rawlinson (New York: Dial, 1928), 5.78; Thucydides, *History,* 3.42–43. T.A. Sinclair, *A History of Greek Political Thought* (London: Routledge and Kegan Paul, 1951), pp. 39, 102–103; Mogens Herman Hansen, *The Athenian Democracy in the Age of Demosthenes: Structure, Principles and Ideology,* trans. J. A. Crook (Oxford: Blackwell, 1991), pp. 57–64; A. H. M. Jones, *Athenian Democracy* (Oxford: Blackwell, 1964); M. I. Finley, *Democracy Ancient and Modern* (New Brunswick, N.J.: Rutgers University Press, 1973); Powell, *Athens and Sparta,* chap. 7.

15. For example, Robert A. Dahl, *Democracy and Its Critics* (New Haven: Yale University Press, 1989), chaps. 8, 9.

16. Jones, *Athenian Democracy,* pp. 13–20, 75–93; Hansen, *Athenian Democracy,* pp. 86–91; Simon Hornblower, *The Greek World, 479–323 B.C.* (London: Methuen, 1983), pp. 172–173; M. I. Finley, *Economy and Society in Ancient Greece,* ed. Brent D. Shaw and Richard P. Salleer (Harmondsworth, England: Penguin, 1983), pp. 102–109; Yvon Garlan, *Slavery in Ancient Greece,* rev. ed. (Ithaca, N.Y.: Cornell University Press, 1988), pp. 59–60.

17. Ellen Meiksins Wood and Neal Wood, *Class Ideology and Ancient Political Theory: Socrates, Plato, and Aristotle in Social Context* (Oxford: Blackwell, 1979), pp. 41–64, 210–214; David Whitehead, *The Ideology of the Athenian Metic* (Cambridge: Cambridge Philosophical Society, 1977); Oswyn Murray, "Life and Society in Classical Greece," in *The Oxford History of the Classical World,* ed. John Boardman et al. (Oxford: Oxford University Press, 1986), pp. 204–233, see pp. 222–223; Garlan, *Slavery;* Davies, *Democracy,* pp. 104–105; Jones, *Athenian Democracy,* pp. 10–19; G. E. M. de Ste. Croix, *The Class Struggle in the Ancient Greek World* (Ithaca, N.Y.: Cornell University Press, 1981); M. I. Finley, *Ancient Slavery and Modern Ideology* (New York: Viking, 1980), esp. pp. 80–82, 100–102; M. I. Finley, *Politics in the Ancient World,* rev. ed. (Cambridge: Cambridge University Press,

1984), pp. 9–11; Ellen Meiksins Wood, *Peasant-Citizen and Slave: The Foundations of Athenian Democracy* (New York: Verso, 1988), chap. 2. See also Demosthenes, *Against Neaera*, 104–107; this and other works are in Demosthenes, *Orations and Letters*, in *Loeb Classical Library*, ed. J. H. Vince and A. T. Murray (New York: G. P. Putnam's Sons, 1926–1949). Isocrates, *Letter to the Rulers of Mytilene*, 4, and *On the Peace*, 50; Plato, *Republic*, 563a (all in *Loeb Classical Library*); Thucydides, *History*, 2.4, 3.73; Diodorus Siculus, *Histories*, 12.41.6.

18. Strategic motives for war: Thucydides, *History*, 2.7, 3.86. See Kagan, *Archidamian*, pp. 182–86; Hornblower, *Greek World*, p. 41. Domestic motives: Diodorus Siculus, *Histories*, 13.2.2, 12.54.1,3; Thucydides, *History*, 6.24. See G. E. M. de Ste. Croix, *The Origins of the Peloponnesian War* (Ithaca, N.Y.: Cornell University Press, 1972), p. 218; M.I. Finley, *Ancient History: Evidence and Models* (New York: Viking, 1985), chap. 5.

19. Geoffrey Blainey, *The Causes of War*, 3rd ed. (New York: Macmillan Free Press, 1988); J. David Singer, ed., *The Correlates of War*, 2 vols. (New York: Free Press, 1979–1980); James E. Dougherty and Robert L. Pfaltzgraff, Jr., *Contending Theories of International Relations: A Comprehensive Survey*, 3rd ed. (New York: Harper and Row, 1990), p. 187; David Kaiser, *Politics and War: European Conflict from Philip II to Hitler* (Cambridge, Mass.: Harvard University Press, 1990); Kalevi J. Holsti, *Peace and War: Armed Conflicts and International Order, 1648–1989* (Cambridge: Cambridge University Press, 1991); Luard, *International Society*, chap. 4.

20. Thucydides, *History*, 3.86, 5.4, 6.6,19; Diodorus Siculus, *Histories*, 12.54,83. See Kagan, *Peace of Nicias*, 176–77; Gomme, *Historical Commentary*, vol. 1, p. 198, vol. 4, p. 221. For generations afterwards: Aeschines, *On the Embassy*, 2.76; Plato, *Menexenus*, 243a, both in *Loeb Classical Library*.

21. For an early statement see Thucydides, *History*, 4.59. Blainey, *Causes of War;* Bruce Bueno de Mesquita and David Lalman, *War and Reason: Domestic and International Imperatives* (New Haven: Yale University Press, 1992).

22. Luis A. Losada, *The Fifth Column in the Peloponnesian War* (Ph.D. diss., Columbia University, 1970), pp. 21–34 and passim; Thucydides, *History*, 3.82.

23. "Violent strife": Thucydides, *History*, 6.17, 20; see Gomme, *Historical Commentary*, vol. 4, p. 250; Plutarch, *Nicias* and *Alcibiades* in Plutarch, *The Rise and Fall of Athens: Nine Greek Lives by Plutarch*, trans. Ian Scott-Kilvert (New York: Penguin, 1960). Syracusan democracy: Thucydides, *History*, 7.55, see also 6.20. All commentators note that Thucydides would stretch for a rhetorical point.

24. Aristotle, *Politics*, trans. Benjamin Jowett (New York: Random House Modern Library, 1943), 1304a27–29. Quite likely fewer than a third of men could vote; besides slaves and metics, Syracuse swarmed with foreign refugees. See Diodorus Siculus, *Histories*, 13.34.6, 13.35, also 11.86.5, 11.87.3–5, and Thucydides, *History*, 6.38. Hansen, *Athenian Democracy*, pp. 66–67; Kagan, *Peace of Nicias*, p. 218–21; M. I. Finley, *Ancient Sicily*, rev. ed. (Totowa, N.J.: Roman and Littlefield, 1979), pp. 61–62, 68–70; Andrew Lintott, *Violence, Civil Strife, and Revolution in the Classical City* (Baltimore: Johns Hopkins University Press, 1962), pp. 189, 191; Hornblower, *Greek World*, pp. 52, 54, 140–141. Thucydides's third-hand account of a Syracusan debate shows, in the most probable interpretation,

that democrats could speak their minds freely but held little power, and an oligarchic clique could execute policies without submitting them to a vote in the assembly. Thucydides, *History,* 6.32–41, 6.72–73; Diodorus Siculus, *Histories,* 13.91.4–5; Gomme, *Historical Commentary* vol. 4, pp. 307, 430–431.

25. Thucydides, *History,* 6.103, 7.2, 7.48–49, 7.73, see Losada, *Fifth Column,* pp. 126–132; Diodorus Siculus, *Histories,* 13.18.4–6; Plutarch, *Nicias,* 18, 21. Conspirators may be connected with democrats by comparing accounts of who demanded executions: Diodorus Siculus, *Histories,* 13.18.5, 13.19.4, 13.33.1; Plutarch, *Nicias,* 28, Thucydides, *History,* 7.86. Ignorance of Syracusan politics: Thucydides, *History,* 6.1, 6.8; see Gomme, *Historical Commentary,* vol. 4, p. 197. Kagan, *Peace of Nicias,* 165, and Hornblower, *Greek World,* pp. 140–141 note that Athenians had campaigned in Sicily with the Leontini, but marching with Syracuse's enemies was a poor way to learn about its domestic politics.

26. I say "Thebans" for Boeotians in general. See Herodotus, *Histories,* 5.82, 6.109, 9.14–15; Thucydides, *History,* 3.62; Plutarch, *Aristides,* 18, in *Nine Greek Lives.* Examples of battles: Thucydides, *History,* 4.101; Herodotus, *Histories,* 5.77–80; Diodorus Siculus, *Histories,* 11.82.5, 12.65.4, 12.70.2–4, 13.72.8–9. Raze Athens: Xenophon, *Hellenica,* 2.2.19–20, see Isocrates, *Plataikos,* 32.

27. "Whole city": Xenophon, *Hellenica,* 3.5.8. Charles D. Hamilton, *Sparta's Bitter Victories: Politics and Diplomacy in the Corinthian War* (Ithaca, N.Y.: Cornell University Press, 1979), p. 145–151; Buckler, *Theban Hegemony,* pp. 36–42; Diodorus Siculus, *Histories,* 14.6.6.

28. Xenophon, *Hellenica,* 5.2.25–36, 5.4.2–11, 5.4.46; Diodorus Siculus, *Histories,* 15.25.1–7. See Cargill, *Second Athenian League,* p. 56; compare the unofficial expeditions that early modern Swiss peasants launched on behalf of their fellows. For subsequent events see general references cited earlier plus J. A. O. Larsen, *Greek Federal States: Their Institutions and History* (Oxford: Clarendon, 1968), pp. 175–180.

29. A good example is Corinth, Xenophon, *Hellenica,* 2.2.19–20, 3.5.1–2, 4.4.1–14; Diodorus Siculus, *Histories,* 14.82.1, 14.86. Most of the twenty-seven betrayals listed in Losada, *Fifth Column,* included switched alliances.

30. Bruce Russett and William Antholis, "Do Democracies Fight Each Other? Evidence from the Peloponnesian War," *Journal of Peace Research* 29 (1992): 415–434 find that wars between democracies were about one-third as common as wars of democracies against nondemocracies. Their methodology suffers, as they note, from their policy of forcing a choice between oligarchy and democracy even when the evidence is only a sentence or two, and from making no discrimination between great wars and trivial skirmishes. They point to some fourteen cases throughout the Peloponnesian War where one could argue that democracies fought one another, but as they recognize, all fourteen are ambiguous; see my appendix for further discussion. For moderately well-documented regimes and serious battles, I find no undoubted wars between democracies. I am grateful to Russett and Antholis for discussion and for sharing the details of data later published in Bruce Russett, *Grasping the Democratic Peace: Principles for a Post–Cold War World* (Princeton: Princeton University Press, 1993) pp. 63–71.

31. Outside the Peloponnesian War we find, for example, democratic Corcyra and Athens vs. oligarchic Corinth; Athens and Platea vs. Thebes when it was an oligarchy; democratic Thebes vs. Sparta; many wars pitting democratic Argos against Sparta and other oligarchies; repeated cases of democracies warring on the Macedonians, Persians, and Romans; etc. An example of one democracy offering another material help is Samos, Thucydides, *History,* 8.21. For a summary see Jones, *Athenian Democracy,* pp. 67–68.

32. A possible exception: support by the Athenian garrison commander for an oligarchic coup in Corcyra in 361 B.C., Aeneus Tacitus, *On the Defense of Fortified Positions,* in *Loeb Classical Library,* trans. The Illinois Greek Club (New York: G. P. Putnam's Sons, 1923), 11.13–15; Diodorus Siculus, *Histories,* 15.95.3. But this was most likely his personal initiative, not a formal Athenian decision; see Cargill, *Second Athenian League,* pp. 172–75. Aristotle, *Politics,* 1307b; similarly Thucydides, *History,* 3:82; Diodorus Siculus, *Histories,* 13.48.4, 14.10. On Spartans see Thucydides, *History,* 1.19, 4.80, 5.14, 8.63; Diodorus Siculus, *Histories,* 15.40.1, 15.45.1; Hamilton, *Sparta's Bitter Victories.*

33. The relative mutual peacefulness of Greek nondemocracies is noted in Russett and Antholis, "Do Democracies Fight," which records some ambiguous cases of wars. These cases all actually involved tribal or monarchical states, or states whose oligarchic status is highly questionable, or apparent hostility without recorded combat. For example, they count a case in which partly oligarchic Athenians marched on conceivably oligarchic Colophon and "won the town over peaceably" (Xenophon, *Hellenica,* 1.2.4).

34. T. Clifton Morgan and Valerie L. Schwebach, "Take Two Democracies and Call Me in the Morning: A Prescription for Peace?" *International Interactions* 17 (1992): 305–320 (which appeared after I reached my conclusions), reports little warfare between 1816 and 1976 between "constrained non-democracies"—close to what I call oligarchic republics— although such regimes did fight democracies.

CHAPTER THREE
Medieval Italy: Wars Without States

1. Envoys: Gida Rossi, *Bologna nella storia, nell'arte e nel costume,* 3rd ed. (Bologna: Forni, 1969), p. 131. For this and the following chapter, general introductions include Daniel Waley, *The Italian City-Republics,* 3rd ed. (London: Longman, 1988); Lauro Martines, *Power and Imagination: City-States in Renaissance Italy* (New York: Knopf, 1979); Denys Hay and John Law, *Italy in the Age of the Renaissance, 1380–1530* (London: Longman, 1989). Overviews of events include Pasquale Villari, *Medieval Italy from Charlemagne to Henry VII,* trans. Costanza Hulton (London: T. Fisher Unwin, 1910); W. F. Butler, *The Lombard Communes: A History of the Republics of North Italy,* 1906 (Westport, Conn.: Greenwood, 1969); Edouard Jordan, *L'Allemagne et l'Italie aux XIIe et XIIIe siècles* (Paris: PUF, 1939). On politics see John K. Hyde, *Society and Politics in Medieval Italy: The Evolution of the Civil Life, 1000–1350* (London: Macmillan, 1973); John Larner, *Italy in the Age of Dante and Petrarch* (London: Longman, 1980); Gene A. Brucker, *Renaissance Florence,* rev. ed. (Berkeley: University of California Press, 1983); Robert Finlay, *Politics in Re-*

naissance Venice (London: Ernest Benn, 1980); Daniel Waley, *Siena and the Sienese in the Thirteenth Century* (Cambridge: Cambridge University Press, 1991).

2. Rinaldo degli Albizzi, *Comissioni di Rinaldo degli Albizzi per il commune di Firenze dal 1394–1433,* 3 vols. (Florence, 1873), vol. 3, p. 206. Similarly, Waley, *Siena,* p. 51; Guidubaldo Guidi, *Il Governo della città-repubblica di Firenze del primo quatrocento,* vol. 2: *Gli istituti "di dentro" che componevano il governo di Firenze nel 1415* (Florence: Olschki, 1981).

3. Marketplace: Antonio Pucci, "Le Proprietà di Mercato Vecchio," in *Delizie degli eruditi toscani,* vol. 6: *Della Poesie di Antonio Pucci,* ed. Fr. Ildefonso (Florence, 1775), p. 270, lines 34–36. "Take into account": Iacopo Nardi, *Istorie della Città di Firenze,* 2 vols., ed. Agenore Gelli (Florence: Le Monnier, 1858), 2 vols., vol. 1, p. 2. See Francesca Klein, "Considerazioni sull'ideologia della Città di Firenze tra Trecento e Quattrocento (Giovanni Villani-Leonardo Bruni)," *Ricerche Storiche* 10 (1980): 311–336, see pp. 324–325. Numbers: Giovanni Villani, *Cronica di Giovanni Villani: A miglior lezione ridotta coll'aiuto de' testi a penna* (Florence: Magheri, 1823), 11.94, pp. 184–185; David Herlihy, *Medieval and Renaissance Pistoia: The Social History of an Italian Town, 1200–1430* (New Haven: Yale University Press, 1967), p. 76.

4. Butler, *Lombard Communes,* p. 202; cf. Rossi, *Bologna,* p. 132.

5. On factionalism see Larner, *Italy in the Age,* pp. 102–110; Jacques Heers, *Parties and Political Life in the Medieval West,* trans. David Nichols (Amsterdam, N.Y.: Nathaniel-Holland, 1977), esp. pp. 101–115; Lauro Martines, ed., *Violence and Civil Disorder in Italian Cities, 1200–1500* (Berkeley: University of California Press, 1972); for examples, see such city histories as Vito Vitale, *Il dominio della Parte Guelfa in Bologna (1280–1327)* (Bologna: A. Forni, 1978).

6. Randolph Starn, *Contrary Commonwealth: The Theme of Exile in Medieval and Renaissance Italy* (Berkeley: University of California Press, 1962).

7. Hyde, *Society and Politics;* Waley, *Italian City-Republics,* pp. 146–149; Jordan, *L'Allemagne et l'Italie.*

8. Jordan, *L'Allemagne et l'Italie;* William M. Bowsky, *Henry VII in Italy: The Conflict of Empire and City-State, 1310–1313* (Lincoln: University of Nebraska Press, 1960).

9. Jordan, *L'Allemagne et l'Italie,* esp. pp. 248, 257, 329–334; for English summary see Bella Duffy, *The Tuscan Republics (Florence, Siena, Pisa, and Lucca) with Genoa* (New York: G. P. Putnam's Sons, 1893).

10. Ferdinand Schevill, *History of Florence from the Founding of the City Through the Renaissance* (New York: Harcourt, Brace, 1936); Ferdinand Schevill, *Siena: The Story of a Medieval Commune* (New York: Scribner's, 1909); for details, G. Villani, *Cronica,* books 5–7; Waley, *Siena,* pp. 114–119; Robert Davidson, *Geschichte von Florenz* (Berlin: Mittler, 1896–1927), book 2, part 1, chaps. 6, 7, supplemented by Davidson, *Forschungen zur Älteren Geschichte von Florenz,* part 4: *13. und 14. Jahrhundert* (Berlin: Mittler, 1908). Siena may actually have been an autocracy (under Salvani). "Resemblance": Jordan, *L'Allemagne et l'Italie,* p. 332.

11. For summary history see John Julius Norwich, *A History of Venice,* 2 vols. (New York: Random House, 1989); W. Carew Hazlitt, *The Venetian Republic: Its Rise, Growth*

and Fall (London: Adam and Charles Black, 1900), esp. chap. 26. For details, Heinrich Kretschmayr, *Geschichte von Venedig,* 3 vols. (Gotha: Perthes, 1905–34), vol. 2; Samuele Romanin, *Storia documentata di Venezia,* 10 vols. (Venice: Naratovich, 1853–61), vols. 2 and 3, pp. 251–292; Roberto Cessi, *Storia della Repubblica di Venezia,* 2 vols. (Milan: G. Principato, 1944), vol. 1. Teofilio Ossian De Negri, *Storia di Genova* (Florence: Giunti Martello, 1986), pp. 309–311, 329–330, 466–468; Gino Benvenuti, *Storia della Repubblica di Genova* (Milan: Mursio, 1977).

12. Jack S. Levy, "Domestic Politics and War," *Journal of Interdisciplinary History* 18 (1988): 658. See J. David Singer, "The Political Origins of International War: A Multi-Factorial Review," in Jo Groebel and Robert A. Hinde, eds., *Aggression and War: Their Biological and Social Basis* (New York: Cambridge University Press, 1989), pp. 202–220. The pioneering study is Lewis Fry Richardson, *Statistics of Deadly Quarrels* (Pittsburgh: Boxwood, 1960), see pp. ix–xiii.

13. Datini quoted in Brucker, *Renaissance Florence,* p. 81.

14. Charles Calvert Bayley, *War and Society in Renaissance Florence: The "De Militia" of Leonardo Bruni* (Toronto: University of Toronto Press, 1961), pp. 55–56; David Herlihy, "Some Psychological and Social Roots of Violence in the Tuscan Cities," in Martines, *Violence and Civil Disorder,* pp. 138–39; Hans Baron, *The Crisis of the Early Italian Renaissance: Civic Humanism and Republican Liberty in an Age of Classicism and Tyranny,* rev. ed. (Princeton: Princeton University Press, 1966), pp. 377–378, 380. Michael Howard, *War and the Liberal Conscience* (New Brunswick, N.J.: Rutgers University Press, 1978), pp. 18–25. There are plausible arguments in David A. Lake, "Powerful Pacifists: Democratic States and War," *American Political Science Review* 86 (1992): 24–37; Mark R. Brawley, "Regime Types, Markets, and War: The Importance of Pervasive Rents in Foreign Policy," *Comparative Political Studies* 26 (1993): 178–197; Dale C. Copeland, "Economic Interdependence and War. A Theory of Trade Expectations," *International Security* 20 (1996): 5–41, includes a good review of theory.

15. John R. Oneal, Frances H. Oneal, Zeev Maoz, and Bruce Russett, "The Liberal Peace: Interdependence, Democracy, and International Conflict," *Journal of Peace Research* 33 (1996): 11–28; Katherine Barbieri, "Economic Interdependence: A Path to Peace or a Source of Interstate Conflict?" *Journal of Peace Research* 33 (1996): 29–49; Copeland, *International Security* (1996).

16. See Levy, "Domestic Politics and War," pp. 663–664; on trade in particular see Bruce Russett, *Grasping the Democratic Peace: Principles for a Post–Cold War World* (Princeton: Princeton University Press, 1993), p. 28.

17. "Delays": Matteo Villani, *Cronica di Matteo Villani* (Florence, 1825), 8.17, p. 26. See Anthony Powell, *Athens and Sparta: Constructing Greek Political and Social History from 478 B.C.* (Portland, Ore.: Areopagitica, 1988), pp. 292–293; Francesco Guicciardini, "Dialogo e Discorsi del Reggimento del Firenze," in Guicciardini, *Opere,* vol. 7, ed. Roberto Palmarocci (Bari: Caterza, 1932), pp. 62–67; Joe D. Hagan, "Domestic Political Stystems and War Proneness," *Mershon International Studies Review* 38 (1994): 138–206.

18. See especially R. J. Rummel, *War, Power, Peace,* vol. 4 of *Understanding Conflict and War* (Beverly Hills: Sage, 1979); R. J. Rummel, *In the Minds of Men: Principles Toward*

Understanding and Waging Peace (Seoul: Sogang University Press, 1984), esp. pp. 160–162, 170–171.

19. Marc Howard Ross, *The Culture of Conflict: Interpretations and Interests in Comparative Perspective* (New Haven: Yale University Press, 1994), chap. 6. On cross-cutting ties see Seymour Brown, *The Causes and Prevention of War* (New York: St. Martin's, 1987), pp. 31, 36. On civil society see Philippe Schmitter in National Research Council, Commission on Behavioral and Social Sciences and Education, *The Transition to Democracy: Proceedings of a Workshop* (Washington, D.C.: National Academy Press, 1991).

20. The Greek men's clubs operated within existing factions; cult associations played no detectible political role. See Ernest Gellner, *Conditions of Liberty: Civil Society and Its Rivals* (London: Penguin, 1994). In medieval Swiss democracies religious associations were absent from the political history and civil society was undeveloped. Even modern Swiss civil society shows little cross-cutting: Arend Lijphart, *Democracies: Patterns of Majoritarian and Consensus Government in Twenty-One Countries* (New Haven: Yale University Press, 1984), pp. 9–16, 53–54, 99–103. Early modern kingdoms: William Doyle, *The Ancien Régime* (Basinsston: Macmillan, 1986). For the Germanies see chapter 14. Nicolai Rubinstein, "Machiavelli and Florentine Republican Experience," in *Machiavelli and Republicanism,* ed. Gisela Bock, Quentin Skinner, and Maurizio Viroli (Cambridge: Cambridge University Press, 1990), pp. 7–8, 11.

21. R. Brian Ferguson and Leslie E. Farragher, *The Anthropology of War: A Bibliography,* Occasional Papers of the Henry Frank Guggenheim Foundation, vol. 1 (New York: Guggenheim Foundation, 1988); R. Brian Ferguson, ed., *Warfare, Culture, and Environment* (Orlando, Fla.: Academic Press, 1984). Other introductions: Peter Matthiessen, *Under the Mountain Wall: A Chronicle of Two Seasons in the Stone Age* (New York: Viking, 1962); Napoleon A. Chagnon, *Yanomamö: The Fierce People,* 3rd ed. (New York: Holt, Rinehart, and Winston, 1983); Mervyn Meggit, *Blood Is Their Argument: Warfare Among the Mae Enga Tribesmen of the New Guinea Highlands* (Palo Alto, Calif.: Mayfield, 1977). Examples from other cultural areas: E. Adamson Hoebel, *The Cheyenne: Indians of the Great Plains,* 2nd ed. (New York: Holt, Rinehart, and Winston, 1978); W. Lloyd Warner, "Murngin Warfare," *Oceania* 1 (1931): 457–494; Ernest Burch, "Eskimo Warfare in Northwest Alaska," *Anthropological Papers of the University of Alaska* 16 (1974): 1–14; Keith F. Otterbein, "Higi Armed Combat," *Anthropology* 24 (1968): 195–213; Robert B. Ekvall, "Peace and War Among the Tibetan Nomads," *American Anthropologist* 66 (1964): 1119–1148. Tribal organization: Elman R. Service, *Primitive Social Organization: An Evolutionary Perspective* (New York: Random House, 1962), chaps. 4, 5; Morton H. Fried, *The Notion of Tribe* (Menlo Park, Calif.: Cummings, 1975).

22. For equality see for example Kenneth E. Read, *The High Valley* (New York: Scribner's, 1965), pp. 89–90.

23. Russett, *Grasping the Democratic Peace,* chap. 5, drawing on Carol R. Ember, Melvin Ember, and Bruce Russett, "Peace Between Participatory Polities: A Cross-Cultural Test of the 'Democracies Rarely Fight Each Other' Hypothesis," *World Politics* 43 (1992): 573–597.

24. For review see R. Brian Ferguson, "Explaining War," in *The Anthropology of War,* ed. Jonathan Haas (Cambridge: Cambridge University Press, 1990), pp. 26–55. On cross-cutting ties see Robert Murphy, "Intergroup Hostility and Social Cohesion," *American Anthropologist* 59 (1957): 1018–1035; R. Brian Ferguson, "Introduction: Studying War," in Ferguson, *Warfare, Culture, and Environment,* pp. 16–17.

25. See Ferguson, *Warfare, Culture,* pp. 19–20, and references above on particular tribes. Also Christopher Boehm, *Blood Revenge: The Anthropology of Feuds in Montenegro and Other Tribal Societies* (Lawrence: University Press of Kansas, 1984), chaps. 6, 11; for the Iroquois see below, chapter 14.

26. For definitions see Service, *Primitive Social Organization,* chap. 4.

27. Anocracy: Ted Robert Gurr, "Persistence and Change in Political Systems, 1800–1971," *American Political Science Review* 68 (1974): 1482–1504, see pp. 1485–1487. See Zeev Maoz and Nasrin Abdolali, "Regime Types and International Conflict, 1816–1976," *Journal of Conflict Resolution* 33 (1989): 3–35, pp. 11–12. "Anarchy" carries too many extraneous implications. "State": an elaboration of Max Weber's definition; for more see Charles Tilly, *Coercion, Capital, and European States, A.D. 990–1992,* rev. ed. (Cambridge, Mass.: Blackwell, 1992), pp. 1–2, 19, and passim; Philip S. Khoury and Joseph Kostiner, eds., *Tribes and State Formation in the Middle East* (Berkeley: University of California Press, 1991).

28. Lebanon: Michael C. Hudson, *The Precarious Republic: Political Modernization in Lebanon* (New York: Random House, 1968), p. 133; see also appendix, 1948 case.

29. Hyde, *Society and Politics,* pp. 104–107; Starn, *Contrary Commonwealth,* pp. 13–16; Marvin B. Becker, *Florence in Transition,* 2 vols. (Baltimore: Johns Hopkins University Press, 1967–1968), vol. 2, chap. 4; Heers, *Parties and Political.* Anarchy: Yves Renouard, *Les Villes d'Italie, de la fin du Xe siècle au début du XIVe siècle* (Paris: Société d'édition d'enseignement, 1969), part 7, p. 166.

30. De Negri, *Storia di Genova,* pp. 454–461, cf. pp. 329–330; Benvenuti, *Storia . . . Genova,* pp. 90–92, cf. pp. 65–66; see G. Villani, *Cronica,* 11.69, p. 142; Hazlitt, *Venetian Republic,* pp. 312–321.

31. "Punitive expedition": Norwich, *History of Venice,* pp. 243–244; see also De Negri, *Storia di Genova,* p. 293.

32. M. Villani, *Cronica,* books 5 and 8, esp. 8.51, vol. 4, pp. 61–62. See William Heywood, *A History of Perugia,* ed. R. Langton Douglas (New York: G. P. Putnam's Sons, 1910), pp. 154–159, 222–241; Pompeo Pellini, *Dell'historia di Perugia,* 1664 (Bologna: Forni, 1968), part 1, book 8, p. 974; for background see Schevill, *Siena,* chap. 7; William M. Bowsky, *A Medieval Italian Commune: Siena Under the Nine, 1287–1355* (Berkeley: University of California Press, 1981).

33. Romanin, *Storia . . . Venezia,* vol. 4, pp. 180–181.

34. Here and below see Gino Benvenuti, *Storia della Repubblica di Pisa* (Pisa: Giardini, 1967), p. 329ff; Becker, *Florence in Transition,* vol. 1; Gisuseppe Rossi-Sabatini, "Pisa al Tempo dei Donaratico (1316–1347)," in *Studio sulla crisi costituzionale del Commune* (Florence: Sansoni, 1938), pp. 232–235; Pietro Silva, *Il Governo di Pietro Gambacorta in Pisa*

e le sue relazioni col resto della Toscana e coi Visconti (Pisa: Nistri, 1911), pp. 14–19. For historiography see introduction by Cinzio Violante in Gioacchino Volpe, *Studi sulli istituzioni comunali a Pisa: Città e contado, communali e podestà secoli XII–XIII,* new ed. (Florence: Sansoni, 1970), pp. xxxvi–xli. On magnates favoring the war see Gene A. Brucker, *Florentine Politics and Society, 1343–1378* (Princeton: Princeton University Press, 1962) p. 112; on Pisan nobles see Benvenuti, *Storia della Repubblica,* p. 324.

35. Besides previously cited works see Ranieri Sardo, "Cronica Pisana," in *Istorie pisana e cronache varie pisanie,* vol. 2, part 1 (Florence, 1845), chaps. 117–121, pp. 132–135; M. Villani, *Cronica,* 5.30–33, p. 3.46–53, and 5.37, p. 3.57–59. After 1356, deaths apparently numbered in the hundreds, Villani, *Cronica,* 6.47, p. 3.168–169; Silva, *Il Governo di Pietro Gambacorta,* pp. 26–27; Sardo, *Cronica,* chap. 131, p. 152. Also Brucker, *Florentine Politics,* pp. 73–74, 183–93; Becker, *Florence in Transition,* vol. 2, p. 122, 122n.

36. Brucker, *Florentine Politics,* p. 268, 268n; François-Tommy Perrens, *Histoire de Florence depuis ses origines jusqu'à la domination des Médicis,* 6 vols., 2nd ed. (Paris: Fontemoing, 1873–1883), vol. 6, pp. 132–154; Benvenuti, *Storia della Repubblica di Pisa,* pp. 378–384; Giovanni di Ser Piero, "Sei capitoli dell'acquisto di Pisa fatto dai fiorentini nel 1406," in *Archivio Storico Italiano,* ser. 1, vol. 6, part 2, ed. Francesco Boniani (Florence, 1845), 245–279, see pp. 248–250; for details, Anonymous, "Cronica volgare di anonimo forentino dall'anno 1385 al 1409 già attributa a Piero di Giovanni Minerbetti," in *Rerum Italicarum Scriptores,* vol. 27, part 2, ed. E. Bellondi (Città di Castello: Lapi, 1915). Some historians attribute Tuscan peace to effective Florentine predominance, but the Florentines were plainly unable to control their neighbors, and wars did erupt when autocrats were involved.

37. After Lucca became a republic around 1370, peace prevailed between these traditional enemies; Florentines noticed "there was not an instance, while Lucca was free, of her having done an injury to Florence." Niccolo Machiavelli, *History of Florence and of the Affairs of Italy* (New York: Harper and Row, 1960), 4.4, p. 180. In 1431 Florence made a grab for Lucca, pointing out that Lucca had fallen to a tyrant. Bayley, *War and Society,* pp. 97–104; Perrens, *Histoire de Florence,* vol. 6, pp. 326–351; Schevill, *History of Florence,* pp. 350–351; Albizzi, *Commissioni,* vol. 3, pp. 192–206.

38. These traditional enemies made peace by the 1370s, each intent that the other maintain a similar republican regime. Bowsky, *A Medieval Italian,* pp. 59–64, 168–173; William M. Bowsky, "The Anatomy of Rebellion in Fourteenth-Century Siena," in Martines, *Violence and Civil Disorder,* pp. 229–272; Gene A. Brucker, *The Civic World of Early Renaissance Florence* (Princeton: Princeton University Press, 1977), pp. 106–108; Schevill, *Siena,* chap. 7. When the Sienese allied with the Duke of Milan, Florence begged them to renounce him, recalling "the identity of our constitutions and our concern for liberty." Nicolai Rubinstein, "Florence and the Despots: Some Aspects of Florentine Diplomacy in the Fourteenth Century," *Transactions of the Royal Historical Society, 5th ser.* 2 (1952): 21–46, see p. 32. But Sienese patricians, fearful of rebellious shopkeepers and artisans, handed the city to the duke in 1391. At just this point petty raiding grew into major warfare with Florence. Perrens, *Histoire de Florence,* vol. 6, book 9, chaps. 1, 2; Anonymous,

"Cronica volgare," in *Rerum Ital Script,* see pp. 102–103, 139 for death counts. In 1404 the Sienese retrieved their liberty; the two republics were soon friends.

39. Despite longstanding rivalries, the cities did not meet in combat until 1466, promptly after Florence fell under the rule of a tyrant. After the Florentines restored their republic, friendship was restored. See appendix for 1447 and 1494. On the 1529 restoration of friendship see William J. Bouwsma, *Venice and the Defense of Republican Liberty: Renaissance Values in the Age of Counter-Reformation* (Berkeley: University of California Press, 1968), p. 102.

40. These traditional enemies kept peace once both became republics, except in the 1390s, when Pisa was under a tyrant. Christine Meek, *Lucca, 1369–1404: Politics and Society in an Early Renaissance City-State* (Oxford: Oxford University Press, 1978), pp. 277–318.

41. Gino Benvenuti, *Storia dell'assedio di Pisa (1494–1509)* (Pisa: Giardini, 1969); Michele Luzzati, *Una Guerra di popolo: Lettere private del tempo del'assedio di Pisa (1494–1509)* (Pisa: Pacini, 1973); Felix Gilbert, *Machiavelli and Guicciardini: Politics and History in 16th Century Florence* (Princeton: Princeton University Press, 1965), pp. 19–25, 38–44, 78–79. See also chapter 13 and appendix.

42. Francesco Guicciardini, *Storia d'Italia,* 3 vols., ed. Silvana Seidel Menchi (Turin: Giulio Einaudi, 1971), vol. 1, 2.1, pp. 137–139 and 2.7, pp. 180–181; Luzzati, *Una Guerra,* esp. chaps. 5, 6. Note how Pisan envoys argued (ibid., p. 28n50) from the democratic concept of equality under natural law, saying God gives to every man a free will and an innate desire, inevitable as the hunger of the wolf, to exercise that free will.

43. "Alla populare": Gilbert, *Machiavelli,* pp. 61–62; see M. E. Mallett, "Pisa and Florence in the Fifteenth Century: Aspects of the Period of the First Florentine Domination," in *Florentine Studies: Politics and Society in Renaissance Florence,* ed. Nicolai Rubinstein (Evanston, Ill.: Northwestern University Press, 1968), pp. 403–441. The Florentines favoring war were the wealthiest and most aristocratic, while lesser tradesmen opposed it. On young patricians as leaders of raids compare Nardi, *Istorie,* 3.17, p. 162 with 3.18, p. 163; see also 2.2, p. 54. On sympathy for Pisans see Piero Vaglienti, *Storia dei suoi tempi, 1492–1514,* ed. Giuliani Berti et al. (Pisa: Nistri-Lischi e Pacini, 1982), p. 223. Sustain cruelty: Guicciardini, "Dialogo," pp. 161–162.

I add up several hundred deaths over the fifteen years, using Nardi, *Istorie,* and Biagio Buonaccorsi, *Diario de'successi piu importanti seguita in Italia . . . 1498–1512,* 1568 (Florence: Libreria SP 44, 1973). The most serious battle was an unplanned melee in which about eighty men died because a river cut off their escape; ibid., p. 100; Vaglienti, *Storia,* p. 196. The ones reluctant to fight were mercenaries, but many of these may have been Florentine commoners. Young patricians were not so reluctant. Buonaccorsi, *Diario* p. 116; Vaglienti, *Storia,* p. 202; Guicciardini, *Storia,* 6.13, pp. 615, 626–627; Luca Landucci, *A Florentine Diary from 1450 to 1516 by Luca Landucci Continued by an Anonymous Writer till 1542,* ed. Iodoco del Badia, trans. Alice de Rosen Jervis (New York: Dutton, 1927).

44. For circumstances and references see appendix.

45. Confined to raiding: Giovanni Cavalcanti, *Istorie fiorentine* (Florence, 1838–1839), 8.3, pp. 483–484. Freebooter brawl: Tommaso Fecini, *Cronache senesi di Tommaso Fecini,*

vol. 15, part 6, no. 10 of *Rerum Italicarum Scriptores, n.s.,* ed. L. A. Muratori (Bologna: Lanichelli, 1939–1947), pp. 841–847.

46. Guicciardini, *Storia,* 2.9, p. 196; 8.14, p. 811; 8.4, p. 749; Buonaccorsi, *Diario,* p. 145. In other wars of the time Italian troops did storm walls.

47. Marino Berengo, *Nobili e mercanti nella Lucca del Cinquecento* (Turin: Einaudi, 1965), pp. 219–228.

48. Quentin Skinner, *The Foundations of Modern Political Thought,* vol. 1 (Cambridge: Cambridge University Press, 1978), chaps. 5, 6; Bouwsma, *Venice and the Defense;* Luigi Villari, *The Republic of Ragusa: An Episode of the Turkish Conquest* (London: Dent, 1904).

49. Garrett Mattingly, *Renaissance Diplomacy,* (1955; reprint, New York: Dover, 1988), chaps. 5–7.

50. Hyde, *Society and Politics,* pp. 166–170, 178–179, 186; Martines, *Power and Imagination,* pp. 168–175; generally see Hay and Law, *Italy in the Age of the Renaissance.* The advent of the Black Death in 1348 was not decisive: the chronicles show a surprising political continuity across these years, and it was a little later that warfare between republics disappeared.

51. Waley, *Italian City-Republics,* pp. 107–115.

52. Lauro Martines, "Political Violence in the Thirteenth Century," in *Violence and Civil Disorder in Italian Cities, 1200–1500,* ed. Lauro Martines (Berkeley: University of California Press, 1972), p. 331; Brucker, *Renaissance Florence,* pp. 91–101, 116–117; Starn, *Contrary Commonwealth,* chap. 4; Becker, *Florence in Transition,* esp. pp. 226–227, 231–233; Marvin B. Becker, "The Florentine Territorial State and Civic Humanism in the Early Renaissance," in Rubinstein, *Florentine Studies,* pp. 109–139; Giorgio Chittolini, "La Crisi delle libertà comunali e le origini dello stato territoriale," in *La Formazione dello stato regionale e le istituzioni del contado* (Turin: Einaudi, 1979), pp. 3–35. For general ideas see Joseph R. Strayer, *On the Medieval Origins of the Modern State* (Princeton: Princeton University Press, 1970). On changing warfare motivations ca. 1400 related to increased state apparatus see Tilly, *Coercion,* pp. 184–185.

CHAPTER FOUR

The Rise of Republican States, Ideals, and Alliances

1. Giovanni Villani, *Cronica di Giovanni Villani: A miglior lezione ridotta coll'aiuto de' testi a penna* (Florence: Magheri, 1823), 11.135, pp. 252–253; cf. 11.30, pp. 234–235.

2. I skip over Villani's nod to the sin of pride. See Louis F. Green, *Chronicle into History: An Essay on the Interpretation of History in Florentine Fourteenth Century Chronicles* (Cambridge: Cambridge University Press, 1972), pp. 7, 141–143.

3. J. H. Burns, ed., *The Cambridge History of Medieval Political Thought, c. 350–c.1450* (Cambridge: Cambridge University Press, 1988), esp. chap. 18; Walter Ullmann, *Principles of Government and Politics in the Middle Ages* (London: Methuen, 1961) pp. 217–218, 227–228; Quentin Skinner, *The Foundations of Modern Political Thought,* vol. 1 (Cambridge: Cambridge University Press, 1978), pp. 44–59; George Holmes, "The Emergence of an Urban Ideology at Florence," *Transactions of the Royal Historical Society, 5th ser.* 23 (1973):

111–134, see pp. 127–129. On autocratic ideology see Hans Baron, *The Crisis of the Early Italian Renaissance: Civic Humanism and Republican Liberty in an Age of Classicism and Tyranny,* rev. ed. (Princeton: Princeton University Press, 1966), pp. 36–38, 134–137, 144.

4. On Florence see also works cited in chapter 3. Peter Partner, "Florence and the Papacy, 1300–1375," in *Europe in the Late Middle Ages,* ed. John Hale, Roger Highfield, and Beryl Smalley (London: Faber and Faber, 1965), pp. 76–121. Epitaph: Bella Duffy, *The Tuscan Republics (Florence, Siena, Pisa, and Lucca) with Genoa* (New York: G. P. Putnam's Sons, 1893), p. 180. In developing an ideology Florence may or may not have been the leader, but it is where we have sources. Francesca Klein, "Considerazioni sull'ideologia della Città di Firenze tra Trecento e Quattrocento (Giovanni Villani-Leonardo Bruni)," *Ricerche Storiche* 10 (1980): 311–336.

5. Nicolai Rubinstein, "Florence and the Despots: Some Aspects of Florentine Diplomacy in the Fourteenth Century," *Transactions of the Royal Historical Society, 5th ser.* 2 (1952): 21–46, see pp. 29–30; D. M. Bueno de Mesquita, "The Place of Despotism in Italian Politics," in Hale, Highfield, and Smalley, *Europe in the Late Middle Ages,* see pp. 304–305; William M. Bowsky, *Henry VII in Italy: The Conflict of Empire and City-State, 1310–1313* (Lincoln: University of Nebraska Press, 1960), chap. 2; Édouard Jordan, *L'Allemagne et l'Italie aux XIIe et XIIIe siècles* (Paris: PUF, 1939), p. 210; John Gilbert Heinberg, "History of the Majority Principle," *American Political Science Review* 20 (1928): 52–68. Since deepest antiquity: not only the assembly of warriors but also village elders, in Homer, *Iliad* 18:566–568.

6. There were forerunners, e.g., in Liége (1253), Ghent (1274), Barcelona (1285), and Rostock (1312); the most famous risings came later, in Florence (1378) and London (1381). An introduction is Guy Fourquin, *The Anatomy of Popular Rebellion in the Middle Ages,* trans. Anne Chesters (Amsterdam: North Holland, 1978). On frequency of German risings, especially in the latter 1300s, see Erich Maschke, "Deutsche Städte am Ausgang des Mittelalters," in *Die Stadt am Ausgang des Mittelalters,* ed. Wilhelm Rausch (Linz: Donau, 1974), pp. 21 and 40n.

7. Daniel Waley, *The Italian City-Republics,* 3rd ed. (London: Longman, 1988), p. 178; Gene A. Brucker, *Renaissance Florence,* rev. ed. (Berkeley: University of California Press, 1983), p. 126; Marvin B. Becker, "The Florentine Territorial State and Civic Humanism in the Early Renaissance," in *Florentine Studies: Politics and Society in Renaissance Florence,* ed. Nicolai Rubinstein (Evanston, Ill.: Northwestern University Press, 1968), p. 115; Lauro Martines, *Power and Imagination: City-States in Renaissance Italy* (New York: Knopf, 1979), pp. 202–205. Marsiglio's work of 1324 was translated into Tuscan around 1362, see James M. Blythe, *Ideal Government and the Mixed Constitution in the Middle Ages* (Princeton: Princeton University Press, 1992), pp. 193–202; J. P. Canning in Burns, *Cambridge History,* pp. 469–476; Ullmann, *Principles,* pp. 266–287; Skinner, *Foundations,* vol. 1, pp. 15–22; John K. Hyde, *Society and Politics in Medieval Italy: The Evolution of the Civil Life, 1000–1350* (London: Macmillan, 1973), pp. 194–196. Based on voting: Matteo Villani, *Cronica di Matteo Villani* (Florence, 1825), 8.24, pp. 34–35; Marvin B. Becker, *Florence in Transition,* 2 vols. (Baltimore: Johns Hopkins University Press, 1967–1968), vol. 1, pp. 60–61, 226; Baron, *Crisis,* pp. 418–424.

8. "Reemerged": Orlando Patterson, *Freedom in the Making of Western Culture,* vol. 1 of *Freedom* (New York: Basic, 1991), p. 368, see chaps. 21, 22. Baron, *Crisis,* pp. 24, 55–57, 196–198, 361–362; Donald Weinstein, "The Myth of Florence," in Rubinstein, *Florentine Studies,* pp. 15–44; Partner, "Florence and the Papacy," p. 97; Nicolai Rubinstein, "Marsilius of Padua and Italian Political Thought of His Time," in Hale, Highfield, and Smalley, *Europe,* pp. 51–52, 62–63; Rubinstein, "Florence and the Despots"; and especially Skinner, *Foundations,* vol. 1, pp. 9–12, 41–47, 53–65. For anti-tyrant rhetoric see M. Villani, *Cronica,* prologues 3.1, 5.1, 6.1, 7.1, and 8.24.

9. The prototypical debate is Herodotus, *The Histories,* trans. George Rawlinson (New York: Dial, 1928), 3.80–82. Note also Euripides, *The Suppliant Women,* lines 399–455, Euripides, *Supplices,* 2 vols., ed. Christopher Collard (Groningen: Bouma's, 1975), vol. 2, pp. 212–233. See A. W. H. Advins, *Moral Values and Political Behaviour in Ancient Greece: From Homer to the End of the Fifth Century* (New York: W. W. Norton, 1972); Ellen Meiksins Wood, *Peasant-Citizen and Slave: The Foundations of Athenian Democracy* (New York: Verso, 1988), pp. 126–137; Mogens Herman Hansen, *The Athenian Democracy in the Age of Demosthenes: Structure, Principles and Ideology,* trans. J. A. Crook (Oxford: Blackwell, 1991), pp. 73–85. On autocracy, James F. McGlew, *Tyranny and Political Culture in Ancient Greece* (Ithaca, N.Y.: Cornell University Press, 1993). On rule by law, M. I. Finley, *Politics in the Ancient World,* rev. ed. (Cambridge: Cambridge University Press, 1984), pp. 135–139. "Never trusting anybody" (Aeschylus) and other remarks: Maurice Pope, "Thucydides and Democracy," *Historia* 37 (1988): 276–296, see p. 285. Pericles: Thucydides, *History of the Peloponnesian War,* trans. Rex Warner (New York: Penguin, 1954), 2.37, 2.41.

10. For background see Christopher R. Friedrichs, "The Swiss and German City-States," in *The City-State in Five Cultures,* ed. Robert Griffeth and Carol G. Thomas (Santa Barbara: ABC-Clio, 1981); Leonard von Muralt, "Renaissance und Reformation," in *Handbuch der Schweizer Geschichte,* vol. 1 (Zurich: Berichthaus, 1972), pp. 405–418, Machiavelli quote p. 410; Thomas A. Brady, Jr., *Turning Swiss: Cities and Empire, 1450–1550* (Cambridge: Cambridge University Press, 1985), pp. 20–21.

11. A summary is Robert D. Putnam, *Making Democracy Work: Civic Traditions in Modern Italy* (Princeton: Princeton University Press, 1993), pp. 87–89. For a typical list see James R. Pennock, *Democratic Political Theory* (Princeton, N.J.: Princeton University Press, 1979), pp. 236–259. Pericles: Thucydides, 2.37.

12. On Greek toleration see, e.g., Thucydides, 7.69, Herodotus, 3.81. For law see Joseph R. Strayer, *On the Medieval Origins of the Modern State* (Princeton: Princeton University Press, 1970), p. 63 and passim. On minority rights see Arend Lijphart, *Democracy in Plural Societies: A Comparative Exploration* (New Haven: Yale University Press, 1977), chap. 2.

13. Baron, *Crisis,* pp. 418–424; John M. Najemy, *Corporatism and Consensus in Florentine Electoral Politics, 1280–1400* (Chapel Hill: University of North Carolina Press, 1982), pp. 308–309; Denys Hay and John Law, *Italy in the Age of the Renaissance, 1380–1530* (London: Longman, 1989), p. 274. "Men fought" quoted in Becker, "The Florentine Territorial State," pp. 138–139.

14. Jane J. Mansbridge, *Beyond Adversary Democracy* (New York: Basic, 1980), chap. 1 and pp. 290–293; Lijphart, *Democracy in Plural,* chap. 3; Hans Daadler, "The Consociational Democracy Theme," *World Politics* 26 (1974): 604–621; Quentin Skinner, "Machiavelli's *Discorsi* and the Pre-Humaninst Origins of Republican Ideas," in *Machiavelli and Republicanism,* ed. Gisela Bock, Quentin Skinner, and Maurizio Viroli (Cambridge: Cambridge University Press, 1990), pp. 121–141. On participation see Andrew J. Nathan and Tianjian Shi, "Cultural Requisites for Democracy in China: Findings From a Survey," *Daedalus (Proceedings of the American Academy of Arts and Sciences)* 122, no. 2 (1993): 95–123. For a sociological perspective see David Knoke, "Incentives in Collective Action Organizations," *American Sociological Review* 53 (1988): 311–329.

15. J. R. Hale, "Contemporary Views on Factional Civil Strife in Thirteenth- and Fourteenth-Century Italy," in *Violence and Civil Disorder in Italian Cities, 1200–1500,* ed. Lauro Martines (Berkeley: University of California Press, 1972), pp. 280–282, 297–299; Jacques Heers, *Parties and Political Life in the Medieval West,* trans. David Nichols (Amsterdam, N.Y.: Nathaniel-Holland, 1977), pp. 54–58; Hyde, *Society and Politics,* p. 187; Rubinstein, "Marsilius of Padua," p. 57; Najemy, *Corporatism;* Skinner, *Foundations* vol. 1, pp. 44, 60–65; for "citizen" see Ullmann, *Principles,* pp. 286, 296; for loyalty see Strayer, *On the Medieval,* pp. 9–10. Statistics: James E. Everett and Donald E. Queller, "Family, Faction and Politics in Early Renaissance Venice: Elections in the Great Council, 1303–87," *Studies in Medieval and Renaissance History* 14 (1994): 1–31.

16. Wilhelm Ebel, *Der Bürgereid als Geltungsgrund und Gestaltungsprinzip des deutschen mittelalterlichen Stadtrechts* (Weimar: Böhlaus, 1958), esp. pp. 24, 43–46. Also Bernd Moeller, *Imperial Cities and the Reformation,* ed. H. C. Erik Midelfort and Mark U. Edwards, Jr., trans. H. C. Erik Midelfort and Mark U. Edwards, Jr. (Philadelphia: Fortress, 1972), pp. 44–49; Hans C. Peyer, *Verfassungsgeschichte der alten Schweiz* (Zurich: Schulthess, 1978), p. 54; *Handbuch der Schweizer Geschichte,* vol. 1 (Zurich: Berichthaus, 1972), pp. 194–196; R. Po-chia Hsia, "The Myth of the Commune: Recent Historiography on City and Reformation in Germany," *Central European History* 20 (1987): 203–215; Heinreich Schmidt, *Die Deutschen Städtechroniken als Spiegel des Bürgerlichen Selbstverständnissn im Spätmittelalter,* Schriftenreihe der Historischen Kommission bei der Bayerischen Akademie der Wissenschaften, vol. 3 (Göttingen: Vandenhoek & Ruprecht, 1958), pp. 76–87. Venetians: William J. Bouwsma, *Venice and the Defense of Republican Liberty: Renaissance Values in the Age of Counter-Reformation* (Berkeley: University of California Press, 1968), p. 54. Saxon tribes: Reginald Horsman, *Race and Manifest Destiny: The Origins of American Racial Anglo-Saxonism* (Cambridge, Mass.: Harvard University Press, 1981), chap. 1.

17. For "upward" vs. "downward" see Ullman, *Principles;* Hans-Christoph Rublack, "Political and Social Norms in Urban Communities in the Holy Roman Empire," in *Religion, Politics, and Social Protest: Three Studies in Early Modern Germany,* ed. Kaspar von Greyerz (London: Allen and Unwin, 1985), pp. 24–60; Erika Uitz, "Zu Friedensbemühungen und Friedensvorstellungen des mittelalterlichen Städtebürgertums," *Jahrbuch für Geschichte Feudalismus* 12 (1988): 27–50, see pp. 28–30.

18. Thucydides, 5.105. A mainstream example is John Spanier, *American Foreign Policy Since World War II,* 12th ed. (Washington D.C.: Congressional Quarterly Press, 1991).

The classic "realist" text is Hans J. Morgenthau and Kenneth W. Thompson, *Politics Among Nations: The Struggle for Power and Peace* (New York: Knopf, 1985), see p. 5, but Morgenthau admits that his "realism" is prescriptive. See also *Neorealism and Its Critics,* ed. Robert O. Keohane (New York: Columbia University Press, 1986); Geoffrey Blainey, *The Causes of War,* 3rd ed. (New York: Macmillan, 1988), esp. p. 150; Evan Luard, *War in International Society: A Study in International Sociology* (London: I. B. Tauris, 1986), chaps. 5, 6; James E. Dougherty and Robert L. Pfaltzgraff, Jr., *Contending Theories of International Relations: A Comprehensive Survey,* 3rd ed. (New York: Harper and Row, 1990), chap. 3.

19. Of the various definitions of "ideology" I use one grounded in cognitive theory and embracing chiefly political, social, and economic thought. See Michael H. Hunt, "Ideology," in *Explaining the History of American Foreign Relations,* ed. Michael J. Hogan and Thomas G. Paterson (Cambridge: Cambridge University Press, 1991), pp. 193–201. For lack of ideology before ca. 1400, see Holmes, "Urban Ideology," pp. 127, 129.

20. Baron, *Crisis,* esp. pp. 22–23, 269–273; "Free peoples federated" quoted p. 395. Also Hans Baron, *In Search of Florentine Civic Humanism: Essays on the Transition from Medieval to Modern Thought* (Princeton: Princeton University Press, 1988), esp. p. 207; Baron, "A Struggle for Liberty in the Renaissance: Florence, Venice, and Milan in the Early Quattrocento," *American Historical Review* 58 (1953): 265–289, 544–570. See Ronald Witt, "The *Crisis* after Forty Years," *American Historical Review* 101 (1996): 110–118.

21. Rubinstein, "Florence and the Despots," pp. 28, 32n5, 39; G. Villani, *Cronica,* 11.48–50, pp. 95–100. M. Villani, *Cronica,* vol. 1, 1.77, pp. 129–130; Gene A. Brucker, *Florentine Politics and Society, 1343–1378* (Princeton: Princeton University Press, 1962), pp. 268, 351; cf. Jerrold E. Siegal, "'Civic Humanism' or Ciceronian Rhetoric? The Culture of Petrarch and Bruni," *Past and Present* 34 (1966): 3–48; Skinner, *Foundations,* vol. 1, pp. 27, 73–76, 82–84; Becker "The Florentine Territorial State," esp. p. 109; George Holmes, *The Florentine Enlightenment: 1400–1450* (New York: Pegasus, 1969), chap. 5; Klein, *Ricerche Storiche* (1980), pp. 316–318.

22. Baron, *Crisis,* pp. 23, 392–395; Christine Meek, *Lucca, 1369–1404: Politics and Society in an Early Renaissance City-State* (Oxford: Oxford University Press, 1978), pp. 140–141. "Defense of Florence" quoted in Baron, "Struggle for Liberty," p. 562.

23. Some crucial dates: formation of Flemish town league (1338), adhesion of Bern to Swiss Confederacy (1353), consolidation of Hanseatic League (1366), formation of Swabian League (1376).

24. Artaxerxes: John Buckler, *The Theban Hegemony, 371–362 B.C.* (Cambridge, Mass.: Harvard University Press, 1980), p. 170. For other cases see appendix: 1443, 1447, 1490, 1494, 1499, 1529, 1652, 1797, 1812, 1847, 1849, 1879, 1899 (Boer), 1941, 1948, 1954, 1994.

25. Niccolo Machiavelli, *Discourses on the First Ten Books of Livy,* trans. Leslie V. Walker and Brian Richardson (Harmondsworth, England: Penguin, 1970), pp. 122–124, 1.59, pp. 259–260, 2.2, pp. 280–281, 2.19, pp. 335–338, 2.21, pp. 342–343; quotes at 2.4, pp. 283–288. See J. N. Stephens, *The Fall of the Florentine Republic, 1512–1530* (Oxford: Clarendon, 1983), p. 157.

26. The best introduction is *From Independence to c. 1870,* vol. 3 of *The Cambridge History of Latin America,* ed. Leslie Bethell (Cambridge: Cambridge University Press, 1985), esp. Frank Safford, "Politics, Ideology, and Society in Post-Independence Spanish America," pp. 347–342. Particularly detailed is Sergio Villalobos R., Fernando Silva V., Osvaldo Silva V., and Patricio Estellé M., *Historia de Chile,* 4 vols. (Santiago: Editorial Universitaria, 1974–1976).

27. 1871 election: Ruben Vargas Ugarte, *La República (1844–1879),* vol. 9 of *Historia General del Perú* (Lima: Carlos Miller Batres, 1971), p. 186. Carbines: Frederick B. Pike, *The Modern History of Peru* (New York: Praeger, 1967). Chilean elections: *Legitimacy and Stability in Latin America: A Study of Chilean Political Culture* (New York: New York University Press, 1969), p. 135n. On the general situation see Ronald H. Berg and Frederick Stinton Weaver, "Toward a Reinterpretation of Political Change in Peru During the First Century of Independence," *Journal of Interamerican Studies and World Affairs* 20 (1978): 69–84.

28. Julio Heise González, *Fundamentos histórico-culturales del parlamentarismo chileno,* vol. 1 of *Historia de Chile: El período parlamentario, 1861–1925* (Santiago: Andres Bello, 1974), pp. 65–66, argues for genuine Chilean "parliamentary liberalism" but finds it strong only after the War of the Pacific.

29. For comparison of caudillo with signor see Richard M. Morse, "Toward a Theory of Spanish American Government," *Journal of the History of Ideas* 15 (1954): 71–93, see pp. 79–80, 88.

30. Glen Caudill Dealy, *The Public Man: An Interpretation of Latin American and Other Catholic Countries* (Amherst: University of Massachusetts Press, 1977); Glen Caudill Dealy, "La tradición de la democracia monista en América Latin," *Estudios Andinos* 4 (1974–1975): 159–201; L. Cecil Jane, *Liberty and Despotism in Spanish America* (Oxford: Clarendon, 1929), chaps. 1, 2, 9; Leopoldo Zea, *The Latin American Mind,* trans. James H. Abott and Lowell Dunham (Norman: University of Oklahoma Press, 1968), pp. 52–53, 72–74; Emilio Willems, *Latin American Culture: An Anthropological Synthesis* (New York: Harper and Row, 1975), chap. 5; Eric R. Wolf and Edward C. Hansen, *The Human Condition in Latin America* (New York: Oxford University Press, 1972), pp. 223–229. For these problems in broader current perspective see Giuseppe Di Palma, *To Craft Democracies: An Essay on Democratic Transitions* (Berkeley: University of California Press, 1990), pp. 134–135, 153–155, 160; Moreno, *Legitimacy and Stability,* esp. chaps. 2, 5; Robert A. Dahl, *Polyarchy. Participation and Opposition* (New Haven: Yale University Press, 1971), pp. 132–138. Piérola quoted in Vargas Ugarte, *La República,* pp. 318–322.

31. Donald L. Horowitz, *Ethnic Groups in Conflict* (Berkeley: University of California Press, 1985), pp. 551–553.

32. Introductions are *Latin America, c. 1870–1930,* vol. 5 of Bethell, *Cambridge History of Latin America;* Walter LaFeber, *Inevitable Revolutions: The United States in Central America* (New York: W. W. Norton, 1983).

33. Daniel M. Masterson, *Militarism and Politics in Latin America: Peru from Sánchez Cerro to Sendero Luminoso* (New York: Greenwood, 1991), pp. 65–71; David W. Schodt,

Ecuador: An Andean Enigma (Boulder: Westview, 1987) pp. 137–144; Philip Mauceri, *Militares: Insurgencia y democratización en el Perú, 1980–1988* (Lima: Instituto de Estudios Peruanos, 1989), pp. 22–23; Jack Child, *Geopolitics and Conflict in South America* (New York: Praeger, 1985), pp. 96.

34. Vargas Ugarte, *La República,* pp. 180–181.

35. John E. Peterson, *The Arab Gulf States: Steps Toward Political Participation* (New York: Praeger, 1988), passim; "chairman" p. 8. Joseph Kostiner, "Transforming Dualities: Tribe and State Formation in Saudi Arabia," in *Tribes and State Formation in the Middle East,* ed. Philip S. Khoury and Joseph Kostiner (Berkeley: University of California Press, 1990), pp. 226–251. Jill Crystal, *Oil and Politics in the Gulf. Rulers and Merchants in Kuwait and Qatar* (Cambridge: Cambridge University Press, 1990); Rosemarie Said Zahlan, *The Making of the Modern Gulf States: Kuwait, Bahrain, Qatar, The United Arab Emirates and Oman* (London: Unwin Hyman, 1989); Fuad L. Khuri, *Tribe and State in Bahrain. The Transformation of Social and Political Authority in an Arab State* (Chicago: University of Chicago Press, 1980); Fred H. Lawson, *Bahrain: The Modernization of Autocracy* (Boulder: Westview, 1989); Ali Mohammed Khalifa, *The United Arab Emirates: Unity in Fragmentation* (Boulder: Westview, 1979), pp. 103–104. On Saudi Arabia see also David Holden and Richard Johns, *The House of Saud* (New York: Holt, Rinehart and Winston, 1981); Robert Lacey, *The Kingdom* (New York: Harcourt Brace Jovanovich, 1982).

36. On rulers forced to step down see Zahlan, *Making of the Modern Gulf,* pp. 88, 93, 113; Arnold Hottinger, "Political Institutions in Saudi Arabia, Kuwait and Bahrain," in *Security in the Persian Gulf: Domestic Political Factors,* ed. Shahram Chubin (Monclair, N.J.: Allanheld, Osmun, 1981), pp. 3–5. For recent deposition of Qatar's ruler see *Washington Post,* 28 June 1995.

37. Abdul-Reda and Kamal Al-Monoufi Assiri, "Kuwait's Political Elite: The Cabinet," *Middle East Journal* 42 (1988): 48–58.

38. Violence in Shariga (Sharijah): Khalifa, *United Arab Emirates,* pp. 102, 105–106; John Duke Anthony, *Arab States of the Lower Gulf: People, Politics, Petroleum* (Washington, D.C.: Middle East Institute, 1975), pp. 186, 213–215.

39. Christian Meier, *The Greek Discovery of Politics* (Cambridge, Mass.: Harvard University Press, 1991); for a description of Greece that could apply almost verbatim to the Italian transition see Ellen Meiksins Wood and Neal Wood, *Class Ideology and Ancient Political Theory: Socrates, Plato, and Aristotle in Social Context* (Oxford: Blackwell, 1979), pp. 23, 26–27, 70–72.

40. George McCall Theal, *History of South Africa from 1795 to 1872,* 5 vols. (London: Allen and Unwin, 1910–1927), vol. 3; Monica Wilson and Leonard Thompson, eds., *The Oxford History of South Africa,* 2 vols. (New York: Oxford University Press, 1969–1971), 2 vols.; "feuds and rivalries": Arthur Conan Doyle, *The Great Boer War,* rev. ed. (New York: McClure, Phillips, 1902), p. 10.

41. Socioeconomic but not political complexity correlates somewhat with wars in the study of Marc Howard Ross, *The Culture of Conflict: Interpretations and Interests in Comparative Perspective* (New Haven: Yale University Press, 1994), chap. 6. On suppressing raids see R. Brian Ferguson, "Explaining War," in *The Anthropology of War,* ed. Jonathan

Haas (Cambridge: Cambridge University Press, 1990), pp. 41, 50; R. Brian Ferguson, "Introduction: Studying War," in *Warfare, Culture, and Environment,* ed. R. Brian Ferguson (Orlando, Fla.: Academic Press, 1984), pp. 16–21. Keith F. Otterbein, *The Evolution of War: A Cross-Cultural Study* (New Haven: Human Relations Area Files, 1970), pp. 29–31; Otterbein's appendices C, D show virtually no feuding in the ten of his fifty "preindustrial" societies that were centralized.

CHAPTER FIVE
The Political Culture of Peace

1. Dante Aligheri, *Inferno* 33: 79–84. Cf. enmity to Pisans in Giovanni Villani, *Cronica di Giovanni Villani: A miglior lezione ridotta coll'aiuto de' testi a penna* (Florence: Magheri, 1823).

2. Matteo Villani, *Cronica di Matteo Villani* (Florence, 1825), 10.83, pp. 108–109, see also 9.78, pp. 274–275 and 10.85, p. 111. "Most of all the Pisans": Antonio Pucci, "Guerra tra fiorentini e' pisani," in *Delizie degli eruditi toscani,* vol. 6: *Della Poesie di Antonio Pucci,* ed. Fr. Ildefonso (Florence, 1775), 2.19, pp. 205–206; see also 1.24–25, pp. 195–196, 2.25, pp. 207, 2.31–34, pp. 209–210; "Vivere all piana," 7.9, p. 258.

3. An overview is Harry Eckstein, *Regarding Politics: Essays on Political Theory, Stability, and Change* (Berkeley: University of California Press, 1992), chaps. 7, 8. On beliefs see Robert A. Dahl, *Polyarchy: Participation and Opposition* (New Haven: Yale University Press, 1971), chap. 8; Gabriel Almond and Sidney Verba, eds., *The Civic Culture Revisited* (Boston: Little, Brown, 1980), especially Gabriel Almond, "The Intellectual History of the Civic Culture Concept," pp. 1–36; Gabriel Almond, "The Study of Political Culture," in *A Discipline Divided: Symbols and Sects in Political Science,* ed. Gabriel Almond (Newbury Park, Calif.: Sage, 1990), pp. 138–156; Gabriel Almond, "The Study of Political Culture," in *Political Culture in Germany,* ed. Dirk Berg-Schlosser and Ralf Rytlewski, eds. (New York: St. Martin's, 1992), pp. 13–26; Sidney Verba, "Comparative Political Culture," in *Political Culture and Political Development,* ed. Lucian W. Pye and Sidney Verba (Princeton: Princeton University Press, 1965), pp. 512–560, see p. 513 for a pioneering definition. For definitions see also Michael Thompson, Richard Ellis, and Aaron Wildavsky, *Cultural Theory* (Boulder: Westview, 1990), pp. 215–218; Akira Iriye, "Culture and Power: International Relations as Intercultural Relations," *Diplomatic History* 3 (1979): 115–128; G. Hofstede in *Processes of International Negotiations,* ed. Frances Mautner-Markhof (Boulder: Westview, 1989), pp. 193–201; Alex Inkeles, ed., "On Measuring Democracy," *Studies in Comparative International Development* 25 (Spring 1990), especially articles by Kenneth A. Bolen, pp. 7–24, Michael Coppedge and Wolfgang H. Reinecke, pp. 51–72, and Mark J. Gasiorowski, pp. 109–125.

4. For meticulous definitions see Marc H. Ross, *The Culture of Conflict* (New Haven: Yale University Press, 1994), pp. 16–23.

5. On mental dissonance and key terms such as "belief" see M. Fishbein and I. Ajzer, *Belief, Attitude, Intention and Behavior* (Reading, Pa.: Addison-Wesley, 1975); H. Markus and R. B. Zajonc, "The Cognitive Perspective in Social Psychology," in *Handbook of Social*

Psychology, 3rd ed., ed. G. Lindzey and E. Aronson (New York: Random House, 1985), pp. 201–204; Susan T. Fiske and Shelley E. Taylor, *Social Cognition,* 2nd ed. (New York: McGraw-Hill, 1991), pp. 467–472. For comments on ideology see Michael H. Hunt, *Ideology and United States Foreign Policy* (New Haven: Yale University Press, 1987), chap. 1.

6. Summaries include Fiske and Taylor, *Social Cognition,* esp. pp. 12–13, 150–152, and chap. 4; Albert Bandara, *Social Foundations of Thought and Action: A Social Cognitive Theory* (Englewood Cliffs, N.J.: Prentice-Hall, 1986); Richard Nisbett and Lee Ross, *Human Inference: Strategies and Shortcomings of Social Judgment* (Englewood Cliffs, N.J.: Prentice-Hall, 1980), esp. chap. 8; Richard R. Lau and David O. Sears, "Social Cognition and Political Cognition: The Past, The Present, and the Future," in *Political Cognition: The 19th Annual Carnegie Symposium on Cognition,* ed. Richard R. Lau and David O. Sears (Hillsdale, N.J.: Erlbaum, 1986); Markus and Zajonc, "Cognitive Perspective," pp. 137–230. For consistency in conflict see R. A. Levine and D. Campbell, *Ethnocentrism: Theories of Conflict, Ethnic Attitudes, and Group Behavior* (New York: Wiley, 1972), chap. 12; Christer Jönsson, *Communicating in International Bargaining* (New York: St. Martin's, 1990); Jonathon Bendor, Roderick M. Kramer, and Suzanne Stout, "When in Doubt . . . Cooperation in a Noisy Prisoner's Dilemma," *Journal of Conflict Resolution* 35 (1991): 691–719, see pp. 714–717.

7. Iriye, "Culture and Power;" Hofstede, "Cultural Predictors;" Y. H. Poortinga and E. C. Hendriks, "Culture as a Factor in International Negotiations," in Mautner-Markhof, *Processes of International Negotiations,* pp. 203–212. For a summary of this cognitive approach to diplomacy see James M. Goldgeier, *Leadership Style and Soviet Foreign Policy* (Baltimore: Johns Hopkins University Press, 1994), pp. 2–8.

8. "Cold-blooded": Henry Kissinger, *Years of Upheaval* (Boston: Little, Brown, 1982), p. 50, see also pp. 168–169. "Fundamentally different," "substantive": Henry Kissinger, "Domestic Structure and Foreign Policy," *Daedalus* (Spring 1966): 503–529, quote on pp. 503–504.

9. Napoleon: Henry A. Kissinger, *A World Restored. Metternich, Castlereagh, and the Problem of Peace, 1812–1822* (1957; reprint, Boston: Houghton Mifflin, 1973), p. 110. Soviets: Kissinger, *Years of Upheaval,* p. 245; see p. 49 for a similar statement on the Chinese Communist leaders; also Kissinger, "Domestic Structure," pp. 520–521. Note that Kissinger is speaking more of individual personalities than of political culture per se.

10. Ancient Athenian: Thucydides, 1.122. See James Davidson, "Isocrates Against Imperialism: An Analysis of the *De Pace,*" *Historia* 39 (1990): 20–36, esp. p. 31; also Plato, *Laws,* trans. R. G. Bury (Cambridge, Mass.: Harvard University Press, 1926), 3.697D.

11. "To be trusted": Niccolo Machiavelli, *Discourses on the First Ten Books of Livy,* trans. Leslie V. Walker and Brian Richardson (Harmondsworth, England: Penguin, 1970), 1.59, pp. 259–260. On republican constancy see also Giovanni Cavalcanti, *Istorie fiorentine,* 2 vols. (Florence, 1838–1839), 3.25, p. 147; and G. Villani, *Cronica*; Garrett Mattingly, *Renaissance Diplomacy* (1955; reprint, New York: Dover, 1988), pp. 70, 81, 99, see also chaps. 5–7; William J. Bouwsma, *Venice and the Defense of Republican Liberty: Renaissance Values in the Age of Counter-Reformation* (Berkeley: University of California Press, 1968), pp. 4–5, 8–17.

12. For example, Immanuel Kant, *Perpetual Peace (Zum ewigen Frieden. Ein philosophisches Entwurf)*, 1795, trans. Lewis White Beck (Indianapolis: Bobbs-Merrill, 1957), pp. 12–13; Michael Howard, *War and the Liberal Conscience* (New Brunswick, N.J.: Rutgers University Press, 1978), p. 25, 27; Felix Gilbert, *To the Farewell Address: Ideas of Early American Foreign Policy* (Princeton: Princeton University Press, 1961), pp. 61–64.

13. Jeremy Black, ed., *The Origins of War in Early Modern Europe* (Edinburgh: John Donald, 1987), esp. p. 205; children on a playground: William Roosen, "The Origins of the War of Spanish Succession," in ibid., pp. 155–156. For examples see Mattingly, *Renaissance Diplomacy*, chap. 18; Paul Sonnino, *Louis XIV and the Origins of the Dutch War* (Cambridge: Cambridge University Press, 1988), esp. pp. 6–7, 23, 192; John Huxtable Elliott, *Richelieu and Olivares* (Cambridge: Cambridge University Press, 1984).

14. United States: Gilbert, *To the Farewell Address*, pp. 65–71. France: Jacques Godechot, *La Grande Nation: L'expansion révolutionnaire de la France dans le monde, 1789–1799*, 2 vols. (Paris: Aubier, 1956), vol. 1, pp. 156–159.

15. For examples see George F. Kennan, *The Fateful Alliance: France, Russia, and the Coming of the First World War* (New York: Pantheon, 1984), pp. 31–32, 55, 66, 70, 153; James L. Garvin, *The Life of Joseph Chamberlain*, 6 vols. (London: Macmillan, 1932–1969), vol. 3, pp. 264, 269, and chap. 58.

16. "Promises": Edgar D'Abernon, *An Ambassador of Peace: Pages from the Diary of Viscount d'Abernon*, 3 vols. (London: Hodder and Stoughton, 1929–1930), vol. 1, p. 317. Nazis: Philip M. H. Bell, *The Origins of the Second World War in Europe* (New York: Longman, 1986), p. 85. Gordon A. Craig, *War, Politics, and Diplomacy: Selected Essays* (New York: Praeger, 1966), pp. 223–224, 229; Gordon A. Craig and Alexander L. George, *Force and Statecraft: Diplomatic Problems of Our Time* (New York: Oxford University Press, 1983), pp. 58, 89–99, 164.

17. Harold Nicolson, *Diplomacy*, 3rd ed. (London: Oxford University Press, 1963), pp. 132, 144.

18. Craig, *War, Politics*, pp. 242–244; Cold War diplomacy: Fred Charles Iklé, *How Nations Negotiate* (New York: Harper and Row, 1964), chap. 12; Leon Sloss and M. Scott Davis, eds., *A Game for High Stakes: Lessons Learned in Negotiating with the Soviet Union* (Cambridge, Mass.: Ballinger, 1986), pp. 6–9; Leon Sloss and M. Scott Davis, "The Soviet Union: The Pursuit of Power and Influence Through Negotiation," in *National Negotiating Styles*, ed. Hans Binnendijk (Washington, D.C.: U.S. Government Printing Office, Foreign Service Institute, U.S. Department of State, 1987), pp. 24–26. Diatribes and barefaced lies: e.g., Strobe Talbot, *The Master of the Game: Paul Nitze and the Nuclear Peace* (New York: Random House Vintage, 1989), pp. 274, 290. Personal struggle: Raymond F. Smith, *Negotiating with the Soviets* (Bloomington: Indiana University Press, 1989), chap. 2 and p. 61, see also pp. 80–92. China: Richard H. Solomon, "Friendship and Obligation in Chinese Negotiating Style," in Binnendijk, *National Negotiating Styles*, p. 10.

19. Andrei Sinyavsky, *Soviet Civilization: A Cultural History*, trans. Joanne Turnbull with Nikolai Formazov (New York: Little, Brown, 1990), chap. 5.

20. Albert O. Hirschman, *The Passions and the Interests: Political Arguments for Capitalism Before its Triumph* (Princeton, N.J.: Princeton University Press, 1977), esp. pp. 10–12,

58–62. See also Charles Tilly, *Coercion, Capital, and European States, A.D. 990–1992,* rev. ed. (Cambridge, Mass.: Blackwell, 1992); Thompson, Ellis, and Wildavsky, *Cultural Theory,* chap. 1.

21. Jane Jacobs, *Systems of Survival: A Dialogue on the Moral Foundations of Commerce and Politics* (New York: Random House, 1992). I slightly modify her wording of precepts to conform with my terminology elsewhere.

22. Raymond Cohen, *Negotiating Across Cultures. Communication Obstacles in International Diplomacy* (Washington, D.C.: U.S. Institute of Peace, 1991).

23. R. J. Rummel, *Death by Government: Genocide and Mass Murder Since 1900* (New Brunswick, N.J.: Transaction, 1994); also R. J. Rummel, "Power, Genocide and Mass Murder," *Journal of Peace Research* 31 (1994): 1–10; R. J. Rummel, "Democracy, Power, Genocide, and Mass Murder," *Journal of Conflict Resolution* 39 (1995): 3–29.

24. Rummel, *Death by Government*; Rummel, "Power, Genocide and Mass Murder"; R. J. Rummel, "Democracies ARE Less Warlike than Other Regimes," *European Journal of International Relations* 1 (1995): 457–479. Insurgencies: e.g., Ted Robert Gurr, "Persistence and Change in Political Systems, 1800–1971," *American Political Science Review* 68 (1974): 1482–1504; Ted Robert Gurr, "Peoples Against States: Ethnopolitical Conflict and the Changing World System," *International Studies Quarterly* 38 (1994): 347–377; Ted Robert Gurr, *Minorities at Risk: A Global View of Ethnopolitical Conflicts* (Washington, D.C.: U.S. Institute of Peace Press, 1993), pp. 137–140, 144–145, 290. Four times less frequent: Stuart A. Bremer, "Dangerous Dyads: Conditions Affecting the Likelihood of Interstate War, 1816–1965," *Journal of Conflict Resolution* 36 (1992): 309–341. Less violence initiation: David L. Rousseau, Christopher Gelpi, Dan Reiter, and Paul K. Huth, "Assessing the Dyadic Nature of the Democratic Peace, 1918–1988," *American Political Science Review* 90 (1996): 512–533. Others arguing for correlations between democracy and nonviolence include Maurice A. East and Charles F. Hermann, "Do Nation-Types Account for Foreign Policy Behavior?" in *Comparing Foreign Policies: Theories, Findings, and Methods,* ed. James N. Rosenau (New York: Wiley, 1974), pp. 209–303; R. J. Rummel, "Libertarianism and International Violence," *Journal of Conflict Resolution* 27 (1983): 27–71; Daniel S. Geller, *Domestic Factors in Foreign Policy: A Cross-National Statistical Analysis* (Cambridge, Mass.: Schenkman, 1985), pp. 148, 153–154; Kenneth Benoit, "Democracies Really Are More Pacific (in General)," *Journal of Conflict Resolution* 40 (1996): 636–657, and especially R. J. Rummel, "Libertarian Propositions on Violence Within and Between Nations: A Test Against Published Research Results," *Journal of Conflict Resolution* 29 (1985): 419–455. For further investigation see James Lee Ray, *Democracy and International Conflict: An Evaluation of the Democratic Peace Proposition* (Columbia: University of South Carolina Press, 1995).

25. A general review is Arthur A. Stein, "Conflict and Cohesion: A Review of the Literature," *Journal of Conflict Resolution* 20 (1976): 143–172. See also Michael Haas, "Societal Approaches to the Study of War," *Journal of Peace Research* 2 (1965): 307–323; Wolf-Dieter Eberwein, "The Qualitative Study of International Conflict: Quantity and Quality? An Assessment of Empirical Research," *Journal of Peace Research* 18 (1981): 19–38; Ross, *Culture of Conflict,* esp. chap. 6; LeVine and Campbell, *Ethnocentrism,* chap. 12.

26. Russell J. Dalton, *Citizen Politics in Western Democracies: Public Opinion and Political Parties in the United States, Great Britain, West Germany, and France* (Chatham, N.J.: Chatham House, 1988); Almond, "Study of Political Culture." For this matter and the German case specifically, see chapter 15 n. 33.

27. For example, in the Crimean and Spanish-American wars, the public was probably more belligerent than the government; in the Mexican, Anglo-Boer, and Vietnam wars, it was probably less so. See Melvin Small, "Public Opinion," in *Explaining the History of American Foreign Policy*, ed. Michael Hogan and Thomas Paterson (Cambridge: Cambridge University Press, 1991), pp. 165–176; Bruce Russett, *Controlling the Sword: The Democratic Governance of National Security* (Cambridge, Mass.: Harvard University Press, 1990), pp. 99–101. On the key role of leaders see Margaret G. Hermann and Charles W. Kegley, Jr., "Rethinking Democracy and International Peace: Perspectives from Political Psychology," *International Studies Quarterly* 39 (1995): 511–533, see p. 515.

28. Early statements are Robert Jervis, *Perception and Misperception in International Politics* (Princeton: Princeton University Press, 1976), p. 283 (Jervis calls for more study, p. 285); Hans J. Morgenthau and Kenneth W. Thompson, *Politics Among Nations: The Struggle for Power and Peace* (New York: Knopf, 1985), pp. 7–8. See also Alexander George, "The 'Operational Code': A Neglected Approach to the Study of Political Leaders and Decision-Making," *International Studies Quarterly* 13 (1969): 190–221; Stephen G. Walker, "The Motivational Foundations of Political Belief Systems: A Re-Analysis of the Operational Code Construct," *International Studies* 27 (1983): 179–201; Alexander L. George, "The Causal Nexus Between Cognitive Beliefs and Decision-Making Behavior: The 'Operational Code' Belief System," in *Psychological Models in International Politics*, ed. Lawrence S. Falkowski (Boulder: Westview, 1979), pp. 95–124; Yaacov Y. I. Vertzberger, *The World in Their Minds: Information Processing, Cognition, and Perception in Foreign Policy Decision-making* (Stanford, Calif.: Stanford University Press, 1990), chap. 5. J. F. Voss and E. Dorsey, "Perception and International Relations," in *Political Psychology and Foreign Policy*, ed. Eric Singer and Valerie Hudson (Boulder: Westview, 1992), pp. 3–30.

29. Italians: Craig, *War, Politics*, pp. 223–224. Japanese: Eul Y. Park, "From Rivalry to Alliance: United States Relations with Japan, 1920–1971," in *Diplomatic Dispute: United States Conflict with Iran, Japan, and Mexico*, ed. Robert L. Paarlberg, Eul Y. Park, and Donald L. Wyman (Cambridge, Mass.: Harvard University Center for International Affairs, 1978), pp. 55–82; Thomas U. Berger, "Norms, Identity, and National Security in Germany and Japan," in *The Culture of National Security*, ed. Peter J. Katzenstein (New York: Columbia University Press, 1996), pp. 317–356.

30. On West Germany see Berger, "Norms"; A. James McAdams, *East Germany and Detente: Building Authority After the Wall* (Cambridge: Cambridge University Press, 1985). On foreign terrorism and assassination see *New York Times Index*, 1991–1992, s.v. "Stasi."

31. Khrushchev quoted in Robert C. Tucker, "The Dictator and Totalitarianism," *World Politics* 17 (1965): 555–583. Christer Jönsson, *Soviet Bargaining Behavior: The Nuclear Test Ban Case* (New York: Columbia University Press, 1979), esp. pp. 201–206, 213; Philip G. Roeder, "Soviet Policies and Kremlin Politics," *International Studies Quarterly* 28 (1984): 171–195; Smith, *Negotiating with the Soviets*, pp. 98, 104–117.

32. For comments see Craig and George, *Force and Statecraft;* Paul Gordon Lauren, ed., *Diplomacy: New Approaches in History, Theory and Policy* (New York: Free Press, 1979); Mautner-Markhof, *Processes of International Negotiations,* especially Hofstede, "Cultural Predictors"; Poortinga and Hendriks, "Culture as a Factor"; I. W. Zartman, "In Search of Common Elements in the Analysis of the Negotiation Process," pp. 241–255.

33. This was no peace between republics—the Mongols were a khanate—but the case is useful to show negotiating styles. Arthur Waldron, *The Great Wall of China: From History to Myth* (Cambridge: Cambridge University Press, 1990), chaps. 7, 8, and pp. 185–186 for foreign affairs; for domestic politics see Ray Huang, *1587, A Year of No Significance: The Ming Dynasty in Decline* (New Haven: Yale University Press, 1981), esp. chaps. 1, 2, pp. 80–82, 108–111, 212–213. "One million lives": Shen Shih-hsing, audience of 25 Aug. 1590, quoted in ibid., pp. 233. See also James Geiss, "The Chia-ching Reign, 1522–1566," in *The Ming Dynasty,* vol. 7 of *The Cambridge History of China,* ed. Frederick W. Mote and Denis Twitchett (Cambridge: Cambridge University Press, 1988), pp. 440–510; Huang, "The Lung-ch'ing and Wan'li Reigns, 1567–1620," in ibid., pp. 511–584; Charles O. Hucker, *The Censorial System of Ming China* (Stanford, Calif.: Stanford University Press, 1966), pp. 41–42 and chap. 7; Charles O. Hucker, "Governmental Organization of the Ming Dynasty," *Harvard Journal of Asiatic Studies* 21 (1958): 1–66, see pp. 64–66 (for voting); Jung-Pang Lo, "Policy Formulation and Decision-Making on Issues Respecting Peace and War," in *Chinese Government in Ming Times: Seven Studies,* ed. Charles O. Hucker (New York: Columbia University Press, 1969), pp. 41–72; Henry Serruys, "Four Documents Relating to the Sino-Mongol Peace of 1570–1571," *Monumenta Serica* 19 (1960): 1–66; Jonathan D. Spence, *The Memory Palace of Matteo Ricci* (New York: Viking, 1989), pp. 210–211, 214–215.

34. On laboratory studies see Margaret G. Hermann and Nathan Kogan, "Effects of Negotiators' Personalities on Negotiating Behavior," in *Negotiations: Social-Psychological Perspectives,* ed. Daniel Druckman (Beverly Hills: Sage, 1977), pp. 247–274. Later surveys are reviewed by Ole R. Holsti and James N. Rosenau, "The Domestic and Foreign Policy Beliefs of American Leaders," *Journal of Conflict Resolution* 32 (1988): 248–294.

35. Historical studies are reviewed by David G. Winter, "Personality and Foreign Policy: Historical Overview of Research," in *Political Psychology and Foreign Policy,* ed. Eric Singer and Valerie Hudson (Boulder: Westview, 1992), pp. 79–101, esp. 87–93; see especially Saul Friedlander and Raymond Cohen, "The Personality Correlates of Belligerence in International Conflict," *Comparitive Politics* 7 (1975): 155–186. Responses to questions: Margaret G. Hermann, "Explaining Foreign Policy Behavior Using the Personal Characteristics of Political Leaders," *International Studies Quarterly* 24 (1980): 7–46. See also Jonathan Wilkenfeld, Gerald W. Hopple, Paul J. Ross, and Stephen J. Andriole, *Foreign Policy Behavior: The Interstate Behavior Analysis Model* (Beverly Hills: Sage, 1980), chap. 8.

36. Lloyd Etheredge, *A World of Men: The Private Sources of American Foreign Policy* (Cambridge, Mass.: MIT Press, 1978), chap. 6; Graham H. Shepard, "Personality Effects on American Foreign Policy, 1969–1984. A Second Test of Interpersonal Generalization Theory," *International Studies Quarterly* 32 (1988): 91–123; Goldgeier, *Leadership Style.*

37. Hermann and Kegley, "Rethinking Democracy," pp. 521–523.

38. Margaret G. Hermann, "Who Becomes a Political Leader? Some Societal and Regime Influences on Selection of a Head of State," in *Psychological Models in International Politics,* ed. Lawrence S. Falkowski (Boulder: Westview, 1979), pp. 15–48.

39. East and Hermann, "Do Nation-Types Account," pp. 295–297; Charles F. Hermann, "Comparing the Foreign Policy Events of Nations," in *International Events and the Comparative Analysis of Foreign Policy,* ed. Charles W. Kegley, Jr., Gregory A. Raymond, Robert M. Rood, and Richard A. Skinner (Columbia: University of South Carolina Press, 1975), pp. 145–158. See also Geller, *Domestic Factors,* pp. 153–154. Study of 278 crises: Michael Brecher, Jonathon Wilkenfeld, and Sheila Moss, *Crises in the Twentieth Century,* vol. 1, *Handbook of International Crises* (Oxford: Pergamon, 1988), pp. 173–174, 246. Study of eighty-eight regimes: Joe D. Hagan, "Regimes, Political Oppositions and the Comparative Analysis of Foreign Policy," in *New Directions in the Study of Foreign Policy,* ed. Charles F. Hermann, Charles W. Kegley, Jr., and James N. Rosenau (Boston: Allen and Unwin, 1987), pp. 339–365. Another massive statistical study which found a distinct but weak tendency for autocratic regimes to be more prone to disputes: Zeev Maoz and Nasrin Abdolali, "Regime Types and International Conflict, 1816–1976," *Journal of Conflict Resolution* 33 (1989): 3–35, see pp. 18–20. For more complex relationships: Margaret G. Hermann and Charles F. Hermann, "Who Makes Foreign Policy Decisions and How: An Empirical Inquiry," *International Studies Quarterly* 33 (1989): 361–387. Kingdoms: Edgar Kiser, Kriss A. Drass, and William Brustein, "Ruler Autonomy and War in Early Modern Western Europe," *International Studies Quarterly* 39 (1995): 109–138.

40. Their term is "norms." Bruce Russett, *Grasping the Democratic Peace: Principles for a Post–Cold War World* (Princeton: Princeton University Press, 1993), pp. 86–93 (with Zeev Maoz); p. 107 (with Carol R. Ember and Melvin Ember). See also T. Clifton Morgan and Sally Howard Campbell, "Domestic Structure, Decisional Constraints, and War: So Why Kant Democracies Fight?," *Journal of Conflict Resolution* 35 (1991): 187–211; Joe D. Hagan, "Domestic Political Systems and War Proneness," *Mershon International Studies Review* 38 (1994): 183–207. T. Clifton Morgan and Valerie Schwebach, "Take Two Democracies and Call Me in the Morning: A Prescription for Peace?" *International Interactions* 17 (1992): 305–320, give a weak statistical argument for structural causation, but actually their "constrained" non-democracies have republican (oligarchic) political culture.

41. For example, Geoffrey Blainey, *The Causes of War,* 3rd ed. (New York: Macmillan Free Press, 1988), esp. chap. 9; Evan Luard, *War in International Society: A Study in International Sociology* (London: I. B. Tauris, 1986); Russell J. Leng, *Interstate Crisis Behavior, 1816–1950: Realism vs. Reciprocity* (New York: Cambridge University Press, 1993), pp. 56–65. Examples of leaders winning politically while the nation loses militarily include the monarchy in the Spanish-American War (see chapter 8) and Egypt's Anwar Sadat in the Suez War.

42. Bruce Bueno de Mesquita and David Lalman, *War and Reason: Domestic and International Imperatives* (New Haven: Yale University Press, 1992), pp. 104–105, see also pp. 154–157. They also claim that the perception of "dovish" tendencies relies on an understanding of high domestic political costs (in democracies) for the use of force; this is not inconsistent with my political culture argument, but the specifics are supported only by

highly indirect and crude measures. See also Woosang Kim and Bruce Bueno de Mesquita, "How Perceptions Influence the Risk of War," *International Studies Quarterly* 39 (1995): 51–65; Bruce Bueno de Mesquita, "The Contribution of Expected Utility Theory to the Study of International Conflict," *Journal of Interdisciplinary History* 18 (1988): 629–652; Bruce Bueno de Mesquita, *The War Trap* (New Haven: Yale University Press, 1981), chap. 2. On perceptions: Luard, *War in International Society,* pp. 224–225. For a general critique of realpolitik see Mary Zey, "Criticisms of Rational Choice Models," in *Decision Making: Alternatives to Rational Choice Models,* ed. Mary Zey (Newbury Park, Calif.: Sage, 1992), pp. 9–31. The role of trust is increasingly considered by social theorists, e.g., Jeffrey Bradach and Robert Eccles, "Price, Authority, and Trust: From Ideal Types to Plural Forms," *Annual Review of Sociology* 15 (1989): 97–118. For games experiments see chapter 11.

43. Thomas Risse-Kappen, "Democratic Peace—Warlike Democracies? A Social Constructivist Interpretation of the Liberal Argument," *European Journal of International Relations* 1 (1995): 491–517, see p. 506.

CHAPTER SIX

The Swiss Republics: Defining an Enemy

1. Here and below: Johannes Dierauer, *Histoire de la Confédération Suisse,* 5 vols., trans. Aug. Reymond (Lausanne: Payot, 1912–1919), vol. 2, book 4, chap. 3; *Nouvelle histoire de la Suisse et des Suisses,* 3 vols., ed. Beatrix Mesmer, Jean-Claude Favez and Romano Broggini (Lausanne: Payot, 1982), vol. 2, pp. 253–265; Gottfried Guggenbühl, *Vom Jahre 1648 bis zur Gegenwart,* vol. 2 of *Geschichte der Schweizerischer Eidgenossenschaft* (Erlenbach-Zurich: Rentsch, 1948), part 1, p. 228ff.

2. Richard Feller, *Von den Anfängen bis 1516,* vol. 1 of *Geschichte Berns,* 4th ed. (Bern: Hubert Lang, 1949), part 3, chap. 4; Paul Bessire, *Berne et la Suisse: Histoire de leurs relations depuis les origines jusqu'à nos jours* (Bern: Libraire de l'Etat de Berne, 1953), p. 61. For 1437 see *Klingenberger Chronik,* ed. Anton Henne von Sargans (Gotha: Perthes, 1861), pp. 237–238. Lucerne and others were at the battle, but "Schwyzers" are identified as the chief participants by Zurich, *Chronik der Stadt Zürich, mit Fortsetzungen,* vol. 18, ed. Allgemeine geschichtsforschende Gesellschaft der Schweiz and Johannes Dierauer, Quellen zur Schweizergeschichte (Basel: Geerig, 1900), pp. 213–214, and Fratri Felicis Fabri, *Descriptio sveviae,* vol. 6 of *Quellen zur Schweizer Geschichte,* ed. Allgemeine geschichtsforschenden Gesellschaft der Schweiz and Hermann Escher (Basel: Felix Schneider, 1884), pp. 195–196.

3. Hans Georg Fernis, "Die politische Volksdichtung der deutschen Schweizer als Quelle für ihre völkisches und staatliches Bewusstsein vom 14.-16. Jahrhunderts," *Deutsche Archiv für Landes- und Volksforschung* 2 (1938): 600–639, see pp. 606–609; Helmut Meyer, *Der Zweite Kappeler Krieg: Die Krise der Schweizerischen Reformation* (Zurich: Hans Rohr, 1976), pp. 68–70, 89.

4. G. Patrick March, *Cossacks of the Brotherhood: The Zaporog Kosh of the Dniepr River* (New York: Peter Lang, 1990); Linda Gordon, *Cossack Rebellions: Social Turmoil in the Sixteenth-Century Ukraine* (Albany: State University of New York Press, 1983); Dmytro

Doroshenke, *A Survey of Ukrainian History,* ed. Oleh W. Gerus (Winnipeg: Trident, 1975), chaps. 12–14; W. E. D. Allen, *The Ukraine: A History* (Cambridge: Cambridge University Press, 1940), pp. 64–123; George V. Gubaroff, *Cossacks and Their Land in the Light Of New Data,* trans. John N. Washburn (Providence: Cossack American National Alliance, 1985), pp. 384–392. For foreign policy decision-making see Erich Lassota von Steblau, *Habsburgs and Zaporozhian Cossacks: The Diary of Erich Lassota von Steblau,* ed. Lubomyr R. Wymar, trans. Orest Subtelny (Littleton, Colo.: Ukrainian Academic Press, 1973), pp. 84–93.

5. Norman Davies, *God's Playground: A History of Poland,* vol. 1 (New York: Columbia University Press, 1982), chaps. 7, 10. "Common menial" quoted in Allen, *Ukraine,* p. 108. No negotiation: Frank Sysyn, *Between Poland and the Ukraine: The Dilemma of Adam Kysil, 1600–1653* (Cambridge, Mass.: Harvard University Press, 1985), p. 154. See Władysław Serczyk, "The Commonwealth and the Cossacks in the First Quarter of the Seventeenth Century," *Harvard Ukrainian Studies* 2 (1978): 78–83; Frank E. Sysyn, "Seventeenth-Century Views on the Causes of the Khmel'nyts'kyi Uprising: An Examination of the 'Discourse on the Present Cossack or Peasant War,'" *Harvard Ukrainian Studies* 5 (1981): 430–466; Andrzej Kamiński, "The Cossack Experiment in *Szlachta* Democracy in the Polish-Lithuanian Commonwealth: The Hadiach (*Hadziacz*) Union," *Harvard Ukrainian Studies* 1 (1977): 178–197; Gordon, *Cossack Rebellions,* esp. pp. 82–87, 181–189, 212.

6. For government see Kurt Messmer, "Zum Luzerner Patriziat im 16. Jahrhundert," in *Luzerner Patriziat: Sozial- und wirtschaftsgeschichtliche Studien zur Entstehung und Entwicklung im 16. und 17. Jahrhunderts,* ed. Kurt Messmer and Peter Hoppe (Lucerne: Rex-Verleg, 1976), pp. 31–214; for Lucerne deaths see p. 61; also Hans Dommann, "Luzern," in Allgemeine geschichstforschende Gesellschaft der Schweiz, *Historisch-biographisches Lexikon der Schweiz,* 7 vols. (Neisenburg: Administration der Hist.-biog. Lexikon, 1921–34), vol. 4, pp. 735. Dierauer, *Histoire Suisse,* vol. 4, pp. 93–96, 243–248.

7. Besides sources cited above see Sebastien Grüter, *Geschichte des Kantons Luzern im 16. und 17. Jahrhundert,* vol. 2 of *Geschichte des Kantons Luzern,* ed. Lucerne Regierungsrat (Lucerne: Räber, 1945), parts 2.2, 6.1, 6.3; Feller, *Geschichte Berns,* vol. 3, pp. 26–28, 300–302; for 1531 battles see Helmut Meyer, *Zweite Kapeller Krieg* (Zurich: H. Rohr, 1976) esp. pp. 153–155, 182–183.

8. Lucerners also had practical reasons: Grüter, *Geschichte Luzern,* pp. 56–61.

9. *Handbuch der Schweizer Geschichte,* 2 vols. (Zurich: Berichthaus, 1972), vol. 1, pp. 491–493, 511–512, 659–660. Diplomacy broke down all across Europe during the Reformation: Garrett Mattingly, *Renaissance Diplomacy* (1955; reprint, New York: Dover, 1988), chap. 21.

10. See Messmer, "Zum Luzerner Patriziat," pp. 68, 73–74, 151–52.

11 Hans Nabholz, Leonhard von Muralt, Richard Teller, and Emil Dürr, *Von den ältesten Zeiten bis zum Ausgang des sechzehnten Jahrhunderts,* vol. 1 of *Geschichte der Schweiz* (Zurich: Schulthess, 1932), pp. 393–394; Bessire, *Berne et la Suisse,* pp. 85; Grüter, *Geschichte Luzerne,* pp. 76–77.

12. Grüter, *Geschichte Luzerne,* part 2.2, esp. pp. 84–85; Meyer, *Zweite Kappeler,* p. 24.

13. Reviews are in R. A. Levine and D. Campbell, *Ethnocentrism: Theories of Conflict, Ethnic Attitudes, and Group Behavior* (New York: Wiley, 1972); Marc Ross, "The Limits to Social Structure: Social Structural and Psychocultural Explanations for Political Conflict and Violence," *Anthropological Quarterly* 59 (1986): 171–176; Marc Howard Ross, *The Culture of Conflict: Interpretations and Interests in Comparative Perspective* (New Haven: Yale University Press, 1994); J. M. Rabbie, "Group Processes as Stimulants of Aggression," in *Aggression and War: Their Biological and Social Bases,* ed. Jo Groebel and Robert A. Hinde (New York: Cambridge University Press, 1989), pp. 141–155. Also Mary Douglas, *How Institutions Think* (Syracuse: Syracuse University Press, 1986), chaps. 1, 4, 5, 8, 9; Vamik D. Volkan, *The Need to Have Enemies and Allies: From Clinical Practice to International Relationships* (Northvale, N.J.: Jason Aronson, 1988).

14. Frans de Waal, *Peacemaking Among Primates* (Cambridge, Mass.: Harvard University Press, 1989), pp. 20–21, 50, 83, 126, 268. Rabbie, "Group Processes," pp. 146–147; Roger Brown, *Social Psychology,* 2nd ed. (New York: Free Press, 1986), chap. 15; William Bloom, *Personal Identity, National Identity and International Relations* (Cambridge: Cambridge University Press, 1990), chap. 2; Michael E. Brown, ed., *Ethnic Conflict and International Security* (Princeton: Princeton University Press, 1993); James E. Dougherty and Robert L. Pfaltzgraff, Jr., *Contending Theories of International Relations. A Comprehensive Survey,* 3rd ed. (New York: Harper and Row, 1990), p. 290; Clark McCauley, "Conference Overview," in *The Anthropology of War,* vol. 3, ed. Jonathan Haas (Cambridge: Cambridge University Press, 1990), pp. 23–24.

15. Steve W. Hoagland and Stephen G. Walker, "Operational Codes and Crisis Outcomes," in *Psychological Models in International Politics,* ed. Lawrence S. Falkowski (Boulder: Westview, 1979), pp. 125–167; Brown, *Social Psychology,* chap. 5.

16. Papal war: François-Tommy Perrens, *Histoire de Florence depuis ses origines jusqu'à la domination des Médicis,* 6 vols., 2nd ed. (Paris: Fontemoing, 1873–1883), vol. 5, pp. 115–116. Florentines and Lucca: Christine Meek, *Lucca, 1369–1404: Politics and Society in an Early Renaissance City-State* (Oxford: Oxford University Press, 1978), pp. 140–141; Hans Baron, *The Crisis of the Early Italian Renaissance: Civic Humanism and Republican Liberty in an Age of Classicism and Tyranny,* rev. ed. (Princeton: Princeton University Press, 1966), p. 23. Anti-Visconti: ibid., p. 447 and passim; also Nicolai Rubinstein, "Florence and the Despots: Some Aspects of Florentine Diplomacy in the Fourteenth Century," *Transactions of the Royal Historical Society,* 5th ser. 2 (1952): 21–46; and Gene A. Brucker, *Renaissance Florence,* rev. ed. (Berkeley: University of California Press, 1983), pp. 162–163.

17. "Seranno sotterati" quoted in Nicolai Rubinstein, "Florence and the Despots: Some Aspects of Florentine Diplomacy in the Fourteenth Century," *Transactions of the Royal Historical Society,* 5th ser., 2 (1952): 21–46, on p. 26.

18. Emile Dürr, *La politique des Confédérés au 14e et au 15e siècle,* vol. 4 of *Histoire Militaire de la Suisse, Part I, 1315–1515: De Morgarten à Marignan* (Bern: Commissariat central des guerres, 1935), chap. 8; "accept everyone" quoted p. 157. Dierauer, *Histoire Suisse* vol. 1, chap. 5, esp. pp. 499–506; Nabholz et al., *Von den ältesten Zeiten*; Johann Caspar Zellweger, *Geschichte des Appenzellischen Volkes,* 3 vols. (St. Gallen: Scheitlin und Zollikosen, 1842), vol. 1, p. 332ff. For 1407, see Henne von Sargans, *Klingenberger Chronik*; also *Nouvelle histoire de la Suisse,* vol. 1, pp. 240–247.

19. Like-minded regime installed: e.g., Plutarch, *Pericles,* 23; Thucydides, *History of the Peloponnesian War,* trans. Rex Warner (New York: Penguin, 1954), 8.21. Treaties: Donald Kagan, *The Outbreak of the Peloponnesian War* (Ithaca, N.Y.: Cornell University Press, 1969), p. 118; Jack Cargill, *The Second Athenian League: Empire or Free Alliance?* (Berkeley: University of California Press, 1981), pp. 44, 64–66, 190–191, 263; Anthony Powell, *Athens and Sparta: Constructing Greek Political and Social History from 478 B.C.* (Portland, Ore.: Areopagitica, 1988), p. 47; Russell Meiggs, *The Athenian Empire* (Oxford: Clarendon, 1972), p. 45; Andrew Lintott, *Violence, Civil Strife, and Revolution in the Classical City* (Baltimore: Johns Hopkins University Press, 1962), p. 102.

20. Yvon Garlan, *Slavery in Ancient Greece,* rev. ed. (Ithaca, N.Y.: Cornell University Press, 1988), pp. 123–126; also T.A. Sinclair, *A History of Greek Political Thought* (London: Routledge and Kegan Paul, 1951), p. 70; A. H. M. Jones, *Athenian Democracy* (Oxford: Blackwell, 1964), esp. pp. 41, 66.

21. Niccolo Machiavelli, *History of Florence and of the Affairs of Italy* (New York: Harper and Row, 1960), 3.3, p. 129; his source is unknown. See Gisela Bock, "Civil Discord in Machiavelli's *Istorie Fiorentine,*" in *Machiavelli and Republicanism,* ed. Gisela Bock, Quentin Skinner, and Maurizio Viroli (Cambridge: Cambridge University Press, 1990), pp. 181–201; J. N. Stephens, *The Fall of the Florentine Republic, 1512–1530* (Oxford: Clarendon, 1983), pp. 254; Thomas A. Brady, Jr., *Turning Swiss: Cities and Empire, 1450–1550* (Cambridge: Cambridge University Press, 1985), p. 18. On antecedents: Guy Fourquin, *The Anatomy of Popular Rebellion in the Middle Ages,* trans. Anne Chesters (Amsterdam: North Holland, 1978), pp. 99–100; Klaus Arnold, "Freiheit im Mittelalter," *Historisches Jahrbuch* 104 (1984): 1–21.

22. Numbers: Randolph Starn, *Contrary Commonwealth: The Theme of Exile in Medieval and Renaissance Italy* (Berkeley: University of California Press, 1962), p. 45; M.I. Finley, *The Ancient Greeks,* rev. ed. (Harmondsworth, England: Penguin, 1977), pp. 89–90.

23. Luis A. Losada, *The Fifth Column in the Peloponnesian War,* (Ph.D. diss., Columbia University, 1970); see also, chapter 2.

24. Douglas, *How Institutions Think,* chap. 9.

25. Polls: Bruce Russett, *Grasping the Democratic Peace. Principles for a Post-Cold War World* (Princeton: Princeton University Press, 1993), pp. 129–130; see also Miroslav Nincic and Bruce Russett, "The Effect of Similarity and Interest on Attitudes Toward Foreign Countries," *Public Opinion Quarterly* 43 (1979): 68–78. Alex Mintz and Nehemia Geva, "Why Don't Democracies Fight Each Other? An Experimental Study," *Journal of Conflict Resolution* 37 (1993): 484–503.

26. For a summary see R. W. Scribner, *The German Reformation* (Atlantic Highlands, N.J.: Humanities Press, 1986), pp. 10–12, 37–39.

27. Violence in 1620–1640 was primitive factional and clan raiding, not confrontation between Swiss state armies.

28. Jack Snyder, *Myths of Empire: Domestic Politics and International Ambition* (Ithaca, N.Y.: Cornell University Press, 1991), pp. 41–42, 317.

29. Stephen Walt, *The Origin of Alliances* (Ithaca, N.Y.: Cornell University Press, 1987), pp. 22–25, 34–40, 183–185. Randolph Siverson and Juliann Emmons, "Birds of a

Feather: Democratic Political Systems and Alliance Choices," *Journal of Conflict Resolution* 35 (1991): 285–306; Michael W. Simon and Erik Gartzke, "Political System Similarity and Choice of Allies," *Journal of Conflict Resolution* 40 (1996): 617–635. See also Ole R. Holsti, P. Terence Hopmann, and John D. Sullivan, *Unity and Disintegration in International Alliances* (New York: Wiley, 1973), pp. 61–64 and chap. 5.

30. "Perverse iniquity": Matteo Villani, *Cronica di Matteo Villani* (Florence, 1825), 11.1, pp. 139–141; see 9.5, pp. 175–176; Giovanni Villani, *Cronica di Giovanni Villani: A miglior lezione ridotta coll'aiuto de' testi a penna* (Florence: Magheri, 1823), 8.2; Marvin B. Becker, *Florence in Transition,* 2 vols. (Baltimore: Johns Hopkins University Press, 1967–1968), vol. 1, pp. 136–137; E. Garin, "I cancelleri umanisti della Repubblica Fiorentina di Coluccio Salutate a Bartolomeo Scala," *Rivista Storica Italiana* 71 (1959): 185–208, see pp. 193–195; Marino Berengo, *Nobili e mercanti nella Lucca del Cinquecento* (Turin: Einaudi, 1965), pp. 263–280; George Holmes, *The Florentine Enlightenment: 1400–1450* (New York: Pegasus, 1969), p. 149. "Popolo libera co' tiranni non stanno insieme" quoted in Pietro Silva, *Il Governo di Pietro Gambacorta in Pisa e le sue relazioni col resto della Toscana e coi Visconti* (Pisa: Nistri, 1911), pp. 327.

31. Peter Partner, "Florence and the Papacy, 1300–1375," in *Europe in the Late Middle Ages,* ed. John Hale, Roger Highfield, and Beryl Smalley (London: Faber and Faber, 1965), pp. 97–98; Rubinstein, "Florence and the Despots," pp. 27–28.

32. Demosthenes, *On the Chersonese,* 40–43; this and other works are in Demosthenes, *Orations and Letters,* in *Loeb Classical Library,* ed. J. H. Vince and A. T. Murray (New York: G.P. Putnam's Sons, 1926–1949). Note also Thucydides, *History,* 8.48.

33. "On any grounds": Demosthenes, *On Organization,* 8–9. Character of oligarchies: Demosthenes, *For the Liberty of the Rhodians,* 17–21. He refers to wars between democracies—possibly the wars against Syracuse and Thebes discussed above plus minor quarrels for which no record survives—but says they were never over vital issues.

34. Old Oligarch (pseudo-Xenophon), *The Constitution of Athens,* vol. 2 of *The Greek Historians,* ed. Francis R. B. Godolphin, trans. H. G. Dakyns (New York: Random House, 1942), 3.11; Lintott, *Violence, Civil Strife,* p. 100; Simon Hornblower, *The Greek World, 479–323 B.C.* (London: Methuen, 1983), p. 29.

35. Thucydides, *History,* 3.27–50, quote from Diodotus is at 3.47. See Ronald P. Legon, "Megara and Mytilene," *Phoenix* 22 (1968): 200–225; David Gillis, "The Revolt at Mytilene," *American Journal of Philosophy* 92 (1971): 38–47. Athenians did kill every man after defeating oligarchic regimes at Scione (421) and Melos (415). Note that Thucydides' account of the Mytilene debate was written or revised after 415, when viewpoints had changed. On the "enormous practical importance of principles" by the end of the Peloponnesian Wars, see Peter J. Fliess, *Thucydides and the Politics of Bipolarity* (Baton Rouge: Louisiana State University Press, 1966), pp. 121–137, esp. p. 127; for ideological development see Maurice Pope, "Thucydides and Democracy," *Historia* 37 (1988): 276–296, see p. 282.

36. On ideology see *Handbuch der Schweizer Geschichte* vol. 1, p. 231; on songs see Fernis, "Die politische Volksdichtung," p. 605.

CHAPTER SEVEN
Oligarchy, Intervention, and Civil War

1. Other cases I have inspected include, for democracies, Yemen and Yugoslavia (see appendix) and some breakaway states of the former Soviet Union in the 1990s; among oligarchic republics, Florence and other Italian cities in the 1200s and Peru and other Latin American states in the 1800s.

2. Ted Robert Gurr, *Minorities at Risk: A Global View of Ethnopolitical Conflicts* (Washington, D.C.: U.S. Institute of Peace Press, 1993).

3. Major recent works, all asserting the centrality of slavery and political culture, include James M. McPherson, *Battle Cry of Freedom: The Civil War Era* (New York: Oxford University Press, 1988); Richard H. Sewell, *A House Divided. Sectionalism and Civil War, 1848–1865* (Baltimore: Johns Hopkins University Press, 1988), chaps. 1–4; Roger L. Ransom, *Conflict and Compromise: The Political Economy of Slavery, Emancipation, and the American Civil War* (New York: Cambridge University Press, 1989); Kenneth M. Stampp, *America in 1857: A Nation on the Brink* (New York: Oxford University Press, 1990), esp. pp. 110–113; Kenneth M. Stampp, *The Causes of the Civil War*, 3rd ed. (New York: Simon and Schuster, 1991); William W. Freehling, *Secessionists at Bay, 1770–1854*, vol. 1 of *The Road to Disunion* (New York: Oxford University Press, 1990). Of older works see Eric Foner, *Free Soil, Free Labor, Free Men: The Ideology of the Republican Party before the Civil War* (New York: Oxford University Press, 1970), esp. chap. 9.

4. See Kenneth S. Greenberg, *Masters and Statesmen. The Political Culture of American Slavery* (Baltimore: Johns Hopkins University Press, 1985); Steven A. Channing, *Crisis of Fear: Secession in South Carolina* (New York: Simon and Schuster, 1970), pp. 155–158; Randall C. Jimerson, *The Private Civil War: Popular Thought During the Sectional Conflict* (Baton Rouge: Louisiana State University Press, 1988), pp. 127–128, 194–195; Freehling, *Secessionists at Bay*, pp. 37–38 and chap. 3; Michael P. Johnson, *Toward a Patriarchal Republic. The Secession of Georgia* (Baton Rouge: Louisiana State University Press, 1977); Eugene D. Genovese, *The Slaveholders' Dilemma. Freedom and Progress in Southern Conservative Thought, 1820–1860* (Columbia: University of South Carolina Press, 1992).

5. James Oakes, *Slavery and Freedom: An Interpretation of the Old South* (New York: Knopf, 1990); *The Ruling Race: A History of American Slaveholders* (New York: Knopf, 1982); Ransom, *Conflict and Compromise;* Drew Gilpin Faust, *The Creation of Confederate Nationalism: Ideology and Identity in the Civil War South* (Baton Rouge: Louisiana State University Press, 1988), pp. 59–60; Carl N. Degler, *The Other South. Southern Dissenters in the Nineteenth Century* (New York: Harper and Row, 1974), p. 122; Eugene D. Genovese, *The Political Economy of Slavery: Studies in the Economy and Society of the Slave South* (New York: Pantheon, 1965). On economics and politics in a "slave society" see Oakes, *Slavery*, pp. 37–38; M. I. Finley, *Ancient Slavery and Modern Ideology* (New York: Viking, 1980), pp. 77–92; G. E. M. de Ste. Croix, *The Class Struggle in the Ancient Greek World* (Ithaca, N.Y.: Cornell University Press, 1981), pp. 29–30.

6. For voting in the secession elections see McPherson, *Battle Cry*, pp. 235, 239, 243–244, 283, 289, 310–311; David M. Potter, *Lincoln and His Party in the Secession Cri-*

sis (New Haven: Yale University Press, 1952), pp. 208–215; Michael F. Holt, *The Political Crisis of the 1850s* (New York: Wiley, 1978), p. 227; Johnson, *Toward a Patriarchal Republic,* p. 63; Robin E. Baker and Dale Baum, "The Texas Voter and the Crisis of the Union, 1859–1861," *Journal of Southern History* 53 (1987): 395–420; and especially Roy R. Doyon and Thomas W. Hodler, "Secessionist Sentiment and Slavery: A Geographic Analysis," *Georgia Historical Quarterly* 73 (1989): 323–348.

7. Clement Eaton, *The Freedom-of-Thought Struggle in the Old South* (New York: Harper and Row, 1964), chap. 15; Sewell, *A House Divided,* pp. 80–81; Johnson, *Toward a Patriarchal,* pp. 108–117; Marc W. Kruman, *Parties and Politics in North Carolina, 1836–1865* (Baton Rouge: Louisiana State University Press, 1983), pp. 210–212; Walter L. Buenger, *Secession and the Union in Texas* (Austin: University of Texas Press, 1984), pp. 143, 160–161. On disaffection see also Paul Escott, "Southern Yeomen and the Confederacy," *South Atlantic Quarterly* 77 (1978): 146–158.

8. Eaton, *Freedom-of-Thought Struggle,* esp. chaps. 5, 8; Freehling, *Secessionists at Bay,* esp. chap. 6; Degler, *The Other South,* chaps. 2, 3; Channing, *Crisis of Fear,* esp. pp. 104–105; Russel B. Nye, *Fettered Freedom: Civil Liberties and the Slavery Controversy, 1830–1860* (East Lansing: Michigan State University Press, 1949), chap. 5; Clarence L. Mohr, *On the Threshold of Freedom. Masters and Slaves in Civil War Georgia* (Athens: University of Georgia Press, 1986), chaps. 1, 2. On slaveholders' "habits of command" see Genovese, *Political Economy of Slavery,* pp. 28–36, 267–270; Greenberg, *Masters and Statesmen,* see pp. 142–143 on rejection of compromise. Abolitionists faced racist mob violence in the North too, but that faded in the 1850s.

9. Holt, *Political Crisis,* chap. 8; Faust, *Creation of Confederate Nationalism,* pp. 34–38; Greenberg, *Masters and Statesmen,* pp. 47–50.

10. Channing, *Crisis of Fear;* Eaton, *Freedom-of-Thought Struggle,* chap. 4; Johnson, *Towards a Patriarchal,* pp. xx, 46–53, 79–90; Jimerson, *Private Civil War,* pp. 8–20; Holt, *Political Crisis,* pp. 222–226; Foner, *Free Soil,* pp. 314–315; Sewell, *A House Divided;* Greenberg, *Masters and Statesmen,* pp. 130–131, 144–146.

11. Holt, *Political Crisis,* esp. pp. 221–222 and chap. 8; Kruman, *Parties and Politics,* chap. 8.

12. Earl Hess, *Liberty, Virtue, and Progress: Northerners and Their War for the Union* (New York: New York University Press, 1988), esp. pp. 14–16, 20–21.

13. A recent review is William E. Gienapp, "The Republican Party and the Slave Power," in *New Perspectives on Race and Slavery in America,* ed. Robert H. Abzug and Stephan E. Maizlish (Lexington: University Press of Kentucky, 1986), pp. 51–78. Also Holt, *Political Crisis,* pp. 189–197 and chap. 8; Jimerson, *Private Civil War,* pp. 131–132; Nye, *Fettered Freedom,* pp. 224–226; James M. McPherson, *Abraham Lincoln and the Second American Revolution* (New York: Oxford University Press, 1991), chaps. 1, 2; Hess, *Liberty, Virtue,* pp. 14–17. "War of a class" quoted in Foner, *Free Soil,* p. 64, see also chap. 2; see also Kenneth M. Stampp, *And the War Came: The North and the Secession Crisis, 1860–1861* (Baton Rouge: Louisiana State University Press, 1950), pp. 253–254. On the role of slaves see Oakes, *Slavery and Freedom,* pp. 170–173.

14. Foner, *Free Soil;* Stampp, *America in 1857.* "Relentless oligarchy" quoted in Gienapp, "Republican Party," p. 62.

15. Here and below: Stampp, *And the War Came;* Ransom, *Conflict and Compromise;* Robert W. Johanssen, *Lincoln, the South, and Slavery: The Political Dimension* (Baton Rouge: Louisiana State University Press, 1991), chap. 3; McPherson, *Battle Cry,* pp. 308–312; Nye, *Fettered Freedom,* pp. 223–240, 243; Jimerson, *Private Civil War,* pp. 33–34; Phillip S. Paludan, "The American Civil War Considered as a Crisis in Law and Order," *American Historical Review* 77 (1972): 1013–1034; Hess, *Liberty, Virtue,* chaps. 1, 2; Freehling, *Secessionists at Bay,* chaps. 17–19.

16. Richard Feller, *Von den Anfängen bis 1516,* vol. 1 of *Geschichte Berns,* 4th ed. (Bern: Hubert Lang, 1949), p. 276. N.b., "union," "confederation" and "league" are all valid translations of the Swiss *bund.* See chapter 8.

17. "Revolvers" quoted in Sewell, *A House Divided,* p. 72.

18. Freethinker majority: Heidi Bossard-Borner, "Luzern im Bundesstaat von 1848," in *Luzern und die Eidgenossenschaft,* ed. Heidi Bossard-Borner (Lucerne: Rex, 1982), pp. 146–150. For other references see appendix.

19. Aristotle, *Politics,* 1279b; Plato, *Republic,* 423a, 551d, where I translate "polis" as regime, state, and city.

20. Andrew Lintott, *Violence, Civil Strife, and Revolution in the Classical City* (Baltimore: Johns Hopkins University Press, 1962), p. 167; Xenophon, *Hellenica,* 1.6.24, 2.4.25; Yvon Garlan, *Slavery in Ancient Greece,* rev. ed. (Ithaca, N.Y.: Cornell University Press, 1988), pp. 163–176. McPherson, *Battle Cry,* pp. 831–837; Mohr, *On the Threshold,* chap. 9. In undoubted oligarchies, e.g., Peru or Britain at certain points, commoners could be so well suppressed that there was little overt fear of revolt. It is in borderline cases that the fear is a telling indicator.

21. Thucydides, *History,* 5.23, see also 1.102.

22. Plutarch, *Lykurgus* 28.4; see Aristotle, *Politics,* 1310a; Garlan, *Slavery,* pp. 153–158.

23. Modern cases in the appendix with an external-internal connection include especially 1847, 1849, 1861, 1899 (Boer), 1948, 1974, and 1991, not to mention rebellions such as 1775, 1828, 1899 (Philippines), 1919.

24. The Transvaal was officially the Republic of South Africa. For war causes see Leonard Thompson, *A History of South Africa* (New Haven: Yale University Press, 1990), chaps. 3, 4; Shula Marks, "Scrambling for South Africa," *Journal of African History* 23 (1982): 97–113; A. Atmore and Shula Marks, "The Imperial Factor in South Africa in the Nineteenth Century: Towards a Reassessment," *Journal of Imperial and Commonwealth History* 3 (1974): 105–139; Andrew N. Porter, "The South African War (1899–1902): Context and Motive Reconsidered," *Journal of African History* 31 (1990): 43–57. Here and below see also Andrew N. Porter, *The Origins of the South African War: Joseph Chamberlain and the Diplomacy of Imperialism, 1895–1899* (New York: St. Martin's, 1980); Thomas Pakenham, *The Boer War* (New York: Random House, 1979); Ronald Robinson, John Galleger, and Alice Denny, *Africa and the Victorians: The Climax of Imperialism* (Garden City, N.Y.: Doubleday, 1968); Johannes S. Marais, *The Fall of Kruger's Republic* (Oxford:

Clarendon, 1961); Peter Warwick and S. B. Spies, eds., *The South African War: The Anglo-Boer War, 1899–1902* (Harlow, Essex: Longman, 1980).

25. Claire Hirschfield, "The Legacy of Dissent: Boer War Opposition and the Shaping of British South African Policy, 1899–1909," *War and Society* 6 (1988): 11–39, see pp. 14–16; Porter, *Origins,* pp. 60–62. Arming blacks: Peter Warwick, "Black People and the War," in Warwick and Spies, *South African War,* pp. 186–209; Byron Farwell, *The Great Anglo-Boer War* (New York: Harper and Row, 1976), pp. 351, 357. Black rights were not a British war aim: ibid., pp. 394–396, 435, 449–450; Porter, *Origins,* pp. 122–124.

26. C. T. Gordon, *The Growth of Boer Opposition to Kruger, 1890–1895* (Cape Town: Oxford University Press, 1970), pp. 155–158.

27. Peter Richardson and Jean Jacques Van-Helten, "The Gold Mining Industry in the Transvaal, 1886–99," in Warwick and Spies, *South African War,* pp. 18–36; Marks, "Scrambling"; Shula Marks and Stanley Trapido, "Lord Milner and the South African State," *History Workshop* 8 (1979): 50–80.

28. Gordon, *Growth of Boer Opposition,* pp. 86–11 on corruption, chap. 7 and pp. 274, 279–282 on election. Valuable if allowance is made for pro-British bias is I. S. Amery, ed., *The Times History of the War in South Africa, 1899–1900,* vol. 1, 2nd ed. (London: Low, Marston, 1900), pp. 128–140 and chap. 5.

29. G. H. L. LeMay, *British Supremacy in South Africa, 1899–1907* (Oxford: Clarendon, 1965), chap. 1; Marais, *Fall of Kruger's Republic,* pp. 159–160, 327–332; Richard T. Shannon, *The Crisis of Imperialism, 1865–1915* (Frogmore, St. Albans, England: Paladin, 1976), pp. 324–325, 328; Ronald Hyam, *Britain's Imperial Century, 1815–1914: A Study of Empire and Expansion* (London: Batsford, 1976), pp. 307–308. For British prejudices, see Arthur Conan Doyle, *The Great Boer War,* rev. ed. (New York: McClure, Phillips, 1902), pp. 38–40; Robinson, *Africa and the Victorians,* chap. 14; Porter, *Origins,* pp. 52–56, 86, 91, 257; Thompson, *History of South Africa,* pp. 133–138; F. H. Hinsley, "British Foreign Policy and Colonial Questions, 1895–1904," in *The Cambridge History of the British Empire,* vol. 3 of *The Empire-Commonwealth,* ed. E. A. Benians, pp. 495–497. On gold see Marks and Trapido, "Lord Milner."

30. Pakenham, *Boer War,* pp. 6, 54, 60–65, 76; Marais, *Fall of Kruger's Republic,* pp. 66–68; Eric Stokes, "Milnerism," *The Historical Journal* 5 (1962): 47–60; J. A. S. Grenville, *Lord Salisbury and Foreign Policy. The Close of the Nineteenth Century* (London: Athlone, 1970), chap. 11.

31. Porter, *Origins,* esp. pp. 140–142, 187–195, 241–247; Porter, "South African War." See also Marais, *Fall of Kruger's Republic,* pp. 234, 248–255; Robinson, *Africa and the Victorians,* pp. 422–423, 443–444 and chap. 14 passim; Alan H. Jeeves, "The Rand Capitalists and the Coming of the South African War, 1896–1899," in Canadian Historical Association, *Historical Papers, 1973* (Ottawa: Canadian Historical Association, 1973), pp. 61–83.

32. Amery, *Times History,* describes repression as seen by the British, e.g. pp. 223–224, 230–231. See also Andrew N. Porter, "Sir Alfred Milner and the Press, 1897–1899," *Historical Journal* 16 (1973): 323–339. Milner quotes in Porter, *Origins,* p. 166. On the introduction of the word "oligarchy" see Edward T. Cook, *Rights and Wrongs of the Transvaal*

War (London: Arnold, 1901), p. 268n. Cf. Doyle, *Great Boer War,* pp. 16, 26. With more space much could be added about Joseph Chamberlain's role, see Richard Koebner and Helmut Dan Schmidt, *Imperialism: The Story and Significance of a Political Word, 1840–1960* (Cambridge: Cambridge University Press, 1964), pp. 181, 185–195; and below, chapter 13.

33. J. P. D. Dunbabin, "Electoral Reforms and Their Outcome in the United Kingdom, 1865–1900," in *Later Victorian Britain, 1867–1900,* ed. T. R. Gourvish and Alan O'Day (Basingstoke, Hampshire: Macmillan, 1988), pp. 93–150; Arno J. Mayer, *The Persistence of the Old Regime: Europe and the Great War* (New York: Pantheon, 1981); Peter Weiler, *The New Liberalism: Liberal Social Theory in Great Britain, 1889–1914* (New York: Garland, 1982), pp. 61, 64.

34. M. C. E. Van Schoor, "The Orange Free State," in *Five Hundred Years: A History of South Africa,* ed. C. F. J. Muller (Pretoria: Academica, 1986), pp. 234–255.

35. Joseph Rothschild, *Return to Diversity: A Political History of East Central Europe Since World War II* (New York: Oxford University Press, 1989); H. Gordon Skilling, *Czechoslovakia's Interrupted Revolution* (Princeton: Princeton University Press, 1976); Zdenek L. Suda, *Zealots and Rebels: A History of the Ruling Communist Party of Czechoslovakia* (Stanford, Calif.: Hoover Institution Press, 1980); Pavel Tigrid, "Czechoslovakia: A Post-Mortem," part 1, *Survey* 73 (1968): 131–164; and ibid., part 2, *Survey* 74–75 (1968): 112–142; Pavel Tigrid, *Why Dubček Fell* (London: MacDonald, 1971); Alexander Dubček, *Hope Dies Last,* ed. Jiri Hochman, trans. Jiri Hochman (New York: Kodansha, 1993). Newly emerged documentation has not changed the picture much; Mark Kramer, "The Prague Spring and the Soviet Invasion of Czechoslovakia: New Interpretations," part 1, *Cold War International History Project Bulletin,* no. 2 (1993): 1, 4–13; ibid., part 2, *Cold War International History Project Bulletin,* no. 3 (1993): 2–13. Poll: Galia Golan, *The Czechoslovak Reform Movement: Communism in Crisis, 1962–1968* (Cambridge: Cambridge University Press, 1971), p. 307, see also chap. 23.

36. Use of "oligarchic" and descriptions of regime: Harry Gelman, *The Brezhnev Politburo and the Decline of Detente* (Ithaca, N.Y.: Cornell University Press, 1984), chap. 2; Jiri Valenta, *Soviet Intervention in Czechoslovakia 1968: Anatomy of a Decision* (Baltimore: Johns Hopkins University Press, 1979), chap. 1; George W. Breslauer, *Khrushchev and Brezhnev as Leaders. Building Authority in Soviet Politics* (London: Allen and Unwin, 1982), esp. pp. 17, 131–133, 264–265, 283; Paul J. Murphy, *Brezhnev: Soviet Politician* (Jefferson, N.C.: McFarland, 1981), esp. pp. 318–323; Grey Hodnett, "The Pattern of Leadership Politics," in *The Domestic Context of Soviet Foreign Policy,* ed. Seweryn Bialer (Boulder: Westview, 1981), pp. 87–118; John Löwenhardt, James Ozinga, and Erik van Ree, *The Rise and Fall of the Soviet Politburo* (New York: St. Martin's, 1992), pp. 62–63; Raymond F. Smith, *Negotiating with the Soviets* (Bloomington: Indiana University Press, 1989), pp. 98, 104–117; Philip G. Roeder, "Soviet Policies and Kremlin Politics," *International Studies Quarterly* 28 (1984): 171–195, see p. 176; and with specific reference to the continuity of domestic and international negotiating styles, James M. Goldgeier, *Leadership Style and Soviet Foreign Policy* (Baltimore: Johns Hopkins University Press, 1994), pp. 25–28.

37. For this and other insights see Václav Havel, "The Power of the Powerless" (1978), trans. Paul Wilson, various reprints, e.g. in Havel, *Open Letters: Selected Writings 1965–1990,* ed. Paul Wilson (New York: Vintage, 1992), pp. 127–214. Cf. the peaceful Confucian stalemate in China under the Wan-li emperor, chapter 5.

38. "Ton of letters": Dubček, *Hope Dies Last,* p. 168; "how can you claim": Radoslav Selucky, "The Dubček Era Revisited," *Problems of Communism* 24 (1975): 38–43, see p. 41. For negotiations see Tigrid, *Survey,* no. 73, pp. 158–164; Tigrid, *Why Dubček Fell,* pp. 82–94; Valenta, *Soviet Intervention,* pp. 71–77, 83–84; Suda, *Zealots and Rebels,* chap. 10 and pp. 341–346; Skilling, *Czechoslovakia's Interrupted Revolution,* pp. 304–309, 881–882.

39. Dubček, *Hope Dies Last,* pp. 157–158; Valenta, *Soviet Intervention,* pp. 37–39, 78–79, 105–106, 123–128, 148. "Handful of rightists": Tigrid, *Why Dubček Fell,* p. 98. Kramer, "The Prague Spring," part 1, p. 35.

40. Valenta, *Soviet Intervention,* pp. 75, 144–145.

41. Skilling, *Czechoslovakia's Interrupted Revolution,* pp. 796–901 and app. D; Dubček, *Hope Dies Last,* chaps. 21–23; Valenta, *Soviet Intervention,* pp. 149–153; Tigrid, "Czechoslovakia," part 2, pp. 119–128; Tigrid, *Why Dubček Fell,* pp. 112–118; cf. Selucky, "The Dubček Era."

42. L. W. Gluchowski, "Poland, 1956"; Mark Kramer, "Hungary and Poland, 1956," *Cold War International History Bulletin* 5 (Spring 1995): 1, 38–56; Mark Kramer, "New Evidence on Soviet Decision-Making and the 1956 Polish and Hungarian Crises," *ibid.* nos. 8–9 (Winter 1996/1997): 358–384.

43. Blainey, *Causes of War;* John G. Stoessinger, *Why Nations Go to War,* 6th ed. (St. Martin's, 1992). Robert Jervis, "War and Misperception," *Journal of Interdisciplinary History* 18 (1988): 675–700; Marc Ross, "The Limits to Social Structure: Social Structural and Psychocultural Explanations for Political Conflict and Violence," *Anthropological Quarterly* 59 (1986): 171–176; J. D. Singer, "The Political Origins of International War," in *Aggression and War: Their Biological and Social Bases,* ed. Jo Groebel and Robert A. Hinde (New York: Cambridge University Press, 1989), pp. 202–220; Yaacov Y. I. Vertzberger, *The World in Their Minds. Information Processing, Cognition, and Perception in Foreign Policy Decision-Making* (Stanford, Calif.: Stanford University Press, 1990); Jack S. Levy, "The Causes of War: a Review of Theories and Evidence," in *Behavior, Society and Nuclear War,* vol. 1, ed. Philip E. Tetlock, Paul C. Stern, and Charles Tilly (New York: Oxford University Press, 1989), pp. 279–289. A general review of related issues is J. F. Voss and E. Dorsey, "Perception and International Relations," in *Political Psychology and Foreign Policy,* ed. Eric Singer and Valerie Hudson (Boulder: Westview, 1992), pp. 3–30.

44. John Malloy Owen IV, "Testing the Democratic Peace: American Diplomatic Crises, 1794–1917," (Ph.D. diss., Harvard University, 1993), pp. 31, 455, and passim.

45. Ido Oren, "The Subjectivity of the 'Democratic' Peace. Changing U.S. Perceptions of Imperial Germany," *International Security* 20 (1995): 147–184, makes the general point, but scarcely differentiates among democracy (U.S.), quasi-oligarchy (Germany in the 1890s), and authoritarian military rule (Germany in 1917).

CHAPTER EIGHT
Republics Versus Autocracies

1. Bradford Perkins, *Prologue to War: England and the United States, 1805–1812* (Berkeley: University of California Press, 1961); Donald R. Hickey, *The War of 1812: A Forgotten Conflict* (Urbana: University of Illinois Press, 1989); should be supplemented (with care) with Henry Adams, *History of the United States of America During the Administration of Thomas Jefferson and James Madison*, 4 vols., 1889–1890 (New York: Boni, 1930). Also Reginald Horsman, *The Causes of the War of 1812* (Philadelphia: University of Pennsylvannia Press, 1962); Bradford Perkins, ed., *The Causes of the War of 1812: National Honor or National Interest?*, (1962; reprint, Malabar, Fla.: R. Krieger, 1983); Ronald N. Hatzenbuehler, "The Early National Period, 1789–1815: The Need for Redefinition," in *American Foreign Relations. A Historiographical Review*, ed. Gerald K. Haines and J. Samuel Walker (Westport, Conn.: Greenwood, 1981), pp. 17–32; Dwight L. Smith, *The War of 1812: An Annotated Bibliography* (New York: Garland, 1985).

2. Linda Colley, "The Apotheosis of George III: Loyalty, Royalty and the British Nation," *Past and Present* 102 (1984): 94–129; Linda Colley, *Britons: Forging the Nation, 1707–1837* (New Haven: Yale University Press, 1992), chap. 5. "Libertine" quoted in J. B. Priestley, *The Prince of Pleasure and His Regency, 1811–1820* (New York: Harper and Row, 1969), pp. 77.

3. Canning quoted in Adams, *History of U.S.*, vol. 2, pp. 180–182; see also Perkins, *Prologue to War*, p. 176.

4. Chilton Williamson, *American Suffrage: From Property to Democracy, 1760–1860* (Princeton: Princeton University Press, 1960), chaps. 7–9; William W. Freehling, "The Founding Fathers and Slavery," *American Historical Review* 77 (1972): 81–93.

5. Jefferson quoted in Perkins, *Prologue to War*, p. 11, see also pp. 58–64. See also Robert W. Tucker and David C. Henderson, *Empire of Liberty: The Statecraft of Thomas Jefferson* (New York: Oxford University Press, 1990); Roger H. Brown, *The Republic in Peril: 1812* (New York: Columbia University Press, 1964), pp. 2–3. On "aristocracy" see Gordon S. Wood, *The Radicalism of the American Revolution* (New York: Knopf, 1992); on view of prince regent see J. C. A. Stagg, *Mr. Madison's War: Politics, Diplomacy and Warfare in the Early American Republic, 1783–1830* (Princeton: Princeton University Press, 1983), p. 64.

6. Robert R. Palmer, *The Age of the Democratic Revolution: A Political History of Europe and America, 1760–1800*, 2 vols. (Princeton: Princeton University Press, 1964), vol. 2, pp. 472–491, 539; Clive Embsley, *British Society and the French Wars, 1793–1815* (London: Macmillan, 1979), pp. 150–159; Frank O. Darvall, *Popular Disturbances and Public Order in Regency England* (London: Oxford University Press, 1934), chap. 16; Malcolm I. Thomis and Peter Holt, *Threats of Revolution in Britain, 1789–1848* (London: Macmillan, 1977), chap. 2; Martin Kaufman, "War Sentiment in Western Pennsylvania, 1812," *Pennsylvania History* 31 (1964): 436–448, see pp. 442–443.

7. Adams, *History of U.S.*, vol. 2, chaps. 10, 11; Brown, *Republic in Peril*, pp. 14–15, 177–181; Richard Buel, Jr., *Securing the Revolution: Ideology and American Politics, 1789–1815* (Ithaca, N.Y.: Cornell University Press, 1972), chap. 12.

8. "Disgusting country" quoted in William H. Masterson, *Tories and Democrats: British Diplomats in Pre-Jacksonian America* (College Station: Texas A&M University Press, 1985), p. 95, see also pp. 4–7 and passim; Perkins, *Prologue to War,* pp. 6–10; Horsman, *Causes of the War,* pp. 190–192. For colonists as "outgroup" see Robert Kelly, "Ideology and Political Culture from Jefferson to Nixon," *American Historical Review* 82 (1977): 531–562, see pp. 534–535. See also, chapter 11.

9. For sources see chapter 6. "Sought other foes": Richard Feller, *Von den Anfängen bis 1516,* vol. 1 of *Geschichte Berns,* 4th ed. (Bern: Hubert Lang, 1949), pp. 283, see also pp. 281–285, 299–301; Leo Alexander Ricker, *Freiburg: Aus der Geschichte einer Stadt* (Karlsruhe: Braun, 1964), pp. 52–53. Chronicle: Zurich, *Chronik der Stadt Zürich, mit Fortsetzungen,* ed. Allgemeine Geschichtsforschende Gesellschaft der Schweiz and Johannes Dierauer, *Quellen zur Schweizergeschichte,* vol. 18 (Basel: Geerig, 1900), p. 216; some fighting with Forest States troops is recorded but there is no evidence of combat directly with Bernese or Lucerners.

10. Besides sources cited in chapter 6 see Anton Largadièr, *Von den Anfängen bis zur Aufklärung,* vol. 1 of *Geschichte von Stadt und Landschaft Zürich* (Erlenbach-Zurich: Rentsch, 1945), pp. 207, 214–215. For a similar case, the Swabian war of 1499, see appendix.

11. As usual, studies refer mainly to Florence; cf. the history of Piero de'Medici. Besides general histories cited above (chapters 3, 4) see J. N. Stephens, *The Fall of the Florentine Republic, 1512–1530* (Oxford: Clarendon, 1983), chap. 1; and John M. Najemy, *Corporatism and Consensus in Florentine Electoral Politics, 1280–1400* (Chapel Hill: University of North Carolina Press, 1982), esp. pp. 299–304. On similar family rule elsewhere see Pietro Silva, *Il Governo di Pietro Gambacorta in Pisa e le sue relazioni col resto della Toscana e coi Visconti* (Pisa: Nistri, 1911); Christine Meek, *Lucca, 1369–1404: Politics and Society in an Early Renaissance City-State* (Oxford: Oxford University Press, 1978), pp. 277–279.

12. Niccolo Machiavelli, *History of Florence and of the Affairs of Italy* (New York: Harper and Row, 1960), 7.4, p. 336, is inaccurate on lack of deaths; cf. François-Tommy Perrens, *Histoire de Florence depuis la domination des Médicis,* 3 vols. (Paris: Quantin, 1888), 3 vols., vol. 1, pp. 331.

13. Perrens, *Histoire de Florence,* vol. 1, pp. 321–329; Machiavelli, *History of Florence,* 7.3, p. 334.

14. Gino Benvenuti, *Storia della Repubblica di Pisa* (Pisa: Giardini, 1967), pp. 355–365; Silva, *Il Governo di Pietro Gambacorta.* Morelli quoted in François-Tommy Perrens, *Histoire de Florence depuis ses origines jusqu'à la domination des Médicis,* 6 vols., 2nd ed. (Paris: Fontemoing, 1873–1883), vol. 6, p. 146; see passim.

15. "Sent to jail": Hannis Taylor, "A Review of the Cuban Question," *The North American Review* 165 (1897): 610–635, see pp. 612–613, 621. Valuable but with disputed interpretations are John L. Offner, *An Unwanted War: The Diplomacy of the United States and Spain over Cuba, 1895–1898* (Chapel Hill: University of North Carolina Press, 1992), and Ernest R. May, *Imperial Democracy: The Emergence of America as a Great Power* (New York: Harcourt, Brace and World, 1961), esp. chap. 9. Also Gabriel Maura Gamazo, *Historia crítica del reinado de Don Alfonso XIII durante su minoridad bajo la regencia de su madre,* vol. 1 (Barcelona: Montanes y Simon, 1919); Fernando Soldevila Zubibaru, *Historia de Es-*

paña, vol. 8 (Barcelona: Ariel, 1959); Raymond Carr, *Spain: 1808–1975,* 2nd ed. (Oxford: Clarendon, 1982), chap. 9; Rhea March Smith, *Spain: A Modern History* (Ann Arbor: University of Michigan Press, 1965), chaps. 38, 39; Carolyn P. Boyd, *Praetorian Politics in Liberal Spain* (Chapel Hill: University of North Carolina Press, 1979), pp. 18–19.

16. "Del casillero caciquil," quoted in Maura Gamazo, *Historia crítica,* p. 275; see Offner, *Unwanted War,* esp. p. 137; French Ensor Chadwick, *Diplomacy,* vol. 1 of *The Relations of the United States and Spain* (New York: Scribner's, 1909), esp. pp. 400–406; for further references see chapter 12.

17. Offner, *Unwanted War;* Louis A. Pérez, Jr., *Cuba Between Empires, 1878–1902* (Pittsburgh: University of Pittsburgh Press, 1983), esp. pp. 170, 175; Manuel Ciges Aparicio, *España bajo la dinastía de los Borbones* (Madrid: Aquilar, 1932), p. 384; Alexander E. Campbell, *Great Britain and the United States, 1895–1903* (London: Longmans, Green, 1960), p. 141; Juan Ortega y Rubio, *Historia de la Regencia de Maria Cristina Hasburgo-Lorena,* vol. 3 (Madrid: Felipe Gonzáles Rojas, 1906), p. 247; Chadwick, *Relations,* pp. 546–549, 568.

18. David Schoenbaum, *Zabern 1913: Consensus Politics in Imperial Germany* (London: Allen and Unwin, 1982). For origins of World War I see chapter 11, n. 27.

19. For the regime as a monarchy see John C. G. Röhl, *The Kaiser and His Court: Wilhelm II and the Government of Germany,* trans. Terence F. Cole (Cambridge: Cambridge University Press, 1994). See also John C. G. Röhl and Nicolaus Sombart, eds., *Kaiser Wilhelm II: New Interpretations: The Corfu Papers* (Cambridge: Cambridge University Press, 1981), especially Nicolaus Sombart, "The Kaiser in His Epoch: Some Reflexions on Wilhelmine Society, Sexuality and Culture," pp. 287–311; Isabel V. Hull, *The Entourage of Kaiser Wilhelm II, 1888–1918* (Cambridge: Cambridge University Press, 1982); Volker R. Berghahn, *Germany and the Approach of War in 1914* (New York: St. Martin's, 1973), esp. p. 168.

20. Berghahn, *Germany and the Approach of War,* esp. pp. 9–10, 164, 187; Hull, *Entourage,* pp. 2–7; John C. G. Röhl, introduction to Röhl and Sombart, *Kaiser Wilhelm II,* pp. 1–22; Paul Kennedy, "The Kaiser and German Weltpolitik: Reflexions on Wilhelm II's Place in the Making of German Foreign Policy," in ibid., pp. 143–168; James Joll, *The Origins of the First World War* (New York: Longman, 1984), chap. 5. On the parliamentary opposition see Hartmut Pogge von Strandmann, "Germany and the Coming of War" in *The Coming of the First World War,* ed. R. J. W. Evans and Hartmut von Strandmann (Oxford: Clarendon, 1990), pp. 87–123; Fritz Fischer, *War of Illusions: German Policies from 1911 to 1914,* 2nd ed., trans. Marian Jackson (London: Chatto and Windus, 1975), pp. 190–191, 248, and chaps. 17, 22; on the socialists, G. D. H. Cole, *The Second International, 1889–1914,* 2 vols. (London: Macmillan, 1960), vol. 1, p. 304.

CHAPTER NINE

Well-Established Republics Versus Authoritarian Regimes

1. "For want": Charles Wilson, *Profit and Power: A Study of England and the Dutch Wars* (London: Longmans, Green, 1957), pp. 156, see also pp. 81, 151. For the following:

Samuel R. Gardiner, *1651–1654,* vol. 2 of *A History of the Commonwealth and Protectorate, 1649–1660* (London: Longmans, Green, 1897); Samuel R. Gardiner, *Letters and Papers Relating to the First Dutch Wars, 1652–1654,* vol. 1 (London: Navy Records Society, 1899); Abraham de Wicquefort, *Histoire des Province-Unies des Païs-Bas depuis . . . la Paix de Munster,* 2 vols. (Amsterdam: F. Muller, 1861–1864), vol. 2; Carl Ballhausen, *Der erste englischholländische Seekrieg, 1652–1654* (The Hague: Nijhoff, 1923).

2. Wilson, *Profit and Power;* R. W. K. Hinton, *The Eastland Trade and the Common Weal in the Seventeenth Century* (Cambridge: Cambridge University Press, 1959); J. E. Farnell, "The Navigation Act of 1651, the First Dutch War and the London Merchant Community," *Economic History Review* 16 (1964): 439–454; George Edmundson, *Anglo-Dutch Rivalry During the First Half of the Seventeenth Century* (Oxford: Clarendon, 1911); K. H. D. Haley, *The British and the Dutch: Political and Cultural Relations Through the Ages* (London: George Philip, 1988), pp. 50–64; Jonathan I. Israel, *Dutch Primacy in World Trade, 1585–1740* (Oxford: Clarendon, 1989), pp. 197–209.

3. Gardiner, *1651–1654,* pp. 107–109; Blair Worden, *The Rump Parliament* (Cambridge: Cambridge University Press, 1974), pp. 257–258, 299; Israel, *Dutch Primacy,* pp. 197–209; Wilson, *Profit and Power,* p. 156; Haley, *British and Dutch,* pp. 80, 89–90. Farnell, "Navigation Act," presents a case for economic motivation which does not fundamentally conflict with these authors.

4. Simon Schama, *Embarrassment of Riches: An Interpretation of Dutch Culture in the Golden Age* (New York: Knopf, 1987), pp. 78, 104, 565–570; K. D. H. Haley, *The Dutch in the Seventeenth Century* (New York: Harcourt Brace Jovanovich, 1972), pp. 52–68; E. O. G. Haitsma-Mulier, "Der Mythos Venedigs und der holländische Republikanismus," in *Der Ost- und Nordseeraum,* ed. K. Fritze, E. Müller-Mertens, and J. Schildhauer (Weimar: Hermann Böhlhausss Nachfolger, 1986), p. 115.

5. Haley, *Dutch in Seventeenth Century* pp. 65–68. For this and the Stadholder's role see also comments in James Geddes, *1623–1654,* vol. 1 of *History of the Administration of John de Witt, Grand Pensionary of Holland* (London: Kegan Paul, 1879), pp. 141, 145–146, 154–155.

6. Derek Hirst, *Authority and Conflict: England, 1603–1658* (Cambridge, Mass.: Harvard University Press, 1986); Worden, *Rump Parliament;* Edmund S. Morgan, *Inventing the People: The Rise of Popular Sovereignty in England and America* (New York: W. W. Norton, 1988), chap. 1; John Morrill, *The Nature of the English Revolution* (London: Longman, 1993), esp. pp. 22–24.

7. Besides references above see D. E. Underdown, *Pride's Purge* (Oxford: Clarendon, 1971). On arrests and executions see Gardiner, *History of the Commonwealth* vol. 1, pp. 399–416.

8. Perez Zagorin, *A History of Political Thought in the English Revolution* (London: Humanities Press, 1954), pp. 12–17. On ideologies see especially Christopher Hill, *The World Turned Upside Down. Radical Ideas during the English Revolution* (New York: Viking, 1972). On millenarian Puritanism see Austin Woolrych, *Commonwealth to Protectorate* (Oxford: Clarendon, 1982), pp. 75, 284–287, 322–324; Worden, *Rump Parliament,* pp. 303–305. Par-

liament's justification: Gardiner, *History of the Commonwealth* vol. 1, pp. 282–284; Underdown, *Pride's Purge,* pp. 263–264; Zagorin, *History of Political Thought,* esp. chaps. 5, 6, 12.

9. Blair Worden, "Classical Republicanism and the English Revolution," in *History and Imagination: Essays in Honor of H. R. Trevor-Roper,* ed. Hugh Lloyd-Jones, Valerie Pearl, and Blair Worden (New York: Holmes and Meier, 1981), pp. 182–200; Zera S. Fink, *The Classical Republicans: An Essay on the Recovery of a Pattern of Thought in Seventeenth Century England,* 2nd ed. (Evanston, Ill.: Northwestern University Press, 1962).

10. "Same form": quoted in Wicquefort, *Histoire des Province-Unies* vol. 2, pp. 114–115. Similarly, Gardiner, *Letters and Papers* vol. 1, pp. 231–232, 270–271. See also Simon Groenveld, "The English Civil Wars as a Cause of the First Anglo-Dutch War, 1640–1652," *Historical Journal* 30 (1987): 541–566, see pp. 544–545; Pieter Geyl, *Orange and Stuart, 1641–1672,* 1939, trans. Arnold Pomerov (London: Weidenfeld and Nicolson, 1969), p. 81; Herbert H. Rowen, *John de Witt, Grand Pensionary of Holland, 1625–1672* (Princeton: Princeton University Press, 1978), pp. 70, 394.

11. William Palmer, *The Political Career of Oliver St. John, 1637–1649* (Newark: University of Delaware Press, 1993); Groenveld, "English Civil Wars"; John Thurloe, *1638–1653,* vol. 1 of *A Collection of the State Papers of John Thurloe,* ed. Thomas Birch (London, 1742), pp. 182–183; Rowen, *John de Witt,* pp. 54–55, 79; Wicquefort, *Histoire des Province-Unies,* vol. 2, p. 79. A plain warning for the Dutch was the unequal "union" that England was forcing upon Scotland.

12. Rowen, *John de Witt,* esp. chap. 4; Geyl, *Orange and Stuart,* pp. 58–80.

13. Dutch ships: Edward Hyde, Earl of Clarendon, *The History of the Rebellion and Civil Wars in England,* vol. 5, ed. Dunn Macray (Oxford: Clarendon, 1888), 8.7, p. 135. "Utmost skill:" Great Britain Public Record Office, *Calendar of State Papers, Domestic Series, 1651–1652,* 1877, ed. Mary Anne Everett Green (Vaduz: Kraus, 1965), p. 136. Embassy: Wicquefort, *Histoire des Province-Unies* vol. 2, p. 81; Ballhausen, *Der erste englisch-holländische Seekrieg,* p. 27. Mistreating diplomats was a common tactic, Garrett Mattingly, *Renaissance Diplomacy* (1955; reprint, New York: Dover, 1988), chap. 27.

14. "Qui n'estoist affectionné de tout son coeur. . . . " Lodewijck Huygens, *The English Journal, 1651–1652,* ed. A. G. H. Bachrach and R. G. Collmer, trans. A. G. H. Bachrach and R. G. Collmer (Leiden: E. J. Brill/Leiden University Press, 1982), pp. 143, 281; note also pp. 37n, 183. See Wicquefort, *Histoire des Province-Unies,* vol. 2, p. 76, and, for English declaration of war, p. 142.

15. James quoted in Edmundson, *Anglo-Dutch Rivalry,* p. 78. Shipping: Israel, *Dutch Primacy,* p. 209; Groenveld, "English Civil Wars," pp. 560–561; Ballhausen, *Der erste englisch-holländische Seekrieg;* Bulstrode Whitelocke, *Memorials of the English Affairs,* vol. 3 (London: Tonson, 1732), p. 359 (folio p. 512). The key role of the search-and-seizure policy in causing the war (see Gardiner, *Letters and Papers,* vol. 1, p. 53), is accepted by most historians.

16. Contemporary historians: Hyde, *History of the Rebellion,* vol. 5, pp. 252; Wicquefort, *Histoire des Province-Unies,* vol. 2, pp. 144–145 and books 5, 6, passim. During war: Woolrych, *Commonwealth to Protectorate,* pp. 281–283, 322. The most significant clause

in the eventual peace terms pledged the Dutch to avoid monarchy, see Haley, *British and Dutch,* p. 94.

17. Schama, *Embarrassment of Riches,* p. 249; Thurloe, *State Papers,* p. 116. Flag: Gardiner, *Letters and Papers* vol. 1, p. 167n; it is also seen in paintings of the period.

18. On the primacy of political division in the English Civil War see Hirst, *Authority and Conflict,* esp. pp. 224–230; David Kaiser, *Politics and War: European Conflict from Philip II to Hitler* (Cambridge, Mass.: Harvard University Press, 1990), pp. 109–137.

19. I pass over some anocratic tendencies (especially overseas) in both cases. For general sources see appendix, 1797. On confiscations see Stanley Elkins and Eric McKitrick, *The Age of Federalism* (New York: Oxford University Press, 1993), pp. 643, 648–652, 670–671.

20. James Morton Smith, *Freedom's Fetters: The Alien and Sedition Laws and American Civil Liberties* (Ithaca, N.Y.: Cornell University Press, 1956); James Roger Sharp, *American Politics in the Early Republic: The New Nation in Crisis* (New Haven: Yale University Press, 1993), esp. pp. 181–182, 188.

21. Donald H. Stewart, *The Opposition Press of the Federalist Period* (Albany: State University of New York Press, 1969), chap. 8; Norman A. Graebner, *Foundations of American Foreign Policy: A Realist Appraisal From Franklin to McKinley* (Wilmington, Del.: Scholarly Resources, 1985), pp. 89, 94; James Alton James, "French Opinion as a Factor in Preventing War Between France and the United States, 1795–1800," *American Historical Review* 30 (1924): 44–55; William C. Stinchcombe, *The XYZ Affair* (Westport, Conn.: Greenwood, 1980), pp. 63, 77, 96–98, 116–118, 125–127; Albert Hall Bowman, *The Struggle for Neutrality: Franco-American Diplomacy During the Federalist Era* (Knoxville: University of Tennessee Press, 1974), chaps. 14–17; E. Wilson Lyon, "The Directory and the United States," *American Historical Review* 43 (1938): 514–532; summary and analysis in John Malloy Owen IV, "Testing the Democratic Peace: American Diplomatic Crises, 1794–1917" (Ph.D. diss., Harvard University, 1993, pp. 98–117).

22. Casualties: George Macaulay Trevelyan, *Garibaldi's Defense of the Roman Republic, 1848–1849,* rev. ed. (London: Longmans, Green, 1908), pp. 345–346. Trevelyan is still the best narrative, but cf. Christopher Hibbert, *Garibaldi and His Enemies* (Boston: Little, Brown, 1966). On antecedents, Emile Bourgeois and E. Clermont, *Rome et Napoléon III (1849–1870): Etude sur les origines et la chute du Second Empire* (Paris: Colin, 1907).

23. George Fasel, "The Wrong Revolution: French Republicanism in 1848," *French Historical Studies* 8 (1974): 654–677; Roger D. Price, ed., *Revolution and Reaction: 1848 and the Second French Republic* (London: Croom Helm, 1975); Roger D. Price, *The French Second Republic: A Social History* (Ithaca, N.Y.: Cornell University Press, 1972); Frederick A. de Lunn, *The French Republic Under Cavaignac, 1848* (Princeton: Princeton University Press, 1969), esp. pp. 382–395; John M. Merriman, *The Agony of the Republic: The Repression of the Left in Revolutionary France, 1848–1851* (New Haven: Yale University Press, 1978); Peter McPhee, *The Politics of Rural Life. Political Mobilization in the French Countryside, 1846–1952* (Oxford: Oxford University Press, 1992), pp. 113–123, 133–134; Peter McPhee, "The Crisis of Radical Republicanism in the French Revolution of 1848," *Historical Studies* 16 (1974): 71–88; André-Jean Tudesq, *L'Election présidentielle de Louis*

Napoléon Bonaparte, 10 décembre 1848 (Paris: Colin, 1965); André-Jean Tudesq, "La Légende Napoléonienne en France en 1848," *Revue Historique* 128 (1957): 64–85; Maurice Agulhon, *The Republican Experiment, 1848–1852,* vol. 2 of *Cambridge History of Modern France,* trans. Janet Lloyd (Cambridge: Cambridge University Press, 1983), pp. 70–73.

24. "Tout ce qu'il peut, il le voudra," quoted in Adrien Dansette, *Louis-Napoléon à la conquête du pouvoir,* rev. ed. (Paris: Hachette, 1961), p. 291, see also pp. 93–94, 286, 309, and passim; Agulhon, *Republican Experiment,* pp. 73–74.

25. Bourgeois, *Rome et Napoléon III,* pp. 10–19; William E. Echard, "Louis Napoleon and the French Decision to Intervene at Rome in 1849: A New Appraisal," *Canadian Journal of History* 9 (1974): 263–274. "Ruffians" quoted in Ross W. Collins, *Catholicism and the Second French Republic (1848–1852)* (Ph.D. diss., Columbia University, New York, 1923), pp. 217–218, see also pp. 214–224. Besides sources cited above, on conditions in Rome see Ferdinand Boyer, "La Vie politique à Rome de Novembre 1848 à avril 1849, d'aprés l'agent vice-consul de France (Lysimaque Caftan-gioglou Tavernier à Civitavecchia)," *Revue d'histoire diplomatique* 86 (1972): 237–246; and the biased but informative Luigi Carlo Farini, *The Roman State from 1815 to 1850,* 4 vols., trans. anon. (London: John Murray, 1852), vol. 4.

26. See Lawrence C. Jennings, *France and Europe in 1848: A Study of French Foreign Affairs in Time of Crisis* (Oxford: Clarendon, 1973), pp. 246–252; here and below see also Collins, *Catholicism.*

27. J. Bouillon, P. Chalmin, et al., eds., *L'Armée et la Seconde République* (La Roche-sur-Yon: Imprimerie centrale de l'Ouest, 1955), esp. Chalmin, "La Crise morale de l'Armée française," pp. 28–76.

28. "Refugees": Bourgeois, *Rome et Napoléon III,* p. 41n, see pp. 22–23, 42–46, 74. Trevelyan, *Garibaldi's Defense,* pp. 127–133.

29. Price, *Second French Republic,* pp. 228–236; Jacques Bouillon, "Les Démocrates-socialistes aux élections de 1849," *Revue française de science politique* 6 (1956): 70–95; Theodore Zeldin, "Government Policy in the French General Election of [May] 1849," *English Historical Review* 74 (1959): 240–248; Bourgeois, *Rome et Napoléon III,* pp. 47–52.

30. Price, *Second French Republic,* p. 247; Collins, *Catholicism and the Second French Republic,* p. 231; Dansette, *Louis-Napoléon à la Conquête,* pp. 303–304.

31. For diplomacy, Bourgeois, *Rome et Napoléon III,* pp. 29–30, 39–40, 107–108, 139, 143, and chap. 6; on diplomatic corps see Jennings, *France and Europe,* pp. 25–26.

32. Harry Hearder, *Italy in the Age of the Risorgimento, 1790–1870* (New York: Longman, 1983), chaps. 7, 8; Harry Hearder, "The Making of the Roman Republic, 1848–1849," *History* 60 (1975): 160–184; Gwilym O. Griffith, *Mazzini: Prophet of Modern Europe* (London: Hudden and Stoughton, 1932); Alberto M. Ghisalberti, *Roma da Mazzini a Pio IX: Ricerche sulla Restaurazione Papale del 1849–1850* (Milan: Giuffrè, 1958), chap. 3.

33. Papal message in Farini, *Roman State,* vol. 3, p. 133, see also 175.

34. "Expedition": Agulhon, *Republican Experiment,* pp. 100–101, see pp. 49, 79. McPhee, *Politics of Rural Life,* esp. pp. 172–175; Merriman, *Agony of the Republic,* chaps. 2, 5, esp. pp. 32, 55–56, 73–74; Price, *Revolution and Reaction.*

35. Helen Chapin Metz, ed., *Iran: A Country Study,* 4th ed., Country Studies, Library of Congress, Federal Research Division (Washington, D.C.: U.S. Government Printing Office, 1989), chap. 4; John W. Limbert, *Iran: At War with History* (Boulder: Westview, 1987), chap. 6. A good summary for Japan is Stephen S. Large, *Emperor Hirohito and Shōwa Japan: A Political Biography* (London: Routledge, 1992).

36. A list of overt military confrontations in post-colonial Africa shows none between a pair of military-oligarchic regimes: Arnold Hughes and Roy May, "Armies on Loan: Toward an Explanation of Trans-National Military Intervention Among Black African States: 1960–1985," in Simon Baynham, ed., *Military Power and Politics in Black Africa* (London: Croom Helm, 1986), pp. 177–202. See Gregory Treverton, "Interstate Conflict in Latin America," in Kevin J. Middlebrook and Carlos Rico, eds., *The United States and Latin America in the 1980s,* pp. 567–568. Arie M. Kacowicz, "Explaining Zones of Peace: Democracies as Satisfied Powers?" (paper presented at International Studies Association meeting, Washington, D.C., March 1994).

37. "Nonrepublican" might be a better term were it not passive and negative. On definitions see Juan J. Linz, "Totalitarian and Authoritarian Regimes," *Handbook of Political Science,* vol. 3, *Macropolitical Theory,* ed. Fred Greenstein and Nelson Polsby (Reading, Mass.: Addison-Wesley, 1975), pp. 175–411; Fareed Zakaria, "The Rise of Illiberal Democracy," *Foreign Affairs* 76 (1997): 22–43.

38. Of the 15 modern wars listed, emigrés or refugees helped instigate war in 1812 (Irish in U.S., royalists in Canada), 1861 (escaped slaves), 1898, 1974, 1991, and also in the conflicts of 1847 and 1954; they were present in 1775, 1849, 1879, 1919. For more on secession see Albert O. O. Hirschman, *Exit, Voice and Loyalty: Response to Decline in Firms, Organizations and States* (Cambridge, Mass.: Harvard University Press, 1970); Bruce Russett, *Grasping the Democratic Peace. Principles for a Post-Cold War World* (Princeton: Princeton University Press, 1993), pp. 113–114 and chap. 5 passim.

39. Survey: Joe D. Hagan, "Regimes, Political Oppositions and the Comparative Analysis of Foreign Policy," in *New Directions in the Study of Foreign Policy,* ed. Charles F. Hermann, Charles W. Kegley, Jr., and James N. Rosenau (Boston: Allen and Unwin, 1987), pp. 339–365.

CHAPTER TEN

Well-Established Republics Versus Newborn Republics

1. Bruce Kent, *The Spoils of War: The Politics, Economics, and Diplomacy of Reparations, 1918–1932* (New York: Oxford University Press, 1989), gives historiography. Also Marc Trachtenberg, *Reparation in World Politics: France and European Economic Diplomacy, 1916–1923* (New York: Columbia University Press, 1980), pp. 41–45, 90–91, 123; Gerald D. Feldman, *The Great Disorder: Politics, Economics and Society in the German Inflation, 1914–1924* (Oxford: Oxford University Press, 1993). On French motives see Denise Artaud, "A propos de l'occupation de la Ruhr," *Revue d'histoire moderne et contemporaine* 17 (1970): 4–5; Walter A. McDougall, *France's Rhineland Diplomacy, 1914–1924: The Last Bid for a Balance of Power in Europe* (Princeton: Princeton University Press, 1978).

2. For diplomacy see especially Heinrich Euler, *Die Aussenpolitik der Weimarer Republik, 1918–1923: Von Waffenstillstand bis zum Ruhr conflikt* (Aschaffenburg: Stock & Körber, 1957), for Spa conference see pp. 161–166. Edgar D'Abernon, *An Ambassador of Peace: Pages from the Diary of Viscount d'Abernon,* 3 vols. (London: Hodder and Stoughton, 1929–1930), vol. 1, p. 61; David Felix, *Walter Rathenau and the Weimar Republic: The Politics of Reparations* (Baltimore: Johns Hopkins University Press, 1971), pp. 10–11, 82; Francis Ludwig Carsten, *The Reichswehr and Politics, 1918–1933* (Oxford: Clarendon, 1966), esp. pp. 104–107.

3. Peter Wulf, *Hugo Stinnes: Wirtschaft und Politik, 1918–1924* (Stuttgart: Klett-Cotta, 1979), pp. 194–207. "Terrier": D'Abernon, *Ambassador,* p. 43, see also p. 64. In service of "Höflichkeit": Euler, *Aussenpolitik der Weimarer Republic,* pp. 170–171.

4. D'Abernon, *Ambassador,* p. 64; Lloyd George quoted in Wulf, *Hugo Stinnes,* p. 297n.

5. "A few business men": Isaac F. Marcosson, "Stinnes," *Saturday Evening Post* 194, no. 13 (24 September 1921): 3ff. and *Saturday Evening Post* 195, no. 20 (11 Nov. 1922): 3ff., 82. Also Wulf, *Hugo Stinnes;* Gerald D. Feldman, *Iron and Steel in the German Inflation, 1916–1923* (Princeton: Princeton University Press, 1977), pp. 213–244, 448–451; Gaston Raphaël, *Le roi de la Ruhr: Hugo Stinnes, l'homme—son oeuvre—son rôle* (Paris: Pazot, 1924).

6. Charles S. Maier, *Recasting Bourgeois Europe: Stabilization in France, Germany, and Italy in the Decade After World War I* (Princeton: Princeton University Press, 1975).

7. On reparations: Georges Soutou, "Der Einfluss der Schwerindustrie auf die Gestaltung der Frankreichpolitik Deutschlands 1919–1921," in *Industrielles System und politische Entwicklung in der Weimarer Republik,* ed. Hans Mommsen, Dietmar Petzina, and Bernd Weisbrod (Dusseldorf: Droste, 1974), pp. 545–546; Hermann J. Rupieper, *The Cuno Government and Reparations, 1922–1923: Politics and Economics* (The Hague: Nijhoff, 1979), pp. 33–34, 37–39; Trachtenberg, *Reparation,* p. 114; Feldman, *Iron and Steel,* p. 327; for French perspective see Jacques Bariéty, *Les Relations franco-allemandes après la première guerre mondiale, 10 Novembre 1918—10 Janvier 1925: De l'exécution à la négociation* (Paris: Pedone, 1977), pp. 189–191. "Herr Stinnes": Wulf, *Hugo Stinnes,* p. 208n; see also Maier, *Recasting Bourgeois Europe,* p. 272.

8. Euler, *Aussenpolitik Weimarer* is the most complete. See also Peter Krüger, *Die Aussenpolitik der Republik von Weimar* (Darmstadt: Wissenschaftliche Buchgesellschaft, 1985), chap. 3; Kent, *Spoils of War.*

9. Pierre Miguel, *Poincaré* (Paris: Fayard, 1961). On attitude toward Germans see McDougall, *France's Rhineland Diplomacy,* p. 114.

10. Feldman, *Iron and Steel;* Marshall M. Lee and Wolfgang Michalka, *German Foreign Policy, 1917–1933: Continuity or Break?* (New York: St. Martin's, 1987), p. 39; Ernst Laubach, *Die Politik der Kabinette Wirth 1921/22,* vol. 402 of *Historiche Studien* (Lübeck: Matthiessen, 1968), esp. pp. 61–66, 145–148; Rupieper, *Cuno Government,* pp. 31, 75; Trachtenberg, *Reparation,* p. 384n49; McDougall, *France's Rhineland Diplomacy,* pp. 170–171; Soutou, "Der Einfluss der Schwerindustrie," pp. 547–551; Euler, *Aussenpolitik der Weimarer Republik,* pp. 305–306; Feldman, *Great Disorder,* esp. pp. 418, 451.

11. D'Abernon, *Ambassador,* vol. 1, pp. 89, 153, 160, 181; vol. 2, p. 59.

12. Jacques Chastenet, *Les Années d'illusions, 1918–1931,* vol. 5 of *Histoire de la Troisième République* (Paris: Hachette, 1960), p. 100; "separated": D'Abernon, *Ambassador,* vol. 2, pp. 111–112.

13. "Masters of Germany": Adrien Dariac, report to French government, 28 May 1922, *Manchester Guardian Weekly* (3 Nov. 1922), pp. 2–3; see also Bariéty, *Relations franco-allemandes,* pp. 97–99; Chastenet, "Les Années d'illusions," p. 108; Trachtenberg, *Reparation,* p. 266, "obstacle" quoted p. 327. Also Rupieper, *Cuno Government,* pp. 49–50; Raphaël, *Roi de la Ruhr,* p. 170; Feldman, *Great Disorder,* pp. 380, 434–435. Stinnes did meet with Lloyd George, to no effect.

14. Wulf, *Hugo Stinnes,* pp. 191–196, 317–343; Bariéty, *Relations franco-allemandes,* pp. 166–170; Feldman, *Iron and Steel,* pp. 328–330; Euler, *Aussenpolitik der Weimarer Republik,* p. 363; Feldman, *Great Disorder,* pp. 378–381. The Rathenau-Loucheur "Weisbaden Accord" of October 1921 was one attempt at oligarchic diplomacy; for brevity I use Stinnes as representative, omitting others.

15. Laubach, *Politik der Kabinette Wirth,* pp. 273, 286–287; Trachtenberg, *Reparation,* pp. 199–200, 382–383; Maier, *Recasting Bourgeois Europe,* pp. 579–594; Feldman, *Great Disorder,* pp. 461–462. Limited competence: Rupieper, *Cuno Government,* p. 75. "Arbitres de notre droit": Miguel, *Poincaré,* pp. 469–470. On French politics see Chastenet, "Les Années d'illusions."

16. "Stinnesy": Raphaël, *Roi de la Ruhr,* p. 169. Rupieper, *Cuno Government,* pp. 68–74; Feldman, *Great Disorder,* pp. 500–504; Alfred E. Cornebise, "Cuno, Germany and the Coming of the Ruhr Occupation: A Study in German-West European Relations," *Proceedings of the American Philosophical Society* 116 (1972): 502–531, see p. 531.

17. Detlef Lehnert and Klaus Megerle, "Problems of Identity and Consensus in a Fragmented Society: The Weimar Republic," in *Political Culture in Germany,* ed. Dirk Berg-Schlosser and Ralf Rytlewski (New York: St. Martin's, 1992), pp. 43–59. On German authoritarianism see McDougall, *France's Rhineland Diplomacy,* pp. 115, 135, 171–172, 190–191, 218, 227; Trachtenberg, *Reparation,* pp. 99–100; Felix, *Walter Rathenau.* Weimar judiciary: Ingo Müller, *Hitler's Justice: The Courts of the Third Reich,* trans. Deborah Lucas Schneider (Cambridge, Mass.: Harvard University Press, 1991), pp. 10–24.

18. Stinnes was aware of all this if not an active participant. Krüger, *Aussenpolitik der Weimarer Republik,* pp. 159–160, 179; Lee and Michalka, *German Foreign Policy,* pp. 56–61; Carsten, *Reichswehr and Politics,* esp. pp. 135–140.

19. "Battallions": Trachtenberg, *Reparation,* p. 203. Euler, *Aussenpolitik der Weimarer Republik,* pp. 173–176, 353; Wulf, *Hugo Stinnes,* pp. 205–206, 212–214; Maier, *Recasting Bourgeois Europe,* p. 244.

20. Besides sources cited above see Stephen A. Schuker, *The End of French Predominance in Europe: The Financial Crisis of 1924 and the Adoption of the Dawes Plan* (Chapel Hill: University of North Carolina Press, 1976), pp. 22–25, 178–179. For another influence, hopes of support from Rhineland separatists, see McDougall, *France's Rhineland Diplomacy,* esp. chap. 2. Speak with Stinnes: Kent, *Spoils of War,* p. 201. Policemen: Bariéty, *Rélations franco-allemandes,* p. 109; see also Kent, *Spoils of War,* p. 207. Belgium participated in the Ruhr occupation for parallel motives (including antagonism against

Stinnes): J. E. Helmreich, "Belgium and the Decision to Occupy the Ruhr: Diplomacy from a Middle Position," *Revue belge de philologie et d'histoire* 51 (1973): 822–839.

21. Feldman, *Iron and Steel,* chap. 6; Kent, *Spoils of War,* pp. 221–227, 235–242; Feldman, *Great Disorder,* pp. 854–858.

22. Friedel Vollbehr, *Die Holländer und die deutsche Hanse,* Hansischen geschichtsverein, Pfingstblätter, no. 21 (Lübeck: Selbstverlag des Vereins Lübeck, 1930), pp. 38–64, 72–73. See Alexander F. Cowan, *The Urban Patriciate: Lübeck and Venice, 1580–1700,* Quellen und Darstellungen zur Hansischen Geschichte, vol. 30 (Cologne: Böhlau, 1986), pp. 28–31. Cf. Lübeck's 1569 attack on Reval after it came under the Swedish monarchy: Philippe Dollinger, *The German Hansa,* ed. D. S. Ault and S. H. Steinberg, trans. D. S. Ault and S. H. Steinberg (Stanford, Calif.: Stanford University Press, 1970), p. 338.

23. Cases listed in the appendix with asterisks. I omit the Greek cases, for which we do not know the duration of one or the other regime, and the anocracies of pre-1380 Italy. New: 1494, 1576, 1652, 1775, 1849, 1861, 1881, 1899 (Philippines), 1919, 1922, 1948, 1974, 1991, 1994. Other: 1656, 1712, 1812, 1879, 1898, 1899, 1914.

24. New (not more than three years old): 1447, 1529, 1797, 1828, 1847, 1923, 1964, 1969, 1981. Others: 1431, 1443, 1490, 1531, 1897, 1941, 1954.

25. Zeev Maoz, "Joining the Club of Nations: Political Development and International Conflict, 1816–1976," *International Studies Quarterly* 33 (1989): 199–231; Edward D. Mansfield and Jack Snyder, "Democratization and War," *Foreign Affairs* 74 (1995): 79–97; Michael Brecher, Jonathon Wilkenfeld, and Sheila Moss, *Crises in the Twentieth Century,* vol. 1, *Handbook of International Crises* (Oxford: Pergamon, 1988), pp. 63, 148, 173–174. John R. Oneal and Bruce Russett, "Exploring the Liberal Peace: Interdependence, Democracy, and Conflict, 1950–1985" (paper presented at annual meeting of International Studies Association, 1996), find the biggest problem comes when a democracy is created among autocracies, its natural enemies.

26. On stability see Kenneth A. Bollen, "Political Democracy: Conceptual and Measurement Traps," *Studies in Comparative International Development* 25 (1990): 7–24; Zeev Maov and Bruce Russett, "Alliance, Contiguity, Wealth and Political Stability: Is the Lack of Conflict Among Democracies a Statistical Artifact?" *International Interactions* 17 (1991): 245–267.

27. James Lee Ray, *Democracy and International Conflict. An Evaluation of the Democratic Peace Proposition* (Columbia: University of South Carolina Press, 1995), pp. 100–102.

28. "Jail smart:" Erazim Kohák, "Ashes, Ashes . . . Central Europe After Forty Years," *Daedalus (Proceedings of the American Academy of Arts and Sciences)* 121, no. 2 (1992): 197–215.

29. "Incapable:" Lenard J. Cohen, *Broken Bonds: The Disintegration of Yugoslavia* (Boulder: Westview, 1993), pp. 199–200, see also pp. 265–266, 274–275; for further references see appendix, 1991.

30. Giuseppe Di Palma, *To Craft Democracies: An Essay on Democratic Transitions* (Berkeley: University of California Press, 1990), see esp. pp. 28, 41–42, 113, 122, 134, 144–145; Harry Eckstein, *Regarding Politics: Essays on Political Theory, Stability, and Change* (Berke-

ley: University of California Press, 1992), pp. 274–281; Philippe C. Schmitter and Terry Lynn Karl, "What Democracy Is . . . and Is Not," *Journal of Democracy* 2 (1991): 75–88; Gabriel A. Almond, "The Study of Political Culture," in Berg-Schlosser and Rytlewski, *Political Culture in Germany,* pp. 13–26. Philip Converse, "Of Time and Partisan Stability," *Comparative Political Studies* 2 (1961): 139–171, argues that stability requires generations, but notes that party systems tend to gel in the first years.

31. Robert D. Putnam, *Making Democracy Work: Civic Traditions in Modern Italy* (Princeton: Princeton University Press, 1993), p. 184, chaps. 2, 5.

32. On plural political subcultures see Michael Thompson, Richard Ellis, and Aaron Wildavsky, *Cultural Theory* (Boulder: Westview, 1990), part 3. On the "republic of letters," especially for the French Revolution, see the conclusion of Margaret C. Jacob, *Living the Enlightenment: Freemasonry and Politics in Eighteenth-Century Europe* (New York: Oxford University Press, 1991).

33. On stereotypes see Aaron L. Friedberg, *The Weary Titan: Britain and the Experience of Relative Decline, 1895–1905* (Princeton: Princeton University Press, 1988), pp. 15–17. Cases in appendix for 1652, 1775, 1849, 1861, 1923, 1954, 1969, 1991; also possibly 415 B.C.

34. Mark Peffley and Jon Hurwitz, "International Events and Foreign Policy Beliefs: Public Response to Changing Soviet-U.S. Relations," *American Journal of Political Science* 36 (1992): 431–461.

CHAPTER ELEVEN

Authoritarian Diplomacy

1. Henry Adams, *History of the United States of America During the Administration of Thomas Jefferson and James Madison,* 4 vols., 1889–1890 (New York: Boni, 1930), vol. 1, book 2, chap. 16; William H. Masterson, *Tories and Democrats: British Diplomats in Pre-Jacksonian America* (College Station: Texas A&M University Press, 1985), pp. 54, 61, 72–78.

2. Fred Charles Iklé, *How Nations Negotiate* (New York: Harper and Row, 1964), pp. 114–117.

3. James D. Fearon, "Counterfactuals and Hypothesis Testing in Political Science," *World Politics* 43 (1991): 169–195. For further methodological references see chapter 1, n. 12.

4. There are few crises for which diplomatic archives on both sides are well investigated. N.b., when I chose cases I was too ignorant to guess whether they would validate my ideas (which anyway were not fully developed at that point).

5. Bruce Bueno de Mesquita and D. Lalman, "The Road to War is Strewn with Peaceful Intentions," in *Models of Strategic Choice in Politics,* ed. Peter C. Ordeshook (Ann Arbor: University of Michigan Press, 1989), pp. 253–266; Woosang Kim and Bruce Bueno de Mesquita, "How Perceptions Influence the Risk of War," *International Studies Quarterly* 39 (1995): 51–65. Bullying strategy: Russell J. Leng, *Interstate Crisis Behavior, 1816–1950. Realism vs. Reciprocity* (New York: Cambridge University Press, 1993), chap. 7.

6. Richard Nisbett and Lee Ross, *Human Inference: Strategies and Shortcomings of Social Judgment* (Englewood Cliffs, N.J.: Prentice-Hall, 1980), p. 188. The classic on the "prisoner's dilemma" is Robert Axelrod, *The Evolution of Cooperation* (New York: Basic Books, 1984). A review is Jonathan Bendor, Roderick M. Kramer, and Suzanne Stout, "When in Doubt . . . Cooperation in a Noisy Prisoner's Dilemma," *Journal of Conflict Resolution* 35 (1991): 691–719, see pp. 713–717. On spirals of distrust the classic is Harold H. Kelley and Anthony J. Stahelski, "Social Interaction Basis of Cooperators' and Competitors' Beliefs About Others," *Journal of Personality and Social Psychology* 16 (1970): 66–91; a review is John A. Vasquez, "Foreign Policy, Learning and War," in *New Directions in the Study of Foreign Policy,* ed. Charles F. Hermann, Charles W. Kegley, Jr., and James N. Rosenau (Boston: Allen and Unwin, 1987), pp. 370–371. On reputations see chapter 5.

7. Barbara D. Slack and John O. Cook, "Authoritarian Behavior in a Conflict Situation," *Journal of Personality and Social Psychology* 25 (1973): 135. Cf. I. W. Zartman, "In Search of Common Elements in the Analysis of the Negotiation Process," in *Processes for International Negotiation,* ed. Frances Mautner-Markhof (Boulder: Westview, 1989), pp. 247–248.

8. Charles F. Hermann, "Comparing the Foreign Policy Events of Nations," in *International Events and the Comparative Analysis of Foreign Policy,* ed. Charles W. Kegley, Jr., Gregory A. Raymond, Robert M. Rood, and Richard A. Skinner (Columbia: University of South Carolina Press, 1975), pp. 145–158. Here is my analysis of data in Maurice A. East and Charles F. Hermann, "Do Nation-Types Account for Foreign Policy Behavior?" in *Comparing Foreign Policies: Theories, Findings, and Methods,* ed. James N. Rosenau (New York: Wiley, 1974), table 6, pp. 295–297: to avoid being swamped by the large number of "small, underdeveloped" nations that were mostly "closed" societies far from democracy, I omitted these. For the rest, I found the average number of acts per pair of nations; for example, the numbers for acts initiated per dyad (sum of relevant cells in their table) between large, developed, closed, similar nations are 24.44 conflictual and 21.17 cooperative, with a ratio of 1.15, i.e., slightly more conflictual than cooperative. Averaging all such numbers one finds the following ratios for acts initiated. Open-open = 0.30; closed-closed = 0.96; closed-open = 1.21. (The last is the average of acts from closed to open (0.71) and open to closed (1.70). Only the average seems reliable, for in bargaining it is often hard to say who really "initiates" an action.)

9. Bruce Russett, *Grasping the Democratic Peace. Principles for a Post-Cold War World* (Princeton: Princeton University Press, 1993), pp. 78–79. Arie M. Kacowicz, "The Problem of Peaceful Territorial Change," *International Studies Quarterly* 38 (1994): 219–254. Cats and dogs: John R. Oneal and Bruce Russett, "Exploring the Liberal Peace: Interdependence, Democracy, and Conflict, 1950–1985" (paper presented at annual meeting of International Studies Association, 1996).

10. Stuart A. Bremer, "Dangerous Dyads: Conditions Affecting the Likelihood of Interstate War, 1816–1965," *Journal of Conflict Resolution* 36 (1992): 309–341, finds democracies much less war-prone than other regimes between 1816 and 1965. T. Clifton Morgan and Valerie Schwebach, "Take Two Democracies and Call Me in the Morning: A Prescription for Peace?" *International Interactions* 17 (1992): 305–320, see p. 312, find non-

democratic pairs nearly twice as war-prone as pairs in which one member is democratic (for 1816–1976), and also notice the relative peace among "constrained non-democracies," mainly oligarchic republics. For total deaths see R. J. Rummel, *Death by Government: Genocide and Mass Murder Since 1900* (New Brunswick, N.J.: Transaction, 1994). Cf. William J. Dixon, "Democracy and the Peaceful Settlement of International Conflict," *American Political Science Review* 88 (1994): 14–32.

11. Randall Schweller, "Domestic Structure and Preventive War: Are Democracies More Pacific?" *World Politics* 44 (1992): 235–269.

12. William D. Coplin, *Introduction to International Politics: A Theoretical Overview* (Chicago: Markham, 1971), pp. 262–269; Mary Douglas, *How Institutions Think* (Syracuse: Syracuse University Press, 1986), p. 126; Iklé, *How Nations Negotiate,* p. 237. On culture in general, Raymond Cohen, *Negotiating Across Cultures: Communication Obstacles in International Diplomacy* (Washington, D.C.: U.S. Institute of Peace, 1991); Hans Binnendijk, ed., *National Negotiating Styles* (Washington, D.C.: U.S. Government Printing Office, Foreign Service Institute, U.S. Department of State, 1987); see also references on misperception cited in chapter 7 n. 43, and on political culture, cited chapter 5 n. 3.

13. On precedence disputes in aristocratic diplomacy see Evan Luard, *Balance of Power: The System of International Relations, 1648–1815* (New York: St. Martin's, 1992), chap. 5. "Mob" quoted in Adams, *History of U.S.* vol. 5, p. 155; tavern-keepers: ibid., vol. 2, p. 184. Bradford Perkins, *Prologue to War: England and the United States, 1805–1812* (Berkeley: University of California Press, 1961), pp. 221, 218–220, 275; Reginald Horsman, *The Causes of the War of 1812* (Philadelphia: University of Pennsylvannia Press, 1962), pp. 47–49, 87; Masterson, *Tories and Democrats,* pp. 147–153, 158. President insulted: J. C. A. Stagg, *Mr. Madison's War: Politics, Diplomacy and Warfare in the Early American Republic, 1783–1830* (Princeton: Princeton University Press, 1983), p. 77.

14. King's influence: John Melish, *Travels in the United States in the Years 1806 and 1807, and 1809, 1810 and 1811,* 2 vols. (Philadelphia, 1812), vol. 1, p. 355. "Insolence": Adams, *History of U.S.,* vol. 5, p. 287.

15. Roger H. Brown, *The Republic in Peril: 1812* (New York: Columbia University Press, 1964), esp. chaps. 1, 4; Perkins, *Prologue to War,* chap. 12; Steven Watts, *The Republic Reborn: War and the Making of Liberal America, 1790–1820* (Baltimore: Johns Hopkins University Press, 1987), pp. 250–270; Sarah McCulloh Lemmon, *Frustrated Patriots: North Carolina and the War of 1812* (Chapel Hill: University of North Carolina Press, 1973), chap. 1; Norman K. Risjord, "1812: Conservatives, War Hawks, and the Nation's Honor," in *The Causes of the War of 1812: National Honor or National Interest?* ed. Bradford Perkins (reprint, Malabar, Fla.: R. Krieger, 1983), pp. 86–95; Donald R. Hickey, *The War of 1812: A Forgotten Conflict* (Urbana: University of Illinois Press, 1989), pp. 26–27, 51; see also Horsman, *Causes of the War.* Note also an outside autocrat, Napoleon, deceitfully provoking conflict: Perkins, *Prologue to War,* pp. 68, 72, 247–248, 253–254; Adams, *History of U.S.,* vol. 3.

16. On American reluctance see Perkins, *Prologue to War,* pp. 413–415, chap. 9; Stagg, *Mr. Madison's War.*

17. Alexander Kinglake, *Eothen: Traces of Travel Brought Home From the East* (1844; reprint, Oxford: Oxford University Press, 1982), pp. 229, 241, and chap. 29.

18. A standard narrative, although partisan, is Harold Temperley, *England and the Near East: The Crimea* (London: Longmans, 1936). Norman Rich, *Why the Crimean War? A Cautionary Tale* (Hanover, N.H.: University Press of New England, 1985); Richard Smoke, "The Crimean War," in *Avoiding War: Problems of Crisis Management,* ed. Alexander L. George (Boulder: Westview, 1991), pp. 36–61; Gavin Burns Henderson, *Crimean War Diplomacy and Other Historical Essays* (Glasgow: Jackson, Son & Co., 1947); Paul W. Schroeder, *Austria, Great Britain, and the Crimean War: The Destruction of the European Concert* (Ithaca, N.Y.: Cornell University Press, 1972); Ann Pottinger Saab, *The Origins of the Crimean Alliance* (Charlottesville: University Press of Virginia, 1977); John Shelton Curtiss, *Russia's Crimean War* (Durham, N.C.: Duke University Press, 1979); Brison D. Gooch, "A Century of Historiography on the Origins of the Crimean War," *American History Review* 62 (1956): 33–58. Also useful are Norman Rich, *Great Power Diplomacy: 1814–1914* (New York: McGraw-Hill, 1992), pp. 101–114; Alan Palmer, *The Banner of Battle: The Story of the Crimean War* (New York: St. Martin's, 1987), chap. 2; Alan Palmer, *The Decline and Fall of the Ottoman Empire* (New York: M. Evans, 1992), pp. 118–125.

19. W. Bruce Lincoln, *Nicholas I. Emperor and Autocrat of All the Russias,* 2nd ed. (Bloomington: Indiana University Press, 1978), see esp. pp. 117–124, 330–338; V. N. Vinogradov, "The Personal Responsibility of Emperor Nicolas I for the Coming of the Crimean War," trans. Hugh Ragsdale, in *Imperial Russian Foreign Policy,* ed. Hugh Ragsdale (Cambridge: Cambridge University Press, 1993), p. 159; David M. Goldfrank, "Policy Traditions and the Menshikov Mission of 1853," in ibid., p. 157.

20. Curtiss, *Russia's Crimean War,* esp. pp. 93–94; Goldfrank, "Policy Traditions." The British ambassador to Constantinople, Stratford Canning, also knew how to browbeat and lie; some said he had spent so many years in the East that he had learned to think like a Turkish pasha. It is debated whether Stratford negotiated in "authoritarian" style and tried to bring war; if so, that was in violation of his instructions. J. L. Herkless, "Stratford, the Cabinet and the Outbreak of the Crimean War," *Historical Journal* 18 (1975): 497–523.

21. See especially Saab, *Origins of the Crimean Alliance,* pp. 40–48.

22. Temperley, *England and the Near East,* p. 513.

23. Quoted in Temperley, *England and the Near East,* p. 367. See Donald Southgate, *"The Most English Minister": The Policies and Politics of Palmerston* (London: Macmillan, 1966), chap. 17 and p. 119; Curtiss, *Russia's Crimean War,* chap. 4 and pp. 110–114.

24. Sacred word: Henderson, *Crimean War Diplomacy,* pp. 10–11, 72; see also Schroeder, *Austria, Great Britain,* pp. 41–43. The tsar likewise put excessive trust in the support of his fellow monarch in Austria; Barbara Jelavich, *Russia's Balkan Entanglements, 1806–1914* (Cambridge: Cambridge University Press, 1991), chap. 3, q.v. for Crimean War generally.

25. The main anti-Russian was Palmerston. Kingsley Martin, *The Triumph of Lord Palmerston: A Study of Public Opinion in England Before the Crimean War,* rev. ed. (London:

Hutchinson, 1963); Schroeder, *Austria, Great Britain,* pp. 414–421; Jack Snyder, *Myths of Empire: Domestic Politics and International Ambition* (Ithaca, N.Y.: Cornell University Press, 1991), pp. 198–201; for the Cabinet's mistakes in general, see Herkless, "Stratford." A more extensive analysis would note how the sultan too was constrained by outraged public opinion and by his council: the Ottoman regime included oligarchic and theocratic quasi-republican elements.

26. For example, George F. Kennan, *American Diplomacy, 1900–1950* (Chicago: University of Chicago Press, 1951), p. 66. For this and related points see Quincy Wright, *A Study of War,* 2nd ed. (Chicago: University of Chicago Press, 1965), pp. 265, 841–848; Jack S. Levy, "Domestic Politics and War," *Journal of Interdisciplinary History* 18 (1988): 653–673, see pp. 659–661.

27. Current views follow Fritz Fischer, "The Foreign Policy of Imperial Germany and the Outbreak of the First World War," in Gregor Schöllgen, *Escape into War? The Foreign Policy of Imperial Germany* (Oxford: Berg, 1990), pp. 19–40; see also Fritz Fischer, *War of Illusions: German Policies from 1911 to 1914,* 2nd ed., trans. Marian Jackson (London: Chatto and Windus, 1975); on controversy over these views see Patrick Glynn, *Closing Pandora's Box: Arms Races, Arms Control, and the History of the Cold War* (New York: Basic, 1992), chap. 1. Most historians hold the German and Austrian leaders responsible less for plotting world conquest than for allowing their political culture to blind them to the consequences of their actions. James Joll, *The Origins of the First World War* (New York: Longman, 1984), gives an entry; also R. J. W. Evans and Hartmut Pogge von Strandmann, eds., *The Coming of the First World War* (Oxford: Clarendon, 1990); David E. Kaiser, "Germany and the Origins of the First World War," *Journal of Modern History* 55 (1983): 442–474; for a broad survey see Oron J. Hale, *The Great Illusion, 1900–1914* (New York: Harper and Row, 1971). The standard diplomatic narrative is Luigi Albertini, *The Origins of the War of 1914,* 3 vols., trans. Isabella M. Massey (London: Oxford University Press, 1952–1957).

On German politics see also references cited chapter 8 n. 19. On Austria see remarks in David Kaiser, *Politics and War: European Conflict from Philip II to Hitler* (Cambridge, Mass.: Harvard University Press, 1990), p. 320; Ralph K. White, "Misperception in Vienna on the Eve of World War I," in *International War: An Anthology and Study Guide,* ed. Melvin Small and J. David Singer (Homewood, Ill.: Dorsey, 1985), pp. 230–239. On Russia see D. C. B. Lieven, *Russia and the Origins of the First World War* (New York: St. Martin's, 1983); David M. McDonald, *United Government and Foreign Policy in Russia, 1900–1914* (Cambridge, Mass.: Harvard University Press, 1992); for criticism of Russian diplomacy see especially Albertini, *Origins;* for relations between tsar and kaiser see George F. Kennan, *The Fateful Alliance: France, Russia, and the Coming of the First World War* (New York: Pantheon, 1984), esp. pp. 120–121, 136, 164. Kennan concludes his fine study by assigning primary causation to political culture; pp. 236–237, 248, 255–257. On France, besides Kennan see John F. V. Keiger, *France and the Origins of the First World War* (New York: St. Martin's, 1983). On Britain see Zara S. Steiner, *Britain and the Origins of the First World War* (London: Macmillan, 1977); Paul Kennedy, *The Rise of the Anglo-German Antagonism, 1860–1914* (London: Allen and Unwin, 1980), esp. pp. 460–462.

28. John G. Stoessinger, *Why Nations Go to War,* 6th ed. (St. Martin's, 1992), chap. 1, asserts the role of personality but actually shows the role of political culture. See Konrad H. Jarausch, "The Illusion of Limited War: Chancellor Bethmann-Hollweg's Calculated Risk, July 1914," *Central European History* 2 (1969): 48–76; Kaiser, "First World War," and references in chapter 8.

29. "Not the kind" quoted in Stephen R. Rock, "Risk Theory Reconsidered: American Success and German Failure in the Coercion of Britain, 1890–1914," *Journal of Strategic Studies (Great Britain)* 11 (1988): 352. Kennedy, *Anglo-German Antagonism,* pp. 253, 436, 453–455; George Monger, *The End of Isolation: British Foreign Policy, 1900–1907* (London: Thomas Nelson, 1963), esp. chap. 2. Linda Brandt Fritzinger, "Friends in High Places: Valentine Chirol, the *Times,* and Anglo-German Relations, 1892–1896," *Victorian Periodicals Review* 21 (1988): 9–14.

30. On the kaiser's pathology see Lamar Cecil, "History as Family Chronicle: Kaiser Wilhelm II and the Dynastic Roots of the Anglo-German Antagonism," in *Kaiser Wilhelm II: New Interpretations; The Corfu Papers,* ed. John C. G. Röhl and Nicholas Sanbart (Cambridge: Cambridge University Press, 1982), pp. 91–119. On Bethmann Hollweg see Jarausch, "Limited War."

31. See references above, especially Albertini, *Origins,* vol. 2, and Steiner, *Britain and the Origins.*

32. "Generous" quoted in Albertini, *Origins,* vol. 3, p. 368. Michael Eckstein and Zara Steiner, "The Sarajevo Crisis," in *British Foreign Policy Under Sir Edward Grey,* ed. Francis H. Hinsley (Cambridge: Cambridge University Press, 1977), pp. 401–403, 409–410; Richard Ned Lebow, *Between Peace and War: The Nature of International Crisis* (Baltimore: Johns Hopkins University Press, 1961), pp. 126–147. Michael Howard, "The Edwardian Arms Race," in *The Lessons of History,* ed. Michael Howard (New Haven: Yale University Press, 1991), p. 95; Glynn, *Closing Pandora's Box,* pp. 7–21 (on appeasement as reflecting political culture see p. x).

33. Paul Kennedy, "The Tradition of Appeasement in British Foreign Policy, 1865–1939," in Paul Kennedy, ed., *Strategy and Diplomacy, 1870–1945* (Boston: Allen and Unwin, 1983), pp. 13–39. Kennedy dates the policy to 1865 but (as we saw preceding the Crimean War) the tendency goes further back, possibly to Napoleonic times. See Wolf D. Gruner, "Europäischer Friede als nationale Interesse: Die Rolle des Deutschen Bundes in der britischer Deutschlandpolitik, 1814–1832," *Bohemia* 18 (1977): 96–128; Wolf D. Gruner, "The British Political, Social and Economic System and the Decision for War and Peace: Reflections on Anglo-German Relations, 1800–1939," *Journal of International Studies* 6 (1980): 189–218. John L. Gaddis, *The United States and the Origin of the Cold War, 1941–1947* (New York: Columbia University Press, 1972). "Assumed that Bethmann": Michael Brock, "Britain Enters the War," in Evans and Pogge von Strandmann, *Coming of the First World War,* pp. 171–172.

34. Ole R. Holsti, Robert C. North, and Richard A. Brody, "Perception and Action in the 1914 Crisis," in *Quantitative International Politics, Insights and Evidence,* ed. J. David Singer (New York: Free Press, 1968), pp. 123–158. The study does not specifically analyze on a scale of democracy; I make use of their table 6, p. 147.

35. On primacy of internal politics in Germany but not Britain see Michael R. Gordon, "Domestic Conflict and the Origins of The First World War: the British and the German Cases," *Journal of Modern History* 46 (1974): 191–226, and references above. That internal separatism helped move Austria against Serbia is generally accepted; the case for Russia needs more study.

36. Conflict strengthens solidarity: see chapter 6. "Giddy minds": William Shakespeare, *Henry IV, Part Two,* 4.5. Openly stated desire for war as a diversion was seen, e.g., in France in 1792, T. C. W. Blanning, *The Origins of the French Revolutionary Wars* (London: Longman, 1986), pp. 106, 210–211; and in 1848; Lawrence C. Jennings, *France and Europe in 1848: A Study of French Foreign Affairs in Time of Crisis* (Oxford: Clarendon, 1973), pp. 99–100; see also Edward D. Mansfield and Jack Snyder, "Democratization and War," *Foreign Affairs* 74 (1995): 93, passim; Geoffrey Blainey, *The Causes of War,* 3rd ed. (New York: Macmillan, 1988), chap. 5; Jack Levy, "The Diversionary Theory of War: A Critique," in *Handbook of War Studies,* ed. Manus Midlarsky (Boston: Unwin Hyman, 1989), pp. 259–288; Levy, "Domestic Politics," p. 666ff.; Bruce Russett, "Economic Decline, Electoral Pressure, and the Initiation of International Conflict," in *Prisoners of War? Nation-States in the Modern Era,* ed. Charles S. Gochman and Alan N. Sabrosky (Lexington, Mass.: Lexington Books, 1990), pp. 123–140; Alex Mintz and Nehemia Geva, "Why Don't Democracies Fight Each Other? An Experimental Study," *Journal of Conflict Resolution* 37 (1993): 484–503; V. P. Gagnon, Jr., "Ethnic Nationalism and International Conflict: The Case of Serbia," *International Security* 19, no. 3 (Winter 1994/1995): 130–166.

37. Quoted in Michael Balfour, *The Kaiser and His Times* (Boston: Houghton Mifflin, 1964), p. 351.

38. Harold Nicolson, *Diplomacy,* 3rd ed. (London: Oxford University Press, 1963), pp. 128, 142.

39. "Always some common:" Kalevi J. Holsti, *Peace and War: Armed Conflicts and International Order, 1648–1989* (Cambridge: Cambridge University Press, 1991), p. 237. Telford Taylor, *Munich: The Price of Peace* (Garden City, N.Y.: Doubleday, 1979), "relied upon" quoted p. 743. Martin Gilbert and Richard Gott, *The Appeasers* (Boston: Houghton Mifflin, 1963); Sidney Aster, " 'Guilty men?': The Case of Neville Chamberlain," in *Paths to War: New Essays on the Origins of the Second World War,* ed. Robert Boyce and Esmonde M. Robertson (London: Macmillan, 1989), pp. 233–268; Paul Kennedy, "Appeasement," in *The Origins of the Second World War Reconsidered,* ed. Gordon Martel (Boston: Allen and Unwin, 1986), pp. 140–161. For background see Philip M. H. Bell, *The Origins of the Second World War in Europe* (New York: Longman, 1986). Even Chamberlain's defender concedes he was too trusting: John Charmley, *Chamberlain and the Lost Peace* (Chicago: Ivan Dee, 1989). Of Chamberlain's colleagues, note Halifax's appeasement; Robin Edmonds, *The Big Three: Churchill, Roosevelt and Stalin in Peace and War* (New York: W. W. Norton, 1991), pp. 76–77, and in general, Irving L. Janis, *Groupthink: Psychological Studies of Policy Decisions and Fiascos* (Boston: Houghton Mifflin, 1982), pp. 187–193. On concessions as fair see A. Lentin, *Lloyd George, Woodrow Wilson and the Guilt of Germany: An Essay in the Pre-History of Appeasement* (Baton Rouge: Louisiana State University Press, 1984), chap. 6.

40. "Worms": William L. Shirer, *The Rise and Fall of the Third Reich: A History of Nazi Germany* (New York: Simon and Schuster, 1960), p. 423; "mask": ibid., p. 618, see also pp. 613–619, 622. Also Donald Cameron Watt, *How War Came. The Immediate Origins of the Second World War* (New York: Pantheon, 1989), pp. 252, 256, 317–318, 328–329.

41. Arthur S. Link, *Woodrow Wilson: Revolution, War and Peace* (Arlington Heights, Ill.: AHM, 1979), chaps. 2, 3; for details of how German hostility toward the United States led to lawless infringements see Reinhard R. Doerries, *Imperial Challenge: Ambassador Count Bernstorff and German-American Relations, 1908–1917,* trans. Christa D. Shannon (Chapel Hill: University of North Carolina Press, 1989), chap. 5.

42. "Correct" diplomacy: Gordon A. Craig and Alexander L. George, *Force and Statecraft: Diplomatic Problems of Our Time* (New York: Oxford University Press, 1983), pp. 195–198. For Japanese self-delusion see James W. Morley, ed., *The Fateful Choice: Japan's Advance into Southeast Asia, 1939–1941: Selected Translations from Taiheiyō sensō e no michi* (New York: Columbia University Press, 1980); Akira Iriye, *The Origins of the Second World War in Asia and the Pacific* (London: Longman, 1987), esp. pp. 78–79, 148–149; Snyder, *Myths of Empire,* pp. 121–123, 127–130. Distrust of Roosevelt: Scott D. Sagan, "From Deterrence to Coercion to War: The Road to Pearl Harbor," in *The Limits of Coercive Diplomacy,* 2nd ed., ed. Alexander L. George and William F. Simons (Boulder: Westview, 1994), p. 85. Also: Dorothy Borg and Shumpei Okamoto, eds., *Pearl Harbor as History: Japanese-American Relations, 1931–1941* (New York: Columbia University Press, 1973), especially Sadao Asada, "The Japanese Navy and the United States," pp. 234, 259; Waldo Heinrichs, *Threshold of War: Franklin D. Roosevelt and American Entry into World War II* (New York: Oxford University Press, 1988), esp. pp. 124–130, 154–155, 159–162, 181; Michael A. Barnhart, *Japan Prepares for Total War: The Search for Economic Security, 1919–1941* (Ithaca, N.Y.: Cornell University Press, 1987), chaps. 10–13, esp. pp. 237–238, 271. Also Herbert Feis, *The Road to Pearl Harbor: The Coming of the War Between the United States and Japan* (1950; reprint, New York: Atheneum, 1962).

43. Peter Lowe, *The Origins of the Korean War* (London: Longman, 1986), pp. 60–63, 118–119; cf. Bruce Cumings, *The Coming of the Korean War,* vol. 2 of *The Roaring of the Cataract* (Princeton: Princeton University Press, 1990), chap. 18. A synthesis is Snyder, *Myths of Empire,* pp. 289–296. On North Korean and Soviet calculations see Sergei N. Goncharov, *Uncertain Partners: Stalin, Mao and the Korean War* (Stanford, Calif.: Stanford University Press, 1993), pp. 141–142, 151–152; Kathryn Weathersby, "New Findings on the Korean War," *Cold War International History Project Bulletin,* no. 3 (Woodrow Wilson Center, Washington, D.C., Fall 1993), pp. 1, 14–18; Weathersby, "Korea, 1949–50: To Attack, or Not to Attack? . . . ," ibid., no. 5 (Spring 1995), pp. 1–9.

Lawrence Freedman and Efraim Karsh, *The Gulf Conflict 1990–1991: Diplomacy and War in the New World Order* (Princeton: Princeton University Press, 1993); Jean Edward Smith, *George Bush's War* (New York: Holt, 1992), pp. 45–62; Elaine Sciolino, *The Outlaw State: Saddam Hussein's Quest for Power and the Gulf Crisis* (New York: Wiley, 1991), chap. 8; Janice Gross Stein, "Deterrence and Compellence in the Gulf, 1990–1991," *International Security* 17 (1992): 147–179; and journalistic accounts, e.g., *New York Times,* 7 June 1992 and 25 October 1992; Theodore Draper, "The Gulf War Reconsidered," *New York Review* 39, no. 1 (16 January 1992), pp. 51–53, and no. 2 (30 January 1992), p. 38.

Serbia: John Newhouse, "Dodging the Problem," *New Yorker,* 24 Aug. 1992, p. 62; Lenard J. Cohen, *Broken Bonds: The Disintegration of Yugoslavia* (Boulder: Westview, 1993), pp. 217–218.

44. Athenians: Thucydides, *History of the Peloponnesian War,* trans. Rex Warner (New York: Penguin, 1954), 3.37. "Not friendly": David D. Newsom, *Diplomacy and the American Democracy* (Bloomington: Indiana University Press, 1988), pp. 112–113.

45. On influence of lawyers, etc., see Henry Kissinger, "Domestic Structures and Foreign Policy," *Daedalus,* Spring 1966, pp. 515–517.

46. Suez: Janice Gross Stein, "Calculation, Miscalculation and Conventional Deterrence: I. The View from Cairo; II. The View from Jerusalem," in *Psychology and Deterrence,* ed. Robert Jervis, Richard Ned Lebow, and Janice Gross Stein (Baltimore: Johns Hopkins University Press, 1985), pp. 34–88, esp. p. 80. Falklands/Malvinas: for a political cultures analysis see William L. Furlong and Craig C. Albiston, "Sovereignty, Culture, and Misperceptions: The Falklands/Malvinas War," *Conflict* 6 (1985): 139–175, also Richard Ned Lebow, "Miscalculations in the South Atlantic: The Origins of the Falklands War," in Jervis, Lebow, and Stein, *Psychology and Deterrence,* pp. 89–124. Korea: Lebow, *Between Peace and War,* pp. 192–216; Chen Jian, *China's Road to the Korean War: The Making of the Sino-American Confrontation* (New York: Columbia University Press, 1994).

47. Study: Joe D. Hagan, "Regimes, Political Oppositions and the Comparative Analysis of Foreign Policy," in Hermann, Kegley, and Rosenau, *New Directions,* pp. 357–358.

48. Margaret G. Hermann and Charles W. Kegley, Jr., "Ballots, a Barrier Against the Use of Bullets and Bombs: Democratization and Military Intervention," *Journal of Conflict Resolution* 40 (1996): 436–460.

49. Edward E. Rice, *Wars of the Third Kind: Conflict in Underdeveloped Countries* (Berkeley: University of California Press, 1988), p. 4; Barbara W. Tuchman, *Stilwell and the American Experience in China, 1911–1945* (New York: Macmillan, 1971); Michael Schaller, *The U.S. Crusade in China, 1938–1945* (New York: Columbia University Press, 1979), esp. p. 161; *The American Image of China,* ed. Benson Lee Grayson (New York: Ungar, 1979), pp. 199–204.

50. "Russian version:" John Spanier, *American Foreign Policy Since World War II,* 12th ed. (Washington, D.C.: Congressional Quarterly Press, 1991), p. 24. See also Edmonds, *Big Three,* pp. 367, 419, 456; Herbert Feis, *Churchill, Roosevelt, Stalin: The War They Waged and the Peace They Sought* (Princeton: Princeton University Press, 1967), esp. pp. 596, 599; Edward M. Bennett, *Franklin D. Roosevelt and the Search for Victory: American-Soviet Relations, 1939–1945* (Wilmington, Del.: Scholarly Resources Books, 1990), pp. 184–187; Martin Gilbert, *Road to Victory, 1941–1945,* vol. 7 of *Winston S. Churchill* (Boston: Houghton Mifflin, 1986); Steven Merritt Miner, *Between Churchill and Stalin: The Soviet Union, Great Britain and the Origin of the Grand Alliance* (Chapel Hill: University of North Carolina Press, 1988). One-sided but useful is Robert Nisbet, *Roosevelt and Stalin: The Failed Courtship* (Washington, D.C.: Regnery Gateway, 1988); cf. Diane S. Clemens, *Yalta* (New York: Oxford University Press, 1970). Daniel Yergin, *Shattered Peace: The Origins of*

the Cold War and the National Security State (Boston: Houghton Mifflin, 1978), p. 119; Gaddis, *United States and the Origin,* pp. 6–7, 34–46, 100–101; Melvyn P. Leffler, *A Preponderance of Power: National Security, the Truman Administration, and the Cold War* (Stanford, Calif.: Stanford University Press, 1992), pp. 52–53; David McCullogh, *Truman* (New York: Simon and Schuster, 1992), pp. 399, 409–410, 418–420, 450–452; Glynn, *Closing Pandora's Box,* pp. 93–110, 118–122.

Debates on Cold War origins will continue until the Soviet archives are well explored. For the Reagan-Gorbachev relationship as another example of American trust in negotiation see Henry Kissinger, *Diplomacy* (New York: Simon and Schuster, 1994), pp. 769–771.

CHAPTER TWELVE

Republican Diplomacy

1. David M. Pletcher, *The Diplomacy of Annexation: Texas, Oregon, and the Mexican War* (Columbia: University of Missouri Press, 1973); Charles Sellers, *James K. Polk: Continentalist, 1843–1846* (Princeton: Princeton University Press, 1966); John Edward Weems, *To Conquer a Peace: The War Between the United States and Mexico* (Garden City, N.Y.: Doubleday, 1974); Jesse S. Reeves, *American Diplomacy Under Tyler and Polk* (Baltimore: Johns Hopkins University Press, 1907); John Schroeder, *Mister Polk's War: American Opposition and Dissent, 1846–1848* (Madison: University of Wisconsin Press, 1973); Carlos Bosch García, *Historia de las relaciones entre México y los Estados Unidos, 1819–1848* (Mexico City: Escuela Nacional de Ciencias Políticas y Sociales, 1961); John S. D. Eisenhower, *So Far from God. The U.S. War with Mexico, 1840–1848* (New York: Random House, 1989); Norman A. Graebner, "The Mexican War: A Study in Causation," *Pacific Historical Review* 49 (1980): 405–426, Norman Graebner, *Foundations of American Foreign Policy: A Realist Appraisal From Franklin to McKinley* (Wilmington, Del.: Scholarly Resources, 1985). Ward McAfee and J. Cordell Robinson, *Origins of the Mexican War: A Documentary Source Book,* 2 vols. (Salisbury, N.C.: Documentary Publications, 1982), 2 vols. conveniently gathers key documents. Glenn W. Price, *Origins of the War with Mexico: The Polk-Stockton Intrigue* (Austin: University of Texas Press, 1967) is useful, although most historians consider his point unproven.

2. On the battle in Congress see Schroeder, *Mister Polk's War,* chap. 1. Grant quoted in Eisenhower, *So Far from God,* p. xvii.

3. Justin H. Smith, *The War with Mexico,* 2 vols. (New York: Macmillan, 1919), vol. 1, chap. 3.

4. Smith, *War with Mexico,* vol. 1, chap. 5; on the press see Gene M. Brack, *Mexico Views Manifest Destiny, 1821–1846: An Essay on the Origins of the Mexican War* (Albuquerque: University of New Mexico Press, 1975), chaps. 8, 9, esp. p. 171.

5. "Glorious" quoted in Miguel E. Soto, "The Monarchist Conspiracy and the Mexican War," in *Essays on the Mexican War,* ed. Douglas W. Richmond (College Station: Texas A & M University Press, 1986), p. 73. See also Brack, *Mexico Views,* p. 166.

6. McAfee and Robinson, *Origins of Mexican War,* quotes in vol. 2, pp. 37–40, 89–90.

7. Worse, some plotted to turn the Mexican regime into a monarchy; see Pletcher, *Diplomacy of Annexation,* chap. 12; Soto, "Monarchist Conspiracy." On United States concern about an alliance with foreign monarchists see Bosch García, *Historia de las relaciones,* pp. 105–106, 109.

8. French Ensor Chadwick, *Diplomacy,* vol. 1 of *The Relations of the United States and Spain* (New York: Scribner's, 1909); and Robert L. Beisner, *From the Old Diplomacy to the New, 1865–1900,* 2nd ed. (New York: Harlan Davidson, 1986) for diplomatic details; on McKinley see Joseph A. Fry, "William McKinley and the Coming of the Spanish-American War: A Study of the Besmirching and Redemption of an Historical Image," *Diplomatic History* 3 (1979): 77–97.

9. On U.S. motives, besides works cited above and in chapter 8 see Lewis L. Gould, *The Presidency of William McKinley* (Lawrence: Regents Press of Kansas, 1980); Louis A. Pérez, Jr., *Cuba Between Empires, 1878–1902* (Pittsburgh: University of Pittsburgh Press, 1983), chaps. 8, 9; Walter LaFeber, *The American Age: United States Foreign Policy at Home and Abroad Since 1750* (New York: W. W. Norton, 1989), pp. 182–190; Walter LaFeber, "That 'Splendid Little War' in Historical Perspective," *Texas Quarterly* 11 (1968): 89–98; Richard E. Welch, Jr., "William McKinley: Reluctant Warrior, Cautious Imperialist," in *Traditions and Values: American Diplomacy, 1865–1945,* ed. Norman Graebner (Lanham, Md.: University Press of America, 1985), pp. 29–52, esp. pp. 36–39; Hugh De Santis, "The Imperialist Impulse and American Innocence, 1865–1900," *American Foreign Relations: A Historiographical Review.,* ed. Gerald K. Haines and J. Samuel Walker (Westport, Conn.: Greenwood, 1981), pp. 65–90.

10. John L. Offner, *An Unwanted War: The Diplomacy of the United States and Spain over Cuba, 1895–1898* (Chapel Hill: University of North Carolina Press, 1992), esp. pp. 17–25. See Pérez, *Cuba Between Empires,* for the role of the rebels. On views of Spain see Marcus M. Wilkerson, *Public Opinion and the Spanish-American War: A Study in War Propaganda* (New York: Russell and Russell, 1967). Also Robert C. Hilderbrand, *Power and the People: Executive Management of Public Opinion in Foreign Affairs, 1897–1921* (Chapel Hill: University of North Carolina Press, 1981), pp. 13–21, 27–28; John Dobson, *Reticent Expansionism: The Foreign Policy of William McKinley* (Pittsburgh: Duquesne University Press, 1988), pp. 24–26. For a different but not incompatible view see Ernest R. May, *Imperial Democracy: The Emergence of America as a Great Power* (New York: Harcourt, Brace and World, 1961), pp. 112–114, 159.

11. Letter quoted in Wilkerson, *Public Opinion,* p. 92. The Spanish word used for "politician" (*politicastro*) is still more insulting. See references above and H. Wayne Morgan, "The De Lôme Letter: A New Appraisal," *Historian* 26 (1963): 36–49.

12. Louis A. Pérez, Jr., "The Meaning of the Maine: Causation and the Historiography of the Spanish-American War," *Pacific Historical Review* 58 (1989): 293–322; John Offner, "President McKinley's Final Attempt to Avoid War with Spain," *Ohio History* 94 (1985): 125–138.

13. On Gulf of Tonkin see Leslie H. Gelb and Richard K. Betts, *The Irony of Vietnam: The System Worked* (Washington, D.C.: Brookings Institution, 1979), pp. 100–104.

14. Richard Sisson and Leo F. Rose, *War and Secession: Pakistan, India and the Creation of Bangladesh* (Berkeley: University of California Press, 1990); also Robert Jackson, *South Asian Crisis: India, Pakistan, and Bangladesh: A Political and Historical Analysis of the 1971 War* (New York: Praeger, 1975), esp. chaps. 2–4; Herbert Feldman, *The End and the Beginning: Pakistan, 1969–1971* (London: Oxford University Press, 1975), chaps. 14, 15.

15. "That woman" (perhaps apocryphal) quoted in John G. Stoessinger, *Why Nations Go to War,* 6th ed. (St. Martin's, 1992), p. 134; "could not get elected" on p. 135, see pp. 128–136.

16. Quoted in Andrew N. Porter, *The Origins of the South African War: Joseph Chamberlain and the Diplomacy of Imperialism, 1895–1899* (New York: St. Martin's, 1980), p. 228.

17. Stuart Creighton Miller, *"Benevolent Assimilation": The American Conquest of the Philippines, 1899–1903* (New Haven: Yale University Press, 1982); Stanley Karnow, *In Our Image: America's Empire in the Philippines* (New York: Random House, 1989); J. David Steinberg, "An Ambiguous Legacy: Years at War in the Philippines," *Pacific Affairs* 45 (1972): 165–190, see pp. 169–178; Richard E. Welch, Jr., *Response to Imperialism: The United States and the Philippine-American War, 1899–1902* (Chapel Hill: University of North Carolina Press, 1979); May, *Imperial Democracy,* esp. pp. 252–254. For U.S. attitudes see also Walter L. Williams, "United States Indian Policy and the Debate over Philippine Annexation: Implications for the Origins of American Imperialism," *Journal of American History* 66 (1980): 810–831, quote pp. 824–825; Emily S. Rosenberg, *Spreading the American Dream: American Economic and Cultural Expansion, 1890–1945* (New York: Hill & Wang, 1982), p. 41.

18. Miller, *Benevolent Assimilation,* chaps. 3, 4. On Filipinos compared with Indians see Williams, "Philippine Annexation." Numbers from Welch, *Response to Imperialism,* p. 155.

19. Thucydides, *History of the Peloponnesian War,* trans. Rex Warner (New York: Penguin, 1954), 1:23–88, esp. 23.

20. Daniel S. Geller, *Domestic Factors in Foreign Policy: A Cross-National Statistical Analysis* (Cambridge, Mass.: Schenkman, 1985), p. 156; Joe D. Hagan, *Political Opposition and Foreign Policy in Comparative Perspective* (Boulder: Rienner, 1993), pp. 180–184. Vietnamese nationalists as "gangs:" Henri Grimal, *Decolonization: The British, French, Dutch and Belgian Empires, 1919–1963,* trans. Stephen De Vos (Boulder: Westview, 1978), p. 242, see also 234ff.

21. The 1881 Anglo-Boer War is another case (see appendix). American military officials preferred giving military aid to clients over political negotiation in post-1945 China, the Philippines, and Vietnam; Douglas J. Macdonald, *Adventures in Chaos: American Intervention for Reform in the Third World* (Cambridge, Mass.: Harvard University Press, 1992), pp. 267–268. General Douglas MacArthur and his staff in Korea biased the information they sent to Washington so as to obscure the danger of provoking Communist Chinese intervention; Richard Ned Lebow, *Between Peace and War: The Nature of International Crisis* (Baltimore: Johns Hopkins University Press, 1961), pp. 155–162.

22. On Milner and the Anglo-Boer War see chapter 7. On Stratford Canning and the Crimean War see chapter 11, n. 20. On the American ambassador who sponsored a Mex-

ican coup in 1913 see chapter 13, n. 3. See chapter 13 also for Guatemala, Chile, etc. On British officers in Palestine in 1948 see appendix.

23. Pletcher, *Diplomacy of Annexation*, chaps. 8–13; Frederick Merk, *The Oregon Question: Essays in Anglo-American Diplomacy and Politics* (Cambridge, Mass.: Harvard University Press, 1967); Wilbur D. Jones, *The American Problem in British Diplomacy, 1841–1861* (London: Macmillan, 1974); Sellers, *James K. Polk,* chap. 9. On the slogan see Edwin A. Miles, "'Fifty-Four Forty or Fight'—An American Political Legend," *Mississippi Valley Historical Review* 44 (1957): 291–309.

24. Thomas R. Hietala, *Manifest Design: Anxious Aggrandizement in Late Jacksonian America* (Ithaca, N.Y.: Cornell University Press, 1985), pp. 75–78. On the Chartist movement see Malcolm I. Thomis and Peter Holt, *Threats of Revolution in Britain, 1789–1848* (London: Macmillan, 1977), chap. 5; Merk, *Oregon Question,* essay 11. "Monarchical" quoted in Frederick Merk and Lois Bannister Merk, *Manifest Destiny and Mission in American History: A Reinterpretation* (New York: Random House, 1963), p. 38; see also Merk, *Oregon Question,* pp. 329–330. "Despotism of democracy" quoted in Richard S. Cramer, "British Magazines and the Oregon Question," *Pacific Historical Review* 32 (1963): 369–382, see p. 379. See also Michael H. Hunt, *Ideology and United States Foreign Policy* (New Haven: Yale University Press, 1987), chap. 2; Pletcher, *Diplomacy of Annexation,* pp. 283, 287; Jones, *American Problem,* p. 9.

25. Remark on stiff public stand: Wilbur D. Jones and J. Chal Vinson, "British Preparedness and the Oregon Settlement," *Pacific Historical Review* 22 (1953): 356; see also Sellers, *James K. Polk,* p. 376, Merk, *Oregon Question,* pp. 222, 275, "same principles" quoted p. 302; John Malloy Owen IV, "Testing the Democratic Peace: American Diplomatic Crises 1794–1917," (Ph.D. diss., Harvard University, 1993), pp. 157–172.

26. "Cordial" quoted in Jones, *American Problem,* p. 223, see also pp. 47–54; Sellers, *James K. Polk,* pp. 235–258; Stuart Anderson, "British Threats and the Settlement of the Oregon Boundary Dispute," *Pacific Northwest Quarterly* 66 (1973): 153–160.

27. Possible confounding factors in such "pseudo-experiments" were reviewed for another comparison (the Fashoda Crisis and the Spanish-American War) by James Lee Ray, *Democracy and International Conflict. An Evaluation of the Democratic Peace Proposition* (Columbia: University of South Carolina Press, 1995), chap. 5.

28. Pletcher, *Diplomacy of Annexation,* p. 599; Jones, *American Problem,* pp. 209–210.

29. Barry M. Gough, "British Policy in the San Juan Boundary Dispute, 1854–1872," *Pacific Northwest Quarterly* 62 (1971): 59–68.

30. Howard Jones, *The Union in Peril: The Crisis over British Intervention in the Civil War* (Chapel Hill: University of North Carolina Press, 1992). On the 1861 Trent affair see Christopher Layne, "Kant or Cant: The Myth of Democratic Peace," *International Security* 19 (1994): 5–49; Layne is answered by John M. Owen, "How Liberalism Produces Democratic Peace," *International Security* 19 (1994): 5–49; see also Owen, "Testing the Democratic Peace," chap. 8. More generally see Charles S. Campbell, Jr., *From Revolution to Rapprochement: The United States and Great Britain, 1783–1900* (New York: Wiley, 1974).

31. For Venezuela I follow especially Beisner, *From the Old Diplomacy,* pp. 98–103, and Michael A. Lutzker, "The Venezuelan Boundary Dispute of 1895 Revisited: The Dy-

namics of Avoiding War" (paper presented to Joint Conference of the Society for Historians of American Foreign Relations, Washington, D.C., Aug. 1984). See also Marsh Bertram, *The Birth of Anglo-American Friendship, the Prime Facet of the Venezuelan Boundary Dispute* (Lanham, Md.: University Press of America, 1992); Charles C. Tansill, *The Foreign Policy of Thomas F. Bayard, 1885–1897* (New York: Fordham University Press, 1940), chaps. 18, 19; Joseph J. Matthews, "Informal Diplomacy in the Venezuelan Crisis of 1896," *Mississippi Valley Historical Review* 50 (1963): 195–212.

More generally see also May, *Imperial Democracy*, chaps. 4–6; Walter LaFeber, "The Background of Cleveland's Venezuelan Policy: A Reinterpretation," *American Historical Review* 66 (1961): 947–967, see pp. 963, 966; Alexander E. Campbell, *Great Britain and the United States, 1895–1903* (London: Longmans, Green, 1960), chap. 7; J. A. S. Grenville, *Lord Salisbury and Foreign Policy: The Close of the Nineteenth Century* (London: Athlone, 1970), chaps. 1, 3; cf. Robert Rhodes James, *From Gladstone to Asquith, 1880–1914*, vol. 1 of *The British Revolution: British Politics, 1880–1939* (London: Hamish Hamilton, 1976), pp. 73–75; Nelson M. Blake, "The Olney-Pauncefote Treaty of 1897," *American Historical Review* 50 (1945): 228–243; Charles S. Campbell, Jr., *Anglo-American Understanding, 1898–1903* (Baltimore: Johns Hopkins Press, 1957), p. 206.

32. Donald F. Bittner, *Lion and White Falcon: Britain and Iceland in the World War II Era* (Hamden, Conn.: Anchor, 1983), esp. pp. 40–48.

33. For conflicts between marginal democracies see appendix. Note too the 1976 nonviolent naval confrontation between Greece and Turkey with Aegean oil at stake, with mediation by NATO democracies much as in the Codfish War. Tozun Bahcheli, *Greek-Turkish Relations Since 1955* (Boulder: Westview, 1990); *New York Times,* 1976, passim.

34. Hannes Jónsson, *Friends in Conflict. The Anglo-Icelandic Cod Wars and the Law of the Sea* (London: Hurst, 1982); Jeffery A. Hart, *The Anglo-Icelandic Cod War of 1972–1973: A Case Study of a Fishery Dispute* (Berkeley, Calif.: University of California Institute of International Studies, 1976). "Pistol": *New York Times,* 11 March 1976; see also London *Times,* 1972–1973, 1975–1976, passim.

35. Gregory A. Raymond, "Democracies, Disputes and Third-Party Intermediaries," *Journal of Conflict Resolution* 38 (1994): 24–42; William J. Dixon, "Democracy and the Management of International Conflict," *Journal of Conflict Resolution* 37 (1993): 42–68. On autocratic mediation see Evan Luard, *War in International Society: A Study in International Sociology* (London: I. B. Tauris, 1986), pp. 281–285; Kalevi J. Holsti, *Peace and War: Armed Conflicts and International Order, 1648–1989* (Cambridge: Cambridge University Press, 1991), pp. 111–112; in general, J. Bercovitch, "International Mediation: A Study of the Incidence, Strategies and Conditions of Successful Outcomes," *Cooperation and Conflict* 21 (1986): 155–168.

36. See Walter A. McDougall, *France's Rhineland Diplomacy, 1914–1924: The Last Bid for a Balance of Power in Europe* (Princeton: Princeton University Press, 1978), and other sources cited in chapter 10; John Gillingham, *Coal, Steel and the Rebirth of Europe, 1945–1955: The Germans and French from Ruhr Conflict to Economic Community* (Cambridge, MA: Cambridge University Press, 1991), chaps. 1, 2.

37. Recent surveys: Richard Mayne, *Postwar: The Dawn of Today's Europe* (New York: Schocken, 1983), chap. 10; Clifford Hackett, *Cautious Revolution: The European Commu-*

nity Arrives (Westport, Conn.: Greenwood, 1990); for details see Gillingham, *Coal, Steel and Rebirth;* Ernst B. Haas, *The Unity of Europe: Political, Social, and Economic Forces, 1950–1957* (Stanford, Calif.: Stanford University Press, 1958); Walter Lipgens, *1945–1947,* vol. 1 of *A History of European Integration,* trans. P. S. Falla and A. J. Ryder (Oxford: Clarendon, 1982); Alan S. Milward, *The European Rescue of the Nation-State* (London: Routledge, 1992).

38. Jean Monnet, *Memoirs,* trans. Richard Mayne (Garden City, N.Y.: Doubleday, 1978), esp. chap. 13; Mayne, *Postwar,* p. 306; Fred Charles Iklé, *How Nations Negotiate* (New York: Harper and Row, 1964), p. 119; François Duchene, "Jean Monnet's Methods," in *Jean Monnet: The Path to European Unity,* ed. Douglas Brinkley and Clifford Hackett (New York: St. Martin's, 1991), pp. 184–209; Gillingham, *Coal, Steel, and Rebirth,* chaps. 4–6.

39. Jacques Freymond, *The Saar Conflict, 1945–1955* (London: Stevens, 1960).

40. Helen Wallace, "Making Multilateral Negotiations Work," in *The Dynamics of European Integration,* ed. William Wallace (London: Pinter, 1990); Haas, *Unity of Europe,* p. 526.

CHAPTER THIRTEEN
Imperialist Aggression by Democracies

1. The most comprehensive account is Piero Gleijeses, *Shattered Hope: The Guatemalan Revolution and the United States, 1944–1954* (Princeton: Princeton University Press, 1991), supplemented by Richard H. Immerman, *The CIA in Guatemala: The Foreign Policy of Intervention* (Austin: University of Texas Press, 1982); and Stephen Schlesinger and Stephen Kinzer, *Bitter Fruit: The Untold Story of the American Coup in Guatemala* (Garden City, N.Y.: Doubleday, 1982). Stephen G. Rabe, *Eisenhower and Latin America: The Foreign Policy of Anticommunism* (Chapel Hill: University of North Carolina Press, 1988) gives context. Although bowdlerized, also useful is *Foreign Relations of the United States, 1952–1954,* vol. 4, *The American Republics* (Washington, D.C.: U.S. Government Printing Office, 1983), henceforth *FRUS, 1952–1954,* vol. 4. Further revelations can be expected (Nicholas Cullather, forthcoming), but the extent of U.S. guidance of the Guatemalan military's takeover may remain uncertain.

2. "War by other means": R. Cohen, "Pacific Unions," *Review of International Studies* 20 (1994): 207–223, see p. 218. A minimum of forty-three "rebels" died according to a recently released report, see *New York Times,* 29 May 1997; casualties on the government side were probably comparable.

3. For example, for secrecy on the 1961 U.S. intervention against the elected leader of British Guiana see *New York Times,* 30 October 1994; for destruction of documents see ibid., 29 May 1997. Cases like the CIA subversion of Iran in 1953 involved fears of Communist takeover of what were not, but might have become, democracies; Mark J. Gasiorowski, *U.S. Foreign Policy and the Shah: Building a Client State in Iran* (Ithaca, N.Y.: Cornell University Press, 1991), chap. 3; for Indonesia (1955), Brazil (1960s), and others see David P. Forsythe, "Democracy, War, and Covert Action," *Journal of Peace Research* 29 (1992): 385–395. He independently reaches conclusions like mine.

A fairly well studied subversion of a potentially democratic government was the U.S. ambassador's encouragement (without Washington's approval) of a violent coup in Mexico in 1913: see Alan Knight, *Porfirians, Liberals, and Peasants,* vol. 1 of *The Mexican Revolution* (New York: Cambridge University Press, 1986); Charles C. Cumberland, *Mexican Revolution: Genesis Under Madero* (Austin: University of Texas Press, 1952); William Weber Johnson, *Heroic Mexico: The Violent Emergence of a Modern Nation* (Garden City, N.Y.: Doubleday, 1968), chap. 12; Graham Stuart and James L. Tigner, *Latin America and the United States* (Englewood Cliffs, N.J.: Prentice-Hall, 1975), pp. 248–255; Martín Luis Guzmán, "Febrero de 1913," in Martín Luis Guzmán, *Obras Completas,* vol. 2 (Mexico City: Fondo de Cultura Económica, 1985), pp. 843–889.

A case especially like Guatemala was the 1953 imposition of military rule in British Guiana by the British government, which had been persuaded by local landholders and the Marxist rhetoric of Guiana's elected leaders that the colony was falling under Communist control. Robert D. Tomasek, "British Guiana: A Case Study of British Colonial Policy," *Political Science Quarterly* 74 (1959): 393–411; Morley Ayearst, *The British West Indies: The Search for Self-Government* (New York: New York University Press, 1960), pp. 112–125.

4. Similar warnings came from the dictators who ruled Guatemala's neighbors. Stephen E. Ambrose, *Ike's Spies: Eisenhower and the Espionage Establishment* (Garden City, N.Y.: Doubleday, 1981), p. 219; Immerman, *CIA in Guatemala,* p. 89, see pp. 124–125 for United Fruit.

5. Memorandum of conversation, 11 May 1954, *FRUS, 1952–1954,* vol. 4, p. 1106.

6. Numbers of Communists: *FRUS, 1952–1954,* vol. 4, pp. 1033, 1098; on their impotence see Gleijeses, *Shattered Hope,* pp. 196–207. Gleijeses, *Shattered Hope,* pp. 141–148, 379

7. Immerman, *CIA in Guatemala,* p. 83; Walter LaFeber, *Inevitable Revolutions: The United States in Central America* (New York: W. W. Norton, 1983), pp. 85–111. On prejudices see David Healy, *Drive to Hegemony: The United States in the Caribbean, 1898–1917* (Madison: University of Wisconsin Press, 1988), pp. 63–68.

8. "Better:" George Kennan quoted in LaFeber, *Inevitable Revolutions,* p. 107, see also p. 115. On motives see Leslie Bethell, "From the Second World War to the Cold War: 1944–1954," in *Exporting Democracy: The United States and Latin America,* ed. Abraham F. Lowenthal (Baltimore: John Hopkins University Press, 1991), pp. 41–70.

9. Immerman, *CIA in Guatemala,* pp. 59–60, 107. See Gleijeses, *Shattered Hope,* pp. 60–67.

10. "Agents:" Dwight D. Eisenhower, *Mandate for Change, 1953–1956,* vol. 1 of *The White House Years* (Garden City, N.Y.: Doubleday, 1963), pp. 424–425, see pp. 83, 421–424. Also Allen Dulles, *The Craft of Intelligence* (New York: Harper and Row, 1963), pp. 122, 221. For evidence that the administration held such views in 1954 see, e.g., Schlesinger, *Bitter Fruit,* pp. 141, 146; Stephen E. Ambrose, *The President,* vol. 2 of *Eisenhower* (New York: Simon and Schuster, 1984), pp. 192–197; *FRUS, 1952–54,* vol. 4, passim. Historians reporting the misperception include Rabe, *Eisenhower and Latin America,* esp. chap. 3; Immerman, *CIA in Guatemala,* p. ix and chaps. 4, 5; Gleijeses, *Shattered Hope,* p. 365; LaFeber, *Inevitable Revolutions,* p. 120; Blanche Weisen Cook, *The Declassified*

Eisenhower: A Divided Legacy (Garden City, N.Y.: Doubleday, 1981), p. 253 and chaps. 6, 7; Ambrose, *Ike's Spies,* p. 222 and chap. 16.

11. Daniel James, "Red Beachhead in America," *Saturday Evening Post* 226 (24 April 1954): 32–34, 125–128. Similarly, *New York Times,* 23 Jan. 1953, 24 Feb. 1954; "The Red Outpost in Central America," *Life* 35 (12 Oct. 1953): 169–177; etc. See Immerman, *CIA in Guatemala,* chap. 5. On United Fruit see Schlesinger, *Bitter Fruit,* pp. 84, 86, 97.

12. Cases include (from appendix) 1652 (Netherlands-Charles II), 1847 (Sonderbund-Austria), 1879 (Peru-Bolivia), 1899 (Transvaal-Germany), 1923 (Germany-Soviet Union).

13. U.S. Department of State, "Penetration of the Political Institutions of Guatemala by the International Communist Movement . . . Information Submitted by the Delegation of the United States of America to the Fifth Meeting of Consultation of Ministers of Foreign Affairs of the American Republics." (Washington, D.C., 1954), pp. 25–30; cf. Gleijeses, *Shattered Hope,* chap. 13, esp. p. 279. On Honduras see *FRUS, 1952–1954,* vol. 4, pp. 1130, 1141–1145, 1164n.

14. U.S. Dept. of State, "Penetration," pp. 14–15. Gleijeses, *Shattered Hope,* p. 317, thinks there may have been at least seventy-five government killings of anti-Communists. Even the few historians who maintain that the U.S. government's primary aim was to protect business interests agree that it failed to perceive the Guatemalan government as a functioning democracy. Cook, *Declassified Eisenhower,* pp. 231, 236; Ambrose, *Ike's Spies,* chap. 16. Envoy's pleas: *FRUS, 1952–1954,* vol. 4, pp. 1040–1041, 1051.

15. Military regime: Susanne Jonas, *The Battle for Guatemala: Rebels, Death Squads, and U.S. Power* (Boulder: Westview, 1991), pp. 34–36 and chap. 3.

16. See references in appendix, also Mary Young, "Racism in Red and Black: Indians and Other Free People of Color in Georgia Law, Politics and Removal Policy," *Georgia Historical Quarterly* 73 (1989): 492–518. The U.S. Supreme Court ruled (fruitlessly) that the Cherokees constituted an independent state.

17. Ward Churchill and Jim Vander Wall, *Agents of Repression: The FBI's Secret Wars Against the Black Panther Party and the American Indian Movement* (Boston: South End, 1988).

18. Correspondent: see Harrison E. Salisbury, *Without Fear or Favor* (New York: Times Books, 1980), pp. 478–482; *FRUS, 1952–54,* vol. 4, p. 1132. See David Caute, *The Great Fear: The Anti-Communist Purge Under Truman and Eisenhower* (New York: Simon and Schuster, 1978); Robert Dallek, *The American Style of Foreign Policy: Cultural Politics and Foreign Affairs* (New York: Knopf, 1983), p. 213.

19. Robert D. Schulzinger, *Henry Kissinger, Doctor of Diplomacy* (New York: Columbia University Press, 1989), pp. 131–140 and William F. Sater, *Chile and the United States: Empires in Conflict* (Athens: University of Georgia Press, 1990), chap. 8, are recent summaries with references. More exhaustive is Poul Jensen, *The Garotte: The United States and Chile, 1970–1973,* 2 vols., trans. Peter Manley (Aarhus, Denmark: Aarhus University Press, 1988). Seymour M. Hersh, Jr., *The Price of Power: Kissinger in the Nixon White House* (New York: Summit, 1983), chaps. 21, 22, indicts Nixon and Kissinger; defenses revealing attitudes are Henry Kissinger, *White House Years* (Boston: Little, Brown, 1979), pp. 654–657, 682–683; Henry Kissinger, *Years of Upheaval* (Boston: Little, Brown, 1982), chap. 9

and p. 405; Nathaniel Davis, *The Last Two Years of Salvador Allende* (Ithaca, N.Y.: Cornell University Press, 1983); see also William Colby with Peter Forbath, *Honorable Men: My Life in the CIA* (New York: Simon and Schuster, 1978), pp. 302–305. Basic documentation is U.S. Senate Select Committee to Study Government Operations with Respect to Intelligence Activities, *Covert Action in Chile, 1963–1973* 94th Cong., 1st sess. (Washington, D.C.: U.S. Government Printing Office, 1985), see esp. pp. 46–48.

20. See also above, note 3. Boer Republic: chapter 7; Ruhr: chapter 10.

21. David Levering Lewis, *The Race to Fashoda: European Colonialism and African Resistance in the Scramble for Africa* (New York: Weidenfeld and Nicolson, 1987); G. N. Sanderson, *England, Europe, and the Upper Nile* (Edinburgh: Edinburgh University Press, 1965); Roger Glenn Brown, *Fashoda Reconsidered: The Impact of Domestic Politics on French Policy in Africa, 1893–1898* (Baltimore: Johns Hopkins University Press, 1969); Christopher Andrew, *Théophile Delcassé and the Making of the Entente Cordiale: A Reappraisal of French Foreign Policy, 1898–1905* (London: Macmillan, 1968), esp. chap. 2 and pp. 91–103; William L. Langer, *The Diplomacy of Imperialism, 1890–1902,* 2nd ed. (New York: Knopf, 1960) pp. 552–561, 574–575; Darrell Bates, *The Fashoda Incident of 1898: Encounter on the Nile* (Oxford: Oxford University Press, 1984); Marc Michel, *La Mission Marchand, 1895–1899* (Paris: Marton, 1972); T. W. Riker, "A Survey of British Policy in the Fashoda Crisis," *Political Science* 44 (1929): 54–78. For diplomacy see Great Britain Foreign Office, *The End of British Isolation,* vol. 1 of *British Documents on the Origin of the War, 1898–1914,* ed. George P. Gooch and Harold Temperley (London: H.M.S.O., 1927).

22. Rachael Arié, "L'Opinion publique en France et l'affaire de Fachoda," *Revue d'histoire des colonies* 41 (1954): 329–367; M. Hugodot, "L'Opinion publique anglaise et l'affaire de Fachoda," *Revue d'histoire des colonies* 44 (1957): 113–137. Great Britain Foreign Office, *British Documents,* vol. 1, pp. 171–172. Public opinion: Langer, *Diplomacy of Imperialism,* p. 556.

23. J. A. S. Grenville, *Lord Salisbury and Foreign Policy: The Close of the Nineteenth Century* (London: Athlone, 1970); on elitist control of foreign policy see Ronald Robinson, John Galleger, and Alice Denny, *Africa and the Victorians: The Climax of Imperialism* (Garden City, N.Y.: Doubleday, 1968), pp. 377–378.

24. For background see Alfred Cobban, *France of the Republics, 1871–1962,* vol. 3 of *A History of Modern France* (Harmondsworth, England: Penguin, 1965), esp. pp. 40–41.

25. "Despotism" quoted in Robinson, Galleger, and Denny, *Africa and the Victorians,* 375. For earlier warnings see James L. Garvin, *The Life of Joseph Chamberlain,* 6 vols. (London: Macmillan, 1932–1969), vol. 3, pp. 213, 215; Great Britain Foreign Office, *British Documents,* vol. 1, p. 146. See also Brown, *Fashoda Reconsidered,* esp. pp. 106–112, 129. If the French went to war, Britain's safety required that its battleships be on station to bottle up the French in their ports; see Aaron L. Friedberg, *The Weary Titan: Britain and the Experience of Relative Decline, 1895–1905* (Princeton: Princeton University Press, 1988), pp. 150–155.

26. Criminals: Hugodot, "L'Opinion publique anglaise." Brown, *Fashoda Reconsidered;* Lewis, *Race to Fashoda,* esp. pp. 86–89.

27. Arié, "L'Opinion publique en France"; "absurd" quoted p. 353; see also E. Malcolm Carroll, *French Public Opinion and Foreign Affairs, 1870–1914* (New York: Century, 1931), pp. 172–182.

28. Susan Peterson, "How Democracies Differ: Public Opinion, State Structure, and the Lessons of the Fashoda Crisis," *Security Studies* 5 (1995): 3–37.

29. Donald Southgate, *"The Most English Minister": The Policies and Politics of Palmerston* (London: Macmillan, 1966), pp. 552–558, puts the turning point toward imperialism at about 1870. Still a good summary is Carlton J. J. Hayes, *A Generation of Materialism, 1878–1900* (New York: Harper and Row, 1941), chap. 7; also E. J. Hobsbawm, *The Age of Empire, 1875–1914* (New York: Pantheon, 1987), esp. pp. 69–71, 88–89. For the following see Arno J. Mayer, *The Persistence of the Old Regime: Europe and the Great War* (New York: Pantheon, 1981), pp. 275–293, 302–306; A. P. Thornton, *The Imperial Idea and Its Enemies: A Study in British Power* (London: Macmillan, 1959), chap. 1; Ernest R. May, *American Imperialism: A Speculative Essay* (New York: H. Wolff, 1968), chaps. 1, 9; Robinson, Galleger, and Denny, *Africa and the Victorians,* chap. 15; Winfried Baumgart, *Imperialism: The Idea and Reality of British and French Colonial Expansion, 1880–1914* (New York: Oxford University Press, 1982), pp. 82–90; Richard Koebner and Helmut Dan Schmidt, *Imperialism: The Story and Significance of a Political Word, 1840–1960* (Cambridge: Cambridge University Press, 1964), pp. 214–216 and chap. 4; Paul Kennedy, *The Rise of the Anglo-German Antagonism, 1860–1914* (London: Allen and Unwin, 1980), pp. 146–151; Friedburg, *Weary Titan,* esp. chap. 2.

30. Sometimes "without reference to ideology there is no explanation" for imperialist expansion, according to Jack Snyder, *Myths of Empire: Domestic Politics and International Ambition* (Ithaca, N.Y.: Cornell University Press, 1991), pp. 312–314 and passim; cf. James E. Dougherty and Robert L. Pfaltzgraff, Jr., *Contending Theories of International Relations: A Comprehensive Survey,* 3rd ed. (New York: Harper and Row, 1990), pp. 202–205. See also Henri Brunschwig, *French Colonialism, 1871–1914: Myths and Realities* (New York: Praeger, 1964); James Morris, *Pax Britannica: The Climax of Empire* (New York: Harcourt Brace Jovanovich, 1968), esp. chap. 23; Ronald Hyam, *Britain's Imperial Century, 1815–1914: A Study of Empire and Expansion* (London: Batsford, 1976), chap. 2. For particular topics see John M. MacKenzie, *Propaganda and Empire: The Manipulation of British Public Opinion, 1880–1960* (Manchester: Manchester University Press, 1984); I. F. Clarke, *Voices Prophesying War, 1763–1984* (London: Oxford University Press, 1966), esp. chap. 4, also pp. 110–115 for Anglo-French antagonism.

31. Hyam, *Britain's Imperial Century,* pp. 39, 78–88; Stuart Anderson, *Race and Rapprochement: Anglo-Saxonism and Anglo-American Relations, 1895–1904* (London: Associated University Presses, 1981), pp. 3–66, esp. pp. 17, 19; for the U.S., Reginald Horsman, *Race and Manifest Destiny: The Origins of American Racial Anglo-Saxonism* (Cambridge, Mass.: Harvard University Press, 1981), esp. p. 298. Salisbury cited in Robert Rhodes James, *From Gladstone to Asquith, 1880–1914,* vol. 1 of *The British Revolution: British Politics, 1880–1939* (London: Hamish Hamilton, 1976), p. 99. "Contest" quoted in Robinson, Galleger, and Denny, *Africa and the Victorians,* pp. 454–455, see chap. 14. "At few times have [political] ideological considerations been less effective in the determination of

European foreign policies," says Alexander E. Campbell, *Great Britain and the United States, 1895–1903* (London: Longmans, Green, 1960), p. 197. Similarly, see Gordon A. Craig, *War, Politics, and Diplomacy: Selected Essays* (New York: Praeger, 1966), pp. 234–235.

32. Eric J. Hobsbawm, "Working-Class Internationalism," in *Internationalism in the Labour Movement, 1830–1940*, 2 vols., ed. Frits van Holthoon and Marcel van der Linden (Leiden: E. J. Brill, 1988), vol. 1, pp. 3–16, see pp. 8–11; G. D. H. Cole, *A History of Socialist Thought*, vol. 3, parts 1–2, *The Second International, 1889–1914* (London: Macmillan, 1960), part 1, pp. 177, 341, 367; James Joll, *The Second International, 1889–1914*, 2nd ed. (London: Routledge & Kegan Paul, 1974), chap. 5; Peter Weiler, *The New Liberalism: Liberal Social Theory in Great Britain, 1889–1914* (New York: Garland, 1982), chap. 2; H. C. G. Matthew, *The Liberal Imperialists: The Ideas and Politics of a Post-Gladstonian Elite* (London: Oxford University Press, 1973), see esp. on Rosebery; Michael Balfour, *Britain and Joseph Chamberlain* (London: Allen and Unwin, 1988), pp. 211–218; Ernest R. May, *Imperial Democracy: The Emergence of America as a Great Power* (New York: Harcourt, Brace and World, 1961), p. 191.

33. Quote from Andrew, *Théophile Delcassé*, p. 57, see also pp. 55–59; M. B. Hayne, *The French Foreign Office and the Origins of the First World War, 1898–1914* (Oxford: Clarendon, 1993), pp. 58–61.

34. Garvin, *Life of Joseph Chamberlain*, esp. vol. 3, extensive but laudatory; Richard Jay, *Joseph Chamberlain: A Political Study* (Oxford: Clarendon, 1981); Balfour, *Britain and Joseph Chamberlain*; Peter Fraser, *Joseph Chamberlain: Radicalism and Empire, 1868–1914* (London: Cassell, 1966); Denis Judd, *Radical Joe: A Life of Joseph Chamberlain* (London: Hamish Hamilton, 1977). On the Niger crisis prefiguring the Fashoda crisis see Garvin, *Life of Joseph Chamberlain*, vol. 3, pp. 204, 208–213, and Robinson, Galleger, and Denny, *Africa and the Victorians*, pp. 402–407.

35. Thucydides, *History of the Peloponnesian War*, 6:6, 6:82, etc.

36. Marcus M. Wilkerson, *Public Opinion and the Spanish-American War: A Study in War Propaganda* (New York: Russell and Russell, 1967); Robinson, Galleger, and Denny, *Africa and the Victorians*, chap. 14, and sources cited in chapter 7.

37. Hutus/Tutsis: Catharine Newbury, *The Cohesion of Oppression: Clientship and Ethnicity in Rwanda, 1860–1960* (New York: Columbia University Press, 1988), pp. 10–15, 51–52. Eugen Weber, *Peasants into Frenchmen: The Modernization of Rural France* (Stanford, Calif.: Stanford University Press, 1976), esp. chaps. 7, 29.

38. Marilyn B. Brewer, "Ethnocentrism and Its Role in Interpersonal Trust," in *Scientific Inquiry in the Social Sciences*, ed. Marilyn B. Brewer and Barry E. Collins (San Francisco: Jossey-Bass, 1981), pp. 345–360; Morton H. Fried, *The Notion of Tribe* (Menlo Park, Calif.: Cummings, 1975); Leroy Vail, ed., *The Creation of Tribalism in Southern Africa* (Berkeley: University of California Press, 1989); Roger Brown, *Social Psychology*, 2nd ed. (New York: Free Press, 1986), chap. 5; Donald L. Horowitz, *Ethnic Groups in Conflict* (Berkeley: University of California Press, 1985).

39. Eric J. Hobsbawm, *Nations and Nationalism Since 1870: Programme, Myth, Reality* (Cambridge: Cambridge University Press, 1990), esp. chaps. 1, 2, 6; Liah Greenfield, *Nationalism: Five Roads to Modernity* (Cambridge, Mass.: Harvard University Press, 1992); for

recent commentary, John A. Hall, "Nationalisms: Classified and Explained," *Daedalus (Proceedings of the American Academy of Arts and Sciences)* 122, no. 3 (Summer 1993): 1–28. Also Anthony D. Smith, *Theories of Nationalism,* 2nd ed. (New York: Holmes and Meier, 1983), preface to the second edition and chap. 10; Anthony D. Smith, *The Ethnic Revival* (Cambridge: Cambridge University Press, 1981), pp. 75–78; Hugh Seton-Watson, *Nations and States: An Enquiry into the Origins of Nations and the Politics of Nationalism* (Boulder: Westview, 1977), pp. 437–440. Groundbreaking works include Benedict Anderson, *Imagined Communities: Reflections on the Origin and Spread of Nationalism,* rev. ed. (London: Verso, 1991); Boyd C. Shafer, *Faces of Nationalism: New Realities and Old Myths* (New York: Harcourt Brace Jovanovich, 1972); Horowitz, *Ethnic Groups,* esp. chaps. 3, 4, 7; Jack Snyder, "Nationalism and the Crisis of the Post-Soviet State," in *Ethnic Conflict and International Security,* ed. Michael E. Brown (Princeton: Princeton University Press, 1993), pp. 79–101; Victor Zaslavsky, "Nationalism and Democratic Transitions in Postcommunist Societies," *Daedalus (Proceedings of the American Academy of Arts and Sciences)* 121, no. 2 (Spring 1992): 97–121; on Africa see Vail, *Creation of Tribalism,* esp. introduction; Elie Kedourie, introduction to *Nationalism in Asia and Africa,* ed. Elie Kedourie (New York: World, 1970), pp. 1–151.

40. Anthony D. Smith, *The Ethnic Origins of Nations* (Oxford: Blackwell, 1986); Smith, *Theories of Nationalism,* pp. 241–242.

41. Saying (my paraphrase) from Frederik Barth, "Pathan Identity and Its Maintenance," in *Ethnic Groups and Boundaries,* ed. Frederik Barth (Boston: Little, Brown, 1969), p. 119.

42. V. P. Gagnon, Jr., "Ethnic Nationalism and International Conflict: The Case of Serbia," *International Security* 19, no. 3 (Winter 1994/1995): 130–166, "Provoking" quoted p. 132; similarly, Warren Zimmerman, "The Last Ambassador," *Foreign Affairs* 74 (1995): 12; further references in appendix. On the diversionary or scapegoat theory of war see also chapter 11, n. 36.

43. Ted Robert Gurr, "Peoples Against States: Ethnopolitical Conflict and the Changing World System," *International Studies Quarterly* 38 (1994): 347–377.

44. Robert Cullen, "Human Rights Quandary," *Foreign Affairs* 72 (1992): 79–88; Greenfield, *Nationalism,* p. 10; David Welsh, "Domestic Politics and Ethnic Conflict," in *Ethnic Conflict and International Security,* ed. Michael E. Brown (Princeton: Princeton University Press, 1993), pp. 56–57. Also Kedourie, *Nationalism in Asia and Africa,* pp. 66–77.

45. "Our city of Pisa": Anonymous, "Cronica volgare di anonimo forentino dall'anno 1385 al 1409 già attribuita a Piero di Giovanni Minerbetti," in *Rerum Italicarum Scriptores,* vol. 27, part 2, ed. E. Bellondi (Città di Castello: Lapi, 1915), p. 338. Similarly, Pisa was *sua possessione;* Francesco Guicciardini, *Storia d'Italia,* 3 vols., ed. Silvana Seidel Menchi (Turin: Giulio Einaudi, 1971), 3.9, vol. 1, p. 299. Note the debate summarized in ibid., 2.1, vol. 1, pp. 139–141. Chamberlain quoted in Garvin, *Life of Joseph Chamberlain,* vol. 3, p. 19, see chap. 48.

46. Warfare directly against a dependency: 412 B.C., 1494, 1576, 1775, 1828, 1881, 1899 (Philippines), 1919, 1968. Intervention by an outside republic: 1431, 1447, 1490, 1494 (Venice), 1531, 1656, 1897, 1898, 1974, 1991. Colonial concerns contributed to additional conflicts, e.g., 1652, 1797 (Caribbean trade), 1812 (Canada), 1914.

47. "Jamais l'Angleterre:" Sanderson, *England, Europe*, p. 362. "Courteous": Great Britain, Foreign Office, *British Documents*, vol. 1, p. 189. For similiar Anglo-French mutual respect in other African disputes see ibid., vol. 1, pp. 157–158, vol. 2, p. 293, and passim; John D. Hargreaves, "*Entente Manquée:* Anglo-French Relations, 1895–1896," *Cambridge Historical Journal* 11 (1953): 65–92.

48. *Times* quoted in Andrew, *Théophile Delcassé*, p. 215. See George Monger, *The End of Isolation: British Foreign Policy, 1900–1907* (London: Thomas Nelson, 1963); Norman Rich, *Great Power Diplomacy: 1814–1914* (New York: McGraw-Hill, 1992), pp. 381–389. Chamberlain quoted in Garvin, *Life of Joseph Chamberlain*, vol. 3, p. 515. On the French, Brown, *Fashoda Reconsidered*, pp. 76, 121–122, 125n; Andrew, *Théophile Delcassé*, pp. 158–179; Hayne, *French Foreign Office*, pp. 95–96, 180–184.

49. "Natural alliance:" *Siècle* quoted approvingly by the London *Times*, quoted in Stephen R. Rock, *Why Peace Breaks Out: Great Power Rapprochement in Historical Perspective*, 2nd ed. (Chapel Hill, N.C.: University of North Carolina Press, 1989), pp. 118–119, see pp. 86–89 for Germany. Andrew, *Théophile Delcassé;* P. J. V. Rolo, *Entente Cordiale: The Origins and Negotiations of the Anglo-French Agreements of 8 April 1904* (London: Macmillan, 1969); Monger, *End of Isolation*. Also Matthew, *Liberal Imperialists*, pp. 156–158, 199–215; Richard Ned Lebow, *Between Peace and War: The Nature of International Crisis* (Baltimore: Johns Hopkins University Press, 1961), pp. 326–330; Hayne, *French Foreign Office*, pp. 100, 103–106, 115. Franco-Russian alliance: George F. Kennan, *The Fateful Alliance: France, Russia, and the Coming of the First World War* (New York: Pantheon, 1984).

50. Friedberg, *Weary Titan*, esp. pp. 169–173, 184–188, 193–199; Stephen R. Rock, "Risk Theory Reconsidered: American Success and German Failure in the Coercion of Britain, 1890–1914," *Journal of Strategic Studies (Great Britain)* 11 (1988): 342–364; Rock, *Why Peace*, pp. 49–56, "innate justice" (Chamberlain) quoted p. 51; see also Garvin, *Life of Joseph Chamberlain*, pp. 66–69, 96; Campbell, *Great Britain and U.S.*, esp. pp. 4, 13, 191–194, 203–205, 208, also Charles S. Campbell, Jr., *Anglo-American Understanding, 1898–1903* (Baltimore: Johns Hopkins University Press, 1957), esp. chap. 2; Anderson, *Race and Rapprochement*, esp. pp. 17–23; Monger, *End of Isolation;* Bradford Perkins, *The Great Rapprochement: England and the United States, 1895–1914* (New York: Atheneum, 1968), esp. pp. 75–83, 310–312; Grenville, *Lord Salisbury and Foreign Policy*, see chaps. 15, 16 for ca. 1901 negotiations; for contrast, Kennedy, *Rise of Anglo-German Antagonism*.

CHAPTER FOURTEEN

Leagues of Republics

1. Jack Cargill, *The Second Athenian League: Empire or Free Alliance?* (Berkeley: University of California Press, 1981), pp. 14, 190–191.

2. Randolph Siverson and Juliann Emmons, "Birds of a Feather: Democratic Political Systems and Alliance Choices," *Journal of Conflict Resolution* 35 (1991): 285–306. The statistical significance of democratic alliance remains even if NATO is excluded, Michael W. Simon and Erik Gartzke, "Political System Similarity and Choice of Allies," *Journal of Con-*

flict Resolution 40 (1996): 617–635. Twice as likely: Michael Mousseau, "Democracy and Militarized Interstate Collaboration," *Journal of Peace Research* 34 (1997): 73–87. Negotiation: Ronald P. Barston, *Modern Diplomacy* (London: Longman, 1988), pp. 102–116; the inspection of Barston's cases in terms of regime type is my own.

3. John A. Vasquez, *The War Puzzle* (Cambridge: Cambridge University Press, 1993), pp. 158–169; Simon and Gartzke, "Choice of Allies."

4. Ivo D. Duchacek, *The Territorial Dimension of Politics Within, Among, and Across Nations* (Boulder: Westview, 1986); Daniel J. Elazar, *Exploring Federalism* (Tuscaloosa: University of Alabama Press, 1987); S. Rufus Davis, *The Federal Principle: A Journey Through Time in Quest of Meaning* (Berkeley: University of California Press, 1978); A. LeRoy Bennett, *International Organizations. Principles and Issues* (Englewood Cliffs, N.J.: Prentice-Hall, 1984). James R. Huntley, *Uniting the Democracies: Institutions of the Emerging Atlantic-Pacific System* (New York: New York University Press, 1980), is exceptional in noting democratic influence, pp. 26–32.

5. Russell Meiggs, *The Athenian Empire* (Oxford: Clarendon, 1972); Benjamin D. Meritt, H. T. Wade-Gery and Malcolm F. McGregor, *The Athenian Tribute Lists,* vol. 3 (Princeton, N.J.: American School of Classical Studies, 1950), vol. 3; and works cited in chapter 2, esp. Anthony Powell, *Athens and Sparta: Constructing Greek Political and Social History from 478 B.C.* (Portland, Ore.: Areopagitica, 1988), chaps. 1–3.

6. References above and G. E. M. de Ste. Croix, "Character of the Athenian Empire," *Historia* 3 (1954): 1–41; T. J. Quinn, "Thucydides and the Unpopularity of the Athenian Empire," *Historia* 13 (1964): 257–266.

7. J. A. O. Larson, *Greek Federal States: Their Institutions and History* (Oxford: Clarendon, 1968); John Buckler, *The Theban Hegemony, 371–362 B.C.* (Cambridge, Mass.: Harvard University Press, 1980), chap. 2. For Arcadian League see also ibid., pp. 70–71; Xenophon, *A History of My Times (Hellenica),* trans. Rex Warner (New York: Penguin, 1966), 6.5.3–12; Diodorus Siculus, *Histories,* in *Loeb Classical Library,* ed. C. H. Oldfather, C. Bradford Welles, and Charles L. Sherman (Cambridge, Mass.: Harvard University Press, 1946–1952), 15.59.

8. Polybius, *Histories,* 2.42, 2.73, from *The Rise of the Roman Empire,* trans. Ian Scott-Kilvert (New York: Penguin, 1979).

9. Thucydides, *History of the Peloponnesian War,* trans. Rex Warner (New York: Penguin, 1954), 1.19, 1.141, 5.30; G. E. M. de Ste. Croix, *The Origins of the Peloponnesian War* (Ithaca, N.Y.: Cornell University Press, 1972), pp. 115–118.

10. For wars involving the anocratic Aetolian League see appendix.

11. Philippe Dollinger, *The German Hansa,* ed. D. S. Ault and S. H. Steinberg, trans. D. S. Ault and S. H. Steinberg (Stanford, Calif.: Stanford University Press, 1970); Konrad Fritze, Johannes Schildhauer, and Walter Stark, *Die Geschichte der Hanse* (West Berlin: Verlage Das Europäische Buch, 1985); Johannes Schildhauer, *The Hansa: History and Culture,* trans. Katherine Vanovitch (Leipzig: Edition Leipzig, 1985).

12. Johannes Schildhauer, "Das soziale und kulturelle Milieu des hansischen Bürgertums," in *Der Ost- und Nordseeraum: Politik—Ideologie—Kultur vom 12. bis zum 17. Jahrhunderts,* ed. Konrad Fritze, Eckhard Müller-Mertens, and Johannes Schildhauer, Ab-

handlungen zur Handels- und Sozialgeschichte, vol. 25 (Weimar: Hermann Böhlaus Nach-folger, 1986), pp. 59–71, on pp. 61–63, 67.

13. A fleet from Lübeck sacked Stralsund in 1249, but neither was a true republic at that early point.

14. Dollinger, *German Hansa,* p. 197. Dollinger sees peace between fellow Germans, which is unconvincing considering the fighting among German princes. Friedel Vollbehr, *Die Holländer und die deutsche Hanse,* Hansischen geschichtsverein, Pfingstblätter, 21 (Lübeck: Selbstverlag des Vereins Lübeck, 1930), pp. 77–79.

15. Fritze, Schildhauer, and Stark, *Geschichte der Hanse,* p. 138; Dollinger, *German Hansa,* p. 108.

16. Reinhard Barth, *Argumentation und Selbstverständnis der Bürgeropposition in städtis-chen Auseinandersetzungen des Spätmittelalters,* Kollektive Einstellungen und sozialer Wan-del im Mittelalter, vol. 3 (Cologne: Böhlau, 1974), pp. 353–354, 361–365; Heinreich Schmidt, *Die Deutschen Städtechroniken als Spiegel des Bürgerlichen Selbstverständnisse im Spätmittelalter,* Schriftenreihe der Historischen Kommission bei der Bayerischen Akademie der Wissenschaften, vol. 3 (Göttingen: Vandenhoek & Ruprecht, 1958), pp. 76–79, 82–86; Karl Czok, "Zur Volksbewegung in der deutschen Städten des 14. Jahrhunderts: Bürgerkämpfe und antikuriale Opposition," in *Städtische Volksbewegungen im 14. Jahrhun-dert,* ed. Deutsche Historiker-Gesellschaft and Erika Engelmann (Berlin: Akademie-Ver-lag, 1960), pp. 157–169. Extension: Horst Wernicke, "Die Stadt in der Städtehanse—Zwischen städtischer Autonomie und bündischer Pflicht-erfüllen," in *Autonomie, Wirtschaft, und Kultur der Hansestädte,* ed. Konrad Fritze, Eckhard Müller-Mertens, and Walter Stark, Abhandlungen zur Handels- und Sozialgeschichte, vol. 23 (Weimar: Hermann Böhlaus Nachfolger, 1984), pp. 34–44.

17. Paul-Joachim Heinig, *Reichsstädte, Freie Städte und Königtum, 1389–1450: Ein Beitrag zur deutschen Verfassungsgeschichte* (Weisbaden: Steiner, 1983), pp. 1–7; Julius Weizsäcker, *Der rheinische Bund, 1254* (Tübingen: Laupp, 1879).

18. Heinz Angermeier, *Königtum und Landfriede im deutschen Spätmittelalter* (Munich: Beck, 1966), pp. 254–287; Wilhelm Vischer, "Geschichte des Schwäbischen Städtebundes der Jahre, 1376–1384," *Forschungen zur deutschen Geschichte* 2 (1862): 1–200; Johannes Schildhauer, "Der Schwäbische Städtebund—Ausdruck der Kraftentfaltung des deutsches Städtebürgertums in der Zweiten Hälfte des 14. Jahrhunderts," *Jahrbuch für Geschichte des Feudalismus* 1 (1977): 187–210.

19. Vischer, "Geschichte des Schwäbischen Städtebundes, pp. 100–103. What matters is not the tale's literal truth but what it reveals about attitudes. On need for cohesion see Hans Delbrück, *Medieval Warfare,* trans. Walter J. Renfroe, Jr. (Lincoln: University of Ne-braska Press, 1990), pp. 447–448, 581–584; John Philippe Contamine, *War in the Middle Ages,* trans. Michael Jones (Oxford: Blackwell, 1984), chaps. 7, 9.

20. Gina Fasoli, "La lega Lombarda: antecedenti, formazione, struttura," in *Scritti di Storia Medievale* (Bologna: Fotocrono Emiliana, 1974), pp. 258–278.

21. "Hermandades," *Diccionario de Historia de España,* vol. 2, 2nd ed. (Madrid: Re-vista de Occidente, 1968), pp. 344–345; Stephen Haliczer, *The Comuneros of Castile: The Forging of a Revolution, 1475–1521* (Madison, Wis.: University of Wisconsin Press, 1981).

22. Harry E. Dembrowski, *The Union of Lublin: Federation in the Golden Age* (New York: Columbia University Press, 1982).

23. See references in chapter 1, n. 17.

24. Ghibellines: Jacques Heers, *Parties and Political Life in the Medieval West,* trans. David Nichols (Amsterdam, N.Y.: Nathaniel-Holland, 1977), p. 146. German knights: Otto Eberbach, *Die deutsche Reichsritterschaft in ihrer staatsrechtlischen-politischen Entwicklung von den Anfängen bis zum Jahre 1495,* Beiträge zur Kulturgeschichte des Mittelalters und der Renaissance, no. 11 (Liepzig: Teubner, 1913), pp. 3–4, 14–18; Vischer, "Geschichte des Schwäbischen Städtebundes" pp. 37–41.

25. Lewis Morgan, *League of the Ho-de-no-san-nee; or Iroquois,* 2 vols., 1851 (New Haven: Human Relations Area Files, 1954); Matthew Dennis, *Cultivating a Landscape of Peace: Iroquois-European Encounters in Seventeenth-Century America* (Ithaca, N.Y.: Cornell University Press, 1993); Asher Wright, "Senaca Indians," *Ethnohistory* 4, no. 1859 (1957): 302–321A; George T. Hunt, *The Wars of the Iroquois: A Study in Intertribal Trade Relations* (Madison: University of Wisconsin Press, 1940), pp. 17–18, 67–68, 159–160.

26. David B. Stout, *San Blas Cuna Acculturation: An Introduction* (New York: Viking Fund, 1947), pp. 28–31. Dennis, *Cultivating a Landscape,* pp. 107–111, 235–236.

27. Dennis, *Cultivating a Landscape,* chap. 7; Francis Jennings, *The Ambiguous Iroquois Empire: The Covenant Chain Confederation of Indian Tribes with English Colonies from its Beginnings to the Lancaster Treaty of 1744* (New York: W. W. Norton, 1984), pp. 8, 95, 160–162. "Hospitality": Francis Jennings, "Iroquois Alliances in American History," in Francis Jennings et al., eds., *The History and Culture of Iroquois Diplomacy. An Interdisciplinary Guide to the Treaties of the Six Nations and Their League* (Syracuse, N.Y.: Syracuse University Press, 1985), chap. 3. Independent of me, this case was pointed out by Neta C. Crawford, "A Security Regime Among Democracies: Cooperation Among Iroquois Nations," *International Organization* 48 (1994): 345–385.

28. Thomas Gregor, "Uneasy Peace: Intertribal Relations in Brazil's Upper Xirgu," in *The Anthropology of War,* ed. Jonathan Haas (Cambridge: Cambridge University Press, 1990), pp. 105–124; Clark McCauley, "Conference Overview," in ibid., pp. 1–25.

29. Bruce G. Trigger, *The Children of Aataensic: A History of the Huron People to 1660,* 2 vols. (Montreal: McGill-Queens University Press, 1976).

30. Ivo D. Duchacek, *Comparative Federalism: The Territorial Dimension of Politics* (New York: Holt, Rinehart and Winston, 1970), pp. 332–335; Duchacek, *Territorial Dimension,* p. 96. On types of union see Karl W. Deutsch et al., *Political Community and the North Atlantic Area: International Organization in the Light of Historical Experience* (Princeton: Princeton University Press, 1957). Sabrina P. Ramet, *Nationalism and Federalism in Yugoslavia, 1962–1991* (Bloomington: Indiana University Press, 1992); Peter Duus, *Feudalism in Japan,* 3rd ed. (New York: McGraw-Hill, 1993), p. 80.

31. Harvey Kantor, "Latin American Federalism: Aspiration and Futility," in *Federalism: Infinite Variety in Theory and Practice,* ed. Valerie Earle (Itasca, Ill.: Peacock, 1968), pp. 185–208, on p. 207. Also Thomas L. Karnews, *The Failure of Union: Central America, 1824–1960,* rev. ed. (Tempe: Arizona State University, 1976).

32. Elazar, *Exploring Federalism,* p. 192, see pp. 91, 108–109; Arend Lijphart, *Democracy in Plural Societies: A Comparative Exploration* (New Haven: Yale University Press, 1977), pp. 9–16, 53–54, 99–103; Karnews, *Failure of Union,* pp. 249–250; Thomas M. Franck, ed., *Why Federations Fail: An Inquiry into the Requisites for Successful Federation* (New York: New York University Press, 1968), chap. 5. Oaths: Davis, *Federal Principle,* pp. 3, 215–216.

33. William J. Bouwsma, *Venice and the Defense of Republican Liberty: Renaissance Values in the Age of Counter-Reformation* (Berkeley: University of California Press, 1968), pp. 507–508, 562; E. O. G. Haitsma-Mulier, "Der Mythos Venedigs und der holländische Republikanismus," in *Der Ost- und Nordseeraum,* ed. K. Fritze, E. Müller-Mertens, and J. Schildhauer (Weimar: Hermann Böhlhausss Nachfolger, 1986), p. 114.

34. Most durable was the peace between the Russian and Austrian empires (as allies against Poland or Turkey). But in 1772 and 1854 they went to the brink of war, in 1812 the Austrians helped Napoleon's invasion of Russia, and between 1914 and 1918 the empires destroyed each other.

35. Daniel N. Nelson, ed., *Soviet Allies: The Warsaw Pact and the Issue of Reliability* (Boulder: Westview, 1984); Daniel N. Nelson, *Alliance Behavior in the Warsaw Pact* (Boulder: Westview, 1986); Dale R. Herspring and Ivan Volgyes, "Political Reliability in the Eastern European Warsaw Pact Armies," *Armed Forces and Society* 6 (1980): 270–296.

36. Burkhart Mueller-Hillebrand, *Germany and Its Allies in World War II: A Record of Axis Collaboration Problems* (Frederick, Md.: University Publications of America, 1980). For success of democracies at war see David A. Lake, "Powerful Pacifists: Democratic States and War," *American Political Science Review* 86 (1992): 24–37.

37. John G. Gagliardo, *Reich and Nation: The Holy Roman Empire as Idea and Reality, 1763–1806* (Bloomington: Indiana University Press, 1980), chaps. 1–3; G. Benecke, *Society and Politics in Germany, 1500–1750* (London: Routledge and Kegan Paul, 1974), chaps. 2, 3, 14; F. L. Carsten, *Princes and Parliaments in Germany from the Fifteenth to the Eighteenth Century* (Oxford: Clarendon, 1959).

38. Carsten, *Princes and Parliaments,* p. 430; Gerhard Ritter, *Frederick the Great,* trans. Peter Paret (Berkeley: University of California Press, 1968), p. 13.

39. The British parlimentary monarchy (a major German power as lord of Hanover) was central in creating and sustaining the German Confederation. Wolf D. Gruner, "The British Political, Social and Economic System and the Decision for War and Peace: Reflections on Anglo-German Relations, 1800–1939," *Journal of International Studies* 6 (1980): 189–218, see pp. 199–200. Frederik Ohles, *Germany's Rude Awakening: Censorship in the Land of the Brothers Grimm* (Kent, Ohio: Kent State University Press, 1992). For liberalism merging with federalism see Leonard Krieger, *The German Idea of Freedom: History of a Political Tradition,* (1957; reprint, Chicago: University of Chicago Press, 1972), chaps. 6, 7; Robert C. Binkley, *Realism and Nationalism* (New York: Harper and Row, 1963), chaps. 9, 12.

40. Kalevi J. Holsti, *Peace and War: Armed Conflicts and International Order, 1648–1989* (Cambridge: Cambridge University Press, 1991), chaps. 6, 7; Norman Rich, *Great Power Diplomacy: 1814–1914* (New York: McGraw-Hill, 1992); Paul Schroeder, *Metter-*

nich's Diplomacy at its Zenith, 1820–1823 (Austin: University of Texas Press, 1962). Also Paul Schroeder, "Did the Vienna Settlement Rest on a Balance of Power?" *American Historical Review* 97 (1992): 683–706, and articles by Enno E. Kraehe, Robert Jervis, and Wolf D. Gruner in "AHR Forum," *American Historical Review* 97 (1992): 707–735. Also Harold Nicolson, *The Congress of Vienna: A Study in Allied Unity; 1812–1822* (1946; reprint, New York: Harcourt Brace, Jovanovich, n.d.); Carsten Holbraad, *The Concert of Europe: A Study in German and British International Theory, 1815–1914* (London: Longman, 1970); Henry A. Kissinger, *A World Restored: Metternich, Castlereagh, and the Problem of Peace, 1812–1822,* (1957; reprint, Boston: Houghton Mifflin, 1973); Paul Schroeder, *Austria, Great Britain, and the Crimean War: The Destruction of the European Concert* (Ithaca, New York: Cornell University Press, 1972), pp. 405–406, gives the Concert of Europe's "rules."

41. Nicolson, *Congress of Vienna,* esp. pp. 216–218, for "legitimacy" see pp. 142–143. Ideals: Schroeder, "Vienna Settlement."

42. Geoffrey Best, *War and Society in Revolutionary Europe, 1770–1870* (New York: St. Martin's, 1982), chaps. 22, 23.

43. Stephen Walt, *The Origin of Alliances* (Ithaca, N.Y.: Cornell University Press, 1987), chap. 6.

44. During the Augsburg peace, in 1609 armies ravaged civilians in Bohemia. The Concert of Europe's peace ended in 1848 with Prussia vs. Denmark and Austria vs. Piedmont, but neither Denmark nor Piedmont was fully monarchical.

45. Krieger, *German Idea of Freedom,* chap. 8.

46. Otto Pflanze, *The Period of Unification, 1815–1871,* vol. 1 of *Bismarck and the Development of Germany* (Princeton: Princeton University Press, 1990), chaps. 7, 8; Lothar Gall, *1851–1871,* vol. 2 of *Bismarck: The White Revolutionary,* trans. J. A. Underwood (London: Allen and Unwin, 1986), chaps. 5, 6; Edward Crankshaw, *Bismarck* (New York: Viking, 1981), pp. 126–138.

47. William Carr, *The Origins of the Wars of German Reunification* (London: Longman, 1991), chap. 3. Bismarck's reliance on force is contrasted with British internationalism by W. N. Medlicott, *Bismarck, Gladstone, and the Concert of Europe* (London: Athlone, 1956), pp. 336–337; Holbraad, *Concert of Europe,* pp. 95–100.

48. David M. Lipset, "Papua New Guinea: The Melanesian Ethic and the Spirit of Capitalism, 1975–1986," in *Asia,* vol. 3 of *Democracy in Developing Countries,* ed. Larry Diamond, Juan D. Linz, and Seymour Martin Lipset (Boulder: Adamantine, 1989), pp. 383–421.

49. Abdullah Omran Taryam, *The Establishment of the United Arab Emirates, 1950–1985* (London: Croom Helm, 1987), chap. 6; John Duke Anthony, *Arab States of the Lower Gulf: People, Politics, Petroleum* (Washington, D.C.: Middle East Institute, 1975). Leonard Thompson, *The Unification of South Africa, 1902–1910* (Oxford: Clarendon, 1960); Leonard Thompson, "The Compromise of Union," in *South Africa, 1870–1966,* vol. 2 of *The Oxford History of South Africa,* ed. Monica Wilson and Leonard Thompson (New York: Oxford University Press, 1971), pp. 349–350; G. H. L. LeMay, *British Supremacy in South Africa, 1899–1907* (Oxford: Clarendon, 1965), chaps. 6–9.

50. Simon Schama, *Patriots and Liberators: Revolution in the Netherlands, 1780–1813* (New York: Knopf, 1977). See also Robert R. Palmer, *The Struggle,* vol. 1 of *The Age of the Democratic Revolution: A Political History of Europe and America, 1760–1800,* 2 vols. (Princeton: Princeton University Press, 1964), esp. vol. 2, chap. 10. On popular forces see Deutsch et al., *Political Community.*

51. Stephen D. Krasner, ed., *International Regimes* (Ithaca, N.Y.: Cornell University Press, 1983), pp. 1–21. On changes see Ethan A. Nadelmann, "Global Prohibition Regimes: The Evolution of Norms in International Society," *International Organization* 44 (1990): 479–526.

52. Charles W. Kegley, Jr. and Gregory A. Raymond, *When Trust Breaks Down: Alliance Norms and World Politics* (Columbia: University of South Carolina Press, 1990), chaps. 8–10.

53. Important contributions to international law did come from German principalities, where republican-style rule of law was valued in the mixed political culture. Arthur Nussbaum, *A Concise History of the Law of Nations* (New York: Macmillan, 1947). Judges: Anne-Marie Burley, "Law Among Liberal States: Liberal Internationalism and the Act of State Doctrine," *Columbia Law Review* 92 (1992): 1907–1996.

54. See Bennett, *International Organizations,* especially for the United Nations.

55. Walter Lipgens, *1945–1947,* vol. 1 of *A History of European Integration,* trans. P. S. Falla and A. J. Ryder (Oxford: Clarendon, 1982), pp. 44–62; Alan S. Milward, *The European Rescue of the Nation-State* (London: Routledge, 1992), pp. 326–333. On Comecon see Huntley, *Uniting the Democracies,* pp. 194–212.

56. Paul Preston and Denis Smyth, *Spain, the EEC and NATO,* vol. 22 of *Chatham House Papers* (London: Routledge and Kegan Paul, 1984), report quoted p. 4. Also Loukas Tsoukalis, *The European Community and Its Mediterranean Enlargement* (London: Allen and Unwin, 1981); Frances Nicholson and Roger East, *From the Six to the Twelve: The Enlargement of the European Communities* (Harlow, Essex: Longman, 1987), esp. chaps. 10, 11, "Freedom and democracy" quoted pp. 214–215.

57. J. Siotis, "The Politics of Greek Accession," in *Spain, Greece, and Community Politics,* vol. 6 of *The Mediterranean Challenge,* ed. G. Minet, J. Siotis, and P. Tsakaloyannis (Sussex, England: University of Sussex, Sussex European Research Center, 1981). Similarly, after a 1980 military coup in Turkey the EEC promptly froze relations; Nicholson and East, *From the Six,* pp. 202–205.

58. Tsoukalis, *European Community,* p. 124, see pp. 105, 128, 145, 159; Nicholas van Praag, "European Political Cooperation and the Southern Periphery," in Minet, Siotis, and Tsakaloyannis, *Mediterranean Challenge,* vol. 1; "osmosis": G. Contogeorgis, "The Greek View of the Community and Greece's Approach to Membership," *A Community of Twelve? The Impact of Further Enlargement on the European Communities,* ed. W. Wallace and I. Herreman (Brussels: DeTempel, 1978), pp. 22–31. U.S. Constitution, art. 4, sec. 4.

59. For example, Thomas Risse-Kappen, "Collective Identity in a Democratic Community: The Case of NATO," in *The Culture of National Security: Norms and Identity in World Politics,* ed. Peter J. Katzenstein (New York: Columbia University Press, 1996), pp. 357–399.

60. See Jeffrey Bradach and Robert Eccles, "Price, Authority, and Trust: From Ideal Types to Plural Forms," *Annual Review of Sociology* 15 (1989): 97–118. For discussing more recent work I thank Wesley Shrum.

61. See Risse-Kappen, "Collective Identity."

62. Ted Robert Gurr, "Persistence and Change in Political Systems, 1800–1971," *American Political Science Review* 68 (1974): 1482–1504. See also references in chapter 5, n. 23.

CHAPTER FIFTEEN
Crusading for Democracy

1. Thomas Carlyle, *The French Revolution* (1837), part 2, book 1, chap. 10.

2. Albert Mathiez, *La Révolution et les étrangers* (Paris: Renaissance, 1918), esp. chap. 6, "crusade" (in speech by Jacques Brissot, 1791), quoted p. 61; Jacques Godechot, *La Grande nation: L'expansion révolutionnaire de la France dans le monde, 1789–1799,* 2 vols. (Paris: Aubier, 1956), 2 vols., esp. vol. 1, chaps. 3, 4; Robert R. Palmer, *The Age of the Democratic Revolution: A Political History of Europe and America, 1760–1800,* vol. 2 (Princeton: Princeton University Press, 1964), vol. 2, pp. 56, 117–120, 219; William Doyle, *The Oxford History of the French Revolution* (Oxford: Clarendon, 1989), pp. 169–173; T.C.W. Blanning, *The Origins of the French Revolutionary Wars* (London: Longman, 1986), pp. 109–111.

3. Thessaly: Xenophon, *A History of My Times (Hellenica),* trans. Rex Warner (New York: Penguin, 1966), 2.3.36. Note also Athenians in the Aegean, A. W. Gomme, *A Historical Commentary on Thucydides* (Oxford: Clarendon, 1950–1956), vol. 1, pp. 293–294, 381; Russell Meiggs, *The Athenian Empire* (Oxford: Clarendon, 1972). For Athenians in Boeotia see Thucydides, *History of the Peloponnesian War,* trans. Rex Warner (New York: Penguin, 1954), 1.108, 1.113, 4.76. For Thebans sponsoring democracy see John Buckler, *The Theban Hegemony, 371–362 B.C.* (Cambridge, Mass.: Harvard University Press, 1980), pp. 70–71, 100; Xenophon, *Hellenica,* 7.1.43. See also chapter 2.

4. See chapters 1 (Flanders), 3 and 4 (Italy), 6 (Switzerland), and 14 (the Germanies).

5. Steven Runciman, *The Kingdom of Jerusalem and the Frankish East, 1100–1187,* vol. 2 of *A History of The Crusades* (Cambridge: Cambridge University Press, 1952), pp. 39–40, 48–55, 112–114.

6. Richard J. Crampton, *Bulgaria, 1878–1918: A History* (New York: Columbia University Press, 1983), chaps. 1–4, esp. p. 80; Mercia Macdermott, *A History of Bulgaria 1393–1885* (London: Allen and Unwin, 1962), pp. 329–333, 341.

7. Isocrates, *Panathenaikos,* in *Orations,* trans. George Norkin and Laurie Van Hook, Loeb Classical Library (Cambridge, Mass.: Harvard University Press, 1928–1945), 15:53–56.

8. Inattention even to the American efforts is discussed in Tony Smith, *America's Mission: The United States and the Worldwide Struggle for Democracy in the Twentieth Century* (Princeton: Princeton University Press, 1994), appendix, esp. pp. 346–348.

9. "Common cause": London newspaper quoted by Pauline Maier, *From Resistance to Revolution: Colonial Radicals and the Development of American Opposition to Britain, 1765–1776* (New York: Knopf, 1972), p. 198.

10. Here and below: Blanning, *Origins*; Palmer, *Democratic Revolution,* vol. 2, esp. chap. 2. Also Doyle, *Oxford History,* esp. pp. 179–183; Conor Cruise O'Brien, "Nationalism and the French Revolution," in *The Permanent Revolution: The French Revolution and Its Legacy, 1789–1989,* ed. Geoffrey Best (London: Fontana, 1988), pp. 17–48.

11. Speech of 24 April 1793, Maximilien Robespierre, *Oeuvres,* vol. 9 (Paris: Presses Universitaires de France, 1910), p. 469. Besides works cited above see Simon Schama, *Citizens: A Chronicle of the French Revolution* (New York: Knopf, 1989), pp. 586–597.

12. John Julius Norwich, *A History of Venice,* 2 vols. (New York: Random House, 1989), vol. 2, pp. 616–634.

13. Surveys are Palmer, *Democratic Revolution,* vol. 2; Godechot, *La Grande nation,* esp. vol. 2, chap. 13 and p. 689. Also Albert Sorel, *L'Europe et la Révolution française,* 10th ed. (Paris: Plon, 1910); Mathiez, *La Révolution et les étrangers,* chaps. 8–11; Harry Hearder, *Italy in the Age of the Risorgimento, 1790–1870* (New York: Longman, 1983); Simon Schama, *Patriots and Liberators. Revolution in the Netherlands, 1780–1813* (New York: Knopf, 1977).

14. Lamb quoted in Charles K. Webster, "Palmerston and the Liberal Movement, 1830–1841," *Politica* 3 (1938): 299–323, see pp. 299–300. A fine survey is William L. Langer, *Political and Social Upheaval, 1832–1852* (New York: Harper and Row, 1969), esp. chap. 3. On Mazzini see chapter 9, n. 32.

15. See Lawrence C. Jennings, *France and Europe in 1848: A Study of French Foreign Affairs in Time of Crisis* (Oxford: Clarendon, 1973) and other works cited in chapter 9.

16. Maier, *From Resistance to Revolution,* pp. 162, 198–199; more generally Palmer, *Democratic Revolution,* vol. 1.

17. James M. McPherson, *Abraham Lincoln and the Second American Revolution* (New York: Oxford University Press, 1991), chaps. 2, 4; James M. McPherson, *Battle Cry of Freedom: The Civil War Era* (New York: Oxford University Press, 1988), pp. 310–312, 494–499; Randall C. Jimerson, *The Private Civil War: Popular Thought During the Sectional Conflict* (Baton Rouge: Louisiana State University Press, 1988), pp. 38–49; James Oakes, *Slavery and Freedom: An Interpretation of the Old South* (New York: Knopf, 1990), pp. 183–191. See also chapter 7.

18. Surveys are William Gillette, *Retreat From Reconstruction, 1869–1879* (Baton Rouge: Louisiana State University Press, 1979); Eric Foner, *Reconstruction: America's Unfinished Revolution, 1863–1877* (New York: Harper and Row, 1988).

19. Arthur S. Link, *Woodrow Wilson: Revolution, War and Peace* (Arlington Heights, Ill.: AHM, 1979); Frederick S. Calhoun, *Power and Principle: Armed Intervention in Wilsonian Foreign Policy* (Kent, Ohio: Kent State University Press, 1986), esp. chaps. 4, 5; Lloyd C. Gardner, *Safe for Democracy: The Anglo-American Response to Revolution, 1913–1923* (New York: Oxford University Press, 1984); Lloyd E. Ambrosius, *Woodrow Wilson and the American Diplomatic Tradition: the Treaty Fight in Perspective* (New York: Cambridge University Press, 1987), chap. 1. Speech: Robert H. Ferrell, *Woodrow Wilson and World War I, 1917–1921* (New York: Harper and Row, 1985), pp. 1–3.

20. Works cited above and Arno Mayer, *Political Origins of the New Diplomacy, 1917–1918* (New Haven: Yale University Press, 1959); Gordon N. Levin, Jr., *Woodrow*

Wilson and World Politics. America's Response to War and Revolution (New York: Oxford University Press, 1968), esp. chap. 7, "dynamite" quoted p. 248; Thomas J. Knock, *To End All Wars. Woodrow Wilson and the Quest for a New World Order* (New York: Oxford University Press, 1992), pp. 171–175; Victor H. Rothwell, *British War Aims and Peace Diplomacy, 1914–1918* (Oxford: Clarendon, 1971), pp. 42–49, 283; David Fromkin, *A Peace to End All Peace: Creating the Modern Middle East, 1914–1922* (New York: Henry Holt, 1989), pp. 290, 561; Jan Willem Schulte, *Woodrow Wilson: A Life for World Peace* (Berkeley: University of California Press, 1991), pp. 259–262.

21. On individual and collective rights see chapter 13.

22. Here and below see Paul W. Drake, "From Good Men to Good Neighbors: 1912–1932," in *Exporting Democracy: The United States and Latin America,* ed. Abraham F. Lowenthal (Baltimore: Johns Hopkins University Press, 1991), pp. 3–40; David Healy, *Drive to Hegemony: The United States in the Caribbean, 1898–1917* (Madison: University of Wisconsin Press, 1988); Karl Bermann, *Under the Big Stick. Nicaragua and the United States Since 1848* (Boston: South End, 1986); Smith, *America's Mission;* Lester D. Langley, *The Banana Wars: An Inner History of American Empire, 1900–1934* (Lexington: University Press of Kentucky, 1983); Lester D. Langley, *America and the Americas: The United States in the Western Hemisphere* (Athens: University of Georgia Press, 1989); Walter LaFeber, *The American Age: United States Foreign Policy at Home and Abroad Since 1750* (New York: W. W. Norton, 1989); Louis A. Pérez, Jr., *Cuba Between Empires, 1878–1902* (Pittsburgh: University of Pittsburgh Press, 1983); Louis A. Pérez, Jr., *Cuba Under the Platt Amendment, 1902–1934* (Pittsburgh: University of Pittsburgh Press, 1986).

23. Richard V. Salisbury, "Good Neighbors? The United States and Latin America in the Twentieth Century," in *American Foreign Relations: A Historiographical Review,* ed. Gerald K. Haines and J. Samuel Walker (Westport, Conn.: Greenwood, 1981), pp. 311–333; Calhoun, *Power and Principle,* chap. 3; Healy, *Drive to Hegemony;* Jules Benjamin, "The Framework of U.S. Relations with Latin America in the Twentieth Century: An Interpretive Essay," *Diplomatic History* 11 (1987): 91–112.

24. On agrarian reform see Smith, *America's Mission,* esp. pp. 18, 52–53, 217–219.

25. Healy, *Drive to Hegemony,* pp. 227–237; Langley, *Banana Wars,* chaps. 5, 6; Theodore Paul Wright, Jr., *American Support of Free Elections Abroad* (Washington, D.C.: Public Affairs, 1964).

26. The best-studied example is Nicaragua; Neill Macaulay, *The Sandino Affair* (Chicago: Quadrangle, 1967); Bernard Diederich, *Somoza and the Legacy of U.S. Involvement in Central America* (New York: E. P. Dutton, 1981).

27. Arthur Hearnden, ed., *The British in Germany: Educational Reconstruction After 1945* (London: Hamish Hamilton, 1978), pp. 77, 101, 108–130.

28. A survey is Joshua Muravchik, *Exporting Democracy: Fulfilling America's Destiny* (Washington, D.C.: American Enterprise Institute, 1991), esp. chap. 8. Here and below also: Edward N. Peterson, *The American Occupation of Germany: Retreat to Victory* (Detroit: Wayne State University Press, 1977); Howard B. Schonberger, *Aftermath of War: Americans and the Remaking of Japan, 1945–1952* (Kent, Ohio: Kent State University Press, 1989); Nicholas Pronay and Keith Wilson, eds., *The Political Re-education of Germany and*

Her Allies After World War II (Totowa, N.J.: Barnes and Noble, 1985); Theodore Cohen, *Remaking Japan: The American Occupation As New Deal,* ed. Herbert Passin (New York: Macmillan, 1987); Toshio Nishi, *Unconditional Democracy, Education and Politics in Occupied Japan, 1945–1952* (Stanford, Calif.: Hoover Institution, 1982); Richard B. Finn, *Winners in Peace: MacArthur, Yoshida and Postwar Japan* (Berkeley: University of California Press, 1992).

29. MacArthur quoted in Nishi, *Unconditional Democracy,* p. 193, and Muravchik, *Exporting Democracy,* p. 100.

30. James F. Tent, *Mission on the Rhine: Re-education and Denazification in American-Occupied Germany* (Chicago: University of Chicago Press, 1982); Gordon Daniels, "The Re-education of Imperial Japan," in Pronay and Wilson, *Political Re-education,* pp. 203–217; Hearnden, *British in Germany,* esp. Robert Birley, "British Policy in Retrospect," pp. 46–63; Nishi, *Unconditional Democracy,* pp. 98–99, 176–186, and chap. 7; Kyoko Hirano, *Mr. Smith Goes to Tokyo: Japanese Cinema Under the American Occupation, 1945–1952* (Washington, D.C.: Smithsonian Institution Press, 1992).

31. Hermann-Josef Rupieper, *Der Wurzeln der westdeutschen Nachkriegsdemocratie: Der amerikanische Beitrag, 1945–1952* (Opladen: Westdeutscher, 1993).

32. Jeffrey M. Diefendorf, Axel Frohm, and Herman-Josef Rupierer, *American Policy and the Reconstruction of West Germany* (Washington, D.C.: German Historical Institute, 1993), especially articles by Rebecca Boehling and Diethelm Prowe.

33. David P. Conradt, "Changing German Political Culture," in *The Civic Culture Revisited,* ed. Gabriel A. Almond and Sidney Verba (Boston: Little, Brown, 1980), pp. 212–272; Kendall Barker, Russell Dalton, and Kai Hildebrandt, *Germany Transformed: Political Culture and the New Politics* (Cambridge, Mass.: Harvard University Press, 1981). Some questioned whether Japan, ruled by a bureaucracy and a single party, was truly a democracy. But Japanese leaders followed the practices that this study finds essential—consensus-seeking rather than violence with no major category treated as an enemy. Gavan McCormack and Yoshio Sugimoto, eds., *Democracy in Contemporary Japan* (Armonk, N.Y.: M. E. Sharpe, 1986); Takeshi Ishida and Ellis S. Krauss, eds., *Democracy in Japan* (Pittsburgh: University of Pittsburgh Press, 1989); Jun-ichi Kyogoku, *The Political Dynamics of Japan,* trans. Nobutaka Ike (Tokyo: University of Tokyo Press, 1987).

34. Paul Ginsborg, *A History of Contemporary Italy: Society and Politics, 1943–1988* (New York: Penguin, 1990), pp. 64–70, 115–118, and chaps. 2, 3; Antonio Gambino, *Storia del dopoguerra: Dalla Liberazione al potere D.C.* (Rome-Bari: Laterza, 1975), esp. pp. 446–457; Muravchik, *Exporting Democracy,* pp. 122–127; Sallie Pisani, *The CIA and the Marshall Plan* (Lawrence: University Press of Kansas, 1991), pp. 66–67. For the 1950s, William Colby with Peter Forbath, *Honorable Men: My Life in the CIA* (New York: Simon and Schuster, 1978), chap. 4.

35. James Morris, *Heaven's Command: An Imperial Progress* (San Diego: Harcourt Brace Jovanovich, 1973), p. 278.

36. Phillip Darby, *Three Faces of Imperialism: British and American Approaches to Asia and Africa, 1870–1970* (New Haven: Yale University Press, 1987); Kenneth Robinson, *The Dilemmas of Trusteeship: Aspects of British Colonial Policy Between the Wars* (London: Ox-

ford University Press, 1965); Emily S. Rosenberg, *Spreading The American Dream: American Economic and Cultural Expansion, 1890–1945* (New York: Hill and Wang, 1982), pp. 208–212; John Flint, "Planned Decolonization and Its Failure in British Africa," *African Affairs* 82 (1983): 389–411; Robert Pearce, "The Colonial Office and Planned Decolonization in Africa," *African Affairs* 83 (1984): 77–93.

37. Robert H. Jackson, "The Weight of Ideas in Decolonization: Normative Change in International Relations," in *Ideas on Foreign Policy: Beliefs, Institutions and Political Change,* ed. Judith Goldstein and Robert O. Keohane (Ithaca, N.Y.: Cornell University Press, 1993), pp. 111–138.

38. Works cited above and Prosser Gifford and William Roger Lewis, eds., *Decolonization and African Independence: The Transfers of Power, 1960–1980* (New Haven: Yale University Press, 1988), esp. Crawford Young, "The Colonial State and Post-Colonial Crisis," pp. 1–31, and Basil Davidson, "Conclusion," pp. 505–514; Henri Grimal, *Decolonization: The British, French, Dutch and Belgian Empires, 1919–1963,* trans. Stephen De Vos (Boulder: Westview, 1978); Ronald Robinson, "Andrew Cohen and the Transfer of Power in Tropical Africa, 1940–1951," in *Decolonisation and After: The British and French Experiences,* ed. W. H. Morris-Jones and Georges Fischer (London: Cass, 1980), pp. 50–72; John Darwin, "British Decolonization Since 1945: A Pattern or a Puzzle?" in *Perspectives on Imperialism and Decolonization,* ed. R. F. Holland and Gowher Rizvi (London: Cass, 1984), pp. 185–209. On post-colonial ethnic strife see Donald L. Horowitz, *Ethnic Groups in Conflict* (Berkeley: University of California Press, 1985), chap. 11 and pp. 186–194. On "waves" of democratization and retrenchment see Samuel P. Huntington, *The Third Wave: Democratization in the Late Twentieth Century* (Norman: University of Oklahoma Press, 1991), chap. 1.

39. On the independence of democracy from culture see Francis Fukuyama, *The End of History and the Last Man* (New York: Free Press, 1992), pp. 219–222. On ethnic vs. democratic identity see Michael E. Brown, ed., *Ethnic Conflict and International Security* (Princeton: Princeton University Press, 1993), esp. David Welsh, "Domestic Politics and Ethnic Conflict," pp. 43–60. On Botswana see John A. Wiseman, *Democracy in Black Africa: Survival and Renewal* (New York: Paragon House, 1990); Michael Crowder, "Botswana and the Survival of Liberal Democracy in Africa," in Gifford and Lewis, *Decolonization,* pp. 461–476. Also: Eliphas G. Mukonoweshuro, "Containing Political Instability in a Poly-Ethnic Society: The Case of Mauritius," *Ethnic and Racial Studies* 4 (1991), pp. 199–224.

40. Wright, *American Support,* chap. 9; Leslie Bethell, "From the Second World War to the Cold War: 1944–1954," in Lowenthal, *Exporting Democracy,* pp. 41–70; Robert Dallek, *The American Style of Foreign Policy: Cultural Politics and Foreign Affairs* (New York: Knopf, 1983); Richard J. Barnet, *Intervention and Revolution: The United States in the Third World* (New York: World, 1968), pp. 169–174.

41. Here and below, summaries are LaFeber, *American Age;* Muravchik, *Exporting Democracy.* See Barnet, *Intervention and Revolution,* esp. chap. 11; Lloyd G. Gardner, *A Covenant with Power. America and World Order from Wilson to Reagan* (New York: Oxford

University Press, 1984); Darby, *Three Faces of Imperialism*, chaps. 8, 9; Dallek, *American Style of Foreign Policy;* John Lewis Gaddis, "New Conceptual Approaches to the Study of American Foreign Relations," *Diplomatic History* 14 (1990): 405–423, see pp. 410–411, and see references on Latin America in chapter 13.

42. A key exploration of this is R. J. Rummel, *Power Kills: Democracy as a Method of Nonviolence* (New Brunswick, N.J.: Transaction, 1996).

43. Stephen G. Rabe, *Eisenhower and Latin America: The Foreign Policy of Anticommunism* (Chapel Hill: University of North Carolina Press, 1988), chaps. 6, 8; Joshua Muravchik, *The Uncertain Crusade: Jimmy Carter and the Dilemmas of Human Rights Policy* (Lanham, Md.: Hamilton, 1986); Smith, *America's Mission*, esp. chaps. 8, 9; Gaddis Smith, *Morality, Reason, and Power: American Diplomacy in the Carter Years* (New York: Hill and Wang, 1986); Zbigniew Brzezinski, *Power and Principle: Memoirs of the National Security Advisor, 1977–1981* (New York: Farrar, Strauss, Giroux, 1983), pp. 124–129, 139–143.

44. "Crusade": 8 June 1982, in U.S. Department of State, *American Foreign Policy: Current Documents* (Washington, D.C.: U.S. Government Printing Office, 1982), pp. 14–20.

45. Thomas Carothers, *In the Name of Democracy: U.S. Policy Toward Latin America in the Reagan Years* (Berkeley: University of California Press, 1991); Brad Roberts, ed., *The New Democracies. Global Change and U.S. Policy* (Cambridge, Mass.: MIT Press, 1990); Susanne Jonas, "Reagan Administration Policy in Central America," in *Reagan and the World*, ed. David E. Kyvig (Westport, Conn.: Greenwood, 1990), pp. 97–118; Lowenthal, *Exporting Democracy.* Huntington, *Third Wave*, reckons the Carter and Reagan administrations gave "critical" help to democratization in ten nations and "contributed" in six more, pp. 77–85.

46. Walesa quoted in Daniel Patrick Moynihan, *On the Law of Nations* (Cambridge, Mass.: Harvard University Press, 1990), p. 125.

47. "Natural friends": Andrei Kozyrev quoted in his "The Lagging Partnership," *Foreign Affairs* 73 (1994): 59–71, on p. 59. "Assure our security:" Bush quoted by James A. Baker 3rd, *New York Times*, 5 Aug. 1992. Clinton: *New York Times*, 26 Jan. 1994. See also Bruce Russett, *Grasping the Democratic Peace: Principles for a Post-Cold War World* (Princeton: Princeton University Press, 1993), pp. 128–129.

48. Lowenthal, *Exporting Democracy;* Muravchik, *Exporting Democracy;* Giuseppe Di Palma, *To Craft Democracies: An Essay on Democratic Transitions* (Berkeley: University of California Press, 1990); National Research Council, Commission on Behavioral and Social Sciences and Education, *The Transition to Democracy: Proceedings of a Workshop* (Washington, D.C.: National Academy Press, 1991); Guillermo O'Donnell, Phillippe C. Schmitter, and Laurence Whitehead, eds., *Transitions from Authoritarian Rule: Prospects for Democracy* (Baltimore: Johns Hopkins University Press, 1986), part 4; Horowitz, *Ethnic Groups*, part 4; a review is Doh Chull Shin, "On the Third Wave of Democratization: A Synthesis and Evaluation," *World Politics* 47 (1994): 135–170; still valuable is Robert A. Dahl, *Polyarchy: Participation and Opposition* (New Haven: Yale University Press, 1971), chaps. 8–11.

49. Huntington, *Third Wave*, pp. 192–207 and chaps. 3, 4.

50. Gary Clyde Hufbauer, Jeffery J. Schott, and Kimberly Ann Elliot, *Economic Sanctions Reconsidered: History and Current Policy,* 2nd ed. (Washington, D.C.: Institute for Economic Relations, 1990).

51. Muravchik, *Exporting Democracy;* Larry Diamond, "Promoting Democracy," *Foreign Policy* 87 (Summer 1992): 25–46. On open markets see Smith, *America's Mission,* pp. 295–297 and passim. On one important private initiative see George Soros, *Underwriting Democracy* (New York: Free Press, 1991), chaps. 1, 7.

52. Huntington, *Third Wave;* Stanley Kober, "Idealpolitik," *Foreign Policy* 79 (1990): 3–24; Horowitz, *Ethnic Groups,* esp. pp. 570–571, 681–684; Douglas J. Macdonald, *Adventures in Chaos: American Intervention for Reform in the Third World* (Cambridge, Mass.: Harvard University Press, 1992), esp. pp. 277–282.

53. See Edward D. Mansfield and Jack Snyder, "Democratization and the Danger of War," *International Security* 20, no. 1 (Summer 1995): 5–38, and Reinhard Wolf et al., "Correspondence: Democratization and the Danger of War," *International Security* 20, no. 4 (Spring 1996): 176–207.

54. George Modelski and Gardner Perry III, "Democratization in Long Perspective," *Technological Forecasting and Social Change* 39 (1991): 23–34; Michael Doyle, "Liberalism and World Politics," *American Political Science Review* 80 (1986): 1151–1161; Russett, *Grasping the Democratic Peace,* esp. pp. 132–138; Huntington, *Third Wave,* chap. 6.

APPENDIX

Military Confrontations Between Approximately Republican Regimes of the Same Kind

1. A reliable secondary source would be a historian who used primary sources, reading and speaking Punic. Carthage was perhaps aristocratic-anocratic. See Serge Lancel, *Carthage: A History,* trans. Antonia Nevill (Oxford: Blackwell, 1995), pp. 115–120.

2. Herodotus, *The Histories,* trans. George Rawlinson (New York: Dial, 1928), 9:86–88.

3. Thucydides, *History of the Peloponnesian War,* trans. Rex Warner (New York: Penguin, 1954), 8:45ff., esp. pp. 90–91.

4. See Donald Kagan, *The Archidamian War* (Ithaca, N.Y.: Cornell University Press, 1974), pp. 270–273; Ronald P. Legon, "Megara and Mytilene," *Phoenix* 22 (1968): 200–225; Ronald Legon, *Megara: The Political History of a Greek City State to 336 B.C.* (Ithaca, N.Y.: Cornell University Press, 1981), pp. 235–247.

5. Thucydides, 3.107–111, 5.69; Kagan, *Archidamian,* pp. 213–214, 334; for further references, G. E. M. de Ste. Croix, *The Origins of the Peloponnesian War* (Ithaca, N.Y.: Cornell University Press, 1972), p. 98. The other chief Spartan allies were from Ambracia, whose Corinthian garrison (Thucydides, 4.42) suggests oligarchic rule.

6. Xenophon, *A History of My Times (Hellenica),* trans. Rex Warner (New York: Penguin, 1966), 1.2.7–13.

7. Thucydides, 8.17, 24–25, 57, 60–61, 99; Xenophon, 1.2.3; Diodorus Siculus, *Histories,* in *Loeb Classical Library* (Cambridge, Mass.: Harvard University Press, 1946–1952), 13.69.2. Chios: Thucydides, 8.14. Thucydides liked to describe one case as representative

of others, and that looks like his method with Chios and Miletus. Xenophon, 1.6.8–12 on fear of the Spartan commander in Miletus; cf. Thucydides, 8.31 on Spartan taking of hostages in Chios and Xenophon, 2.4.9–10 on intimidation of voters.

8. Thucydides, 2.25.

9. Thucydides, 3.94–98; J. A. O. Larsen, *Greek Federal States: Their Institutions and History* (Oxford: Clarendon, 1968), pp. 79–80, 135–136, 195–203.

10. Thucydides, 4.120–122, 129–131.

11. Thucydides, 4.104–106, cf. 4.88, 4.123; Kagan, *Archidamian*, pp. 294–298.

12. Thucydides, 4.84–88; see A. W. Gomme, *A Historical Commentary on Thucydides*, 3 vols. (Oxford: Clarendon, 1950–1956), vol. 3, pp. 554–557.

13. Simon Hornblower, *The Greek World, 479–323 B.C.* (London: Methuen, 1983), p. 169; Diodorus Siculus, 14.97.

14. Diodorus Siculus, 15.23–39; on Phocis see Larsen, *Greek Federal States*, pp. 44–47.

15. Polybius, *The Rise of the Roman Empire (Histories)*, trans. Ian Scott-Kilvert (New York: Penguin, 1979), passim; Julius Beloch, *Griechische Geschichte*, vol. 3 (Strasbourg: Trübner, 1904), pp. 642, 645–660, 744–746; F. W. Walbank, "Macedonia and the Greek Leagues," in *The Hellenistic World*, vol. 7, part 1 of *The Cambridge Ancient History*, ed. F. W. Walbank et al. (Cambridge: Cambridge University Press, 1984), pp. 446–481; Larsen, *Greek Federal States*, pp. 195–214, 313–314, 327–354.

16. Charles Calvert Bayley, *War and Society in Renaissance Florence: The "De Militia" of Leonardo Bruni* (Toronto: University of Toronto Press, 1961), pp. 97–104; François-Tommy Perrens, *Histoire de Florence depuis ses origines jusqu'à la domination des Médicis*, 6 vols., 2nd ed. (Paris: Fontemoing, 1873–1883), vol. 6, pp. 326–351; Rinaldo degli Albizzi, *Comissioni di Rinaldo degli Albizzi per il commune di Firenze dal 1394–1433*, 3 vols. (Florence, 1873), vol. 3, pp. 192–206; Giovanni Cavalcanti, *Istorie fiorentine*, 2 vols. (Florence, 1838–39), sections 6–8.

17. Cecelia M. Ady, *A History of Milan Under the Sforza* (London: Methuen, 1907), pp. 37–57; William Pollard Urquhart, *Life and Times of Francesco Sforza*, 2 vols. (Edinburgh: Blackwood, 1852), vol. 2, book 5; *Storia di Milano*, 16 vols. (Milan: Fondazione Treccani degli Alfieri, 1953–1962), vol. 6, part 2; Bernandino Corio, *Storia di Milano*, 2 vols., 1554, ed. Anna Morisi Guerra (Turin: Unione Tipigrafico, 1978), pp. 1216–1303; Samuele Romanin, *Storia documentata di Venezia*, 10 vols. (Venice: Naratovich, 1853–61), vol. 4, pp. 213–221. "As free men" quoted in Hans Baron, *The Crisis of the Early Italian Renaissance: Civic Humanism and Republican Liberty in an Age of Classicism and Tyranny*, rev. ed. (Princeton: Princeton University Press, 1966), p. 398.

18. *Storia di Milano*, vol. 6, p. 404; Gaetano Cozzi and Michael Knapton, *La Repubblica di Venezia nell'età moderna dalla guerra di Chioggia al 1517*, vol. 12, book 1 of *Storia d'Italia (Galasso)* (Turin: Unione Tipigrafico, 1986), pp. 207–209.

19. Corio, *Storia di Milano*, pp. 1235–1237, 1278–1279.

20. Francesco Guiccardini, *Storia d'Italia*, 3 vols., ed. Silvana Seidel Menchi (Turin: Giulio Einaudi, 1971), vol. 1, passim; Piero Vaglienti, *Storia dei suoi tempi, 1492–1514*, ed. Giuliani Berti et al. (Pisa: Nistri-Lischi e Pacini, 1982), p. 52; Iacopo Nardi, *Istorie della Città di Firenze*, ed. Agenore Gelli (Florence: Le Monnier, 1858), 3.7, pp. 145–147; Gino

Benvenuti, *Storia dell'assedio di Pisa (1494–1509)* (Pisa: Giardini, 1969), pp. 72–73. The republics of Lucca, Siena, and Genoa also gave nominal support to Pisa.

21. Besides the general histories such as Johannes Dierauer, *Histoire de la Confédéra-tion Suisse,* 5 vols., trans. Aug. Reymond (Lausanne: Payot, 1912–1919), vol. 2, book 5, chap. 4, see Thomas A. Brady, Jr., *Turning Swiss: Cities and Empire, 1450–1550* (Cambridge: Cambridge University Press, 1985), esp. pp. 35–38, 55–70, 222–230; Heinrich Ulmann, *Kaiser Maximilian I,* vol. 1 (Stuttgart: Cotta, 1884), chap. 6. On politics see Christopher R. Friedrichs, "The Swiss and German City-States," in *The City-State in Five Cultures,* ed. Robert Griffeth and Carol G. Thomas (Santa Barbara: ABC-Clio, 1981). For imperial intervention see, e.g., Helmut Maurer, *Konstanz im Mittelalter,* vol. 2 (Constance: Stadler, 1989), pp. 213–246. "Only in obedience" quoted in Brady, *Turning Swiss,* p. 67. On South German towns see also chapter 14.

22. Ernst Bock, "Der Schwäbische Bund und sein Verfassung (1488–1534)," in *Untersuchungen zur deutschen Staats- und Rechtsgeschichte,* vol. 137 (old series) (Breslau: Marcus, 1927), esp. pp. 88–90; Wilhelm Martens, *Geschichte der Stadt Konstanz* (Konstanz: K. Gess, 1911), pp. 190–192; Ulmann, *Kaiser Maximilian I,* vol. 1, pp. 716–718, 725–726. Richard Feller, *Geschichte Berns* (Bern: Herbert Lang, 1949), vol. 1, pp. 473–491, describes Bern's reluctance and combat losses, apparently against imperial troops; Peter F. Kramml, "Die Reichsstadt Konstanz, der Bund der Bodenseestädte und die Eidgenossen," in *Die Eidgenossen und ihre Nachbarn im Deutschen Reich des Mittelalters,* ed. Peter Rück (Marburg an der Lahn: Basilisken, 1991), describes Constance's reluctance and 130 deaths, probably against Forest States; Joseph Bader, *Geschichte der Stadt Freiburg im Breisgau,* vol. 1 (Freiburg: Herder, 1882), pp. 492, 498–502 describes Freiburg's bloodless role; for Nuremberg's avoidance of combat and other research I thank Johannes Wolfart, who checked through Willibald Pirckheimer, *Der Schweizerkrieg,* trans. E. Münch (Berlin: Militärverlag der DDR, 1988); see esp. pp. 79, 106, and 151–153; also Karl August Klüpfel, *Urkunden zur Geschichte des Schwäbischen Bundes (1488–1533),* vol. 1, Bibliothek des Literarischen Vereins in Stuttgart, 14 (Stuttgart, 1846), see p. 319. I have not studied all the combats in full detail.

23. Cecil Roth, *The Last Florentine Republic* (London: Methuen, 1925); Guicciardini, *Storia d'Italia,* vol. 3, 19.15, pp. 2024–2025.

24. Paul Simson, *Geschichte der Stadt Danzig, 1517–1626,* vol. 2 of *Geschichte der Stadt Danzig,* 1918–1924 (Aalen: Scientia, 1967), pp. 270–319. "I wish to rule," quoted in Norman Davies, *The Origins to 1795,* vol. 2 of *God's Playground: A History of Poland* (New York: Columbia University Press, 1982), p. 424; also see pp. 421–425. On the Polish oligarchy see chapter 6.

25. Robert Middlekauff, *The Glorious Cause: The American Revolution, 1763–1789* (New York: Oxford University Press, 1982); Peter D. G. Thomas, *Tea Party to Independence: The Third Phase of the American Revolution, 1773–1776* (Oxford: Clarendon, 1991); Pauline Maier, *From Resistance to Revolution: Colonial Radicals and the Development of American Opposition to Britain, 1765–1776,* (New York: Knopf, 1972); Jerrilyn Greene Marston, *King and Congress: The Transfer of Political Legitimacy, 1774–1776* (Princeton: Princeton University Press, 1987); Robert W. Tucker and David C. Hendrickson, *The Fall of the First*

British Empire: Origins of the War of American Independence (Baltimore: Johns Hopkins University Press, 1982); Garry Wills, *Inventing America: Jefferson's Declaration of Independence* (Garden City, N.Y.: Doubleday, 1978), pp. 310–319. "Royal brute:" Tom Paine, *Common Sense* (London: Penguin, 1976); Paine found it "difficult to find a proper name" for the English government but argued that it was "nearly as monarchical as France or Spain," p. 81.

26. Oaths: Gordon S. Wood, *The Radicalism of the American Revolution* (New York: Knopf, 1992), p. 215.

27. Ira D. Gruber, "The American Revolution as a Conspiracy: The British View," *William and Mary Quarterly* 26 (1969): 360–372; Paul Langford, "British Correspondence in the Anglo-American Press, 1763–1775: A Study in Anglo-American Misunderstanding Before the American Revolution," in *The Press and the American Revolution,* ed. Bernard Bailyn and John B. Hench (Boston: Northeastern University Press, 1981), pp. 273–313. On the political cultures see David Hackett Fischer, *Paul Revere's Ride* (Oxford: Oxford University Press, 1994), pp. 3–43.

28. Albert Hall Bowman, *The Struggle for Neutrality: Franco-American Diplomacy During the Federalist Era* (Knoxville: University of Tennessee Press, 1974), see chap. 5 for ambassadors; Alexander DeConde, *The Quasi-War: The Politics and Diplomacy of the Undeclared War with France, 1797–1801* (New York: Scribner's, 1966); William C. Stinchcombe, *The XYZ Affair* (Westport, Conn.: Greenwood, 1980); Richard Buel, Jr., *Securing the Revolution. Ideology and American Politics, 1789–1815* (Ithaca, N.Y.: Cornell University Press, 1972), chaps. 7–10; Stanley Elkins and Eric McKitrick, *The Age of Federalism* (New York: Oxford University Press, 1993), chap. 8 and passim; Albert Sorel, *Bonaparte et le Directoire, 1795–1799,* vol. 5 of *L'Europe et la Révolution française,* 10th ed. (Paris: Plon, 1910), esp. chap. 6.

29. William Doyle, *The Oxford History of the French Revolution* (Oxford: Clarendon, 1989), chap. 14; Georges LeFebvre, *From 1793 to 1799,* vol. 2 of *The French Revolution,* trans. John H. Stewart and James Friguglietti (London: Routledge & Kegan Paul, 1964), chaps. 5–8. Franchise: Peter Campbell, *French Electoral Systems and Elections, 1789–1957* (London: Faber and Faber, 1958), p. 53.

30. "Enemy" quoted in Bowman, *Struggle for Neutrality,* p. 241, see also chap. 10; also Robert R. Palmer, *The Age of the Democratic Revolution: A Political History of Europe and America, 1760–1800,* vol. 2 (Princeton: Princeton University Press, 1964), pp. 266–268; "British party" quoted in Buel, *Securing the Revolution,* p. 163; see Robert W. Tucker and David C. Hendrickson, *Empire of Liberty: The Statecraft of Thomas Jefferson* (New York: Oxford University Press, 1990).

31. "Catacomb": Stanley Elkins and Eric McKitrick, *The Age of Federalism* (New York: Oxford University Press, 1993), p. 569, see also pp. 549–582; Michel Poniatowski, *Talleyrand et le Directoire, 1796–1800* (Paris: Librarie académique Perrin, 1982), chap. 18.

32. If we include men killed after Napoleon seized dictatorial power in 1799, the total reaches several hundred. *Naval Battles of the United States* (Boston: Higgins, Bradley and Dayton, 1859); Gardner W. Allen, *Our Naval War with France* (Boston: Houghton Mifflin, 1909).

33. William G. McLoughlin, *Cherokee Renascence in the New Republic* (Princeton: Princeton University Press, 1986), chaps. 18–21; Marion L. Starkey, *The Cherokee Nation* (New York: Knopf, 1946); Louis Filler and Allen Guttmann, *Removal of the Cherokee Nation: Manifest Destiny or National Dishonor?* (Boston: D.C. Heath, 1962); Thomas Wilkins, *Cherokee Tragedy: The Ridge Family and the Decimation of a People,* 2nd ed. (Norman: University of Oklahoma Press, 1986); Grant Foreman, *Indian Removal: The Emigration of the Five Civilized Tribes of Indians* (Norman: University of Oklahoma Press, 1932); John Ehle, *Trail of Tears: The Rise and Fall of the Cherokee Nation* (New York: Doubleday, 1988); Special Issue Commemorating the Sesquicentennial of Cherokee Removal, *Georgia Historical Quarterly* 73, nos. 3–4 (Fall 1989).

34. Theda Perdue, "The Conflict Within: The Cherokee Power Structure and Removal," *Georgia Historical Quarterly* 73 (1989): 467–491; Wilkins, *Cherokee Tragedy.* On suspension of elections see Starkey, *Cherokee Nation,* pp. 190, 222.

35. Clement F. Goodfellow, *Great Britain and South African Confederation, 1870–1881* (Cape Town: Oxford University Press, 1966); D. M. Schreuder, *Gladstone and Kruger: Liberal Government and Colonial "Home Rule," 1880–1885* (London: Routledge & Kegan Paul, 1969); Theal George McCall, *History of South Africa from 1873 to 1884,* 2 vols. (London: Allen and Unwin, 1919); Leonard Thompson, "The Compromise of Union," in *The Oxford History of South Africa,* vol. 2, ed. Monica Wilson and Leonard Thompson (New York: Oxford University Press, 1971), pp. 325–364; Michael Streak, *The Afrikaner as Viewed by the English, 1795–1854* (Cape Town: Struik, 1974).

36. Besides references in chapter 12 see Milagros C. Guerrero, "The Provincial and Municipal Elites of Luzon During the Revolution, 1898–1902," in *Philippine Social History. Global Trade and Local Transformations,* ed. Alfred W. McCoy and Ed. C. de Jesus, Asian Studies Association of Australia Southeast Asia Publications Series no. 7 (Honolulu: University of Hawaii Press, 1982), pp. 156–190.

37. Jill Crystal, *Oil and Politics in the Gulf. Rulers and Merchants in Kuwait and Qatar* (Cambridge: Cambridge University Press, 1990), p. 166; Rosemarie Said Zahlan, *The Making of the Modern Gulf States: Kuwait, Bahrain, Qatar, The United Arab Emirates and Oman* (London: Unwin Hyman, 1989), pp. 141–142.

38. See general sources cited in chapter 6, esp. Johannes Dierauer, *Histoire de la Confédération Suisse,* 5 vols., trans. Aug. Reymond (Lausanne: Payot, 1912–1919), vol. 5, part 2, book 13. Also Remak, *A Very Civil War;* Gordon A. Craig, *The Triumph of Liberalism: Zurich in the Golden Age, 1830–1869* (New York: Scribner's, 1988), pp. 66–75; Erwin Bucher, *Die Geschichte des Sonderbundskrieges* (Zurich: Breithaus, 1966); Jean-Charles Biaudet, "Der Modernen Schweiz Entgegen," in *Handbuch der Schweizer Geschichte,* 2 vols. (Zurich: Berichthaus, 1972), vol. 2, pp. 871–986.

39. G. N. Sanderson, *England, Europe, and the Upper Nile* (Edinburgh: Edinburgh University Press, 1965), pp. 318–323; Alf Andrew Heggoy, *The African Politics of Gabriel Hanotaux, 1894–1898* (Athens: University of Georgia Press, 1972), chaps. 9, 10; Ronald Robinson, John Galleger, and Alice Denny, *Africa and the Victorians: The Climax of Imperialism* (Garden City, N.Y.: Doubleday, 1968), pp. 402–407; James L. Garvin, *The Life of Joseph Chamberlain,* 6 vols. (London: Macmillan, 1932–69), vol. 3, chap. 55.

40. On Léopold see David Levering Lewis, *The Race to Fashoda: European Colonialism and African Resistance in the Scramble for Africa* (New York: Weidenfeld and Nicolson, 1987).

41. Joseph M. Curran, *The Birth of the Irish Free State, 1921–1923* (University: University of Alabama Press, 1980), "murder gang," p. 28, casualties, p. 62; Dorothy Macardle, *The Irish Republic. A Documented Chronicle of the Anglo-Irish Conflict, 1916–1923,* 2nd ed. (New York: Farrar, Straus and Giroux, 1965), esp. pp. 436–437; George Dangerfield, *The Damnable Question: A Study in Anglo-Irish Relations* (Boston, Mass.: Little, Brown, 1976), part 5; Piaras Béaslai, *Michael Collins and the Making of a New Ireland,* 2 vols. (London: Harrap, 1926), vol. 1, esp. chap. 22 and pp. 270–278; Michael Hopkinson, *Green Against Green: The Irish Civil War* (New York: St. Martin's, 1988), chap. 2. On the IRA see Jeffrey Prager, *Building Democracy in Ireland: Political Order and Cultural Integration in a Newly Independent Nation* (Cambridge: Cambridge University Press, 1986), pp. 46–57; Maryann Gialanella Valiulis, *Portrait of a Revolutionary: General Richard Mulcahy and the Founding of the Irish Free State* (Lexington: University Press of Kentucky, 1992), pp. 38–71; J. Bowyer Bell, *The Secret Army: The IRA, 1916–1979* (Cambridge, Mass.: Cambridge University Press, 1979), esp. p. 19; David Fitzpatrick, *Politics and Irish Life, 1913–1921: Provincial Experiences of War and Revolution* (Dublin: Gill and Macmillan, 1977), chaps. 5, 6 and p. 234.

42. Hans Peter Krosby, *Finland, Germany and Soviet Union: The Petsamo Dispute* (Madison: University of Wisconsin Press, 1968); R. Michael Berry, *American Foreign Policy and the Finnish Exception,* vol. 214 of *Studia Historica* (Helsinki: Suomen Historiallinen Seura, 1987), esp. chap. 4; Ernest Llewellyn Woodward, *British Foreign Policy in the Second World War,* vol. 2 (London: HMSO, 1971), pp. 47–54.

43. C. Leonard Lundin, *Finland in the Second World War* (Bloomington: Indiana University Press, 1957); Anthony Upton, *Finland in Crisis, 1940–1941: A Study in Small-Power Politics* (London: Faber and Faber, 1964), pp. 54–58 and passim; Krosby, *The Petsamo Dispute,* pp. 172–176, 182–184.

44. Harold M. Sachar, *A History of Israel from the Rise of Zionism to Our Time* (New York: Knopf, 1976); Michael C. Hudson, *The Precarious Republic: Political Modernization in Lebanon* (New York: Random House, 1968). Israeli casualties: Simha Flappan, *The Birth of Israel: Myths and Realities* (New York: Pantheon, 1987), p. 199n. Kevin Downing provided research support in additional sources for this section.

45. Jon Kimche and David Kimche, *Clash of Destinies: The Arab-Jewish War and the Founding of the State of Israel* (New York: Praeger, 1960); Ilan Pappé, *Britain and the Arab-Israeli Conflict, 1948–1951* (New York: St. Martin's, 1988); Ilan Pappé, *The Making of the Arab-Israeli Conflict, 1947–1951* (New York: St. Martin's, 1992), pp. 100–101; Allan Bullock, *Ernest Bevin* (London: Heineman, 1983), pp. 594–595, 649–650.

46. Here and below: Tozun Bahcheli, *Greek-Turkish Relations since 1955* (Boulder: Westview, 1990), chap. 3; Polyvios G. Polyviou, *Cyprus: Conflict and Negotiation, 1960–1980* (New York: Holmes and Meier, 1980), pp. 13–25, 47–50; Kyriacos C. Markides, *The Rise and Fall of the Cyprus Republic* (New Haven: Yale University Press, 1977), pp. 86–97; Zaim M. Necatigil, *The Cyprus Question and the Turkish Position in International Law* (Oxford: Oxford University Press, 1989), chap. 1.

47. Halil Ibrahim Salih, *Cyprus. The Impact of Diverse Nationalism on a State* (University: University of Alabama Press, 1978), p. 16; Markides, *Rise and Fall*, pp. 32–33 and chap. 3.

48. "Abbot": Markides, *Rise and Fall*, p. 52, see also chap. 2. Stanley Mayes, *Makarios: A Biography* (New York: St. Martin's, 1981).

49. Metin Tamkoç, *The Warrior Diplomats. Guardians of the National Security and Modernization of Turkey* (Salt Lake City: University of Utah Press, 1976); Barbara Hoffmann and C. Balkan, *Militär und Demokratie in der Türkei* (Berlin: Express, 1985), pp. 57–58; William Hale, "The Turkish Army in Politics, 1960–1973," in *Turkish State, Turkish Society*, ed. Andrew Finkel and Nückhet Sirman (London: Routledge, 1990), pp. 53–77. For American intervention see Parker T. Hart, *Two NATO Allies: At the Threshold of War. Cyprus: A Firsthand Account of Crisis Management, 1965–1968* (Durham, N.C.: Duke University Press, 1990), pp. 14–15 and app. 4.

50. For failed negotiations see Polyviou, *Cyprus,* chap. 6, and other sources cited above; Christopher M. Woodhouse, *Karamanlis: The Restorer of Greek Democracy* (Oxford: Clarendon, 1982), pp. 214–220; Necatigil, *Cyprus Question,* pp. 82–87; *New York Times,* 15 Aug. 1974. For brevity I omit the important role of Greece.

51. Renewed fighting in 1994 brought under a hundred deaths. The political culture of Peru's regime then might be classified as authoritarian, but this case is too recent for analysis.

52. Some scholarly writings: Lenard J. Cohen, *Broken Bonds: The Disintegration of Yugoslavia* (Boulder: Westview, 1993); Sabrina P. Ramet, *Nationalism and Federalism in Yugoslavia, 1962–1991,* 2nd ed. (Bloomington: Indiana University Press, 1992); *The Tragedy of Yugoslavia. The Failure of Democratic Transformation,* ed. James Seroka and Vukasin Pavlovic (Armonk, N.Y.: Sharpe, 1992); Norman Cigar, "The Serbo-Croatian War 1991: Political and Military Dimensions," *Journal of Strategic Studies* 16 (1993): 297–338; V. P. Gagnon, Jr., "Ethnic Nationalism and International Conflict: The Case of Serbia," *International Security* 19, no. 3 (Winter 1994/1995): 130–166; Cvijeto Job, "Yugoslavia's Ethnic Furies," *Foreign Policy* 92 (1993): 52–74; Dusko Doder, "Yugoslavia: New War, Old Hatreds," *Foreign Policy* 91 (1993): 3–23. I also use journalistic accounts, including Misha Glenny, *The Fall of Yugoslavia: The Third Balkan War* (London: Penguin, 1992), esp. chap. 2; Warren Zimmerman, "The Last Ambassador: A Memoir of the Collapse of Yugoslavia," *Foreign Affairs* 74, no. 2 (March–April 1995): 2–20; see also Zimmerman, *Origins of a Catastrophe: Yugoslavia and Its Destroyers* (New York: Times Books-Random House, 1996); Ivo Banac, "Post-Communism as Post-Yugoslavism: The Yugoslav Non-revolutions of 1989–1990," in *Eastern Europe in Revolution,* ed. Ivo Banac (Ithaca, N.Y.: Cornell University Press, 1992), pp. 168–187; Mark Thompson, *A Paper House: The Ending of Yugoslavia* (New York: Pantheon, 1992), esp. chap. 8; Branka Magaš, *The Destruction of Yugoslavia: Tracking the Break-Up, 1980–1992* (London: Verso, 1993), esp. part 5; and numerous accounts in the news media.

53. Besides sources cited above see Juan J. Linz and Alfred Stepan, "Political Identities and Electoral Sequence: Spain, The Soviet Union, and Yugoslavia," *Daedelus* 121, no. 2

(1992): 123–139; Sabrina P. Ramet, *Nationalism and Federalism in Yugoslavia, 1962–1991* (Bloomington: Indiana University Press, 1992), p. 251.

54. "Caudillo": *Time,* 13 January 1992, p. 24. On Milošević see Aleksa Djilas, "Profile of Slobodan Milosevic," *Foreign Affairs* 72, no. 3 (1993): 81–96; Cohen, *Broken Bonds,* esp. pp. 151–156; Thompson, *Paper House,* pp. 206–214; Stephen Engleberg, "Carving Out a Greater Serbia," *New York Times Magazine,* 1 Sept. 1991, p. 18ff.

55. See Stephen Kinza, "Croatia's Founding Chief," *New York Times,* 5 Aug. 1993; Zimmerman, "The Last Ambassador," pp. 7–8; Thompson, *Paper House,* pp. 281–282.

56. On all this see especially Cohen, *Broken Bonds.*

57. Deaths: John Zamatica, *The Yugoslav Conflict,* Adelphi Paper 270 (London: Brassey's for the International Institute of Strategic Studies, 1992), p. 15. Zimmerman, "The Last Ambassador," p. 13, gives a total of 49.

58. Chuck Schmitz, "Civil War in Yemen: The Price of Unity?" *Current History* 94 (1995): 33–36; *The Economist,* 14 May 1994, pp. 16–17; *New York Times,* 10 May 1994, 29 May 1994.

Index

Aberdeen, Lord, 190, 213, 214

Abolitionists: as outgroup, 116–18, 133

Acarnanian League, 246, 300

Achaean League, 246, 247, 300

Adams, John, 305

Aetolian League, 300

Afghanistan: anocracy in, 12; Pathans of, 236; "tribal" warfare in, 47

Aguinaldo, Emilio, 308

Alexander (tsar of Russia), 259

Allende, Salvador, 227

Alliances: of ancient Greek democracies, 244–47; anocratic confederations, 250–55; autocracies' attempted confederations, 255–62; based on shared ideals, 64–67, 248–49; Concert of Europe, 259, 260–61, 396n44; confederations distinguished from, 246; democratic federations, 262–63; durability of republican alliances, 267–69; German Confederation, 258–59, 260, 261, 264, 395n39; Hanseatic League, 247–50; and ideology, 107–11; and international regimes, 264–67, 269; of oligarchies, 247–50; and the propagation of republican regimes, 271–72; realpolitik explanation for, 64, 107, 244; and republican political culture, 262–63; and transnational political beliefs, 101–7, 264

Alsace, 142

Ancient Greece: alliances in, 66, 109–10, 244–45; belligerence of democracies in, 35, 327n31, 327n32; causes of wars in, 31–34; changing relations in as regimes changed, 34–35, 73, 326n30; democracies propagated in, 271; ideology of solidarity in, 102–3; oligarchy defined in, 121; peace among democracies of, 13; peace among oligarchies of, 35, 327n33; transition from anocracy to republican regimes in, 73. *See also individual city-states*

Anglo-Dutch War *(1652)*, 146–47, 152–53, 304

Anocracies, 12, 47–48; aggressive response of republics to, 207–12; confederations of, 250–55; kinship loyalty in, 69; in Peru, 70–71; transition to republic statehood from, 71–74

Antholis, William, 326n30, 327n33

Antiphon, 103

Appeasement trap, 195–200

Appenzell, 10, 102, 271; vs. Schwyz *(1490)*, 13, 26, 304

Araña, Francisco, 223

Arbenz, Jacobo, 220, 222, 223, 224

Arcadian League, 246, 247

Argentina, 198

Aristotle, 33, 35, 121

Artaxerxes of Persia, 66

Athenian League, 246

Athens: alliances of, 244, 246; in the ambiguous zone between democracy and oligarchy, 119–20; changing relations with Thebes as regimes changed, 34; citizen body of, 30–31; oligarchic faction in, 35; as republic, 28; surrenders to Sparta, 34; vs. Mantinea *(426 B.C.)*, 298; vs. Megara *(427 B.C.)*, 298; vs. Miletus *(412 B.C.)*, 299; vs. Sparta *(411 B.C.)*, 298; vs. Syracuse *(409, 415 B.C.)*, 24, 31–34, 110, 298; vs. Thebes *(362 B.C.)*, 25–26, 299, 323n7; vs. various states *(431–355 B.C.)*, 299–300

Austria: Habsburgs of, 255; Prussian invasion of *(1866)*, 261–62; World War I belligerence of, 192, 193, 376n35